the Macintosh™ Bible

Second Edition

thousands of basic and advanced
tips, tricks and shortcuts
logically organized and fully indexed

edited by
Arthur Naiman

Goldstein & Blair
Box 7635
Berkeley, California 94707

Design—Arthur Naiman
Illustrations—Sandra Speidel, Esther Travis, WetPaint, Gerry Clement
Index—Arthur Naiman
Margin icons—Thomas Friesch, Esther Travis, WetPaint,
          Arthur Naiman, Ken Milburn

This book was written in Microsoft Works and Word, edited in Works on a Mac II with a Radius Two Page Display and a PCPC internal hard disk drive, and poured into PageMaker. Final pages were printed on a LaserWriter II NTX in ITC Benguiat Book, 11/13, with tables in Optima, 11/13, and running heads in 14-point ITC Zapf Chancery Medium Italic (all three fonts from Adobe). Program listings and Hyper-Card scripts are in 9-point Courier. Color separations were made by Color Media of Dublin, California. The book was printed by Consolidated Printers of Berkeley, California.

The Macintosh Bible is distributed to bookstores and book wholesalers by Publishers Group West, Box 8843, Emeryville CA 94662, 800/982-8319 (in California, 415/658-3453).

Individual copies are available for $28 (+ $4 for shipping and tax, if any, to any US address) from Goldstein & Blair, Box 7635, Berkeley CA 94707, 415/524-4000, who also sell in quantity to computer stores and to other retailers and wholesalers outside the book trade.

Printed in the United States of America   printing #   2 3 4 5 6 7 8 9

<u>More rave reviews</u>

One fantastic book.

Max Vizsla, The MACazine

If I hadn't received a review copy, I would have cheerfully paid money to get it.   Bruce Webster, BYTE magazine

Biblical in proportion...contains a wealth of information.

John Barry, Computer Currents

Rating: 95 out of 100.

Doug Miles, MacGuide magazine

Well organized and well written...If you are new to the Mac, The Macintosh Bible is an excellent reference to own.

Gordon Firestein, Bay Area Mac Classifieds

No Mac user should be without this easy-to-use, comprehensive survey.

The Midwest Book Review

For more reviews, see the back cover
and the last page of the book.
For readers' comments, see pages 752–59.

This edition of The Macintosh Bible is dedicated to

Bonnie Edwards, Ann Jauregui and Linda Spangler,

who know when to think, when to feel

and how to do both superbly.

Contents

Each chapter also has a table of contents of its own.

Trademark notice

Because a major purpose of this book is to describe and comment on various hardware and software products, many such products are identified by their tradenames. In most—if not all—cases, these designations are claimed as legally protected trademarks by the companies that make the products. It is not our intent to use any of these names generically, and the reader is cautioned to investigate a claimed trademark before using it for any purpose except to refer to the product to which it is attached.

In particular: *Apple* and *Macintosh* are registered trademarks of Apple Computer, Inc. *The Macintosh Bible* is a trademark of Goldstein & Blair, which is not affiliated with Apple Computer, Inc.

Disclaimer

We've got to make a disclaimer that common sense requires: Although we've tried to check all the tips, tricks and shortcuts described in this book to make sure they work as described, we can't guarantee that they do. Don't try anything except on a backup file. Satisfy yourself that the technique you're trying works before using it on your valuable files.

We can't be—and aren't—responsible for any damage or loss to your data or your equipment that results directly or indirectly from your use of this book. We make no warranty, express or implied, about the contents of this book, its merchantability or its fitness for any particular purpose. The exclusion of implied warranties is not permitted by some states. The above exclusion may not apply to you. This warranty provides you specific legal rights. There may be other rights that you may have which vary from state to state.

Preface

Most computer books are out-of-date a few months after they're published. But not this one. To keep the information in it current, we include two *free* updates in the price of the book. And they're not chintzy little flyers, either, but substantial booklets—in fact, the first edition's updates were each 59 pages long!

To get your free updates to *this* edition, all you have to do is send us your name and address. (It's easiest to use the card in the back of the book, but anything is fine. See the inside front or back cover for details.)

The Macintosh Bible is a collection of thousands of basic and advanced tips, tricks, shortcuts and product evaluations that help you get the most from your Mac. The information is logically organized and fully indexed, so it's easy to find what you're looking for.

This second edition has been *completely* revised and updated, and contains hundreds of pages of new material. In fact, there's more completely new material in this edition than there is in most books that are published for the first time.

This is a reference book and isn't meant to be read from beginning to end—although we get letters from readers that say, "once you start reading it, you can't put it down", "as good as curling up with a good novel" and "I've read it from cover to cover—twice!". Naturally, we'll be delighted if you have the same reaction; if not, use the table of contents and the index to dip into the book wherever you want (but first read the section called *How to use this book* that begins on page 6).

If you want to try out some of the best shareware and public-domain programs mentioned in the book, as well as a few things of our own devising, take a look at *The Macintosh Bible Disk* (described in the last chapter).

Acknowledgments

The book wouldn't exist without the incredible effort expended on the first edition by Dale Coleman. Sharon Zardetto Aker, Eric Alderman, Tom Bennett, Brad Bunnin, Raines Cohen, Steve Costa, Allen Glazer, Paul Hoffman, Dennis Klatzkin, Don McCunn, Roxie Lum McCunn, Steve Michel, Carol Pladsen, Steve Rosenthal, Charles Rubin and Harry Sadler offered advice whose brilliance was only surpassed by the generosity with which it was given.

Byron Brown did a terrific job of pouring the book into Page-Maker (with help from Kerry Golemon and Geoff Geiger). Julia DeMuth proofed much of the book, worked on Dictionary Helper and made dozens of other contributions, all in addition to her work at Goldstein & Blair. Jan Brenner and John Grimes kept the business going while the second edition was being written, working with exceptional diligence and dedication under difficult circumstances. Carol Pladsen held the whole thing together, as only Carol Pladsen can.

I'm particuarly grateful to Peter Lewis, Andy Hertzfeld, Bruce Webster, Bob LeVitus, Wendy Woods, John Barry, Joost Romeu and all the other reviewers who were kind enough to take the time to look at and comment on the book. Julie Bennett, Randy Fleming, Bill Hurst and Charlie Winton keep astounding me with their monthly sales reports (a tradition I sincerely hope they'll continue). I also want to thank the contributors to this edition (for brief biographical notes on them, see pp. 10–11) and the illustrators whose Mac-created drawings beautify what would otherwise be boring blank pages: Esther Travis, Gerald Clement and various artists from the WetPaint collection.

I can't tell you how much the letters we get from readers brighten our days at Goldstein & Blair. (Quotes from some of them are reprinted at the end of the book.) We all wish we had time to answer each letter personally, and not only because it would be a lot more fun than what we otherwise spend our time doing. But since there are thousands of letters, and since we seem to be in a permanent state of catastrophic overload, please accept our thanks here and believe me when I say, we *really love* your letters.

Now for my favorite part of the acknowledgments—the exotic names club! (Who says acknowledgements have to be dull? You just have to know people with interesting names.) Fokko Du Cloux checked most of the first edition for out-of-dateness, organized Chapter 10 and made many substantial contributions. He really should have been listed as a contributor instead of just having his name attached to a few entries. Xenia Lisanevich and Lila Dargahi did a very conscientious job of proofreading and worked on a number of other crucial projects as well. Nancy Krompotich got the book off to a flying start. Tanta Rivoli (née Rebele) provided unfailing support, as she has since time immemorial. The talented and glamorous Gloria Zarifa was a continual inspiration.

I also want to thank the following people for favors too various to specify, but which were greatly appreciated in every case: Larry Abel, Carole Alden, Eric Angress, Bonnie Beren, Simone Biase, Dave Brast, Tom Brockland, Nenelle Bunnin, John Boeschen, Tony Bove, Brent of Computer Literacy, Michael Castleman, Tom Cottingham, Brian Davis, Dan Doernberg, Richard Dunsay, Dan Farber, Sherrin Farley, Caitlin Fisher, Vic Fisher, Matt Foley, Ruth Gendler, George at Computerland of Oakland, David Goldman, Reese Jones, David Jouris, Chris Kafitz, Diana Kehlmann, Ed Kelly, Peggy Kilburn, Art Kleiner, Scott Kronick, Renee Larson, Lyon Leifer, Sarah Levin, Ron Lichty, Susan McCallister, Yvette Manson, Malcolm Margolin, Albert Naiman, Nettie Naiman, Dave Nee of Another Change of Hobbit, Cheryl Nichols, Nick of Cody's, Sandy Niemann, Guy Orcutt, Alan Orso, Harold Patterson, Marianne Petrillo, Nevin Pfaltzgraff, Gloria Polanski, Larry Press, Susan Quinn, Kal Rabinowitz, Phil Reese, Cheryl Rhodes, Richard at the Swiss National Tourist Office in San Francisco, Mark Richardson, Ira Rosenberg, Ed Rosenthal, Phil Russell, Tom Santos, Marty Schiffenbauer, Scott Schwartz, Nancy Shine, Gar Smith, Denny Smithson, David Socholitzky, Joani Spadaro, Martha Steffen, Jean-Luc Szpakowski, Levi Thomas, Lou Tomafsky, Paul Towner, Lisette van Vliet, Anne Walzer, Esther Wanning, Roy Webb, Malka Weitman, Neil Wilkinson and, last but not least, the charming and witty Rachelle DeStephens, formerly of Lima, Ohio.

As always, I'd like conclude by thanking my ophthalmologist, Rod Cohen. (To show the intensity of my gratitude, I've spelled *ophthalmologist* right this time.)

Introduction

It's a common saying that the best source of tips is the manual that comes with a product. To this is often added a mild reproach: "if only people would take the trouble to read it."

Of course manuals contain a lot of good tips. There are also a lot of needles in that haystack over there. The trick is to *find* them.

The typical manual buries its useful information beneath tons of idiotic over-simplification ("Lift your hand into the air, using your arm and shoulder muscles, and lower it onto the mouse, palm down"), ridiculous warnings ("Do NOT grasp the back of the picture tube with the power on and jump into a bathtub full of water") and unintelligible computerese (*"Guess* is an optional argument that specifies the starting value of the iteration"—this last, as you may have guessed, is an actual quote from a manual).

You have better things to do with your time than read hundreds of pages of this sort of stuff every time you want to use a new product. So we've tried to do some gleaning for you.

Needless to say, this book can't cover the ground it does and still do a comprehensive job in each area (although the size of the book shows you we tried). It's inevitable that some areas will be covered more thoroughly than others. Still, within each area, we've tried to be selective and concentrate on the most useful stuff.

One thing I felt the first edition needed more of was introductory material. I've added a lot to this edition (for example, a tutorial for beginners in Chapter 1 called *A Guide for the Perplexed),* along with a new icon to highlight it:

**esp. for
beginners**

Product evaluations are an important part of the book but you have to take them with a grain of salt, if for no other reason than that they may be out-of-date by the time you read them. (That's what the updates are for, so be sure to send for your free copies.)

A certain amount of subjectivity is bound to creep into product evaluations; in an attempt to combat that, I've sometimes had more than one person review (or comment on) a product.

We recommend what we think are the best products but we give you tips on the most popular, whether we like them or not. For example, I can't stand Word, but a lot of people use it, so we spend almost forty pages helping you get the most out of it.

Some of you who bought the first edition didn't get the updates, books or disks you ordered from us as quickly as you should have. We had some people working for us who weren't doing a very good job; they've left and this hopefully won't be a problem anymore. We aim to ship orders out within 24 hours. (Updates take longer, because they go by bulk mail and that requires a minimum quantity of 200.)

It really pains me when orders go out late or get screwed up. If there's any problem, please feel free to take advantage of our money-back guarantee (just return the book or disk in resellable condition within 30 days). I want you to be totally satisfied in your dealings with us.

Finally, a company called STAX! has published a HyperCard version of the first edition and may be doing one of the second edition. If you're on our mailing list, we'll let you know about it if it happens. (To get on the list, just send for your updates.)

How to use this book

This book covers a wide range of subjects and a wide range of Mac experience. No matter how much or how little you know, there will be stuff in here that's either too easy or too hard for you. So just skip over the stuff that obviously isn't meant for you—there'll be plenty that is.

Margin icons are one way we help you find items you're likely to be interested in. We use nine of them:

esp. for beginners

If you're new to the Mac, it might make sense for you to check out all of these first. (They're listed in the index.) Unlike other icons, this one usually refers to a whole page or entry, rather than just to a single paragraph.

very hot tip

All our tips are hot, but these are particularly hot.

shortcut

Isn't that a beautiful icon? It comes from the WetPaint clip art collection.

very good feature

We're critical enough when that's what's called for, so we like to also give credit where credit is due.

very bad feature

These two icons are a subtle plug for left-handers.

bargain

We use this to indicate particularly good values.

This one is pretty self-explanatory.

Nobody can predict the future, but we try.

This icon is for stuff that's more interesting than useful. Look for it when you need a break.

The table of contents at the start of the book tells you the general area each chapter covers; in addition, each chapter has a more detailed table of contents of its own.

The index, as you can see by its length, is a *real* one, not one of those imitation indexes that's just there so the publisher can say the book has one. You can really *find* things in this index.

Appendix A is 43-page glossary of Macintosh terms. Don't say, "Oh, yeah, a glossary, OK." I worked *very* hard to make it as useful and complete as possible. If you run across a term you're not sure of, that's the place to look first.

Appendix B lists addresses and phone numbers for the products, companies, Mac consultants and artists mentioned in the book, as well as the contributors to it (except those who didn't want to be listed).

Except for the first chapter and the appendices, the book is made up of *entries* (whose titles look like this: **⌘ *entry title***). Each entry contains at least one tip, often dozens.

With rare exceptions, entries are meant to stand on their own—although I've grouped them into subject areas and have also put them into logical order wherever possible. I've tried to put the more basic entries toward the start of each section, but sometimes grouping by topic made this difficult.

The initials of whoever wrote the intial draft for each entry appear in parentheses after its title (except for people who just contributed one or two items, whose names are written out in full). To find out who SZA, CR and all the rest are, see *Notes on contributors* on pp. 10–11.

When I add a comment to someone else's entry, it either starts with *Editor's note:* or ends with *—AN,* depending on my mood and the position of the planets. When something isn't signed, I wrote it (all this introductory stuff, for example).

Regardless of who wrote the original drafts, I rewrote them, often with a fairly heavy hand, to try to make the whole book speak with one voice (mine—for better or worse). So if something is wrong (and isn't a typo), it's the fault of the person whose initials you see; if something is *unclear,* it's my fault. Naturally except but other than whether not it should be—oh my God, I'm doing it already. (If the jokes aren't funny, that's my fault too.)

Thanks to a new LaserWriter with more memory, I can use more fonts in this edition. The first one I added was World Class Font's Manhattan, which contains a number of useful symbols: Tab, Shift, Caps Lock, Option, ⌘, Return, Enter, Backspace, Click and Double-Click. (Manhattan is a bit-mapped font—that is, it's designed for use on dot-matrix printers like the ImageWriter. Why no one has come out with these symbols in a laser font is completely beyond me.)

I use those symbols throughout the book to make it easier for you to enter key combinations. When doing that, I always list them in the order shown above (which is how the keys are arranged on Apple's standard ADB keyboard)—so you don't sometimes see Option ⌘ –A and sometimes ⌘ Option –A (except when a contributor prepared a diagram the other way). This also makes it easier for you to put your fingers down on the keys left to right as you read a command.

(On most keyboards, the Backspace key is actually labelled *delete.* But I stuck with Backspace for a very simple reason—Manhattan, designed several years ago, doesn't have a key-caps symbol for *delete.)*

One other note about keys: the ⌘ key, for which many names contended when the Mac first came out (including *cloverleaf* and *pretzel)* is now quite generally called by its official name, the *command* key. Now some third-party keyboards just label that key *command* and don't even put the ⌘ symbol on it. *O tempora! O mores!* (Who says computer books can't be literate?)

Prices, when shown, are just to give you a *very* general idea of what things cost, at list. Prices change rapidly and discounts are almost always available, so don't rely too heavily on the prices we quote. Since this book is written for people with IQs in *three* figures, all prices are rounded up ("Oh, it's only $995? What a relief! I thought I was going to have spend at least a thousand dollars.").

Notes on contributors

AN—Arthur Naiman's ten books about personal computers have sold more than half a million copies. He's also the author of *Every Goy's Guide to Common Jewish Expressions* and is working on a book about Central America.

BB—Brad Bunnin is an attorney who restricts his practice to literary law. He's the principal author of *The Writer's Legal Companion* and teaches at the University of California's Graduate School of Journalism.

CJW—C.J. Weigand is Senior Editor at both *MACazine* and *Personal Publishing*, a frequent contributor to many other publications and an independent Macintosh consultant.

CR—Charles Rubin is Executive Editor of *Macintosh Business Review* and the author of six books, the most recent of which is *Macintosh Hard Disk Management*.

DC—Dale Coleman is *MacWEEK's* Editor-at-Large, working with the news and reviews sections. He currently ponders the meaning of HyperCard and the future of UNIX.

DK—Dennis Klatzkin is a San-Francisco-based consultant and writer. His articles and reviews appear frequently in *MacWEEK*, where he is acting Reviews Editor.

EA—Eric Alderman is the author of several computer books and has written for *Macworld, Macintosh Today, PC World* and other computer publications. He's a contributing editor of *MacWEEK*, where he cowrites the *StackWEEK* column.

FT—Fred Terry, a writer and microcomputer consultant, specializes in word processing, page layout and hardware solutions.

KM—Ken Milburn is a freelance writer and microcomputer consultant specializing in graphics. His articles and reviews have appeared in *InfoWorld, MacWEEK, Personal Computing* and many other publications.

LP—Larry Pina is a regular contributor to *The MACazine* and the author of Test Pattern Generator.

MB—Michael Bradley has been a technical writer since 1982. Before that he was everything from a carpenter to a video producer. He's active in the National Writer's Union.

PH—Paul Hoffman is the author of many popular microcomputer books, including *Microsoft Word Made Easy—Macintosh Edition.* He's also News Editor at *MicroTimes.*

SB—Scott Beamer has published more than a hundred articles in various Macintosh magazines. He specializes in the areas of accounting, word processing, spelling checkers, monitors, color and the Mac II.

SH—Steve Herold is a calligrapher, graphic artist and publisher who currently teaches, writes on publishing technology and operates Lasergraphics, a computer-aided publishing and graphics company in Seattle.

SM—Steve Michel is the author of *HyperCard: The Complete Reference* and *IBM PC and Macintosh Networking.* He's a contributing editor of *MacWEEK,* where he cowrites the *StackWEEK* column.

SS—Steve Schwartz has been a freelance writer, editor and reviewer since 1978. A former editor of *Software Digest,* he's currently Business Applications Editor for *MACazine.*

SZA—Sharon Zardetto Aker makes a living playing with the Macintosh day and night. To make it look like work, she designs software and writes Mac books, magazine articles and documentation.

TR—Tim Ryan is an independent consultant and certified developer specializing in desktop publishing and font-related Macintosh software. He's the author of *The Macintosh Book of Fonts.*

You'll find contact information
(for those who wanted it listed)
in Appendix B.

Chapter 1

General principles

The Ten Commandments
(AN)

I. This is the Mac.
It's *supposed* to be fun.

For years, most businesspeople treated the Mac as a toy, while those of us who'd already had a bellyful of the deranged command structure of more primitive computers romped happily in the fields of Macintosh. Now that the Mac has gotten some corporate acceptance, there seems to be a campaign on to make it as dull as the IBM PC. What a great idea!

The rigid dichotomy between work and fun—and the acceptance of that dichotomy as inevitable and necessary—is, to quote Dr. "Happy" Harry Cox, "Old Age thinking." More clearly than any other computer, the Mac demonstrates that aesthetics enhance, rather than detract from, efficient work.

So don't let them turn the Mac into an expensive version of the PC. Demand fun as your birthright!

II. Easy is hard.

There's a macho attitude among some computer jocks (although certainly not among the best of them) that the harder something is to deal with, the more advanced it is. That's what usually lies behind the absurd idea that the PC is a more powerful machine than the Mac.

Actually, of course, it's very hard to make things easy. The more work you put into something, the less work the person who uses it has to do.

So if you find yourself beating your head against a wall erected by someone's laziness (or greed), look around for a different wall that someone else took the trouble to put a door in. And if anybody mocks what you're using as a toy, just smile and say, "Easy is powerful. Hard is primitive."

III. It's not your fault you're confused.

Over the years, manuals have gotten better and programs are designed more sensibly than they used to be, but that's a little like saying how much nicer Himmler has been since his lobotomy. The standard is still abysmally low.

If you're confused, it's not because you're stupid—it's because the people who designed that product, or wrote that manual, or rushed people so they couldn't do a good job, are stupid. Just make sure they, not you, pay for it.

IV. You can't do it all.

Some experienced Mac users can make you feel like a loser because you're not up on the new products and techniques they're always discovering. But it's really just that you have different interests. Theirs is exploring the Mac and yours (if you're like most people) is simply using it.

Each approach has its virtues and neither is inherently superior to the other. So feel free to restrict yourself to a small number of Mac programs that you master and use intensively. Remember—you can't do it all and, unless you're a Mac fanatic, you shouldn't even try.

V. Make the Mac your own.

There's never been a computer you could, as Omar put it, mold "nearer to the heart's desire." So give yourself time to customize it. Find the software you like best. Spend hours rearranging the Desktop or the files on your disks. The more the Mac feels like your own creation, the more efficient and enjoyable your work on it will be.

Think of the Mac as your home. You wouldn't try to move every different kind of furniture in the world into it, just because you could. (Virtually any individual piece would fit, but not all of them together. That's just the point.) You have furniture you feel comfortable with, appliances you need and use, decorations and toys that amuse you. Treat your Mac the same way.

VI. A file saved is a file saved.

What shall it profit you if you create the greatest piece of work in the world but lose it because you forgot to save?

Despite how wonderfully easy it is to use, the Mac has as many traps and pitfalls as any other computer—maybe more. These don't have to be a problem, if you save your work! Of course it's a pain and interrupts the flow of your thoughts, but that's nothing compared to what it feels like to lose work.

People are always telling you to save, as if it mattered to them. It's too bad saving has acquired this taint of moralism. Saving your work isn't something you should do because some authority tells you to. The appeal here is pure pleasure principle—you'll be a lot happier if you get in the habit.

VII. Two, three, many backups.

Saving is only half the battle. Disks crash all the time. If you don't make regular backups, you may as well not save your work at all.

VIII. Combat the tragedy of the commons.

In English villages, the "commons" was (or is) a piece of land on which everyone can graze livestock. (This is what the Boston Commons originally was.)

It's clearly in each villager's individual interest to graze as many head of, say, sheep on the commons as he or she can. And yet if all the villagers follow their own best interest, the common gets grazed bare and all the sheep starve. This is called "the tragedy of the commons."

The solution, of course, is simple: limit the number of sheep each villager can graze (hopefully in some sort of equitable way). But that can be hard to enforce since, even when a quota exists, it's still in each villager's individual interest to graze as many sheep as possible on the commons. It requires some social and environmental consciousness on the part of all the villagers, some long-range, unselfish thinking, to avoid the ecological tragedy.

Just the same thing is true on the Mac. It's no big deal if one person doesn't pay for a shareware program, but if a lot of people don't, good shareware stops getting written. It's no big deal if one person copies a commercial program and uses it for free, but if a lot of people do that, software developers have trouble making money and start cutting corners. In both cases, slowly but surely, the commons becomes a barren patch of dirt.

IX. Allow for Murphy's Law (since you can't avoid it).

Here's a piece of trivia few people know—the origin of Murphy's Law. In 1949, Captain Ed Murphy was an engineer working at Edwards Air Force Base in California. When a technician working in his lab miswired something, Murphy said, "If there's any way to do it wrong, he will." A coworker of his, George E. Nichols, dubbed this Murphy's Law.

Murphy's Law has evolved into, "If anything can go wrong, it will," but it's interesting to note that it originally referred to incompetence, not to some sort of impersonal malevolence on the part of the cosmos.

For whatever reason, things certainly do go wrong with distressing regularity. This happens less on the Mac than elsewhere, thanks to the care and dedication of its original designers. In fact, the Mac's ease of use can lull you into the dangerous delusion that Murphy's Law has been banished from its realm.

No sooner do you assume this than reality disabuses you of the notion—usually more abruptly than you'd like. It works sort of like the Greek concept of hubris: Pride—or, in this case, complaisance—goeth before a fall.

X. That goes double for Sturgeon's Law.

In the late 50's, Theodore Sturgeon (1918–85) wrote a book-review column for a magazine called Venture Science Fiction. It was there he first enunciated Sturgeon's Law. "It's well known," he wrote (I'm paraphrasing), "that 90% of all science-fiction writing is crap. But then, 90% of <u>everything</u> is crap."

When I first started writing about computers, I wasted a lot of time railing at some of the more wretched products popular back then, and at the brain-damaged ways they went about things. Today, you hardly ever hear their names. (In Bach's day, Hasse's music was more popular than Bach's. You remember Hasse, right?)

Natural selection is going on at a blinding pace in this field, so just find some good stuff, use it until something better comes along and forget about the rest.

The trick, of course, is _finding_ the good stuff. That's one of the things this book is designed to help you do. So stop browsing and buy it already. (This is the famous Lost Eleventh Commandment.)

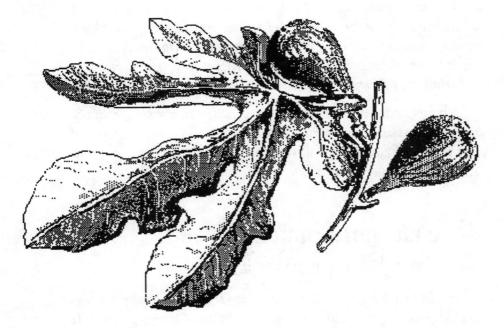

Hardware buying tips *(AN)*

The extent to which computers are sold like cars never ceases to amaze me. (But then, the extent to which cars are sold like cologne never ceases to amaze me.)

Hard disk manufacturers advertise access times as if a millisecond or two is going to make any difference to the average user (not to mention the fact that access time is seldom the main determinant of how fast a hard disk is). It's just like choosing a car because its top speed is 130 instead of 120.

The three most important things to look for in a piece of computer hardware, as with a car, are whether it can do what you want it to, how reliable it is and (with a nod to Commandment IX above) how easy it is to get it fixed.

very hot tip

One way to maximize your chances of getting a reliable (and repairable) piece of hardware is to buy from a company with a commitment to quality. (Granted, that commitment can evaporate like the morning dew, but you still stand a better chance from a company that's had it in the past than one that hasn't.)

It's astounding how little a company can care about its customers. For example, I couldn't get a Bering hard disk I was evaluating to install correctly, so I called the company's tech support line. They said their techs were busy and took my number. I got a call back a *week* later. Needless to say, I was glad I was only testing this drive and hadn't been foolish enough to buy it.

very bad feature

Two hardware companies whose products I know and whose reputations are good are Jasmine (hard disks) and Farallon Computing (networking, sound recording, etc.). Steve Herold recommends Computer Friends, a small company on the outskirts of Portland with some very innovative and reasonably priced products, including color video boards, a color paint program called Modern Artist, printer buffers, re-inkers for dot-matrix printer ribbons (including the four-color kind) and two- and four-way

very good feature

switches. They also distribute Shinko color printers and Dunn film recorders.

very good feature

In a refreshing departure from the norm, Computer Friends has always sold their products as inexpensively as possible, rather than trying to see what the market will bear.

There are a lot of other excellent companies out there. Look for a long warranty, good support policies and a place where you'll feel comfortable bringing something back if it breaks.

There's one other important consideration—price. How important that is depends on how your budget, of course, but let me say this: Don't underestimate the Mac's importance in your life. This is not some trivial plaything—this is the most powerful tool for personal expression ever invented.

If you *want* something—a laser printer instead of a dot-matrix printer, say, or a Mac II instead of an SE—you'll usually be happier if you figure out some way to justify having it. I've seldom if ever heard anyone say, "I really shouldn't have bought this *(expensive piece of computer equipment)*. I really could have gotten by with *(something simpler and less expensive)*." But I can't count the number of times I've heard people who've gotten some powerful new piece of hardware say, "How did I live without this?"

important warning

On the other hand, don't buy something you plan to grow into; by the time you grow into it, you'll be able to buy something better for less. (There's one exception to this rule: If you're about to buy your first hard disk, get twice as much capacity as you think you'll need. You'll fill it up before you know it.)

Because computer technology is still on the steep upslope of its growth curve, technological advances that provide more power for less money have—so far—always greatly outstripped increasing material and labor costs. Sometimes prices go down a lot and sometimes they go down a little, but they almost always go down.

Because of that, people will sometimes advise you to wait and buy later, when whatever you're buying will cost you less. This advice doesn't always make sense. For one thing, if you followed it faithfully, you'd never buy anything. For another, it fails to consider the value of owning and using the equipment, which, in my experience, has almost always outweighed whatever money I might have saved waiting for tomorrow's lower price.

very hot tip

So, if you have a use for something right now, and you *want* it, do without the new drapes or the new car—the Mac is more fun.

Software buying tips (AN)

This book is filled with evaluations and comparisons of specific Mac programs. Here are some general guidelines on what to look for and avoid:

Ease of use

A lot of software—with its impenetrable manuals, commands reminiscent of Shiners' initiation rites and what Michael Ward calls "unpleasant surprises"—isn't worth the trouble it takes to learn it.

One of the major reasons people buy the Mac is to avoid all that intimidating, user-hostile gobbledygook. Fortunately, most companies that publish software for the Mac seem to realize that. But not all. Some let their programmers' bizarre thinking mold the final product and others let dollar-crazed marketing executives make the decisions.

very hot tip

You shouldn't have to put up with any of that, so *don't* — not even for a second. The Mac is an inherently easy-to-use machine. If you find yourself having *any trouble at all* learning how to use a program for the Mac, stop wasting your time and find another program that doesn't give you the same trouble.

Logical hierarchy of commands

For software to be easy to use, it should be hierarchically organized. This means that most basic operations are simple and central to how the program works and the more advanced operations are off to the side, so you don't even know about them until you need them.

Mac software should be Mac-like

Aside from being easy-to-use, the Mac's interface has another major virtue: you don't have to learn a new set of commands and procedures for each program. At least you shouldn't have to.

very good feature

Fortunately, most Mac programs have all the standard Mac features: pop-down menus, icons, windows, a mouse-controlled pointer, dialog boxes and buttons, scroll bars, cut-and-paste, etc. Some also have an *Undo* command (and the more circumstances it works in, the better). But other programs have simply been converted slap-dash from a version that runs on inferior computers like the PC and these should be avoided.

There is a third category, however—programs that take advantage of the Mac's features but do so in a nonstandard way. Whether you like one of these programs or not depends on whether you find the features it offers spiffy enough to justify switching gears between it and other Mac programs (and hitting a lot of wrong keys in the process).

If there's a standard program, you probably want it

In certain areas, one piece of software has more or less become the standard. When this happens, it makes sense to get that program. But watch out for false, or premature, standards. Don't be lured into getting a program until it's clearly a standard (or is just what you want anyway).

Speed

As many people have learned to their sorrow, ease of use ain't everything. How fast a program runs can be even more important. Unfortunately, that's seldom mentioned in ads or by salesclerks and it's one of the hardest things to evaluate in an in-store tryout.

But delays of even a few seconds can be very annoying if you keep running into them. Because of that, speed is one of the prime things to look for in a program. Many computer novices tend to ignore this consideration—since doing something on a computer is always so much faster than doing it by hand. But, believe me now or believe me later, if you buy a slow program, you'll live to regret it. (Steve Michel says no one *ever* realizes this; they just go for the power.)

very
hot
tip

Take reviews (including ours) with a grain of salt

*important
warning*

One problem with reviews is that most reviewers aren't like most users. They tend to have much more experience with Mac programs and to be much more interested in exploring them as an activity in itself.

Another problem is that reviewers seldom have enough time to really get to know the ins and outs of the software they're evaluating. Lots of programs are complicated enough that you don't really get a feeling for their strengths and weaknesses until you've used them fairly heavily for a couple of months.

A third problem is that magazines are supported by advertising revenues, and while I'm always surprised by how tough they're willing to be in spite of that fact, no magazine's reviews are going to be, on the average, 75% or even 50% negative.

Still, reviews are a great place to learn about products. Just don't treat them as the holy gospel—even when they appear in the Bible.

Shareware is worth trying

*esp. for
beginners*

To be absolutely sure you're going to want a program before you buy it, you need to use it for some reasonable period of time. The best way to do that is *shareware*— software you're allowed to copy freely and only pay for if you like it and continue to use it. As you'll discover from reading this book, some of the best Mac programs are shareware.

bargain

In order to encourage this proconsumer approach to software distribution, always give shareware a try before spending money for a commercial program that does the same thing, and *always* pay for any shareware you end up keeping and using.

*important
warning*

If you don't, the people who write it will have to find some other way to make a living and will no longer be able to update their programs or create new ones. In the short run, you'll save a little money; in the long run, you'll lose a lot, as you end up paying more for programs you're not even sure you'll use, because no good shareware alternatives are available.

Public-domain software

Lots of programs are available absolutely free, thanks to the generosity of their authors. You can get this software from good computer stores (if you've done business with them), *user groups or bulletin boards.* You often have to put up with skimpy documentation, or none at all, and early versions of most programs have bugs. But there's a lot of terrific public-domain software, some of it better than commercial programs.

bargain

(You can get a sampling of great Mac shareware and public-domain programs on *The Macintosh Bible disk,* which has a money-back guarantee. See Chapter 16 for details.)

In-store tryouts

Any decent computer store will let you sit and play with software for hours at a time, as long as no one else wants to use the machine (unfortunately, someone almost always will). Trying a program in a store will often (but not always) give you enough of a feeling for it to decide if you want to buy it.

Money-back guarantees

If you're buying a program mail order and sight unseen, try to get a money-back guarantee. Remember—a lot of software isn't worth using, no matter how good it sounds.

important warning

You want a great manual you don't need

No matter how great a program is, it doesn't do you any good unless you know how to use it. Mac software should be so clear, its menu commands so understandable, that you don't even need a manual. If you *do* need a manual, at least it should be a good one.

Ironically (but predictably), the easiest programs to learn tend to have the best manuals and the hardest to learn tend to have the worst manuals.

Support, support, support

very
hot
tip

There's a saying in real estate that the three most important things to consider when buying property are *location, location and location.* Likewise, the three most important things to consider when buying a computer product are *support, support and support.* (*Support* is the availability of someone to answer your questions, usually on the phone, and to fix things if they go wrong.)

Support is the reason it often makes sense to pay a little more to buy from a vendor whose staff knows something (whether it's a local store or a mail-order distributor). Don't imagine you can depend on the publisher's telephone support line. Although there are some exceptions, most of them are so understaffed that you might as well just play a tape recording of a busy signal and not tie up your phone.

Don't use a hammer to kill a fly

very
hot
tip

You should use a computer to do things you can't do more easily in some other way (with pencil and paper, for example). The Mac can't make you organized or creative (although it can certainly help you organize and create).

Thou shalt not steal

In the case of some programs, there are more illegal copies in existence than legal ones. (Not that this is always bad for the publisher. WordStar became an industry-standard word processing program at least partly because so many people had bootleg copies of it.)

Most of the problem is that people give copies to their friends; few computer hackers are despicable enough to steal someone else's work and then *sell* it. Still, the average program represents many person-years of labor, and you can't blame a publisher for wanting to protect that investment.

As a result, most Mac software used to be *copy-pro-tected.* (There are many ways to make it difficult to copy a disk and no way to make it impossible, so it becomes a question of percentages: "How many hackers can we outsmart.")

Copy-protection is a real drag and virtually all Mac software publishers have stopped doing it. This puts the burden on us. If people can't make money developing software because everyone is stealing their software instead of buying it, soon there won't be any good programs at all. (I know I'm repeating myself. This bears repeating.)

important warning

Beware of vaporware

So much software has been promised that never saw the light of day (or saw it on a day many months after it was supposed to) that there's even a name for it—*vaporware.*

important warning

So when some salesclerk (or ad, or friend) tells you that a new product will be along "real soon now," don't depend on it. Few computer products come out on time, and lots of software ends up being nothing more than vaporware.

Don't pay to be a beta tester

When software publishers get a product to a certain stage, they hand out copies to people on the outside and ask them to test it. This work, called *beta testing,* is unpaid; the testers are motivated by the advantage (or prestige) of being the first to know about something.

esp. for beginners

That's all fine, but don't *pay* to beta-test a product that's already been released. Vaporware is bad enough, but it's much worse to spend your good money on a product that's full of bugs.

So wait a while when a new product comes out. Go to a user group meeting or two and see if anyone's having problems with it. If you telecommunicate, ask about it on a bulletin board. Remember: feeling impatient is a lot less painful than feeling victimized.

important warning

Avoid companies with growth disease

important warning

In certain companies that are lousy with MBAs, talking about what consumers *need* will get you snickered at. (Talking about what consumers *want* is usually tolerated, because that's related to what they'll spend money on.) These companies are out to conquer the world (quite openly—that's the way they talk) and they can't see any farther than their bottom line.

Needless to say, companies with growth disease should be avoided like the plague. The libel laws prevent me from mentioning any by name, but I can talk about their opposites:

Trust good publishers

Since movie reviewers spend most of their time telling you the plot (and usually can't even do that with any accuracy), one of the best ways to tell if a movie is worth seeing is to find out who directed it. Similarly, one of the best ways to tell if a program is worth buying is to judge by the company that publishes it.

very hot tip

Here are the names of some companies that produce intelligent, useful products at reasonable prices, have kept them updated and seem likely to continue in that good tradition (their addresses and phone numbers are in Appendix B):

CasadyWare (Fluent Fonts)

CE Software (DiskTop, QuicKeys, CalendarMaker, etc.)

Dubl-Click Software (WetPaint, World Class Fonts, Calculator Construction Kit, etc.)

Solutions (SmartScrap & The Clipper, Curator, SuperGlue, etc.)

There are many other excellent software publishers, so please don't think of this as an exclusive list.

A guide for the perplexed (AN)
(things that often confuse beginners)

esp. for
beginners

The Mac is the most intuitive computer ever sold, but that's not saying much. There are still things about it that confuse beginning users, and Apple's manuals, while better than most, tend to make you wade through a lot of stuff you already know—or that's obvious—to get to the useful information.

Here's a very brief introduction to the Mac that's designed to get beginning users started off on the right foot and to guide them around some of the more common pitfalls. You can supplement it with Apple's manuals to get more details on various points, but it should get you up and running a lot faster than they will.

One word of caution: Apple is always updating and changing the Mac's basic software, so what appears on your screen may not exactly match the screen shots printed in this book. Don't let that throw you—the basic principles will be the same.

The pointer

The Mac's way of communicating with people is the *pointing interface* (sometimes also referred to as the *graphical* or *visual interface*). As its name implies, the pointing interface lets you control a computer by pointing at *icons* (little pictures) or at clear, simple, English words, instead of forcing you to memorize a bunch of abbreviated commands.

You do your pointing with an on-screen symbol called (with simple elegance) the *pointer*. Although it can take many shapes, its basic one is a left-leaning arrow (▶). When you're dealing with text, it takes the shape of an *I-beam* (⌶). Graphics programs like MacPaint have a whole slew of specialized pointers; for example, 🖌 , 🖐 , 🖊 , 🖑 and 🔍 .

esp. for
beginners

You typically control the pointer with a *mouse*—a small box with a ball on the bottom and a button on the top, connected to the rest of the system by a cord. When you roll the mouse around, the pointer moves in the same direction on the screen (although not normally the same distance). You get so used to it after a while, it begins to feel as if you're moving the pointer directly with your hand.

The Desktop

A basic Apple program called the Finder creates a gray area that covers the screen. Because most of the kind of work that's done on a Mac is otherwise done at a desk, this gray area is called the *Desktop*.

The things you point to are arranged on the Desktop. Just as on a real desktop, you can open folders and files and read what's in them, throw things in the wastebasket and so on. Here's what the Desktop looks like:

Menus

The only thing on the Desktop that doesn't follow this real-world analogy is the line of words across the top. This is called the *menu bar* and the words on it are called *menu titles*. If you put the pointer on a menu title and hold down the mouse button, a menu pops down over the Desktop.

esp. for beginners

(As you probably know, a *menu* is a list of commands available to you at a particular time. *Commands*, of course, are things you can tell the computer to do.)

Apple insists on calling these *pull-down menus*—presumably on the theory that, in real life, things pop *up* (like toast) but *pull* down (like window shades). Well, first of all, that isn't always the case; for example, those oxygen masks stewardesses demonstrate before a flight pop *down* from overhead if the air pressure in the cabin drops (at least you hope they do.)

But even if nothing in the real world ever popped down, that's *still* what the Mac's menus do. You don't grab the menu title and pull the menu down over the Desktop; you *touch* the menu title with the pointer, press the mouse button and the menu *pops* down over the Desktop. The pointer stays up at the menu title, not down at the bottom of the menu where it would be if you were pulling it.

I could go on for days about this important point, but I'll control myself and move on. Here's what a pop-down menu looks like:

This is called the *Apple menu* (since so few people can pronounce). The first command on it always tells you about the software you're using—what version it is, who wrote it, etc. Sometimes you also get other information—it depends on the program you're using.

To select a command on this or any other menu, you slide the pointer down

About the Finder...
Suitcase ⌘K
Alarm Clock
Artisto
AutoSave
Calculator
Chooser
Control Panel
DiskTop
Find File
Key Caps
LaserStatus
Scrapbook
Super Note Pad

*esp. for
beginners*

it, keeping your finger on the mouse button. As you pass each command, it *highlights*—that is, instead of appearing as black letters on a white background, it appears as white letters on a black background. When the command you want is highlighted (as *About the Finder...* is above), you just release the mouse button and the command executes.

(All the other commands on the menu are for *desk accessories*—programs you can use without having to exit whatever software you're working with at the time.)

Here's the next menu on the menu bar:

As you can see, some of the commands on this menu are *dimmed* (or *grayed).* This means you can't use them at the present time—if you slide the pointer past them, they won't highlight. For example, *Print* is dimmed because we haven't picked a document to print.

File	
New Folder	⌘N
Open	⌘O
Print	
Close	⌘W
Get Info	⌘I
Duplicate	⌘D
Put Away	
Page Setup...	
Print Catalog...	
Eject	⌘E

Icons

The icon in the upper right corner of the Desktop shown on page 32 represents the hard disk that I'm running off of (on the Mac SE where I made these screen shots)—which, as you can see, is called *SEmore.* (You can change the names of most things on the Mac and make them whatever you want.) In the lower right corner is the *Trash* icon; this is where you put things when you don't want them any more.

There are various Desktops on the Mac, but the way to tell that you're at the basic one, the one created by the Finder, is to look for that Trash can in the lower right corner. Only the Finder's Desktop has it.

On the Desktop above, the Trash icon is white with black lines and lettering—which is the normal way for icons to look. But the disk icon is black with white lines and lettering; as with a command on a menu, that means it's *selected*.

Selecting

esp. for beginners

Selecting is the single most important concept for understanding how Mac software works. The basic two principles are:

1. *You always have to select something before you can do anything with it. (Apple calls this the "noun, then verb" or "hey, you—do this" approach. Another way to remember it is "select, then affect.")*

2. *Selecting, in and of itself, never alters anything.*

Trying to do something when nothing is selected, or with something different from what you think selected, is the cause of 90% of the confusion people have when learning to use the Mac.

I didn't have to select the *SEmore* icon because a hard disk is automatically selected when you start up from it. But let's say you want to select something else. To do that, you just put the pointer on it, then press and release the mouse button (this is called *clicking*).

In the screen on the next page, I've clicked on Trash; now it's selected and *SEmore* has been automatically deselected. (That's not inevitable, however—you can select more than one icon at a time by holding down the Shift key while clicking on them. This is called *shift-clicking*.)

You can also move icons around the Desktop. To do that, put the pointer on an icon, then press and hold the mouse button as you move the mouse. The icon will stick to the pointer until you release the mouse button. This is called *dragging*.

You can also rename icons, just by typing the new name while the icon is selected. You can use any character but the colon (:) in an icon name, including spaces. (More primitive computers like the PC normally don't let you use spaces in file names.)

Now you're ready for another basic concept: *Icons can (and often do) contain things.*

Windows

To see what's in an icon, you *open* it. To open an icon, you point to it and click the mouse button twice in rapid succession. This is called *double-clicking*.

You can also click once on the icon, go up to the File menu and choose the *Open* command, but that's a whole lot more trouble than double-clicking. There's also a third possibility. If you look at the *Open* command on the File menu above, you'll see that ⌘–O follows it. That cloverleaf symbol appears on a special key on the Mac keyboard and is called the *command* key.

⌘–O means that instead of moving the pointer up to the File menu, clicking the mouse button to make the menu pop down, going down the menu to the *Open* command, then releasing the mouse button, you can just hold down the ⌘ key, hit the O key and get the same result.

esp. for beginners

Double-clicking on the Trash icon (or using either of the other two techniques just described) produces this:

This is called a *window*. It's empty, because nothing has been thrown into Trash since we began working.

When you throw a file icon into Trash, it's kept there for a while in case you change your mind. If you do, you just open the Trash window (as we have here) and retrieve it. Icons only disappear from Trash when you do one of several things (which are described in the entry called *flushing the Trash* in Chapter 4).

In order to do anything with—or to—a window, it has to be *active* (selected). When it is, you'll see six horizontal lines in the *title bar* (which runs across the top of the window with the title in the middle).

A window is always active when it first opens (this is only logical, since you have to select its icon to open it). To select a different window—that is, to make a different window the active one—all you have to do is click anywhere in it. (The first click just activates the window; to select something in the window, you have to click again.)

A window must also be active for you to close it. You do that by clicking in the little *close box* at the left end of the title bar or choosing the *Close* command from the File menu.

esp. for
beginners

Another indication that a window is active is the gray _scroll bars_ that appear along the right side and across the bottom when the window contains more information than can be shown in it. Since there's nothing in the Trash window, we'll need to open another one to show you scroll bars.

To do that, we just go back to our old friend _SEmore,_ the hard disk icon, and ⌜Double-Click⌟ on it. That produces this:

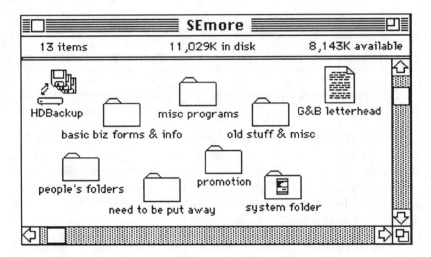

The gray area in the scroll bars, the small white boxes and the arrows are all tools for bringing the other icons in a window into view. (Sometimes you just get one scroll bar and not the other; it depends on where the missing information is.)

Programs, documents and folders

Now let's talk about the icons in the window. _HDBackup_ is a _program_ (in this case, a _utility_ that backs up the data from a hard disk). ⌜Double-Click⌟ on it and HDBackup will be _launched_ (put into memory). You'll be asked some questions about what you want to backup and where you want to put the copy.

G&B letterhead is a *data file* or *document* (in this case, a template for writing business letters that was created by the program Microsoft Works). Double-Click on it and it will first launch Works, then open itself so you can edit it, print it, etc. (More primitive machines won't automatically launch a program when you open a document created by it; you have to open the program first, then the document.)

The rest of the icons in this window are *folders*. You use them to organize your icons. Double-Click on any of them and it will open into a window that contains more icons—like the one below. You can put folders within folders to your heart's content—whatever you need to organize your work and make it easy to find.

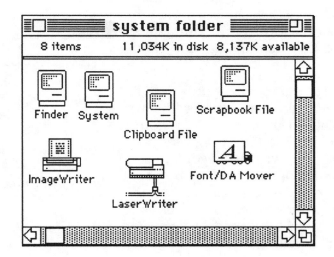

The system folder

The *system folder* is treated specially by the Mac. It's where the Mac looks for the basic software that tells it how to operate: the System file, the Finder, MultiFinder, the *drivers* that tell it how to control various kinds of printers, etc. (By the way, this tutorial assumes that you're running the Finder, not MultiFinder, which is what you should do when you're a beginner.)

Apple has announced plans to update the System and Finder every six months. (It's changes in these two programs that will make the screen shots and some of the things I say in this section out-of-date.)

You can modify the System yourself, by adding or removing *fonts* or *desk accessories* (see the chapters on these topics for more details).

Cutting and pasting

Two other files in the system folder are worth mentioning: the *Clipboard* and the *Scrapbook*. They're used for holding stuff you want to transfer from one place to another. You put things in and take things out of the Clipboard and the Scrapbook with three commands on the Edit menu: *Cut, Copy* and *Paste.*

To *cut* something, you select it (how you do that varies with the application), then pick the *Cut* command from the Edit menu—or just hit ⌘–X. Whatever you've selected disappears from its original location and is stored in Clipboard. (Many programs let you check the contents of Clipboard by choosing *Show Clipboard* from the Edit menu.)

Edit	
Undo	⌘Z
Cut	⌘X
Copy	⌘C
Paste	⌘V
Clear	
Select All	⌘A
Show Clipboard	

Copy (⌘–C) works the same way as *Cut,* except that the selected material stays in the original location in addition to moving to the Clipboard. To *paste* what you've cut or copied, you just indicate where you want it and hit ⌘–V— or select *Paste* from the Edit menu.

When you're working with text, a flashing vertical line called the *insertion point* marks the spot where the pasted material will be inserted. The insertion point is deposited by clicking with the I-beam pointer (⌶) .

You can cut and paste between most Mac programs. The amount of material you can transfer is usually only limited by the amount of memory that's free on your Mac. But since the Clipboard will only hold one selection at a time, each time you cut or copy something new, the previous material is flushed (lost irretrievably).

esp. for
beginners

On the other hand, since things stay in the Clipboard until you flush them, you can paste the same thing many different places—as long as you remember not to cut or copy anything else in the interim.

If you simply want to get rid of something, you can just cut it and never paste it; it will disappear the next time you cut or copy. Or you can just hit the [Backspace] key after it's selected and it will disappear without even passing through the Clipboard.

A good definition for the Clipboard is *a temporary holding area for cut or copied material.* The *Scrapbook*, on the other hand, is a permanent file for cut or copied material. What you put in the Scrapbook stays there not only when you add more stuff but also when you turn the machine off. (You can, of course, remove things from the Scrapbook whenever you want.) Since you use *Cut, Copy* and *Paste* to get things into and out of the Scrapbook, they all pass through the Clipboard on the way.

If you're transferring just a few things, it's easier to move them one at a time with the Clipboard (that is, to simply cut and paste them). If you have several things to transfer at one time, or if you want them to be available for pasting for more than one work session, the Scrapbook is more convenient.

Ways to view files

Files are only represented by icons on the Desktop (that is, in the Finder); in most other places, they're identified simply by their names. The View menu lets you display documents by names instead of icons on the Desktop as well.

esp. for beginners

As you can see, you can list them:

- in alphabetical order *(by Name)*

- in order of when you last changed them, with the most recent one first *(by Date)*

- *by Size,* from biggest to smallest

- *by Kind,* with all the documents of a particular sort (applications programs, folders, MacWrite documents, MacPaint documents, etc.) grouped together

- *by Small Icon* (just the same as by icon except that the icons are smaller)

Dialog boxes

When you choose the *Print* command from the File menu, the Mac gives you what's called a *dialog box* (called that because the Mac is telling you something and asking for a response). Dialog boxes look a little like windows but what you can do in—and with—them is much more limited.

Here's an example of a print dialog box. (They vary depending on what printer, and also what version of the *printer driver* software, you're using.)

```
┌──────────────────────────────────────────────────────────────┐
│ LaserWriter  "LaserWriter II NTX"          v5.1   │   OK    │ │
│ Copies: 1          Pages: ● All ○ From:     To:   │ Cancel  │ │
│ Cover Page:  ● No ○ First Page ○ Last Page        │  Help   │ │
│ Paper Source: ● Paper Cassette  ○ Manual Feed                │
└──────────────────────────────────────────────────────────────┘
```

The circular and oval areas are called *buttons.* You click on them to tell the Mac what you want. The three rectangles are called *text boxes;* you type information into them (numbers, in this case, but in other dialog boxes, words as well).

Dialog boxes can get more complex than this. For example, if you choose the *Open* command from the File menu while inside Works, you'll get something that looks like this:

esp. for beginners

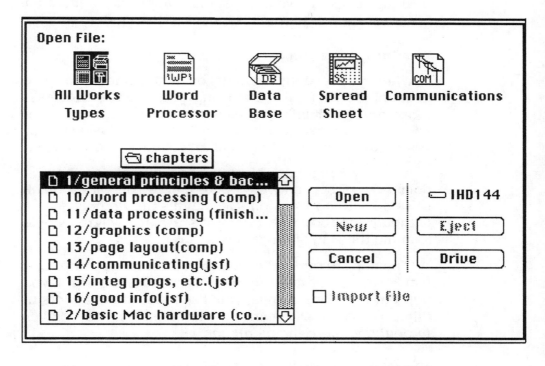

In the lower left corner of this dialog box is a smaller *list box.* You can scroll through the documents listed in it and open them, either by double-clicking on their names or by using the *Open* button on the right.

There are several ways to scroll through the document names. The two most basic are to use the scroll bar or to drag down through the list of names. (For other ways, see the entry titled *keyboard shortcuts in dialog boxes* in Chapter 4.)

Above the list box is the name of the folder which contains these documents (it's called *chapters*). On the right is the name of the disk on which the *chapters* folder

**esp. for
beginners**

is located *(IHD144)*. Clicking on the *Drive* button switches
you between disks. When the disk or folder changes, so do
the names in the list box.

The Open dialog box isn't as elegant as the Finder's
Desktop, but once you're inside an application, it's a lot
faster to use it than to go back out to the Finder.

The "nothing screen"

When you're done working on a document, the File
menu of the program you're using gives you two choices—
Close or *Quit*. Quitting takes you out of the program and
back to the Finder (that is, to the Desktop). Closing leaves
you in the program, so you can open another document.

In many programs, closing a document (or the last
document, if several were open) leaves you with a blank
Desktop with no icons on it. I call this the *nothing screen*
(although nobody else does); it's a place where people
learning the Mac often get lost.

The thing to remember is that no Desktop is completely
blank—there's always the menu bar across the top. If you
pop down various menus, you'll see that there are lots of
things you can do. So here's the last basic principle: *When
in doubt, explore the menu bar.*

Shutting Down

When you're done working and want to turn off the Mac,
the first thing to do is to get back
to the Desktop (to the Finder, in
other words). Then choose *Shut
Down* from the Special menu. In
a second or so, the Mac will tell
you it's OK to turn off your machine.

Summary

esp. for
beginners

Here's a recap of the most important principles to keep in mind when using the Mac:

- You have to select something before you can do something.

- By itself, selecting never alters anything.

- To open icons, `Double-Click` .

- When in doubt, explore the menu bar.

(For a discussion of the theory and principles behind the Mac's user interface, a good book is *Human Interface Guidelines: The Apple Desktop Interface,* written by people at Apple and published by Addison-Wesley. Although it's primarily aimed at programmers, it's quite accessible and very interesting.)

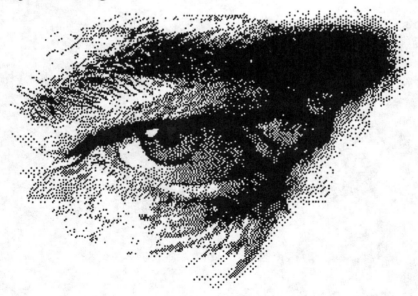

From the WetPaint clip art collection.
Copyright © 1988–89 by Dubl-Click Software Inc.
All rights reserved.

Chapter 2

Basic Mac hardware

Tips on the Mac II

⚫ *the opening chord* (AN)

When you turn a Mac II on—by pushing the button in the center top of the keyboard (it may be elsewhere on third-party keyboards)—it makes a musical sound. (I wanted to tell you exactly what chord it is, but I never got around to finding out. If you know, write and tell me.)

This chord tells you that all is right with the machine (or at least that certain basic things are right). If something's wrong, the notes sound separately rather than together.

⚫ *a choice of beeps* (AN)

The Mac II lets you choose a different sound for the beep (by changing the Alert Sound Setting in the Sound section of the Control Panel). As of this writing, Apple gives you a choice of three sounds beyond the Mac's normal beep: a monkey's screech, a *Clink-Klank* (which sounds just like its name) and a *Bong,* which probably should be called a *Boing,* since it sounds a lot like Gerald McBoing Boing's favorite sound.

very good feature

I favor Bong, because it's the funniest and also the softest. Bong lets me set Speaker Volume to 7, so I can hear music and sound effects nice and loud but still not be startled by loud beeps while I'm working. (The Simple Beep is the loudest of the four sounds, followed by Clink-Klank and Monkey.) You can install many more choices for beep sounds with a piece of $10 shareware called SoundMaster.

⚫ *the II's fan* (AN)

Before I got a Mac II, I was afraid the fan was going to drive me crazy (the one on the original SE certainly did). But I've found the Mac II's fan to be a lot better—not nearly as nice as silence, you understand, but quite bearable.

That's because it puts out *white noise* (sounds at all frequencies) or something pretty close to it. White noise drowns out other noises and is even considered soothing by some. I wouldn't go that far, but you can actually work in front of a Mac II.

🍎 *don't double-up on disks* (AN)

important warning

It's a lot less obvious when there's a disk in the Mac II's floppy drive than it is on the SE or the Plus. Several times I've tried to stick a second one in and once or twice I've actually succeeded (the second disk slides in over the first at an angle).

I've always been able to get the second disk out, but this can't be good for the drive, so pay special attention to whether that drive slot is occupied before you blithely shove a disk into it.

🍎 *opening the case* (AN)

Because the Mac II has those six lovely expansion slots, you're probably going to end up using them. To do that, you'll have to pull the cover off, and that's slightly more difficult than it should be.

The first thing to do is remove the small screw in the center top of the back of the machine. Then push in the two latches at either side of the top (also on the back of the machine) and tilt the cover forward. At a certain point, you'll hear a cracking noise, like you broke something. Don't worry, you didn't—that's just the normal sound the II's cover makes when opening.

important warning

However—make sure you didn't accidentally leave an ejected floppy in the disk drive. If you did, you won't be able to get the top off, and trying will pry the disk up inside the drive.

When you put the cover back on, you have to take some care to line up the front of the cover with the front of the case. After a while you'll see what goes where, but it's not terribly obvious. Sometimes the cover catches in the back but not the front; when that happens you can usually just push down on the front and snap it into place (even after you've reattached the little screw in the back).

⚫ *too fast?* (AN)

The II's speed is usually a delight (see *tech specs* below for the reasons behind it) but one place where it's actually annoying is in list boxes. The names go by so fast you sometimes have to go back and forth several times to get the one you want in the window.

⚫ *here's a trick that will amaze your friends* (AN)

Because the Mac II can take very large screens (see the monitors section below for details), it's actually possible to lose track of where the pointer is. The easiest way to find it is simply to move it around a bunch, but a much more dramatic approach is to hold down the following four keys all at once: *control-*Option ⌘ *-spacebar.*

gossip/ trivia

(I could tell you what happens, but that would be like giving the plot of a movie away. It's much more fun to actually see it on the screen.)

⚫ *clearing parameter RAM on the Mac II* (CJW)

The Mac's battery provides power to a special area of memory called *parameter RAM* (or *PRAM*). It addition to keeping track of the date, time and various Control Panel settings, parameter RAM also remembers what's connected to the printer and modem ports on the back of the Mac.

Early versions of the Mac II had a bug that messed up *parameter RAM* when an application crashed, and other things can confuse PRAM as well. One result can be that your Mac will lose track of an internal hard disk; its icon won't show up on the screen. You can often recover from

very hot tip

this dilemma by "zapping" the PRAM—that is, making it revert to its default settings.

On all Macs up to and including the Plus, you did that by removing the battery for about ten minutes. But this won't work on SEs and Mac IIs because their long-life (seven-year) lithium batteries are soldered onto the machine's mother-board. Here's what to do instead:

Restart from a floppy that contains a System file and Finder. Pop down the ⌘ menu, then hold down Shift Option ⌘ while choosing Control Panel. You'll get a message tells you you're about to zap the PRAM and gives you a chance to cancel. Just click on OK—the only problem with zapping the PRAM is that you'll have to reset a few settings on the Control Panel.

The next time you restart the machine, the icon for your internal hard disk will reappear (unless there's something seriously wrong with the disk) and most—but usually not all—of the settings in parameter RAM will revert to their default values (time and date are never affected).

⌘ *installing the programmer's switch* (AN)

very
hot
tip

How is the Mac II different from all other Macs? On all other Macs, we install the programmer's switch on the left side of the Mac with the loose end of the buttons facing down, while on the Mac II we install it on the right side with the loose ends of the buttons facing up. (On both machines we insert it in the rearmost vents.)

⌘ *tech specs* (DC)

very good
feature

The Mac II's processor chip is a 68020 running at 16 MHz (the SE and the Plus use a 68000 running at about 8 MHz). In addition, it has a numeric coprocessor chip that speeds up any task that involves a lot of computation—like graph-ics processing or reformatting text.

Unlike the SE, which has only one expansion slot, the II is a completely open machine, with high-speed NuBus expansion slots for additional coprocessors, video boards and the like. NuBus is designed to accommodate multiple processors running together in the same machine—so you could, for example, run a DOS program concurrently with a Mac program, each in its own window. NuBus will also let you use the II to control devices like cameras and video disks.

very good feature

Apple's video board for the II has a resolution of 640 by 480 pixels and accommodates both color and monochrome monitors. (Video boards from third parties offer much more than that.) By expanding its memory, you can display as many as 256 colors simultaneously.

There are color QuickDraw routines in the II's ROMs and any program that uses them will work with any monitor, thus freeing the developer from having to write dozens of separate drivers. You can hook up several monitors at one time and the Mac II will automatically treat them as one large screen (the way Radius monitors do). So, for example, you could have a full-screen color image on one monitor and monochrome text on another.

Like the SE and the Plus, the II comes with one meg of RAM standard, but it can address up to sixteen megs (as opposed to four). Sixteen megs isn't a gigabyte, but you can do some pretty amazing stuff with that much memory, including some fairly sophisticated artificial intelligence.

Tips on the SE

♦ *quieting the SE* (FT)

The fans on early SE's were very noisy because Apple used a cheap "squirrel cage" fan (a rotating drum with slots in it). As if the noise weren't enough, the fans caused some very annoying screen jitters. Apple never admitted the

very bad feature

screen problems were caused by the fan, but quietly replaced it with a better one.

If you have an old SE with the cheap fan, you can replace it with a new one; the Apple kit (part number 076-0311) runs about $90. But here's at least one cheaper alternative—the $50 SE Silencer from Mobius, a bladed fan that runs slower than the original fan and has a two-year warranty.

The installation is relatively simple and should take about 15 or 20 minutes. But be careful not to zap any chips with static electricity; watch out for high voltage around the picture tube; and make sure you don't break the neck off tube (as one friend of Arthur's—who shall, to his great relief, remain nameless—did twice). Also be aware that once you open the SE, its warranty is voided.

I was amazed at how quiet my SE was after I installed the fan. I could even hear the fan on my external monitor.

🍎 *installing the programmer's switch* (AN)

See this same entry title in the Mac II section above.

🍎 *how to open the SE's case* (DC)

The original designers of the Macintosh never imagined that users would want to open their machines to add the hard disks, fans and other goodies that many of us consider necessities. In fact, you need special tools just to open the case.

important warning

(There's a good reason for this. The Mac contains high-voltage components that can give you the shock of your life, and possibly even end it. Continue reading this tip only if you know where they are and how to avoid them. We provide this information because it's both useful and commonly available, and because many Mac owners do routinely open the case on their Macs. But we don't recommend this practice.)

The screwdriver used to open the Mac case needs to have a Torx T-15 tip and an 8" shaft. Apple sells this tool to dealers along with a "splitter" to pry apart the two parts of the case. The splitter is not commonly available. The next best tool is an architect's three-sided ruler.

To open the case, set the Mac on its face on a smooth surface. Use the long screwdriver to remove the five screws on the back. Two are deep in the handle (hence, the long shaft), two are just above the cable connectors and the fifth is hidden behind the battery cover.

Then use the architect's ruler to gently separate the two parts of the case. An aluminum RF shield fits over the cable connectors and may come off when you remove the case. Just replace it before you replace the back of the case.

clearing parameter RAM on the SE (AN)

See the equivalent entry in the Mac II section above (ignore the stuff that only applies to the II).

tech specs (DC)

The SE is built around a 68000 processor chip running at 7.83 MHz. The system board contains one custom chip that integrates the tasks of nineteen chips on its predecessor, the Mac Plus. This makes the SE both faster and more reliable. In addition to the Mac's basic software, the SE's 256K ROMs contain the Mac's system fonts (12-point Chicago, 9- and 12-point Geneva, 9-point Monaco) and twelve other fonts for use with European languages and Japanese.

very good feature

There's also an expansion slot for plugging in cards that let the SE run DOS, drive a large external monitor or connect to an expansion box with several more slots. It has a 100-watt power supply (the Plus's was inadequate and was always blowing) and seven-year lithium battery soldered onto the motherboard.

You can buy an SE with two internal 800K floppy drives or with one floppy drive and a 20MB internal SCSI hard disk. (To discourage third-party internal hard disks, Apple doesn't sell the SE without a drive in the second spot.) The floppy drives are quite fast, but sometimes the data they write can't be read by other drives.

very bad feature

Far and away the worst feature of the original SE was its cheap, noisy, "squirrel-cage" fan, which made the machine sound like a a beehive someone just hit with a stick. Responding to a roar of protest about the racket made by this SE fan, Apple finally replaced it with a much quieter one.

The SE was an evolutionary product, correcting some of the deficiencies of the original Mac while maintaining many of its nice features—small footprint, ease of use, attractive appearance and affordability (but not silent operation!).

Tips on the Plus and earlier Macs

⁜ *upgrade path to a Mac Plus* (DC)

If you have an original 128K or a 512 Mac and want to upgrade it to a Plus, you may be confused about what's involved. There are three steps, but you can choose to take only one or two of them.

The first step involves upgrading from the 64K to the 128K ROMs and from the 400K to the 800K drive; to do it, you must also have at least 512K of RAM. Any Apple dealer can do this step, usually while you wait (if you call a few days ahead to make an appointment).

very hot tip

This step is definitely worth taking; it will make your machine run more quietly (the 800K Sony drives are wonderful) and faster (because both the drives and the QuickDraw routines in the ROMs are faster). It's also a prerequisite for either of the next two steps.

The second step is to replace the original motherboard (main circuit board) and to go up to 1 meg of RAM. The back of the Mac's case also gets replaced with one that has a SCSI port and the small, round connectors.

This third step is to get a Mac Plus keyboard, which has arrow keys and a built-in numeric keypad. (You can do this without step 2, but not without step 1.) Some people love the Mac Plus keyboard; other people can't stand how big it is, and the fact that some keys are missing and others are smaller. In any case, your get to keep your old keyboard, so you can always go back to it.

When you've done all three steps, the only thing you'll be missing is the Macintosh Plus logo that goes on the front of the machine.

◉ *how to open the case* (AN)

The entry in the previous section on how to open the SE's case applies to all earlier Macs as well.

◉ *replacing the battery* (DC)

The battery in the back of a Mac Plus, 512K or 128K Mac will eventually run down and need to be replaced. (Usually it's good for about two years.) The proper replacement batteries are: DuraCell PX21, Eveready 523BP, Panasonic PX21 and Ray-O-Vac RPX21. They should cost about $5 and should be fairly easy to find.

If you can't replace the battery immediately, you can still continue to use your Mac. Turn it off, take out the battery, turn it back on, reset the time, date and other Control Panel settings and reselect the serial ports. You'll have to repeat this every time you turn on the Mac, until you replace the battery. (For more on what the battery does, see the entry on *parameter RAM* in the Mac II section above.)

⚫ *alternative keyboard cables for pre-SE Macs* (DC)

The keyboard cable for the Mac Plus, 512K Mac and 128K Macs looks just like a telephone cord but it isn't—the wires in the Mac keyboard cable connect straight through from one end to the other, while in a telephone cord, they twist. So if you want a longer keyboard cable, you can't just substitute a phone cord.

Lon Poole recommends Your Affordable Software Company (see Appendix B for their address). They sell a 12-foot and 25-foot keyboard cable (though why anyone would want to type 25 or even 12 feet away from a 9-inch monitor is beyond us).

⚫ *worn feet on the pre-SE mouse* (DC)

The two small feet on the bottom of the old, pre-ADB mouse will wear down eventually. You can extend the time this takes by moving your mouse on a surface softer than the average desktop—like a mouse pad (which are available for less than $10 at just about any computer store).

very hot tip

But what if the feet on your mouse are already worn? One solution is to attach small pieces of Velcro (the loop, not the hook, kind) on either side of the worn feet, with the fuzzy side facing down.

Monitors

⚫ *bit-mapping and QuickDraw* (AN)

very good feature

One of the Mac's greatest features, and one that Mac users tend to take for granted, is how quickly all the graphic elements on its screen can be manipulated—created, redrawn, moved around. For example, windows can be shrunk, stretched, squeezed, overlapped and moved around with amazing rapidity, especially given how much detail there is in them.

This is possible because the Mac's screen is bit-mapped—
that is, for every little dot on the screen (called a *pixel),*
there's a little switch in memory that controls it. Since you
can control the screen directly, you can change it quickly.

But it takes more than hardware to get a screen image as
responsive and fast as the Mac's. Software is the key and in
this case the software is QuickDraw. Developed by Apple
programming genius Bill Atkinson (also the creator of
HyperCard), QuickDraw is certainly a milestone in the
history of personal computers. It makes your life more
pleasant every time you touch the mouse.

❤ *black-and-white* (AN)

The Mac displays black letters on a white background,
thank God. I've never been able to understand the supposed advantage of all these green (or amber) screens. It's
not natural, nor any good for your eyes, to look at one color
all the time. People suggest putting some red object near a
green screen to compensate, but why bother with all that?
A white surface reflects all colors, black contains all colors,
and black on white is what we're used to looking at on
paper.

❤ *black-on-gray* (AN)

One problem with black-on-white is that, because of the
large white area on the screen, it increases the amount of
flicker (see the entry on refresh rate below); that makes it
harder to look at the screen for a long time. This is
particularly troublesome on very large monitors, where it
would be a relief to be able to switch to white-on-black, at
least some of the time.

One thing you can and should do to make the screen
easier on your eyes is turn the brightness down. A bright
white background is very hard to look at—you want black
on gray, not black on white. Most people keep their
computer screens too bright, which puts a real strain on
their eyes.

**very
hot
tip**

Another important step is to keep your room as dark as possible, and eliminate glare (reflections on the screen). If daylight does seep in, or if there are lights you can't turn off, turn the brightness up to compensate. But a dimly lit room and a black-on-gray screen are ideal.

⬛ *protecting the phosphor* (AN)

⚠
important
warning

The phosphor that's painted on the inside of your screen and glows when the electron beam hits it can become exhausted from too much use, leaving dark spots on your screen. So it's a good idea not to leave an image visible on your screen except when you're actually using the computer. But you don't want to be constantly turning the Mac on and off, because that's hard on the electronics.

That's where programs called *screen blankers* come in. They keep track of how long it's been since you hit a key or the mouse button and black out your screen automatically after a certain amount of time—which you select—has passed. They also create some sort of moving pattern on the screen (fireworks, stars, a clock that moves around) so you know the Mac is on. Hitting any key or the mouse brings back the image.

The bigger the screen is, the more important a screen blanker is. Fortunately, most big monitors come with their own built in.

If you telecommunicate, make sure any screen blanker you use checks the modem port for activity. If it doesn't, and you're sending or receiving a file when it goes into action, the connection will be lost and you'll have to start the file transfer all over again.

AutoBlack is one shareware screen blanker that does check the modem port. It bounces an analog clock (the kind with hands) around your screen to let you know it's there. AutoBlack only costs $5 (the address is in Appendix B), but if you end up using the program, send $10 or $20; no useful piece of software is worth just $5.

If you don't want to use a screen blanker, you can simply turn the brightness down when you get up from the Mac. On all Macs through the SE, the brightness control is on the front of the machine, to the left, just underneath the Apple logo (🍎).

*esp. for
beginners*

Now don't feel that I'm patronizing you by telling you something as basic as that. I was once at the house of a (very intelligent) writer friend who uses her Mac extensively. I saw an image on the Mac's screen, so I casually walked over and turned the brightness down to black. She had no idea what had happened and totally freaked out. I showed her how to adjust the brightness, but she wouldn't calm down until I turned it back up and left it there. Even then she had the sneaking suspicion that I'd done some sort of subtle but irreparable damage to her machine.

*gossip/
trivia*

External monitors almost always have brightness controls as well (although often they're not as conveniently located). But screen blankers are really the way to go.

🍎 *refresh rate* (AN)

One of the most important characteristics in a monitor is its *refresh rate*—how often it redraws the image on its screen. The refresh rate is measured in *hertz* (times per second), which is abbreviated *Hz*.

If the refresh rate is too slow, you get *flicker* (also called *strobe)*—which means you can actually see the image being redrawn. Your peripheral vision is particularly sensitive to flicker; another good way to bring it out is to wave your hand in front of the screen.

*very
hot
tip*

Regular house current alternates at 60 Hz; if you can see the flicker in fluorescent lights, a refresh rate of 60 Hz may be too slow for you. The refresh rate for the regular 9" screen found on all Macs through the SE is 60 Hz, but because the screen is small, most people find this acceptable.

The larger a monitor is, the more critical the refresh rate is. Apple uses 67 Hz on its 12" and 13" monitors, and other companies go up to 72 Hz on their larger monitors.

● *screen filters* (AN)

Many people feel that it's important to put a glass or mesh filter over the Mac's screen to cut down on glare and on certain low-frequency radiation that may have harmful health effects. This is a big subject and we're not going to go into it here, but if you want to find out about it, write or call Ergonomic Computer Products in San Francisco. They sell excellent products at good prices and are extremely well informed. Their customer service is great too.

● *monochrome, gray-scale, color* (LP)

Monitors can either be monochrome, gray-scale or color. On a monochrome monitor, each pixel (dot) on the screen is either black or white. Gray patterns are simulated by varying the number of black-and-white pixels in a particular area.

On a gray-scale monitor, the shade of *individual* pixels can be varied. This allows for true halftones and real shading. You can easily tell a gray-scale monitor from a monochrome monitor by checking the ● in the upper left corner of the screen. If it's black, it's a monochrome monitor; if you see the six bands of gray in the ●, it's a gray-scale monitor.

On a color monitor, both the shade and the hue of each pixel can be varied. Color monitors require a color video card and color QuickDraw ROMs (or some other way of converting color QuickDraw calls to color).

● *big-screen basics* (AN)

I was never one who thought the Mac's screen was too small. I love its crisp, readable image and recognize that resolution (the number of *pixels*—dots—on the screen) is what's important, not the physical size of the screen. (To realize that, all you need to do is walk up close to a big-screen color TV—one of those room-filling monsters, I mean—and watch the snarling, boiling lines battle each other. It's a real 20th-century nightmare image.)

Still, it's annoying only to be able to see about a third of a standard 8-1/2 x 11 page at a time (although no more annoying than the screen on most PCs, where you see no more than that—and sometimes even less). With a Mac II, larger external monitors are standard equipment, and you can also get them for the SE, Plus and other Macs.

Like TVs, the size of monitors is given in diagonal inches—the distance from one corner of the tube to another. Since not all tubes are the same shape, however, two 19″ screens can be very different. The basic distinction is between tall and wide screens—or *portrait* and *landscape,* as they're sometimes called.

So you'll actually know more about a screen if you measure its width and height rather than simply rely on its advertised (diagonal) size. But even the width and height won't tell you what you want to know about a screen's capacity, because the size of the pixels—and therefore the number of them—also varies from monitor to monitor. In other words, they have different numbers of *dots per inch (dpi).*

So now let's say you know a monitor's dpi and the height and width of its screen. You still need to know how wide a border it leaves around the image (it can be half an inch or more). So my advice is to leave your measuring tape at home and think in terms of pixels.

The first and most basic thing you want to know about a screen (aside from obvious things like whether it's black-and-white or color) is how many pixels it displays horizontally and vertically. The original Mac screen (used on the 128K, 512K, Mac Plus and SE) has 512 pixels across and 342 down, and displays them at 72 dpi. Simple division tells you, therefore, that it will display an image 7.1 inches wide and 4.8 inches high. Just think of it as 7 x 5.

(4.8 inches is actually about 44% of the 11-inch length of a standard sheet of paper, not a third. But by the time you allow for the menu bar, the horizontal scroll bar and so on, it takes just about three screenfuls to display a page.)

What size the 7 x 5 image on the original Mac screen ends up actually being on paper is a complex matter and depends both on what software and what printer you're using. But, in general, the screen image corresponds fairly closely in both size and shape to the image on paper.

The best measure of a screen's capacity is the total number of pixels it displays. If you calculate that for the original Mac screen (512 x 342), you get 175,104. Monitors available as of this writing are capable of displaying up to two million pixels—more than *fourteen* times the capacity of the original Mac screen—although they usually do it at more dots per inch than 72.

I personally think 72 dpi is too large. Once you get used to 82 dpi or 92 dpi (and it just takes a hour or two), 72 dpi looks ridiculously big and clunky.

very hot tip

When comparing the price of monitors, forget about screen size (unless you have some particular reason for caring about it). What you're interested in is how many pixels you get per dollar. Just multiply the number of pixels across by the number of pixels down, then divide the price of the monitor into that. The bigger the resulting number, the better.

Pixels per dollar can vary quite widely. Among the four monitors reviewed below, the figures range from less than 200 to more than 800 (based on list prices).

That's about all I have to say about how much a screen can display. The next question is, how good does that display look? I originally planned to talk about all sorts of technical issues, but monitors are a lot like speakers—you can look at specs all day long, but the only way to buy speakers is to listen to them, and the only way to buy monitors is to look at them, ideally side-by-side.

What you're looking for is a crisp, high-contrast, rock-solid image—one that isn't washed-out and that doesn't waver or flicker. There are some pretty good monitors out there, but there's still room for improvement.

⚫ *Apple's "High-Resolution" monitors* (AN)

Despite their names, these monitors for the Mac II (a 13" color and a 12" monochrome) are low-resolution compared to the competition. Both display 640 x 480 pixels at 72 dpi—not even twice the resolution of the regular Mac screen.

These monitors also are more expensive than third-party equivalents. The monochrome monitor only gives you 195 pixels per dollar (based on its current list price of $900).

⚫ *Radius monitors* (AN)

Radius makes a line of monochrome monitors designed by two Mac wizards, Burrell Smith (hardware) and Andy Hertzfeld (software). They're the crispest and most con-trasty of any Mac monitors I've seen; next to them, other big screens tend to look washed out.

very good feature

Hertzfeld's software is a real plus. You get tear-off menus in all applications, a built-in screen saver you can set in one-minute increments from 1 minute to 59 minutes (or for 5 seconds), screen dumps you can crop, and menus in larger-than-normal type (the one feature I don't use).

very good feature

The monitor displays 1152 x 882 pixels on its 19" screen (1,016,064 pixels total—5.8 times the regular Mac screen's). This gives you an effective display area 10.75" high by 14" wide. This isn't quite enough for two 8-1/2 x 11 pages, but it is if you don't need to see the margins (don't forget that many publications are smaller than 8-1/2 x 11).

There are 82 dots to the inch (better than the normal 72 dpi, I think) and the refresh rate is a refreshing (sorry) 72 Hz—the highest available on any Mac monitor at the present time.

very bad feature

One negative feature of the Two Page Display is that the brightness and contrast controls are in the back. Even though I have long arms, it's still a reach to get my hand back to the controls while keeping my eyes where they can see the screen from anything like the same angle at which I normally look at it. For many people, it'll be so hard they'll have to alternate between adjusting the control and looking at the result—a ridiculous inconvenience.

The Two Page Display currently lists for $2400, which gives you about 425 pixels per dollar. There's also a gray-scale version (current list, $3600) and a line of single-page displays ($1700 for the Plus and SE, $1800 for the II).

I produced this book on a Mac II with a Radius Two Page Display because I was convinced it had the crispest picture around. (The Full Page Display's picture is just as good.)

● *Moniterm's Viking monitors* (AN)

very good feature

For great resolution, try the Viking 1 from Moniterm, a two-page monochrome display that works with either the SE or the II. It gives you 1280 by 960 pixels, for a total of 1,228,800—more than seven times the regular Mac screen. This is more than enough to display two full 8-1/2 x 11 pages; in fact, when you ask whatever software you're using to fit both pages on the screen instead of showing them actual size, they *expand!*

Pixels are displayed at 92 dots per inch, which means the characters on the screen are about 70% the size they'll end up on paper. So 12-point type appears as 8.5-point, 10-point as 7-point and 9-point as 6.5-point. In general, type down to about 6-point is readable (that's even true of small fonts like Times; big fonts like Helvetica and Benguiat are readable even smaller). *Greeking* (indicating the type rather than showing the actual letters) isn't the end of the world for type below 9-point, so I don't see any problem with 92 dpi.

At its current list price of $2000, the Viking 1 gives you about 615 pixels per dollar.

There's also a 24" version, the Viking 2400. It has the same number of pixels (who'd need more?) but they're at the regular 72 dpi instead of the Viking 1's 92 dpi. And I also think a 24" screen would be overpowering—not to mention that it costs $3000 vs. the Viking 1's $2000 (there's also a 19" gray-scale Viking for $2400).

The image on the Viking monitors isn't as crisp and contrasty as on the Radiuses, but it's certainly adequate for most applications. The refresh rate is 66 Hz. The monitors are made by Moniterm itself, which also supplies them to many other monitor companies.

very good feature

The Viking monitors seem to be well-made and Moniterm appears to be a well-run company, staffed by competent people (even the receptionist knew the answer when I called with a question).

🍎 *LaserView monitors* (AN)

This two-page monochrome display for the SE and the II, available in both 15" and 19" sizes, has a fairly crisp picture (but not as crisp as on the Radiuses). The refresh rate is only 60 Hz, so you may have a problem with flicker.

The software lets you choose between two resolutions— 832 x 600 (about 500,000 pixels; 2.85 times the normal Mac screen) or 1664 x 1200 (about 2,000,000 pixels; more than *eleven!* times the regular Mac screen). That's a lot of pixels, but they're awfully small; at high resolution, things can get awfully hard to read.

At current list prices of $2300 for the SE and $2400 for the II, the LaserView (at high resolution) offers about 850 pixels per dollar.

⬤ *MacLarger* (LP)

MacLarger is a 12" Apple IIGS monitor that's been modified to work on a Mac with a 9" screen (SE, Plus, etc.). Since those Macs don't have external video connectors, Power R (MacLarger's maker) supplies an adapter to plug into the logic board. Everything you need to do the job (including tools) is supplied and the directions are very easy to follow. Even if you've never had your Mac apart before, the job should take no more than half an hour.

MacLarger doesn't give you any more pixels, just bigger ones. The diagonal measurement of your screen increases from 8.55" to 11.09", giving you a picture that's 70% bigger. It lists for $450 with the video adaptors. When you want several monitors all displaying the same thing (as in a classroom situation), you can easily chain them. Additional monitors without the video adaptors are $350 and you can connect them with a couple of dollars' worth of cables from Radio Shack.

If you're looking for something with the official Apple brand name that's a piece of cake to install, this is the one. But if you want better quality for $50 less, see the next entry.

⬤ *Nuvotech EasyView* (LP)

This monitor is designed to work with any 9"-screen Mac, from the 128K to the SE. Installing its video adapter is somewhat more complicated than MacLarger's; no tools are supplied and dealer installation is recommended. But unlike the MacLarger, which is a composite monitor, the EasyView uses *TTL* (transistor-transistor logic), which is more expensive but produces a better picture. (Here again, you just get bigger pixels, not more of them.)

Although it's called a 14" monitor, the EasyView displays exactly the same size picture as MacLarger; it just has a much larger black border. The picture is sharper than MacLarger's and exceptionally linear (i.e., the lines it displays are straight). It also has a reverse video switch and a nice swivel base. The list price is $400.

Assuming your dealer employs competent technicians, and assuming you're willing to pay for professional installation, you'll see the difference with this set.

⌘ *Sher-Mark Anti-Glare Magnification Screen* (LP)

This isn't a monitor at all; it's a Fresnel lens that enlarges the screen to the same 11" diagonal size the two sets above do. Manufactured by Polaroid, it doesn't give you anywhere near the the same picture quality as a real monitor, but consider the advantages:

- Installation takes less than a minute.

- You don't have to open your Mac.

- The lens is completely portable.

- It doesn't tie up an electrical outlet.

- It doesn't take up valuable desk space.

- It only costs $90.

⌘ *Stepping Out II* (AN)

For yet another approach to stretching the Mac's screen, see the entry on this program in Chapter 8.

⌘ *Test Pattern Generator* (AN)

If you really want to compare monitors, you need this nifty piece of software written by *Macintosh Bible* contributor Larry Pina. In addition to testing a monitor every way you can imagine (and several you can't), it also lets you measure the speed of printers.

very good feature

This piece of shareware is very well done. You can get it in all the regular places (bulletin boards, user groups, etc) or by sending $10 (a real bargain) to Larry at 47 Meadow Road, Westport MA 02790.

bargain

❡ Computer Friends' color video boards (SH)

In early 1987, this small Portland company introduced the SuperChroma color system (which works on any Mac except the 128K and the XL) and a basic but adequate color paint program. The screen flickers, but it's wonderful to be able to see and use color on a 512K Mac. The video board is $1500, the color monitor $650 and the optional *genlock* board (for freezing video frames) is $1500.

bargain

Computer Friends also had the first video board for the Mac II; called TV Producer, it's still the least expensive one. TV Producer lets you import images from a VCR or video camera and export them to a VCR. Prices run from $600 to $1500, depending on the quality of the signal. Genlock will be available soon (probably by the time you read this).

❡ multiple screens(AN)

If you have two or more monitors connected to a Mac, icons for them will show up in the Monitor section of the Control Panel. To get more control over them, hold down the [Option] key when you click on the Monitor cdev. Make sure you keep the happy-face icon on the same screen as the menu bar. To move both screen icons together, hold down the [Option] key.

Keyboards

❡ Apple's ADB keyboards (DC/AN)

Since the original small Mac keyboard was the best either Dale or Arthur had ever typed on, it was inevitable that Apple would discontinue it. It was replaced by the somewhat inferior ADB keyboards, which work on the SE, Mac II, Apple II GS and, no doubt, on future machines as well.

There are two varieties—the standard keyboard and the extended, which has fifteen special-function keys and is designed specifically for connecting to mainframe computers. Both have a control key (so you can run DOS software, should you take leave of your senses and wish to do that), arrow keys (for all five or six people who prefer them to a mouse) and a numeric keypad (another thing most people don't need). Because of their width, both these keyboards make operating the mouse more uncomfortable.

very bad feature

The keyboards are called *ADB* because they connect to the *Apple Desktop bus.* There are a couple of advantages to this approach. The computer doesn't have to spend as much time scanning the keyboard for input and you can hook up multiple keyboards and mice to the same computer, which can be useful for one-on-one training.

the impossible dream—a NIBMO keyboard (AN)

Apple's habit of changing of keyboards without sufficient reason is very annoying. It's hard to get used to a new key layout; the slightest variation in key placement is very disruptive. Keyboards should only be changed when they absolutely have to be, not just when somebody in marketing thinks it might be sexy to have a new product. And when new machines come out, old keyboards should work on them too (or at least there should be new keyboards with the same layouts).

On the other hand, people should be able to choose from a variety of key layouts. One of the most annoying things about Apple's ADB keyboards is their slavish pandering to the world of the IBM PC. On the regular ADB keyboard, for example, the *control* key (which no Macintosh lover with a shred of self-respect would ever use) is twice the size of the Option key (which gets used *all* the time). An *esc* key and four arrow keys further clutter up the keyboard.

very bad feature

I have nothing against people who need those keys for compatibility with PC software. But why should the rest of us (hey, that's a catchy phrase), who wouldn't get within fifty yards of a PC unless it was downwind and hidden behind a bush, have to suffer along with them? Why can't

things to come

Apple make a *non-IBM-obsequious* keyboard for us to use? (And if Apple won't, who will?)

✦ *Data Desk Mac 101 keyboard* (AN)

This third-party keyboard has become very popular because, for less than the price of Apple's extended keyboard, it gives you the ability to create custom command keys (in other words, to assign *macros* to them). But I had some problems with it.

I use a lot of em dashes—they look like that—so I'm always hitting the `Shift`, `Option` and hyphen key simultaneously to generate them. But on the MAC-101, you have to hold down `Shift` and `Option` first, *then* hit the hyphen key (I assume the same problem occurs with all `Shift` `Option` characters). That doesn't sound like much of a problem, but when a certain procedure is totally ingrained, it's really maddening to have it changed on you.

Cables attach to the back of the MAC-101 (an inconvenient place) and go in upside down (the opposite of how they go into a regular Apple keyboard).

Finally, the keyboard is very sensitive to being plugged in when the power is on. This is never a good idea, but Apple keyboards seldom have problems with it. Still, if you want macro keys, this keyboard gives you a lot of bang for the buck.

Mice and mouse substitutes

✦ *Apple's ADB mouse* (AN)

very good feature

The ADB mouse (standard on the SE and the II) is a joy to use. Smaller and with a much lighter and more delicate touch, it's a great improvement over its predecessor, which was clunky and stiff. It also moves more easily, thanks to its

Teflon bearings, and uses a heavier ball, which gives it more stability.

Unfortunately, it doesn't seem to last very long at all. When you buy a replacement, be sure to bring the old mouse with you; Apple dealers charge less for a new mouse if you trade in your old one.

very hot tip

✎ *quadLYNX Trackball, Turbo Mouse* (SS)

Since a mouse comes with every Mac, manufacturers have been understandably reluctant to offer alternatives. But Asher Engineering's quadLYNX Trackball and Kensington's Turbo Mouse are two mouse replacements that—in some ways—improve on the original concept.

Although mice (the computer variety) are a fairly hardy species, there are two significant disadvantages to using them. First, they get dirty easily—their feet get covered with black gunk and the little rubber ball picks up dust and debris as it rolls along. Although cleaning a mouse is relatively straightforward, there *are* sensitive parts that can be damaged.

Second, using a mouse requires a fair amount of uncluttered desk space. Even with the small footprint of the standard Mac, space can still be at a premium if you aren't a tidy sort.

A trackball is a stationary device that was made popular in video arcade machines; it's sort of like a mouse upside down. Rather than rolling the entire unit around to move the pointer, you use your fingertips to roll a ball that's mounted in the unit. The ball is the only moving part; there are no feet to wear out or get dirty. And since the unit is sealed, no dismantling for cleaning should ever be necessary.

very good feature

It only takes a short time to become comfortable with a trackball. The only major difference is that to move the pointer diagonally across the screen usually requires two or three rolls of the trackball, while with a mouse you can often reach your destination in a single motion. *(I've had a very different experience. I could never get used to trackballs.—AN)*

The quadLYNX Trackball measures about 8" x 3" and is the same color and texture as the Mac. It has a comfortable resting place for your wrist, an elevated trackball and two buttons—the larger one a standard mouse button and the smaller one a lock button.

very good feature

Instead of having to hold down the mouse button (when dragging, say, or resizing a window), you can hit the lock button, perform the task and then hit either button on the trackball when you're done. This sounds like a pretty trivial convenience (if any at all) but once you've gotten used to the lock button, you'll find it hard to get along without it.

For example, to choose a command from a menu, all you have to do is move the pointer to the menu bar and click the lock button. This locks the menu in the open position. Next, move the pointer to the desired command and press either button to choose it. This makes it much more difficult to slip and choose the wrong command than it is when you're using the mouse.

With its base as a resting place for the hand, the quadLYNX is more comfortable to use than a mouse; your palm isn't dragged around the surface of the desk. Games, particularly the "shoot 'em up" variety, are a breeze with the quadLYNX. And you can use the lock button to fire repeatedly.

Only one problem has surfaced with the quadLYNX—the lock button can go on the fritz, requiring that you really jam it down. Fortunately you can get that fixed under the unit's one-year warranty.

The Turbo Mouse is 4" x 6", somewhat smaller than the quadLYNX. It fits alongside either Mac keyboard (there are two models), perfectly matching its size, slope and color. The Turbo Mouse has two large buttons, to accommodate both left- and right-handers; both work the same as the mouse button.

Turbo Mouse has a built-in port for plugging in a mouse. With one connected, you can switch between trackball and mouse at will, just by moving your hand from one to the other. Kensington has thoughtfully included a plastic pocket with an adhesive strip that you can stick to the side of your Mac and store your mouse in.

Unlike the quadLYNX, the Turbo Mouse is speed-sensitive—if you roll the ball faster, it moves further. Cross-screen motions are almost as easy as with a mouse. *[Not for me they're not.—AN]* Small movements, such as those needed during word-processing, are equally simple. *[Not for me they're not.—AN]*

After a year, too many games of Crystal Quest finally killed one of the Turbo Mouse buttons. Although the unit only comes with a 90-day warranty, out-of-warranty repairs are very reasonable (in this case, $15).

Although the two trackballs are similar in price, performance and durability, there are several noteworthy differences. The quadLYNX Trackball has a lock button, a comfortable resting place for your wrist and a superior warranty. Turbo Mouse requires less space, has a mouse port and is sensitive to speed changes. Because of this last advantage, I found it slightly easier to use for heavy-duty editing. But, oh, I miss the quadLYNX's lock button!

Although trackballs usually cost more than mice (these both list at $130), they have some real advantages. So when your mouse is ready to be buried (under a little cross made out of matchsticks in the pet cemetery behind your house), you should definitely consider replacing it with a trackball.

Felix (BB)

The mouse is a lovable but maddening creature. It picks up lint and grunge, it wobbles when you want it to roll straight and it takes up a lot of valuable desktop real estate. But the alternatives haven't been much better. Track balls, for example, are better suited to games than to text editing or precise control of graphics. Now, however, there's Felix.

Felix consists of a six-inch-square base shaped like a squat pyramid, its point replaced with a sunken well. A plastic block about an inch square slides around in the well. On the block is a button. Your hand rests on the sloped side of the pyramid, your thumb and middle finger lightly grip the sides of the little block and your forefinger finger rests on the button. Move the block and the pointer moves. Click the button and the usual happens.

Felix solves many mouse problems. It laughs at dirt, because the moving parts are protected. It requires less than half the desk space a mouse does. And it's responsive. Because both Felix and your fingers are designed to make small, precise movements, your control of the pointer becomes more precise. For graphics applications, there's a precision mode that takes pointer movements right down to one-pixel increments.

Is Felix the perfect replacement for the common desktop rodent? For some users, it may be. It's precise, quick and efficient, and requires very little hand movement to move the pointer. But it also requires a light touch and refined movement, not everyone's style. My wife and my daughter each rests her hand on the mouse; they thought Felix made them tense.

The tactile sensation isn't as slick and linear as I'd like it to be. (The problem is to find just the right combination of plastic and manufacturing technique. They're working on it.) Finally, Felix probably isn't as good as a tablet and stylus for freehand graphics (but it's much cheaper).

🍎 Dale's cheap mouse pad *(DC)*

very hot tip

Dale's favorite mouse pad is a sheet of heavyweight paper inside a good-quality spiral-bound notebook. Unlike the cloth surfaces on commercial mouse pads, it doesn't attract dust and cat hairs, and it sells for a fraction of the cost. Best of all, when you want a new pad, all you have to do is turn the page.

If you already have a commercial mouse pad, you can prolong its life by covering its surface with a piece of heavy paper cut to size.

bargain

Miscellaneous basic hardware tips

♠ *the best way to ship a Mac* (Paul Blood)

The best box to ship a Mac in is the one Apple shipped it to you in—except for one thing: it lets everyone know that a valuable computer is inside. The solution? Pull the box apart, then reassemble it inside out. All the same styrofoam packing materials will fit.

very hot tip

♠ *setting up a workstation* (AN)

If you put a one-piece Mac (one with the screen built into the CPU) and its keyboard on the same surface, either the screen will be too low or the keyboard too high. This is less true of Macs where the monitor is separate, like the Mac II, but sometimes even putting the screen on top of the CPU doesn't get it high enough.

For comfortable typing, your wrists should never be higher than your elbows. Depending on your height and the height of your chair, this means the keyboard should be on a surface 24–27 inches from the floor.

very hot tip

The screen should be 4-8 inches higher than the surface the keyboard is on, so that you can look at it comfortably without having to bend your head. And don't strain your eyes by putting it too close—allow at least a foot between the back of the keyboard and the front of the Mac.

One way to put together a comfortable workstation is to use two tables—a low typing table and one of normal height. Put them together with the low one in front, then put the keyboard on it and the Mac on the higher table in the back. A good swivel (like Ergotron's MacTilt) can help raise

very hot tip

the Mac to where you want it, or just put it on a thick book or a sturdy box.

bargain

Another inexpensive approach is to find a used desk with a typing well in it. Fasten the well in the open position and use it for the keyboard, then build a higher platform behind it for the Mac to rest on. (The platform doesn't have to be anything fancy, just a piece of plywood and few boards)

For information on a highly recommended workstation that's made specifically for the Mac, see the entry on MacTable in Chapter 7.

Chapter 3

Memory and storage

🍎 *memory vs. storage* (AN)

These two words are often used interchangeably. That's a pity, because they make a very convenient distinction when used the way they are in this book.

By *memory*, we mean the short-term retention of information electronically, on chips; by *storage*, we mean the long-term retention of information, typically on magnetic media like disks and tapes or on optical media like CD ROMs. Memory is fast but disappears when you turn your machine off; storage is slower but survives when you turn your machine off.

Now isn't that a simple distinction? Too simple, apparently, because many people in the field are constantly muddying it.

In this chapter, we discuss storage devices (hard disks and floppies) first, then memory.

Disk drives

🍎 *you need a hard disk* (AN)

You may not be able to afford one, but you need one all the same. Hard disks used to be seen as great luxuries, something lusted after by the great masses of computer users (myself among them) but owned by few. Now they're pretty much standard equipment. A Mac running off floppies isn't useless but it's hard to do any kind of serious work without a hard disk.

esp. for beginners

So, if there's any way you can afford a hard disk, get one. If you're like most people, once you have it, you won't know how you lived without it.

🍎 *$/meg* (AN)

That's the best way to evaluate the price of a hard disk. Just take the cost and divide it by the number of megs the

**very
hot
tip**

drive holds (but don't rely on the advertised capacity—see the next entry for more on that). The lower the number, the better. Once you know the actual cost of what you're getting, you can compare other factors like reliability, support, length of warranty and speed.

⚫ *untruth in labelling* (AN)

**very bad
feature**

With very rare exceptions, the number of megabytes a manufacturer says you get is a lot more than the actual capacity of the drive. It's really a disgrace how completely unprincipled this has become.

First they call a megabyte a million characters instead of 1024K. (1024K = 1,048,576 characters, which is 47K—almost 5%—more than a million characters. If you don't think that's significant, I'll be happy to take a 5% commission on everything you buy.) But even assuming these million-character *minimegs* (as I like to call them), they lie.

I know of one "144MB" hard disk that holds 133.5 megs (136.7 minimegs) and a "45MB" hard disk that holds 41.7 megs (42.7 minimegs). I'd tell you the brands but it wouldn't be fair to them, because virtually everyone (including Apple) does the same thing.

**very
hot
tip**

So—just ignore a drive's advertised capacity. Get its *actual* capacity and use that in your $/meg calculations. Don't think for a moment that you can compare the prices of two "70MB" or "150MB" drives until you've determined what each one really holds.

⚫ *internal vs. external hard disks* (AN)

The advantage of an internal hard disk (one that's mounted inside the Mac itself) is that you don't have to lug a separate hard disk around when you're moving your Mac. Internal hard disks also tend to be somewhat cheaper than an equivalent external hard disk and of course they take up no desk space.

There are several disadvantages to internal hard disks, however. A Mac with an internal hard disk is both more fragile and heavier than a normal Mac. If the disk needs to be repaired, you'll be without your Mac for the interim (unless you want to pull it out). If you want to diagnose whether the hard disk or something else in the Mac is causing the problem, it's a lot easier to disconnect an external hard disk and plug in a different one than it is to remove an internal hard disk.

For these reasons, I think an external hard disk is generally a smarter move. You should take that statement with a grain of salt, however, since I used an internal hard disk while writing this book. The point is: everything else being equal, an external hard disk is preferable. When everything else isn't equal (as is usually the case), you have to use your judgment.

**very
hot
tip**

● *which brand to buy* (AN)

We're not big enough to set up a comprehensive program of hard disk testing, so I talked to someone at a large user group and asked him what the experience of its thousands of users has been. Here's what he told me:

Jasmine drives are great and so is their support; they're the only company that says they'll try to recover your data if your drive crashes. PCPC's drives are, if anything, even better, but their support is minimal and their drives are expensive.

**very
hot
tip**

La Cie makes a good drive but their support is problematic. Peripheral Land now makes a pretty good drive but has had some *very* serious problems in the past (my informant knows someone who went through *nine* Peripheral Land drives before she got one that works).

He didn't recommend SuperMac, Rodime or CMS drives—particularly the CMS drives for the Mac II (in that particular case, it seems to be a problem with the ROMs rather than the drive itself). But my informant reserved his harshest words for Bering, which he said discontinued a drive rather than fix some problems with it and left owners in the lurch.

**very bad
feature**

This is, of course, only one person's opinion at one point in time, but it's based on lots of feedback from lots of people calling the user group's help line and sharing experiences at meetings. It also accords with my own experience and that of many people I know. For example, I couldn't get a Bering drive I was evaluating to install properly. I called their tech support number and had my call returned *a week later*.

bargain

Here's some more information on the two manufacturers that were recommended most highly. Jasmine sells direct to the public at low prices (I know there isn't much air in them because when they sell to developers, they only knock 10% off retail). They offer a 30-day money-back guarantee and a one-year parts-and-labor warranty.

very good
feature

Jasmine drives come loaded with many megabytes of public-domain software (17 megs as of this writing, but the number keeps increasing). We've got a couple of Jasmine disks at the office (a 45-meg and a 70-meg) and they've been completely trouble-free. All in all, they're one of the best—if not *the* best—deal around.

PCPC (Personal Computer Peripherals Corporation) is one of the oldest manufacturers of hard disks for the Mac. I used a 144-meg internal hard disk in my Mac II while working on this edition of the book and had no problems with it.

very bad
feature

I do have a complaint, however. PCPC included a laser printer spooler on the disk that they *knew* would hang up the whole system in a very bizarre way whenever you used it with AppleTalk connected (hardly the most exotic circumstance imaginable). Thanks to their thoughtlessness, I wasted a whole evening of my life trying to track down the problem.

PCPC's MacBottom external drives are designed to sit directly underneath the Mac, thus raising the screen to the correct height. Charles Rubin has had good experience with one of these (see the next entry). PCPC also publishes a hard-disk backup utility called HFS Back-Up and a file-finding utility called Eureka!

♠ _MacBottom hard disks—a personal testimonial_ (CR)

I used a MacBottom hard disk with my Mac for almost three years, and was very happy with both the product and its manufacturer.

PCPC prides itself on fast service. Soon after I got my MacBottom drive, I had a compatibility problem between its ROM and the original version of Microsoft Word. I sent the drive to Florida and I got back a completely new drive (with my files on it) via Federal Express in three days. To minimize delays when you send a disk in to be upgraded to a larger size (PCPC has a discount upgrade program), the service department waits until it knows it can turn the job around in a day, then gives you a call.

very good feature

Other than the initial problem, my MacBottom has survived many system updates and crashes, several power failures and the indignity of being shoved into my briefcase for a trip to the office every day for a year.

very good feature

♠ _removable hard-disk cartridges_ (AN)

This is the best backup system I've seen. The removable 45-meg Winchester hard disks look like giant floppies; you stick them in the drive and they act like hard disks.

These have a 25-millisecond access time, which is faster than a lot of fixed hard disks—although Fred Fowler, the company's president, tells me that getting data in and out over the the SCSI connection, not access time, is what really slows drives down.

Custom Memory Systems' drives have 8K data caches to help compensate for the slowness of the SCSI connector. Whatever the reason, these drives are _fast._ I backed up 68 megs of data in less than 27 minutes, and that includes switching disks.

very good feature

These drives have other impressive technological features. The platter is made from a nickel-cadmium slurry, which is very hard stuff, and is coated with a fluorocarbon that's many times more slippery than Teflon. To get dust

very good feature

and other junk off it, it spins up to 4200 rpm when you turn it on, then back down to its operating speed of 3260 rpm. The drives have DC voice coil servos imbedded, which are much more expensive than the normal stepper motors.

Other companies make a similar product but Custom Memory Systems (not to be confused with CMS, which is a different company) was the first out with them. We use these drives for backup and haven't had a lot of problems with them.

The only reason I can think of for not using a drive of this sort is the price (about $1800 for the drive and $125 per disk). But that may come down and, as Fowler points out, you don't have to use them just for backup—they work great as your only hard disk too.

gossip/
trivia

(This just in: Custom Memory Systems has been driven into Chapter 11 by a lawsuit from Sun Microsystems. From what I can gather, Custom Memory Systems couldn't afford the expense of fighting the suit in court, so they agreed to binding arbitration. This greatly limited their ability to appeal the decision, which went against them.

If the Chapter 11 reorganization doesn't put Custom Memory Systems back on its feet, you'll have to look to other manufacturers who make the same kind of drives.)

❤ arrivederci SCSI *(AN)*

things
to come

SCSI is on the way out. The much-faster drives of the future will use a DMA channel direct to the NuBus card (which you'll have to buy from Apple).

❤ DaynaFile *(SM)*

If you need to exchange data between Macs and PCs, you have two hurdles to overcome. *(Those of you who've fallen into the dreadful habit of referring to all personal computers as "PCs" please note that what we mean by the term is "an IBM Personal Computer or a clone thereof." —AN)*

First you have to get the data onto a disk a Mac can read, then you have to convert the data into a format that Mac programs can read.

One way to solve the first problem is to have a PC around—which is a dreadful waste of money and space that could be used for Mac hardware or software. The DaynaFile is a much more elegant solution—it's a disk drive that reads PC disks. All you have to do is connect it to the Mac's SCSI port. Then, when you put a PC disk into the DaynaFile, the disk's icon appears on the Mac's desktop.

There are DaynaFiles to read both kinds of 5-1/4" floppies—the 360K ones used by the original PC or the XT and the 1.2 MB ones used by the AT—as well as both the 720K and 1.44MB 3-1/2" disks used by the PS/2 series and many portable PCs. (You can get any of the four drives alone and there are also many different two-drive combinations.)

Now that you've got the data on the Mac, you have to read it. Many Mac programs can do that. For example, Excel for the Mac can read 1-2-3 files and the Mac versions of Word, PageMaker and Word Perfect can all read files created by their PC counterparts. To read the data produced by other PC programs, you can use a specially modified version of MacLink Plus that's supplied by DaynaFile for an extra $100. It can convert many kinds of PC text files to MacWrite format.

Installation of both the DaynaFile and its software is very easy *(even Arthur could do it)*. Unfortunately, the manual isn't much good for anything more advanced than installation—it's repetitive, poorly organized and poorly indexed.

The unit I tested worked very well, saving and copying PC disks quite efficiently and easily. But there are a few things that take some getting used to. For example, 5-1/4" disks don't eject themselves; after dragging the disk to the trash, you have to remove them manually. This is standard

very good feature

practice in the PCs that use these disks but it takes some getting used to on the Mac.

Also unexpected was the fact that the 1.2MB drive won't read 360K disks; in fact, when you insert a 360K disk in the 1.2MB drive, you're asked if you want to initialize it. This isn't a bug—the different ways the PC and the Mac work make it necessary. But it did confuse me at first, and the manual didn't explain it.

If you need to transfer data between PCs and Macs on a regular basis, DaynaFile may be just what you need. When used with MacLink Plus or with the Apple File Exchange utility, there isn't much it can't do.

As of this writing, prices range from $600 for a single 360K (5-1/4") drive to $1030 for a unit with two 1.44MB (3-1/2") drives—plus $100 for MacLink Plus, if you need it. That's not much cheaper than buying a low-priced PC clone and running TOPS or something on it; if you have a use for a PC, that's probably the way to go. If you don't, DaynaFile can save you money, trouble and desk space.

Basic disk tips

✎ *how many backups to make* (AN)

esp. for beginners

An 800K floppy disk costs less than $2 and holds at least 40 hours' work. So if you value your time at more than 5¢ an hour, the moral is simple: you should always have enough disks around to make multiple copies of your work.

important warning

I make three copies, each on a separate disk, of every piece of work I do (so that when I'm working on a document, I actually have four copies—one on the hard disk, two on floppies and one in memory). Tony Pietsch got me into that habit years ago, when he described the following scenario: "Let's say you only have two copies of something and your disk drive screws up. You insert the first disk and see garbage on the screen. Naturally you assume there's something wrong with that disk, but you're not worried, because you have a second disk with the same document on it. So you insert the second disk and the drive zaps that too. At that point you realize the problem is with the drive, not the disk, but it's too late—unless you have a third copy."

🍎 *backup of previous entry* (CJW)

I second what Arthur just said. Two backups let you recover from losses caused by program crashes, system crashes, undetected errors, viruses or disk failure. (The shelf-life of a diskette is two to three years at most and the potential for random media problems can increase dramatically as time goes by.)

esp. for beginners

If you really want to be safe, rotate in a third backup and keep it in a separate building, so you can recover your files even if you suffer a fire or a burglary. (For more on guarding against fire, see the entry titled *disks melt before paper burns* in the floppy disk section below.)

very hot tip

🍎 *two ways to back up disks* (DC)

There are two ways to back up disks. One is to select all the files on the source disk (using ⌘–A is the fastest way) and drag them as a group to the backup disk. The second way is to drag the icon of the source disk onto the icon of the backup disk.

The second method erases anything that was previously on the backup disk—so if you only want files copied into the blank spaces on the backup disk, use the first method. When you use the second method, the Desktop of the backup disk ends up looking exactly the same as the source disk's, with all the icons in the same places. Any invisible (but unprotected) files on the source disk get copied too.

🍎 *more backup tips* (PH)

Here are two more reasons to back up your hard disk: a virus may erase your hard disk (or parts of it) or someone may steal your Mac and hard disk. With a backup, you can rent another Mac and start working again.

As C. J. suggested a couple of entries ago, you should store at least one set of backups away from your computer and probably in a different building. If the building burns down, having a stack of backups next to the computer won't do you much good. Also, if someone steals the computer, the thief may steal all the disks near the computer as well.

Backup systems like removable hard disks are fast and efficient but they're also expensive. Most Mac users have avoided them due to the cost. If you don't have one, you should back up your hard disk regularly on floppies, even though it takes time and money.

very hot tip

If your Mac is on a network, you might consider backing it up by copying to unused space onto the hard disks of other computers. For example, if you're networked to a minicomputer with a large disk, filling up 20 megabytes may be perfectly acceptable to the system administrator. This is usually much, much slower than backing up to floppies, but it doesn't cost anything since no floppies are used.

important warning

Be sure to label your backup disks with the complete date of the backup, including the year. Since it's likely that you will own your Mac for more than a year, finding information on old backups is almost impossible otherwise.

✎ *backup programs* (PH)

very good feature

DiskFit is by far the most popular and easy-to-use program for backup. It's designed for speed, so doing a daily backup takes much less time (and uses fewer floppies) than other programs. Doing a daily *incremental backup* (where only the files that have been changed are backed up) will usually take less than a minute and DiskFit can run in the background under MultiFinder.

very bad feature

You can choose to back up all files or just documents, but DiskFit's major drawback is that you can't get more specific than that—for instance you can't back up a single file. You can, however, leave certain folders out of the backup by surrounding their names with square brackets.

[With removable hard disks, there's another drawback: it takes DiskFit forever to read a 45MB disk full of files—and I mean <u>forever</u>!—AN]

❡ *backup programs* (AN)

As Paul mentioned in the previous entry, DiskFit is widely used, and if you're backing up to floppies, it's probably fine. But as I mentioned in the previous entry, I found it completely unusable for removable hard disks, because of the amount it takes to read a 45-meg disk full of files. What I use instead is DM Capture, which you get free with Custom Memory Systems' removable hard disk drives.

Like DiskFit, DM Capture does incremental backups; unlike DiskFit, it does an *archival* backup—that is, it doesn't replace the last version of a file with a new one. This is ideal if, like me, you've sometimes wiped out your backups by saving a damaged new version over them, but it does require a lot of space, so it's not for floppies.

DM Capture can be set to automatically backup each day at a certain time (you just leave your machine on when you leave and when you come back to work on it, the backup has been done). Because it puts each backup in its own folder, reading a 45MB disk only takes it a few seconds, even when it's full.

**very good
feature**

❡ *one disk, one system* (DC/AN)

You can avoid a lot of problems by always remembering this simple rule: Never put more than one system file on any one disk. If you have two or more system files on a disk, you're almost guaranteed crashes, bombs and data loss. (This can happen on floppies, but it's much more likely on hard disks and thus much more of a problem there.)

!

**important
warning**

While most people wouldn't consciously add a second system file, it's pretty easy to do accidentally, especially on a hard disk (as we can tell you from personal experience). It usually happens when you're putting new software on the disk. It seems natural just to select all the files on the distribution disk and drag them over, but don't, because most distribution disks contain a system folder.

✎ *quick hard-disk recovery* (CJW)

esp. for beginners

If you regularly use a hard disk, be sure to keep a floppy disk with a duplicate System and Finder on it. Every time you add or delete desk accessories or fonts to the System on your hard disk, do the same to your backup. *(Or, better yet, use Suitcase or Font/DA Juggler (described in Chapter 8).—AN)*

Since the System is easily corrupted, there's sure to come a day when you'll start to notice random System errors, a sudden increase in how long it takes you to access a file, or a crash. You may not even be able to start from your hard disk.

If you get any of those problems, choose *Shut Down* (on the Special menu) and then start up again from your backup floppy. Drag the hard disk's System and Finder files to the Trash and drag the System and Finder from the backup floppy into your hard disk's system folder. (If you have your System and Finder where they belong, you could eliminate the first step, but this way is the safest.) When the copy is complete, choose *Restart* (also on the Special menu).

Usually you'll find you're back in business again, and your total lost time will amount to less than a couple of minutes.

✎ *changing the startup disk* (DC/AN)

You can change the startup disk (the one the Mac looks to for the System file, DAs, fonts, etc.) simply by choosing *Restart* from the Special menu and inserting the disk you want to be the new startup disk into the internal drive. To make a hard disk the startup, just choose *Restart* and put no disk in the internal drive.

But there's an easier way to do it (and the only way if you have more than one hard disk). Just `Double-Click` on the Finder icon of the disk you want to be the new startup disk while holding down the Option and ⌘ keys. You can use this same trick to launch MultiFinder from the Finder (but not vice-versa).

⚫ *preventing startup disk changes* (DC)

Launching an application that resides on a disk other than the startup disk makes the disk the application is on the startup disk (assuming, of course, it contains a System file and a Finder). To prevent this from happening, drag the Finder on the application's disk out of the system folder.

Hard disk tips

⚫ *care and feeding of hard disks* (DC)

Hard disks are remarkably tough, but cruel and unusual punishment can damage them. The most important rule is not to move a hard disk when it's turned on. And when you move it, pick it up—never scoot it across the desk surface.

important warning

Another thing to avoid is rapid temperature changes. Don't carry a hard disk around in your trunk all day in the dead of winter, bring it inside and start it up; give it a couple of hours to warm to room temperature.

important warning

⚫ *putting hard disks where you can't hear them* (AN)

Hard disks are great, but even the ones without fans make a fair amount of noise. If you're sensitive to noise and love the fact that the all Macs through the Plus were virtually silent, a hard disk is likely to bother you.

Fortunately, the solution is simple. Just attach a long cable to your hard disk and put it in a closet or some other place where you can't hear it (for a long time I kept them on a shelf outside—and above—the door to my work room).

SCSI drives are designed to accept cables up to 7 meters, or 21 feet (7 meters is equal to 23 feet, not 21, but don't blame us—we're just quoting from the box Apple's cables come in). But hardware pundit C. J. Weigand says you shouldn't go more than 15–18 feet (see his entry below on chaining SCSI devices).

Since it seems unlikely that you can physically harm a drive by putting it on a long cable, it makes sense to at least experiment with one; if you do have problems, you'll only be out the price of the cable. I think long cables may somewhat increase the number of crashes you experience, but since you *always* back up your work every fifteen minutes or half hour (right?), you won't lose much data.

SCSI devices must be on (AN)

important warning

Every device that's connected in a SCSI chain must be turned on or the whole chain won't boot.

SCSI cables (AN)

There are two kinds of SCSI connectors—25-pin and 50-pin—and thus many possible kinds of SCSI cables (25-pin male to 25-pin male, 25-pin male to 25-pin female, 25-pin male to 50-pin male, etc. etc.—not to mention various lengths). Depending on what you're connecting together, you might need a some special cable configuration. Whatever it is, rest assured that your local computer store won't have it in stock.

ID numbers on SCSI devices (MB)

important warning

Some hard disks allow you to set their SCSI ID numbers with software. This isn't a good idea, because if any two SCSI devices in a chain (hard disks, QuickDraw printers or whatever) have the same ID number, your system will crash. (It doesn't matter whether you've changed the numbers or they came that way.)

Even if you disconnect all of the devices except one, you won't be able to change its ID number because it will be "in use by the System" (since you booted off it). In fact, even if you boot off another SCSI disk, and put the device whose number you want to change behind it in the chain, you can sometimes get that message when you try to change the ID number of the nonbooting disk (it shouldn't happen, but sometimes it does).

This isn't a problem if the ID numbers are set with actual physical switches on the hardware. Your system will crash just the same but you'll be able to turn it off, reset one of the switches and then restart.

very good feature

🍎 *chaining SCSI devices* (CJW)

Daisy-chain more than a few SCSI devices together and you're bound to run into problems. The types of devices installed, the manner in which they're terminated, the order in which they're hooked up, the SCSI addresses assigned to each device and the total length of the interconnecting cables all play a role in determining whether or not the system will function properly. (For a supposed standard interface, SCSI needs a lot of work.)

Some devices won't work correctly if installed together on the same bus. For example, if you use a tape drive for doing periodic backups, don't also try to hook up a removable hard-disk drive. Apple, in its infinite wisdom, gave us only one backup channel on the SCSI bus and both types of drives are considered backup devices. If you connect both, only one will work. They may both *appear* to work, but you'll discover, probably too late (as I did), that one of them really isn't doing the job.

important warning

I thought I'd backed up my hard disk successfully on tape, but found when restoring that no files were visible or accessible, even via MacTools. Then I tried a different arrangement of the drives. The result? Only half a backup was made before the tape froze in the drive. A third arrangement resulted in the removable-media drive not even appearing on the Desktop.

Contrary to expectations, some SCSI devices function properly only if connected in a certain order; at least one tape drive manufacturer (MDIdeas) requires their unit to be

important
warning

at the other end of the chain from the Mac. So you may have to experiment a bit to hit upon a satisfactorily working combination. If all else fails, sometimes changing a SCSI address to a higher or lower number can get a balky drive working again. Make sure no two devices are assigned the same number, though, or you might wipe the contents of both disks.

important
warning

Although almost all SCSI devices come terminated (Toshiba's CD-ROM drive is an exception), only the first and last in the chain should remain so. Those in between should have their terminating resistors removed. Otherwise, your data transfer may be messed up by signal *echoes*, or you may be unable to boot, or one or more devices on the chain won't be recognized.

Generally, you have to open the case and lift out the internal mechanism to get at a device's terminating resistor, a job best reserved for a qualified technician. If you're fearless enough to try it yourself, however, you should know that terminating resistors are usually burnt yellow or robin's-egg blue. Most are socketed and snap out easily, although you'll occasionally find some, like the ones in the MacScan interface box, that are permanently soldered in place.

important
warning

If you use too much cable, you'll experience the same kind of problems improper termination can cause. The total cable length, from the back of your computer to the last device in a SCSI chain, shouldn't exceed eighteen feet (to be extrasafe, fifteen feet).

Officially, the standard is seven meters (about 23 feet), but that's a dream. The fail length seems to vary slightly according to the type of cables, connectors and devices used. In my experience (I generally have all SCSI addresses in use with a variety of devices), it usually turns out to be about eighteen feet, but I lost the chain once with as little as fifteen feet.

important
warning

When experimenting with different SCSI arrangements, be sure that you turn off all power before connecting or disconnecting cables. If you do it with the power on, you can get transient voltage spikes that can damage the equipment.

❤ *a fleet is only as fast...* (DC)

If you have more than one hard disk connected to your Mac, you'll find that returning to the Desktop from an application will only be as fast as the slowest drive connected. You can speed things up somewhat by keeping all the windows on the slower drive(s) closed.

❤ *starting and turning off hard disks* (DC/AN)

In general, you should turn on your hard disk(s) first and then turn on the Mac, but if both are connected to a surge suppressor or a power strip, it's fine to turn them on simultaneously.

When the smiling-face-inside-the-Mac icon appears, it means that the Mac has discovered the disk and is talking to it. Never turn off a Mac or a hard disk when the smiling face is on the screen. Don't even hit the reset button on the programmer's switch, because it will take much longer for the disk to restart. If you need to shut off the system, wait until the Desktop appears, then choose *Shut Down* from the Special menu, turn off the Mac and then the disk(s).

important warning

❤ *defragmenting hard disks* (AN)

Hard disks write data wherever there's room and this results in files being *fragmented*—that is, parts of the same file are written in different places on the disk. When this happens often enough, the access speed on your disk slows way down. Then it's time to *defragment*.

This involves rewriting all the files to your disk so they occupy contiguous portions of the disk. There are a couple of programs that do that—DiskExpress and PowerUP. DiskExpress has been around longer and costs less ($40 vs. $60, as of this writing) but PowerUP works faster.

🍎 *organizing a hard disk* (AN)

*gossip/
trivia*

The general principles of good organization apply to hard disks as much as they do to anything else. Prime among these, of course, is *apfeaeiip*. By an incredible coincidence, the letters that make up this word (which, as you undoubtedly know, means *good housekeeping* in Fijian) are also the initials of the English phrase *a place for everything and everything in its place.*

*very
hot
tip*

Apfeaeiip is, of course, an unattainable ideal. That's why you need a *wrong-place box.* I came upon this concept when living with four roommates. We'd take turns straightening up but that was an impossible task when all kinds of stuff, of indeterminate ownership and importance, lay randomly about the house.

So we got a big cardboard box and put it in a central location. Then we had a meeting and agreed where things belonged. From that point on, if anything wasn't in its place, whoever was straightening up put it in the wrong-place box. If you couldn't find something where you left it, you just looked there. (This sounds sort of fascistic, but it was actually a very simple and easy way to deal with the problem.)

If you share your hard disk (and probably even if you don't), you need a wrong-place box—a folder called *need to be put away, left in the wrong place* or the like. You just pop things in there when they're in the way and then periodically, when you don't have anything more pressing to do, you open that folder and figure out where all the stuff in it really belongs.

There are two basic ways to organize folders on a hard disk—by type of application (graphics, word processing, databases, etc.) and by type of work (Project A, Project B, budget, personal, etc.). In general, it makes sense to use both kinds of folders, even though you'll sometimes forget whether a given document is filed away under a work category or under the kind of application that created it.

Don't lay down a rigid organizational scheme and then be afraid to break out of it. For example, if you use a particular program frequently, it's fine to put its icon by itself out in the disk window (also known as the *root directory*) even if all the related programs and documents are in a folder. By the same token, if you use one particular document most of the time you use a given application, put its icon, rather than the application's icon, somewhere easy to get to—not where related programs and documents are kept.

*very
hot
tip*

I like to view folders and programs by name and documents by date (so the ones you worked on most recently rise to the top of the list). Viewing by name or date also gives you nice, small icons that don't take up a lot of room. Combining that with careful positioning and "staircasing" of nested windows allows the maximum amount of data to be viewed.

One last general rule: *it's your Desktop.* You can do whatever you want with it. There's no right or wrong way to organize things. In particular, remember that you can name your folders whatever you want. (I have one called *dealing with psychopaths* which, unfortunately, is chock full of stuff.) Feel free to reorganize and rename folders and files often—a good Desktop is constantly evolving.

*very
hot
tip*

There's a good book on all aspects of dealing with a hard disk. Written by Charles Rubin, who's contributed many brilliant tips to this book, and Ben Calica, it's called *Macintosh Hard Disk Management* and is published by Howard W. Sams.

Floppy disk tips

➤ *ejecting floppy disks* (DC)

There are several ways to eject floppy disks. The most straightforward method is to drag the disk's icon to the Trash. You can also choose *Eject* from the Finder's File menu, or hit the Eject button in the Save As or Open dialog box. Or you can use the following keyboard commands; they'll eject any disk, including the startup disk, regardless of whether you're on the Desktop or in an application.

*esp. for
beginners*

⌘–E   ejects the selected disk(s).

Shift ⌘–1   ejects the disk in the internal drive.

Shift ⌘–2   ejects the disk in the external drive.

When you use these keyboard commands from the Finder (or choose *Eject* from the File menu), a dimmed version of the disk's icon—and of any of its windows that happened to be open—remains on the Desktop. When you throw a disk's icon in the trash (or eject a disk from within an application), all trace of it disappears from the Desktop.

If you try to close the dimmed window of an ejected disk, you'll be asked to reinsert the disk, so if you're not going to be using the disk again, drag the dimmed disk icon to the Trash. The Finder will remove any of that disk's windows that happen to be open (unless it's the startup disk); if you insert the disk again, it will remember which windows were open and put them back where they were.

important warning

Never turn off your Mac without first ejecting any floppy disks that are in either drive. The correct procedure is to close any application that may be running, then choose *Shut Down* from the Special menu. Failing to heed this warning is an excellent way to lose data.

❦ *escaping from switch-disks nightmares* (MB)

very hot tip

To escape from one of those interminable switch-disks nightmares (the kind that make you want to scream at your Mac, "You want that disk *again?* There's something sick about your obsession with that disk!"), just press ⌘–period. (Unfortunately, this little trick doesn't work with versions of the Finder earlier than 4.0.)

❦ *disks stuck in drives* (SM)

important warning

The heads in the Mac's double-sided floppy disk drives break easily. One thing that will definitely wipe them out is forcing disks in and out of the drive. So if a disk gets stuck in your drive—which seems to happen more often with

older floppies and with disks with several labels on them—
bring your Mac to your local dealer to have it repaired.

They'll need to take the machine apart, so you may even
have to leave it, but the time, hassle and money will all be
less than if you have to have a new disk drive installed—as
you almost certainly will if you try to force the disk out.

❖ *where to put an external floppy drive* (DC)

Don't put the external floppy disk drive on the left side
of an SE, Mac Plus or earlier Mac. The Mac's power supply
is there and can interfere with reading and writing to disk.
(This will probably be true of future all-in-one Macs as well.)
The best place for the drive is on the Mac's right side, either
sitting flat on the table or sideways against the side of the
Mac in a bracket like the one that comes with Ergotron's
MacTilt (described in Chapter 7).

**important
warning**

You may also be tempted to put the external drive on top
of the Mac, but don't. The Mac generates enough heat after
an hour or two to expand the surface of a disk, and this can
cause errors. Even if you don't get errors immediately, any
information written to a disk that is warmer than normal
might not be readable when the disk has cooled to normal
temperatures. (If, in spite of this warning, you still insist on
putting the external drive on top of the Mac, at least make
sure it's right in the center, so it doesn't block the cooling
vents.)

**important
warning**

❖ *recovering data from trashed disks* (DC)

If a disk bombs when inserted, you still may be able to
recover the information it contains. Hold down the ⌘ and
[Option] keys while inserting the disk and keep them held
down. A message will appear asking if you want to rebuild
the Desktop. [Click] on *Yes*. If the recovery succeeds, the
Desktop will appear after a minute or two (how long it takes
depends on how many files are on the disk).

**very
hot
tip**

(If you're using a version of the Finder earlier than 5.0,
all icon positions, folder titles, window sizes and positions

will be lost, but all the actual data in your files will be preserved.)

very hot tip

If the above technique doesn't work, you still may be able to save some or all of the documents. Insert a disk that contains the application that created the documents you want to save, launch the application and choose *Open...* from the application's File menu. Then eject the application disk and insert the problem disk.

In most cases, the Mac will accept the problem disk and present you with a list box containing the documents you want to save. Load them into memory and save them to another disk. If the documents on the problem disk were created by more than one application, just repeat the process for each application.

very hot tip

If that doesn't work either, try rotating the disk's hub a quarter-turn or so and then reinsert it.

These tricks won't work with every disk that goes bad, but they're worth a try. If none of them works, remember the entire episode the next time you think you just don't have time to make backups of your documents.

❤ *recycling trashed disks* (DC)

If you can't—or don't need to—recover the data from a trashed disk, here's a way to at least try to recycle it, so you can use it for new data. (If you *do* need to recover the data, see the last entry.)

very hot tip

Hold down the [Tab], [Option] and [⌘] keys while inserting the trashed disk. You'll get the standard dialog box asking you if you want to initialize the disk Single-Sided or Double-Sided. Click on whichever one you prefer. The trashed disk should now initialize with no further problems.

If this doesn't work, your disk is really trashed and you should recycle it as a high-tech coaster for drinks.

✦ *formatting single-sided disks as double* (AN)

Every Mac expert I know reformats single-sided (400K) floppies as double-sided (800K); in fact, BMUG buys single-sided disks exclusively and reformats them double-sided for their booming shareware and public-domain disk business. (Most individuals don't go that far; they buy double-sided disks but reformat their old single-sided ones.)

On some small percentage of the disks, the double-sided initialization will fail; you just reformat those single-sided and use them that way. But on most single-sided disks the double-sided initialization will work. Everyone seems to agree that if a disk will take double-sided initialization, it will then be as reliable as a double-sided disk you buy.

very hot tip

✦ *protecting confidential data* (DC/AN)

If you keep confidential data on disk, be aware that deleting the file doesn't actually remove the data. It's still there and a clever hacker can recover your secrets using any one of several utility programs. Writing another file to the disk may remove the old file; reformatting the disk certainly will. (For other approaches, see the review of Complete Delete in Chapter 8 and the entries on security software at the end of Chapter 15.)

✦ *disks melt before paper burns* (AN)

Paper burns at 451° Fahrenheit (whence the title of Ray Bradbury's book). Floppy disks melt at about 160° F. (the disk itself, that is, the part that actually holds the data). So a normal fireproof safe won't protect the data on your disks. There *are* safes that are designed to keep their contents below 160° but they cost an arm and a leg.

I have another approach, which is to put a fireproof storage box inside a fireproof safe. I don't know if this will work but it ought to (if my house burns down, I'll let you know the results). It certainly costs less, since both fireproof safes and fireproof storage boxes (the regular ones, for paper) are relatively inexpensive.

bargain

✿ *floppy disks and magnets* (DC)

important warning

The information on disks is stored magnetically and magnets placed near disks can hopelessly scramble that information. So keep magnets as far away as possible from disks (and disk drives). And remember that most of the magnets you're going to run across are going to be in small appliances and other devices—telephones, for example— not lying around loose on your desk.

For example, the cover of the ImageWriter I has a magnet underneath the left side. Put your disks there at your own risk. The cover of the ImageWriter II has a much smaller magnet on the right side, but since the surface is slanted at an angle, disks will probably slide off if you try to put them there.

✿ *removing old disk labels* (CJW)

very hot tip

Ordinary lighter fluid will quickly remove old, stubborn labels from your disks without causing damage. (Even if it seeps inside, it just evaporates.) I've even used lighter fluid to clean fingerprints and sticky, dried soft drink off the actual floppy-disk surface itself.

Saturate the label for a few seconds, then gently remove it using an inexpensive razor-blade scraper (you can get one in any hardware store). The label should lift off pretty much in one piece. You can then use a cloth moistened with lighter fluid to scrub off any leftover residue.

✿ *cheap disk labels* (SS)

I don't know about you, but I'm a stickler for clean, legible labels on my floppies. But if you've priced Mac disk labels lately, you may have decided to make do with scratching out and reusing the old ones. The prices are outrageous!

A better solution is as close as your local stationery store. You probably won't find any labels there that fit the disks exactly but you can cover the surface with a couple of them.

⬢ *ultracheap disk storage* (CJW)

The average (men's) shoe box will comfortably hold 200 diskettes in two side-by-side rows of 100 each. Shoe boxes stack neatly and can be decorated on the outside in a variety of ways.

bargain

⬢ *airport X-ray machines* (DC)

Since 1977, I've been shlepping disks in my carry-on luggage. I've run them through the security X-ray machines at airports all over the world and I've never lost so much as a bit. I recently heard a Mac enthusiast describe his trip to Australia and New Zealand, disks in tow. His experience is the same as mine.

In spite of all that, airport security can be dangerous to disks. The problem isn't the X-rays but the powerful magnetic motors in the X-ray machines. So if you want to play it completely safe, have your disks hand-checked.

Memory upgrades

⬢ *memory upgrade overview* (LP)

There are three different types of memory upgrades—board swaps, daughter boards and SIMMs. Which you use depends on which Mac you have.

The original 128K Mac contained sixteen 64K RAM (memory) chips—for what, at the time, seemed a whopping amount of memory. A year later, Apple substituted 256K chips and was able to produce essentially the same machine with four times as much memory. In both cases, the chips were soldered (not socketed) to the *motherboard* (the main printed circuit board in the Mac).

Rather than having to desolder and resolder 256 connections (sixteen pins times sixteen chips), dealers took your old board in trade (it went back to the factory to become someone else's upgrade) and sold you a new one. This is called a *board swap.*

To upgrade the 512K Mac, you need a *daughter board* (so called because it mounts on top of the motherboard). MacSnap models from Dove Computer snap into place without soldering but only work with absolutely perfect motherboards; if there's been any previous upgrade or repair work, the snaps may not line up properly.

Other daughter boards, like Sophisticated Circuits' Macs-a-Million, come with a wiring harness that solders onto the motherboard. These units are much harder to install but are more tolerant of previous upgrades.

An important consideration when buying a daughter board is whether the extra memory is socketed or soldered. Socketed is always easier to deal with.

Beginning with the Mac Plus, Apple started supplying RAM chips on *SIMMs* (short for *single in-line memory modules).* Upgrading a Plus or an SE is simple—all you have to do is replace two or four of the standard 256K SIMMs that come with the machine with 1-meg SIMMs. (You may also have to clip a resistor, but that's about it.) Some upgrades provide a second set of connectors so you can use your old memory as well.

Like the SE and the Plus, the Mac II comes with four 256K SIMMs (making one meg) and slots for four more. The slots are arranged in two banks of four and you have to fill the whole bank with chips of the same size. This gives you just four options:

1. You can leave the first bank filled with 256K SIMMs and leave the second bank empty. This gives you the 1 meg of memory the computer comes with.

2. You can leave the first bank filled with 256K SIMMs and fill the other with 256K SIMMs. This gives you 2 megs of memory total.

3. You can leave the first bank filled with 256K SIMMs and fill the other with 1-meg SIMMs. This gives you 5 megs of memory total.

4. You can fill both banks with 1-meg SIMMs. This gives you 8 megs of memory total—the maximum you can get without special fiddling.

The speed of SIMMs is measured in *nanoseconds* (abbreviated *NS*). The lower the number on the chip, the faster it is. The Plus and the SE need SIMMs rated at less than 200NS (they usually come with 150NS) but the Mac II needs ones rated at less than 140NS (it usually comes with 120NS). Using SIMMs from a Plus or an SE (or off a dealer's shelf) that are slower than 140NS will cause what are called *soft errors* if you put them in a II.

important warning

[Some SEs (and maybe even some Pluses) are shipped with 120NS SIMMs and these will work fine in a II. I'm using a couple I got from a friend in my II and haven't had any problems.—AN]

❤ *acceleration too* (LP)

Sometimes extra memory is combined with a higher-speed CPU chip on an accelerator board. Speed is especially important when you plan to use an external monitor. As screen size increases, so does the time it takes to draw a screen. Most monitors have extra memory on their video cards to take care of this problem but even so, an accelerator board usually speeds things up.

Some accelerators have sockets for math coprocessor chips, which cost about $300 as we go to press. These won't do much for you unless you work with complex formulas and large spreadsheets. If you're not absolutely sure that you need a math coprocessor, it generally means you don't.

very hot tip

Accelerators come in all shapes and sizes, and they're available for every model of the Mac from the 512K on up. Some of the older accelerators, like Levco's Monster Mac, use a special kind of daughter board. Others designed for the Macintosh SE and the Macintosh II are properly referred to as *cards* because they plug into expansion slots.

♦ *what to look for in an accelerator board* *(FT)*

bargain

If you need color, or if money is no object, the Mac II is the Mac to buy (at this point in time, at any rate). But if neither of those statements applies to you, an SE or a Mac Plus with a third-party accelerator board will give you the power and speed of a Mac II at a fraction of the cost. There are even accelerator boards for 512K Macs.

When shopping for an accelerator board, the first thing to think about is what chip it uses. The 68000 chip the Plus and SE (and all earlier Macs) are built around runs at a speed of about 8 MHz. The more powerful 68020 chip the II is built around runs at 16 MHz. Some manufacturers of accelerator boards for the SE or the Plus use a 16 MHz version of the 68000 to give you the speed of the 68020 without the expense. And some boards use a 25MHz version of the 68020.

very hot tip

Some accelerators have a socket for a 68881 math coprocessor chip. As mentioned in the previous entry, math coprocessors are for *very* heavy number crunching. If you don't know what a *floating point* operation is, you don't need a 68881 (even if you do know, you probably don't need one).

very hot tip

You can also get a 68551 "paged-memory-management" chip that allows up to eight megabytes of contiguous memory (as opposed to the four megs possible on an unmodified SE). But right now A/UX, Apple's version of Unix, is the only environment that can use eight megs of contiguous memory, and A/UX only runs on the Mac II. The 68030 chip has the functions of the 68551 built-in, and by the time the SE could make use of eight megabytes, the 68030 might be shipping in quantity and might even be affordable.

Some accelerator boards for the SE have a connection that lets you add another card (in effect, they create another slot to replace the one they're taking up).

If you're planning to purchase a large screen at some point, you should know that not all external monitors work with all boards. For example, the Radius accelerator boards are only compatible with Radius's Full Page and Two Page Displays while the Prodigy board works with several different monitors.

important warning

Accelerator boards aren't always compatible with memory upgrades. If you don't have surface-mount SIMMs, the board may push against the chips. I have two MacMemory SIMMs that are only slightly taller than Apple SIMMs, but their height kept me from installing the Prodigy board. The Radius accelerators have a cutout over the SIMMs to deal with this problem.

important warning

Another way in which accelerator boards obviously vary is cost. As of this writing, they range from SuperMac's SpeedCard ($400 without the math coprocessor) to the Levco 4MB Prodigy board for the Plus and the 512K Mac ($3500).

The chart below compares the speed of three accelerator boards I tested (all running on an SE) and two unmodified Macs. I timed how long it took to scroll from the top to the bottom of a 245-page Word document, to read that same document into PageMaker 3.0, and to autoflow 128 pages of it. To test the 68881, I calculated the amortization of a $200,000 loan.

	scroll Word doc.	open in PM 3.0	auto- flow 128p.	calc. amor- tiz.
stock SE	20:46	13:23	10:50	1:28
5MB Mac II	8:52	6:40	8:48	:19
Prodigy SE	8:58	7:08	4:12	:15
Radius 16	9:18	4:31	4:11	:22
Radius 25	8:18	3:33	3:55	:14

(But remember that disk drives, external monitors and different amounts of memory can all affect these speeds.)

important warning

Installing most accelerator boards is simple enough that you can do it if you have the correct tools and a smattering of knowledge about the inside of the Mac—although some board manufacturers require installation by an authorized technician. You should be aware that once you (or anyone but an Apple-authorized technician) opens the case of an SE or a Plus, you void the warranty.

very good feature

Most software has been updated to work on the Mac II, so it should also work with any 68020 accelerator board; you shouldn't have any compatibility problems with a board based on a 16MHz 68000 either. I ran all of the popular programs on the Radius and Prodigy boards and everything worked fine. Even MacWrite 4.5, which isn't compatible with the Mac II or the other accelerator boards, ran on the Radius boards.

But you can't depend on that. Sometimes the only way to check if an accelerator board is crashing a piece of software is to turn the board off. So being able to do that easily is a real plus.

An idiosyncrasy of the accelerators I tested is that they make sounds (the Mac's beeps, music, etc.) fuzzy. This is less of a problem on 68000-based boards. I've heard that the Novy boards come with a software patch that eliminates this problem.

♠ *Radius Accelerator & Accelerator 25* (FT)

The Accelerator has a 16MHz 68000 and the Accelerator 25 a 25MHz 68020; as of this writing, they cost $1000 and $1400. A 16MHz 68881 chip is an optional feature on both, adding $400–800 to the price. Turning either board off is very easy and accomplished with software. Both have a 32K RAM cache to supplement the one on the Control Panel.

Although the installation manual is very clear and even has photographs of the major steps, Radius requires that an authorized dealer with Apple certification install the board. The user manual is very thorough and contains a trouble-shooting section. Both boards have a 90-day warranty.

🍎 *Prodigy* (FT)

The Prodigy board comes in 1MB ($1500), 2MB ($2000) and 4MB ($2800 on the SE, $3500 on the Plus and 512K) configurations, with the 68881 standard on all. (The SE versions of the board are sold by SuperMac, the Plus and 512K by Levco, who originally designed all of them.)

The RAM on the boards is proprietary and if you upgrade your board later, you have to buy the chips from SuperMac or Levco. There's a socket on the board for a 68551 chip, but it's not offered as an option. An optional connector lets you use E-Machines, SuperMac, Viking or LaserView monitors with the board.

You can turn off the board or the 68881 with software but returning to 68000 mode isn't as easy as on the Radius boards—you have to close all programs and desk accessories, press and hold down the interrupt button on the programmer's switch, then press and release the reset button.

The Prodigy board ran all major programs without problems, but the AutoBlack screen blanker didn't work. I also ran into trouble with the ImageWriter LQ. When I tried to print from any program, the program crashed just as the document finished printing. SuperMac's tech support told me to connect the printer to the modem port and, amazingly enough, that fixed the problem.

The Prodigy's software lets you use the RAM on your SE's motherboard as a RAM disk. Though you can't have eight megs of contiguous memory, you can have a four-meg RAM disk and another four megs of regular RAM.

Although the installation manual is well illustrated, SuperMac requires that an authorized dealer install the Prodigy. The board has a one-year warranty.

Chapter 4

Basic system software

Tips about windows

⚫ *opening windows temporarily* (DC)

If you're using a hard disk, you probably have some files that are buried several folders deep. When you exit from one of these files after working on it, there's a long wait as the Finder recreates the cluttered Desktop you left, with all the windows still open that you opened to get down to the file.

There's a way to avoid this delay. Hold down the Option key while working your way down through all of those folders on the way to the file. Then when you exit from the program, the Finder will forget that they were ever open and return you to the Desktop much more quickly.

very hot tip

In other words, if you hold down Option when you open a window, it won't stay open after you leave the Desktop to run an application. When you come back to the Desktop, the window will be closed. You can use this technique for as many windows as you want, and for disk windows as well as folder windows. (For other variations on this theme, see the next two entries.)

⚫ *speedy return to the Desktop* (DC)

Even if you didn't hold down the Option key while opening windows (as per the previous entry), you can tell the Mac to close them from within an application. Just hold down Option when you choose *Quit* from the File menu; you'll be returned to an empty Desktop—with no open windows—in much less time than it would otherwise take.

shortcut

⚫ *closing all the windows on the Desktop* (DC)

To close all the windows open on the Desktop, just hold down Option when you close a window. Every other window on the Desktop will close too. (For other variations on this theme, see the two previous entries.)

shortcut

✦ *moving inactive windows* (DC)

very
hot
tip

It can be annoying to always have to select a window before moving it. To move a window that's not active (not selected), just hold down the ⌘ key while dragging it.

✦ *shrinking windows* (FT)

By letting you keep several applications open at the same time, MultiFinder has emphasized how painfully small the 9-inch screen is. In or out of MultiFinder, if you have more than half a dozen windows open, you can get lost in the thicket of scroll bars. An Fkey called ShrinkWindow can reduce some of this overcrowding.

ShrinkWindow shrinks the active window so that only the title bar shows. With all of the windows shrunk to just the title bar (you just cycle through them to do that), you can quickly tile the windows so they're all visible at once. Then you only have to click on the zoom box of the document you want to work on and zoom it back down when you're done. This makes switching between documents and programs much faster.

✦ *moving icons into windows Viewed by Name, etc.* (DC)

**important
warning**

Be careful when you move a file to a window that's displayed in any mode other than by Icon, especially if a number of names on the list are for folders rather than for files. It's very easy to select one of those folders by accident, and then the file you moved will be hidden away inside of it, rather than out in the larger window where you meant to put it. You can have quite a time trying to find it, opening one folder after another.

The best way to avoid this problem is to drag the icons you want to copy to the part of the window just below the title bar (the rectangular space where the words *Name, Size, Kind* and *Last Modified* appear). Since no icons can appear there, there's no danger of the icons you're dragging disappearing into a folder.

♠ *the zoom box* (AN)

At the right end of an active window's title bar there's a small box with an even smaller box within it. That's the *zoom box* (the whole icon—both boxes). Click on it and the window expands to fill the screen; click on it again and it resumes its former size and shape.

esp. for beginners

This is a nice feature, but it could be implemented better. On a large monitor, for example, the whole screen option is ridiculous; it looks as if someone has suddenly opened a bedsheet in front of your screen. The size and shape of the larger size should be user-adjustable, in the Control Panel.

♠ *keyboard shortcuts in dialog boxes* (DC/AN)

↑	moves you up through a list of folders
↓	moves you down through a list of folders
~ (tilde)	takes you to the end of the list
(Shift isn't necessary)	
Backspace , → or ←	takes you to the beginning of the list (although, for some reason, you often have to hit the arrows more than once)
⌘– ↑	moves you up through a hierarchy of folders
⌘– ↓	moves you down through a hierarchy of folders
Tab	same as clicking on the Drive button (if there is no Drive button, Tab steps you through whatever text boxes there are)

very hot tip

♠ *a nonkeyboard nonshortcut* (AN)

If you click on the disk icon in a dialog box (it's next to the name of the disk, over on the right, above the Eject button), it will move you up through a hierarchy of folders.

gossip/ trivia

Of course, if you're going to use the mouse, it's easier simply to *scroll* through the hierarchy of folders directly (using the menu that pops down over the list box), so this is really more a curiosity than a tip.

shortcut

⚫ *cancelling Save... or Open...* (DC)

You can cancel a Save or Open dialog box by pressing ⌘-period.

⚫ *using Clean Up to rearrange icons* (DC)

There are two ways to have the Mac automatically organize a window in which the icons are strewn messily about.

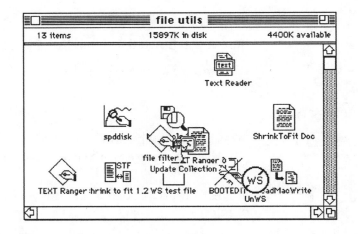

If the icons are more or less where you want them, choose *Clean Up* from the Special menu. The icons will move to the nearest available location along an invisible grid.

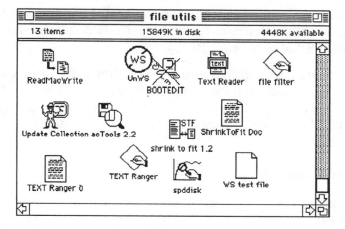

If the icons are totally disorganized, you can do a more thoroughgoing rearrangement by holding down the Option key when you choose *Clean Up.* The icons will then be moved from wherever they are and placed in neat horizontal rows, beginning in the upper left corner of the window.

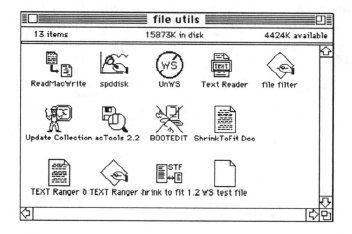

For an even better way to organize your icons (although one that requires more of your personal attention), see the entry on Naimanizing below.

🍎 *organizing icons alphabetically* (DC)

Here's a way to organize all the icons in a window alphabetically. Open the folder you want to organize.

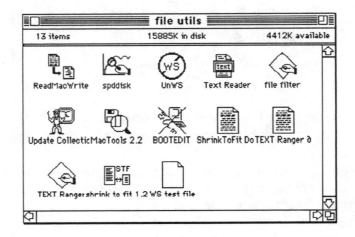

**very
hot
tip**

Choose *by Name* from the View menu. Now choose *Select All* from the Edit menu (or hit ⌘–A). Drag all the icons out of the folder and onto the Desktop.

Now select *by Icon* from the View menu and drag the still-selected icons back from the Desktop to the folder. Finally, hold down Option and choose *Clean Up* from the Special menu. Your files and folders will now be arranged alphabetically, from left to right.

🍎 *selective Clean Up* (DC)

If no icons are selected within a window, the command appears as *Clean Up Window* on the menu. If one or more icons are selected, the command changes to *Clean Up Selection* and only the selected icons are rearranged.

🍎 *Naimanizing* (AN)

On most icons, the name is wider than the picture, giving them the shape of stovepipe hats (with the name as the brim). In addition, the names usually vary in length, so that some icons have very wide brims, some narrower ones and some no brim at all.

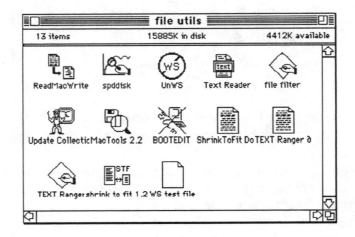

If you simply ignore this fact when you line icons up (as the *Clean Up* command does), the names will either interfere with each other, or you'll be forced to put icons farther apart than you'd like.

Here's a simple way to neatly organize your icons so that none of the names overlap, and so that you can get the maximum number of icons possible on the screen. First, choose *Clean Up* from the Special menu (if your icons are really scrambled all over the window, hold down the Option key while choosing *Clean Up)*. This will organize your icons in neat rows along the invisible grid. They will also be aligned in neat columns, and that's the key to this trick.

Use the selection rectangle to select the second column of icons. Now move the column down just enough so that its icon names don't overlap with the icon names in the first column. Repeat this procedure with all the other pairs of columns. Now your window will look something like this:

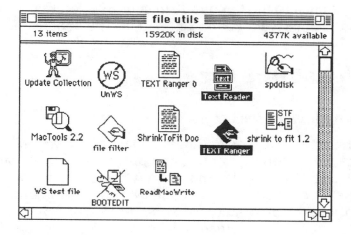

If you want to fit as many icons as possible into the window, you can also move the columns closer together and switch icons around to accommodate unusual shapes. This tightest possible packing looks something like this:

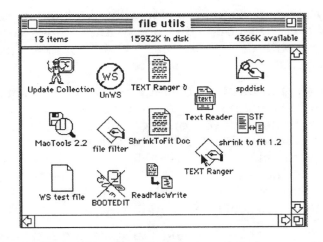

This technique of tucking the name of an icon under the names of its neighbors is known as *Naimanizing (NAY-mun-eye-zing)*. The origins of this term are lost in the mists of history. Some scholars suggest that it's a play on the word *name,* but that wouldn't account for the spelling. Others trace it back to the famous 17th-century explorer, philosophe and bon vivant Balthasar Naiman. The debate goes on.

Tips about files

✎ *two kinds of files* (AN)

**esp. for
beginners**

There are two basic kinds of files: *documents,* which contain data you've created, and *programs,* which you use to create documents and to run the system. Because application programs are far and away the most commonly used kind of programs, we sometimes write *documents and applications* instead of the more precise *documents and programs.* In any case, both phrases are equivalent to *files.*

✎ *easy way to tell if a file is locked* (DC)

Just select the icon and put the pointer over its name. If the pointer changes to an I-beam, the file isn't locked; if it stays an arrow, the file is locked.

🍎 *easy way to put away files* (DC)

If you have a file icon out on the Desktop that you want to put away, you don't have to drag it back to its original folder (which can be quite a task if it's nested several folders deep). Just select the icon, then choose *Put Away* from the File menu. The file will scurry back to wherever it was you got it from.

🍎 *printing multiple documents* (DC)

You can only do this from the Desktop. All you have to do is select the documents you want to print (either by shift-clicking or using the selection rectangle) and then choose *Print* from the File menu. The documents will be printed one after the other, in the order in which you selected them.

esp. for beginners

This technique will work only if the application that created the documents is on an active disk. For example, if you insert a MacPaint data disk in the external drive but MacPaint itself is not on a disk in any of the drives, the files will not print.

🍎 *no colons in file names* (AN)

You can use just about any symbol you want in the name of a Mac file, except for the colon (:). If you try to put it in, the Mac automatically turns it into a hyphen.

🍎 *keeping filenames at the top of a list* (MB)

I once tried to make a table of characters showing how the Mac sorts things like filenames and database records— *a* before *z*, *0* before *9*, *æ* before *œ*, things like that. It turned out to be impossible, because the Mac sorts things differently at different times. For example, in Finder windows, file names starting with a delta symbol (Δ) are sorted to the bottom of lists but in dialog boxes they're sorted to the top.

But if you start filenames with three particular special characters, they'll sort to the top of lists in all situations. A blank space always goes to the very top, followed by an exclamation mark, followed by the number symbol (#).

So if the files you want most often always seem to be down at the bottom of the list, with names like *second draft* and *Word utilities.* simply stuck a space or an exclamation mark in front of their names and they'll pop to the top of the list.

*very
hot
tip*

There is one wrinkle: the Finder won't let you begin a file name with a space. But there's a simple way around this limitation—just add a letter, followed by a space, to the beginning of the name, then delete the letter.

❖ *correcting mistaken icon names* (DC/AN)

*esp. for
beginners*

Sometimes when you're renaming a file or folder, you realize that you were better off before you start changing the name. Even more often, you accidentally hit a key while an icon is selected and rename it *z* or / or something.

If either of these things happens, all you have to do is hold down the [Backspace] until all the characters in the new name have been deleted, then hit [Return]. Voila! The original name is back. (You can also hit [⌘]–Z, which saves you having to backspace.)

❖ *pointers' hot spots* (AN)

You can't just use any part of a pointer to click on something and select it (or otherwise affect it). With each pointer shape there's a *hot spot,* a part of the pointer that counts; other parts of the pointer have no effect. For example, the arrow pointer's hot spot is its tip; the crosshairs pointer's hot spot is its center (where the two lines cross).

❖ *comparing files with Get Info* (DC)

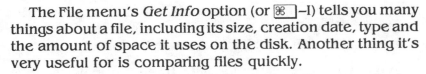

*esp. for
beginners*

The File menu's *Get Info* option (or [⌘]–I) tells you many things about a file, including its size, creation date, type and the amount of space it uses on the disk. Another thing it's very useful for is comparing files quickly.

You may want to compare files for a variety of reasons— for example, to determine which copy of a document is the most recent. You can open several Get Info windows on screen at one time, and you can move them all around. But you can't shrink them, which is too bad, because they're kind of large.

⚫ *locking documents with Get Info* (DC)

To lock a file, simply click on the box marked *Locked* in the Get Info window. When a document is locked, you can only save it to disk if you use *Save As...* to give it another name, and you can't throw it in the Trash.

esp. for beginners

To unlock a document, simply choose *Get Info* again and click on the Locked box. The *X* in the box will disappear and you'll be able to modify the document and save it under its own name. You can lock and unlock documents as often as you like.

⚫ *using templates to change defaults* (MB/DC)

All applications have default settings for things like font and type size, ruler, print quality, spreadsheet size and data format. Sometimes you can change the defaults, but often you can't. This means every new document will always start out formatted the standard way, whether you like it or not. If you don't like it, you should try using templates to format new documents the way you want them.

esp. for beginners

A *template* is a document with a special format that you use repeatedly—for example, one containing your letterhead, so you don't have to recreate the letterhead every time you want to write a letter. They're easy to make. All you have to do is open a new document choose the formatting you want. When you're done, save the document with a name like *biz ltr, memo* or *standard Excel template.* There's no limit to how many different kinds of templates you can make.

To format a new document like one of your templates, don't use the *New...* command on the File menu. Instead, open the template and immediately save it with the name you want to give your new document (*Save As...* on the File menu). This automatically transfers the template's format-ting to the new document.

Because of the way templates are used, they run a special risk of being overwritten. You can avoid this risk by locking them (see the last entry for details on how to do that). This will prevent you from saving a modified template under the original name and will force you into the correct habit—always Saving As as soon as you open the template.

If you need to change the template itself, it's easy enough to unlock it. But don't forget to lock it again when you've finished making changes to it.

✎ finding the size of folders (DC)

esp. for beginners

One annoying feature of the Finder is that when you're Viewing by Size, Kind or Date, the size of folders isn't listed (unless the folder's window is open). One solution is to select a folder, then choose *Get Info* from the File menu (or, easier, hit ⌘ –I). The Get Info window will give you, in K, the total size of all the files and folders contained in the folder.

✎ duplicating a file between folders (DC)

very hot tip

The Mac only duplicates a file if you move it from one disk to another (leaving a copy on the source disk as well as on the destination disk); when you drag it from one folder to another on the same disk, the file actually moves (that is, it disappears from the source folder).

Sometimes that's what you want, but you do have a choice: if you hold down the Option key when dragging the icon, the Mac will leave a copy of the file in the source folder as well as in the destination folder.

✎ be careful when replacing folders (CR)

Roger Galliett wrote in with a good, common-sense suggestion:

When you drag a folder from one disk onto a folder with the same name on another disk, the contents of the first completely replace the contents of the second. This can be a problem if the folder on the destination disk contains some extra files that the dragged folder doesn't.

important warning

For example, if you have a folder called *dogs* on one disk that contains two files, *dobermans* and *retrievers*, and you drag a folder called *dogs* from another disk that contains two files, *dobermans* and *poodles*, the *retrievers* file will be irretrievably lost. So be careful!

MultiFinder Tips

♠ *Set Startup...* *(SZA)*

To start up in MultiFinder, use the *Set Startup...* command on the Finder's Special menu and then reboot. (To go back to the Finder, use the same command.) You can choose to start up with MultiFinder alone, or with applications that are selected when you choose *Set Startup...*, or with the applications and documents that are currently open; just click the appropriate buttons in the Set Startup dialog box.

esp. for beginners

♠ *temporarily disabling MultiFinder* *(SZA)*

If MultiFinder is the startup and for some reason you want to disable it, hold down the `Option` key as the Mac starts up. This forces the Finder to take over, but leaves MultiFinder still set for startup the next time. (Note that this may cause some inits not to load.)

esp. for beginners

♠ *shutting down with applications open* *(AN)*

If you choose *Shut Down* from the Finder's Special menu while in MultiFinder with other applications open, you'll get the standard *Save changes...?* dialog box for all open documents (a piece of idiot-proofing for which idiots like myself are quite grateful).

esp. for beginners

⚫ cycling through applications *(SZA)*

esp. for
beginners

Click on the little icon at the right end of the menu bar to switch to another active application; the icon will change as you cycle through all the programs you have open.

⚫ opening multiple applications *(SZA)*

Even if you don't set multiple applications to start up automatically, you can open several at the same time (as opposed to one after the other). Just click on the first application you want, shift-click on the others and then double-click on any one of them (or choose *Open...* from the File menu). Note that for this to work, the applications have to be in the same window, because you can't shift-click between windows.

⚫ getting DAs out of the way *(SZA)*

very
hot
tip

If you've used Suitcase or Font/DA Juggler Plus to cram your ⚫ menu full of desk accessories, it can be a real drag (excuse the pun) to scroll through them all when you want to get to the applications listed at the bottom of the menu. To make all of them (except Suitcase or Font/DA Juggler) temporarily disappear, hold down the Option key when you open the ⚫ menu.

⚫ making DAs application-specific *(SZA)*

Not all DAs add their own menus to the menu bar, but you can assign those that do to specific applications, rather than having them appear on the menu bar all the time. You do that by holding down the Option key while you choose the DA from the ⚫ menu.

From then on, that DA will be available only when you're working in the application you were in at that time. Quitting or closing the DA as usual while you're in that application is all it takes to remove it from the menu bar.

At first glance, it would seem that you can't use this trick when you're using Suitcase or Font/DA Juggler Plus, since both programs hide the DAs on the ⚫ menu when you hold down the ⌈Option⌋ key. But there's a way around this. Just pop down the ⌘ menu without pressing the ⌈Option⌋ key, *then* press it and choose the DA you want to assign.

There's another advantage to this: it lets the DA use the memory already set aside for the application, instead of having to carve out an additional chunk for itself.

⌘ *solving "not enough memory" problems* (SZA)

esp. for beginners

Sometimes an application running under MultiFinder will tell you that it doesn't have enough memory. You can fix that by changing how much memory MultiFinder gives the application.

To do that, quit the application, then select its icon in the Finder and *Get Info* on it. The Get Info box will list a Suggested Memory Size and an Application Memory Size; unless you've changed the latter, they'll be the same. All you have to do is make the Application Memory Size larger, as we've done below:

If your initial guess isn't big enough, repeat the process until you get it right. At some later point, when you're trying to squeeze more applications into existing memory, you may want to make the Application Memory Size smaller again. But never go lower than the Suggested Memory Size, since that's the minimum for safe operation.

✿ *memory fragmentation* (SZA)

Programs need *contiguous RAM* to run in; that means that the memory they use has to be all in one place and not split apart by other pieces of memory used by other programs. If you open and close lots of applications during a work session, the memory gets *fragmented.* This can be a problem, because a segment initially set aside for one application may not be big enough for another, and you may wind up with lots of unusable memory.

Fortunately, all you have to do to unfragment the memory is quit all the open applications and launch them again. You don't have to restart your Mac.

✿ *MultiFinder and memory* (SM)

Under MultiFinder, *About the Finder...* (on the ✿ menu) won't always accurately tell you how much memory you have available, because it simply reports the size of the largest single block of unoccupied memory. (By the way, it's always *About the Finder...*, never *About the MultiFinder....*)

For example, let's say you start up SuperPaint, which uses 200K of RAM (these are just dummy numbers). Then you go to the Finder and start up Microsoft Works. With both those programs (and the Finder) running, let's say you have 175K of memory left. Then you go back to SuperPaint and quit it. *About the Finder...* will report that the Largest Unused Block of memory is 200K (the space left where SuperPaint was, which is now the largest block of unoccupied memory). But actually you have 375K left (200K + 175K). Multifinder can't find both blocks, because they're separated by the portion of memory occupied by MacWrite.

The solution is to quit MacWrite—or whatever program is separating the unoccupied portions of memory—then start it up again (if you still want to use it). It will now occupy the lowest available portion of memory.

To avoid this problem in general, you should always try to first load the program you expect to be using for the longest time, then the program you expect to be using for the next longest time and so on.

Obviously, the real solution to this problem is for Apple to teach MultiFinder to either move things around when a program is quit so that all memory is contiguous, or to find and total all unoccupied portions of memory, whether they're contiguous or not.

✎ *the right edge* (SZA)

Here's a MultiFinder housekeeping tip: move the right edges of your application windows in a little from the right edge of the screen. Otherwise, you'll find that when you're in the Finder, you won't be able to get to the disk icons or the Trash. You'll have to click on the offending windows, thus activating them and putting you back in their applications, just so you can move them out of the way.

Miscellaneous basic tips

✎ *shift-clicking* (SM)

One way to select a number of different objects is with the *selection rectangle* (if you don't know what that is, see the glossary). Shift-clicking is another essential technique. Normally when you click on something to select it, the thing you selected last is automatically deselected. But if you hold the ⒮⒣⒤⒡⒯ key down, previously selected items stay selected.

esp. for beginners

You can see how useful this would be. Let's say you're working with the Font/DA Mover and want to copy fifteen fonts into the System file. Instead of having to select one, click on the Copy button, select another, hit the Copy button and so on, you just select all fifteen by shift-clicking on each one, hit the Copy button once and go do something else while the copying takes place.

Shift-clicking is also useful in object-oriented graphics programs like MacDraw, MacDraft, Mac 3D and Filevision, and on the Desktop to select several icons for copying, moving, deleting or putting into a folder. (There's another way to select multiple objects in these contexts—you draw a box around them with the selection rectangle. If objects you don't want fall into the rectangle, just shift-click on them and they'll be deselected.)

Shift-clicking can also be used to select large portions of continuous material like text. Let's say you want to select the whole of a MacWrite document. You'd click in front of the first character in the document, then use the scroll bar to move to the end of the document, position the I-beam after the last character, hold the [Shift] key down, and click again. This causes everything between the two clicks—the whole document, in this case—to be selected.

(This same technique works in Microsoft Word, but with Word it's sometimes easier to use the selection bar. See our tips on Word in chapter 10 for more details on this and other Word tricks.)

Shift-clicking works in a similar manner in spreadsheets: If you click in one cell, then shift-click in another, a rectangle of cells will be selected, with those two cells in the corners.

After you've selected a large hunk of text, you can use shift-clicking to deselect some of it (in other words, make your selection smaller without having to do it all over again), or to extend the selection. Position the I-beam at either the beginning or end of the selected text, hold down the [Shift] key, [Click] and drag in the appropriate direction.

About the only drawback to this technique is that you can just use it at one end or the other of a given selection. So, for example, if you've dragged at the end of a selection and then go to the beginning to drag there, the Mac will treat your click as the beginning of a new selection (even though you're holding down the Shift key) and you'll have to start over from scratch.

You can deselect objects in a similar manner, because if you shift-click on an object that's already selected, it deselects. In fact, you can toggle an object between selection and deselection by shift-clicking on it repeatedly.

escape from tear-off menus (AN)

More and more Mac programs are giving you *tear-off menus*—that is, menus you can detach from the menu bar and move around the screen like windows. Generally, they're a delight to use, but until you get used to them, you can feel trapped in them when you want to get out without choosing a command.

esp. for
beginners

The problem is, you can't get out by moving to the side, because that tears off the menu. The solution? Go out the bottom.

what to do when the lights go out (DC)

If your Mac's power supply goes out, the first thing to do (even before slashing your wrists) is to hit ⌘ –S. This will probably save the document you were working on, even if the whole screen has dwindled into one vertical line. (Obviously this only works with programs where ⌘ –S saves the file.) We're not guaranteeing anything, but it's certainly worth a try.

very
hot
tip

avoid first releases of system software (AN)

The first releases of Mac system software are often pretty buggy. Unless you enjoy being a pioneer (and the arrows through the hat that go with it), you should generally avoid versions of the System and Finder that end in *.0*. Wait for *.1* or *.2* before switching over, or at least until the *.0* version has been out for a couple of months and seems to be problem-free.

important
warning

(This will become even more important now that Apple says it plans to release new versions of the System and Finder every six months or so.)

❡ *preserving the contents of the Clipboard* (DC)

*esp. for
beginners*

The contents of the Clipboard are lost if you use Cut (⌘–X) to delete text, but if you use Backspace , the Clipboard remains unchanged.

If you accidentally cut when you didn't want to flush the Clipboard, choose *Undo* immediately (or hit ⌘–Z). The contents of the Clipboard will be restored, along with the text in your document.

❡ *flushing the Clipboard to free up memory* (DC)

If you run low on memory while using any application that supports the Clipboard (and all good applications do), you may be able to free up some memory by clearing out the Clipboard's contents. You do that by Copying a single character to the Clipboard, then doing it again.

The reason that you have to do it twice is that the first time you copy to the Clipboard, its previous contents remain in memory, in an area called the Undo Buffer. This is so you can undo the last copy, in case you didn't actually want to flush the buffer. When you copy the single character to the Clipboard the second time, the first letter you copied is placed in the Undo buffer (thus flushing out its previous contents), so that between them they only take up two bytes of memory.

❡ *... after a command name* (AN)

*esp. for
beginners*

When the name of a command on a menu is followed by an *ellipsis* (...), choosing it usually brings up a dialog box. (I shouldn't have to say *usually* but not everyone follows the convention.) When a command name isn't followed by an ellipsis, choosing it usually makes the command execute immediately (ditto for *usually*).

Option Trash (DC)

very hot tip

Holding down the Option key when dragging a file to the Trash has two effects: It lets you throw away locked files (so they don't bounce back from the Trash) and if you're throwing away an application, you won't be asked to confirm that that is indeed what you wanted to do.

flushing the Trash (DC)

Files placed in the Trash are not actually deleted from the disk until you do one of the following things:

- empty the Trash
- launch an application
- drag the disk's icon to the trash.
- copy a file to the disk
- Shut Down the system

If you haven't done any of those things, you can open the Trash and retrieve whatever you put in it.

retrieving files from the Trash (DC)

The best way to ensure that files retrieved from the Trash are put back where they came from is to open the Trash, select the files, and then choose *Put Away* from the File menu. Anytime *Put Away* is not dimmed, you can use it to return any selected file to its original folder.

recovering from some crashes and system hangs (DC)

Every Mac user experiences the dreaded bomb message from time to time. Most users have also experienced a system hang (that's when the Mac simply decides to ignore the mouse and the keyboard). In either case, your options are limited. You can click on the Restart button (if you have a bomb message), push the *reset* (front) button on the programmer's switch (if you have it installed) or turn the Mac's power switch off and on.

But if you do any of those things, all the information you hadn't saved to disk is lost forever. If you're using a hard disk, you'll also have to wait from one to five minutes while the hard disk checks to make sure everything is all right before putting you back on the Desktop.

So we always try the following technique first, even though it fails most of the time (often giving you a bomb message from a system hang, for example). But you have nothing to lose, because if it doesn't work, you're no worse off than when you started. Here's what to do:

The *interrupt* button is in the back of the programmer's switch, behind the *reset button*. (You have to have the programmer's switch installed for this trick to work.) When you hit it, a large rectangular box with a > in the upper left corner appears on the screen. (If it doesn't, just give up and push the reset button. If your system wasn't hung, it will be now.)

This box is the command area for the Mac's internal debugger. It's used primarily by Mac software developers, but this is an instance when regular users like us can use it too. Type in: sm fa700 a9f4 and hit Return . Then type in: pc fa700 and hit Return again. Now type in: g and hit Return one last time.

You'll get a bunch of numbers on the screen each time you hit Return , but the > will be there with room after it for your commands, so just ignore the numbers and type in the next command line.

Be sure to type in exactly what's shown here, with spaces and line breaks where indicated. The characters you type will show up as caps, but we've written them lowercase because that's how you should type them; you gain nothing by holding down the Shift key. All the 0's are zeros, not capital O's.

As we said above, we don't guarantee that those commands will work; in fact, most of the time they probably won't. We can't even promise you that they won't damage your files, although we've never experienced anything like that and we use this technique ourselves all the time. We think you have nothing to lose by trying it, but feel free to be conservative and just restart the system.

✦ *silencing alert beeps* (DC)

There are two ways to turn off the beep the Mac makes when it wants your attention. One way is to open the Control Panel and set the volume level to zero. Now, instead of beeping at you, the menu bar will flash silently to get your attention. (Some programs may override this.)

A surer way to silence the alert beeps is to plug a mini jack (like the one used for headphones on a Walkman) into the music socket on the back of the Mac. You can get a mini jack for about $2 at Radio Shack and similar places.

✦ *init files—finding the troublemakers* (SM)

Init files are wonderful (if you don't know what they are, see the glossary) but they can sometimes cause crashes or other problems (sometimes they can even prevent the Mac from booting). To see if an init is at fault, create a new folder called *inits* (or whatever) and copy all the inits to it. This will inactivate them, even if you keep the new folder in your system folder, because inits need to be right out in the system folder to work. Then restart your Mac. (Until you do that, they're still in effect from the last time you started the Mac.)

If an init was causing the problem, you should now be OK. If you are, start putting the init files back into the system folder one at a time, beginning with the most necessary/important ones. Restart each time you move an init. When the difficulties reappear, you'll have isolated the problem init.

✦ *where Get Info info is stored* (AN)

The information you type into a Get Info box is stored in the Desktop file, an invisible file that keeps track of things like window sizes and locations. If you copy files to a disk and don't also copy the Desktop file, the note space in their Get Info boxes will be blank.

■ *grammar alert* (AN)

*gossip/
trivia*

When you choose the *Shut Down* command from the Finder's Special menu on any Mac that has a conventional on/off power switch (unlike the one on the Mac II's keyboard), you get a message that reads: *You may now switch off your Macintosh safely.* What that means is: *you* can *now switch off your Mac safely.*

The person who wrote this message obviously never recovered from grade school teachers telling him to say *May I go to the bathroom* instead of *Can I go to the bathroom?* (they assumed, probably correctly, that he had the *ability* to go to the bathroom pretty much whenever he wanted to).

Well, *may* is correct in that case (although it smacks of a sort of mundane fascism, as does so much of what was pounded into our heads in grammar school). But when you're asking for information about whether it's safe to shut off your Mac, and not permission to do so, *may* is incorrect. (It's also a perfect example of *overcompensation*—as epitomized by Anita Loos's classic line, *a girl like I.*)

The Mac is full of poorly written and often confusing messages. Apple ought to get a good writer in to clean them up.

■ *Easy Access* (DC)

Easy Access is a free system software designed for disabled people who have difficulty using the mouse or issuing multiple key commands ([Shift] [Option] –8, say). To make it work, you simply put it in your system folder and follow the instructions below. It offers two new features: Sticky Keys and Mouse Keys.

Sticky Keys lets you type key combinations one at a time instead of having to press the keys simultaneously. You turn Sticky Keys on by pressing the ⌈Shift⌉ key five times in a row. (Be sure not to move the mouse while you're doing this or you'll have to start over.) You turn it off by pressing the ⌈Shift⌉ key five times again or by pressing any two of the following keys simultaneously: ⌈⌘⌉, ⌈Shift⌉, ⌈Option⌉ or the SE's *control* key. (Apple recommends using ⌈Option⌉⌈⌘⌉ because they're close together.)

Mouse Keys lets you use the numeric keypad to do all the things you usually do with the mouse. (You have to have the Mac Plus or SE/II keyboard to use Mouse Keys; it doesn't work with the separate Apple Numeric Keypad sold for the original Mac keyboard.) To turn on Mouse Keys you press ⌈Shift⌉, ⌈⌘⌉ and the *clear* key (on the numeric keypad) simultaneously (or sequentially, if you're using Sticky Keys).

Keys 1–4 and 6–9 on the numeric keypad move the pointer up, down, left, right and diagonally. Pressing the 5 key is the same as clicking the mouse. The 0 key is the equivalent of holding the mouse button down, and the decimal point is equivalent to releasing it.

So, for example, if you wanted to open a menu with Mouse Keys, you'd use keys 1–4 and 6–9 to move to its title, then hit 0 to make the menu drop down. The 8 and 2 keys would move you up and down the menu. When the command you wanted was selected, you'd execute it by hitting the decimal point. To leave the menu without selecting anything, you'd simply move the pointer outside of it, then hit the decimal point.

When you use the keypad to move the cursor, you'll notice that the longer you press a key, the faster the pointer moves. If you want to adjust the speed, use the Control Panel to change the mouse speed (the option labeled Tablet is the slowest).

You can get very precise control of pointer movement by tapping the keys. Each brief tap will move the pointer one pixel.

Here's how to shift-click with Easy Access. (If you don't know what shift-clicking is, see the entry above.) First, turn on Sticky Keys, then press [Shift] twice to lock it down and use the 5 key to click where you want your selection to begin. Use the keypad to move the pointer to where you want the selection to end and press the 5 key again. Everything between the two positions will now be selected.

From the WetPaint clip art collection.
Copyright © 1988–89 by Dubl-Click Software Inc. All rights reserved.

Chapter 5

Fonts

Font basics

⌘ *what is a font?* (AN)

*esp. for
beginners*

In regular typesetting, a font is a particular typeface in a particular size and a particular style (bold, italic, etc.) On the Mac, however, *font* has come to mean a typeface in every size and every style (what a regular typesetter calls "a type family").

For example, Geneva comes supplied in six sizes and, on the ImageWriter, it can be transformed into sixteen different type styles (bold, italic, etc—see the entry below on font styles for details). A regular typesetter would call that 96 different fonts; to a Mac user, it's all one font—Geneva.

With the introduction of the LaserWriter, which much more closely approximates regular typesetting, there's a move on to bring the two terminologies closer together. In the glossary in the LaserWriter manual, for example, the definition for *font* is followed by one for *font family*—"a font in various sizes and styles."

But I think Mac users have gotten too used to their own meaning of the word to be pushed back into line with the old terminology. When you change the size or style of some type, you don't think of it as changing the *font*. So, throughout this book, I use *font* in the classic Mac sense: a typeface in every size and style.

⌘ *font styles* (AN)

*esp. for
beginners*

On dot matrix printers like the ImageWriter, every font can be made bold, italic, outline, shadow and any combination thereof—which amounts to bold italic, bold outline, bold shadow, italic outline, italic shadow, outline shadow, bold italic outline, bold italic shadow, bold outline shadow, italic outline shadow, bold italic outline shadow and, of course, plain—sixteen possible combinations in all.

Some of these combinations may seem foolish to you, but it's not just a case of meaningless overkill—quite often one variation will have just the look you want and no other variation will be quite right. And you'll find that in another font, that particular variation will look terrible and a different one will be just right. (For an easy way to see them all, see the entry on font templates below.)

Type styles (except for some on the LaserWriter) are derived *algorithmically*—that is, by the application of a rules like *increase the width 15%* (to create boldface) or *slant right 11°* (to create italics).

On laser printers, you don't get all sixteen variations; how many you do get depends on the font. For more details, see the entry *type styles on laser printers* in the printer chapter.

❤ *the two kinds of Mac fonts* (AN)

esp. for beginners

Every Mac comes equipped with fonts designed for printing on dot-matrix printers like the ImageWriter. They're called *bit-mapped fonts,* because they're made up of dots; *ImageWriter fonts* is another name. They're also what's used on the Mac's screen; Geneva and Chicago are two well-known examples.

There are 72 dots per inch in the pictures of the characters that make up a bit-mapped font—or, to say it a different way, bit-mapped fonts have a resolution of 72 dpi. (Actually, in a normal ImageWriter text printout, there are 80 dots per inch across and 72 down; to get 72 x 72, you have to ask for Tall Adjusted.)

Bit-mapped fonts will print out on the LaserWriter and, with *Smoothing* on (you choose it in the *Page Setup...* dialog box), they look pretty good. But *laser fonts* (so called because they're designed for printing on laser printers) look better.

The characters in laser fonts aren't made up of dots—they're composed of *instructions,* usually in a page-description programming language called PostScript, which was specifically designed to handle text and graphics and their placement on a page. For this reason, they're also known as *PostScript fonts.* (Some laser fonts don't use PostScript; they use QuickDraw or something else.)

Because PostScript fonts are formed of outlines which are then filled in, they're also sometimes called *outline fonts.* (Technically, not all PostScript fonts are outline fonts. For example, when you send a bit-mapped font to the LaserWriter, a special, bit-mapped PostScript version of it is created. But when people speak of a PostScript font, they're virtually always referring to an outline font.)

When you send a laser font to a laser printer or typesetting machine, the printer reads the instructions (in PostScript or whatever) and then draws the characters in as much detail—as high a resolution—as it's capable of. On the LaserWriters and most other laser printers (as of this writing), that's 300 dpi, which amounts to 90,000 dots per square inch (300 across by 300 down), or about 16 to 17 times the resolution of an ImageWriter printout.

But 90,000 dpsi is nothing compared to what regular typesetting machines can do. For more information on them, see the entry about relative resolutions in the *Basic laser printer tips* section of the printer chapter.

Since the Mac's screen isn't a PostScript device, it can't display laser fonts directly. So each comes with a 72-dpi, bit-mapped *screen font* that's used to represent it on the screen. (Like any bit-mapped font, screen fonts will print out on the ImageWriter, but they won't look a whole lot like the actual laser font does when printed on the Laser-Writer—both because of the lower resolution and because the person who designed the font knew it was only going to be used as an approximation, and therefore probably didn't spend a lot of time fine-tuning it.)

For tips on using fonts on the LaserWriter, see the printer chapter.

ɝ *font sizes* (AN)

The sizes of Mac fonts are measured in points, which are 72nds of an inch. (Actually, to be more precise, a point is

esp. for beginners

.0138" and 72 of them only make .9936", but since the difference between a point and a 72nd of inch is less than .0001", the distinction is pointless...so to speak.)

Bit-mapped fonts come supplied in various sizes and, on dot-matrix printers, they should be used in those sizes only, because scaling them—shrinking or enlarging them from one size to another—looks really dreadful. (Scaling them and printing them on laser printers, however, usually looks fine.)

You can tell what sizes of bit-mapped fonts (and screen fonts) are installed in the System file you're using by looking on the font size menu (which is usually part of another menu); the installed sizes are listed in outline type.

Laser fonts scale beautifully, since they're composed of instructions, not bit maps, and are designed to print at any size you say. But remember that the smaller the type size, the more the resolution of the device you're using matters. (At any given resolution, it's obviously easier to form a nice-looking 72-point character than a 6-point one, because you have more dots to work with.)

The standard type sizes that almost every application gives you are 9-, 10-, 12-, 14-, 18- and 24-point; other standard sizes—available in some applications—are 36-, 48-, 60- and 72-point. Microsoft Word lets you generate type of any size from 4-point to 127-point (whole numbers only), but the results will occasionally look a little funny (for more details, see the entry titled *Word on laser printers* in the printer chapter).

**very
hot
tip**

Point sizes aren't consistent and vary dramatically from font to font. For example, the type you're reading is 11/13— that is, 11-point type sitting on 13-point lines (called 11 on 13). The headers (the text at the top of the page, above the solid line) are in 14-point type, but they hardly look bigger than this 11-point type. (For more on this, see the entry below called *a template for viewing fonts.)*

● *picking fonts* (AN)

Which fonts to use is a matter of personal taste, of course, but there are a couple of general principles that will help you do it efficiently. The first rule is that it takes a while to learn which fonts you like, so spend some time playing with them before making your choices.

Second (and this may also be obvious), be aware that different kinds of jobs require different fonts. You might choose one group of fonts you use for your business letters, another for your personal letters, a third for your drawings, and so on.

● *font packages* (AN)

If you're working on a floppy disk system, it makes sense to put together a package of fonts for each purpose, and create separate System files with different font packages on them. Then, when you set up a new disk, you just transfer the appropriate System onto it. But make sure you keep at least two backup copies of each font on a pair of archive disks (called *font library* or something like that), so you'll always have them to use in the future.

very hot tip

On a hard disk, you may still want to put together various font packages and put them in different *suitcase* files (see the glossary if you don't know what that means).

In either case, it will be worth your while to reduce the number of fonts on each of your disks to the number you really need; messages telling you the disk is full can get really frustrating.

● *a template for viewing fonts* (AN)

Most font publishers don't give you full printouts of their fonts, so in order to evaluate which fonts you want to use, it makes sense to make up a template like the one below. Once you've set it up—which might take twenty minutes—all you have to do is select the entire template and then change the font in order to get a printout of every character

esp. for beginners

a given font can produce, as well as samples of the sixteen possible type styles in that font. (You can also get this template on disk, in MacWrite 4.6 format. See the end of Chapter 16 for details on *The Macintosh Bible disk.)*

It doesn't matter which font you choose to make the original template, since you're going to be changing it when you use the template anyway. I've picked the one this book is set in.

font: ITC Benguiat (BENG-gat)   from: Adobe

9 point: 1234567890 abcdefghijklmnopqrstuvwxyz

ABCDEFGHIJKLMNOPQRSTUVWXYZ

10 point: 1234567890 abcdefghijklmnopqrstuvwxyz

ABCDEFGHIJKLMNOPQRSTUVWXYZ

12 point: 1234567890 abcdefghijklmnopqrstuvwxyz

ABCDEFGHIJKLMNOPQRSTUVWXYZ

14 point: 1234567890
abcdefghijklmnopqrstuvw

ABCDEFGHIJKLMNOPQRSTUVWXYZ

18 point: 1234567890

abcdefghijklmnopqrstuvwxyz

ABCDEFGHIJKLMNOPQRSTUVW

24 point: 1234567890

abcdefghijklmnopqrstu

ABCDEFGHIJKLMNOPQR

unshifted symbols: ` - = [ ] \ ; ' , . /

shifted symbols:

~ ! @ # $ % ^ & * ( ) _ + { } | : " < > ?

option keys:

` ¡ ™ £ ¢ ∞ § ¶ • ª º – ≠

œ ∑ ´ ® † ¥ ¨ ^ ø π " ' «

å ß ∂ ƒ © ˙ ∆ ˚ ¬ … æ

Ω ≈ ç √ ∫ ~ µ ≤ ≥ ÷

shift-option keys:

Ÿ / ¤ ‹ › fi fl ‡ ° · , — ±

Œ „ ‰ Â Ê Á Ë È Ø ∏ " ' »

Å Í Î Ï Ì Ó Ô Ò Ú Æ

Û Ù Ç ◊ ı ˆ ˜ ¯ ˘ ¿

This is bold. *This is italic.* Outline. Shadow. ***Bold italic.*** Bold outline. **Bold shadow.** *Italic outline. Italic shadow.* Outline shadow. *Bold italic outline.* ***Bold italic shadow.*** Bold outline shadow. *Italic outline shadow. Bold italic outline shadow.*

In most programs, the outline shadow variations look just the same as the shadow variations. (PageMaker, as you can see, is an exception.) This is a peculiarity of laser fonts; see *type styles on laser printers* in Chapter 6 for more details. (At least one laser font—Zapf Chancery—has only three style variations: plain, outline and shadow.) Bit-mapped fonts printed on dot-matrix printers like the ImageWriter have all sixteen variations—but not when they're printed on laser printers from most programs.

very bad feature

Here are some pointers on how to set this template up for yourself. You might as well begin by just typing in ours, or copying it from *The Macintosh Bible Disk*. Then you can customize it any way you want.

The shifted and unshifted symbols are shown in the order in which they appear on the keyboard, from left to right and top to bottom. Because the characters produced by the Option key (with and without the Shift key) don't appear on the keyboard, I've set it up so that each row under the *option keys* and *shift-option keys* headings represents a row of keys. This makes it easy to find the symbol on the keyboard.

Although all fifteen type styles are shown at the bottom of the template (plain text is omitted because most of the rest of the template is in it), it makes sense to give yourself a bit more of a look at the three most useful ones: bold, italic and bold italic. So I've put the title (font and publisher) in **bold italic**, the type sizes in *italic*, and the subheads below the type sizes *(unshifted symbols, shifted symbols,* etc.) in **bold**. I've also underlined those subheads and the type sizes, so you can see how underlining looks with the font.

Because the 8-1/2 x 11 page you'll use to print out the template is wider than this 7 x 9 page, the template we supply on disk completes the 18-point and 24-point alphabets that are cut off above. It also puts the Option and Shift Option keys side by side. You should do both things yourself if you're typing it in.

In either case, you may also want to make the special characters or the style variations bigger, so you can see them better; with most fonts, the whole template will still fit on a page.

Each time you select the template and change it to a different font, you may have to readjust line breaks and even lop a few letters off some of the larger alphabets. That's because fonts of the same nominal point size vary quite a bit in actual size, both in height and width.

For example, compare the size of these fonts, all technically 24-point:

Times

Benguiat

With a font like Dream (from CasadyWare), you'll have to do more than lop off a few letters of the alphabet to make the template fit on a single page. (On the other hand, it doesn't have any lowercase letters, numbers or symbols.)

When using the template for a bit-mapped font, it makes sense to only show the sizes it's actually supplied in, because scaled sizes of bit-mapped fonts generally look wretched. (The one exception to this rule is when a scaled size is exactly half of a supplied size.) You might want to underline the supplied sizes, so you know which are which. (In the template above, all the sizes are underlined, because laser fonts are—in effect—supplied in all sizes.)

With a bit-mapped font, you'll only want the supplied sizes anyway, so that will save some room. And you certainly don't need to see Dream in bold italic outline shadow.

Like Benguiat in the sample template above, most laser fonts have special characters for every possible slot. Bit-mapped fonts almost never do. When a bit-mapped font doesn't have a given special character, it will produce the missing character box: □ (its appearance varies with the font, but it always looks pretty much like that). But it will only do that on a dot-matrix printer; laser printers won't print the missing character box (I had to paste that one in from the ImageWriter).

✦ *Font Charter* (AN)

very good feature

The Font Charter is an application that comes on World Class Fonts disks (from Dubl-Click Software). It prints charts of all the characters in a font, arranged either by their location on the keyboard or by ASCII number, on either an ImageWriter or a laser printer.

This is quite handy for comparing fonts (if for some reason you don't like the template described in the previous entry). It's a good idea to make a printout of all the fonts you use, either with Font Charter or our template, and put them in a notebook. Then you can refer to them when deciding which font to use.

✦ *DefaultFont* (AN)

very good feature

This DA is another application that comes on World Class Fonts disks. It lets you change the font that many applications default to when they're first opened. So if you're tired of having to change from Geneva every time you select *New* from the File menu, you love this desk accessory. (The World Class Font disks are almost worth the money just for the utilities that come on them—never mind the terrific fonts.)

✦ *Font/DA Mover, Suitcase and Font/DA Juggler* (AN)

These are the key programs for handling fonts, but since they handle DAs as well, they're discussed in Chapter 8 rather than here.

✦ *where to put what* (PH)

very hot tip

Due to the way the Mac looks at fonts, all sizes for a font have to be in the same file. This means that all sizes of Geneva, Monaco and Chicago (Apple only provides it in 12-point, but World Class Fonts has it in 9-, 10- and 24-point as well) should be in the System file, even if you want it stripped down to bare bones. (There's no reason to have any other fonts in there; put them all in suitcase files and have Suitcase or Font/DA Juggler load them.)

When you upgrade your system, Apple's Installer program will put a copy of Helvetica and Times 10- and 12-point into the new System file. If you have other sizes of Helvetica and Times in your suitcase files, they won't be usable. So after upgrading, use the Font/DA Mover to remove Helvetica and Times from your System file.

🍎 *Set Paths* (PH)

This utility program (described in Chapter 8) is incredibly handy for dealing with laser fonts. Here's why:

Each laser font has three parts: the screen font, the printer font and the AFM file, the last two of which you have to put in the system folder. Keeping all those files around the system folder can get really messy, but all you have to do is create a folder called *printer fonts* and another called *AFM files* and use Set Paths to direct software to them. This really cuts down on clutter.

very good feature

🍎 *hyphens and en dashes in different fonts* (MB)

Hyphens should always be shorter than en dashes ([Option]–hyphen) but sometimes they're not (see the entry on this in Chapter 6 for more details). It varies with the font and sometimes even with the type size. For example, it's true in Benguiat but not in Chicago, in 10-point Geneva but not in 12-point:

	hyphen	*en dash*
Benguiat	-	–
Chicago	–	-
Geneva 10-point	–	-
Geneva 12-point	–	–

The only way to tell for sure with any font is to type a hyphen and an en dash and compare them.

Special characters

 *the standard special characters (AN)*

very good feature

There are some pretty bizarre characters on the Mac's—or just about any computer's—keyboard. For example, there's the backslash (\ ), the vertical bar (|), the lesser than and greater than signs (<   >) and so on. But when people talk about special characters on the Mac, they mean ones that aren't shown on the keyboard at all. To get one of these special characters, you hold down the Option key while hitting another key (or keys).

Let's say you want to type: "Hein, salopard! Parlez-vous français?" To get the special character ç in "français," you hold down Option while hitting c. To get certain other special characters, you have to hold down the Shift key as well. For example, if you hit Shift Option –c, you get an uppercase Ç instead of a lowercase one. (In this case, the two characters are related, but sometimes the Option and Shift Option characters have nothing to do with each other.)

Some fonts have idiosyncratic special characters of their own, but there's a set of standard special characters that virtually all fonts share. No bit-mapped font contains all of them—Geneva and Chicago seem to have the most—but most laser fonts have the full set. (You can see it—arranged by keyboard rows—in the font template for Benguiat in the previous entry, under the headings *option keys* and *shift-option keys*.)

In the following entries, I've listed these standard special characters by category. I show the special character first, followed by the regular character used to generate it in outline type. I don't bother putting Option in front of each of the regular keyboard characters, and I also don't use the Shift symbol—since it's simpler just to show you the capital letter instead. So when you see Å followed by A, it means that to get Å, you need to hit Shift Option –a.

Sometimes I have to clarify which regular keyboard character I'm indicating—for example, when there might be a confusion between the capital letter O and the numeral 0 (or, for that matter, between a small o and a capital O, since standing alone, they can be hard to tell apart). For maximum legibility, I've set both regular and special characters in larger type.

Unless you're a whole lot more knowledgeable than I was, you won't know what half these characters are, so I provide the name—and, when appropriate, the common foreign name—for most of them.

Some special characters do double duty; for example, the square root sign can serve as a check mark. When a character has more than one function, I list it under each category where it can be used.

I've shown the characters that are generally available in laser fonts; the 🍎 and a few other characters usually aren't available in bit-mapped fonts (and of course many fonts of both types don't implement all the characters).

accent marks for foreign languages

Two foreign accent marks—the tilde (~) and the accent grave (`)—are regular characters on the Mac's keyboard, marked right on the key. But it's not clear what you're supposed to use them for, since if you just press those keys, the characters always appear on a space of their own, not above another character.

The accent marks listed below—which include a different tilde and a different accent grave—work the way they should: when you hit ⎡Option⎤ plus the regular character indicated, nothing shows up on the screen; then, when you type the next character, the appropriate accent mark appears above it.

These accent marks won't appear over just any letter you type—it has to be one the Mac thinks makes sense. If you try to put an accent over a different letter, the accent appears by itself on one space and the letter on the next—like this: ´A.

In the table below, I've listed the letters that work with each accent in curly brackets after it. If you want to produce an accent over a blank space, you can always do that simply by hitting the appropriate key, then the space bar.

´   acute accent; accent aigu {á é í ó ú É}   e

`     grave accent; accent grave {à è ì ò ù}                      `
      (In other words, if you just hit the ` key by
      itself, you get ` on a space of its own; if you
      use Option , ` appears above the next letter
      you type.)

^   circumflex; circonflexe {â ê î ô û}   i

··   dieresis; umlaut {ä ë ï ö ü Ä Ö Ü}   u

~   tilde {ã ñ õ Ñ}   n

foreign letters, letter combinations & abbreviations

å   a   Å   A

æ   ′ (apostrophe)   Æ   ″ (regular quote mark)

ç   c   Ç   C

ø   o (small o)   Ø   O (capital O)

œ   q   Œ   Q

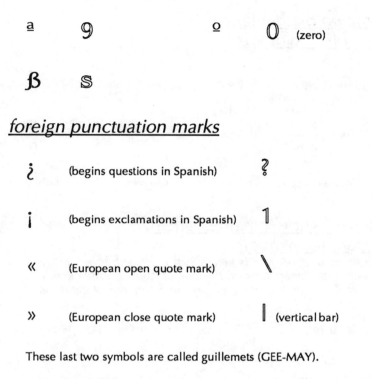

<u>a</u>   9   <u>o</u>   0   (zero)

ß   s

foreign punctuation marks

¿   (begins questions in Spanish)   ?

¡   (begins exclamations in Spanish)   1

«   (European open quote mark)   \

»   (European close quote mark) | (vertical bar)

These last two symbols are called guillemets (GEE-MAY).

monetary symbols

£ (pound sign) 3   ¥ (yen sign)   y   ¢ (cent sign) 4

legal symbols

§   (section mark)   6   ¶ (paragraph mark)   7

™   (trademark)   2   ® (registered mark)   r

© (copyright symbol)   g

well-known mathematical & scientific symbols

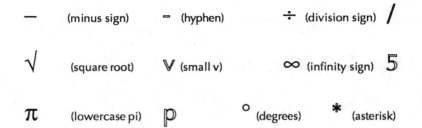

— (minus sign)   ⁻ (hyphen)   ÷ (division sign) /

√ (square root)   V (small v)   ∞ (infinity sign) 5

π (lowercase pi) p   ° (degrees)   * (asterisk)

not-so-well-known mathematical & scientific symbols

Since some of the symbols below can represent about a dozen different things, depending on the field of study, I simply give you their Greek names and/or what they most commonly stand for.

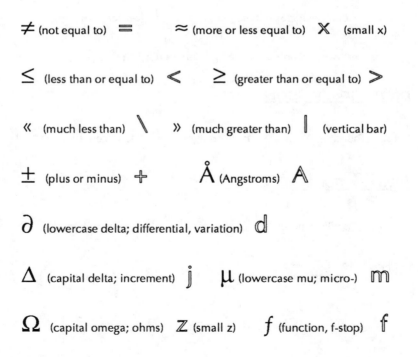

≠ (not equal to) ≡   ≈ (more or less equal to) X (small x)

≤ (less than or equal to) <   ≥ (greater than or equal to) >

≪ (much less than) \   ≫ (much greater than) | (vertical bar)

± (plus or minus) +   Å (Angstroms) A

∂ (lowercase delta; differential, variation) d

Δ (capital delta; increment) j   μ (lowercase mu; micro-) m

Ω (capital omega; ohms) Z (small z)   ƒ (function, f-stop) f

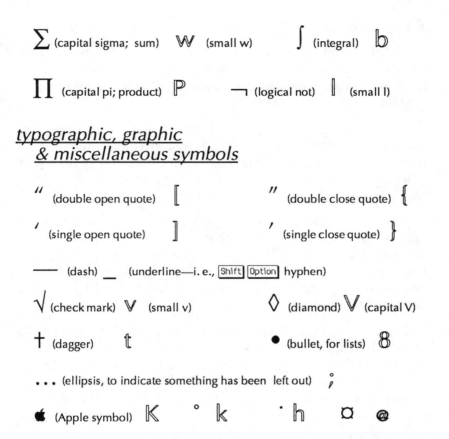

∑ (capital sigma; sum)   W   (small w)   ∫ (integral)   b

∏ (capital pi; product)   P   ¬ (logical not) | (small l)

typographic, graphic
& miscellaneous symbols

″   (double open quote)   [″   (double close quote)   {

′   (single open quote)   ]   ′   (single close quote)   }

⸺ (dash)   _   (underline—i. e., Shift Option hyphen)

√ (check mark)   V   (small v)   ◊ (diamond) V (capital V)

† (dagger)   t   • (bullet, for lists)   8

... (ellipsis, to indicate something has been left out)   °ρ

 (Apple symbol)   K   °   k   ·h   ◌   @

Finally, there's the missing character box: □ . This is produced by any Option or Shift Option key that has no special character assigned to it in the particular font you're using (or even a regular key with no character assigned to it). Apple's bit-mapped font London, for example, has only three special characters, so almost any Option or Shift Option key you hit in it produces the box.

You can't get this character in laser fonts, for several reasons: many laser fonts have special characters assigned to all the Option and Shift Option keys; some laser fonts use a different missing character symbol; and even if the missing character box shows up on the screen, a laser printer won't print it.

♠ **Key Caps** *(AN)*

It's often hard to remember which key combination to hit to produce the special character you need, or even whether the font you're using has that character. That's what Apple's Key Caps desk accessory is for.

When you choose Key Caps from the ♠ menu, it displays a representation of the Mac's keyboard and puts a new menu title, Key Caps, at the right end of the menu bar. You select the font you're interested in from that menu and the Key Caps display switches over to it.

very good feature

When you hold down the Option key, Key Caps displays the special characters that font gives you when you hold down Option and press another key. Likewise, when you hold down the Shift and the Option key, Key Caps displays the special characters that font gives you when you hold down Shift Option and press another key.

If you use a lot of special characters and have trouble remembering which keys generate them, you can resize your text window to leave room at the bottom of the screen for Key Caps to be displayed at all times. But it's probably easier just to make a copy of the previous entry and put it on your wall.

♠ **BigCaps** *(AN)*

very good feature

BigCaps is a replacement for Key Caps that comes on World Class Fonts disks (from Dubl-Click Software). It has two advantages: it displays a wider variety of font styles and sizes, and it will display fonts in files other than the System (like those in *suitcase files* created by Suitcase or Font/DA Juggler).

If you have any World Class fonts (and you should, as the bit-mapped font sampler below should make obvious), you'll have this program, and there's really no reason to use Key Caps if you do.

✎ *pictorial characters* (AN)

One of the best features of the Macintosh is the availability of pictorial characters—little images you can place in a document with nothing more than a keystroke or two. The best-known pictorial fonts are Cairo and Mobile (formerly know as Taliesin), bit-mapped fonts published by Apple.

**very good
feature**

CasadyWare offers some useful pictorial fonts for the ImageWriter, including one that contains architectural symbols and drawings (like a little toilet, or an overhead shot of a person walking), and a whimsical one called Images. Dubl-Click Century Fonts publishes several pictorial laser fonts, including laser versions of Cairo and Mobile. (See the bit-mapped font sampler section below for more details.)

The best way to arrange a pictorial font for reference is by categories, rather than by the keys that generate the characters, so you can look for what you want instead of having to scan a whole list or table. Every publisher of a pictorial font ought to provide a printout of it by logical categories, but since they don't, the next three entries give you some. They cover two of the most used pictorial fonts, Adobe's Zapf Dingbats and Apple's Cairo, and another useful font, Adobe's Carta.

One final note: if a pictorial character (or any other kind of nonstandard special character) uses one of the foreign accent mark keys, you'll have to hit the key twice to generate the character (because normally that key waits for you to type a letter to put the accent mark over). So, for example, to get the character ① in Zapf Dingbats, you have to hit [Option]–u (which normally generates an umlaut, ¨) twice; hit it once and nothing will happen.

**important
warning**

✎ *Zapf Dingbats by categories* (AN)

When Zapf Dingbats is the selected font, all you have to do to generate any of the pictorial characters shown is hit the key(s) indicated below it.

arrows (fat tails)

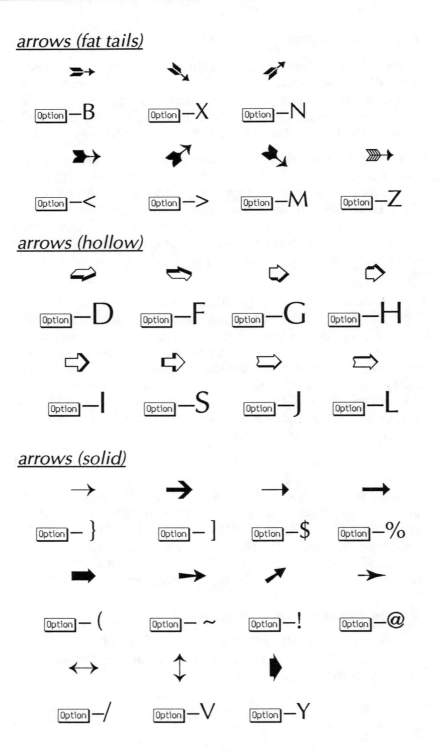

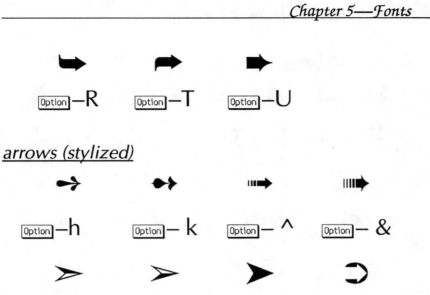

Option—R   Option—T   Option—U

arrows (stylized)

Option—h   Option—k   Option—^   Option—&

Option—W   Option—)   Option—E   Option—:

asterisks (florettes, snowflakes, starbursts)

a   b   c   d   e   f   g   h

i   j   k   `   [   ]   \   B

C   D   E   Q   R   S   T   U

V   W   X   Y   Z   ^   _

boxes and bars

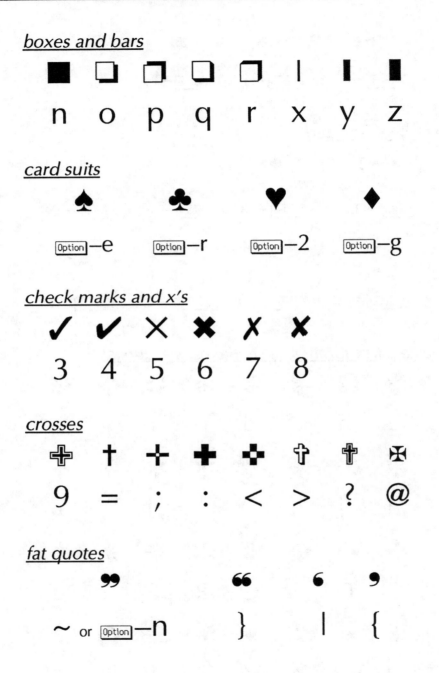

n o p q r x y z

card suits

Option—e   Option—r   Option—2   Option—g

check marks and x's

3 4 5 6 7 8

crosses

9 = ; : < > ? @

fat quotes

~ or Option—n   } | {

geometric shapes (miscellaneous)

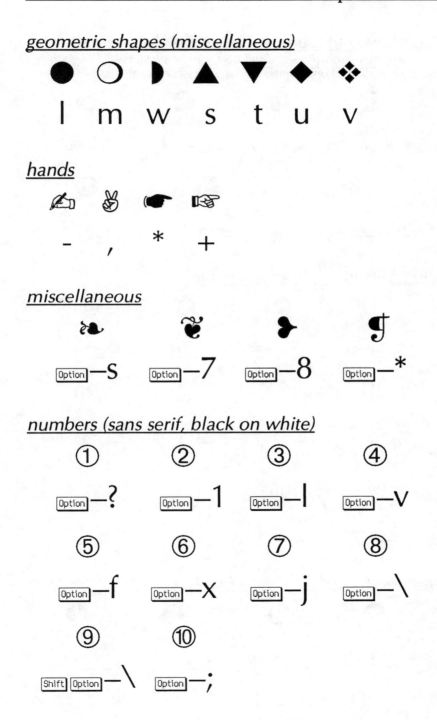

● ○ ◗ ▲ ▼ ◆ ❖

l m w s t u v

hands

✍ ✌ ☛ ☞

- , * +

miscellaneous

Option—s   Option—7   Option—8   Option—*

numbers (sans serif, black on white)

① ② ③ ④

Option—?   Option—1   Option—l   Option—v

⑤ ⑥ ⑦ ⑧

Option—f   Option—x   Option—j   Option—\

⑨ ⑩

Shift Option—\   Option—;

numbers (sans serif, white on black)

For some reason, this set of numbers is incomplete, even though the font has lots of unassigned keys and key combinations.

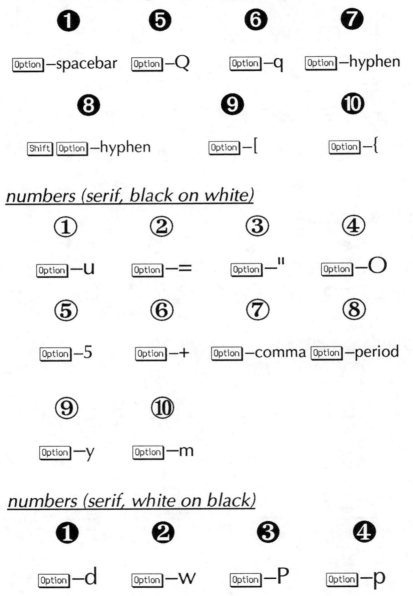

❶   ❺   ❻   ❼

Option —spacebar   Option —Q   Option —q   Option —hyphen

❽   ❾   ❿

Shift Option —hyphen   Option —[Option —{

numbers (serif, black on white)

①   ②   ③   ④

Option —u   Option —=   Option —"   Option —O

⑤   ⑥   ⑦   ⑧

Option —5   Option —+   Option —comma   Option —period

⑨   ⑩

Option —y   Option —m

numbers (serif, white on black)

❶   ❷   ❸   ❹

Option —d   Option —w   Option —P   Option —p

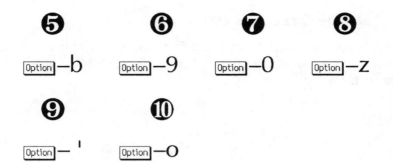

❺ ❻ ❼ ❽

[Option]–b   [Option]–9   [Option]–0   [Option]–z

❾ ❿

[Option]– '   [Option]–O

objects (miscellaneous)

✂ ✄ ✂ ✂ ☎ ✆ ✈ ✉

!   #   " $ %   &   (   )

pens and pencils

✒ ✒ ✐ ✐ ✐

1   2   0   .   /

stars

✡ ✦ ✧ ★ ☆ ✪

A   F   G   H   I   J

✭ ✪ ✭ ✪ ✭ ☆

K   L   M   N   O   P

⚫ *Cairo by categories* (AN)

When Cairo is the selected font, all you have to do to generate any of the pictures shown is hit the key(s) indicated below it.

animals

z   ~   U   c   e

"   K   ]   d

arrows

h   -   =   [+

art tools

a   j   i   /

buildings

E   Q   R   T   W   %

celestial objects

☀ ☽ ☆ ♄

@   7   8   g

electrical symbols

⊣⊢   ⊣⊩   ⌇   ∕

q   r   s   0

everyday objects—bigger than a breadbox

🏴   📺   🪑   🧳   🔔   ⚓

;   D   3   _   {   t

everyday objects—smaller than a breadbox

🔑   ✉   ☐   💡   🕯   🧨

f   S   '   ?   l   u

🌏

Option‑u, then A

food and drink

🍳   🍦   🍰   ☕   🍾   🍷

`   !   5   \   4   6

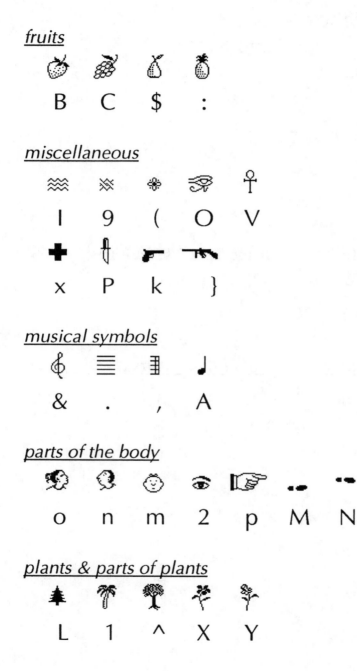

fruits

B   C $:

miscellaneous

I   9   (O   V

x   P   k   }

musical symbols

&   .   ,   A

parts of the body

o   n   m   2   p   M   N

plants & parts of plants

L   1   ^   X   Y

Z   )   #   w   *

things you wear

b   <   v   >   y

transportation

H   F   G   J   I   Option–A

🍎 *Carta by categories* (TR/AN)

Carta is a font of map-making symbols designed by Lynne Garell and published by Adobe. The list below groups the symbols into logical categories and tells you what they normally represent.

The characters to the left of each symbol indicate the keys you hit to get it (S = Shift, O = Option) and its ASCII number (some programs—like Dubl-Click's BigCaps, described below—let you insert characters by using the ASCII code rather than the keyboard).

arrows

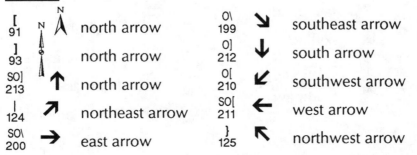

[91	north arrow
] 93	north arrow
SO] 213	north arrow
I 124	northeast arrow
SO\ 200	east arrow
O\ 199	southeast arrow
O] 212	south arrow
O[210	southwest arrow
SO[211	west arrow
} 125	northwest arrow

buildings, etc.

SOx 244	✚	hospital
x 120	✛	hospital
Ow 183	✱	police
Oz 189	⊠	post office
Z 90	☎	telephone
Q 81	🏛	bank
q 113	⚖	courthouse
SOq 206	⊞	prison
V 86	🚩	school
v 118	🎓	university
Oq 207	🏛	museum
b 98	⛪	church
B 66	⛪	mission
Ob 186	☪	mosque
SOv 215	⛩	pagoda
Ov 195	✡	synagogue
- 45	🗼	lighthouse
95	🌬	windmill
0, 178	📡	satellite dish
C 67	🏙	skyline
SOb 245	†	cemetery
= 61	⚑	landmark

+ 43	∴	ruin
SO= 177	⌂	site

cities and towns

t 116	◉	city
T 84	◎	town
SOt 230	○	village
R 82	✪	national capital
Or 168	✪	state capital
E 69	☆	county seat

geometric shapes (large)

P 80	▽	triangle
253	▼	filled triangle
Op 185	▷	triangle
254	▶	filled triangle
I 108	□	square
SO7 224	■	filled square
Ol 194	▭	rectangle
SO3 220	▬	filled rectangle
L 76	▭	rectangle
OnA 204	▬	filled rectangle
p 112	◇	diamond
O(SP) 202	◆	filled diamond

Oo 191	⬡	octagon
Ouy 216	⬢	filled octagon
o 111	◯	circle
SO4 221	●	filled circle
O 79	⬭	oval
SO5 222	⬬	filled oval

geometric shapes (small)

! 33	○	circle
SOw 227	•	small filled circle
01 193	●	filled circle
SO1 218	●	larger filled circle
# 35	△	triangle
O3 163	▲	filled triangle
$ 36	◇	diamond
O4 162	◆	filled diamond
% 37	⬡	hexagon
O5 176	⬢	filled hexagon
@ 64	□	square
O2 170	■	filled square
e 101	★	star
SOe 228	☆	inline star
OeOe 171	✬	half-filled star
SOr 229	☆	circle in star

r 114	✪	star in circle
SO' 174	+	thin plus
O' 190	×	thin cross

highway signs

i 105	⛨	Interstate hwy
SO2 219	⬛	Interstate hwy
u 117	⬡	US highway
U 85	⬭	US highway
SO' 217	⬛	US highway
SOo 175	⬠	California hwy
OnO 205	⬟	California hwy
l 73	⬠	county highway
252	⬟	county highway
OuOu 172	⬓	hwy in nat'l forest
O'A 203	⬛	hwy in nat'l forest
SOu 232	⬙	hwy on Ind. reserv.
SO8 161	⬛	hwy on Ind. reserv.
Y 89	🍁	Trans-Canada hwy
y 121	⬡	Mexican hwy
SO9 225	⬛	Mexican hwy
Oy 180	⬡	Mexican hwy
SO0 226	⬛	Mexican hwy
SOy 231	⬠	hwy school sign

SOk 240		hwy school sign
SOl 241		hwy RR crossing
SOz 243		hwy RR crossing

mining and industrial

. 46		mining
> 62		placer
0. 179		gravel pit
? 63		mine shaft
< 60		metals
' 44		gold
SOm 247		gems
n 110		uranium
N 78		radiation
SOn 246		nuclear reactor
Ox 197		chemicals
Om 181		coal
m 109		oil
SO, 248		refinery
M 77		oil well
SO/ 192		gas well
SO; 242		dry well
SO. 249		factory

miscellaneous symbols

\ 92		compass
{ 123		scale
SOp 184		registration mark
X 88		handicapped
` 96		pedest. crossing
~ 126		children crossing
SOi 233		traffic light
O/ 214		tunnel
SOh 238		bridge
K 75		dam
Oj 198		large airport
J 74		small airport
SOj 239		heliport
k 107		Amtrak
Ok 251		port of entry
W 87		maple leaf
w 119		hammer & sickle
c 99		world

outdoor recreation

Oh 250		boat
H 72		boat launching

h 104	⚓	marina
SOf 236		golf
Og 169		state park
d 100		campsite
D 68		campsite
Od 182		picnic area
f 102		hostel
SOd 235		pack station
SOs 234		fire
F 70		hiking
Of 196		bicycle trail
SOg 237		horse trail
a 97		skiing
A 65		winter sports
s 115		game preserve
S 83		bird refuge
Os 167		fish hatchery
g 103		ranger station
G 71		US Fire Svc facil.

surveying and land use

; 59	⊙	benchmark
: 58		boundary

0; 201	△	control
/ 47		gauging station (USGS)
' 39		lookout
" 34		lookout control

warfare

0- 208		battlefield
SO- 209		fort
0= 173		castle
00 188		soldier
09 187		tank
06 164		aircraft carrier
08 165		tanker
07 166		battleship
j 106		military airbase
) 41		ICBM
(40		IRBM
SO6 223		flat explosion
^ 94		explosion
* 42		filled explosion
& 38		filled explosion

♦ *non-Roman alphabets* (AN)

very good feature

Another exciting aspect of fonts on the Mac is the ability to generate foreign—that is, non-Roman—alphabets, especially since you can mix them in freely with regular text. (Roman alphabets—like the ones used for English, French and Spanish—have more or less the same characters as Latin does. Non-Roman alphabets—like the ones used for Greek, Russian, Hebrew, Japanese and Chinese—have different characters.)

There's a wide variety of both laser and ImageWriter non-Roman fonts available—everything from common ones like Greek, Hebrew, Katakana (Japanese phonetic characters) and Cyrillic (Russian, etc.) right down to totally obscure ones like Linear B (an early form of Greek writing dating from around 1500 BC).

This last was designed by Gary Palmer, who teaches anthropology at the University of Nevada in Las Vegas and also helps run the Center for Computer Applications in the Humanities Department there. Here's a short sample of it:

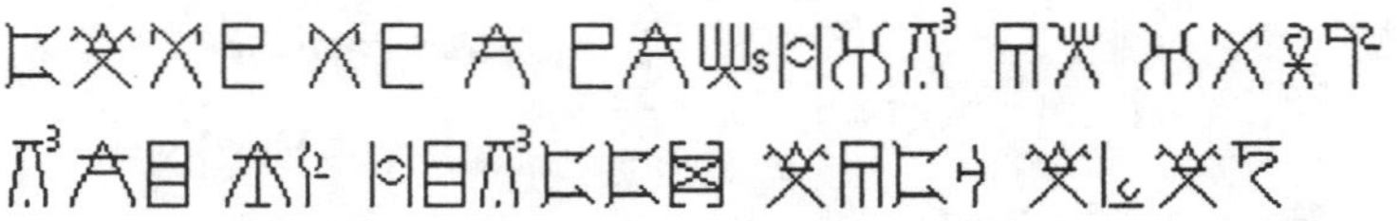

ᚷᚷᚷᛈ ᚷᛖ ᚠ ᛈᚪᛃᛶᚺᚷᚷᛚᚫ ᛗᚷ ᚺᚷᚷᛈ�

Pretty hot, huh?

One last note about non-Roman alphabets: remember that generating the characters may be only half the battle. For example, unless a Hebrew font comes with a word processor that lets you write from right to left, you'll have to type out the Hebrew text backwards (from left to right).

A bit-mapped font sampler

♦ *Apple's bit-mapped fonts* (AN)

One of the standard fonts used by the Mac, Geneva, is a bit-mapped version of the classic, standard typeface

Helvetica. It's called Geneva because Helvetica is a Swiss font, which in turn gets *its* name from the official name for Switzerland, *Confoederatio Helvetica,* "the Swiss Confederation" (that's why the international license plate tag for Switzerland is CH).

gossip/ trivia

The Swiss use a Latin name so as not to favor any of their four official languages—German, French, Italian and Romansch—over the others. *Helvetica* comes from the name of a Celtic people, the Helvetii, who inhabited Switzerland during the time of Julius Caesar. I don't know how they came by *their* name, but tell me, what other computer book gives you trivia of this caliber?

gossip/ trivia

Unlike New York—a bit-mapped version of Times, the font Stanley Morrison designed for the *London Times* in 1922—Geneva is quite pretty and pleasant to read (which is fortunate, because it's used by the System to display things). But it doesn't hold a candle to **Chicago.**

You look at Chicago so much on menus and the titles of windows that it's easy to forget what an attractive font it is. Created by master type craftsman Charles Bigelow specifically for use on the Mac, it's probably the most beautiful and functional bit-mapped font ever designed. To get this kind of style out of 72 dots per inch is an incredible accomplishment.

very good feature

(Chicago looks great on the screen and in ImageWriter printouts, but for some reason it doesn't look so good in this printout. The Laser-Writer makes it too skinny. It looks more like the screen font in boldface.)

Apple only supplies Chicago in 12-point, but Dubl-Click Software's World Class fonts gives you 9-point, 10-point and 24-point versions of it as well.

𝕬nother 𝕬pple font 𝕀 love i𝕾

𝕾an Franci𝕾co. 𝕎hen the 𝕸ac

first came out, a lot of grave warnings were issued about not using this "ransom note" (or "circus poster") font for business letters—as if most Mac users had IQs down in the room-temperature range.

WEll, you shouldn't use San Francisco for your will, either—unless you want it challenged on the grounds that you weren't of sound mind when you made it. But that doesn't mean you should *never* use San Francisco. Remember the first commandment: This is the Mac. It's *supposed* to be fun.

⚫ *an easy choice* (AN)

CasadyWare and Dubl-Click Software produce such beautiful fonts and sell them for such reasonable prices that they make your decision easy. Just look through their Fluent Fonts and World Class Fonts collections and buy what you like (buy them all, if you can afford it). Fonts are one of the cheapest luxuries I know.

very good feature

⚫ *Fluent Fonts* (AN)

But the bit-mapped fonts I use the most come on a two-disk Fluent Fonts set from CasadyWare ($50). In addition to fonts of architectural, astronomical, astrological, biological, chemical, electronic, mathematical, meteorological and even a few yachting symbols, it includes some of the most useful and beautiful bit-mapped typefaces I've seen.

bargain

My personal favorites are:

Nordic (Isn't this a beauty? I could look at it all day. It was all I could do to control myself and not set the whole book in it.)

Oblique (a great substitute for, and improvement on, Apple's Athens. This is another font you never get tired of looking at.)

Chubby Shadow (for when you want

TO GET REALLY DRA-
MATIC) and last, but certainly not least,

CasadyWare also has a font of borders called Border-line. Here are a few samples from it:

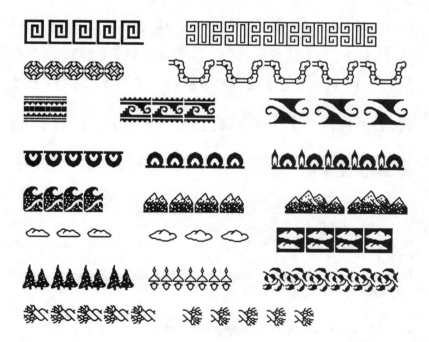

✦ *World Class Fonts* (AN)

Dubl-Click Software puts out a series of bit-mapped fonts that boggle the mind and dazzle the eye. They go by the name of World Class Fonts; there are three sets of three 800K disks and each set only costs $80—about $1 a font!

very good feature

World Class Fonts give you Chicago in three other sizes than the 12-point Apple supplies, and Venice in two other sizes than the 14-point Apple supplies. You also get several foreign alphabets (Greek, Hebrew, Japanese, Russian) and a vast quantity of unique special characters that are hard— or impossible—to find elsewhere.

Other fonts give you chess pieces (a black set and a white set), postal labels, religious symbols (34 separate crosses, among much else), architectural symbols and border designs.

The Manhattan font gives you Macintosh symbols like ⌘ and ☞; it's what I've used in this book to indicate keys. **Hollywood gives you what must be the ultimate in special characters—not merely 🏃, 🎥 and 🍸 but also**

very good feature

There are dozens of other useful and interesting fonts and, as if all that weren't enough, you get some great utilities with the disk. (See the entries on BigCaps, Font Charter and DefaultFont above). The manual is terrific (except that the type is too small), the selection is astounding and the value is incredible.

🍎 public-domain bit-mapped fonts *(AN)*

bargain

There are a lot of public-domain bit-mapped fonts available, but my favorite is Santa Monica, designed by Paul Hoffman. As you can see, it's just about the widest font you'll ever find (this is just 12-point, believe it or not), which makes it a little hard to use, but I love the way it looks.

A laser font sampler

● *Apple's laser fonts* (AN)

The original LaserWriter came with four fonts built in:

Times—the standard, boring serif typeface. Look at how much smaller it is than Helvetica at the same type size (11-point).

Helvetica—the standard, boring sans serif typeface. Look at how much bigger it is than Times at the same type size (11-point).

Courier—an excellent choice if you want to make your laser printer look like a typewriter. To be fair, Courier is also useful when you need a monospaced font for some reason. Even I use it to display programming listings and HyperCard scripts, where precise spacing is important.

Finally, there's Σψμβολ—that is, Symbol, which supplements the other fonts by supplying symbols to them (although you can also get some great stuff by using it directly).

The LaserWriter Plus, II NT and II NTX contain a bunch of other fonts that Adobe also sells separately on disk (Bookman, Palatino, Zapf Chancery, Zapf Dingbats, Helvetica Narrow, etc.) In general, it's a useful and sensible selection—if not terribly exciting.

● *Adobe's laser fonts* (AN)

Adobe's fonts typically cost $185, which is much more than the competition, and that's only for a license to use them on one printer. Before I actually used Adobe fonts, I couldn't imagine how they could possibly be worth the extra expense. Now I know and you see the result: this book is set in Adobe's ITC Benguiat, with tables in their Optima and headers in their ITC Zapf Chancery.

very good feature

(The ITC you see before the names of various fonts stands for the International Typeface Corporation of New York City, a powerful force for excellence and innovation in typography. They've been responsible for many beautiful new fonts and for tasteful redesigns of classic fonts like Garamond as well. Part of their agreement when they license a typeface to Adobe (or anyone else) is that their initials be part of the name.)

I haven't made a side-by-side comparison of each Adobe font with each of its competitors, but my subjective impression is that—at least for the most part—Adobe's fonts often look better. (See *Adobe's home-court advantage* in the *Advanced font tips* section below for the probable reason why.)

The difference in quality may not matter all that much to you, you may not be in a position where you can afford to let it matter, or you may prefer to spend your money on a lot of fonts rather than a few fine ones. But there is an argument to be made for quality versus variety and price, and that's an argument Adobe often wins.

very good feature

The first Adobe font I'll talk about is the ineffably beautiful Benguiat. BENGUIAT IS MOST OFTEN USED AS A DISPLAY FACE— THE CAP A, B and Q ARE PARTICU- LARLY LOVELY—but for all its sensuous lushness, it's also an extremely readable font. Aren't you glad I used it for the book instead of something pedestrian like Times or New Century Schoolbook?

gossip/ trivia

Benguiat is named after the man who created it, Ed Benguiat (BENG-gat), who is certainly one of the greatest type designers who's ever lived. (I love names, so I took the trouble to find out that his is Spanish, originally from Cordoba. Actually, going all the way back, it's Moorish, *ben* meaning *son of* in Arabic.)

Anyway, Ed Benguiat, who was born in 1927, is responsible for more than five *hundred* typefaces, including classics like Bookman, Souvenir, Korinna, Tiffany and Charisma. In addition to being a designer and a vice-president at ITC, he's a pilot and a jazz drummer who's played with Stan Kenton and Woody Herman.

Benguiat says, "in designing an alphabet, each letter should almost be like a painting or a piece of sculpture—that is, beautiful within itself." This approach is evident in all his typefaces, but nowhere more than in the one he put his name to.

very bad feature

Adobe's version of Benguiat—of Benguiat Book, to be precise—is fine as far as it goes—which isn't far enough. No italic or italic bold is provided, so everywhere you see those type styles in this book, they're algorithmic. (See the entry on font styles at the beginning of this chapter if you don't know what that means.) That's a pity, because *real* Benguiat italic—the kind they use on phototypesetting machines—is *beautiful.*

If Adobe's going to offer this gorgeous face (and I'm certainly glad they do), why don't they do a complete job of it? (I've been asking them that for years.) And if they won't finish the job, who will?

If there's a prettier sans serif typeface than Optima, I've never seen it. It was designed by another master type craftsman, Hermann Zapf (1918–). Why anyone would ever use Helvetica when they could use Optima is something I'll never understand.

Optima is much smaller than Benguiat in a given size (11-point, in this case). IT'S A GREAT DISPLAY FACE TOO, AND LOOKS EVEN BETTER ON A LINOTRONIC TYPESETTER.

As its name implies, Zapf Chancery was also designed by Hermann Zapf. Adobe's version is of the medium italic and is really quite deficient. It's somewhat understandable that you can't make it italic, since it's <u>already</u> italic, although that's still annoying—look how I had to underline that word because I couldn't put it in italics. But why shouldn't you be able to make it bold? Ah, well.

Notice how much smaller Zapf Chancery is even than Optima (this is 11-point). Zapf Chancery also works nicely as a display font. For example, we use it for our logo: Goldstein & Blair. *How do you like that ampersand?*

A third Adobe face designed by Zapf is Dingbats. There's a whole chart of the symbols in it, arranged by categories, in the *Special characters* section above.

Another Adobe offering is Korinna, a beautiful redesign by Ed Benguiat of a turn-of-the-century typeface. It has the sensual grace that marks all his fonts—not to mention a really great capital U and lowercase italic *f*. It's also very readable (this is 18-point). Here's how it looks in **bold**, *italic and* ***bold italic.***

A third Adobe font of Benguiat's is Souvenir (in Light and Demibold). I once wrote a book for kids that was set in Souvenir and it worked great. It has an informal feel but, at the same time, it's elegant. Here's how it looks in **bold,** *italic and* ***bold italic.***

A fourth Adobe font of Benguiat's is Tiffany and it's a beauty too. You can make it bold but if you really want some weight, **use Tiffany Heavy, which comes on the same disk. (You can't make *that* bold, though.)**

Cooper Black is one of my favorite display faces and Adobe has done a fine implementation of it. *I think Cooper looks best in italic. You can't make Cooper bold, because it's already "black," which is bolder than bold.*

Brush Script is another terrific display face, and on the same disk you get STENCIL, WHICH COMES IN CAPS ONLY, and the much-beloved (and much-used) Hobo.

Hobo is unusual in that it has no descenders (parts of letters that extend below the baseline). This cuts down on legibility but gives it a great lowercase g. Unfortunately, you can't

make the Adobe version of Hobo italic or bold.

Anyway, these three fonts make quite a nice package (I can't bear to leave Hobo just yet). Adobe has lots of other fonts and a great, free catalog that shows them all.

● *CasadyWare's Fluent Laser Fonts* (AN)

Richard Ware, the designer at CasadyWare, has come up with some really beautiful laser fonts (to go along with his really beautiful bit-mapped fonts).

One of those is Monterey, an adaptation of a classic face called Peignot (pain-yoh). Isn't it exquisite? I use it in my letterhead. There's also a Monterey Medium (slightly heavier and wider) and you can make either the regular font or the Medium bold (but the two look the same. *Here's how it looks in italic.*

My favorite CasadyWare font is Dorovar. I use it for memos (it gives them a more personal touch). Isn't it gorgeous? Sometimes I find myself trying to think of what else I can put in a memo, just so I can keep on looking at this font.

Another favorite of mine is Gazelle. It's got a great lowercase ð (which doesn't do a lot for readability, however). Gazelle really looks dramatic on the page. Here's how it looks in **bold**, *italic and* ***bold italic.***

CasadyWare also has an Old English font called Gregorian which you may remember from The Ten Commandments at the beginning of the book.

Another medieval font of theirs is Kells. It's what's called an *uncial (UN-chul)* font—that is, it resembles the lettering used in Irish and English manuscripts during the Middle Ages.

Another useful font is Ritz, a version of a classic (and classy) typeface called Broadway. If you find yourself suddenly transported back in time to

the 30's (you never know when that might happen), this is the face to use.

Finally, there's Gatsby Light, which, as you can see, is an elegant face ideally suited for a fancy invitation or an ad for a store that sells very expensive women's clothing. But it's nice sometimes to work against the grain of a font; for example, isn't the next sentence an interesting juxtaposition of form and content? Hey, baby, let's boogie!

bargain

There are a lot of other beautiful Fluent Laser Fonts. They come on disks that each contain one or two fonts in one to four styles and only cost $70. You really should send for their catalog; at those prices, you can afford to be tempted.

☀ *Century's laser fonts* (DC)

very good feature

Michael Mace's Century Software offers a wide selection of laser fonts that are both very inexpensive and loaded with features. For example, he's remapped the keyboard to provide you with all the accents you need to type in more than thirty languages—including Polish, Czech, Turkish, Hungarian and Esperanto.

very good feature

Even better, the keys that normally produce square brackets ([ ]) and, when shifted, curly brackets ({ }) produce true single quotes ' ' and, when shifted, true double quotes " " in Century Fonts (the brackets are shifted to the Option and Shift Option positions). If, like most people, you use quotation marks more often than brackets, this is great. The remapped Century keyboard also gives you commas and periods when the ⬚Shift⬚ key is down, as well as when it isn't.

Another great Century product is Special Effects—unusual style variations on Times and Helvetica, two fonts that are built into every LaserWriter. (We'd love to show them to you but for some reason PageMaker had trouble bringing them in.) Because they're algorithmic, Century's Special Effects hardly take up any of the LaserWriter's precious memory and, on top of everything, they only cost $2.50 each! At this price, I recommend them to virtually any LaserWriter user.

very good feature

bargain

🍎 *Complementary Type laser fonts* (AN)

A company called Software Complement has come up with a number of very interesting and beautiful fonts that they sell for $70 a disk under the name of Complementary Type (each disk contains up to three separate fonts). They have a version of Hobo called Hobnob, a version of Stencil called Cut Outs that has lowercase letters as well as caps, and a bunch of other fonts I'm about to show you.

bargain

One problem is that there's only one printer font for each typeface. That means that all the bold, italic and bold italic type has to be algorithmically derived. You can judge from the samples below how well that works (pretty well, I think).

Fluent Fonts has a nice bit-mapped Art Nouveau (turn-of-the-century) font, but I've longed for a laser version. Here's a pretty one from Software Complement called simply Nouveau. Bold. *Italic. Bold italic.*

A different sort of Art Nouveau font is Fletcher Gothic. Feast your eyes on these caps! ABCDEFGHIJKLMNOPQRSTUVWXYZ. Gorgeous, aren't they? Look how the L and M cross. Mmm! The lowercase letters are beautiful too; for example, look at the c and h combination in a word like Fletcher—it almost makes a heart. **Bold.** *Italic.* ***Bold italic.***

MICHELLE IS ANOTHER ALL CAPS FONT, WITH VARIANTS FOR SOME OF THE LETTERS (S AND ſ, FOR EXAMPLE). YOU MIGHT USE IT TO RESPOND TO AN IRS AUDIT NOTICE. THEY'LL PROBABLY THINK YOU'RE SO CRAZY THEY'LL DROP THE WHOLE THING. **BOLD.** *ITALIC.* ***BOLD ITALIC.***

FATTI PATTI IS A THIRD ALL-CAPS FONT. IT'S AN IMITATION OF A FAMOUS TYPEFACE CALLED BABY TEETH. *ITALIC LOOKS OK, BUT BOLD FILLS IN TOO MUCH.*

Our final Complementary Type selection this evening is Kasse, a sleek, modern, European face that manages to be elegant without being the least bit old-fashioned. **Bold.** *Italic.* ***Bold italic.***

 throw away that clay tablet (AN)

Sure, this chapter has shown you a lot of interesting and useful fonts. But what if your job calls for something in cuneiform (perhaps a memo to the main office back in Babylon)? Sure, you could just haul out the old clay tablet and knock one off, but you're wearing your good light suit and you're afraid you'll get the cuffs dirty.

No problem. Just use cuneifont, the public-domain laser font you're reading right now. It's missing some characters, like an em dash, curly apostrophe and curly quotes, but when you really need cuneiform, nothing else will do.

Advanced font tips

🍎 Adobe's home-court advantage (SH)

The outlines that create the Mac's PostScript fonts are described by mathematical equations called *Bezier spline curves.* Adobe has a proprietary program that uses Bezier curves to tweak letter shapes in a very detailed and precise way.

Linotype is allowed to use this program for jointly developed fonts, and it's rumored that a Japanese company also uses it. At least two other Bezier font programs exist—Fontographer from Altsys and a program written by Michael Mace, publisher of Century fonts, that he hasn't released commercially yet.

In large sizes, fonts produced by all of these programs print well, especially on high-resolution devices like typesetting machines. But in small sizes, funny things start happening to non-Adobe fonts, especially on relatively low-resolution devices like 300-dpi laser printers.

The problem arises when the font wants to place a dot where the output device can't put one. The font has *rounding routines* to decide where to put the dot, but if they're not good enough, you get things like a baseline that rises and falls unevenly, or an *n* with one leg narrower than the other.

Adobe puts little tricks into their fonts to avoid these problems. To prevent others from following in their footsteps, they've kept some PostScript programming secrets to themselves. As a result, the PostScript in your printer and typesetter will only recognize and respond to Adobe's tricks. Other font publishers can program in equally good tricks, but PostScript printers will ignore them.

Although this ploy may enable Adobe to sell more of their fonts in the short run, it's pretty short-sighted, because it stands in the way of PostScript becoming a true graphics standard.

very bad
feature

🍎 *some good font utilities* (SH)

There are a number of utilities you can use to get a font's ID numbers. Older ones such as Font Librarian and Font Manager provide the IDs of installed fonts (and Font Librarian does that for fonts in any suitcase file as well). But since these programs don't support FOND resources, which are essential with PostScript fonts, they should be used *only* to read ID numbers.

You can also get font ID numbers from ResEdit, FONTastic Plus, FontDisplay, PDFontEdit, Font/DA Utility or DAFont3. Some of these will also let you change ID numbers of fonts to avoid conflicts, but this should only be done with great care when you are *sure* of what you are doing. (See the entry below called *the font-numbering mess* for a discussion of the pitfalls of irresponsible font ID renumbering.) Of these programs, FONTastic Plus is the most powerful for

important
warning

nontechnical people, since it lets you redesign screen fonts as well as change parameters.

very good feature

For everyday use, my favorite font utility is FontDisplay, because it gives me ID numbers, better keyboard layouts than Key Caps, sample text in any size or style and character count per pica for any font or size (the typesetter's dream). It also prints out wonderful reference sheets containing any or all of this information.

✦ *sharing printer fonts* (SH)

There are two very useful utilities that let a single set of fonts be shared on a network like TOPS or AppleShare so you don't have multiple copies around wasting disk space.

bargain

A $20 shareware program called Set Paths is the more powerful—and by far the cheaper—of the two. As described in the utilities chapter, Set Paths lets you tell the Mac five other places to look for something than the normal places it looks (which are the folder you're in, the System folder and the window of the disk you're on). This is called setting a *search path.*

very good feature

This capability makes it possible for you to share one set of screen fonts and/or printer fonts over a network. (Using TOPS, for example, you'd just publish the font folder on the network.) Version 1.3 of Set Paths is a little shaky with MultiFinder, but that should be corrected by the time you read this.

very good feature

FontShare is more limited, because it only lets you set search paths to printer font files (Set Paths works for all sorts of data files) but does that very well and works with MultiFinder. Whenever a printer font isn't available in the printer or system folder, it asks you where it is and remembers from then on, downloading it automatically.

The drawbacks are that you have to individually set the path for every single printer font (bold, italic, etc.)—a lengthy process. Fortunately, you can copy the resulting file to other machines on the network so it only has to be done once. It's also very pricey at $300.

❡ *fractional character widths* (TR)

A FOND resource can contain fractional character-widths—that is, you can specify the width of a character as 4.53 units instead of being limited to 4 units or 5. This precision lets you pack characters more tightly on a line, which makes them look and read better.

*very
hot
tip*

Though fractional information is built into virtually every PostScript font and supported by ROMs on all machines after the Mac 512, it's still largely ignored by most software; for example, Ready,Set,Go! 4 and Cricket Presents 1.0 don't support it.

The following software seems to use fractional spacing: Cricket Draw 1.1, Freehand 1.0, FullWrite 1.0, Illustrator 88 1.5, MacDraw II, PageMaker 3.0, PowerPoint 1.01, Scoop, WriteNow 1.00 and XPress 1.10L. Sometimes the feature has to be turned on in an obscure way—for example, in WriteNow you have to choose *Use Printer Spacing* in the Page Setup dialog box.

FOND resources can also contain kerning information. PageMaker, ReadySetGo 4 and XPress can all use FOND kerning information if you specifically request it, Scoop doesn't. Freehand uses FOND kerning information automatically but Illustrator 88 doesn't give you any way to access it.

❡ *the font-numbering mess* (SH)

The ability to use a variety of typefaces was part of Apple's plan for the original Macintosh, and it was a major step forward from the typewriter mentality of previous personal computers.

*very
hot
tip*

Apple decided that each font would be assigned a unique ID number. Whatever a font was called, its ID number would be the only way printers would identify it (in fact, the ID number is the only indication saved with a file as to what fonts are intended).

Because Apple had no idea of the flood of fonts that would follow, they chose to reduce the strain on the original 64K ROMs and 128K memory by allowing for only 512 ID numbers. Due to flaws in the original ROMs, only the first 256 of those font IDs could be reliably used, and they had to serve for both bit-mapped (ImageWriter) and laser fonts.

Since Apple developed the first fonts, they assumed they'd have to keep doing that for some time. And they also used font resources for other purposes, such as the icons on MacPaint's and MacDraw's tool palate. So they reserved the first 128 numbers for their own use. This only left 128 font ID numbers for everybody else.

Still, since most other computers at the time only had one font, 128 seemed like a lot. Apple certainly had no intention of restricting the use or development of the Macintosh typefaces. But back then no one at Apple seriously thought of using the Mac for typesetting. In fact, many of the original fonts were invented for the Mac, rather than being based on commercial typefaces (of which there are thousands).

very bad feature

As soon as the Mac was released, users and developers began flooding the market and bulletin boards with fonts. By the time well-designed fonts arrived, many of the available numbers were already taken. By now, the 128-number limit has become a catastrophe. (For a list of about 500 fonts and their ID numbers, both alphabetically by font name and numerically by ID number, see the next two entries.)

very bad feature

And yet, although Apple is long gone from the font market and has acknowledged Adobe as their de facto successor in that role, they jealously protect those first 128 ID numbers from commercial use. Adobe reports that when they began using some of these IDs last year in an attempt to prevent the confusion of multiple fonts with one ID number, Apple angrily ordered them to stop doing so or risk losing Apple's cooperation. And so, with a few rare exceptions, IDs 35 to 128 remain off-limits—wasted by Apple in a pointless display of corporate power.

It was problems with the original Mac's ROMs of the 128K Mac that limited us to only 256 font ID numbers. The 128K Mac is long gone from the commercial scene, and it can't even run the new layout programs, but Apple still insists on keeping compatibility among all its machines for as long as possible. Many programs and even some font utilities will not recognize fonts with IDs greater than 256. Apple should at least let us use ID numbers 257–512 by abandoning this out-of-date nostalgia.

Since the Mac Plus, there's been a wholly adequate alternative to the original font ID numbers. Called NFNT numbers (for *new FONT*), there are 32,768 of them—which is enough for the foreseeable future. But to retrofit all PostScript fonts to NFNT would require upgrading many of the programs and virtually all of the fonts already available.

things to come

Version 6.0 of the System and version 3.8 of the Font/DA Mover support NFNT numbers. (For other software that does, see the entry below titled *NFNT compatibility.*) But for this approach to work, a standard utility has to be made available to all font owners that tags each existing font with a *unique* NFNT number. Font publishers will need to get together to make sure there will be no duplication of NFNT numbers, and such an agreement may be some time off.

All this may seem like a programmer's academic exercise, but it isn't. The everyday difficulties that font ID number conflicts create for heavy users of fonts are a rapidly-growing nightmare. The following typical ID conflict will demonstrate how ugly it can get.

important warning

Let's take ID number 153. Adobe uses this for *American Typewriter Bold* and *News Gothic,* Century uses it for *Thin Helvetica,* Electric Typographer uses it for *Flourish* and Dubl-Click uses it for the bit-mapped font *Stuttgart.*

Suppose you've created a document in *News Gothic* and want a headline in *American Typewriter Bold.* You load that font into the System file with the Font/DA mover, type the headline and proof it on your LaserWriter. Everything looks great. Then you go to your local Linotype service bureau and are startled to see the headline in *Melior Italic.*

Unknown to you, when you installed *Typewriter*, the Font/DA mover renumbered it to ID 200, because ID 153 was already taken by *News Gothic*. In your own closed world this didn't matter, but anywhere else you no longer have *American Typewriter Bold* (since fonts are called by their ID number, not their names).

You call up the page on screen, correct the headline on their machine, things print out correctly and you go home.

Phase two is even more bizarre. Since the *Typewriter Bold* has taken the ID slot for *Melior Italic*, when you want to use *Melior Italic* and load it into your System file it, in turn, is renumbered. Now two fonts are misnumbered. Like an infectious disease, ID conflicts spread throughout your entire font collection.

Then one day you remove the *Typewriter Bold* from your System file. Someone points out that using a clean copy of *Melior Italic* might solve the problem, so you remove and reinstall it. It works, at home and at the service bureau.

But the next time you install *Typewriter Bold* its new, changed ID is taken, so it's given yet another ID number. It still prints out OK on your machine but it's a disaster at the service bureau. When you go home you load up the first file to see if it's still OK, and *American Typewriter Bold* is now *Melior Italic* on your screen and prints that way. The same font, in different files, shows and prints differently.

very good feature

Recognizing this problem, Aldus has written a resource into PageMaker that tags fonts with their *names* rather than their numbers. (Pretty obvious and simple, isn't it? If Aldus can do this, why not everyone?).

If you change System files or have font ID conflicts, the fonts previously tagged will display incorrectly on the screen but will still print correctly—providing the proper printer fonts are available. (If, however, you edit an improperly displayed font it will lose its original PostScript identity and print to match the displayed font.)

Since MacPaint, FullPaint and MacDraw all use fonts as the source of their tool palate icons, you can get strange

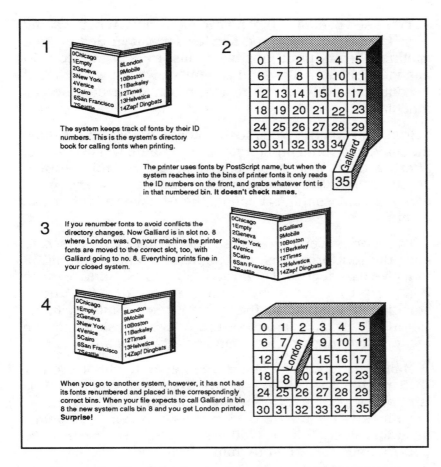

1

0Chicago
1Empty
2Geneva
3New York
4Venice
5Cairo
6San Francisco
7Seattle
8London
9Mobile
10Boston
11Berkeley
12Times
13Helvetica
14Zapf Dingbats

The system keeps track of fonts by their ID numbers. This is the system's directory book for calling fonts when printing.

2

0	1	2	3	4	5
6	7	8	9	10	11
12	13	14	15	16	17
18	19	20	21	22	23
24	25	26	27	28	29
30	31	32	33	34	Galliard 35

The printer uses fonts by PostScript name, but when the system reaches into the bins of printer fonts it only reads the ID numbers on the front, and grabs whatever font is in that numbered bin. **It doesn't check names.**

3 If you renumber fonts to avoid conflicts the directory changes. Now Galliard is in slot no. 8 where London was. On your machine the printer fonts are moved to the correct slot, too, with Galliard going to no. 8. Everything prints fine in your closed system.

0Chicago
1Empty
2Geneva
3New York
4Venice
5Cairo
6San Francisco
7Seattle
8Galliard
9Mobile
10Boston
11Berkeley
12Times
13Helvetica
14Zapf Dingbats

4

0Chicago
1Empty
2Geneva
3New York
4Venice
5Cairo
6San Francisco
7Seattle
8London
9Mobile
10Boston
11Berkeley
12Times
13Helvetica
14Zapf Dingbats

When you go to another system, however, it has not had its fonts renumbered and placed in the correspondingly correct bins. When your file expects to call Galliard in bin 8 the new system calls bin 8 and you get London printed. **Surprise!**

0	1	2	3	4	5
6	7 London	9	10	11
12	8	15	16	17
18	20	21	22	23
24	25	26	27	28	29
30	31	32	33	34	35

characters in place of the tool icons, and it can take some guesswork to figure out which font is conflicting with the program's icon font. *Bodoni Roman*, for example, conflicts with MacDraw's icons and *Franklin Gothic Heavy Italic* conflicts with FullPaint's.

Some people have tried to avoid font ID conflicts by sticking to one publisher's fonts. Unfortunately, the number of ID numbers is so limited that both Adobe and Century have had to start reusing the same numbers for different fonts, and CasadyWare is almost at that point.

This is not a theoretical problem. I see people every day who have these problems—some with their font ID numbers

very bad feature

so confused over time that no two files print a font the same way. I know one Linotype service bureau in Seattle that routinely has to print jobs twice, just to deal with font ID changes. This is a slow and expensive way to work, and if it continues will doom the Macintosh as a commercial machine.

things to come

Ironically, as the Macintosh catches on as a publishing machine and fonts proliferate, the problem will get worse. There are thousands of fonts announced from Adobe, Linotype, Varityper, Compugraphic and many other companies and, unless things change, they'll have to fit into 128 ID numbers.

There are several interim solutions that can be used to ease the font problems, and some programs and utilities that give us a degree of control over font IDs. None of these is a perfect fix and many require a more detailed understanding of fonts than the general user wants to have. Unfortunately, this is one of the prices of using such an inexpensive machine for complicated layout work.

Many frustrated users have threatened to change to MS-DOS machines which do not have ID number conflicts. This isn't any sort of solution, as anyone who has used these machines is aware. MS-DOS has its own font problems, including a very small selection and (often) bizarre installation routines for each program.

Since the PC's Intel CPU chips (8088, etc.) were not designed for graphics (unlike the 68000 and other Motorola chips used by the Mac), PCs are at least a generation behind Macs in ease of use and power. Many users switch from MS-DOS to the Macintosh, but in four years of training and consulting I've never met anyone who's gone the other way.

very hot tip

A better solution is to bring (or send) your System file along when you want to print at a service bureau. Then boot from your System disk and print. One possible problem: if you use a program on the hard disk at the service bureau to print the file, simply starting up that program may switch you over to the hard disk's System file.

If you use lots of fonts and DAs and thus have a big System file, or if you use PageMaker 3.0, which no longer fits on an 800K disk, it may be easiest to simply bring your computer or hard disk and plug it into their network (if they'll let you).

Another way to avoid font conflicts is to save all files for printing as PostScript files (if the program you're using lets you do that). PageMaker is one program that lets you save files as pure PostScript or as an EPS file. With most other programs, choosing *Print...* and then pressing ⌘]–F will print the file to disk as an Apple PostScript file.

very
hot
tip

Since PostScript files contain font names in place of ID numbers, they'll print correctly on any PostScript printer. Unless the file is huge, you can do this instead of bringing in your own System file and program disks. PostScript files print faster as well, so if your service bureau adds time charges to the print bill, this approach will save you money as well.

Another straightforward, but somewhat tedious, way to control the problem is to be aware of ID numbers of all of your fonts (using the lists in the next two entries) and to avoid using conflicting ones together.

very
hot
tip

This approach is easier if you use Suitcase or Font/DA Juggler instead of Font/DA Mover. Font/DA Mover renumbers conflicting fonts and then loads them, causing some of the problems described above. Suitcase and Font/DA Juggler don't renumber fonts; if numbers conflict, they simply don't let you use one of the fonts.

They give priority first to fonts installed in the System file (rather than in suitcase files), then to the last font used. So if you carefully choose the order in which you load fonts, you can use ones with conflicting numbers.

There is one solution to this problem that would make font ID numbers irrelevant, but it hasn't been developed yet. Suppose someone wrote a simple init program that creates an ID number/font name lookup table for the

things
to come

current System file. This table would be invisibly appended to every file you create and would be referred to, by every program, whenever you print. That way, you'd always end up with the right printer font, no matter how the screen fonts' IDs might change.

(Cricket Draw does something similar: when you save a file in QuickDraw format, the program saves the PostScript description of the file and attaches it to the QuickDraw version. This can be partly seen in the garbage characters that often appear in the corner of the saved image when you place it in another program. The PostScript substitutes for the QuickDraw description when printing, giving full Post-Script resolution and effects—and proper font calls.)

very hot tip

You could also give the lookup table to your local service bureau along with the file to be printed—a far better solution then sending them your whole System file.

We need such a utility, so we won't have to rewrite every program in order to use a new font resource number like NFNT. Where is the programmer who will rescue the Mac from the font-numbering mess?

✦ *font ID numbers in alphabetical order* (SH)

very hot tip

This is an updated version of a list that CasadyWare was kind enough to supply me. It gives you the ID numbers of about 500 Macintosh fonts, in alphabetical order by font name.

Note that more than one company may have a font with the same name; for example, both Adobe and CasadyWare offer a version of Bodoni. Fonts in italics are from Adobe; (CW) = CasadyWare, (Cn) = Century.

Varityper fonts are not included because they appear to all use the same ID numbers! The two I was able to examine—Varitimes and Aristocrat—both used 128 for Roman, 129 for Bold, 130 for Italic and 131 for Bold Italic.

✪ *font ID numbers in numerical order* (SH)

This list gives you the same information as the previous one, but in numerical order by font ID number rather than in alphabetical order by font name. See the beginning of the previous entry for information that applies to both lists.

ID #	Fonts
0–12	Original Apple System Imagewriter fonts
13	*Zapf Dingbats*
14	*Bookman Light*
15	*Helvetica Narrow*
16	*Palatino Roman*
17	*American Typewriter Medium*
18	*Zapf Chancery Medium Italic*
19	*Souvenir Light*
20	*Times*
21	*Helvetica*
22	*Courier*
23	*Symbol*
24	Mobile (Cn)
25	none...
26	*Lubalin graph*
27	*Benguiat Book*
28	*Friz Quadrata*
29	*Glypha*
30	*Machine*
31	*Optima*
32	none...
33	*Avant Garde Book*
34	*New Century Schoolbook Roman*
35–47	none
48	none...
49–74	none...
75	Szwajcarskie
76–78	none...

79	none...
80	Zip Helvetica (Cn), Tempora Fake
81	Triangle Helvetica (Cn)
82	Slant Helvetica (Cn)
83	Random Helvetica (Cn)
84	Line Helvetica (Cn)
85	Inline Helvetica (Cn), Tempora Roman
86	Grid Helvetica (Cn)
87	Gray Scale Helvetica (Cn)
88	Fountain Helvetica (Cn)
89	*Goudy Roman*, Diamond Helvetica (Cn)
90	Circle Helvetica (Cn)
91	Burst Helvetica (Cn)
92	Slant Times (Cn)
93	Gray Scale Times (Cn)
94	Zip Times (Cn)
95	Burst Times (Cn)
96	Inline Times (Cn), Structure
97	Grid Times (Cn), Thompson
98	Random Times (Cn), Haber
99	Diamond Times (Cn)
100	Circle Times (Cn)
101	Line Times (Cn)
102	Triangle Times (Cn), Czasy Roman
103	Fountain Times (Cn)
104–109	none...
110	Czasy fake
111–127	none...
128	Acropolis
129	*Avant Garde Book Oblique, Aachen*, Ironworks, Thin Extralight Willamette (Cn)
130	*Avant Garde Demi*, Kimberley, Thin Devoll (Cn)
131	*Avant Garde Demi Oblique, Freestyle*, Parthenon, Fat ExtraLight Willamette (Cn)
132	*Bookman Light Italic, Revue*, Sirius, Fat Devoll (Cn)

133   *BookmanDemi, Lucida Sans Bold,* Trisse, Thin Medium Willamette (Cn)

134   *Bookman Demi italic, University Roman,* Cumberland (Cn)

135   *Courier Oblique, Carta,* Alexandra, Fat Medium Willamette (Cn)

136   *Courier Bold, Letter Gothic Bold Italic,* Serotype, Thin Cumberland (Cn)

137   *Courier Bold Oblique, Letter Gothic Italic,* New East, Micro Times (Cn)

138   *Helvetica Oblique, Prestige Elite Bold Italic,* Patriot

139   *Helvetica Bold, Prestige Elite Italic,* Blackjack, Thin Times (Cn)

140   *Helvetica Bold Oblique, Orator Slant,* Light Manistee (Cn)

141   *Narrow Helvetica Oblique, Lucida,* Fat Times (Cn)

142   *Narrow Helvetica Bold, Lucida Italic,* Moonlight, Bold Manistee (Cn)

143   *Helvetica Narrow Bold Oblique, Lucida Bold,* Newbaby, Micro Courier (Cn)

144   *New Century Schoolbook Italic, Bodoni Bold,* Benatar, Extralight Willamette (Cn)

145   *New Century Schoolbook Bold, Bodoni Italic,* Kadmos, Milliways, Thin Courier (Cn)

146   *New Century Schoolbook Bold Italic, Bodoni Poster,* Devoll (Cn)

147   *Palatino Italic, Bodoni Bold Italic,* Fat Courier (Cn)

148   *Palatino Bold, Lucida Bold Italic*

149   *Lucida Sans, Palatino Bold Italic,* Micro Helvetica (Cn), *Lucida Sans Roman,* Kells (CW)

150   *Lucida Sans Bold Italic, Times Italic,* Fat Cumberland (Cn)

151   *Lucida Sans Italic, Times Bold,* Fat Helvetica (Cn), Meath (CW)

152   *Times Bold Italic, News Gothic Bold,* Spokane (Cn)

153   *American Typewriter Bold, News Gothic,* Flourish, Thin Helvetica (Cn)

154   *Benguiat Bold, Cooper Black,* Thin Spokane (Cn)

155   *Friz Quadrata Bold, Cooper Black Italic,* Fat Spokane (Cn)

156   *Garamond Light,* Thin Yukon (Cn)

157   *Garamond Light Italic,* Fat Yukon (Cn), *Lucida Sans Italic*

158	*Garamond Bold*, Thin Hudson (Cn)
159	*Garamond Bold Italic*, Fat Hudson (Cn)
160	*Glypha Oblique*, Thin Rhine (Cn)
161	*Glypha Bold*, *Hobo*, Fat Rhine (Cn)
162	*Glypha Bold Oblique*, *Brush Script*, Thin Potomac (Cn)
163	*Lubalin Graph Book Oblique*, *Stencil*, Fat Potomoc (Cn)
164	*Lubalin Graph Demi*, *Tiffany Roman*, Shady Times (Cn),College Black (CW)
165	*Lubalin Graph Demi Oblique*, *Tiffany Demi*, Shadow Times (Cn), College Outline (CW)
166	*Optima Oblique*, *Tiffany Heavy*, Fill Times (Cn), Desperado (CW)
167	*Optima Bold*, Stack Times (Cn), Dry Gulch (CW)
168	*Optima Bold Oblique*, *Futura Book*, Light Gray Times (Cn), Abilene (CW)
169	*Souvenir Light Italic*, *Futura Book Oblique*, Dark Gray Times (Cn), Collegiate (CW)
170	*Souvenir Demi*, *Tiffany Italic*, Thin Bold Manistee (Cn)
171	*Souvenir Demi Italic*, Fat Bold Manistee (Cn), *Futura Extra Bold*, Gazelle (CW)
172	*Tiffany Bold Italic*, Thin Light Manistee (Cn), Jott (CW)
173	*Tiffany Heavy Italic*, *Futura Light*, Fat Light Manistee (Cn), Jott Italic (CW)
174	*News Gothic Oblique*, Fat Columbia (Cn), Jott Bold (CW), *Futura*
175	*News Gothic Bold Oblique*, *Futura Bold*, Thin Columbia (Cn), Jott Bold Italic (CW)
176	Fat Bold Neosho (Cn), *Eurostyle*, *Futura Heavy*
177	*Helvetica Condensed Bold*, Thin Bold Neosho (Cn), *Eurostyle Demibold*, *Futura Oblique*
178	Fat Light Neosho (Cn), *Eurostyle Bold*, *Futura Condensed*
179	*Futura Bold Oblique*, Thin Light Neosho (Cn)
180	Bold Neosho (Cn), Alexandria (CW), *Futura Condensed Bold*
181	Light Neosho (Cn), Alexandria Bold (CW), *Eurostyle Oblique*, *Futura Condensed Extra Bold*
182	*Galliard Bold*, After Times (Cn), Alexandria Italic (CW), *Futura Condensed Light*

183   *Galliard Bold Italic,* After Helvetica (Cn), Alexandria Bold Italic (CW), *Eurostyle Demibold Oblique*

184   *Galliard Italic,* Shadow helvetica (Cn), Campanile (CW), *Eurostyle Bold Oblique*

185   *Galliard roman, Universe Light Oblique,* Shady Helvetica (Cn), Giottot (CW), Giotto (CW)

186   *Goudy Bold, Universe Oblique,* Fill Helvetica (Cn), Giottot Bold (CW), Giotto Bold (CW)

187   *Goudy Bold Italic, Universe Black Oblique,* Stack Helvetica (Cn), Galileo Roman (CW)

188   *Goudy Italic, Universe Bold Oblique,* Light Gray Helvetica (Cn), Galileo Bold (CW)

189   *Universe Cond. Light Oblique,* Dark Gray Helvetica (Cn), Galileo Italic (CW)

190   *Helvetica Condensed Light Black,* Trent (Cn), Galileo Bold Italic (CW)

191   *Helvetica Condensed Bold Oblique,* Fat Trent (Cn), Sans Serif Bold Condensed (CW)

192   *Helvetica Condensed Light,* Thin Trent (Cn), Sans Serif Bold Condensed Italic (CW)

193   *Helvetica Light,* Thingamajigs (Cn), Sans Serif Extra Bold Condensed (CW)

194   *Korinna Bold, Stone Serif,* Sans Serif Extra Bold Condensed Italic (CW)

195   *Korinna Kursiv Bold, Stone Serif Semi-Bold,* Doodads (Cn), Micro Laser (CW), Micro (CW)

196   *Korinna Kursiv Regular, Stone Serif Bold,* Micro Italic (CW)

197   *Korinna, Stone Serif Light,* Micro Bold (CW)

198   *Melior Bold,* Stone *Serif Semi-Bold Italic,* Gimcracks, Micro Bold Italic (CW)

199   *Melior Bold Italic, Stone Serif Bold Italic,* Sans Serif Shadow (CW)

200   *Helvetica Compressed, Melior Italic, Stone Sans,* Liberty Font Outline, Frontier, Goudy Newstyle, Goudy Oldstyle (Altsys), Fontographer default ID, *Memphis Light*

201   *Helvetica Extra Compressed, Melior, Stone Sans Semi-Bold,* Rubber Stamp Gray, Fat Congo (Cn), Micro Extended, *Memphis Light Italic,* Micro Extended (CW)

202   *Helvetica Ultra Compressed, New Baskerville Bold, Stone Sans Bold*, Macintosh Font Extended, Paint Brush Font, Fat Styx (Cn), Micro Extended Italic (CW), *Memphis Bold*

203   *New Baskerville Bold Italic, Stone Sans Italic*, Surfstyle, Fat Thames (Cn), Micro Extended Bold (CW), *Memphis Bold Italic*

204   *New Baskerville Italic, Stone Sans Semi-Bold Italic*, Thin Congo (Cn), Micro Extended Bold Italic (CW), *Memphis Medium*

205   *New Baskerville Roman, Stone Sans Bold Italic*, Mechanical font, Thin Styx (Cn), Dorovar (CW), *Memphis Medius Italic*

206   *Trump Medieval Bold, Stone Informal*, Mechanical Outline, Thin Thames (Cn), Dorovar Italic (CW), *Memphis Extra Bold*

207   *Trump Medieval Bold Italic, Stone Informal Semi-Bold*, Crome Font, Thin Colorado (Cn), Cyrillic Bold Italic (CW)

208   *Trump Medieval Italic, Stone Informal Bold*, Modern, Colorado (Cn), Cyrillic Italic (CW)

209   *Trump Medieval, Stone Informal Italic*, Fat Colorado (Cn), Cyrillic Bold (CW)

210   *Helvetica condensed Light Black Oblique, Stone Informal Semi-Bold Italic*, Medium Willamette (Cn), Sans Serif (CW)

211   *Helvetica Condensed Light Oblique, Stone Informal Bold Italic*, Sans Serif Italic (CW)

212   *Helvetica Light Oblique,*Rhine (Cn), Sans Serif Book (CW)

213   *Universe Cond. Oblique*, Sans Serif Book Italic (CW)

214   *Universe Cond. Bold Oblique*, Columbia (Cn), Sans Serif Demi Bold (CW)

215   Sans Serif Demi Italic (CW)

216   Sans Serif Bold (CW)

217   Sans Serif Bold Italic (CW)

218   *Futura Light Oblique*, Yukon (Cn), Sans Serif Extra Bold (CW)

219   Sans Serif Extra Bold Italic (CW), *Futura Extra Bold*

220   Thames (Cn), Monterey (CW), *Futura Condensed Light Oblique*

221   Monterey Medium (CW), *Futura Heavy Oblique*

222   Hudson (Cn), Monterey Bold

223   *Cheltenham Roman*, Fat Seine (Cn), Monterey Italic (CW), *Futura Condensed Bold*

224   *Cheltenham Bold*, Seine (Cn), Monterey Bold Italic (CW), *Futura Condensed Extra Bold*

225   *Cheltenham Italic, Universe,* Thin Seine (Cn), Calligraphy (CW)

226   *Cheltenham Bold Italic, Universe Black,* Macntosh Font, Gatsby Demibold Italic (CW)

227   *Franklin Gothic, Universe Bold,* Liberty Font, Gatsby Demibold (CW)

228   *Franklin Gothic Demibold, Universe Cond. Bold,* Aria Font, Rubber Stamp, Gatsby Light Italic (CW)

229   *Franklin Gothic Heavy, Universe Cond.,* Aria Thin, Surfstyle Shadow, Gatsby Light (CW)

230   *Prestige Elite, Universe Light,* Brass Plate, Scanning Font, Regency Script (CW)

231   *Prestige Elite Bold,* Lynz Grey Font, Coventry Script (CW)

232   *Century Old Style Roman,* Lynz Font, Congo, Zephyr Script (CW)

233   *Century Old Style Bold,* Castle Gray Font, Cunei, Gregorian (CW)

234   *Century Old Style Italic,* Castle Font, Bullets & Boxes, Cyrillic (CW)

235   *Letter Gothic,* PaintBrush Gray Font, Prelude Script (CW)

236   *Letter Gothic Bold,* Paint Brush, Bodoni (CW)

237   *Orator,* Tipe Heavy Grey Font, Fat Chancery (Cn), Prelude Bold (CW)

238   *Helvetica Condensed,* Tipe Condensed Font, Styx (Cn), Prelude Light Slant (CW)

239   *Helvetica Condensed Oblique,*Tipe Heavy Font, Thin Chancery (Cn), Prelude Bold Slant (CW)

240   Tipe Thin Font, Thin Avant Garde (Cn), Ritz Laser (CW)

241   *Helvetica Black,* Fat Avant Garde (Cn), Ritz Condensed (CW)

242   *Helvetica Black Oblique,* Sonata, Thin Bookman (Cn), Ritz Italic (CW)

243   Fat Bookman (Cn), Bodoni Ultra Condensed Italic (CW)

244   *Park Avenue,* Thin Schoolbook (Cn), Bodoni Ultra Condensed (CW)

245   Fat Schoolbook (Cn), Right Bank (CW), *Corona*

246	Thin Palatino (Cn), Logo Font (CW), *Corona Italic*
247	Fat Palatino (Cn), Bodoni Ultra (CW), *Corona Bold*
248	*Excelsior*
249	MacPaint Icon Font, *Excelsior Italic*
250	FullPaint Icon Font, *Franklin Gothic Heavy Italic*, Thin Dingbats (Cn), Bodoni Laser (CW), *Excelsior Bold*
251	*Franklin Gothic Oblique*, Fina Font, Fat Dingbats (Cn), Bodoni Italic (CW)
252	*Franklin Gothic Demi Oblique*, Fina Font Extended, Micro Avant Garde (Cn), Bodoni Bold (CW)
253	Sofa font, Micro Palatino (Cn), Bodoni Bold Italic (CW)
254	MacDraw Icon Font, *Bodoni Roman*, Sofa Extended Font, Micro Chancery (Cn)
255	Micro dingbats (Cn)

NFNT compatibility *(TR)*

Y means the program can use fonts with NFNT numbers. *M* means that fonts with NFNT numbers will be missing from the program's font menu. *P* means there's some other problem.

very hot tip

Acta 2.02 ....Y	DeskPaint 1.05 ....Y
ApFont 3.0 ....Y	Double Helix 2.0 ....Y
Draw v2.5 ....Y	Easy Envelopes+ 1.0.............Y
BigCaps 3.0...........................Y	Excel 1.06 & 1.5 ....M
Biplane 1.0 ....M	Expressionist 2.0 ....M
Bulk Mailer+ 3.2 ....Y	Facelift 1.01 ....M
CalendarMaker 2.2.1 ....Y	File 1.00.............................M
Canvas 1.01 ....Y	FileMaker 4 ....Y
C.A.T. 2.0 ....Y	FileMaker Plus 2.1 ....Y
CheapPaint ....Y	Filevision 1.0 ....Y
Cricket Draw 1.1 ....M	Fontastic Plus 2.0 ....Y
Cricket Presents 1.0..............Y	Font Charter 2.0 ....Y
DAFont 3 ....M	Font/DA Juggler Plus 1.04 .....Y
dbase Mac 1.0 ....Y	Font/DA Mover 3.8 ....Y
Design 2.0 ....M	FontDisplay 5.35 ....P

FontMaster88	Y	MegaForm 1.0	Y
Font Mover DA	Y	Micro Planner 5.7	Y
Font Resolver 1.00	P	MindWrite 1.0	Y
Fourth Dimension 1.0.1	Y	Minicad 3.06	Y
Freehand 1.0	Y	MiniWriter 1.42	Y
FullPaint 1.0	Y	Modern Artist .5	Y
FullWrite 1.0	Y	Multiplan 1.1	M
Glue SuperViewer 1.02	Y	Omnis 3.22	Y
GraphicWorks 1.1	Y	PageMaker 3.0	M
Guide 1.0	Y	PixelPaint 1.0	Y
HyperCard 1.1	Y	PosterMaker Plus 2.5	P
Illustrator '88 1.5	Y	PowerDraw 11/87	Y
Jazz 1.0a	P	PowerPoint 1.01	Y
JoliWrite 2.0	Y	Prototyper 1.0	Y
Key Caps 2.2	Y	Qued/M 2.01	Y
Kiwi Envelopes 1.02	Y	Ragtime 1.0	Y
Layout 1.3	Y	ReadySetGo 4	Y
MacAuthor 1.05	P	RecordHolderPlus 3.0	Y
MacBillboard 4.0	Y	Red Ryder 10.3	Y
MacDraft 1.2a	P	Reflex 1.0	Y
MacDraw II	Y	ResEdit 1.1b3	P
MacΣqn 2.1.3	Y	Scoop	Y
MacFlow 2.02	Y	Silicon Press 1.0	Y
MacPaint 2.0	Y	Suitcase 1.2.4	Y
MacProject II	Y	SuperPaint 1.1	Y
MacPublisher III	Y	Trapeze 1.0b	Y
Mac3D 2.1	M	Voila! 1.0	Y
MacWrite 2.2, 4.5, 4.6, 5.0	Y	WordHandler 1.6	Y
Mangle 1.0A1	Y	WordPerfect 1.0	Y
MathType 1.52	M	Word 3.01	Y
MathWriter 1.4	Y	Works 1.1	Y
MDC II 2.1	Y	WriteNow 1.00	Y
Medit 1.53	Y	XPress 1.10L	Y

Chapter 6

Printers

Printer evaluations and comparisons

⚫ *types of printers* (AN)

Two types of printers are commonly used with a Mac—dot-matrix and laser. A *dot-matrix printer* forms characters out of a pattern of dots, the way the Mac forms images on the screen. Typically, each dot is made by a separate pin pushing against a ribbon and then against the paper, although there are other ways of getting the image on the paper. *ImageWriter* is the name Apple gives to its line of dot-matrix printers.

esp. for beginners

Laser printers create images by drawing them on a metal drum with a beam of laser light. The image is then made visible by electrostatically attracting dry ink powder to it, as in a photocopying machine. *LaserWriter* is the name Apple gives to its line of laser printers.

There are many other kind of printers—ink jet, formed-character, etc.—but as of this writing, none has assumed much importance on the Mac. This section discusses dot-matrix printers first, then laser printers (after the next two entries.

⚫ *relative resolutions of various devices* (AN)

In a normal ImageWriter text printout (from a word processing program, say), there are 80 dots per inch across and 72 down (5760 dots per square inch). If you choose Tall Adjusted, there are 72 dots per inch in both directions (5184 dpsi).

The LaserWriter's resolution is 300 dpi, which amounts to 90,000 dpsi—about 16 to 17 times the ImageWriter's. But 90,000 dpsi is nothing compared to what typesetting machines can do.

The 1270-dpi Linotronic 100 phototypesetter, for example, produces 1.6 million dpsi—about 18 times the resolution of a LaserWriter and almost 300 times that of an ImageWriter.

The 1690-dpi Linotronic 500 produces 2.85 million dpsi—almost 32 times the LaserWriter's and about 520 times the ImageWriter's.

The 2540-dpi Linotronic 300 produces 6.45 million dpsi—more than 70 times the LaserWriter's and well over 1000 times the ImageWriter's.

❖ *"letter-quality" printers* (AN)

Letter-quality was a name commonly given to formed-character printers before the advent of laser printers. Though it's now more often used to refer to the output of high-resolution dot-matrix printers like the ImageWriter LQ, I've retained this entry from the first edition because some people still do think formed-character printers are the only professional way to go.

Formed-character printers produce images the same way typewriters do—by pushing something the shape of a character against an inked ribbon and then into the paper. The something they push is a daisywheel or thimble containing all the available characters—sort of like the type ball used by IBM's Selectric typewriters.

Because formed-character printers work like typewriters, they're able to produce pages that look like they were typed on a typewriter. The question is: why would anyone want to work on a machine as sophisticated as the Macintosh and then try to fool the world into thinking the work was done on something as primitive as a typewriter?

Whenever you hear someone say that only a (formed-character) letter-quality printer will do for their work, imagine you're back in the late 1800s. You've just suggested to the president of your company that he invest in a typewriter. His response: "What!? Send out a letter that isn't hand-written? Never!"

Even a regular ImageWriter can produce documents that are much more pleasant to look at than those from a typewriter or formed-character printer; a laser printer or a 24-pin dot-matrix printer like the LQ simply leave typewriters and formed-character printers in the dust. Fortunately, most businesspeople and academics have finally come to realize this. In fact, thanks mostly to the Mac, expectations about the visual quality of documents have risen markedly.

very good feature

◆ *models of the ImageWriter* (AN)

The first model of the ImageWriter spelled its name with a lowercase *w* and was never called the *ImageWriter I,* but by now everyone calls it that, so we do too. It's easy to tell the machines apart: the ImageWriter I is beige and rectangular while the ImageWriter II is white or gray (what Apple calls "platinum") and looks sort of like a flattened version of R2D2 doing pushups.

It may be hard to find any ImageWriter I's around anymore but some people swear by them. They're very cheap and very rugged. If you're on a limited budget and want low-tech reliability, it may make sense to look for one. But you'd probably be better off with one of the Imagewriter substitutes described in the next entry.

There's also a letter-quality version of the ImageWriter called—appropriately enough—the LQ. It's also discussed in the next entry.

◆ *ImageWriter substitutes* (LP)

The ImageWriter II is the best-selling printer in the world but it's hardly the best bargain. Not only is its list price ($625 as of this writing) high for its capabilities but discounts on it are usually a lot shallower than on third-party competitors, which often sell for 40–50% off.

Here are three substitutes for the ImageWriter, one of which—the ProWriter—is really more equivalent to the ImageWriter LQ, Apple's expensive (currently $1430 list), 24-pin, letter-quality printer.

The ProWriter is distributed by C. Itoh, which buys them from TEC (Tokyo Electric), the same company that supplied Apple with the original ImageWriters. There are two models of ProWriter—the standard carriage, which lists for $750, and the $950 wide carriage.

very good feature

In letter-quality mode, the ProWriter's output looks just as good as an ImageWriter LQ's. The characters don't show jagged edges, even under a magnifying glass, and vertical lines print straight and true. Graphics have a maximum resolution of 240 dpi and are closer in appearance to laser-printer output than to what you're used to on a dot-matrix printer. And you get all this from a 9-pin printhead just like the one in an ImageWriter II.

Like the ImageWriter LQ, the ProWriters come with both push and pull tractors. In the push mode (which is what's used on the ImageWriter II), the paper is pushed under and around the platen and comes out the rear of the printer, in a hairpin pattern. In the pull mode, the paper enters the printer through a slot in the bottom and is pulled around the platen in an L pattern.

The pull mode provides more reliable paper handling, the push mode higher-quality printouts. Normally, you'd use the push mode for business correspondence and the pull mode for labels and envelopes.

For envelopes, letterhead stationery and other single sheets of paper, the ProWriter's cover tilts 45° and serves as a semiautomatic sheet feeder. This feature works re-markably well—you just insert the paper one sheet at a time. Since this mode disengages the tractor feed, individual sheets of paper can easily be alternated with pin-feed forms. (You can also do this on the ImageWriter II but awkward paper handling makes it impractical.)

very bad feature

Unfortunately, the ProWriter's manual is terrible. Many of the printer's parts are not as pictured. Critical setup instructions are contradictory. The self-test requires 15"-wide paper but the instructions don't tell you that. Use regular letter-size paper and the ProWriter prints right onto the platen—not something you want to happen.

The Macintosh section of the manual is completely wrong. Several pages describe setting up the MacEnhancer, a $300 peripheral, together with various serial drivers and an IBM-type printer cable, when in fact none of that equipment is necessary.

If you can ignore the manual, and if the price is right (given the healthy discount you should be able to get), you should give these super-fast, letter-quality printers a real hard look. If the price still isn't right, consider the Seikosha SP-1000AP. It's an inexpensive ($350 list) printer that uses an ordinary ImageWriter I cable and works off the standard ImageWriter print driver.

bargain

Built by the makers of Seiko watches and Epson printers, the SP-1000AP is very reliable; unlike my ImageWriters, this unit's never jammed on me and I use it almost every day. Another advantage: If you need a ribbon at 8 o'clock at night or on a Sunday, you'll be happy to know that the SP-1000AP uses the same ribbons as Radio Shack's DMP-130 printer (which you can get for 3/$13).

very good
feature

As with the ProWriters, the paper separator rotates 45° and doubles as a sheet feeder. And like the ProWriters, the Seikosha is refreshingly quiet (less than 55db). So what's wrong with it? Well, it's slow. Draft-quality printing is only 75 characters per second (compared to the ImageWriter II's 250 cps) and near-letter-quality is really slow, only 15 cps (compared to the ImageWriter II's 45 cps).

The flip side of this is that the 1000AP's slow printout is much straighter. And when you stop to think that you can buy two, possibly three, Seikoshas for less than the price of a single ImageWriter, even the speed difference becomes negligible. At well under $200 mail order, the slow, reliable Seikosha 1000AP is hard to beat for value per dollar and it may be all the printer you need.

There's at least one other printer you should consider—the Olympia NP30APL. It lists for $370—slightly more than the Seikosha and a lot less than ProWriters and the ImageWriter II. In performance, it's more or less equivalent

bargain

to an ImageWriter I and slightly faster than the Seikosha (150 cps draft, 26 cps near-letter-quality).

Because it works just as well connected to a PC as a Mac, the Olympia is an excellent choice for office environments with mixed equipment. Parallel and serial ports are standard; so are a push-type tractor feed and semiautomatic sheet feeding. A pull-type tractor feed ($50) and a true sheet feeder ($170) are available as options. It uses inexpensive Epson LX80 ribbons that you can get anywhere, even at stationery stores.

very good feature

The printer is guaranteed for a year, and after that you can order individual parts and service manuals directly from Olympia. They've sold typewriters and office machines since 1904, and they still do business the old-fashioned way; they won't make you buy a $200 board when all you really need is a $2 part.

very good feature

All three of these printers are 100%-compatible with the ImageWriter. Having any one of them at the end of the cable is just like having an ImageWriter there, with one exception—they handle the top margin differently. Unless you adjust for the difference, the first line of whatever you print will always be two lines too low.

One solution is to waste the first page and manually wind the second page back until its top is just even with the printhead (as you have to do with dot-matrix printers that work with the PC). A better solution is to reset the margins in your software to .67" (four lines) for the top and 1.33" (eight lines) for the bottom, instead of the Mac standard of 1" (six lines) top and bottom.

things to come

The three printers discussed here are all 9-pin, but a whole slew of 24-pin competitors to the ImageWriter LQ (including the NEC P2200) will be coming out right about when this book does. (Actually, the printers are already here; what's coming is an inexpensive disk of printer drivers that makes them ImageWriter-compatible.) Watch the updates to this book for more about this.

❦ *inexpensive color printers* (SH)

Shinko PanChroma color dot-matrix printers (available from Computer Friends) cost $4500 for the 200-dpi model and $9000 for the 300-dpi model. Their output is essentially as good as the much-publicized $25,000 QMS.

bargain

❦ *the ImageWriter II's sheet feeder* (DC/AN)

Using fan-fold paper is a lot of trouble. It often gets jammed (particularly on the ImageWriter II, whose tractor feed isn't very good) and when the job is done, you're faced with the task of removing the perforated edges with the holes in them, separating the individual pages and collating them.

A sheet feeder frees you from all that. You can use virtually any kind of paper you please and change it as often as you want. When the printing is finished, the pages of your document are not only separated but also collated. One final advantage: regular 8-1/2 by 11 paper is less expensive than fan-fold paper.

So why doesn't everyone use sheet feeders? Because they're usually expensive and not very reliable. The sheet feeder Apple sells for the ImageWriter II isn't expensive (it lists for $230) but we've found it to be not very reliable. If you need one, it may still be worth buying; just make sure you take out an AppleCare extended warranty on it.

❦ *laser printers and typesetters* (AN)

There are two basic kinds of laser printers—those that use PostScript (Adobe's page-description programming language) and those that don't. PostScript devices let more than one machine share the printer and give you access to PostScript fonts, which are scalable to any level of resolution without loss of detail. (For more on this, see the section below called *text on laser printers and typesetters.)*

esp. for beginners

Laser printers that don't use PostScript, like General Computer's Personal Laser Printer and Apple's LaserWriter

II SC, rely on QuickDraw, the Mac's built-in imaging software, to scale bit-mapped fonts like those used on the Mac's screen. The output looks great but there are two problems: because they can't connect to LocalTalk, only one Mac at a time can use these non-PostScript printers, and because they use the Mac to do their calculations, they're usually much slower than PostScript printers.

Not all PostScript devices are laser printers; some are phototypesetters (machines that print a high-resolution on film rather than paper). The most widely used of these are the Linotronics. For info on their outputs, see the entry on relative resolutions above.

⚫ *models of the LaserWriter* (AN)

The first laser printers Apple sold were the LaserWriter and the LaserWriter Plus. Both were built around the Canon's CX *marking engine* (the part of the printer that actually makes the image). The CX works fine for most things but it can't produce a solid black area (it ends up gray or streaked). The LaserWriter IIs are built around a second-generation marking engine, the SX, which produces much solider and darker blacks—in fact, sometimes they're too dark.

very bad feature

Both these early LaserWriters were hamstrung with just 1.5 megabytes of RAM, which greatly (and very annoyingly) limits the number of fonts you can use.

Both generations of LaserWriters produce eight pages a minute, but that doesn't take into account the time the printer (and/or your Mac) spends figuring out what to put on the page. To speed that up, you need a faster chip and more memory. That's what the LaserWriter II NT and particularly the II NTX give you, and believe me, the NTX is a *lot* faster than the original LaserWriter (I know, because I moved directly from one to the other). For more about the LaserWriter II line, see the next entry.

✎ *the printer with three brains* *(AN)*

I could have incorporated this entry into the one above but then I wouldn't have been able to use that title. It refers, of course, to a wonderful Steve Martin movie called *The Man with Two Brains,* which is worth seeing just to hear Kathleen Turner hiss at her rich husband (who she's trying to give a heart attack so she can inherit his money), "You just hate me because I'm so young and *hot!*"

gossip/ trivia

Anyway, the LaserWriter II comes in three models. The lowest-priced ($2800 as of this writing) is the SC (called that because it connects to the Mac through the SCSI port, like a hard disk). The SC's brain is built around a 68000 chip like the one in the SE, the Plus and earlier Macs.

The SC can only be accessed by one Mac; it's not a PostScript device and uses bit-mapped fonts (although they look great on a laser printer). It only has one meg of RAM, but since it isn't using PostScript fonts, this isn't much of a disadvantage.

The intermediate model is the NT (for *new technology),* Its brain (also known as a *controller card)* is built around a 68020 chip like the one in the Mac II, which makes it a lot faster than the SC. It's a PostScript device, so it can be shared by several Macs, and comes with eleven Adobe font families built-in. The current list price is $4600.

very good feature

The high-end LaserWriter II ($6600 list) is the NTX (the *x* stands for *expandable).* Like the NT, its brain is built around the 68020 and like the NT, it comes with two megs of RAM standard (as opposed to the SC's one meg). But the NTX also lets you expand RAM up to twelve megs just by popping in some SIMMs. And you can connect a SCSI hard disk (for keeping fonts on) directly to it (but so far, only Apple disks can be used for this purpose).

very good feature

You can upgrade an NT to an NTX and an SC to either. You just buy them new brains.

🍎 *General Computer's Personal Laser Printer* (BB)

The General Computer Personal Laser Printer uses Apple's QuickDraw routines (the same ones that form the image on your screen) to describe the pages it prints, rather than Adobe's PostScript programming language, which is used in many other laser printers. This brings its price down two ways: the printer needs much less memory (since the Mac itself, rather than the printer, figures out what the page should look like) and there's no PostScript license fee to pay.

With a list price of $2000, the PLP is a bargain—if you can accept its limitations. Here's a brief rundown:

Since the PLP doesn't have its own built-in processor, you can't print in the background; the Mac's sole function while printing is printing. For the same reason, the PLP is a lot slower than the LaserWriter.

You can speed up the process by printing in draft mode, which produces printing like the ImageWriter's (but blacker). Or you can buy an accelerator board, more RAM or both; the additional speed and memory will benefit other work as well as printing.

Because the PLP attaches to the SCSI port, not to LocalTalk, you can only connect one Mac to it at a time. General Computer offers a board swap for the printer that gives it PostScript and an external device that gives it LocalTalk compatibility. These last two come at a price, of course, but you can choose what's important to you and pay only for what you need.

The PLP uses the Mac's memory to process pages, so unless your Mac has at least 2MB of RAM, you can't print directly from programs (like Hypercard) that require a lot of memory. Instead, you must quit the application and print using the special print manager program that comes with the printer. You might find that a nuisance, although it's one I don't much mind.

Because the PLP uses QuickDraw to describe what it prints, PostScript-based programs like Illustrator and Cricket

Draw won't produce images at 300 dots per inch on it. You're also restricted to QuickDraw fonts (which look good but are far fewer in number than PostScript fonts) or fonts designed for the ImageWriter (which look surprisingly good with Smoothing on).

The documentation is a model of clarity, with two exceptions: its failure to tell you how to print envelopes and its treatment of terminators, a subject no one has handled well.

very good feature

Terminators are little devices that filter signals in chains of SCSI devices; if there are more than two terminators, they can damage your hardware. Some SCSI devices have terminators and others don't; unfortunately, many manuals don't give you that information. If in doubt, ask the dealer or the manufacturer before plugging in a new device. And read both the Macintosh manual and the PLP manual carefully to see where the terminators belong.

important warning

Envelopes feed right down the middle of the PLP but the printer thinks the envelope is really a sheet of letter-size paper, 8 1/2" x 11". So you have to fool it by getting the first line of text to fall where you want it. Experiment with sheets of paper until you get it right. (I print my return address on my envelopes. Seven carriage returns precede the first line of the return address; five come between it and the first line of the recipient's address.)

The machine functions just the way the manual says it will. Setup instructions are simple, understandable and effective, perhaps because the setup itself is so easy. My 18-year old daughter, who likes but doesn't love computers, assembled the printer herself in fifteen minutes. Paper handling is direct and effective. You can pick a curved paper path for pages stacked in normal page order or a straight path for heavier stock. When the machine does jam (it's rare), clearing it is easy.

If its limitations don't bother you, the PLP may be the answer to your prayers for higher-quality printing. Thanks to its Ricoh marking engine, the PLP's output looks great, with fine detail and good solid blacks. All in all, the PLP's low price, ease-of-use, good documentation, impressive performance and modularity (which lets you only pay for the features you want) make it a good choice for many Mac users.

General printer tips

☀ *stopping printouts* (DC)

esp. for beginners

If you need to stop printing from within an application and clicking on the *Cancel* button doesn't work (or if the application you're using has no *Cancel* button to stop printing), try ⌘-period.

If that doesn't work, you can always just turn off the ImageWriter. Most programs will continue for a while as if they were still sending output to the printer, then realize it's no longer responding and give you the opportunity to exit from print mode.

☀ *printing the screen* (AN)

Printing the image currently on your Mac's screen is easy—if you want to print it on the ImageWriter. All you have to do is hit Shift Caps Lock ⌘-4. But the only way to print a screen on a laser printer is save it to disk with Shift ⌘-3 (or with a desk accessory like Capture or Camera). This creates a MacPaint file which you can then print.

☀ *switching between printers* (AN)

esp. for beginners

If you use more than one printer on a Mac (say an ImageWriter and a LaserWriter), be sure to choose *Page Setup...* when you switch between them. The ImageWriter and the LaserWriter have different print areas on the page, so applications need to be told, via Page Setup, that you've switched.

You should also choose *Page Setup...* the first time you print from an application after installing a new version of a *printer driver* program. You don't have to change anything in it if you don't want to—you can just click OK as soon as the dialog box appears—but you do need to enter and exit Page Setup to activate the new driver.

✦ *proofing LaserWriter text on the ImageWriter* (DC)

If you're using an ImageWriter to proof documents that will ultimately be printed on a LaserWriter, choose *Tall Adjusted* in the Page Setup dialog box. This will cause line and page breaks to print on the ImageWriter exactly as they will on the LaserWriter.

*very
hot
tip*

ImageWriter tips

✦ *best quality text* (DC)

When you select Best print quality from an application's print dialog box, the Mac looks for a font size double the one you've specified and then reduces it 50% to create a high-quality image on the ImageWriter. If the double-size font isn't installed in your System file, the print quality won't be much better than Faster quality. So for the highest-quality printouts, make sure that a font twice as large as the one you've requested is installed.

*esp. for
beginners*

✦ *continuing to work while printing* (DC)

If you use the ImageWriter often, you know that print time is break time. Time to stretch your legs, get a cup of coffee or—if the document's long enough—even go to the store. The problem is, of course, that you may not want to take a break then. You may want to go on working and take a break some other time. But there's no way to do that, because printing takes all the Mac's attention.

What you need is something that lets the Mac generate output as fast as possible, without having to wait for the relatively slow ImageWriter, stores that output somewhere until it's needed and then spoon-feeds it to the ImageWriter on demand, thus freeing up the Mac so you can go on to other things.

These requirements can be met by either hardware or software. The hardware solution is called a *print buffer*, and it's basically just a bunch of memory that stores the computer's output before sending it to the printer.

The hardware approach works well on simple computers, but the Mac's lovely fonts and graphics take up a lot of room. To be able to handle a Mac's huge print files, a print buffer needs to have more than a meg of memory, and that can easily cost more than you paid for your ImageWriter.

One of the best print buffers available is MacBuffer by Ergotron, the same people who make the MacTilt swivel. There are 256K and 512K models, but for use with the Mac, I recommend the 1MB model. MacBuffer has the added advantage of allowing two Macs to be connected to one ImageWriter.

The software solution to the working-while-printing problem is called a *print spooler* (the name is a leftover from the archaic world of CP/M and stands for *simultaneous print operations on-line)*. Spoolers intercept the print file on its way to the printer and reroute it to the disk, where it's held until the printer is ready for it.

A good print spooler should let you continue to use your Mac while printing, without significantly hampering the performance of either of the printer or the computer. It should also be totally transparent to you, the user—i.e., no special commands or options, just the standard print dialog box.

very hot tip

A third feature to look for is control over the spooling process. Let's say you've spooled several documents for printing, but decide that the second or third document shouldn't be printed after all, or that the last document in the queue needs to be printed right away. A good print spooler should let you change the order of the documents in the queue and cancel the printing of any document without affecting the others.

One good ImageWriter print spooler is SuperSpool. It comes standard with DataFrame hard disks and is also available separately for $75. Installing SuperSpool is easy: you just place the file in the system folder (if you intend to use it regularly—and you probably will—make it the startup application), then install a desk accessory called Print Queue.

That's all there is to it. When you print from an application you won't notice anything different—the print dialog box will look the way it always does. But as soon as the printer output is written to the disk (which takes about two minutes for a fifteen-page Word document), control of the Mac is returned to you.

I've discovered one disappointing bug in SuperSpool version 2.0. When used with the ImageWriter II with a sheet feeder, it occasionally prevents a sheet of paper from feeding. The ImageWriter then proceeds to print the entire page on the platen. Because this can seriously damage the platen over time, I recommend that you not use SuperSpool with the ImageWriter sheet feeder.

✎ *printing envelopes on the ImageWriter II* (BB)

Printing envelopes on an ImageWriter can be a troublesome process. They tend to jam and minimum margin settings make it difficult to print a return address in its usual location in the upper left corner. There are more complicated ways around this problem, but here's the simplest: just feed the envelope into the printer with the flap open and compensate by adding as much length as you need to the top margin.

very hot tip

My return address is already printed on my envelopes, so all I need to print is the recipient's address. I set my top margin by measuring down from the top of the closed envelope to the first line of the address (1.75" on my envelopes) and adding another inch for the flap (for a setting of 2.75").

If you need to print your return address, just measure how far you want its top line to come below the top edge of the envelope and add an inch to that figure—or whatever distance works for the flaps on your envelopes. (I think the response of the ImageWriter's paper sensor depends on where the edge of the flap meets the sensor.)

The natural curl of the envelope flap can cause the envelope to wrap around the platen. To avoid that, just bend the tip of the flap back a little before you feed it.

⬤ *mimeo stencils* (MB)

very hot tip

If you use an ImageWriter to cut mimeograph stencils, you may run into trouble; with some brands, the wax backing gums up the pins in the ImageWriter's print head. Try leaving an old, faint, fabric ribbon in the printer, to shield the print head from the stencil wax. Some stencils are made especially for computer printers—A.B. Dick's part #2060, for example.

very hot tip

When you make drawings for mimeo stencils, use dotted lines instead of solid ones. Solid lines can tear the stencil and/or smear the image, especially if they're closely spaced.

very hot tip

When you fill an image, using light pattern instead of a dark one. Areas filled with dark or solid black patterns can smear the drum of the mimeo printer with ink. This also means being careful about using font symbols that are solid images, like ⬤.

⬤ *alternative ribbons* (DC)

very hot tip

From time to time your local supplier may run out of ImageWriter ribbons. This will probably happen late Saturday afternoon, just before you plan to begin a marathon weekend of printing to meet Monday morning's deadline. But don't panic: ImageWriter ribbons are completely interchangeable with ribbons for the C. Itoh 8510, the NEC 8023 and DEC LA50 printers. You shouldn't have any trouble finding one or another of these ribbons.

♦ *speeding up draft mode on the ImageWriter II* (PH)

According to its manual, the ImageWriter II will print at 250 cps. Needless to say, that's only in draft mode, and even then you need to know a couple of tricks to get that kind of speed out of it.

*very
hot
tip*

The first trick concerns fonts. The font the ImageWriter uses in draft mode is Monaco 10. If your document is in any other font, the ImageWriter will try to adjust the spacing between the letters and the words to make them match how the text looks on the screen. It will fail—miserably—but it will try, and the trying takes time.

If you put your document into Monaco 10 before printing it, that exercise in futility will be spared you. (You can also write and edit your documents in Monaco 10, but it's ugly and hard to read on the screen.)

Here's the other trick: for the fastest speed, you not only have to select draft mode in the Print dialog box but you also have to select it on the print quality switches on the ImageWriter itself. (These switches only have an effect when you're printing in draft mode).

shortcut

By doing those two things, you'll get printouts in the shortest time possible.

♦ *draft printing on the ImageWriter I* (DC)

The spacing between the words on documents printed in draft mode on the ImageWriter I is usually quite irregular. You can avoid that by changing the font of the entire document to Monaco (which is a monospaced font). For this technique to work, you have to convert the whole document; if any line of text includes more than one font, or if there are graphics in the document, spacing will be irregular.

♦ *turning your Mac into a typewriter (sort of)* (DC)

There's nothing like a typewriter for addressing envelopes but many Mac users would like to put the ancient old beast in the closet and forget about it. The desk accessory TypeNow might be just the tool to let you do that. With TypeNow, when you type a line in a window on the screen and press `Return`, the ImageWriter prints in one its built-in draft fonts (Pica, Pica Proportional, Elite or Elite Proportional—you choose which one in TypeNow).

The only real limitation—and it's a big one—is that the ImageWriter can only print a line at a time, not a character at a time. So while TypeNow is great for envelopes, it won't do for forms that require you to fill in several blanks on the same line.

❤ *print-head overheating on the ImageWriter I* (DC)

Printing documents that are more than 25% solid black can cause the print head on the ImageWriter I to overheat and fail. Replacing the print head is not only expensive but a major hassle, since many dealers don't stock adequate spare parts. So—never print more than one page of a document that contains large black areas without giving the print head a chance to cool.

This precaution isn't necessary with the ImageWriter II, because it has built-in protection against print-head overheating.

Laser printer tips

❤ *printing multiple copies* (AN)

esp. for beginners

Because most laser printers take a long time to figure out a page but not very long after that to print it, it's much faster to ask for multiple copies of a document than to reprint it several times.

❤ *laser printer hangups* (AN)

Laser printers get confused and hang up quite regularly. When this happens, just reset the printer (with LaserStatus or some other utility program). If that doesn't help, restart your Mac (with *Restart* on the Special Menu).

If there's still a problem, turn both the Mac and the printer off and wait five minutes before turning them back on (check all the cable connections while they're both off). If even that doesn't help, replace your System and Finder files with ones from the disk you got from Apple (or a copy thereof).

If you're *still* having a problem, it may actually be in the hardware.

⚫ *let us now praise a clearly written manual* (AN)

The LaserWriter manual has an excellent section on all aspects of setting up and maintaining the printer; it's clearly written and full of helpful illustrations.

very good feature

⚫ *feeding single sheets on the LaserWriter II* (AN)

The LaserWriter II will pull a sheet from the single-sheet feed on the top of the paper tray whether you tell it to or not. So all you have to do is put a sheet of paper in the slot; you don't gain anything by clicking the *Manual Feed* button in the Print dialog box.

⚫ *where to put your laser printer* (AN)

Most laser printers make a fair amount of noise. They're nothing like the average PC, which tends to sound like a commercial jet testing its engines, they still can be pretty annoying. (This is particularly true if you're lucky enough to have a quiet place to work; in the typical office environment, you may barely be able to hear a laser printer.)

One way around this problem is to put the laser printer in a closet. Since it's connected on LocalTalk, there's no problem with the cables not reaching, and most closets are large enough. I've kept two different models of LaserWriters in a closet with just 8" to the front, 7" to the rear and a couple of feet to each side, and have had no problems with insufficient ventilation or heat buildup. (Because closets usually have no windows and often have no external walls, they tend to vary in temperature less than regular rooms.)

If you're really worried about heat buildup, hang a thermometer on the closet wall and check it regularly. I do that and mine has never registered above 80°—even on days when it was hotter than that outside and when the LaserWriter had been on for many hours (although, admittedly, it never gets really hot where I live—the average high temperature during the hottest month is just 72°).

The LaserWriter's manual says the temperature of the air around the printer shouldn't get over 90°, which means that if you live in New Orleans or some other place where the sidewalks melt in the summer, you're going to need air conditioning to stay within their specs (which also call for humidity of 80% or less). But if you live in a place like that, a laser printer in your closet isn't going to be the only reason you need an air conditioner.

There is, of course, one major disadvantage to putting your laser printer in a closet—you have to get up and walk over to it each time you want to look at the output. I don't find this bothersome; in fact, I enjoy the break and exercise (if walking ten feet can be called exercise). But it could get annoying, particularly if you're doing a lot of trial-and-error futzing with a document.

♠ *LaserWriter page-setup options* (AN)

The LaserWriter driver gives you a number of useful features in the Page Setup dialog box. One of these is Faster Bitmap Printing, which preprocesses bit-mapped images before they're sent to the LaserWriter. Apple states that "in rare cases, some documents may not print with this option turned on," but this has never happened to me. If it happens to you, just turn the option off and try again.

There's a button called Options. Clicking on it gives you several additional choices. You can flip the entire image on your page either vertically or horizontally, or "invert" it (print a negative of it, changing whites to blacks and blacks to whites).

Precision Bitmap Alignment improves pictures pasted in from MacPaint or FullPaint by reducing the entire image on the page to 96% of its normal size. This gets around the incompatibility between the 72 dots per inch of the Mac's screen and the 300 dots per inch of the LaserWriter's output (300 divided by 72 is 4.1666, but 96% of 300 is 288, into which 72 goes exactly 4 times).

Larger Print Area lets you cover slightly more of the page—but only if the application you're using lets you. Doing this limits the number of fonts you can use, which may or may not be a problem, depending on how much RAM your printer has.

A dog of indeterminate breed helps you see the effect of all these options by acting them out for you as you select them.

✎ *versions of the LaserWriter driver* (DC)

You can find out what version of the LaserWriter driver you have by looking in the dialog box that comes up when you choose *Print...* from the File menu (with every program but PageMaker). The number appears just to the left of the OK button.

esp. for beginners

✎ *suppressing the LaserWriter's startup page* (AN/CR)

Every time you turn on the LaserWriter, it spits out a rather attractive test page that tells you how many copies have ever been printed on the machine. While it's possible to get into this constantly mounting total as a measure of your productivity (and therefore your general worth as a human being: *I've printed 3000 pages on my LaserWriter— I must be doing something useful with my life)*, it does cost you about 3¢ in toner, some fraction of a cent in paper and some hard-to-figure but probably significant amount of wear-and-tear on the machine.

very hot tip

So it's sometimes nice to be able to turn off the startup page, at least for a while. The easiest way to do that is to use Widgets, which comes as part of DiskTop (see the review in Chapter 8). Century Software also has a pair of programs called Start-up On and Start-Up Off that...well, I'm sure you can figure it out.

Below are two short PostScript programs that also do the same thing. Just type them out exactly as you see them (only the last two lines are essential; the others are comments), save them as a text-only file with a name that's easy to remember and send them to the LaserWriter with any of the downloading programs that come on laser font disks.

```
%Disable LaserWriter from Printing Startup Page upon Powerup
% John Monaco Compuserve 73317,3677 %%GEnie J Monaco
%%EndComments
serverdict begin 0 exitserver statusdict begin false
setdostartuppage

%Enable LaserWriter to Print Startup Page upon Powerup
% John Monaco Compuserve 73317,3677 %%GEnie J Monaco
%%EndComments
serverdict begin 0 exitserver statusdict begin true
setdostartuppage
```

Neale Hall wrote from Alexander Hill, Australia to suggest yet another (very simple) way to suppress the startup page; unlike the approaches above, you have to do it each time · you turn the printer on, which makes it somewhat tedious. You just pull out the paper tray before you turn the LaserWriter on each time and don't push it in again until the LaserWriter's warmed up.

But how do you know when that is? One function of the startup page is to tell you exactly when the LaserWriter is ready to begin printing. If you turn off the startup page, you need to know the following:

When you turn the LaserWriter on, it tests itself; while it's doing that, the green light blinks (on the LaserWriter II, some other lights come on first, but just ignore them). When the green light stops blinking, wait a few seconds and the machine is ready to use. In a cold room, this warmup and test procedure may take about a minute. If you've used the machine recently and/or the room is warm, it may take much less time than that.

⁤ *printing custom stationery* (AN)

Access to a LaserWriter can not only save you the expense of buying stationery, it can allow you to modify your stationery as often you like. You can change the text, the fonts, the graphics or the paper you print it on. (On the LaserWriter, it's just as economical to produce five sheets of letterhead with matching envelopes as it is to produce five hundred.) Custom stationery makes a wonderful present, particularly if you use fancy paper and spend some time making the stationery match the recipient's personality.

very hot tip

There's no special trick to doing letterhead on the LaserWriter. (There are some general tips on the subject in the *General word processing tips* section of chapter 10; also see the entry below on special typographic effects). But envelopes can be tricky. You have to hand-feed them into the LaserWriter, face up and against the back edge of the manual feed guide. Certain kinds of envelopes don't feed very well—like ones made from "parchment"-type paper.

If you print your name and return address along the length of the envelope—that is, in the same direction as the name and address of the person you're sending it to—you'll only have to run the envelope through the Laserwriter once. If you want your name and address to run across the end of the envelope—which looks snazzier—you'll either have run the envelopes through a second time, print labels and stick them on or address the envelopes by hand. (There's a tip in Chapter 10 on how to set up Word to print across the end of envelopes on the LaserWriter.)

Whichever direction you use for your address, you may find yourself frustrated by the LaserWriter's inability to print closer than a quarter of an inch to the edge of the envelope. But a reader named Mike Chan wrote in with a cunning trick. He uses Post-It notes to trip the paper guide (he sticks them on the envelope with about a quarter of an inch protruding).

very hot tip

He says he's only had to open the LaserWriter two or three times to retrieve Post-Its that have fallen off inside.

important warning

Mike also said that a toner cartridge recharging company told him that running envelopes through the LaserWriter will do in the drum in the cartridge and that they didn't recommend recharging cartridges if envelopes have been run through them.

✎ *getting the most from toner cartridges* (AN)

Before installing a new toner cartridge in a LaserWriter, you should rotate it gently from side to side (that is, lift the right side, then the left—it's roll you want, not yaw). If you don't do this, the images you get may not be dark enough. (You may also have to break in the cartridge by printing thirty pages or so.)

very hot tip

If you rock the cartridge whenever pages start to look light and keep the print-density dial set as low as it will go until the cartridge is really on its last legs, you should easily be able to get 4000 pages and more from each cartridge, with perfectly acceptable quality (except, of course, for solid blacks on LaserWriter I's, which you can't get even with a new cartridge).

Using those techniques, I've been able to average almost 5000 copies on my LaserWriter I cartridges and have gotten more than 4000 from my first LaserWriter II cartridge. Go then and do likewise.

✎ *buying toner cartridges* (AN)

If you can't find an Apple-brand toner cartridge for your LaserWriter, a Hewlett-Packard LaserJet cartridge should work just as well. The cost to the dealer for both brands is the same, so the price you pay should be too. In theory, a toner cartridge made for any other laser printer that uses the Canon CX or SX marking engine (depending on which model laser printer you have) should also work, but I haven't tried any.

⚫ *refilling toner cartridges* (Byron Brown)

very hot tip

Toner cartridges are far and away your greatest expense in operating a laser printer. Fortunately, there are ways to cut the cost of them. The easiest is to sell your empty cartridges to a company that refills them. You'll find ads offering $10 for empty cartridges in the back of most Mac magazines.

But the most profitable approach is to have your cartridges refilled. If done by a reputable company, refilling won't hurt your printer and will provide printouts that are just as good as you get from new cartridges (in fact, the image is often darker). One refilled LaserWriter I cartridge gave me blacks almost as solid as a Laserwriter II's.

In general, cartridges shouldn't be refilled more than three times, and most companies mark them so they can discard them after the third refill. I'd guess my LaserWriter I refills give me about 90% of the life of new cartridges, and they only cost $45–70 instead of $90–105.

very good feature

I've been using Encore Ribbon in Petaluma, California for two years and have been very satisfied with their service. They have an 800 number, are there to answer it when you call, know their product well and make every effort to keep their customers happy. Whenever a refill of mine has had a problem, they've replaced it free of charge.

bargain

Encore picks up and delivers free in the (San Francisco) Bay Area. They charge only $45—the best price I've seen by far—for a LaserWriter I refill + $3 for replacing the felt on the green wand that keeps the rollers clean. Refilling takes about two weeks, so I rotate between three cartridges (that way I always have a spare, even when one's out being refilled).

very bad feature

Donna at Encore tells me that the first LaserWriter II cartridges had a corrosive chemical in the toner that ate out the inside of the cartridge—so you couldn't refill them and had to buy new ones. Wasn't that thoughtful?

Although this practice has been abandoned, you may still find yourself with one of the old, corrosive cartridges. If you do, Encore has a workaround. For $10, they'll refill it with noncorrosive toner, thus making it possible for you to refill it later.

Encore charges $50 to refill LaserWriter II cartridges. So if you figure $110 for the new cartridge and $50 for each of the three subsequent refills, $270 buys you what would otherwise cost you about $440.

🍎 *throwing toner cartridges out* (AN)

If you take a used toner cartridge out of a laser printer and toss it immediately into a plastic waste basket (as I have), you may end up with a melted waste basket (as I have). Those suckers are *hot* when they come out of the machine. So unless you want your waste baskets to look like not-very-inspired modern art, let the toner cartridge cool down before throwing it away.

🍎 *what kind of paper to use* (AN)

Laser printers put images down on paper in exactly the same way as photocopiers do; in fact, the guts of the LaserWriters (and of several other PostScript laser printers) are identical to those of many Canon copiers. So the kind of paper specifically designed for use in copiers—often labeled *xerographic*—is what you want for laser printers.

Copier paper comes in more than one grade. When you're preparing originals for presentation, you'll naturally want to use a nice-looking, heavy, opaque paper. But for everyday use, and when you're preparing documents to be reproduced, use the cheapest kind you can find. Here's why:

When the humidity is high, pieces of paper tend to stick together. To help them separate more easily, paper manufacturers put powder between the sheets. This is called dusting, and the more expensive a paper is, the more dusting it tends to have. The problem with dusting is that particles of the powder tend to get bonded to the paper along with the image, producing a rough, uneven surface. So cheap paper, with little or no dusting, is best.

Cheap paper has another advantage: because of its low fiber content, it has a smoother surface than most expensive paper (except those specifically designed to be ultra-smooth). The smoother the surface, the more precise the image bonded to it will be.

If there's a discount paper supply house in your area that sells retail, you should be able to buy inexpensive copier paper for about $3 a ream (500 sheets). If there isn't (and you live on the West Coast), try a local Copy-Mat outlet. They sell the standard paper they use in their machines for $3.75 a ream. (I don't know if other copy shops also sell paper, but it's worth asking.) Copy-Mats also have a fairly good selection of other kinds of paper (colored, "parchment," "laid," etc.), although a paper supply house's stock will obviously be much more extensive.

The best source for paper we've found is the Costco wholesale discount chain. You have to be a member (small businesses, independent professionals, government workers, organization members, etc. qualify) and be willing to buy ten reams at a time, but if you are, you can get plain 20-lb. bond for about $2 a ream.

bargain

Except in an emergency, it makes absolutely no sense to go into a stationery store and pay $6–$7 a ream when you can get the same paper at half the price or less elsewhere.

❡ autofeed labels for the LaserWriter *(AN)*

Avery makes labels specifically designed to feed through laser printers from the paper tray. Because a special adhesive is used, the labels don't peel off when subjected to the high heat inside the printer. We've been using them and haven't had any problems with jamming. They come in three sizes: 1" x 2-5/8" (product codes 5160 and 5260),

1″ x 4″ (product codes 5161 and 5261) and 1-1/2″ x 4″ (product codes 5162 and 5262) and are available at most office supply stores.

PhoneNET *(AN)*

Laser printers and Macs are connected together by an LocalTalk network but I don't know anyone who actually uses Apple's LocalTalk cables and connectors to do it. We all use PhoneNET, from Farallon Computing.

PhoneNET networks use regular telephone wire, which costs a whole lot less than LocalTalk cable. You can even use the yellow and black wires on your existing phone wiring and avoid running any new cables at all.

bargain

Farallon makes an adaptor for connecting LocalTalk connectors to PhoneNET systems, so you won't lose whatever you have invested in hardware. If you have a network of any size, PhoneNET can save you a lot of money.

LaserWriter print spoolers *(DC)*

Spooling a LaserWriter print file is a much bigger job than spooling an ImageWriter print file, because they're much, much larger. You can spend several minutes waiting for them to be sent to the disk and if your job is fairly long, you'll probably run out of disk space.

very bad feature

[Not only that, but I've never found one that works often enough to be usable. I don't know if it's the inits I have in my system folder or what, but they all act screwy and crash all the time. I'd love to find a good one, but so far I haven't.—AN]

flashing messages and lights on LW I's *(AN)*

esp. for beginners

When a Mac is collaborating with an original LaserWriter or a LaserWriter Plus to figure out how to print a document, a message appears on the Mac's screen that lists its *status* as *processing job*. Every five seconds or so this message flickers. *Do not panic* (as I, of course, did). The periodic flashing doesn't mean that the power pole outside your house is about to fall over, or that enemy aliens from Saturn are trying to destroy your Mac by sending power surges through the house wiring. It's perfectly normal, just a way of reminding you that the Mac is thinking.

The LaserWriter lets you know it's thinking by flashing its yellow light every two seconds. (Double-flashing indicates a *wait state,* which usually doesn't last more than 30 seconds.)

When the Mac's role in the printing collaboration is done, the status message will disappear from the screen, but a page still may not have emerged from the LaserWriter. *Do not panic* (as I, of course, did). The LaserWriter is still thinking on its own about how exactly to print the document; you know that because the yellow light is still flashing.

You're free to continue editing the document, to close it, to quit the application or whatever. The LaserWriter will print the document eventually, all in its own good time.

⚫ *maximum image areas on LW I's* (AN)

The maximum area an original LaserWriter or a Laser-Writer Plus will print on a standard US letter-size (8.5 x 11) sheet of paper is 8 by 10.92 inches, centered on the page. The width limitation is the most significant; it means you must always have a margin of at least a quarter inch on each side. (The required .04-inch border top and bottom is, of course, trivial.)

*very
hot
tip*

What's more, few programs are capable of filling the entire area. MacDraw, for example, can only fill an area of 7.68 by 10.16 inches, and MacWrite requires a left margin of 1".

The image-size restriction is even more dramatic on legal-size paper (8.5 x 14). There the LaserWriter can only fill an area 6.72 inches wide by 13 inches deep, thus requiring margins of more than 7/8" on each side and 1/2" borders top and bottom. (There are similar restrictions for the common European paper sizes, A4 and B5.)

very bad
feature

The reason for these limitations is the LaserWriter I's memory. A megabyte and a half is only enough to image between 87 and 88 square inches of page (which is what both 8" x 10.92" and 6.72" x 13" amount to). To really process a page adequately with PostScript, a printer should have at least 2 megs of memory. Many other PostScript printers and typesetters do have that much memory (the LaserWriter II NT and NTX among them).

One time it's important to remember these size limitations is when you're proofing something on the ImageWriter that will ultimately be printed out on the LaserWriter. Because the ImageWriter can print wider than the Laser-Writer, be sure to leave adequate margins; otherwise your image will get cropped on the edges when you put it on the LaserWriter.

❤ *how to get rich, deep blacks* (DC/AN)

Buy a LaserWriter II or some other laser printer built around Canon's SX *marking engine*. The original Laser-Writer, the LaserWriter Plus and other laser printers built around Canon's CX marking engine simply can't do it. Black areas of any significant size will contain small white splotches or streaks, regardless of where you put the print density dial.

This is only a problem with areas of black, not regular text—which tends to look good no matter how low you set the print density dial. And it's also only a problem if the printer's output is used as the final product. The film used by printers will almost always fill the black areas in and you can even get the same result from a photocopy machine (usually).

But if you aren't going to print or photocopy what comes out of a CX-based laser printer, it makes sense to follow these rules:

1. Try to avoid graphics with black backgrounds or other dark areas.

2. If, like most people, you'll mostly be printing text, use a page of text, not a graphic image, as your sample when you're adjusting the print density dial.

3. Don't bother turning the dial all the way to high— you'll just be wasting toner for no purpose.

❦ *proofing on the LaserWriter before typesetting* (DC)

The Macintosh and the ImageWriter use QuickDraw routines to create their images, while the LaserWriter and many other laser printers and typesetters use PostScript. Although a lot of brilliant work has been done to allow QuickDraw and PostScript to talk to each other, what you see on the Mac and on an ImageWriter is always going to vary somewhat from the output of a PostScript-driven device.

This means there's no substitute for hard copies. If you're planning to do final output on a PostScript-driven typesetter like the Linotronic, you definitely should proof your work on the LaserWriter. The differences between its output and the typesetter's will be negligible. (The resolution will, of course be higher on the Linotronic—that's why you're using it in the first place—but the position of all the elements and the overall look of the page will be the same.)

There are two exceptions to that rule. First of all, the Linotronic can print all the way to the edges of the roll of paper it's using (which can be either 8.5" or 11" wide) while the LaserWriter can't print wider than 8". Secondly, the Linotronic won't smooth bit-mapped images. If you want the images smoothed, print them out on a LaserWriter and then paste them manually over the equivalent unsmoothed images in the Linotronic output.

❦ *halftoning on the LaserWriter* (AN)

The LaserWriter handles text so nicely, it's tempting to use it to produce everything that goes on the page, including pictures. But certain kinds of images have to be processed before you can print them. Here's why:

esp. for beginners

All printed material is made up of either text or art (which is what every graphic element except text is called). There are two kinds of art—*line,* which contains no grays, and *continuous-tone,* which does (the name comes from the fact that the tones form a continuum, from black through gray to white).

Continuous-tone art presents a problem: since printing ink is black (or whatever) and paper is white (or whatever), how can the grays be represented?

Far-and-away the most common solution involves putting a *screen* over the photograph. (It's called a screen because the original ones were made of fine metal mesh, although most screens today are sheets of plastic with dots printed on them.) The screen converts light grays to tiny black dots on a white background, and dark grays to tiny white dots on a black background. From a normal reading distance, these dots—in many different sizes—look like various shades of gray.

Once a continuous-tone image has been screened, it's called a *halftone.* If you hold a magnifying glass to a halftoned picture (virtually any printed picture will do), you'll see the little halftone dots, but you won't find them on a continuous-tone photograph like a snapshot.

If you use the traditional screen approach to halftoning, you won't be able to integrate your graphics with your text and print them both out on the LaserWriter at the same time; you'll have to leave a space for the graphics and add them at a later stage. To integrate halftones with text, you need a device called a *scanner* that can capture continuous-tone images and halftone them electronically.

Scanners vary in sampling density (how many times per inch they evaluate the picture) and in how many levels of gray they'll pick up. They also vary in quality and price. ThunderScan is an inexpensive scanner ($230) that can produce images suitable for use in an informal newsletter—or maybe somewhat better than that, if you really know how to use it.

The next level of scanners have a resolution of 300 dpi and cost quite a bit more; their software makes it easy to capture an image as a PostScript file. Apple's scanner is one example among many.

Once a scanner has captured the image, you can use various programs—usually software that comes with the scanner—to play with it. One unbundled program that does a great job with halftones is Silicon Beach's Digital Darkroom.

very good feature

Everything else being equal, the quality of a halftone depends on the frequency of the screen you use (how many lines per inch it breaks the picture into). The higher the number of lines, the better the photograph looks. The coarsest screen in general use is 65 lines per inch. Newspapers typically use an 85-line screen and magazines a 120-line screen. The finest screen in general use is 150 lines per inch.

Laser printers and typesetters each have a default screen frequency that the manufacturer has picked to produce the best output on that particular device. On a 300-dpi printer like the LaserWriter, it's usually 60 lines per inch (lpi); on the Linotronic 100, 90 lpi; on the Linotronic 300, 120 lpi. You can vary this frequency somewhat (using simple PostScript programming), but if you go too far from the default, the results may not look very good.

The LaserWriter's resolution of 60 lpi is just below the usual minimum standard for halftones, and you can't expect an image printed at that resolution to look like the ones in magazines and books. But the quality is good enough for some purposes.

❡ *renting time on a PostScript device* (AN)

Businesses have sprung up all over (particularly in big cities and near universities) that let you come in with your Mac disk and print it out on one or more kinds of PostScript-compatible printers. Renting time can be surprisingly inexpensive: there's a place near me that charges just $5 an hour and 15¢ a page.

bargain

If you can't find a place in the phone book, check with a local Mac user group (in fact, do that first; unlike the Yellow Pages, they can tell you which businesses know what they're doing, charge the least and so on). If there's no user group in your area or they don't know of a rental place, check out the entry below on remote typesetting services; many of those services also provide LaserWriter output.

✎ *getting your disks ready for a rented LaserWriter* (DC)

When you're planning to rent time on a LaserWriter, you might as well format your documents and set up your disks as completely as possible ahead of time, to cut down on the amount of time you have to pay for.

important warning

The first step is to make sure that the disk you bring with you has the software you need on it; the rental place will obviously have some software but they may not have what you used to create your document (or the same versions of it). Call beforehand to make sure they have the laser fonts you want to use installed on their printer; if not, be sure that the System file on the startup disk you bring has the appropriate screen fonts installed, and that the system folder contains the font files you need for the printer.

If you haven't already done so, change the fonts in your document to laser fonts by selecting the text and choosing the screen fonts just the way you would any other font. (We're assuming you proofed your document on the ImageWriter.) Next, open Chooser (on the ✎ menu) and select the LaserWriter icon. Then open the Page Setup window (on the File menu), make any changes you want (or no changes) and click on OK.

Now go through your document. ImageWriter page setup has different margins from LaserWriter page setup, and there are other incompatibilities, so there may be changes you need to make.

important warning

There's one other hangup that gets more and more likely as time goes by—font ID conflicts. This complex issue is discussed in the *Advanced font tips* section at the end of Chapter 5.

When you've done that, you're ready for the shortest possible time rental on the LaserWriter.

⚫ *remote typesetting from Mac disks* (DC)

Let's say you've proofed your document on a LaserWriter until it's just the way you want it. Now you want to typeset it. But your budget's a little tight and you can't afford to buy a Linotronic this month (it probably wouldn't fit in the closet anyway). Don't despair. There are several services that will accept your Mac disks and print out from them on their own PostScript-driven typesetters or laser printers.

The costs usually run from $5 to $15 a page (some places also have a one-time registration charge of about $50). Many of these services let you send data via modem—although if your document is at all long, it's going to take forever. Another advantage of mailing the disk (or, if you're in a hurry, sending it by Federal Express) is that you can send a printout along with it as a proof, so there won't be any questions about how you want the finished document to look.

bargain

Even if you send the document on the phone, you should send a message with it detailing exactly what you want. This is always a good idea, but with version 1.9 and earlier of MacDraw, it's an absolute necessity. MacDraw remembers fonts in the order in which they were installed in the system (other applications may do this too), and since the odds that the typesetting service will have installed the same fonts in the same order that you did are about one in a trillion, you'll need to tell them what fonts you want.

important warning

(This is not a problem with MacDraw drawings after they've been pasted into documents created by other applications—as long as the same System was used to create those documents as was used to create the MacDraw drawings.)

As mentioned in the previous entry, there's one other potential problem—font ID conflicts. See the *Advanced font tips* section at the end of Chapter 5 for a discussion of this complex issue.

important warning

To find the names and addresses of services that offer typesetting from Mac disks, check out the various magazines on the Mac and on desktop publishing; they sometimes run updated lists of such services.

● *viewing PostScript code* (DC)

To see the actual PostScript code that gets sent to the LaserWriter, give the *Print...* command, [Click] OK when the print dialog box comes up, then immediately hold down [⌘]–F. When you see the message that reads *creating PostScript file,* you can let up on the keys.

very hot tip

The PostScript code generated to print the document will be placed in a file on disk, rather than being sent to the printer. This file will be named *PostScript* and it's a good idea to rename immediately, because if you use [⌘]–F again, a new file named *PostScript* will overwrite the old.

Text on laser printers and typesetters

● *bit-mapped fonts on PostScript printers* (AN)

If you turn *Font Substitution* on in the Page Setup dialog box, a PostScript printer will convert four basic bit-mapped fonts to laser fonts when it runs across them in a document. The conversions are New York to Times, Geneva to Helvetica, Monaco to Courier (they deserve each other) and Seattle to a modified version of Helvetica. But the character spacing produced with *Font Substitution* leaves a lot to be desired.

If you turn *Font Substitution* off, or use any bit-mapped fonts other than the four mentioned above, the printer creates special PostScript versions of the bit-mapped fonts it finds in a document. (Most people don't realize that PostScript can create bit-mapped fonts as well as outline fonts.)

These PostScript versions of bit-mapped fonts print more smoothly than the original fonts do on the ImageWriter and they also scale much better. But rotation doesn't work too well (which means that they may not look great in italic, for example). Two other disadvantages of the PostScript versions: they take much longer to print and they strip out most of the type style variations you get on the ImageWriter. (For more information on that, see the entries below called *type styles on laser printers* and *how fonts affect laser printers' speed.)*

❡ *downloadable fonts* (AN)

PostScript laser printers almost always come with some fonts built into their ROMs. If you want other laser fonts, you have to buy them on disk and *download* (send) them to the printer.

esp. for beginners

Downloadable fonts have several advantages over fonts in ROM. The main thing is that there's a much greater selection of them (see Chapter 5 for a sampling of just a few of the thousands that are available). Downloadable fonts also tend to be cheaper, with some selling for as little as $30. And they're much easier for the publisher to enhance, upgrade or update.

bargain

The only disadvantages of downloadable fonts is that they take longer to print and use up some of the printer's RAM, which is in short supply on the original LaserWriter and LaserWriter Plus. Still, downloadable fonts are where it's at. Don't restrict yourself to what some printer manufacturer thinks you need.

❡ *two ways to download fonts* (AN)

Laser fonts that reside on disk rather than in ROM can be sent to the printer two ways. You can "manually" download them to the LaserWriter before printing or you can have them downloaded automatically during printing (you just use the screen fonts in your document and the Mac sends the fonts' print files to the LaserWriter as it runs across them). Most applications support automatic downloading.

esp. for beginners

(Apple and Adobe refer to manual downloading as "permanent" downloading, which is pretty confusing, since the fonts only stay in the LaserWriter until you turn it off. "Manual"—which is obviously based on an analogy to automatic and manual transmissions in cars—isn't exactly the right word either, but I can't think of a better one.)

Manual downloading is done with a program that comes on the disk with the fonts. Once the fonts are downloaded, printing is faster, because they don't have to be downloaded over and over again each time you print (automatic downloading takes about 5–15 seconds per font).

The main advantage of automatic downloading is that it's easier (manual downloading is an annoying chore, even though it only takes a few minutes). Another advantage is that the fonts get flushed out after each printing job, making room for new fonts on the next printing job.

very
hot
tip

As a rule, manual downloading isn't worth the trouble unless you're going to be using the same font(s) in three or more printouts (which might be the same document revised and reprinted three times). On the other hand, it almost always makes sense when you're printing from PageMaker, which flushes automatically downloaded fonts after each text block, rather than at the end of the printing job, and thus has to reload them for each subsequent text block.

❡ *how fonts affect laser printers' speed* (AN)

Laser printers process some kinds of fonts much faster than others. Laser fonts in ROM are the fastest. Downloadable laser fonts are slightly slower (in addition, ones that are downloaded automatically take 5–15 seconds longer than ones that are manually downloaded). Bit-mapped fonts are far and away the slowest, because the printer not only has to download them but also has to create a PostScript version of them.

Obviously, the more fonts (of any kind) you use, the longer it will take to print a page. So you'll get the very fastest speed out of a laser printer if you use just one font in ROM in just one style and, because scaling also takes time, in just one size. But that's quite a sacrifice to make for a little speed.

shortcut

If you use more fonts than a laser printer's RAM can accommodate, it won't print the page at all. This is particularly a problem on the original LaserWriter and the LaserWriter Plus, with their skimpy 1.5 megs of RAM.

⚫ *where to store downloadable fonts* (AN)

Put the *printer files* for downloadable laser fonts either in the system folder (that's the best place for them) or in the startup disk's window—also known as the *root directory.* (*Screen fonts* should, of course, be installed in the System file with the Font/DA Mover.) If the printer font files are stuck away in a folder anywhere else, the Mac won't be able to find them and they won't be downloaded to the printer.

important warning

Why those restrictions? Because there can be so many files on a hard disk that the Mac could spend forever looking for the fonts, if it didn't limit its search to just those locations. (The public domain program Set Paths, by Paul Snively, lets you put printer files wherever you want them. For details, see the entry on it in Chapter 8.)

By the way, don't change the names of printer font files; the automatic downloading process depends on their staying the same. (Sometimes the icon for a printer font file will change when you copy it from the disk you get from the publisher, but don't pay any attention to that.)

important warning

⚫ *installing screen fonts* (AN)

Some versions of the System and Finder limit the number of bit-mapped fonts (including screen fonts) you can install in the System file to about 200. The simplest solution to this problem is just to use the latest system software but if for some reason you're not (you have an old machine, say), here's more on the problem:

You may think you'd never need to have anything like 200 fonts installed, but each different size counts as a different font; in other words, it's the listing in the Font/DA Mover window that counts (with the sizes alongside the names), not the one on the Font menu (where the sizes aren't listed). So if you have twenty fonts installed, each in 9-, 10-, 12-, 14-, 18- and 24- point, you're already up to 120.

Needless to say, you don't need to install every size of a font, unless you're going to be printing it out on the ImageWriter. Since the laser printer does its own scaling and doesn't depend on the screen fonts, you only need enough sizes installed to keep the screen display legible.

very
hot
tip

One way to keep the number of screen fonts down is to only install the ones for plain text, not bold or italic or whatever. Choosing a plain text font and then making it bold (say) will produce exactly the same effect as if you choose the bold screen font. (For more on this, see the entry on type styles below.)

✦ *special characters on laser printers* (AN)

important
warning

As a general rule, laser fonts give you a wider selection of special characters than bit-mapped fonts (for more details, see Chapter 5). But many laser fonts borrow some of their special characters from the Symbol font. So if you want the full range of special characters, make sure Symbol's printer file is in the system folder on your startup disk.

✦ *type styles on laser printers* (AN)

very bad
feature

On the ImageWriter, every font can be transformed into bold, italic, outline, shadow and any combination thereof—which comes to sixteen possible variations. On laser printers, however, no font I've seen can produce all sixteen variations. For example, Zapf Chancery (from Adobe) only gives you three: plain, outline and shadow (bold, italic and bold italic print out as plain and all the other variations print out as either outline or shadow).

Times and Helvetica do much better. Although outline shadow looks the same as shadow, eliminating four possibilities, the other twelve variations are there. (I've yet to see a laser font that will make the distinction between shadow and outline shadow—although with some type sizes in Word, characters are spaced farther apart in outline shadow than in shadow.) Adobe's Benguiat has the same twelve combinations, as does CasadyWare's San Serif. Casady-Ware's Ritz provides eight of the possibilities—exactly half.

Bit-mapped fonts lose most of their style variations when they're translated into PostScript bit-map fonts. For example, when printed on a laser printer, Chicago retains just five of the sixteen styles it has on the ImageWriter. The only way to tell what variations a particular font will give you on the a laser printer is to try them out.

All type styles on the ImageWriter are produced algorithmically—that is, by the application of a rule like *increase the width 10%* (to create boldface) or *slant right 11°* (to create italic). But on the LaserWriter, many fonts have their own separate *cuttings* for bold, italic and bold italic—that is, all the characters in those styles were individually designed, as if for a separate font.

If a font does have separate cuttings for certain styles, you'll have to load a separate printer file in the system folder for each one. But, as a rule, you'll get better-looking characters than with an algorithmically derived style. You can always tell whether the style you're using is algorithmic by looking to see if there's a separate printer file for it. (In some cases, you don't need to bother—for example, type styles called *oblique* rather than *italic* are almost always algorithmic.)

Fonts with separate cuttings usually come with screen fonts to match but you can save room in your System file by not installing them. Just select the type style you want from the style menu and PostScript will know to look for the font file before making the change algorithmically. But if you do install the special screen fonts, you'll get a cleaner representation of the characters on the screen.

very good feature

Some fonts also have separate cuttings for variations with different names than bold, italic, outline or shadow (the next entry discusses some examples). In these cases, you do have to install the screen font—unless the style is basically a variation on bold or italic. If it is, it will normally be "mapped" to the menu option. For example, *demi* type is bolder than regular, so selecting text set in Souvenir and then choosing *Bold* from the menu will give you Souvenir Demi.

Generally, font publishers try to do what makes sense; if a font comes with four variations, you can usually get them by choosing plain text, bold, italic and bold italic.

Although *oblique* is the only other name in common use for italic type (both are slanted, but italic letters are also redrawn in other ways), there are many names for various levels of boldness. The common ones are listed below, going from lightest to boldest:

very hot tip

Ultra Light
Extra Light
Light
Roman, Book or no adjective (just the name of the typeface)
Medium
Demi
Bold
Extra Bold, Heavy or Black
Ultra Bold

❡ *special type styles on laser printers* (AN)

Some laser fonts offer exotic type styles far beyond the standard sixteen (only on the Mac could you call bold italic outline shadow "standard"). In addition to all the different levels of boldness mentioned at the end of the last entry, there's condensed or "thin" (letters squeezed together and stretched vertically) and expanded or "fat" (letters spread apart and stretched horizontally).

Century's Special Effects use some really fancy algorithms—stack, fill, reflect, and so on. For samples of these, see Chapter 5. To get special type styles like condensed and expanded, stack and fill, you obviously have to install the screen fonts, since there are no menu items that correspond to them.

❡ *creating special typographic effects* (AN)

To distort a headline or other piece of display type for special effect, type it first in MacDraw, MacDraft or any other *draw* (object-oriented graphics) *program*. Then paste it into a word processor or page layout program, either through the Clipboard or the Scrapbook.

very hot tip

Once it's there, select it and reshape it to stretch the type horizontally, vertically or both. It will look terrible on the screen but when you print it out, the characters will have the same crisp, clean edges that laser fonts normally do. Here

are some examples of the kinds of effects you can get:

(The fonts being distorted are Adobe's Cooper Black italic, CasadyWare's Kells and their Gazelle.)

very hot tip

You can also use a draw program to *drop out (reverse out)* type—that is, to give you white type on a dark background. First create a solid shape filled with black (or gray, or any other pattern you want for the background). Then either drag some outline type on top of it or, with the filled-in shape selected—choose *Outline* from the Style menu and start typing.

You can combine both these techniques, creating white writing on a dark background and stretching it once it gets into your word processing program. (I had an example to show you but for some reason it's not printing. Well, it's more fun to do it yourself anyway.)

These typographic special effects also work on the ImageWriter, but you don't get smoothing and the results don't look anywhere near as good.

❡ *sticky header files* (DC)

Most Macintosh applications send header files of Post-Script instructions to the LaserWriter at the beginning of each document to be printed. Sometimes these header files stay in the LaserWriter and force it to reset (and spit out a startup page) before letting you print a document from a different application. This is a bug. If you find the Laser-Writer resetting every time you switch from a given application, contact the publisher of that application for a fix.

❡ *using lots of fonts on the LaserWriter I* (AN)

**important
warning**

Don't. (I'll resist the temptation to make this the shortest entry in the book.)

After the original LaserWriter or the LaserWriter Plus finishes imaging the page and doing other necessary tasks, it only has about 210K of RAM available for downloading fonts and other necessary information.

To give you an idea of just how limiting that is, consider that PageMaker takes about 50K for its header (the Post-Script instructions it gives to the printer) and that the necessary QuickDraw information takes another 90K. This leaves only 70K for your downloadable fonts, which usually require between 20K and 35K each. (Other programs often have somewhat smaller headers and thus leave slightly more room for fonts to be downloaded.)

In addition to the space the fonts themselves take up, another 10K or so has to be downloaded along with the first font. This one-time hit contains information that applies to all fonts.

PageMaker offers you a way around the problem. It flushes out the fonts after each text block, instead of at the end of the document, so the limitations that normally apply to fonts per document apply to fonts per text block. Since you can have as many text blocks as you want in a document, you can also have as many fonts as you want (within reason, that is; things can get pretty tedious with dozens of text blocks on a page).

very good feature

But in most applications, you only have room to download three or four fonts; under some extreme circumstances, there may only be room for two. And remember that if bold, italic, bold italic or some other style comes in its own cutting (that is, if it's been separately designed and comes as a separate font file), it counts towards the total just like a completely different typeface.

(One exception to this is special cuttings labeled *oblique*. They're usually derived algorithmically—that is, by the application of a rule—and take up much less of the LaserWriter's memory. For example, ITC Glypha Oblique only takes up 3K if you already have Glypha Roman loaded, since all that needs to be added are the PostScript instructions on how to tilt the letters.)

If you use too many fonts, the Mac will show you one or more messages that tell you you're running short of memory. In a classic case of boneheaded design, these messages neither beep nor stay on the screen for very long.

very bad feature

So if you happen not to be completely catatonic and have therefore chosen to get up and do something rather than to stare blankly at the screen for the five or ten minutes it takes the LaserWriter to print a document with a lot of fonts, you'll miss the messages. When you come back into the room, the LaserWriter will be humming innocently away (*What do you mean, "Where's your printout?" What print-out?*), with no indication on the screen of what happened.

(The above assumes your fonts are being automatically downloaded. If you're manually downloading fonts—sending them to the LaserWriter one by one with a downloading program prior to printing—and you overrun the LaserWriter's RAM, it will probably just restart itself and spit out a new startup page.)

very hot tip

If a document won't print, it's always worth trying to print it again; it often works the second time. If that doesn't work, try printing the document one page at a time. If that doesn't work, try breaking it into smaller documents.

very hot tip

If you're not sure that too many fonts is the reason the LaserWriter won't print your document, the easiest way to find out is to make a copy of it, change the entire copy to Times or Helvetica, and try printing that. If that works, your problem is almost certainly too many fonts.

To get around this limitation, some applications use note format, which gives half-inch margins all around (on the assumption that you're not going to want to print anything closer to the edge of the paper than that). This gives you room for more fonts, theoretically as many as eight or ten. But don't count on it.

The LaserStatus DA (described in the DiskTop entry in Chapter 8) tells you how much RAM is left in the LaserWriter and what fonts—both downloadable and ROM-based—are already there; it also lets you reset the LaserWriter—that is, flush its memory—without turning off the power. Adobe, CasadyWare and Century offer similar software on their font disks.

All in all, the limitation on how many fonts you can use is the LaserWriter I's most annoying shortcoming. The best way around this problem, of course, is to get a laser printer with at least 2MB of RAM, like the LaserWriter II NT or II NTX.

🍎 *laser fonts in MacPaint* (AN)

Bit-mapped paint programs like MacPaint and FullPaint won't output laser fonts. What you get instead is the screen font, just the way you see it on the screen.

To get around this, use a draw program like MacDraw or, even better, a draw/paint program like SuperPaint that lets you combine bit-mapped and object-oriented graphics.

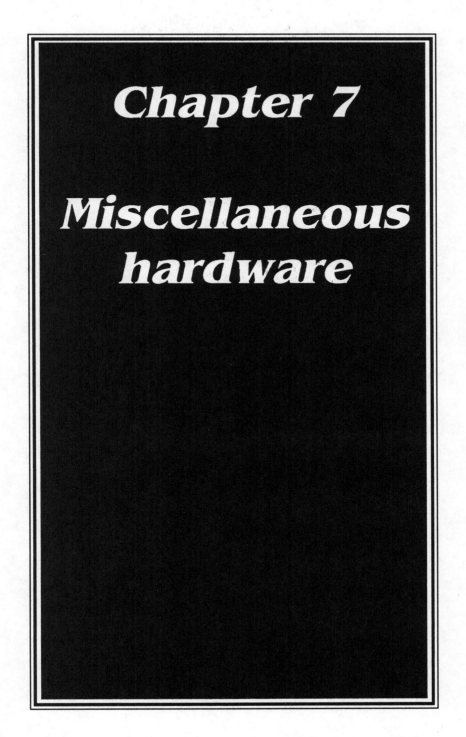

Chapter 7

Miscellaneous hardware

CD players, scanners, etc.

ᘓ CD players—Apples and others *(AN)*

Compact disks can hold about 550–600 *megabytes,* depending on how they're formatted, which is equivalent to more than 700 800K disks and well over a quarter of a million typewritten pages. This incredible capacity makes them the ultimate mass storage device for computers (*ultimate* for the next couple of years, anyway),

esp. for beginners

Apple makes a player call the AppleCD SC (because it connects over the SCSI port). It lists for $1200 and is described by my team of experts as slow. A whole slew of competitors are waiting in the wings, so watch the updates for details.

ᘓ prolonging the life of CDs *(CJW)*

Although CDs are ballyhooed as being indestructible, don't believe it. The thin plastic coating can be easily scratched and that can cause data to drop out during the read cycle. Dirt can do the same thing, as can warping of the disk caused by excessive heat.

important warning

So keep your CDs out of direct sunlight, away from heat and in their protective cases when you're not using them. It's bad enough to ruin a $12 music CD but it's a lot worse to ruin a CD ROM that cost you $200.

ᘓ scanners—Apple's and others *(AN)*

Scanners are devices that convert images to digital form so they can be stored and manipulated by computers. Scanners very in terms of how many *bits per pixel* they can store; those that store more than two can capture gray tones and are thus called *gray-scale scanners.* Some gray-scale scanners can have as many as 256 bits per pixel. This gives you really high-quality pictures but also costs a bundle.

esp. for beginners

Among the non-gray-scale scanners, the least expensive is ThunderScan ($250). It attaches to an ImageWriter printer and can only scan loose sheets of paper. There are a bunch of faster and more powerful 300-dpi scanners like Apple's (which is simply called the Apple Scanner); they tend to cost $1000+.

None of these non-gray-scale scanners produce pictures that are of book or magazine quality, but this is a field where both software and hardware development is proceeding at a furious pace, so we'll probably have some news to give you in an update.

🍎 *ThunderScan output on the LaserWriter* (DC)

very hot tip

Since the ThunderScan digitizer reads a picture on the ImageWriter, printouts on the LaserWriter often look no better than a MacPaint document at 72 dots per inch. But there's a way around this. Scan the image at 400%, then print it at 25%. That will give your image a resolution of 288 dpi.

But be prepared to wait a while. Scanning a whole page at 400% takes over an hour.

🍎 *avoiding stair-stepping on the ThunderScan* (DC)

One way to improve the quality of a ThunderScan image is to make sure you insert the original into the ImageWriter as straight as possible. If it contains horizontal lines, try to align them with the roller shaft. You can test the alignment quite easily—if the horizontal lines in the digitized image are slightly "stair-stepped," the alignment is off.

🍎 *vertical lines on the ThunderScan* (DC)

very hot tip

If the image you are digitizing with ThunderScan contains lots of vertical lines, put it in the ImageWriter sideways (but see the previous entry about aligning it precisely). You can then use MacPaint's *Rotate* command to properly orient the digitized image.

✎ *best video cameras for digitizers* (DC)

bargain

Less expensive black-and-white video cameras with high-quality lenses will provide much better images on camera-based digitizers like MacVision than the more expensive color cameras.

✎ *creating depth with camera-based digitizers* (DC)

When using a camera-based digitizer like MacVision, you can give the image dramatic depth by angling the object slightly. Be careful, though—just a little is enough.

✎ *Dunn film recorders* (SH)

Film recorders are what you use to made slides (or prints) from what's on your computer's screen. In my experience, those from Dunn (available from Computer Friends) are reliable and produce high-quality output. They start at $7500. *Filmbacks* (the things you put the film in) run from $900 for 35mm to $2,000 for 8 x 10.

Protecting your Mac

✎ *AppleCare* (AN)

Apple's extended service contracts, which go under the name of AppleCare, provide the same coverage you get during the initial warranty period (free parts and labor for whatever goes wrong—unless, of course, you drop your Mac out a window, open its case or do something else Apple doesn't approve of). AppleCare isn't cheap ($420/year for a LaserWriter I, for example) and it's not as essential as it was back in the days of the power supply that blew more frequently than Old Faithful.

Macs have gotten to be a lot more reliable since then, so whether or not you get AppleCare basically depends on your temperament and your finances. If you're a cautious type and/or can't afford a big, unexpected repair bill, get it; if you're a gambler and/or can absorb that big bill in the unlikely event it comes along, save your money. (Since there's profit built into AppleCare, the odds are in your favor if you don't buy it. But that's usually less important than peace of mind.

🍎 *lightning only has to strike once* (CJW)

important warning

A surge suppressor is a good way to protect your computer from sudden variations in electrical current, and every Mac (and major peripheral, like a disk drive or a printer) should be on one. But don't rely on it during a thunderstorm. Lightning can arc across open contacts and do extensive damage to your equipment.

So get in the habit of pulling the plug out of the wall whenever you shut down your system for any length of time. That's the only way to make sure it's safe. If you have a modem connected to your Mac, also unplug the incoming telephone line or disconnect the cable. Your computer can be zapped just as easily by lightning striking your telephone line.

🍎 *MacGard* (LP)

important warning

In the middle of a dry New England winter, just walking across the room can build up a terrific static charge, especially around synthetic fabrics, rubber-soled shoes and wall-to-wall carpeting. Under these conditions, touching anything connected to an electrical ground results in a painful shock. Sometimes it's so bad, it triggers an instant lockup.

very good feature

One solution is to use a $90 surge suppressor called MacGard. Besides superior surge protection (in lab tests I ran, it outperformed several units costing twice as much), it has an integral static-draining touch pad. When you tap it, you hear the same crackling noise that's normally associated with a painful shock but the discharge is much slower and completely painless. You can then touch your Mac safely.

☼ *covering the Mac* (AN)

To paraphrase an old saying, dust never sleeps, and the more of it that gets into your Mac, the worse off you are. Many people sell covers for the Mac, but the ones we like best are sold by Computer Cover Company (how's that for a straightforward name?). They come in several colors, are attractive and well made, and are available for various models of the Mac, its peripherals, the keyboard, and even the mouse. Best of all, they're made of high-quality woven nylon, instead of vinyl with its nauseating, carcinogenic fumes.

very good feature

☼ *fans, pro and con* (AN/DC/Tom Swain)

All Macs since the SE have fans, so the following tips only apply to the Mac Plus and earlier models. (For a tip on how to quiet the loud fan in early SEs, see *silencing the SE* in Chapter 2.)

Fanless Macs are cooled by convection—the basic principle of which is that hot air rises. The Mac's designers put hot components like the power supply near the vents on the top of the case, where they create an upward flow of air that cools things below.

According to Apple, fanless Macs can maintain an internal temperature no higher than 15° C. (27° F.) above the room temperature. While a 15° C. difference is within Apple's guidelines and normally won't present a problem, the cooler a computer runs, the better (within reason).

Heat is a problem in a computer for two main reasons. First, cool chips last longer. For example, a chip that's fated to die after one year of operation at 170° F. will last two at 80° F.

Second, heat generated can warm and therefore expand floppy disks in the internal drive. If a file is written to the disk in this condition—say on a hot summer afternoon after your machine has been on for several hours—it can disappear the next morning when you turn your machine on. The disk

important warning

drive will be searching for a track that moved a little during the night as the disk cooled. (If this happens to you, the file can most likely be recovered by letting the machine—and therefore the disk—warm up for a few hours and then trying to reread it.)

Here's a simple test of the temperature inside your Mac: Leave the machine on for at least an hour with a disk in the internal drive and then eject it. Immediately hold the top side of the disk's shutter mechanism (the sliding metal piece) to your face. The warmth (or lack thereof) will give a benchmark against which to gauge the effectiveness of any subsequent cooling strategy.

So—a fan certainly isn't going to hurt the performance of any fanless Mac, and if yours has third-party additions (memory expansion upgrades and/or internal hard disks), a fan may well be a necessity. Unfortunately, fans have their own set of problems.

If they draw power from the Mac's power supply (as most of them do), then you're asking a component with an already questionable track record to do even more work. (This is only a problem with pre-SE power supplies.)

important warning

When Tom installed a fan, he felt that his friendly, unobtrusive Mac had been transformed into a "hissing and obnoxious desktop troll." Many people find the noise from a fan much more annoying over hundreds or thousands of hours in a quiet home or office than they think they will when listening to it for a few minutes in a noisy computer store. So if you decide to get a fan, spend some time listening to it first and make sure you have the right to return it.

important warning

Some fans for the Mac are external; they mount on top of the case and boost the Mac's normal convective cooling. Because they're relatively powerful, they also draw dust, dirt and smoke particles into the Mac. You open the case after six months and it looks like the lint sock on a dryer vent. This isn't great for disk drives.

So use external fans with caution if you're a smoker or work in a relatively dusty environment. They also tend to be the noisiest type of fan for the Mac. (See the next entry for a review of one external fan.)

You should definitely avoid any external fan that draws air in and forces it downward into the Mac's case. Since the power supply is the major source of heat in the Mac, and since it's near the top, these fans actually blow hot air down onto the delicate (and expensive) motherboard.

important warning

Internal fans usually cost less than external ones. There are three basic kinds—*rotary* (blades twirling around), *piezoelectric* (two thin plastic flaps that vibrate back and forth) and *squirrel-cage* (a spinning cylinder with slots and fins on it).

Squirrel cages are junk; avoid them at any cost. Internal rotary fans are less noisy than external fans and piezoelectric fans are quieter still, making only a slight, dull hum (MacMemory sells one called MaxChill for $50). They're powerful enough to cool the circuit boards but it's not clear how much they cool the disk drive.

Dale installed a 2MB memory upgrade in a Mac Plus. Since the clip-on daughterboard mounted directly over the motherboard, he was skeptical that the little piezoelectric fan provided would be adequate. But after using the upgraded system for about five hours, the top of the unit was barely warm to the touch, dramatically cooler than a fanless Mac. This made him a piezoelectric fan fan. (Sorry.)

very good feature

In Arthur's opinion, the ideal solution comes from a completely different direction. The MacChimney, developed by Tom Swain, is a totally silent. It's primarily suited for people who tend to keep their Mac in one place, prefer to leave it on much of the time and are sensitive to sound. On the next page is a picture of how it looks on the Mac.

very good feature

Basically, the MacChimney works the same way as a fireplace chimney. Cool air enters the Mac through the vents in the bottom and gets heated by the electronics. As it enters the MacChimney, it acts as a buoyant mass and sucks about 60% more air in through the bottom vents than if the MacChimney weren't there.

very good feature

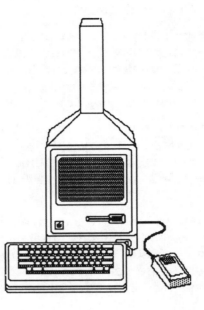

(I'm so sensitive to noise that even a piezoelectric fan got on my nerves after a while (although, oddly enough, I can tolerate the Mac II's fan, because it puts out white noise). But rather than put an ordinary fan on a fanless Mac, I use MacChimney. It makes the Mac look a little strange—sort of like the Tin Woodman in The Wizard of Oz—but that gives it a certain charm.

MacChimney cools the Mac very efficiently, is totally silent, costs only $18 (which includes shipping, handling, tax and a ten-day money-back guarantee) and makes a great conversation piece. I have one on both my fanless Macs and love them.—AN)

🍎 *System Saver Mac* (SS)

If you have a fanless Mac (prior to the SE), you know how hot it can get. If you don't, try resting your hand on the top vents for a few seconds after it's been on for several hours.

As mentioned in the previous entry, extremes in temperature can prematurely age the chips in your Mac, so a good fan can be considered preventative maintenance.

System Saver Mac is more than a fan. It also provides protection from power surges that can cripple your Mac and trash data files. The unit sits atop the Mac, fitting neatly between the two vent areas. Installation is as easy as sliding the unit forward until its lip clicks into the groove near the front of the Mac.

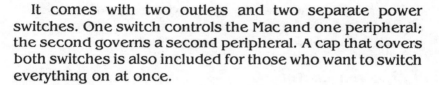
very good feature

It comes with two outlets and two separate power switches. One switch controls the Mac and one peripheral; the second governs a second peripheral. A cap that covers both switches is also included for those who want to switch everything on at once.

In my experience, System Saver Mac works nicely and its design doesn't detract from the sleek, slim appearance of the Mac. But it's a bit pricey at $100. *(And it does turn the wonderfully silent Mac into something that sounds like a PC. For some other alternatives, see the discussion of piezoelectric fans and the MacChimney in the previous entry.—AN)*

the Ergotron Muzzle *(AN)*

What with *viruses* running rampant, leaving a Mac unattended at a trade show or in a store can be an invitation to disaster. Ergotron has the answer. Called The Muzzle, it's a piece of metal that covers the floppy drive slot, thus preventing anyone from putting software on your hard disk without your knowledge. There's even a model that prevents the Mac from being turned on.

Miscellaneous hardware

MacRecorder *(AN)*

Steve Michel thinks this dandy sound-capturing hardware-and-software package is the greatest thing since sliced bread. (Actually, he thinks it's even better than sliced bread, which he really doesn't like all that much.

very good feature

Created by Farallon Computing and sold for $200 list, MacRecorder lets you capture any sound (at 22,000 samples per second), mix it and add special effects. Once you have the sound the way you want it, you can use it in HyperCard stacks, as a replacement for normal Mac beeps (so your Mac will talk—or sing—tot you) and in many music and sound programs.

The hardware works very well and the software is generally slick and easy to use. But be aware that digitized sound takes up a *lot* of room in RAM or on a disk.

⬥ *Ergotron MacTilt* (AN)

As I said in Chapter 2, a computer screen should be 4–8" higher than the surface the keyboard rests on, so you can look at it comfortably without having to bend your head. Some people also like to be able to change the viewing angle during long sessions.

MacTilt is an ergonomic stand for the Macintosh that both raises the Mac 4" and lets you position it just about any way you can imagine. It tilts 15° forward and 15° back, and rotates 360°. You can adjust the Mac with the touch of a finger, and it stays where you put it.

very good feature

MacTilt is built so tough you can stand on it. That kind of construction doesn't come cheap and MacTilt costs $90— which really isn't so much when you consider that it's probably the best tilt/swivel device on the market. (If you have three times that much to spend, see the next entry.)

⬥ *MacTable* (LP)

When you're not straining your body to work, everything goes faster and easier. Nothing proves that statement better than a day at the MacTable, a full-sized workcenter designed exclusively for Macintosh computers.

Functionally, the MacTable is everything you could ask for and that's true structurally as well; made of beechwood and Formica-like plastic laminate, it's double-doweled and metal-fastened for extra stability. Thanks to knock-down design and well-written directions, setting it up is easy and the special tools you need to do that are included.

The MacTable comes with two shelves—one that's 56" x 15" and another made up of three parts, each 12" deep. Either shelf can be put in the front or back of the table to accommodate various kinds of Macs and can be tilted 15°— to minimize screen glare or to make for easier typing. (This idea of tilting the screen back is very clever and means you don't have to raise it as much.) You can also adjust the height of the front shelf from 26" to 28.5".

So much thought has gone into this table that after just a short while, you begin to experience it and the Mac as one, integrated system. Satisfied users include *The MACazine's* editor-in-chief and managing editor and *MacUser's* chief scientist. There are reportedly more than forty MacTables at *MacWEEK*.

I've used my MacTable for over two years. It's the only workcenter I'd ever consider for my Mac, and at its list price of $290, it's a real bargain.

⁴ APG cash drawer *(LP)*

This handsome, well-constructed cash drawer ($300 and up) connects to the Mac's modem port. Combine it with the ShopKeeper software reviewed in Chapter 11 (also $300) and you can turn your Mac into a sophisticated electronic cash register like those in big retail chains, at a fraction of what that would otherwise cost.

The APG cash drawer is a proven performer; in fact, many MacDonald's outlets use them. (It comes with a BASIC routine for writing your own software, if you prefer doing that to getting ShopKeeper.)

⚫ *X-10 CP290* *(LP)*

bargain

We're now entering a new era of computerized home control. Everything from the heat to the stereo can now be programmed, timed and controlled with a $50 X-10 CP290 Interface that plugs right into your Mac's modem port. (In addition, modules are required for every device you want to control; they cost about $15 each.) Discounted starter systems run about $100. I've had my system for over two years and use it every day.

⚫ *Lisas and Lisa parts* *(AN)*

bargain

The Lisa, also known for a brief period as the Mac XL, is now being sold at super-low prices. You sacrifice upward compatibility but you get a lot of computer for your money. Two sources for Lisas and Lisa parts are Sun Remarketing in Utah and The Lisa Shop in Minneapolis (their addresses and phone numbers are in Appendix B).

⚫ *Kensington accessories for the Mac II* *(FT)*

Wonderful as the Mac II is, it's big and noisy. One way to deal with both those problems is to get the CPU off of your desk. To help you do that, Kensington Microware sells a 7-foot keyboard cable, 6-foot power cord and 6-foot video cable.

Kensington also has an aluminum floor stand for the Mac II that lets you stand it vertically next to your desk. It provides a stable support for the II and puts it about 2" above the floor, but it ignores the Mac II owner's manual warning to "keep your computer main unit flat, sitting on its rubber feet. Standing it on edge defeats the cooling design and is likely to make your computer overheat." Apple technical support confirms this warning but Kensington (not surprisingly) claims that the stand provides enough clearance for convective cooling.

important warning

If you do use the stand, put the Mac II on it with the right side down. The power supply is on the left and if you put that side on the bottom, all of the heat from it will flow up over the motherboard and the chips. Unfortunately, putting the right side down places the floppy disk drive(s) near the floor and also deprives you of access to the programmer's switch (if you have it installed).

⚫ *MacCable* (AN)

For some reason I'm not clear on, most sources for Macintosh cables are flakes. One that isn't is Monster Cable of San Francisco. Their MacCable line is extensive, and if they don't have what you'll want, they'll make it for you.

From the WetPaint clip art collection.
Copyright © 1988–89 by Dubl-Click Software.
All rights reserved.

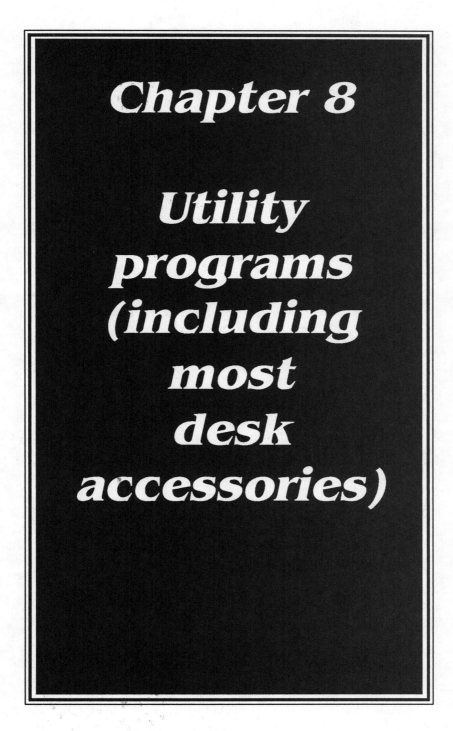

Chapter 8

Utility programs (including most desk accessories)

Basic terms

❡ *what utilities are* (AN)

Utilities are programs that perform relatively simple tasks—like searching for a specific file on a disk, setting an alarm, clipping a picture or counting the words in a document. They come in various forms—as stand-alone programs, *desk accessories* (see the next entry for a definition), *inits*, *cdevs* or *FKeys* (see the glossary for definitions).

*esp. for
beginners*

Many utilities are covered in the other chapters; for example, Acta—an excellent outliner in the form of a DA— is covered in the word processing chapter. Those that don't fit neatly into one category or another—or that span categories, like programs used for clipping art from paint files and pasting them into word processing documents—are covered here.

❡ *what desk accessories are* (DC/AN)

You open most programs by clicking on their icons on the Desktop. But you open *desk accessories* by choosing them from the ❡ menu. The advantage is that DAs can be used without leaving the application you're in, since no matter what you're doing on the Mac—with a few rare exceptions—the ❡ menu will be in the upper left corner of the screen and will contain all the items it does on the Desktop.

*esp. for
beginners*

For example, you can open up Apple's Calculator desk accessory in the middle of a MacWrite session and use it to add up a column of figures. (As a matter of fact, you can copy the column directly into the calculator and then paste the result into your document.)

Some desk accessories are complex enough to be considered applications, but most are utilities. They let you to take notes, dial the phone, open documents created by other programs than the one you're in, create new folders, check spelling, play games and move, rename and delete files; there's even one that will nag you about your work habits.

Officially you're limited to sixteen DAs installed in any one system file—in other words, at any one time—but you can get around that with programs like Suitcase and Font/DA Juggler Plus, both discussed below.

DAs—particularly big, powerful ones—can take up a lot of space on disk. This isn't a problem on a hard disk but if you're using floppies, you'll have to weigh the advantages offered by a particular DA against how much space it will take up on your system disk(s).

❡ *public-domain and shareware utilities* (DC)

There are thousands of utility programs and most of them are either *shareware* (you get to try them out before paying) or in the *public domain* (i.e., free). The ones listed below are some of the best and are often more powerful than their commercial competitors. (Some good commercial programs are described below as well.)

You can get shareware and public-domain DAs from information services like CompuServe and from many bulletin boards (for a list of a few of the best, see Chapter 16). If you don't have the modem—or the patience—you need to access a BBS, most user groups also sell disks full of DAs.

You can also usually order a shareware DA directly from its author. Of course, this means you have to pay for it before you're sure you like it, but the price is typically so low that it hardly makes a difference.

A final source of good shareware and public-domain programs is *The Macintosh Bible disk,* described at the end of Chapter 16. It contains some of the best software around and comes with a 30-day money-back guarantee.

bargain

Shareware and public-domain desk accessories are certainly the greatest bargains there are on the Mac. So make sure you always pay for (register) any shareware program you end up using. Be selfish—keep these people writing software.

✎ *possible utility/System conflicts* (DC)

Some utilities can cause problems with certain versions of the System and Finder. If you begin to have problems when you start using a utility, try removing it. It's not likely that it's the cause of your problem, but it's worth checking out.

File handlers and Finder substitutes

✎ *Dir-Acta-ry* (DC)

This useful program creates an Acta outline of all the files on a hard disk (Acta is reviewed in Chapter 10). Each level in the file hierarchy is shown as a different level on the outline.

Dir-Acta-ry was written by David Dunham, who also wrote Acta; it's free, but only useful if you have Acta. You can find it on various bulletin boards and information services.

✎ *DiskInfo* (DC/AN)

From within any application DiskInfo will tell you how much memory and how much disk space you have available, plus the name, size, type and creator of any file on any disk (even ones you've ejected), including files that are invisible on the Desktop.

It will also locate any file on a disk (even ones you've ejected). You can search for a file by its full name, by the beginning of its name, or by any part of its name.

Although most people I know now use DiskTop, which has more features, DiskInfo only costs $10—quite a low price for such a useful program. So if you're not ready to

bargain

plop down $50 for DiskTop, send a fifth that much to Maitreya Design, Box 1480, Goleta CA 93116.

gossip/
trivia

Maitreya, by the way, is the name of the next Buddha to arise (according to the traditional doctrine, there are many Buddhas, and we're due for one more in this cycle). Now, I ask you—what other book on the Mac goes behind the scenes to give you this kind of in-depth information?

🍎 *DiskTop* (CR)

very good
feature

DiskTop is a desk accessory that does so many things so well that it's hard to describe them all. For openers, it lets you find, open, delete, copy, move and rename files or folders (and eject disks) from inside any program. It also gives you information on files—either the kind provided in the Finder's Get Info window or more technical information that's useful to programmers. You can even switch applications from within an application, without having to go back to the Finder; DiskTop will close the current program and give you a chance to save your files before launching the new program. DiskTop performs all these operations at least twice as fast as the Finder—sometimes much faster.

shortcut

DiskTop is a delight to use. If you install a special init file in your system folder, you can call up the DiskTop window by typing from the keyboard, rather than by selecting it from the Apple menu, and you can even choose the keystroke combination you want to use to do that.

Instead of simply showing you disk icons, DiskTop tells you the capacity of each disk and how much free space remains on it.

Clicking on a disk icon displays its contents, just as with the Finder. You can navigate into and out of folders by double-clicking on them, and you can also search for files by name, type, creator, date created, date last modified or size—and in the case of these last three categories, you can enter ranges (e.g., *find me all the files that were modified in the last two weeks, or that are between 10 and 20K*). You can search for files whose names begin with, contain or exactly match the letters you type.

shortcut

DiskTop can search multiple disks at the same time. When it finds a file, it lists it and keeps on going. When you select the name of a file it's found, DiskTop displays a graphic map of where that file is located. You can launch the application straight from that map by double-clicking on its name (and when you do, DiskTop quits the application you're in, giving you a chance to save if necessary).

very good feature

Ah, but that's only the beginning of what you can do with DiskTop. You can also set a default folder, so the application you're running always looks for files in the same place. You can add up to 20 documents or applications to the DiskTop menu, so you can simply select them from the menu bar instead of having to root around for them. You can set preferences for how DiskTop sorts files, whether it shows file sizes in K or in bytes, and which level (technical or normal) of information you see when you get information about a file.

very good feature

DiskTop comes with a really decent 130-page manual and two bonus utilities. One of these, LaserStatus, is a desk accessory that tells you:

- what kind of printer you have (LaserWriter, for example)

- what name you've given it

- what version of PostScript it contains

- which fonts are built into it

- whether or not it's set to print a startup page whenever you turn it on

- how many pages have been printed since the printer was new

- how much memory it has available for page images, down-loaded fonts, etc.

- how much of that memory is currently being used

When you begin printing, the LaserStatus window shows the progress of your print job. There's a button that lets you download fonts or PostScript code to the printer and another that lets you reset it. There's even an option for creating PostScript files on the fly.

very good feature

Used along with the Widgets program, LaserStatus becomes even more powerful; for example, you can use it to assemble laser fonts into groups and then use LaserStatus to download them together. Widgets also lets you turn off the LaserWriter's startup page.

Widgets does a lot of other things too. For example, it lets you substitute any MacPaint document for the standard Welcome to Macintosh startup screen. It lets you create various custom DiskTop menus, with sets of documents or applications on them, and save them for later use—and you can sort the contents of these menus by name or by type.

Widgets lets you change the format of graphic files from bit-mapped (as in MacPaint) to PICT (as in MacDraw). Finally, it lets you change the size of your Mac's system heap, which is an area of memory set aside for storing system information. If you have a lot of DAs, fonts, chooser resources and init files installed in your System file and are having problems with large applications crashing occasionally, you may be able to remedy things by making the system heap larger.

bargain

All this cost just $50!—an incredible bargain. Disktop is sold by CE Software, one of the best small software publishers around.

◆ *DiskTop and PowerStation* (PH)

shortcut

DiskTop's *Find* function runs much faster than Apple's Find File DA. I also prefer copying files with DiskTop to dragging icons around on the Desktop. I tend to change my mind about what I want to name files after I create them; DiskTop makes it easy to change the names, since it normally opens up right to the directory to which the last save was made.

I prefer PowerStation over DiskTop for launching programs, however, because PowerStation is more flexible for installing documents.

❡ *Find File* (DC)

The Find File desk accessory (free from Apple) is very well thought out and contains several useful features. For example, it doesn't stop every time it finds a match; instead, it continues until all matches are found, then gives you the freedom to scroll through the list of files to examine the one you want.

Select a file from the list, and Find File will display a mini Get Info box (in the bottom left of the window) and will show you the path to get to the file in the bottom right. You can also drag the file to the Desktop (when you're through with it, you can use *Put Away* to return it to its original folder).

Another nice touch is that you can stop Find File at any point during a search and explore the matches found thus far. Finally, Find File will continue to search in the background while you work with an application.

very good feature

❡ *Findswell* (CR)

Findswell is a file-finding utility that appears as an extra button in the Open dialog box. Click thee button and a window opens that lets you search for files; when you find one, its path name (all the folders it's in) is shown. You can also navigate through files and folders the way you do in an Open window, and you can open any file you come across that was created by the application you're currently running (which saves you the trouble of quitting Findswell and going into the application's own Open window).

A number of other file-finding programs, including Apple's Find File, are available free or for less than $20 from user groups or bulletin boards. So why pay $50 for Findswell? Well, it has a few advantages that most of the competition doesn't.

Findswell will match a complete file name, the first part of a file name or any part of a file name; these choices let you specify a search more precisely, so you don't have to look at a whole slew of files with similar names. Another (somewhat minor) advantage is that you don't have to go up to the ⬛ menu to access it. Because it's an *init file* (see the glossary if you don't know what that is), it autoloads when you start up your Mac, and then whenever you select *Open...* or *Save As...*, its button is there.

But Findswell's nicest—and most unusual—feature lets you mark frequently used files so that they always appear in the Findswell window; if they're stuck deep inside two or three folders, this gets you to them much faster.

⬛ *PowerStation* (PH)

This is the easiest Finder substitute to use and by far the most useful. Its most powerful feature is the ability to launch documents. Instead of putting all your choices on one screen, PowerStation gives you sixteen screens of buttons, so that you can group your buttons by type (such as graphics programs or utilities) or by project (all of the documents for one project on each screen).

PowerStation works particularly well with MultiFinder, and since it takes up much less memory than the Finder, it leaves more memory for your programs.

⬛ *SkipFinder* (DC)

SkipFinder is a desk accessory that does just what the name implies: it lets you skip the Finder (and thus not wait for the Mac to reconstruct all the open windows on the DeskTop) when you quit an application. Instead of the Desktop, you're presented with a list box that displays just applications. If you decide you need to go back to the Finder after all, there's also a button that lets you do that.

SkipFinder is particularly handy if you're using a hard disk and frequently change applications. After using it just a few times, you won't want to be without it.

The program's author, Darin Adler, asks that you try it, then send him what you think it's worth. His address is 2765 Marl Oak Dr, Highland Park IL 60035.

Font and DA handlers

⚫ *Font/DA Juggler 2.0* *(CR)*

This competitor to Suitcase is better in some ways and worse in others. Like Suitcase, it can automatically open and close font and DA files as you work. The problem is that you can only have two files open at once. Assuming you have one standard font/DA file that opens automatically whenever you start up your Mac (if you don't understand the advantage of that, see the Suitcase review below), you can only have one other file open, which really cramps my style and may cramp yours.

But Font/DA Juggler goes beyond Suitcase in several ways. It lets you compress font (but not DA) files on disk by as much as 40% (the files are automatically uncompressed when you open them with Font/DA Juggler).

very good feature

There's a bonus program that comes with it that lets you install Fkeys (see the glossary if you don't know what they are). A custom Fkey that comes with it lets you install an unlimited number of Fkeys on a pop-up menu (so you aren't restricted to the six available number keys). Another custom Fkey pops up a menu of available DAs and lets you select one by typing its name. A final bonus is a file containing about fifty public-domain DAs and about twenty public-domain Fkey programs.

very good feature

Like Suitcase, Font/DA Juggler costs $60. While its Fkey utilities are nice, I prefer Suitcase for managing fonts and DAs, because it doesn't limit you to two open font or DA files.

⚫ *Suitcase* *(CR)*

Suitcase is an init file and desk accessory that lets you:

• add or remove fonts and desk accessories from the ⚫ and Font menus at any time, without having to exit to the Finder and use the Font/DA Mover

very good feature

- overcome the normal limit of fifteen DAs

- load fonts and DAs automatically at startup without cluttering up your System file with them (this makes it much easier to install a new System file when a new version comes out or when your old one has gotten munched for some reason)

Suitcase gives you a whole new way to approach fonts and DAs. You can assemble custom files of fonts or DAs for different projects, and then swap them on and off your menus as you move from one job to another. You can try out new fonts or DAs without quitting the application you're running. You can access Suitcase at any time by typing (as long as your current application program doesn't use ⌘ –K for something else) as well as by choosing it from the menu.

Suitcase is such a clever, simple piece of software that Apple should buy it and bundle it with every Mac. Until they do, it'll cost you $60. *[It's worth it. Once you've used Suitcase, you can't imagine how you lived without it. —AN]*

Suitcase vs. Font/DA Juggler Plus (SH)

Personally, I prefer Suitcase because of its greater simplicity and compatibility with other utilities like Set Paths, which I find essential. Font/DA Juggler Plus uses more complex, hierarchical menus and some of its extra features are of no interest to me, but to many users, these extra features are important. Unlike Suitcase, Font/DA Juggler is copy-protected to a single machine.

You'll have to judge for yourself which program suits your style better. Both work well and you can't go wrong with either.

Suitcase and MultiFinder—the good news (SM)

Suitcase is one of the most useful desk accessories ever written for the Macintosh. And one nice feature of it comes in very handy when working with MultiFinder.

When you load an application into memory (that is, when you enter it), MultiFinder lists it at the end of the menu. This makes it easy for you to get back to that application at some later point. But Suitcase lets you load so many desk accessories at startup that those application names may be far off the bottom of the screen.

The solution? Hold down the Option key when you open the menu. All DAs except Suitcase itself will disappear from the menu, thus bringing the list of MultiFinder applications within easy reach.

very
hot
tip

Suitcase and MultiFinder—the bad news (CR)

Without giving developers a lot of warning, Apple made the space available for DAs a lot smaller in MultiFinder than it was in Finder. As a result, some early versions of Suitcase won't let you open font or DA files on the fly under MultiFinder. (This doesn't affect Suitcase's ability to install fonts and DAs automatically on startup; it does that just fine under MultiFinder.)

custom font & DA files (CR)

When creating custom font/DA sets for Suitcase or Font/DA Juggler, you can install both fonts and DAs in the same file. To do that, hold down the Option key while clicking the Open button in the Font/DA Mover. You'll be able to open (and copy from) both font and DA files, instead of just one or the other.

Font/DA Mover tips

Option *at launch* (DC)

When the Font/DA Mover opens, it normally displays fonts. If you want to install or remove a desk accessory, you have to click on that button and sit around while it dumps the fonts and loads the desk accessories. A faster way is to hold down the Option key when clicking on the Font/DA

shortcut

Mover icon; keep it held down until the Font/DA Mover window appears. It will come up with desk accessories rather than fonts displayed.

● *attaching fonts & DAs to applications* (DC)

Although the Font/DA Mover normally installs fonts and desk accessories in the System file and makes them available to all applications, you can avoid clutter in your system file (and save disk space) by attaching fonts to specific applications. To do that, hold down the [Option] key when clicking on the Font/DA Mover's Open button. You'll then be free to choose the application you want to attach the fonts to.

You can also attach desk accessories to applications (which is particularly useful with DAs that only work with one or two specific applications). To do that, hold down the [Option] key while clicking on the Open button to place desk accessories in the program's resource file instead of in the System file.

This technique will help you get around the nasty limit of only sixteen desk accessories in the system file, and you won't have to listen to the Font/DA Mover beep at you when you try to choose a desk accessory after you've reached the limit. (For an even better approach, see the programs discussed in The *Font and DA handlers* section above.)

● *ejecting disks from within Font/DA Mover* (DC)

There are two ways to eject disks from within the Font/DA Mover. The most obvious is to click on the eject button (it's in the dialog box that appears when you click on the Open button). But you can also eject a disk from the Font/DA Mover's main window by holding down the [Option] key while clicking on the Close button. This second method will save you some time if you need to use Font/DA Mover to work on several disks.

⚜ *getting file info from within Font/DA Mover* (DC)

You can see how much memory a desk accessory uses from within the Font/DA Mover. Just hold down the [Option] key while clicking on the desk accessory. The Font/DA Mover will then display the size of the desk accessory's data and resource forks, and will also tell you if the desk accessory has a PICT resource.

⚜ *Font/DA Mover* [Option] *command summary* (DC)

[Option] *key*	*effect*
at launch	opens DAs instead of fonts
+ [Click] on Open	opens applications
+ [Click] on Close	closes the open file & ejects the disk
when selecting DA in list box	shows data and resource forks
when quitting	exits, ejects both disks

very hot tip

⚜ *quick exit* (DC)

When you launch the Font/DA Mover, it can take what seems like minutes for it to read in the System file. This can be a real annoyance when it's not opening the file you want (you wanted desk accessories instead of fonts, say, or the System fonts from a different disk). Well, just click on the Quit button.

shortcut

Even though the Font/DA Mover hasn't finished reading in the file, and the list box is blank, Quit will work. The Font/DA Mover will immediately stop reading in the System file and will return you to the Desktop.

⚜ *improved handling of font and DA names* (DC)

Beginning with version 3.2 of the System, you no longer have to remove a desk accessory from the System file when

shortcut

you're installing a later version with the same name; Font/DA Mover is now smart enough to know that you want to substitute the new one. This can save you a fair amount of time.

✎ *don't use any Font/DA Mover earlier than V. 3.0* (DC)

There were some very serious problems with versions of the Font/DA Mover earlier than 3.0. They can screw up your system file but good, so don't use them.

General system utilities

✎ *recommended Control Panel settings* (AN)

When you first see the Control Panel (accessed via the ✎ menu), you may think it gives you more choices than you want. But in time you'll be glad to have them. Here's a brief discussion of what some of the controls do and my recommendations on how to set them:

In the General section, there's a setting for Desktop Pattern. The rectangle on the right shows what the background of the Desktop is currently, and the two small arrows at the top cycle you through the other available patterns. The box on the left shows an enlargement of the "tile" that makes up the pattern (the pattern is created by repeating the tile over and over again). You can modify the tile of any pattern by the normal Mac method of clicking on dots to turn them on and off.

You should probably stick with the default pattern, a medium gray, because it's quite pleasant for daily use. If you use a floppy-based system (and therefore have a variety of system files), you may find it convenient to use a different Desktop pattern to identify the different systems. You can also get fancy; for details, see the entry called *changing the Desktop pattern* below.

Not surprisingly, Rate of Insertion Point Blinking controls how fast the insertion point blinks. This is a totally subjective matter, so set it wherever you like (but do try Slow some time and see if you don't find it less distracting—I certainly do).

A RAM cache (pronounced *cash*) is a portion of memory that has been set aside to store information that's recently been read in from the disk. If the Mac needs the information again, it gets it from the RAM cache rather than from the disk. This works transparently—after you've set the RAM cache, the Mac does all the work for you. Since memory access is much faster than disk access, RAM caching can significantly speed up performance.

The larger the RAM cache, the more information can be held in it, and the longer it will be before new information read in from the disk flushes it out. On the other hand, the larger the RAM cache, the less RAM you have left for other purposes.

That all makes a lot of sense and the Control Panel's RAM Cache should be one of the Mac's more useful and powerful features. Unfortunately, Apple has apparently implemented it in some brain-dead way so that every Mac expert I know advises simply leaving it turned off.

**important
warning**

If you do use it, however, be aware that any changes you make in the RAM cache only take effect when you restart the Mac, either by choosing Restart from the Special menu or by turning the machine off and then on again. This is true both for turning RAM caching on or off, and for changing the size of the RAM cache.

Speaker Volume controls how loud the Mac's beeps (and any other sounds it makes) will be. There are eight settings, 0 through 7, with 7 being the loudest. If you don't want to hear any beeps at all, slide the control to 0; instead of making sounds, the Mac will flash the menu bar when it wants your attention (except when starting or restarting—the Mac always makes noise then).

When you change the Speaker Volume setting, the Mac gives you a sample of what the new beep sounds like, making it easy to find the volume level you want. I recommend starting with 1, then trying 2 or some higher number if you want it louder. After you've been using the Mac for a while and have a good feel for how it works, you may also want to try 0.

very good feature

On Mac II's you can choose a different sound for the beep, by changing the Alert Sound Setting in the Sound section of the Control Panel. As of this writing, Apple supplies you with three choices beyond the simple beep, but you can install many other choices with a piece of $10 shareware called SoundMaster. For more information on the three standard choices, see *a choice of beeps* in Chapter 1.

In the Mouse section of the Control Panel, there's a setting for Double-Click Speed. This tells the Mac how long it should wait after one click to see if you're going to double-click. With the long interval set, the Mac will treat clicks that are fairly far apart as double-clicks; with the short interval set, you'll have to double-click pretty fast or the Mac will think you're giving two separate clicks rather than double-clicking.

I recommend either the short interval or the medium one; if you use the long interval, you'll always be accidentally double-clicking on things and opening them when you only wanted to select them.

As for Mouse Tracking, I like this set to the fastest setting, which really helps you get the pointer where you want it quickly. It may take a little getting used to but it's worth it in the long run.

In the Keyboard section of the Control Panel, Delay until Repeat controls how long it takes before a key you're holding down begins to automatically repeat, and Key Repeat Rate controls how fast the key repeats after it begins repeating. I recommend that you set Key Repeat Rate at either of the two fastest speeds and Delay until Repeat at either of the two middle choices.

All of these Control Panel settings, plus the system time and date, are kept in a portion of memory called *parameter RAM* (also called *PRAM*)—except for the Desktop pattern, which is stored on disk. Because parameter RAM is powered by the Mac's battery, these settings aren't lost when you turn the Mac off. And because these settings are held in memory, not on disk, they stay the same regardless of what disk you're using (until you change them).

◉ *who's responsible* (AN)

For the names of the people responsible for the version of the Control Panel you're using, click in the space at the bottom where the version number is.

◉ *changing the Desktop pattern* (MB)

Backdrop and StartupDesk are two public-domain programs that let you substitute any MacPaint-format graphic for the Mac's regular gray Desktop background. (The Control Panel lets you select other patterns too, but they're all pretty boring.)

The next page shows what my Desktop now looks like, thanks to Backdrop. (Your taste may vary, but you get the idea.)

Both Backdrop and StartupDesk work OK, and neither screwed up my system. (That's saying quite a bit, since half a dozen init files, three Fkeys, a dozen DAs and more than a dozen fonts get loaded into my System file at startup.) But in ease-of-use and documentation, Backdrop is clearly superior.

To make Backdrop work, all you have to do is put it in your system folder, along with a new folder named *Screens* into which you put the MacPaint-format files you want to use. Then, every time you start your Mac, Backdrop randomly chooses one of the drawings in the Screens folder to use as a background for the Desktop. (To make it always choose the same one, only put one in there.)

very good feature

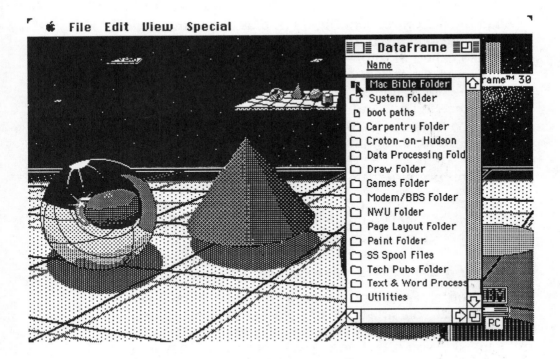

If it's a full-page drawing, Backdrop uses the top of it, so edit the files to take this into account. (Of course if you have a full-page display, you'll *want* a full-page drawing.)

StartupDesk, on the other hand, has to be installed with ResEdit, and requires that you convert your MacPaint files to a special format called StartupScreen. (The only programs I know of that can save in that format are Screen Maker and SuperPaint.)

very bad feature

Backdrop has good documentation, but StartupDesk's says, "simply install the resource in your System file (using ResEdit)," as if everyone has ResEdit and knows how to use it. It took me an hour to figure out what the developer could have explained in two minutes.

As a bonus, Backdrop also comes as a DA that lets you try out various drawings on the Desktop without having to put them in the Screens folder and then restart your Mac. (The reason Backdrop is so much better than StartupDesk is probably that it was developed as a bonus for buyers of TOPS, so there was some monetary motivation to make it a slick product.

🍎 *Complete Delete* (CR)

When you put a file in the Trash or use a standard *delete* command from inside a program, you only remove the file's directory listing from your disk—the file is still on the disk, and it can be recovered with an undelete utility like the one in MacTools. Complete Delete is a public-domain program that completely erases a file from the disk, so that there's no way it can be recovered.

🍎 *Layout* (MB)

Tired of the standard 9-point Geneva font used in the Finder? A public-domain program called Layout lets you change the font and/or type size to any in your System file. It also lets you change other defaults like the size and shape of new windows, the spacing of icons and text, and how files are Viewed in windows (by Icon, by Name or whatever).

Layout is good, bug-free software. It's available through the usual public-domain channels—bulletin boards, user groups, etc. We haven't given you the author's address in Appendix B because, according to the program's help file, he doesn't want to handle sales.

🍎 *On Cue* (PH)

If you use MultiFinder, you'll love On Cue. Even if you don't, you'll probably find this inexpensive utility very handy.

On Cue sits in the right corner of the menu bar and holds a list of applications and documents that you normally run. Under MultiFinder, selecting an application on the On Cue menu starts up that application; in the regular Finder, it quits the current application and starts up the selected one. Not having to go to the Finder each time you want to start an application is a godsend.

Installing On Cue is simple (just put it in your System Folder), and so is adding your own applications and documents.

Graphics tools

⬧ *Artisto* (DC)

If you deal with a large collection of clip art and often find yourself searching for just the right picture, you'll really appreciate the flexibility that Artisto provides. This desk accessory allows you to open any MacPaint or FullPaint document on any disk, copy all—or any portion—of it to the Clipboard (using a standard selection rectangle) and paste it directly to any application that accepts pictures.

Tom Taylor, the program's author, asks only that if you find Artisto useful, you send him a donation in any amount you like. His address is #137, 3707 Poincianna D., Santa Clara CA 95051.

⬧ *The Curator* (EA)

very good feature

The Curator is a tool for managing graphic files on disk. It lets you browse through folders and look at thumbnail versions of all the graphic images in them. You can also search by filename or by keyword (to do that, of course, you first have to attach keywords to the images). The Curator automatically reads and displays graphic images in a variety of formats—paint (i.e., bit-mapped), PICT, EPS, TIFF and Glue—and can also convert between some of them (TIFF to paint, for example, or EPS to PICT).

The Curator comes both as a DA and an application. While some of its interface tends toward the cute side, it's nonetheless a useful and clever utility for those of us whose graphic libraries are starting to get—or have already gotten—out of hand.

❡ *Camera* (DC)

You can't print a screen (with Shift Caps Lock ⌘ –4) or save it to disk (with Shift ⌘ –3) while the mouse button is pressed. This means you can't show what a screen looks like with a menu down (since the minute you release the mouse button, the menu disappears). Fortunately Keith A. Esau has written a desk accessory called Camera that gets around this problem.

Camera works like the shutter delay on a camera. You specify how many seconds you want it to wait until the screen is printed (either to the ImageWriter, or to disk as a MacPaint file). When the time has elapsed, the screen image is captured, regardless of whether the mouse button is down or not.

One neat application of Camera suggested by one of our readers, Riley Willcox of Los Altos CA, is to use it to take screen shots of key caps displays.

The only problem I've had with Camera is where it puts the MacPaint files it creates. The Shift ⌘ –3 method puts them in the window for the disk (i.e., in the root directory), but Camera puts them in the system folder. In spite of that little quirk, Camera is a terrifically useful program.

Best of all, Camera is a public-domain program. It's available on bulletin boards and information services, and from many user groups.

❡ *Capture* (AN)

Like Camera (see the previous entry), this $60 init file lets you capture areas of the Desktop even while menus are down or dialog boxes are open. You can save them in MacDraw's PICT format, which maintains their quality better than MacPaint format when you resize them. Capture works great, even with color monitors.

✦ **SmartScrap and The Clipper** *(DC)*

These two desk accessories (from Solutions International) will quickly spoil you if you use the Scrapbook a lot or if you do a lot of page layout work.

very good feature

SmartScrap replaces Apple's Scrapbook and overcomes most of its limitations. In addition to being much faster than the Scrapbook, SmartScrap lets you keep multiple Scrapbook files instead of just one. It also lets you copy just part of an image with a selection marquee. But those of us who keep large scrapbooks love the Table of Contents feature the best; it lists the contents of the scrapbook and lets you open any page just by clicking on the entry.

very good feature

The Clipper is designed specifically for page layout work; it uses a transparent window to let you size and trim the contents of the Clipboard—either by eye or by specifying precise measurements—before you paste them into your document. Once you see The Clipper in action, you'll never want to paste an image without it.

bargain

At $60, these two DAs are among the best bargains around.

Macro programs

✦ **macros defined** *(AN)*

A *macro* is a command that incorporates two or more other commands and/or text. A macro can be as simple as a keyboard equivalent to a menu command (⌘–S for *Save,* for example) or so complex that it really amounts to a miniprogram. (The name comes from the idea that the macro command incorporates "micro" commands.)

Macro programs create macro commands by recording your keystrokes and mouse clicks or by giving you a sort of pseudo programming language to write them in. Entries on some of the more popular ones follow.

◆ *AutoMac III* (TR)

This is by far the easiest to use and most elegantly designed of the macro programs I've tried. Completely rewritten from an earlier incarnation, it's now an *init* that can utilize function keys, keypad keys, the [Shift], [Option] and [⌘] keys, pauses, exact-match menu selections, precision mouse tracking, relative mouse positioning and recursive combinations of macros. Real-time recording is also an option. It's compatible with MultiFinder, and its list price is $50.

◆ *QuicKeys* (AN)

I've been using this macro program to generate "dumb quotes" (see the entry on that in Chapter 10 for more details). I found its setup instructions too complicated to do much more than that, but it's very widely used among the computer experts I know, so it must have something going for it.

In the limited way I use it, it's performed flawlessly. The keys I hit for my dumb quotes, etc., respond as quickly as any unmodified key. QuicKeys is a *cdev,* so you access it through the Control Panel. It costs $100, and with it you get DialogKeys, which gives you keyboard equivalents for buttons and check boxes in dialog boxes.

◆ *Tempo* (AN)

Tempo (from Affinity Micro-systems) lets you assign complex series of commands to [⌘]–key sequences, thus speeding up, and making less tedious, often-repeated procedures. It's also useful for simple commands for which there's no [⌘]–key sequence. The program lists for $100.

◆ *Tempo II* (TR)

With this top-of-the-line product you can not only record continuously but you can also use logical branching to control the action of macro or use a counter to repeat an action a specified number of times. Tempo comes as both a desk accessory and an init and it can also be activated with an FKey.

● *Tempo vs. QuicKeys* (PH)

I prefer Tempo II to QuicKeys because it's easier to define a macro in it. Tempo lets you define any combination of keystrokes and mouse clicks as a macro, which you can execute by pressing a ⌘ –key combination.

shortcut

A real time-saving macro for Word is one that copies all of the paragraphs with a particular style from one document to another. Because I hate programs that make you click on their opening dialog boxes before you can do any work, I create Tempo macros which start the program and then click on the opening dialog box.

Text tools

● *JoliWrite* (PH)

very good feature

This little-known DA is a $20 shareware gem from France. Like the Note Pad, it lets you create and edit text-only documents while running other programs. It's much more powerful than miniWRITER and is compatible with more software, because it doesn't take up any space on the menu bar.

● *Lookup* (CR)

very good feature

Lookup is a desk accessory that lets you search through Spellswell's 60,000 or 90,000-word dictionary (it gives you a choice) from inside any program, so you don't have to quit a program to run Spellswell itself. This is handy for checking the spelling of individual words as you're typing and editing.

In most word processor, spreadsheet and database programs—we tried Word, MacWrite, Excel and Microsoft Works—you can highlight a word to be checked and then automatically replace it with an alternative Lookup suggests (it often gives you several choices). In some programs—

MacPaint, for example—you can look up words but you can't automatically replace them.

If you don't like the alternate word Lookup suggests, you can scroll through Spellswell's dictionary to find another. You can also add words to, or delete them from, the dictionary. When you add a word, you can specify variants such as plurals, adjectives and adverbs in one dialog box, so you don't have to add all these separately.

You have to choose Lookup from the DA menu and locate the Spellswell dictionary for it the first time, but after that you can check words during the same work session by typing [Option] [⌘]–tilde (~) from the keyboard.

It's nice to have access to a large dictionary from inside any application, but Lookup only checks individual words. For the same $50 you could buy Thunder, a desk accessory that will check the spelling of whole documents from inside most applications, and which includes a glossary feature to boot.

⌘ *McSink* (PH)

This is another shareware wonder (just $25). If there's anything you want to do with text—capitalize or uncapitalize all the words in a file, sort lines, add line numbers, cut columns of text, convert tabs to spaces, etc., etc.—you can probably do it with McSink.

very good feature

⌘ *miniWRITER* (AN)

This is most people's favorite note-taking DA. Written by David Dunham of Maitreya Design, it's fast, slick and has a great (and accurate) word-count function.

very good feature

⌘ *MockWrite* (DC)

MockWrite is a favorite desk accessory of mine. If you've ever needed to take a note or two during a database or spreadsheet session, or needed to compose a message off-line for uploading to information services that charge by the minute (CompuServe, etc.), this is one of the first DAs you should get.

MockWrite provides all the standard Macintosh editing functions (Cut, Copy, Paste, etc.). The MockWrite documents you create can be printed and saved. About the only thing the program lacks is the ability to change fonts (everything is displayed in boring 12-point Monaco).

MockWrite is another great shareware bargain—it only costs $30 to register the entire MockPackage, which also includes MockPrint, a print-spooling utility, and MockTerminal, a somewhat limited communications desk accessory. If you don't have access to a BBS, an information utility or a user group, you can get the MockPackage directly from CE Software (their address is in Appendix B).

reading the unreadable with Qued/M (SS)

Have you ever had the extraordinarily frustrating experience of obtaining an exciting new program only to find that the documentation file is written for a word processor you don't own? I've sometimes gone so far as to try to read the hex pattern of the file with MacTools.

If you have a copy of Qued/M, a text editor from Paragon Concepts, there's a much easier solution. (If you don't have a copy, Appendix B tells you where you can get one.) Just enter Qued/M, select _Open...,_ Click on the Other button and turn off the _text only_ default. Qued/M will now be able to read many proprietary file formats, including Word, Works and WriteNow. The file will contain some gibberish, but the text will be there.

QuickDEX (PH)

**very good
feature**

This is the ultimate note-taking DA—so intuitive I can't even imagine using the manual. You write on the equivalent of index cards and then toss them in the card box. The Find command works at lightning speed and searches for any word on the card. You can easily create different card stacks; QuickDEX keeps track of all of them at once. It costs $60.

❡ *Quote Init* (AN)

As you type, this public-domain program substitutes true open and close quotation marks (" ") for the Mac's standard vertical quotation mark (") and a right-leaning apostrophe (') for the Mac's standard vertical one ('). It also supplies open and close single quotation marks (' ')— even when they're nested within double quotes.

very good feature

Quote Init is very smart about what to do when (for example, it can recognize the continuation of a long quotation through multiple paragraphs) and on the rare occasions when it makes a mistake (usually when you're inserting punctuation into existing text), corrections are easy— you just backspace over the character and type it again.

Once active, Quote Init works in every application (including the Finder). You can choose to have it automatically install itself at startup or wait for your command, and you can toggle it on and off with [Shift] [⌘]–apostrophe (or another [Shift] [⌘] combination of your choice) as you work. The toggling is very rapid, so it's no trouble going back and forth.

Toggling is useful for removing the vertical apostrophes from existing text. You just call up the find-and-replace dialog box (in whatever program you're in), hit [Shift] [⌘]–apostrophe (or whatever key combination you've assigned to Quote Init), type ' in the Find field, tab to the Replace field, hit [Shift] [⌘]–apostrophe again, type ' and proceed to replace.

important warning

Toggling Quote Init on and off also lets you work with programs that use [⌘]–" (i.e., [Shift] [⌘]–apostrophe) to duplicate information—a common choice, since " is a symbol for *ditto*. (You have to assign Quote Init a different key combination in those cases, of course.)

You can get Quote Init from all the usual places (CompuServe, bulletin boards, user groups, etc.). The program's author, Lincoln D. Stein, asks that you write him (at #2, 44 Boynton St., Jamaica Plain MA 02130) if you think of ways that Quote Init might be improved.

I used to be a great Quote Init fan, but now I've switched strategies. For my new one, see the entry called *dumb quotes* in Chapter 10.

text-search programs (SS)

Apple's Find File desk accessory is great when you know which file you're looking for. But what do you do when all you can remember is the topic you're looking for, or a phrase?

Well, you can use Roundup!, which searches documents by their *contents*. Version 2.0E can search Word, Works, MacWrite, More, WriteNow, Trapeze, Ready Set Go! 4 and text-only files, in whatever folder (or on whatever disk) you specify. When it finds the word or phrase you've asked it to search for, it displays it in context (within a line of text).

If you then want to open the file, Roundup! lets you move it to the Desktop for easy access. If you're not sure, you can check for the next occurrence within the same document. You can also ask Roundup! to check the next file or look at the last occurrence again.

Roundup! is both a good idea and a good start, but it has some problems and limitations. First of all, for some strange reason, it's a stand-alone program instead of a desk accessory. If I'm *already* in a word processing program, I really don't want to have to quit it to find another word processing file.

Second, there's no option to limit the file types checked. If I know that I'm looking for a MacWrite document, I don't want to waste time looking through every Roundup!-compatible file—especially if I have to search the whole hard disk for it.

Third, if you choose to move a found file to the Desktop, Roundup! automatically continues searching for another file—which isn't normally what you'd want to do. Making this the default instead of just an option is a mistake.

Finally, Roundup! is short on features. There's a full-featured text search program for the IBM PC called ZyIndex that puts it to shame. ZyIndex lets you do wildcard, and/or/not and proximity searches (e.g., find the word *disk* whenever it occurs within fifteen words of the word *duplication*). Instead of giving you a line of text for a context, ZyIndex shows an entire page. And there's a procedure for clipping text from the found document. Finally, search results are presented almost instantly because each document is preindexed by the program. (It is a bit of a pain to have to index a document before searching it, but it's worth it for the search speed it provides).

Any or all of these features would find a welcome home in Roundup!, which I don't really think is worth $50 in its present form. If you want a text-search program, you might check out GOfer, a competitor that was unavailable for review by press time. It seems to have a lot more power (at least according to the specs in its ad).

⚫ *Word Count* (DC)

Word Count is a simple desk accessory that does one thing very well: it counts, with lightning speed, the number of characters, words and lines in any Word document, or any other document saved as text only. It's another free offering from Léo Laporte.

Miscellaneous utilities

⚫ *Amortize 2.1* (CR)

Anyone can figure loan payments with a spreadsheet if you know the formulas, but this little program does all the calculations for you. All you have to do is enter the loan amount, interest rate, number of payments, payment period and starting date, and Amortize 2.1 creates a complete table showing payments, principal, interest and the remaining balance for the life of the loan.

❡ *AutoSave DA* (AN)

For all its wonderful creativity and ease of use, the Mac crashes a lot (at least mine does). And although I'm pretty diligent about backing up, it's not something I think of when I get really involved in working. So I believe that every Mac application should automatically save your work at set intervals (or should at least remind you to save). You should be able to choose the intervals between saves (or reminders) and you should be able to turn the function off when you want.

No Mac applications do that (the closest any come are several databases which automatically save each record when you go on to the next). So I was delighted to discover a desk accessory that does the job. Called AutoSave, it generates the ⌘ –key command of your choice at any interval you choose. Thus you can not only use it for automatic saves (⌘ –S on most systems), but for any other command you want to issue.

The version of AutoSave I have had some problems with MultiFinder. And then, of course, it won't work with programs that don't have a ⌘ –key equivalent for the *Save* command. In those cases, you can install a ⌘ –key equivalent with ResEdit or some other utility designed specifically for that purpose. This isn't hard, but if it feels beyond your capabilities, the store where you bought your Mac should be happy to do it for you.

By the way, if you install a ⌘ –key equivalent for *Save* in MacWrite 4.6 (or an earlier version), use ⌘ –A rather than ⌘ –S; ⌘ –A is slightly easier to reach, and you won't lose ⌘ –S's normal function (it gives you the Shadow type style).

AutoSave lists for $50. For another utility that does the same sort of thing, see the entry below on Bookmark.

❡ *BatteryPak* (DC)

BatteryPak (from a company called Batteries Included) is another useful collection of DAs. Probably the best of these is a Note Pad that holds up to 250 pages and lets you dial any phone number directly from the NotePad.

A DA called Disk Tools lets you do things from within applications that you normally have to be on the Desktop to do: create folders, copy and delete files, and Get Info on a file or a disk.

BatteryPak also includes two Hewlett-Packard-like (Reverse Polish Notation) scientific calculators, one a scaled-down version of the other. The package is not copy-protected. At $50, BatteryPak is well worth the money.

⁜ *Bookmark* (SS)

By now everyone should know the importance of saving and backing up. But you're still going to lose work if there's a power failure. My dog, for instance, has a nasty habit of wagging the Mac's power cable out of the wall.

Bookmark, a little-known utility from Intellisoft International, is just the thing for that added layer of data protection. Once installed, it saves the entire contents of RAM at any time interval or after any number of keystrokes you specify.

very good feature

You can also specify a mandatory interval at which a backup *has to* occur, a "do not disturb" interval (seconds of keyboard inactivity that have to pass before a backup is made, so you won't be rudely interrupted in the middle of a sentence), whether one or two copies are kept and whether you get an audible indication that the process is taking place.

You can even make restorations dependent on a password. A multifile option allows Bookmark to operate correctly with database and accounting programs—making sure it doesn't try to do a save during normal disk activity.

Bookmark has another use—with it, you can just turn off the Mac whenever you want, instead of having to quit the program you're in, return to the Finder and choose *Shut Down* from the Special menu. Since the Bookmark file is an

very good feature

exact copy of what was in memory, restoring from it automatically brings you back to where you left off—with the same application open, the same file loaded and the pointer where it was.

Bookmark is relatively unobtrusive. The ⌘ in the menu bar flashes to let you know when it's time to place a new bookmark. As soon as you stop typing and the *do not disturb* interval passes, the ⌘ changes to a bookmark icon and the program does its thing. Completion of the save is signaled by a double tone or, if you have that turned off, by the bookmark icon changing back to an ⌘.

There are several ways to turn Bookmark on and off or to force a save or restore. There's even a DA that shows the current program settings and lets you control most Bookmark activities while you're working.

I've only discovered a few problems with Bookmark. One is that the DA window occasionally comes up garbled in MacWrite 5.0 (closing and reopening it usually fixes it).

Second, Bookmark isn't compatible with MultiFinder. Intellisoft says they've delayed releasing a compatible version until Apple releases a more final version of MultiFinder itself. At that point, all registered Bookmark owners will receive a free copy of the compatible version.

Finally, because Bookmark works by making an exact disk-file image of RAM, you need as much free space on your hard disk as your Mac has memory—twice as much if you want to use the double backup option. If disk space is a problem, forget about Bookmark.

Bookmark works quickly on most systems, taking between three and nine seconds to perform a backup or a restore. This $100 program is flexible, easy-to-use and is bound to be a real life-saver, sooner or later.

⌘ *Calculator Construction Set* (AN/PH)

If Apple's regular calculator DA is a bit too primitive for you, Calculator Construction Set is what you want. Published by Dubl-Click Software, it lets you assemble the ultimate monster calculator of your dreams (you can stretch it to any size you want and keep loading in the keys). Then when you're done, you can install it as a desk accessory.

Rather than go into endless detail about all the functions Calculator Construction Set makes available, we'll just say that if you want it, they've almost certainly got it. And the user interface is good, so you won't have any trouble creating what you want.

very good feature

Here's a calculator Paul Hoffman put together that should give you some idea of what's possible:

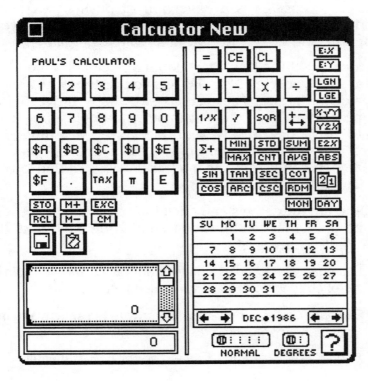

 CalendarMaker *(DC)*

This shareware program from CE software lets you create personalized calendars. You can choose any MacPaint or FullPaint image as an illustration and you can enter special

very good feature

events like birthdays, anniversaries and appointments for each date. The beauty of CalendarMaker is that you can revise a calendar as often as you like, and if you're low on funds but rich in thoughtfulness, a personalized calendar makes a great gift.

To get the most recent version of the program, along with a manual, send $20 to CE Software at the address in Appendix B. If you already have it and want to register it, just send $15.

✢ *Desk Necessities* (SS)

bargain

Desk Necessities is a collection of desk accessories, stand-alone applications and FKeys designed to make your computing life easier. At $30, it's really a bargain.

It includes three DAs. The Global Search DA will quickly find any file you specify; it also lets you restrict your search to a specific file type. FileMaster lets you copy, move, delete or rename files, or create new folders, without having to return to the Finder. DeskWriter is a Note Pad substitute that offers single or double-spacing, an adjustable left margin, a search function and near-letter-quality printing on an Imagewriter II).

There are four FKeys and each includes its own installation program that can be used to add or delete it from the System file. They are:

- *Calendar,* which shows a single month at a glance and can be scrolled forward or backward one month at a time

- *QuickInfo,* which shows free memory in the system and free space on any mounted disk volume

- *PrinterReset,* resets an Imagewriter I or II to its defaults

- *ShutDown,* same as choosing Shut Down from the Finder

Finally, there are a couple of stand-alone applications. CopyMassTer is a backup program for single-drive Macs. If you have at least a meg of memory and an 800K drive, it can save you from the disk-swapping morass. Formatter Deluxe is a utility that helps you format a lot of disks. If your system has two floppy drives, it lets you insert disks in both of them to speed things up. Although the formatting time is about the same as you'd get via the Finder, the various features and options Formatter Deluxe offers really reduce aggravation.

Desktop Help (SS)

Whenever you're working on the Mac, on-line help should be no more than a keystroke or menu command away. But even when it's provided, it's often not very good and you have to refer to the manual for the depth of information you need. This can particularly be a problem in a business where inexperienced workers are using software they're not very familiar with.

Desktop Help offers a way around that problem. It consists of two desk accessories—one called Help Editor in which you create and edit help messages, and one called simply Help, which is used to read and display the messages (when someone chooses the Help DA and then a menu command, the message you created is displayed, instead of the program executing the command).

If you're ambitious and have a programming background, you can also add context-sensitive help. Then, whenever a user clicks on an icon on the Desktop (say), your help message will appear. You can even link help information to alert dialog boxes. The program lets you create up to 10,000 of these context-sensitive help messages.

Documenting menu commands is easy with Desktop Help. At the simplest level, all you have to do is choose each menu command and write some related text. The Help Editor can read MacWrite and text files in addition to messages it creates itself, and they can include all type styles (boldface, italics, superscripts and subscripts, etc). Pictures can be created with MacPaint and pasted in. Cross-references can also be added.

But determining how all the components of Desktop Help work together will take some thinking and digging. Expect to read the manual several times and carefully examine the sample help files before undertaking your project. This is the price for the power and flexibility that Desktop Help offers. Still, a reasonably talented nonprogrammer should be able to handle the task.

There is one limitation to the program: because you can't call up any other DA while the Help Editor is active, Desktop Help can't be used to document desk accessories.

The $400 price may seem steep, but not if you consider the increased productivity you'll get as a result. One great use for this program is to add help messages to software you're selling. The price includes a one–year license to ship the Help DA with your program and free support and updates for the same period. After the first year, there's an annual license fee of $150.

⌘ *Icon-It!* (SS)

Even though pop-down menus are easy-to-use, I've often wanted a quicker way to choose commands. (Memorizing sets of command keys isn't much easier than using menus if you have more than a few programs you use regularly.) Wouldn't it be nice to have your most frequently used commands available at the click of a button? Icon-It! helps you do just that by letting you design miniature icons to represent any command in any program (and FKeys and desk accessories as well).

Icon-It! provides templates of icons for the Finder and for about forty major word processors, databases, graphics programs and programming languages. Even though the templates may not have every option you want, they're a good place to start. You can replace any icon with one of your own design or copy one in from another template.

You modify icons (or build them from scratch) in Icon-It!'s FatBits-like editor. Another part of the editor lets you specify the number of icons in the menu, as well as their height, width, spacing and screen placement. Each icon can be assigned to a menu position, a menu name or a macro command.

Icon-It! won't run on a Mac XL/Lisa or a 512K Mac with the old ROMs, and it doesn't work with MacDraw 1.9, SuperPaint 1.0, MacTerminal 2.0 or Switcher.

Icon-It! is a well-designed product and many people will find it worth the $80 it costs.

⚫ *Set Paths* (AN)

This incredibly useful $20 shareware utility helps prevent clutter in your system folder (and interminable waits when you open it). With it you can specify up to five additional folders that programs will look in when they normally look in the system folder. This lets you put away all those things that *have* to be in the system folder, like help files, printer fonts, AFM files, etc. (but be aware that some kinds of files—printer drivers, for example—have to be right out in the system folder).

very good feature

bargain

Normally you put the additional folders in the system folder, but they can be anywhere on the disk. All you have to do to set them up is open the Set Paths DA and click on them.

very good feature

Most expert users I know couldn't live without Set Paths. I certainly couldn't. Paul Snively wrote it, and you can get it directly from him by sending $20 to: Apt E, 3519 Park Lodge Ct, Indianapolis IN 46205.

⚫ *using Set Paths on a network* (SH)

Set Paths will only find one search path when used over a network.

very hot tip

⚫ *Stepping Out II* (SS)

If you've been drooling over large-screen displays but can't justify their cost, here's a $100 alternative. Stepping Out II will make the standard Mac screen act like a big

bargain

screen (or a window onto one). You can choose from a variety of preprogrammed screen sizes or create and save custom-sized screens of your own.

When you move the pointer to the edge of the screen, the view automatically scrolls over. There are also options to view the screen at a magnification of 2–16 times its original size, and at a 25%, 50% or 75% reduction. The menu bar and tool palettes stay in place no matter where you scroll, and the type on them stays normal Mac size.

Stepping Out can be set to run automatically whenever you turn on your Mac, or you can switch it on and off from the Control Panel or by holding down the Option key when launching an application. (Since some applications, like Font/DA Mover, use the Option key during launch for other purposes, you'll occasionally get a change in screen size as a side-effect.)

However you turn the program on, keep an eye on how much memory you have available. It takes a fair amount to emulate a big screen—from 100K for the simplest to over 600K for a 3' x 2' blueprint layout.

Although extremely handy, Stepping Out takes getting used to. For example, if you're in the Finder and use the Control Panel to turn off Stepping Out, your disk icons will occasionally be stranded somewhere off-screen. To get to them, you'll have to reactivate the program temporarily. Also, when you're working on a very large screen or with MultiFinder, zooming icons open or closed occurs in slow motion.

The screen-locking function is quite useful when you want everything to hold still for awhile (and not scroll)—when you're editing a detailed drawing, say. Unfortunately, there are certain display modes where it doesn't work.

If your work demands a large display and you're willing to take the time to learn the ins and outs of Stepping Out II, I think you'll find it one of the most useful programs you own.

🍎 *Talking Moose* (DC)

Talking Moose is the only desk accessory we've seen that makes almost everyone laugh out loud the first time they encounter it. When you activate it by choosing it from the 🍎 menu, Talking Moose monitors your keyboard and mouse activity. When a certain amount of time (which you specify) has elapsed without any activity, a small moose pops up in the upper left corner of the screen and says things like *What's holding things up?*, *Don't fall asleep!* and *Why don't we ever go out anymore?*

gossip/ trivia

The program's author points out that all this isn't quite as trivial as it seems. A more sophisticated program of the same type could monitor keyboard and mouse activity for content, and comment accordingly. The possibilities for self-regulating, context-sensitive, on-line tutorials are mind-boggling.

Talking Moose was written by Steve Halls of Edmonton, Canada. There's no charge for this public-domain delight. A great companion to Talking Moose is Moose Frazer, written by Jan Eugenides. This program lets you add phrases to the Talking Moose's vocabulary and is also free.

bargain

Tips on miscellaneous utilities

🍎 *FKeys* (DC)

Few people realize that the Mac has an equivalent to the function keys on an IBM PC or clone. They're called *FKeys* (*EF-keez,* short for *function keys)* and you get them by holding down [Shift], [⌘] and one of the ten number keys (1–0) that run across the top of the keyboard (the ones on the numeric keypad don't work).

esp. for beginners

Like desk accessories, FKeys are available from within applications. Five are programmed into the Mac:

[Shift][⌘]–1 ejects the disk in the internal drive.

[Shift][⌘]–2 ejects the disk in the external drive.

⇧Shift ⌘ —3 takes a snapshot of the screen and saves it as a MacPaint document on disk.

⇧Shift ⌘ —4 prints out whatever's in the active window on the Imagewriter (but not on the LaserWriter or on an ImageWriter connected on AppleTalk).

If you hold down the Caps Lock key along with ⇧Shift ⌘ —4, you get a printout of the entire screen, instead of just the active window.

That leaves ⇧Shift ⌘ —5 through ⇧Shift ⌘ —0 available for commands you choose yourself (apparently Caps Lock ⇧Shift ⌘ —4 is the only instance in which you can add to the standard ⇧Shift ⌘ —number combination).

To install an FKey, you need a program like Dreams of the Phoenix's FKey Installer, which is included in their Quick & Dirty Utilities Volume 2, and is also available free of charge on many bulletin boards with their blessings.

Many ready-made shareware and public-domain FKeys are available on bulletin boards and electronic information services like CompuServe (see Chapter 16 for information about these services). They do things like send commands to the printer, customize the keyboard and automatically blank the screen when you're not using the Mac (so you don't exhaust the phosphor). I use and like the FKey version of Q&D's desk accessory SetFile, which allows you to change file attributes and also provides the same information you get with Get Info.

❦ putting a DA at the top of the ❦ menu *(PH)*

very hot tip

If you have a copy of Apple's ResEdit program, you can make any desk accessory appear at the top of the list by putting a space at the beginning of the name. To do that, enter ResEdit and then open your System file (or the file which contains the DA) by double-clicking on it.

The window that opens lists the Macintosh resources in that file; double-click on the DRVR resource. This opens a window with the names of each desk accessory in the file.

Select the one you want to rename by clicking on it, then give the *Get Info* command from the File menu. Add a space before the name.

Close the Get Info dialog box, close the DRVR window and close the file's window. ResEdit asks if you want to save your changes; click Yes. Quit ResEdit and you'll see that DA at the top of the ⚫ menu. You don't have to reboot.

⚫ *SideKick on floppy-disk systems* (DC)

Because SideKick is a large program, it works best on a hard disk system. But there are several strategies that allow you to use it successfully on a system with floppy drives, even if they're both 400K. Here's how to do it:

If you use SideKick more than half the time you use your Mac, create a disk with the System, the Finder, the printer drivers, and SideKick and its data files on it. Then create disks that contain various applications and their data files, but no System or Finder.

If you use SideKick infrequently, it makes more sense to set up a disk with the system software and your utilities on it, and put SideKick and its data files on a separate disk. SideKick will prompt you to insert that disk as needed.

⚫ *text attributes are preserved in the Scrapbook* (DC)

When you copy or cut text into the Scrapbook, it looks like it's been converted to 12-point Geneva plain text, but in reality, none of the text formatting characteristics are lost. You get them back when the text is pasted into any application that can handle them.

esp. for beginners

⚫ *Scrapbook index* (DC)

If your Scrapbook is crammed full of stuff, you can reduce the time you spend scrolling through it by creating an index for it in your word processor and printing it out. Then you can use the scroll bar at the bottom of the Scrapbook to move directly to the page you want.

♦ copying to and from the Calculator (DC)

Few people realize that you can copy and paste to and from the Calculator DA with the same standard techniques used with other Macintosh applications. If you're dealing with a complex calculation within a word processor or some other application that doesn't do math, copy the calculation into the Calculator and paste the result to your document.

♦ speeding up Tempo macros (DC)

Tempo macros run much faster if you create them using ⌘ –key sequences (whenever possible) instead of menu choices.

♦ Tempo macros with Word (PH)

shortcut

Tempo is quite useful for assigning single-key macros to various Word 3.01 commands. Some of the ones I find handiest are for style names (normally Shift ⌘ –S style name), hide/show hidden characters, page preview (why on earth didn't they give this a ⌘ –key equivalent?) and page setup.

very
hot
tip

If your document normally has margins that make the page wider than 6.25", it's annoying to have to jump left and right as you enter or edit text. Use Tempo to create a macro that calls Page Setup and changes the right margin to a larger or smaller number.

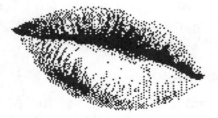

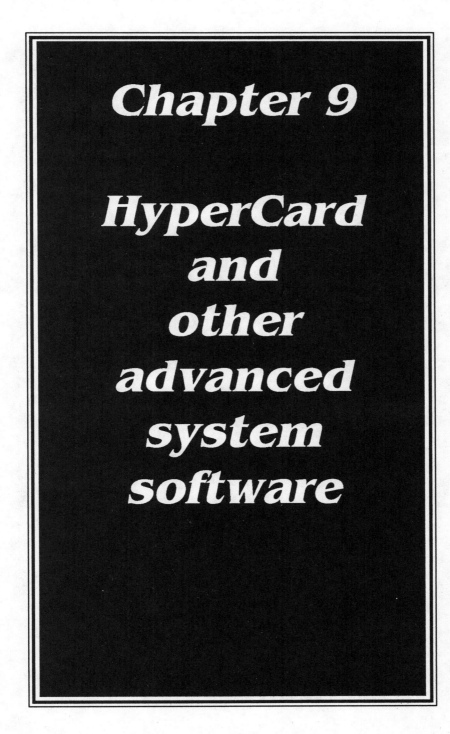

Chapter 9

HyperCard
and
other
advanced
system
software

HyperCard tips

✪ *quitting from an application* *(MB)*

When you open an application from within HyperCard, quitting the application takes you back to the card you were at. To quit to the Finder, press <kbd>Option</kbd> when you choose *Quit* and hold it down until the Finder's menu bar is displayed. (You have to choose *Quit* from the menu; pressing <kbd>Option</kbd> <kbd>⌘</kbd> –Q won't work.)

shortcut

✪ *attaching fonts & DAs* *(MB)*

You can attach fonts and desk accessories to HyperCard stacks with the Font/DA Mover in just the same way you can attach them to applications. Just hold down the <kbd>Option</kbd> key when you click the *Open* button in the Font/DA Mover's window and then select the stack you want to add them to. (For more details, see *attaching fonts & DAs to applications* in the previous chapter).

✪ *HyperDA* *(AN)*

This extremely useful desk accessory is a stripped-down version of HyperCard that lets you access stacks without having to either exit the application you're in or buy enough memory to run HyperCard and other applications under MultiFinder. It's designed for people who aren't techie but who still want to be able to refer to stacks.

✪ *improving HyperCard's dialer tones* *(MB)*

HyperCard's Address Directory stack (and stacks like it) can output touch-tone dialing sounds through the Mac's speaker. This means you can hold your phone's handset up to the speaker and have HyperCard dial for you. (On a Mac Plus, hold the handset to the lower left side of the computer; on the SE, to the lower front; and on the Mac II, to the lower right front.)

For some phones, however, the Mac's speaker isn't good enough. There are two ways around this problem. One is to use an external speaker. Get the kind that's sold for Walkman-type personal stereos; it will plug right into the Mac's sound port. But a more effective and convenient solution is to buy HyperDialer—a $35 gizmo that connects the Mac to your phone.

❡ *The HyperMedia Group* (AN)

If you'd rather have someone else create stacks (Hyper-Card demos, etc.) for you, I recommend The HyperMedia Group. In the spirit of full disclosure I should say that many of its members are friends of mine, but I've seen their work (done for clients like Apple, Claris and Novell) and been impressed by it. Contact info is in Appendix B.

❡ *simulating grayed-out buttons* (EA)

**very
hot
tip**

One Macintosh interface feature that isn't provided in HyperCard is the ability to disable—or *gray-out*—buttons. But you can achieve the same basic effect by following these steps:

1. Create the button.

2. Make a screen dump with [Shift] [⌘]–3.

3. Use a paint program to load the dump, and copy out the image of the button (you can use a new card in HyperCard to import the dump, if you want).

4. Return to the card with the button and paste the image of the button behind the button itself. Carefully align them.

5. Now hide the button and gray out the text of the image by using FatBits and the paint bucket with a gray pattern, and clicking on each letter.

6. Now you can enable the button by showing it and disable it by hiding it.

♠ *simulating list boxes* (EA)

The key to simulating a list box in HyperCard is setting
the lockText of a field to true, so the field will read the
mouse click. Once clicked, the script of the field will set the
lockText of the field to false and will use the mouse location
to decide which line to select. (This technique has been
used by several people, most notably by Frank Patrick in his
XRef-Text stack.)

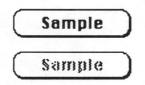

By checking for the mouseClick in the mouseUp handler,
you can sense a double-click on the field. (A more depend-
able way to sense a double-click would be to keep track of
the elapsed ticks since the original click and then vary that
number based on the desired delay for the second click.
But checking for the mouseClick usually works just fine,
and it's a lot easier.)

In the field script:

```
on mouseUp
   get the clickLoc
   put item 1 of it into Hmouse
   put item 2 of it into Vmouse
   set the lockText of me to false
   -- allow the handler to edit the text
```

```
    get the rect of me
    -- click at the same vertical location
    -- but 1 pixel inside the left edge
    click at item 1 of it + 1,Vmouse
    -- figure out how high the field is
    put item 4 of it - item 2 of it - 2 into fieldHeight
    -- based on field height and textHeight, calc num. of lines
    put fieldHeight / the textHeight of me into numLines
    -- next, check for last line (special case)
    if Vmouse > (numLines - 1) * the textHeight of me + item 2¬
      of it then
        click at item 1 of it + 1,item 4 of it - 1 with shiftKey
    else
        click at item 1 of it + 1,Vmouse + the textHeight of me¬
        with shiftKey
    end if
    set the lockText of me to true -- enable clicking again
end mouseUp
```

Version 1.2 of HyperCard provides some new commands which make this routine a little cleaner. Here's a handler you can use in 1.2 to perform the same function:

```
on mouseUp
    set the lockText of me to false
    -- allow the handler to edit the text
    click at the clickLoc
    -- place insertion point at the same position
    get the selectedLine
    -- use new "the selectedLine" to find line number
    select it  -- select the entire line (all except RETURN)
    get the selectedChunk
    -- get a chunk expression of the selection
    add 1 to word 4 of it
    -- add 1 to the end character (to include RETURN)
    select it  -- select the line with RETURN
    set the lockText of me to true  -- enable clicking again
end mouseUp
```

You can see that this is a lot more elegant than the first handler.

With either one of the handlers, be sure you size the field so that it's the correct height for the size of text you plan to use. You can determine the height of a field in HyperCard 1.2 by checking the *height* property of the field; in previous versions, subtract the top of the field's rectangle from the bottom of its rectangle. The height should be equal to the *textHeight* of the field times the number of lines that you want it to contain, plus 2 for the top and bottom borders.

After you've selected a line with either of these handlers, you can use the command *get the selection* to determine what was selected. In HyperCard 1.2, you can also use the functions *the selectedLine, the selectedChunk* and *the selectedText.*

For information on how buttons with autohiliting get along with selected text, see the next entry.

✎ *problems with selected text & autohilite buttons* (EA)

Clicking on a button which is set to autohilite causes the program to deselect any text which happens to be selected. This means that the script of the button can't do a *get the selection* to determine what text has been selected, and that means you have to use buttons that don't autohilite (which is really too bad—I prefer buttons that autohilite).

One possible alternative is to place the contents of the selection into a global variable as soon as it's selected (in the script of the field). Then it wouldn't matter if the text is deselected when a button is pressed, since the button's script could simply access the value of the global variable.

There's another possible solution: Instead of using the *Auto hilite* check box in the Button Info dialog box, you can simulate the autohiliting in the script after the selection has been grabbed. Here's a handler you can place in a button (with autohilite set to off) that puts the selection into a variable (which I call—quite cleverly—*aVariable):*

```
on mouseUp
  put the selection into aVariable
  set the hilite of me to true
  wait 5 ticks
  set the hilite of me to false
  -- continue with other steps that use the contents of¬
  "aVariable"
end mouseUp
```

✎ *hiding field scroll bars* (EA)

Field scroll bars in HyperCard don't act like normal Mac scroll bars—they're always displayed, no matter how much

very
hot
tip

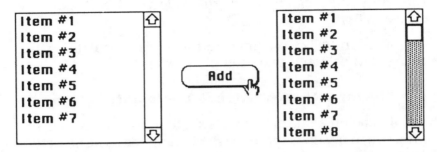

text is in the field. This is disconcerting to most Mac users, who expect the scroll bars to disappear (become blank) when there isn't more text than will fit in a field or window.

The way I've gotten around this is to create narrow, opaque fields (with lockText set to true) that cover the scroll bars when they should be blank; I call them *cover fields*. Once they're created, all that's left to do is to show or hide them as needed. Here's a script that does that:

```
on cover fieldtoCover
   get the rect of field fieldtoCover
   put item 4 of it - item 2 of it - 2 into fieldHeight
   put fieldHeight / the textHeight of field fieldtoCover¬
   into numLines
   put "Cover" && fieldtoCover into coverField
   if the number of lines in field fieldtoCover > numLines¬
   then
      hide field coverField
   else
      show field coverField
   end if
   set the scroll of field fieldtoCover to 0
end cardCover
```

Cover fields work best in list-box type fields like the ones shown above for a couple of reasons: since the text is usually inserted into the field in a controlled manner by a script, you can call the cover fields as needed; and since each line usually ends with a [Return] (rather than being word-wrapped), it's simple to ask for *number of lines*.

With wrapped text, there's no way to determine the number of "lines," since a line by definition is a string of text ending in a [Return]. So it's very hard to sense when the number of lines has changed as you're typing. *On idle* doesn't work either, because it's too disruptive.

I developed a klugy but workable solution. I found that if you *set the scroll* of a wrapping field to some very large number, then did a *click at* to click the up arrow, the field would scroll to its bottom (using *drag* to drag the scroll box would have been better, but I couldn't get it to work). Once at the bottom of the field, you can tell whether the cover field is needed by checking to see if the scroll is now greater than 0 (that is, if any text is scrolled off the top).

Hey—it works, OK?

Here's the script for wrapped fields:

```
on cover fieldtoCover
  get the rect of field fieldtoCover
  set the scroll of field fieldtoCover to 10000
  click at item 3 of it - 5,item 2 of it + 5
  put "Cover" && fieldtoCover into coverField
  get the scroll of field fieldtoCover
  if it > 0 then
    hide field coverField
  else
    show field coverField
  end if
end cover
```

Both of these handlers assume that the name of the cover field (the one that's used to cover the scroll bar) is named *Cover,* followed by a space, followed by the name of the field it will affect. To use the routine, you place one of these handlers into the card, background or stack script of your stack. Then a command like *cover "card field 1"* will perform the cover routine on any given field.

¢ *hiding dialog boxes* (EA)

When you want to hide a dialog box you've popped up over a screen, it's best to set lockScreen to true. (If you don't, you get a much messier effect as each element of the dialog box disappears.) If there are many elements to the dialog, you might also *set cursor to 4,* which changes the pointer to a watch. (With version 1.2, use *set cursor to "watch").*

⚫ *locking up stacks* (EA)

*very
hot
tip*

I fully believe in the knowledge-sharing orientation of HyperCard. Like most HyperCard programmers, I encourage others to look at and learn from my scripts and techniques. I know I've learned a lot by looking at other people's scripts.

But...there may be some applications where you prefer that the user not be able to take control of the stack. You can, of course, set a userLevel for the stack, and password-protect it. But if you want to go beyond that level, you can also make a stack look like a self-running program.

You do it by placing the handlers shown below into the stack script. For example, the doMenu handler catches all menu choices, including keyboard equivalents like ⌘–M for the Message window. It allows a menu choice to go through only if the userLevel is set to 5 (useful while you're developing a stack) or when you've chosen Protect Stack.

With key handlers like returnKey, you can decide whether or not you want to allow the keys to be active during development (for example, when userLevel is set to 5). Just the existence of the handler without a pass command means that the key won't do anything, not even beep.

Using ⌘–spacebar simply sends a *show menuBar* or *hide menuBar* command. So, you can use the show handler listed below to actually prevent the menu bar from being displayed. Three checks are made for this handler—one for the userLevel and two more to see if what was being shown is a field or a button. (HyperCard sends *<field>* when a field has been shown and *<button>* for a button. Showing buttons and fields is needed for putting up dialogs and so on.)

There's no way to trap for ⌘–period, which interrupts a script while it's executing. So the best way to protect against a script being prematurely aborted is to write an *on idle* handler which checks out what's happening—for example, what card is current, or the state of a global variable—to determine whether a script was rudely interrupted. If one was, the *on idle* handler can recover. (There'll be a pause of about three or four seconds after the ⌘]–period until the *on idle* handler picks up.)

Here are the handlers described above:

```
on doMenu choice
   if the userLevel is 5 or choice is "Protect Stack..." then
      pass doMenu
   end if
end doMenu

on returnKey
   if the userLevel is 5 then
     pass returnKey
   end if
end returnKey

on enterKey
   if the userLevel is 5 then
     pass enterKey
   end if
end enterKey

on arrowKey
end arrowKey

on tabKey
end tabKey

on show what
   if (the userLevel is 5) or (what is "<field>") or¬
   (what is "<button>") then
     pass show
   end if
end show
```

Be very careful with these handlers—one mistake and you can lock yourself out of your own stack. (It's very frustrating, believe me.) There is a way around it, however—which shows that you can't really lock up a stack completely (not yet anyway).

Let's say that the stack you've locked yourself out of is called *Locked*. First be sure you're in another stack, then type the following line into the message box:

```
edit script of stack "Locked"
```

When you press Enter , HyperCard will look for the stack called *Locked* and display its stack script. Now you can modify the script, removing any handlers—like the *doMenu* handler above—that were causing a problem.

🍎 *simulating variable arrays* (EA)

The lack of *variable arrays* in HyperTalk is a shortcoming that quickly becomes apparent to someone proficient in other programming languages like BASIC. Arrays are useful anytime you have a collection of related values you need to store. For example, in BASIC you can define a variable array to store ten salary values called SALARY(1) through SALARY(10), and wouldn't need to develop unique variable names for each of them.

So how might you use this ability in HyperCard? One way would be when you need to transfer all of the values on a given card to the same fields on another card.

For example, let's assume you have a database-style stack for which you want to create a special data entry/edit screen. This screen will contain the same background fields as the rest of the cards in the stack but it will be embellished with little tricks to facilitate entering the data, like pop-up menus to select from a list of options, check boxes, radio buttons and so on. (These types of accouterments may be difficult to tote around for use on just any card.)

Your goal is to write a script which will transfer all of the values from the input screen onto a new card at the end of the stack. Normally, you would use either just one local variable (and then jump back and forth between the input card and the data card) or individual variables (with each one stored using a separate *put* command).

The first option can easily become quite slow and the second one is inflexible and a bit long-winded. A better solution would be to build a variable array to store all of the field values for the transfer.

Even though HyperTalk doesn't provide an array function, you can fool it into creating "numbered" variables—

thereby achieving the same basic effect. You just use HyperTalk string concatenation functions to build a command for the *do* command to execute. Let's take a simple *put* statement as a model:

```
put field 1 into fieldVal
```

Here, the contents of Field 1 are placed into a variable called *fieldVal.* By using a *repeat* loop to rotate through all of the fields, you can place the contents of each field into a matching variable called *fieldValn* (where *n* is the number of that field).

For example, if you're using the variable *i* as a repeat counter, the following *do* command will build and execute the correct *put* command:

```
do "put field" && i && "into fieldVal" & i
```

For the first field, this executes the command *put field 1 into fieldVal1;* for the second field, it executes *put field 2 into fieldVal2;* and so on. A new variable is automatically created for each field.

A similar routine can then reverse the operation to place the values of the variables back into the fields of the new card. The script shown below is an example of a routine which extracts the value of all fields on an input card and then places them on a new card.

```
on mouseUp

   -- start on the input card, put values into array
   put the number of fields into fieldCount
   repeat with i = 1 to fieldCount
     do "put field" && i && "into fieldVal" & i
   end repeat

   -- create a new card at end of stack
   go last card
   doMenu "New Card"

   -- Put array values into fields
   repeat with i = 1 to fieldCount
     do "put fieldVal" & i && "into field" && i
   end repeat

end mouseUp
```

It's easy to get lost among all of the ampersands and lose track of what the final command will look like when it's built. To check it, first select the text of the command, starting with the first quote after *do*, and copy it to the Clipboard (with ⌘–C). Then close the script window and call up the message box. Put some value into the counter variable (for example, type *put 1 into i*).

Next, type *put* in the message box, type a space, paste the command you copied and press Return . This creates a *put* command that evaluates the expression to be executed by *do* and displays the result in the message box, so you can see what the command will look like after HyperCard has evaluated the string expression.

❖ *pre-1.2 script-editing shortcuts* (EA/SM)

If you aren't using HyperCard 1.2, you should be. But if, for some reason, you're still using a previous version, here are some ways to quickly edit the scripts of objects in your stack (1.2 has several tricks like these built-in).

You can place the following handlers into your Home stack script to make it easy to edit the scripts of all of your stacks.

```
on mouseDown
   if the Option Key is down then
     edit script of the target
     exit to HyperCard
   end if
end mouseDown

on controlKey num
   if num is 3 then edit script of this card
   else if num is 2 then edit script of this background
   else if num is 19 then edit script of this stack
   else pass controlKey
end controlKey
```

The *mouseDown* handler checks to see if the Option key is being held down. If it is, the script of the object is edited. This allows you to quickly call up the script of any button, locked field or card with Option Click .

The controlKey handler calls up the script for the card, background or stack when you press *control-*C, *control-*B, or *control-*S, respectively. (Note that this will only work on an SE or Mac II.) If you don't have one of these, the following handlers produce the same result:

```
on c
  edit script of this card
end c

on b
  edit script of this bkgnd
end b

on s
  edit script of this stack
end s
```

These three handlers call up the scripts of the card, background or stack when you type *c, b* or *s* (respectively) into the Message box and press ⸢Enter⸣ .

❡ *zooming fields* (EA)

You can simulate the action of a zooming window with a HyperCard field. For example, you might want to have a small field on a card that can expand to a larger size and then contract back to its original size. Here's a script that will do that:

very hot tip

```
on mouseUp
  global oldRect
  -- the variable oldRect tracks the field's original size
  if the rect of the target is not "3,23,509,339" then
    -- time to zoom
    put the rect of the target into oldRect
    -- remember orig. size
    visual effect zoom open
    go to this card
    -- produces visual effect without going anywhere
    set the rect of the target to 3,23,509,339 -- zoom
  else -- unzoom the field
    visual effect zoom close
    go to this card
    -- produces visual effect without going anywhere
    set the rect of the target to oldRect -- unzoom
  end if
end mouseUp
```

By placing this script into any locked field, you can zoom it to full size by simply clicking on it and then return it to normal size by clicking again. Of course, you could modify this to only work when, for example, the field was [Option]-clicked.

If you want to be able to zoom a field which isn't locked, use the same script but hold down [⌘] when you click on the field.

The rectangle used in the script is about full size in the HyperCard window, but you can easily modify it to make the field expand to any size and position you wanted.

You'll have to watch out for other cards or fields that appear in front of the zoomed field. To deal with that, either use the Bring Closer menu command to bring the zoomed field closer to the front or hide some of the buttons and fields each time you zoom the field.

♦ *changing the pointer while over a button* (EA)

very hot tip

You may want the pointer to change its shape when it is moved over a button on the screen, as a way of letting the user know when to press the mouse button. For example, you might want to turn it into a picture of a mouse or of a finger pointing.

You can do this by placing a *mouseWithin* handler in the card, background or stack script of your stack which changes the pointer as long as it's within the rectangle of a button. Here's the handler:

```
on mouseWithin
   if "button" is not in the target then exit mouseWithin
   set cursor to 4  -- or whatever you want
   put the rect of the target into buttonrect
   put item 1 of buttonrect into left
   put item 2 of buttonrect into top
   put item 3 of buttonrect into right
   put item 4 of buttonrect into bottom
   repeat while ¬
      the mouseH > left and the mouseH < right and ¬
      the mouseV > top and the mouseV < bottom
      if the mouseClick then
         click at the loc of the target
```

```
        exit mouseWithin
      end if
   end repeat
end mouseWithin
```

As soon as the pointer is placed within the rectangle of a button, this script begins a loop to watch where the mouse goes. If the pointer leaves the rectangle of the button, the script is ended. If the user clicks the mouse button, the script is ended, and the button click is passed through to the button.

This script can be greatly simplified in HyperCard 1.2, due to its *is within* operator:

```
on mouseWithin
   if "button" is not in the target then exit mouseWithin
   set cursor to "watch"  -- or whatever you want
   repeat while the mouseLoc is within the rect of the target
      if the mouseClick then
         click at the loc of the target
         exit mouseWithin
      end if
   end repeat
end mouseWithin
```

⚫ *repeat loops* (SM)

I wanted to replace all the *returns* in the text with *linefeeds*. The first way I thought of doing that was:

```
on cleantext theText
   repeat while theText contains return
      put linefeed into char offset(return,theText) of
theText
   end repeat
end cleantext
```

But it turned out that a faster way was to use a repeat loop:

```
on cleantext theText
   repeat with x = 1 to the number of chars in theText
      if char x of theText is return then
         put linefeed into char x of theText
      end if
   end repeat
end cleantext
```

shortcut

Even though this second routine has to step through every character in the text, it still seems to be quite a bit faster than the other way.

✎ *FullPaint default for Export Paint pictures* (SM)

To make *Export Paint* pictures FullPaint instead of MacPaint files, open Fedit, then open (a copy of) HyperCard (the program file itself). Do an ASCII search for MPNT (all caps) and replace it with PANT. Then just write the sector to disk and quit.

(This works fine, but actually, I now find MacPaint 2.0 easier to use than FullPaint.)

ResEdit tips

✎ *using ResEdit* (MB)

esp. for beginners

Macintosh software contains *resources* that control how various things appear on the screen. Here are some examples:

ALRT	alert boxes (the boxes themselves)
CURS	"cursors" (insertion point, various pointer shapes)
DITL	text in alert and dialog boxes
DLOG	dialog boxes (the boxes themselves)
FKEY	Fkeys
FOND	ID number for a font and the font's dimensions
FONT	characters of a font
ICN#	icons for an application and its documents
ICON	other icons, especially in the System file
MENU	menus
STR#	text of screen messages

A free Apple program called ResEdit (pronounced *REZ-ed-it,* short for *Resource Editor)* lets you edit all of these, graphics as well as text, so you can thoroughly customize and personalize your Mac. I'll describe how to use ResEdit by running through a couple of examples.

In many fonts, it's hard to distinguish zeros from capital O's. This can be a problem in technical fields like accounting, engineering and programming and is normally avoided by putting slashes through the zeros. ResEdit lets you add a slashed zero to any font. Here's how to add one to Courier 12:

First, duplicate your System file (or whatever file the Courier font is in) and put it somewhere safe. This is *very* important. Never use ResEdit on the System file you're using. Always work on a copy.

Next, open ResEdit. You'll get a list box. Find the System file (I'll assume from now on that that's where Courier 12 is) and Double-Click on it. ResEdit will display a list of two font resources, FOND and FONT. Click on FONT and you'll get a font-editing window like the one shown here:

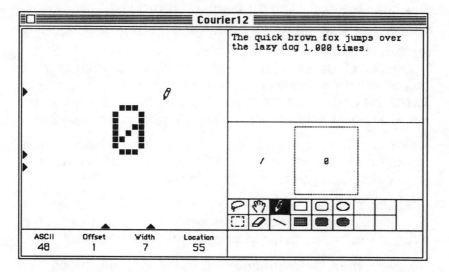

Type in a character and it will appear in the FatBits display on the left and actual size in the dashed box on the right.

(In this case, the window shows a slashed zero, but that's getting ahead of ourself; if the font already had a slashed zero, we wouldn't need to create one.)

The font-editing window also gives you a sample of the font *(The quick brown fox...)* and a palette of graphics tools. The little triangles in the FatBits display show (starting from the top left) the maximum permissible height of a character above the baseline, the baseline, the maximum permissible distance below the baseline, the left limit of a character and the right limit. When you click on a triangle, it puts a line across the window showing the limit.

important warning

In the space below the FatBits display there's the ASCII code for the character, the offset (the distance, in pixels, from the left limit to the first pixel of the character), the character's width (in pixels) and its location in the font. When you edit a character, you shouldn't change its offset or width. If you do, other characters in the font will be shifted to the left or right and will look terrible.

Fortunately, you don't have to worry about all this technical stuff to add a slash like the one shown above. All you have to do is click on pixels with the $\emptyset$.

You can edit other characters while you're at it—just remember to preserve their offsets and widths. Start by typing the character you're want to edit in the sample text box on the right. ResEdit will continually update the sample in the box while you're changing the FatBits display, so you'll be able to keep track of your changes as you go along.

When you're done, close the font editing window, then close the whole font. When ResEdit asks if you want to save your changes, click on the *Yes* button.

very good feature

ResEdit usually comes with half a dozen folders of replacement icons and pointer shapes, and you can have a lot of fun customizing your system software with them.

Unless there's documentation in the ResEdit folder that tells you which existing icons the new ones are meant to replace, you'll have to begin by opening the replacement icon and noting its resource type and ID number. Then open your own files and look for the same resource type and ID number.

For instance, a file named Random Resources came with my copy of ResEdit but there wasn't any documentation. When I opened the file, it listed three resource types— CURS, ICN# and ICON. I clicked on ICON and got the small window shown below. Clicking on the first icon produced the larger window.

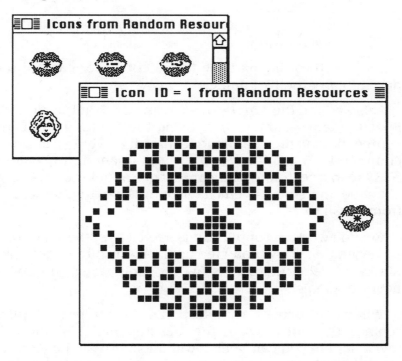

This icon's ID number is 1, so I opened the System file with ResEdit and found that the ICON 1 is the talking head icon—the one that gives you messages in a balloon that issues from its mouth.

To replace it with the lips, I made a copy of my System file and opened its ICON resources (ResEdit lets you open more than one file at a time). Then I just pasted the lips icon over the talking head icon, closed Random Resources and the copy of the System file (saving changes, of course) and quit from ResEdit. That's all there was to it.

I replaced the Trash icons (in the Finder) the same way. The empty Trash icon is ICN# 130 and the full one is ICN# 134. I started by replacing 130 with an icon named Kurt's Trash, then edited both to make them look like this:

(Empty
Trash PC)   (Full
IBM PC)

(I figure throwing garbage into a computer earns it the right to carry the IBM name.)

I also edited the *Empty Trash* command on the Finder's Special menu—simply by opening the Finder's MENU resource, finding the command, cutting it and typing in a new command—*Trash Files in PC*. Then I opened the Finder's STR# resource, found all the messages about the Trash and changed them too. I even changed the label under the icon from *Trash* to *PC*.

ResEdit works on applications as well as system files (but be aware that copy-protected applications often don't take kindly to being edited. As always, only work on copies, never originals.

When you change an application's icons, you should also replace the old ones in the Desktop file (it's normally invisible, but you can open it with ResEdit). All the icons of all the applications on your startup disk will be in the Desktop file's ICN# resource.

**important
warning**

When you edit messages and dialog boxes, keep these *Don't's* in mind.

Don't remove any items.

Don't change an item's resource type.

Don't use the DITL menu's *Send to Back* or *Bring to Front* command. (ResEdit displays a special DITL menu when you open this resource. It also displays special menus for the ALRT and DLOG resources.)

Don't edit or remove characters like *( )*, *^0* or *^1*. These are markers for meaningful text that will be added by the Mac when it displays the box.

Don't move items in the boxes, especially the items that show around the edges of the boxes when you choose the DITL menu's *Full Window* command.

Several versions of ResEdit are in circulation. Differences between versions are usually minor but it's always wise to have the latest.

Here's how I rate ResEdit (on a ten-point scale):

speed of operation	7	
grace of operation	9	
freedom from bugs	9	
error-trapping, idiot-proofing	6	(no monitoring of dumb mistakes)
intuitiveness	8	
Maclikeness	10	
ease of learning	5	(see the next item)
documentation	2	
support	8	(through user groups)
commitment to updates	5	

There's no support except through user groups, but that can be quite adequate.

don't run ResEdit under MultiFinder (SM)

Opening ResEdit while running MultiFinder is a dangerous proposition. Restart with the Finder and, as always, make sure you only work on copies.

important warning

⚫ *changing the number of open windows* (SM)

very hot tip

The Finder normally only lets you have a dozen windows open at the same time but in versions of the Finder from 6.1 on, you can change that. Open ResEdit, then (a copy of) the Finder. Find the LAYO resource, open it and scroll down to the last item. Just change the number from 12 to whatever you want, then save and exit.

⚫ *pseudoNaimanizing with ResEdit and Layout* (CR)

Shepherd Mead and Roger Galliett both wrote in to suggest ways to get the Mac to automatically tuck icons into each other—a process better known as Naimanizing. They touted ResEdit, Apple's resource editing utility, and a public-domain program called Layout.

Both Layout and ResEdit let you alter the vertical and horizontal spacing between icons or rows of icons in the Finder, so that when you use the *Clean Up* command, the icons will automatically move to staggered locations along an invisible grid without their names overlapping. You can even set the Finder so that icons always "snap to" this invisible grid and stay tidy without your having to use *Clean Up.*

gossip/ trivia

[Please note: the results produced by Layout or ResEdit will never conserve space—or please the eye—the way icons hand-Naimanized by a skilled practitioner can. No mere machine can hope to master a craft that has been refined for centuries and into which living human beings have poured their hearts and souls, their hopes and dreams.—AN]

Layout gives you other powers as well. It lets you change:

- the default in the Finder from View by icon to something else

- the formats used in View by name, date, kind and size

- the default font used in windows in the Finder

- the default size or location of windows.

It also lets you turn off the warning message that asks if you're sure you want to toss applications or system files into the Trash.

Layout is essentially a friendly user interface stuck on top of ResEdit. It lets you drag icons and grid lines around, and type information into dialog boxes; using ResEdit is much more like programming.

very good feature

Whichever program you use, make your changes to a copy of the Finder. Once you're sure everything works right, you can replace the Finder you've been using with the new, customized one. (But don't throw the old one away; put it on a floppy somewhere just in case.)

[To use ResEdit for pseudo-Naimanizing, open the Finder file, then resource type LAYO (there will only be one, with resource ID #128). Look at the vertical phase entry. If your Finder isn't pseudo-Naimanizing yet, this will read 0. Change it to the number of pixels you want the icons to be shifted (12 or 16 are good values). That's all there is to it.—Fokko Du Cloux]

very hot tip

Other advanced system software tips

🍎 clearing memory *(DC)*

The *reset* button on the programmer's switch (it's the one in the front) is handy for restarting your system, but be aware that it doesn't completely clear memory or start the Mac's self-diagnostic routines. You have to actually turn off the power switch to start with a completely reset system.

important warning

🍎 file descriptor flags *(DC)*

The Mac's file directory keeps a description of each file, which includes a set of file flags (or *bits*). These can be turned on or off with several programs, including Fedit ($30), a DA called SetFile ($10) and ResEdit (choose *Get*

Info for the file). Here's a list of the flags and what they mean:

Bozo

This file is copy-protected. (This is an obsolete method of copy protection, ignored by Finder versions 5.0 and later.)

Bundle

The Finder won't display this file's icon unless it's set to ON.

Busy

This file is open (currently being used).

Changed

This file has been changed since the very first time it was saved. (As you can imagine, most files have this flag set ON.)

Inited

(pronounced *in-IT-ed)* This file's icon has been given a specific location on the Desktop. (If you create a document from within an application, it won't be inited until you quit the application and return to the Desktop.

Invisible

The Finder won't display this file's icon.

Locked

The Finder can't delete, rename or replace this file. (This is the only flag that can be changed without a special utility like Fedit or SetFile.)

Protected

The Finder can't move or duplicate this file.

System

This is a system file.

◉ *FullPaint default for screen shots* (SM)

To save screen shots as FullPaint instead of MacPaint files, open Fedit, then open the System file. Do an ASCII search for MPNT (all caps) and replace it with PANT. Then just write the sector to disk and quit.

(This works fine but, as mentioned above, I now find MacPaint 2.0 easier to use than FullPaint.)

● *compilers vs. interpreters* (AN)

esp. for
beginners

There are two ways to implement a programming language—with a *compiler* or with an *interpreter*. Interpreters execute each line of a program individually each time the program is run, while compilers translate the whole program at once, before it's run. From that point on, you can run the compiled program whenever you want, without having to use the compiler to translate it again.

Compiling is more time-consuming when you're editing a program for mistakes, because you have to recompile the whole program each time you want to check out the effect of a change you've made (and large programs can take an hour or more to compile). But compilers are less time-consuming when you want to use the finished program over and over again.

Interpreters are better for learning, because there's no compilation time, but they run more slowly each time through.

● *the Toolbox* (DC)

One thing that makes the Mac's programming environment stand head and shoulders above that of other computers is a built-in feature called the Toolbox. It's part of the ROMs and works like this:

very good
feature

Let's say you want to draw a circle on the screen. With old-fashioned computers, you'd have to write a great deal of code specifying every aspect of making a circle. On the Mac, you simply have your program call the Toolbox and use the code already written there to draw the circle. Many wonderful things are included in the Toolbox, including all the information the Mac needs to create windows and pop-down menus.

● *out of memory message in Mac Pascal* (DC)

Macintosh Pascal programs sometimes give you an *out of memory* error. To get around it, try hiding all the windows (with the *Hide All* command) and then only use the windows as needed by the program.

❹ *keyboard shortcuts in Microsoft BASIC 2.x* (DC)

shortcut

Microsoft BASIC offers a variety of keyboard shortcuts for common commands. It makes more sense to type out some of the simple commands rather than to try to memorize all the keyboard shortcuts but some of the more commonly used ones, like PRINT or STRING$, can be quite useful.

These keyboard shortcuts are case sensitive; that is, it makes a difference whether you type in a lowercase or a capital letter. That's particularly important to remember if you usually enter your BASIC programs all in caps.

A command won't execute until you press Return. For example, if you press Option–L, the letter L will appear on your screen; only when you hit Return will the L change to AND (which is the command Option–L stands for).

this statement produced by:	*this key sequence:*	*this statement produced by:*	*this key sequence:*
AND	Option –L	ASC	Option –A
ATN	Option –C	CVS	Option –a
DATA	Option –c	EQU	Option –X
IMP	Option –B	LOC	Option –*
LOF	Option –4	LOG	Option –3
LSET	Option –6	MID$	Option –8
MKD$	Option –7	MKI$	Option –s
MKS$	Option –r	MOD	Option –N
NEXT	Option –g	NOT	Option –Y
ON	Option –2	OPEN	Option –e
OR	Option –:	PRINT	Option –u

PUT	Option –=	READ	Option –"
REM	Option –O	RETU	Option –5
RIGHT$	Option –+	RND	Option –,
RSET	Option –.	SGN	Option –y
SIN	Option –m	SPAC	Option –d
SQR	Option –w	STATIC	Option –W
STRING$	Option –p	STR$	Option –P
TAN	Option –b	THEN	Option –T
TO	Option –R	USING	Option –E
VAL	Option –0	XOR	Option –Z
WEND	Option –z	WHILE	Option –'
WRITE	Option –o		

From the WetPaint clip art collection.
Copyright © 1988–89 by Dubl·Click Software Inc.
All rights reserved.

Chapter 10

Word processing

Word processors

❡ the import/export test *(AN)*

One very important (but often overlooked) consideration when choosing a word processor is what formats it will accept files in, and what formats it's capable of exporting files in. Some programs can take text from just about any other program, and give it back just as generously. Others make you jump through hoops to export and import or only recognize a limited variety of formats.

very hot tip

❡ *FullWrite Professional 1.0* *(PH)*

Until Ashton-Tate comes out with a major fix to this program and its documentation, don't bother with it. It has many nice features, but the first release was premature (even though it was more than a year after they said it would be ready). The manuals are poorly organized and don't discuss important features. Even worse, some of the notes and hints in the manual are just plain wrong.

very bad feature

Documentation aside, the program has numerous serious bugs that were known to Ashton-Tate before the product was released, but they released it anyway. Until it works better with the LaserWriter (if you underline a word at the beginning of a line, the underline extends into the margin) and doesn't crash, it should be ignored.

very bad feature

❡ *MacWrite (AN)*

Although MacWrite was the standard Mac word processor from the Mac's inception, it no longer fills that niche very well. Microsoft Works is a better entry-level program.

Most page layout and word processing programs accept text in MacWrite 4.5 or 4.6 format, and many are being revised to accept it in MacWrite 5.0 format (which is different) as well. But MacWrite 5.0 isn't as much of an improvement as it should have been, and MacWrite seems bound to lose its privileged place as the standard low-end word processing program and text format.

⌘ *MacWrite 5.0* (AN)

This Claris update of the classic Mac word processor contains some nice enhancements, but it's mostly a case of too little, too late. It still only allows you one window, and you can't resize it to fill a large screen. It still scrolls long files very slowly. You still have to use zillions of rulers to format text.

The 5.0 file format is distinctly different from that of 4.6 and earlier versions and lots of programs can't import it (although that's likely to change). There are a lot more keyboard equivalents for commands on the menus, and that's a welcome addition.

Like earlier versions of MacWrite, 5.0 is an easy-to-use, accessible, intuitive program. But there's better stuff out there. I recommend you look at Works and WriteNow or, if you want more power, WordPerfect.

⌘ *MindWrite* (CR)

MindWrite does a lot of things other word processors don't. It offers incredibly smooth integration between outlining and word processing. You can move from outline to text views with a single command, and outline markers disappear automatically when you move to a text view (as they should but don't in Word 3.01).

MindWrite lets you open as many documents as there's room for in memory, and you can open multiple windows on the same document—a substitute for split-screen editing. MindWrite has a terrific window-management system that lets you zoom, overlay or tile windows on the screen, and you can select windows from a menu as well as by clicking. There's also a *Preferences* command so you can set the font, size, heading markers and other default options you want to have with each new document you create.

MindWrite's outliner is as capable as More, Acta or any of the other stand-alone or DA outliners when it comes to entering, sorting, arranging, expanding, collapsing and searching through outline headings (although it doesn't do the charts or calculations that More does). You can perform most functions with either the keyboard or the mouse. There's also a table of contents generator that creates a new document window listing the section headings in an outline. If you've been using ThinkTank, you can read the files directly into MindWrite.

very good feature

MindWrite's word processor has a lot of extras that show thought has gone into the program. There's an accumulating clipboard that stores everything you cut until you specifically delete it; this is very handy when you want to rearrange a lot of text. MindWrite will keep track of the date you enter text and then let you select portions of a document that were changed since a certain date or between two dates. (This is great if you collaborate with other people on your writing.) You can also get an instant word count at any time.

very good feature

The search commands are particularly impressive. For example, you can search for sections of documents that have changed since a particular date, and you can have MindWrite automatically copy all the occurrences it finds of a string and place them in a new document window. (This is handy for gathering all pieces of text marked with a special character—for indexing, for example.) You can search through text in headers and footers, or you can limit searches to open sections of outlines.

very good feature

MindWrite's formatting capabilities are like MacWrite's. You use multiple rulers to format everything, but you can set MindWrite's rulers to affect only certain levels of outlines and not others. You can put graphics into headers and footers as well as into the text itself, but you can't have text and a graphic on the same line. You can't display or print text in multiple columns, and you can't alternate headers or footers on left and right pages.

There is no built-in spelling checker, and because Mind-Write uses a proprietary file format, you have to save files as text before using a third-party spelling checker on them (in other words, it isn't worth the trouble).

very bad feature

But the biggest problem with MindWrite is its speed—or rather, its slowness. It's at least as slow as MacWrite at entering text and scrolling, especially when paragraphs get longer than fifteen lines or so. The performance also bogs down when you have a lot of stuff on the Clipboard or when you have the automatic repagination feature turned on. MindWrite is a lot slower than Word, not to mention really fast word processors like WriteNow and Works.

MindWrite used to sell for a very reasonable $125, but now it's $200. It was a bargain at $125; at $200, it's still worth serious consideration, if the unique features it offers are worth enough to you to ignore the features it doesn't have.

⌘ *a few words about Word* (AN)

Microsoft Word is the word processor most Mac experts use but I've never been able to warm up to it. It has a very unMaclike feel (which isn't surprising, since it's a patched-together imitation of Word on the PC) and it isn't very carefully thought out.

For example, it was only recently that fonts were shown alphabetically on the menu and, as of version 3.02, you still had to put them there manually or go into a dialog box to get them—they don't show up automatically.

very bad feature

Word's command hierarchy is a shambles. Basic commands (like ⌘–B for bold and ⌘–I for italic) are assigned to Shift ⌘ keys while commands you use much less often (if ever) are given simple ⌘ equivalents. In the Page Setup dialog box, tabbing takes you to text fields in this order: *Left, Top, Right, Bottom* (just the way you think of them, isn't it?).

The program is riddled with examples of this kind of thoughtlessness. Even so, it wouldn't be so bad if other programs, like PageMaker, didn't follow Word's lead, but they do—as if Word were the standard and every other Mac program some sort of aberration.

Microsoft's lack of concern for users also shows up in their manuals (which are virtually useless but totally necessary, since the program is so counterintuitive) and their selling of programs before they're done (Word 3.0 had more bugs than a New York apartment with peanut butter smeared on its walls; one wag summed it up on Compu-Serve by writing: *Word 3, Users 0*).

very bad feature

Version 4 of Word will be out soon after this book is and will undoubtedly offer many new features. But it's unlikely that it will significantly alter the program's basic feel.

❖ *Word 3.01/3.02* (DC/AN)

Word has many powerful features in these versions (3.01 and 3.02 are virtually the same program). They include:

- an index and table of contents generator

- a built-in spelling checker with an 80,000-word dictionary

- the ability to open up to sixteen windows at one time

- the ability to keep your document in RAM, instead of constantly writing it to—and reading it from—disk

- a Fast Save option that appends changes to the end of a document rather than taking the time to save the whole file (which it only does periodically)

- three unusual character styles—double underline, strike-through and "hidden" (which might be used for comments in a complicated document worked on by several people)

- customizable menus

very good feature

- an outliner you can have open in one window with the associated document open in another (they're linked, so when you scroll through the outline, the document scrolls too)

- extensive use of keyboard equivalents for menu commands (you can use the Mac without ever touching the mouse—just what you've always dreamed of, right?)

- the ability to save files in seven formats: Mac Word 3.0 (the default) , PC Word 3.0, Word 1.05, MacWrite, text only, text only with line breaks and RTF *(rich text format),* a new standard—developed by Microsoft and said to be supported by other vendors—that allows you to retain font, style and graphic information when transferring text between applications

- vertical rules (lines) at specific tab stops

- boxes around paragraphs that get bigger as you add text

- easy manipulation of columns

- the ability to do simple math on numbers in your documents

very good feature

- style sheets.

A *Style* in Word is a way of assigning formatting settings to a particular kind of text—all subheads, say, or all regular text paragraphs. (We capitalize it to distinguish it from *type styles* like bold and italic.) When you change the Style, all such pieces of text throughout the document change automatically. A *style sheet* is a collection of Styles (we don't capitalize that because there's no danger of confusion).

esp. for beginners

Word 3.01 lets you incorporate one style sheet within another. For example, you can define headlines as *normal style + centered + 24 point.* This nesting of style sheets makes it very easy to change the formatting of your document in major ways.

very good feature

For example, let's say almost all of a document is in Times (in other words, that's the normal style and several other style sheets are based on it), except for one other font that's scattered throughout. You decide you want to change Times to Bodoni. In virtually any other program, you'd have to select the whole document, change it all to Bodoni, then go back and manually insert the second font where needed. But in Word, you just change the normal font, and all the other changes ripple through.

You can even specify which style you want to immediately follow another style. Let's say you want your headlines to always be followed by a paragraph in normal style. Word will let you automatically switch back to normal style as soon as you hit the Return key at the end of the headline.

For all its powerful features, Word 3.01 (they're virtually the same program) has some serious problems. Primary among them is memory management. Dale once tried to merge a 42-record name-and-address file with a 3-page letter. That shouldn't push the limits—or even come within sight of the limits—of a $400 program. But Word couldn't do it.

very bad feature

Many of 3.01's features were already available in the DOS version of Word 3.0 and Microsoft seems to have imported them with little thought to the Mac interface. For example, you can't search for question marks because in DOS they function as *wild cards* (i.e., they stand for any character). And why do question marks stand for any character in DOS? Because they did in CP/M! And so Word beats on, a boat against the current, borne back ceaselessly into the past.

very bad feature

¢ *WordPerfect 1.0* (SB)

Thanks to its sophisticated features, quality performance and excellent technical support (an 800 number staffed by more than a hundred people), WordPerfect is the largest-selling word processor on the PC. I predict that within a year or so, it will be for the Mac as well—at least among people who feel they need an industrial-strength word processor.

things to come

The truth is, even at the office, most people don't need one. They'll never use most of the high-powered features in WordPerfect, FullWrite and Word. Many professional writers I know work in WriteNow—a less expensive, leaner program.

very hot tip

The WordPerfect screen looks a lot like MacWrite's. In fact, you can just sit down and start using it, pretending you're in MacWrite, and go on for hours without opening the manual (which, by the way, is pretty good—except for its index). *[I had a couple of problems with the manual. The page numbers are so faint you can barely read them in the low light you should have around a computer, and the ink smells so bad I can barely stand to open the manual. But at least it doesn't have a smelly vinyl cover.—AN]*

But sooner or later, your curiosity is going to get the better of you and you're going to start exploring all those menu choices. You'll find that while MacWrite 5.0 has 46 of them, WordPerfect has 154 (including those on 18 hierarchical menus—which, by the way, stay open, making them much easier to use). MacWrite gives you 29 command keys, WordPerfect 67 (all available without the extended keyboard).

If that still doesn't motivate you to tackle the 700-page manual, the on-line Help is the best I know of in any Mac program. Not only is it exhaustive, it allows you to customize command keys or execute directly from the Help files.

WordPerfect, which costs $400, has an impressive list of features unique among Macintosh word processors. Probably the most important of these is its macro recorder. You just turn it on and show it what you want it to do. Two other rare features are auto save and kerning.

very good feature

Other Mac word processors offer newspaper-style columns (where the text snakes from one column to the next). As of this writing, WordPerfect is the only one that also has screenplay-style columns, where adding material or spaces in one column causes the material in other columns on the page to move down the same distance. Up to 24 columns per page are permitted (a few more than you'll need) and they can all be different widths if you want.

The formatting characters, which are normally invisible, can be made visible on a split screen, so you can see the text as it will print on the top and with the codes in place at the bottom, where they can be edited. To help with this, there's a scrollable list of formatting codes in all three dialog boxes accessed through the Search menu.

WordPerfect has most of the features found in other top-end word processors, like leading control, mail merge, indexing, table of contents generation, an outliner, thesaurus and spelling checker. I'm especially fond of the spelling checker, one of the best available on the Mac, with a 115,000-word dictionary and a word counter. There's also an excellent file-management function that lets you to rename or delete files, create folders, Get Info, etc., without leaving the program.

very good feature

Not only is the page number visible at all times, but also the line number . If you can't remember how to get a special character, the *Insert Literal...* command gives you a window that shows the entire character set for the font you're using. Clicking on a character inserts it.

Other unusual features include vertical centering (for one-page documents) and dot leader tabs (e.g., *Ties............$2.39 ea.*). You can customize the date and time stamps and even freeze them at a certain point in time (in all other Mac programs I know of, the date and time stamps are automatically updated every time you open the document).

Unfortunately, all is not yet perfect with WordPerfect on the Mac. Some performance is disappointing and import and export are weak. WordPerfect can only bring in MacWrite, text and WordPerfect files (from the PC or whatever) and can't even export to MacWrite. Some formatting is lost when you transfer text between WordPerfect on different machines (PC to Mac, etc.).

very bad feature

But my chief complaint is that the screen is still rather jumpy. Good typists will get ahead of the program, especially when editing existing text, and characters and even lines will sometimes disappear from the screen. Usually it's only a display problem, and the missing text will come back when the word wrap changes; if not, you can restore them with the three-level Undelete function (that is, you can go back three steps instead of just one).

very good feature

The best thing about WordPerfect is its stupendous telephone support. That alone might be reason enough to choose WordPerfect over the competition.

✦ *other opinions on WordPerfect* (AN)

One Word Perfect expert I know says that the Mac version feels too PC-like to him; he only recommends it to people who are going back and forth between it and WordPerfect on the PC.

Some people really love WordPerfect's ubiquitous submenus; others find them distracting and clumsy (although everyone agrees that they're better than dialog boxes).

very good feature

In my opinion, an adequately staffed, toll-free telephone support line (not just one for orders) is an enormous advantage. And they tell you about it on the first page of the manual. With WordPerfect, you feel that you're in the hands of professionals, and ones that care about you. In the long run, that counts for more than just about anything else.

✦ *word processing with Works* (AN)

Because I do a lot of work with the programs I use, I'm very slow to change them; I don't have time to waste learning the ins-and-outs of a new program unless it has some real advantages. In the first seven years I had a personal computer, I used just two word processors— WRITE (which runs on CP/M machines) and MacWrite. But then I switched to Microsoft Works.

The advantage? It scrolls much faster than MacWrite, especially on long files. Other than that, the two programs are more or less equivalent (considered solely as writing tools, that is; Works also gives you a database, a spreadsheet and a communications module). Works makes it much easier to work with rulers and pictures, but MacWrite has better find-and-replace techniques and many more keyboard equivalents for common commands.

One thing that used to bother me about Works is its use of ⌘–P for printing rather than for plain text, which is the Mac standard. If you think that's a quibble, wait till you see how hard it is to get out of the habit of using a keyboard command that works in virtually every other Mac application. (Printing happens so seldom it doesn't need a keyboard equivalent anyway.) But then MacWrite 5.0 decided to use ⌘–P for printing as well, so I guess there really isn't a standard Mac command for plain text any more.

Although Works is marketed by Microsoft, it was developed independently. Version 2.0 (described in Chapter 15) incorporates Spellswell, one of the better spelling checkers around. All in all, Works is an impressive program. It's what I recommend to people who are buying a Mac because it's all most users need in the four areas it covers.

very good feature

❖ *WriteNow* (AN)

This is a fast, easy-to-use word processor with a slew of useful features, including nonstandard type sizes and leading control. It appeals to people who like programs that resemble sports cars rather than those that resemble 12-cylinder Bulgemobiles with electric rear-view mirrors.

very good feature

WriteNow's built-in spelling checker is particularly good at suggesting alternate spellings. Most spelling checkers use a rather simple algorithm that begins by looking at the first letter of the suspect word to determine the range of possibilities. If you type the first letter wrong, all their suggestions will be useless. WriteNow uses a much more sophisticated method for finding alternate spellings.

Despite its many good points, WriteNow had a major drawback that prevented us from recommending it: you couldn't read in files from other word processors without going out to the Desktop and using a separate file-conversion utility. This has been fixed in version 2.0, which is described in the next entry.

⚫ *WriteNow 2.0* (SB)

very good feature

Bigger isn't always better. When I'm asked to recommend a word processor, I usually suggest WriteNow. Version 2.0 imports and exports files from within the program, like other word processors. The otherwise excellent spelling checker will increase its dictionary from 50,000 to 100,000 words (although the 50,000 word dictionary will also be included for people without hard disks). A sophisticated word-count function has been added.

Other features in 2.0 include a window menu (for moving between open documents), mail merge, decimal tabs, smart quotes, fixed or variable line spacing, variable or fixed time or date stamping, upper- to lowercase conversions (and vice versa, of course), moving the pointer with arrow keys and support for MultiFinder and networks. You'll also be able to hide pictures so you can scroll faster through documents with lots of graphics.

very good feature

WriteNow 2.0 is a *free* upgrade for registered owners (way to go, T/Maker!). It hasn't shipped as I write this, so I can't tell you how well the new features work, but if you're curious about it, get the free demo disk from a dealer or user group. It's fully functional but prints *This is a Sample* across every page.

bargain

WriteNow costs a lot less than Word or WordPerfect, usually just a little over $100. This is a program definitely worth checking out.

Spelling checkers

⚫ *finding the right spelling checker* (SB)

Everyone who does word processing on a Mac should use a spelling checker. It doesn't make much difference whether you consider yourself a good speller, because most errors are typos. Spelling checkers not only help you to find these, they let you correct them quickly and efficiently.

(But remember: Since no spelling checker can find errors in which you inadvertently substitute a valid word for the one you intended (*form* for *from,* say, or *tow* for *two),* you should proofread a document one last time after running it through a spelling checker.)

I have about 25 Macintosh spelling checkers in my collection. Don't worry, you don't need to consider them all to choose one. Most of them are out-of-date (though some unscrupulous merchants still sell them). Below are thumbnail reviews of the four stand-alone products I consider active and viable in the Mac market. Pick among these and you'll be all right.

More and more Macintosh software comes with built-in spelling checkers, a trend I expect to continue. In general, these built-ins are pretty good (I discuss a few of them below), but some people may still want a stand-alone spelling checker to use with other applications, and to get features not included in a particular built-in.

things to come

All the spelling checkers discussed here offer *batch checking,* which processes an entire document, or a selected portion of it, at once. Some also offer *interactive checking,* which means the program interrupts you every time you type something it doesn't understand. Interactive checking makes me lose my concentration, but you may prefer it.

A big dictionary is one of the most important features of a good spelling checker, because it cuts down on the number of "false alarms"—correctly spelled words it doesn't recognize. The fewer of these, the faster you'll finish checking a file. Another advantage of a large dictionary is that it's more likely to offer a correct spelling as an option, which is the fastest way to make a correction.

very hot tip

I like a dictionary of at least 80,000–100,000 words. Much smaller than that and there may be more false alarms than actual spelling errors—which is an annoyance.

Most stand-alone checkers offer statistics, including word count (a feature which, as a journalist, I'm very fond of; among the built-ins discussed below, only Quark XPress and WordPerfect do.

very good feature

Many programs of both types offer extras. A glossary function is one of the more useful of those. This allows you to make a list of abbreviations and the full text they represent. Type the abbreviation and the full text appears (e.g., you type *td* when you want today's date). The text to be substituted can be quite long, so whole paragraphs of boilerplate can be put in the glossary. Some glossaries even accept carriage returns, which makes it possible for you to insert your whole address by typing a simple abbreviation.

Other extras offered by some programs include the ability to recognize the entire ASCII character set, not just the standard alphabet. This lets you put words with foreign accents and even mathematical formulas into the dictionary.

Another useful extra feature is flagging double words (like *and and*), which are both very common and among the most difficult mistakes to spot when proofreading. Some spelling checkers also look for correct capitalization and simple punctuation errors such as unmatched parentheses or quotation marks.

Automatic hyphenation and hyphenation checking are offered by many programs. PageMaker 3.0 checks hyphenation but not spelling.

very good feature

Being able to view the actual dictionary and make changes in it is very useful (especially since virtually all dictionaries contain some errors).

A final consideration when choosing a spelling checker is how many different applications it can work with without having to change the formatting. Both the DA spelling checkers discussed below have some problems with formatting, because they use the clipboard as part of their correction routine. This will cause problems with applications that don't follow Apple's guidelines (Microsoft products, for example).

✎ *Spelling Coach* (SB)

This is the direct descendant of MacLightning, a popular spelling checker of yesteryear. You get both a DA and a regular application on the disk. The DA isn't much improved over MacLightning; it's a clumsy guesser and the slowest checker discussed here. But the application version, called Coach Speller, is among the fastest (though it's just as slow at guessing).

The 154,000-word dictionary, the largest available for the Mac, comes as several modules, including ones of medical and legal terms which were previously sold separately, and also geographical and biographical names. If you're using a hard disk, install all the modules—it won't slow down the corrections (in fact, it actually speeds them up, by eliminating false alarms).

very good feature

This version of the program costs $100; Spelling Coach Professional costs $200. It's the same program but it contains two additional modules—a thesaurus (also sold separately) and a dictionary with actual definitions—which, though it takes up over a meg, only provides definitions for about half of the words in the spelling checking dictionary. All the dictionaries are supplied by Merriam-Webster and are guaranteed to be error-free.

These modules seem to be popular, because Spelling Coach Professional outsells the other version ten to one, even though it costs twice as much.

✎ *Spellswell* (SB)

One of the most popular spelling checkers, Spellswell ($75) also works with the greatest number of applications. Options include medical and legal dictionaries (expensive at $100 each) and LookUp, a DA that allows you to look up the spelling of a word from anywhere you have access to the ✎ menu. It will also paste a word selected from the dictionary into almost any program.

Spellswell checks homonyms, double words, capitalization and some punctuation (as well as spelling, of course), but it's only an average guesser. Its dictionary will soon be 105,000 words and it will be offered in a DA version too. Here's a review of it from Arthur:

⚫ *Spellswell* (AN)

Is it Spells Well or Spell Swell? Only its publisher knows for sure. Either way, their spelling checker is one of the better ones on the market (although its dictionary isn't as good as Spelling Champion's).

I used Spellswell for a while but fell afoul of its inability to ignore special characters like dashes—which, as you can see, I use all the time—and foreign accents (I was writing a book on Central America and got tired of adding words like Jos to the dictionary because Spellswell couldn't deal with the é in José).

But aside from that, this is an efficient, well-written program. If for some reason you can't use—or don't like—Spelling Champion, you definitely should take a look at it.

⚫ *Spelling Champion* (SB)

bargain

This program is an unusual combination: it's the cheapest of these four stand-alone programs ($40), has the second largest dictionary (but takes up the second smallest amount of space on disk) and is probably the fastest at actual corrections.

Spelling Champion seems more like shareware than a commercial product. The two-man company runs the business and updates the program in their spare time from their homes. Tech support is by mail or by leaving a message on their answering machine.

I like Spelling Champion very much, but some will find it too bare-bones. It has the fewest additional features of any of the four stand-alone programs discussed here. Here's what Arthur thinks of it:

✦ *Spelling Champion* (AN)

bargain

I like to work with programs that are lean and fast, even if that means sacrificing a few features, and that's why I like this stand-alone spelling checker, published at the bargain price of $40 by a small company in Wisconsin called Champion Software.

I've found that how long a spelling program takes to check a file matters a lot less than how many correctly spelled words it presents to you as suspected misspellings. One Mac spelling checker I used didn't recognize *affords, buzzer, magnify, modesty, shouldn't, sticker* and *tab.* You can, of course, add all these words to its dictionary, but that can take forever, and besides—why are you doing the work the people who wrote the program should have done?

very good feature

Spelling Champion queries me about fewer correct words than any other spelling checker I've used (except WorksPlus Spell) and it's fast, intuitive and easy-to-use. When you correct a spelling, it automatically corrects the word in the document you're checking and saves the corrected document when you're done (if you want it to). I don't like the fact that it won't check hyphenated words or add them to the dictionary (it treats them as two separate words) and I wish it were a desk accessory so I wouldn't have to keep going out to the Desktop. But basically I love it.

Champion Software offers no telephone support (although you can write them with questions). This sounds like a major drawback, but since the program is so simple to learn and use, and so inexpensive, I really don't think it makes much of a difference. Besides, the phone lines of some companies that supposedly offer support are so understaffed that they might as well not offer phone support; the effect is the same.

✦ *Thunder* (SB)

This DA spelling checker is distinctly underpowered compared to the other programs discussed here. Yet, with a major update, it could be one of the best. Though Electronic Arts has promised that rewrite for over a year, it still hasn't appeared.

very bad feature

The dictionary is too small, contains major errors and can't be corrected. The user interface is sometimes clumsy. There is a good glossary feature. This is the second slowest of these four programs and also the second cheapest ($50).

very bad feature

(I found Thunder clumsy to use and its dictionary way too small. Responding to all the false alarms was very tedious. And the word count function is totally unreliable. I was using it to pay contributors to this book by the word until I happened to recheck the count of a particularly long piece. Then I rechecked it again. And again. I got different word counts—hundreds of words different—several times in a row. Since then I've used miniWRITER to count words.—AN)

⁜ *built-in spelling checkers* (SB)

very good feature

WordPerfect's spelling checker is fast and an excellent guesser; it has a large dictionary that includes many legal terms. There's also a thesaurus and a word counter. I thought it was the best, but FullWrite Professional's and MacWrite 5.0's (both use the same program) is just about as good. It has a good-sized dictionary, is an excellent guesser and is very fast at corrections. FullWrite Professional also includes a thesaurus.

very bad feature

Word 3.01's spelling checker was frequently mentioned on the list of complaints about Word 3.0. Microsoft promised to fix it, but a year and a half later nothing had been done. Perhaps when Word 4 comes out they'll get around to it. It needs an Ignore button, so that it will not question the same word repeatedly throughout a document. Another annoying feature: if it doesn't have a guess for a misspelled word, it pops up a dialogue box in the middle of the screen telling you that, and you have to click on its OK button to continue.

WriteNow 1.09's spelling checker has long been the model for me; it's fast and efficient, and requires a minimum of motion on the user's part. There's just one problem—the dictionary is only 50,000 words. Hopefully, by the time you read this, version 2.0 will be out, which T/Maker promises will have a 100,000-word dictionary. If it does, I'd consider WriteNow the best combination of word processor and spelling checker, dollar for dollar, available on the Mac.

bargain

HabaWord has a nice spelling checker in a pretty good word processor—if it weren't for the price ($400) and the weak support of the eccentric company behind it.

Ready, Set, Go 4 has the only built-in spelling checker I really don't like. A big improvement over the one in RSG 3.0 (they've increased the dictionary to 100,000 words and added a guessing feature), it is still too bare-bones, not a very good guesser and awkward to use. Maybe with RSG 5.0 they'll finally get this part of their program right.

very bad feature

XPress 1.4 has a first-rate spelling checker. It's got a large dictionary, a word count feature and a nice interface. It's also very fast and an excellent guesser.

WorksPlus Spell (which works only with Works) is one of the best spelling checkers available on the Macintosh. The only criticism I have for it is that its dictionary is only 73,000 words. However, Works 1.1 comes bundled with Spellswell and Works 2.0 will incorporate it as a menu choice.

very good feature

(I've had a much more serious problem with WorksPlus Spell. It has a tendency to completely erase files as you're in the process of saving them! (how's that for a insidious bug?). It only happens intermittently, but how often does something like that have to happen to turn you off a program for good?

important warning

This bug was supposed to be fixed in later versions, so I eventually gave the program another shot. I thought at first the later version—1.1a2—had solved the problem, until one day it ate another one of my files. I don't have time for that kind of nonsense. So I (reluctantly) had to give up on WorksPlus Spell.—AN)

❡ *spelling checkers of the future* (SB)

things to come

In the near future, expect to see foreign-language dictionaries offered as options for both stand-alone and built-in spelling checkers. More specialized dictionaries, (technical, geographical, biographical, etc.) will also become more common.

bargain

[For a small—but free!—bibliographical and geographical dictionary, see the entry on Dictionary Helper below. (Well, all right, it's only free if you're willing to type it in. If you want it on disk, it's merely very inexpensive.)—AN]

things to come

Dictionary size will not increase greatly until floppy disk size doubles, RAM increases and/or CD ROM drives become common. At that point we'll see electronic dictionaries equivalent to the unabridged paper ones.

❡ *WorksPlus Spell* (CR)

This program fills in some of the gaps in Microsoft Works by integrating spelling checking, automatic hyphenation and a glossary feature directly into Work's word processing module. When you install it in a copy of Works, fourteen new commands show up on the Search and Format menus.

WorksPlus Spell works like most spelling checkers, flagging suspect words in context, displaying a dictionary window and offering alternative spellings (it's pretty good at guessing them). You can either select a bunch of text to be checked—the whole file, if you want—or tell it to check your spelling as you type (it beeps whenever you type a word it doesn't recognize). When checking in the batch mode, it gives you a word count of the selected text.

very good feature

Both the interactive and batch methods are quite fast. It took Spellswell over three minutes to go through a 30K file with no spelling errors in it, but WorksPlus Spell checked it in fifteen seconds, and it checked a clean 180K file (24,500 words) in about a minute. (The program does slow down, however, when it's looking for alternative spellings to suggest.) You can add your own words to the 73,000-word dictionary and you'll need to; a few of the words it doesn't contain are *accident, Asia, leaky, males, markings* and *understands.* There's a screen that lets you quickly add other forms of the word—the plural, adjective, adverb and so on.

WorksPlus Spell's hyphenation feature also works either interactively (automatically hyphenating each line as you type) or in batch mode (going back after the fact and hyphenating a selected portion of the file). The glossary feature lets you set up special abbreviations for long phrases you use frequently and then automatically replaces the abbreviation with the longer phrase as you type; it happens so quickly you barely notice. The phrase can be up to 255 characters long and can include carriage returns.

very good feature

You need a hard disk to run this program efficiently. While the program itself only takes up 65K, its spelling and hyphenation dictionaries require 146K each and Works needs about 380K. That's a total of 737K, so if you don't have a hard disk, you'll have to put your System and Finder on a second floppy and your workfiles on a third (unless they're pretty small).

If you use a lot of init files, you may find that you can't install WorksPlus Spell into Works. If you don't know what an init file is, you don't need to worry about this. But if you do have the problem, you'll have to decide if WorksPlus Spell's capabilities or those of your favorite init are more important to you.

[Sounds pretty good, doesn't it? Well, it is; in fact, it's the best spelling checker I've ever used. Unfortunately, every version of that I've tested has a brutal bug that totally destroys files. See the end of the entry before last for details.—AN]

important warning

⬥ *Word Finder* (AN)

Word Finder isn't a spelling checker, it's a thesaurus in the form of a desk accessory, but I didn't know where else to talk about it. Anyway, it's another one of those products that makes everyone who uses it wonder how they lived without it.

very good feature

Word Finder's thesaurus contains 220,000 synonyms for 15,000 words. That sounds like a lot, but I'd like it to be even more extensive. Still, it's so useful to have a thesaurus as a DA that I hardly ever consult my paper one anymore.

very good feature

Word Finder's operation is slick and obvious; it finds words fast and usually gives you a lot of them. If you need the manual to use this program, you don't know much about the Mac. At $60, this is a must-own product.

❖ Dictionary Helper (LP/AN)

very good feature

Dictionary Helper is a file of 1313 words (how's that for a lucky number?) that normally aren't found in the dictionaries of spelling checkers. Instead of having to add these words to the dictionary one by one whenever you happen to use them in something you write—which can be an incredible nuisance—just open Dictionary Helper, run your spelling checker on it and add all the words at one sitting.

That's a tedious task but it's a lot better than doing it piecemeal. Some spelling checkers will let you import all the words in bulk, so you don't have to click *OK* or *Add* for each one.

Dictionary Helper adds less than 9K to your spelling checker's dictionary(ies) but it greatly reduces the number of "false alarms"—flagged words that are actually correct. Here's what it contains:

- contractions (with both straight and curly apostrophes)
- everyday abbreviations like Thurs, Apr, St, etc.
- the 26 letters of the alphabet as stand-alone words
- the names of the 50 states, their standard two-letter abbreviations, their capitals and other major US cities
- the names of foreign countries and large foreign cities
- common US first names and nicknames

- common US last names

- common brand names

- the names of some famous people (inevitably a very subjective—and incomplete—list)

In all the above categories, names are omitted when they're also words. So, for example, the first names list omits *Art, Bill, Bob, Dawn, Frank, Pat, Ray,* etc.; the cities and states lists omit *Little Rock, New, South,* etc.; and the days of the week abbreviations omit *Sat* and *Sun.*

We may have missed a few, or decided to err on the side of caution, but it doesn't matter—if words on this list are already in your spelling checker's dictionary, all that will happen is you won't be queried about them (or, if you're importing the whole file in bulk, your dictionary(ies) will contain a few extra words).

Names are also omitted when they're in some other list. So, for example, *Jan* isn't in the list of first names because it's in the list of month abbreviations, and Lincoln, Jefferson and Madison aren't in the list of famous people's names because they're in the list of state capitals.

If you want to type out the file yourself, here it is (we don't envy you). For those of you who can't handle the boredom, we've included Dictionary Helper on the *Macintosh Bible Disk* (see Chapter 16 for ordering details). Feel free to add and/or delete words from the file to make it fit your particular needs.

bargain

aren't can't couldn't didn't doesn't don't hasn't haven't he'd he'll he's I'd I'll I'm I've isn't it'd it'll it's she'd she'll she's shouldn't should've that'd that'll that's there's they'd they're they've they'll wasn't we'd we'll we're weren't we've who've won't wouldn't would've you'd you'll you're you've

aren't can't couldn't didn't doesn't don't hasn't haven't he'd he'll he's I'd I'll I'm I've isn't it'd it'll it's she'd she'll she's shouldn't should've that'd that'll that's there's they'd they're they've they'll wasn't we'd we'll we're weren't we've who've won't wouldn't would've you'd you'll you're you've

Mon Mo Tues Tue Tu Thurs Thur Thu Th Fri Fr Sa Su Jan Feb Mar Apr Jun Jul Aug Sep Oct Nov Dec Ave Av bldg Blvd Cir Ct dept Dr hwy Ln

Rd Sq St Ste Wy NW NE SW SE amp avg cc cm ext ft gal lb ml mm mph mpg pkg pp qt tel yd yr TV VCR UHF VHF Mr Mrs Ms Jr Sr II III IV MD DDS BA AB BS MA PhD meg megs MB cps dpi Hz MHz CP/M MS DOS PC el le la los las de des di von van der San Santa a b c d e f g h i j k l m n o p q r s t u v w x y z

AL AK AZ AR CA CO CT DE DC FL GA ID IL IA KS KY LA MA MD MI MN MS MO MT NE NV NH NJ NM NY NC ND OH OK PA PR RI SC SD TN TX UT VT VA VI WA WV WI WY

Montgomery Alabama Juneau Alaska Phoenix Arizona Arkansas Sacramento California Denver Colorado Hartford Connecticut Dover Delaware Tallahassee Florida Atlanta Georgia Honolulu Hawaii Boise Idaho Springfield Illinois Indianapolis Indiana Moines Iowa Topeka Kansas Frankfort Kentucky Louisiana Augusta Maine Annapolis Maryland Boston Massachusetts Lansing Michigan Minnesota Jackson Mississippi Jefferson Missouri Helena Montana Lincoln Nebraska Carson Nevada Concord Hampshire Trenton Jersey Fe Mexico Albany York Raleigh Carolina Bismarck Dakota Columbus Ohio Oklahoma Salem Oregon Harrisburg Pennsylvania Rhode Columbia Carolina Pierre Nashville Tennessee Austin Texas Utah Montpelier Vermont Richmond Virginia Olympia Washington Charleston Madison Wisconsin Cheyenne Wyoming Columbia Juan Puerto Rico

Angeles Chicago Francisco Philadelphia Detroit Dallas Houston Nassau Pittsburgh Baltimore Minneapolis Newark Anaheim Cleveland Diego Miami Seattle Tampa Bernardino Cincinnati Milwaukee Portland Orleans Antonio Lauderdale Tucson Memphis Jacksonville Paso Tulsa Toledo Oakland Albuquerque Omaha Charlotte Louisville Wichita Birmingham Norfolk Corpus Christi Fresno Rochester Petersburg Akron Jose Ana Shreveport Lexington Yonkers Dayton Arlington Vegas Lubbock Huntington Knoxville Riverside Spokane Chattanooga Wayne Syracuse Stockton Tacoma Worcester Greensboro Berkeley Cambridge Jolla

Afghanistan Albania Algeria Andorra Angola Argentina Australia Austria Bahamas Bahrain Bangladesh Barbados Belgium Belize Benin Bhutan Bolivia Botswana Brazil Bulgaria Burma Burundi Cambodia Cameroon Canada African Chad Chile Colombia Congo Costa Rica Cuba Cyprus Czechoslovakia Denmark Dominican Ecuador Egypt Salvador Ethiopia Fiji Finland France Gabon Gambia Germany Ghana Greece Grenada Guatemala Guinea Guyana Haiti Honduras Hungary Iceland India Indonesia Iran Iraq Ireland Israel Italy Jamaica Japan Jordan Kenya Korea Kuwait Laos Lebanon Lesotho Liberia Libya Liechtenstein Luxembourg Madagascar Malawi Malaysia Maldives Mali Malta Mauritania Mauritius Monaco Mongolia Morocco Mozambique Nauru Nepal Netherlands Zealand Nicaragua Niger Nigeria Norway Pakistan Panama Paraguay Peru Philippines Poland Portugal Qatar Romania Rwanda Marino Saudi Arabia Senegal Sierra Leone Singapore Solomon Somalia Africa Spain Sri Lanka Sudan Swaziland Sweden Switzerland Syria Taiwan Tanzania Thailand Togo Tonga Trinidad Tobago Tunisia Uganda USSR SSR Volta Uruguay Vatican Venezuela Vietnam Samoa Yemen Yugoslavia Zaire Zambia Zimbabwe

Addis Ababa Ahmedabad Alexandria Algiers Amman Amsterdam
Ankara Antwerp Athens Auckland Baghdad Baku Bandung Bangalore
Bangkok Barcelona Barranquilla Beijing Beirut Belfast Belgrade Belo
Horizonte Berlin Bern Birmingham Bogotá Bogota Bombay Brisbane
Brussels Bucharest Budapest Buenos Aires Cairo Calcutta Calgary Cali
Canton Caracas Casablanca Chittagong Chongqing Cologne Copen-
hagen Cordoba Cuenca Dacca Damascus Delhi Dhaka Dnepropetrovsk
Donetsk Dresden Dublin Düsseldorf Dusseldorf Edinburgh Edmonton
Essen Frankfurt Fukuoka Geneva Genoa Glasgow Gorky Guadalajara
Guayaquil Hague Haifa Hamburg Harbin Havana Helsinki Ho Chi
Minh Hyderabad Ibadan Istanbul Jakarta Jerusalem Johannesburg
Kanpur Karachi Kharkov Kiev Kinshasa Kobe Kuala Lumpur Kuilbyshev
Lagos Lahore Paz Lausanne Leipzig Leningrad Liege Lima Lisbon
Liverpool Lódz Lodz London Lyons Madras Madrid Managua Manch-
ester Manila Marseilles Mecca Medellin Melbourne Milan Minsk
Monterrey Montevideo Montreal Moscow Munich Nagoya Nanjing
Nantes Naples Novosibirsk Odessa Osaka Oslo Ottawa Oxford Palermo
Paris Peking Porto Alegre Prague Pusan Pyongyang Quebec Quezon
Quito Rangoon Recife Rio Janeiro Riyadh Rome Rosario Rotterdam
Saigon José Santiago Santo Domingo São Sao Paulo Sapporo Seoul
Seville Shanghai Sheffield Shenyang Singapore Sofia Stockholm
Stuttgart Surabaja Sverdlovsk Sydney Taipei Tashkent Tbilisi Teheran
Tel Aviv Tianjin Tokyo Toronto Tripoli Tunis Turin Valparaiso Valencia
Vancouver Venice Vienna Volgograd Warsaw Wellington Winnipeg
Yokohama Zurich

Aaron Adam Alan Albert Alexander Alfred Alice Alicia Allen Allison
Amanda Amber Amy Andrea Andrew Andy Angela Angie Ann Anna
Anne Annie Anthony Arnie Arnold Arthur Artie Ashley Audrey Barbara
Barry Beckie Becky Ben Benjamin Benjy Bennie Bernard Bernie Beth
Betty Beverly Billy Bobby Bobbie Bonnie Bradley Brandi Brandon
Brenda Brent Brian Bruce Caitlin Candace Candice Carl Carol Carole
Carolyn Carrie Catherine Cathy Chad Charlie Charles Chelsea Cheryl
Chris Christina Christine Christopher Christie Christy Corey Cory
Courtney Craig Cynthia Dale Dan Dana Daniel Danielle Danny
Darlene Darryl Dave David Deborah Denise Dennis Derek Derrick
Diana Dick Don Donald Donna Doris Dorothy Douglas Dustin Earl Ed
Eddie Edith Edward Edwin Elaine Eleanor Elizabeth Emily Eric Erica Erin
Ernest Esther Ethel Eugene Eva Eve Evelyn Florence Frances Francis
Franklin Fred Frederick Gail Gary George Gerald Gerry Glenn Gloria
Gordon Greg Gregory Harold Harry Harvey Helen Henry Herbert
Howard Jackie Jacob Jacqueline James Jamie Jane Janet Janice Jared
Jason Jean Jeff Jeffrey Jennifer Jenny Jeremy Jerome Jerry Jesse Jessica
Jessie Jill Jim Jo Joan Joanne Joe John Johnny Jon Jonathan Joseph Joshua
Josie Joyce Judith Judy Julia Julie Juliet Juliette Justin Karen Karl Kate
Katherine Kathleen Kathy Katie Keith Kelly Ken Kenneth Kevin Kim
Kimberly Kristen Kristin Kyle Lacey Lakisha Larry Latoya Laura Lauren
Lawrence Lenny Leonard Lewis Linda Lindsay Lisa Liz Lizzy Lois
Lorraine Lou Louie Louis Louise Lori Lynn Lynne Maggie Malcolm
Mandy Marcia Marc Marcus Margaret Maria Marianne Marie Marilyn
Marion Marjorie Mark Marsha Martha Martin Marty Marvin Mary Matt
Matthew Maureen Megan Melissa Michael Michelle Mick Mickie

Micky Mike Mildred Mollie Molly Monica Nancy Natalie Nathan Ned
Nicholas Nick Nicole Norma Norman Pamela Patricia Patrick Paul Pete
Peggy Peter Phil Philip Phillip Phyllis Rachel Ralph Randy Raymond
Rebecca Renee Renée Rhonda Richard Richie Rick Ricky Rita Robert
Roger Ron Ronald Ronnie Ronny Ross Russ Russell Ruth Ryan Sally
Samantha Samuel Sandra Sarah Scott Sean Shane Shannon Sharon
Sherry Shirley Stacey Stacy Stanley Stefanie Stephan Stephanie Stephen
Steve Steven Stewart Stu Stuart Sue Susan Susie Suzanne Suzy Tammy
Tara Ted Teddy Teri Theodore Theresa Thomas Tiffany Tim Timothy
Tina Todd Tom Tommy Tony Tracy Travis Tricia Tyler Vic Victoria
Virginia Walter Warren Wendy William Yvette Zachary

Smith Johnson Williams Jones Miller Davis Martin Anderson Wilson
Harris Harrison Taylor Moore Thompson Clark Roberts Robertson
Walker Robins Robinson Peters Peterson Allen Morris Morrison Wright
Nelson Rodriguez Richards Richardson Lee Adams Mitchell Phillips
Campbell Gonzalez Carter Garcia Evans Turner Collins Parker Edwards

Macintosh Mac Sony Motorola IBM DEC NEC GE Toshiba Panasonic
Toyota Honda Acura Nissan Mazda Chevrolet Buick Pontiac Cadillac
Oldsmobile Chrysler Plymouth Jeep Porsche Volkswagen Audi BMW
Saab Volvo

Sigmund Freud Einstein Marx Engels Darwin Plato Socrates Isaac
Newton Pascal Kant Ludwig Beethoven Johann Sebastian Bach
Wolfgang Amadeus Mozart Brahms Mendelssohn Corelli Vivaldi
Ellington Armstrong Parker Gillespie Coltrane Goodman Basie Pablo
Picasso Orson Welles Humphrey Bogart Marlon Brando Hepburn Ali
Shakespeare Milton Dickens Orwell Eliot Auden Yeats Whitman Kafka
Dante Goethe Nietzsche Hugo Shelley Keats Byron Dylan Hemingway
Fitzgerald Reagan Carter Nixon Kennedy Eisenhower Truman Roosevelt
Hoover Coolidge Taft Monroe Adams Paine Gorbachev Stalin Lenin
Winston Churchill Adolph Hitler Napoleon Bonaparte Jesus Christ
Moses Jehovah Mohammed Allah Buddha Confucius Luther Brahma
Vishnu Shiva Krishna Rama

Outliners

🍎 *Acta* (DC/AN)

Outlining programs have been available on the Mac for
some time; in fact, one of the first Mac programs available
was an outliner called ThinkTank. Unfortunately, ThinkTank
doesn't follow the standard Mac interface and it isn't a desk
accessory (an outliner should be available from within your
word processing application so you can switch between it
and the text you're organizing with minimal effort).

Acta, from Symmetry Corporation, is the answer to many of ThinkTank's shortcomings. It's a desk accessory that follows the Mac interface to such an extent that you don't really need its brief but excellent manual (except possibly to look up some basic outlining terminology). That's very rare in a powerful program, and very praiseworthy.

very good feature

Acta also allows you to paste MacPaint pictures into your outline. (We can't think of any compelling reason to paste pictures into an outline, but it's the kind of thing you want to be able to do on a Mac.)

The real power of any outlining program is the ability it gives you to organize your thoughts. You just enter ideas as they occur to you, then go back and shuffle them around until they're in a logical order (or at least the order you want them to be in). In Acta, doing this shuffling is as simple as clicking on an entry (called a *topic)* and dragging it where you want it.

The terminology Acta uses is quite sensible. Topics on the same level are called *sisters*. Topics on the next level down are called *daughters* of the ones they're under. And topics on the level above—but not directly over—a topic are called its *aunts*.

Another feature that's useful in organizing your thoughts is the ability to see both the forest and the trees, the big picture and all the details. Acta accommodates this need by letting you *collapse* a topic—that is, show only the main topic, but none of the topics below it.

A triangle that precedes each topic tells you whether any subtopics are hidden under it. If the triangle is solid, there aren't any; if it's hollow, there are. If you want to see the hidden subtopics, you simply click on the hollow triangle and they're displayed instantly.

Acta files can be saved in Text, Acta or MacWrite format. Saving in MacWrite format allows you to transfer the outline to most word processing programs with all formatting intact (including any pictures you may have pasted in).

very good feature

Acta's publisher, Symmetry Corporation, distributes a public-domain program that reads the names of all the files and folders on a disk and makes an Acta outline of them. Each folder becomes a topic, and each file or folder in it becomes a daughter topic. When combined with Acta's ability to store outlines in MacWrite format, you have a handy tool for creating floppy disk labels. But it's probably most useful for keeping track of what's on a hard disk.

bargain

Although it's a bargain at $75, and is all most people need, Acta isn't the ultimate outliner. For one thing, it only lets you use eight of the fonts installed in your system file. While this isn't a devastating deficiency for an outliner, it's certainly annoying. And it's strange, too, because Acta was written by David Dunham, the author of miniWRITER, a note-pad desk accessory that looks and feels a lot like Acta but gives you access to all the installed fonts. (On the other hand, miniWriter doesn't have tabs.) Hopefully this shortcoming will be fixed in a later version.

Another drawback of Acta's is that you have to save an outline as text or a MacWrite document before you can print it. And here's a more minor complaint: when you close an Acta file and you're asked if you want to save the changes, your only options are *Yes* and *No;* the standard *Cancel* option is missing.

Acta won't do organizational charts. It won't do cloning, hoisting or a lot of other esoteric stuff. And it won't do mathematical calculations. If you need an outliner with more power than Acta, check out the next entry.

🍎 *more praise for Acta* (PH)

very good feature

I used to think I didn't like outline processors, but Acta changed my mind; it's much, much easier to use than Word's outliner. I like to begin writing projects in Acta, then convert them to Word once they're organized.

🍎 *More* (DC)

More, from Living Videotext, goes far beyond basic outliners like Acta or ThinkTank. Not only does it offer a very rich collection of features, it also adheres the Mac interface better than virtually any other program we've seen (which is particularly refreshing in view of the fact that the company's earlier product, ThinkTank, did just the opposite).

More is also one of the fastest Mac programs you'll ever use. This is mostly due to the fact that it uses a sophisticated technique called off-screen bit-mapping. After you've scrolled through a large More document, many word processors will feel positively lethargic).

very good feature

More retains ThinkTank's powerful features, like *hoisting* and *cloning*. Hoisting is useful when you're working on a particularly long or complex outline. You select a topic, hoist it, and all the rest of the outline disappears; just that topic, along with its subtopics, remains. (You can, of course, get the rest of the outline back when you want it, but it's out-of-the-way until then.) When you clone a topic, any changes you make in it are immediately reflected in the clone as well.

With a simple menu selection, More lets you create a chart of almost any kind, including bullet charts, organizational charts and tree charts, and then gives you powerful but easy-to-use tools for modifying them. You can save More outlines and charts in several formats.

You can even use More to do simple animation. Steve Michel used the Phoenix 3D program to create a globe, rotated it incrementally (saving the image with each rotation), then read the saved files into More to create an animated spinning globe.

More does math and can even be used as a simple spreadsheet. It also lets you dial phone numbers from within an outline.

For all its virtues, More does have some defects; for example, you can only work in one font at a time. Much more seriously, there's no *Undo* command—which is not only a treacherous omission but a real departure from the Mac interface.

A final drawback is the program's $300 price. That's a lot of money to pay for even the sexiest outliner imaginable—but then, More is a lot more than just an outliner.

General word processing tips

Unless otherwise noted, these tips apply to Word 3.01 and to both version 4.6 and version 5.0 of MacWrite—although most of them should also work with other versions of these programs and with other word processing programs as well.

⚫ insertion point vs. I-beam pointer *(AN)*

esp. for beginners

A common confusion among beginning Mac users (and even some who've been using the machine for a while) is between the *insertion point*—the thin, blinking, vertical line that indicates where the next character of text will appear (or disappear)—and the *I-beam pointer*, which looks like this: Ⅰ .

Basically, the I-beam pointer places the insertion point. You move it to where you want the insertion point to be and click the mouse button once.

(Unlike more primitive machines, the Mac has no *cursor*. But this term from the prehistoric world of the PC is sometimes incorrectly applied to either the pointer or the insertion point.)

⚫ em dashes, en dashes and hyphens *(AN)*

very hot tip

Em dash is the technical name for what people normally just call a dash—there's one right there. (It gets its name from the fact that it's more or less the same width as a capital *M*).

An *en dash* is half the length of an em dash and is used to indicate ranges of numbers (1926–66) or as a minus sign. (It gets its name from the fact that it's more or less the same width as a lowercase *n*.

Hyphens are shorter than either. Here's a comparison of the three:

em dash   —

en dash   –

hyphen   -

On the Mac, you get an em dash by holding down the `Shift` and `Option` keys while hitting the hyphen key, and you get an en dash by holding down the `Option` key and hitting the hyphen key.

✦ *editing italicized text* (DC)

Because of the fairly gross way italicized text is displayed on the Mac's screen, it's sometimes difficult to tell just where a given character falls. If you try to select it, you often get one of its neighbors.

esp. for beginners

The more you work with italicized text, the better your eye gets and the less this problem bothers you, but it's often easier just to change the text to plain, do your editing and then change it back to italic again.

Another useful technique is double-clicking to select words. You may not be able to see exactly where they begin and end, but the Mac knows.

very hot tip

✦ *spacing after italics* (DC)

On the ImageWriter (and the Mac's screen), italics bend so far over that they crowd, or even run into, the plain-text characters that follow them. This is particularly a problem when the last italic character and/or the first plain character is a capital letter or a lowercase *b, d, f, h, k* or *l.* (On the LaserWriter, things are easier. Laser fonts are designed so that the italic characters don't crowd the following plain text.)

Putting two spaces after the italics gives you too much room. The solution is to use the option space, which usually produces a space that's larger than a regular one but

very hot tip

smaller than two (you get it, of course, by holding down the [Option] key while hitting the space bar). See the next entry for more details.

🍎 *the option space* (AN)

very good feature

This character, generated by holding down the [Option] key while hitting the space bar, has two unique features. The first is that it's always a *hard* space—which means that if it falls at the end of a line, it won't break; instead, it will drag the word before and after it down to the next line. This is useful when you want to keep phrases like WW II and J. B. S. Haldane all on the same line, but can make for a very uneven right margin (or, if your text is justified, for lines with very loose spacing).

The second feature is that, in some fonts, the option space is wider than a regular space (but narrower than two). This is also useful for keeping italic characters from leaning into the plain text that follows them on the ImageWriter (see the previous entry for details).

The easiest way to see if a font makes the option space wider is to type a character (let's say you use *X),* hit the space bar five times, type another *X,* hit [Return] , type *X,* hold down the [Option] key and hit the space bar five times, and type a final *X.* If the option space is wider than regular spaces, the second *X* on the second line will be to the right of the second *X* on the first line; if the option space is the same width as the regular spaces, the *Xs* will line up.

The wider option space only occurs in proportionally spaced fonts (which is what most Mac fonts are); in mono-spaced fonts like Monaco, hard spaces are always the same width as regular spaces.

This combining of two features into the option space is far from ideal. When you want a hard space, you normally don't want a wide space, and when you want a wide space, you normally don't want a hard space. Eliminating the wider space only solves half the problem. Hopefully some savvy font designer will soon start providing hard spaces and wide spaces as separate characters (Option –space and ⌘ –space, say).

🍎 *curly quotes in Benguiat* (AN)

In Benguiat, the font used for regular text in this book, left- and right-leaning quotes don't look very different: " " (they actually are slightly different—one's narrower at the top and the other's narrower at the bottom—but it's very subtle). So when we're talking about curly quotes, I'll sometimes put them in Times, where they look more different: " "

🍎 *dumb quotes* (CJW)

Using smart-quote utilities like Quote Init can be annoying, because backspacing over or selecting a quote or apostrophe and then retyping it can leave it facing the wrong direction.

I prefer the "dumb quote" approach. Using QuicKeys from CE Software, I reassign the curly apostrophe (') to the straight apostrophe key and the curly quotes (" ")to the left and right curly bracket keys (i.e. Shift left and right square brackets). This way I'm always sure of typing the correct symbol. If I ever need to type a straight apostrophe or curly brackets, all I have to do is temporarily turn QuicKeys off. (Also see the entry on left and right quotation marks in the *Basic Word tips* section below.)

very hot tip

(Editor's note: Although I've been a fervent Quote Init fan, I have to admit that CJ's approach makes more sense. As soon as I get my copy of QuicKeys, I'm going to do what he suggests—except I'm going to assign the quotes to the square bracket (unshifted) keys, to make them even easier than quotes are normally.

While I'm at it, I'm going to make Shift comma and period stay comma and period, instead of becoming < and > . I'll put < and > on the \ and | key, and I'll move the square brackets to where the curly brackets are. I may even get rid of the letter Z. I hardly ever use it. *But zees may be fooleesh.* Yeah, I guess I was getting carried away. Z can stay.)

(This late-breaking news: I've done it and I love it. Dumb quotes and shifted period and comma are definitely the way to go. And I was right to keep the Z. Film at 11, showing it in use.—AN)

🍎 *custom letterhead* (AN)

There are no particular tricks for creating a letterhead— although creating a nice one requires a great deal of skill and taste. But here's a trick on how to deal with one once it's been created:

Assuming you have access to the Mac and a laser printer on a regular basis, don't waste your time printing out blank sheets of letterhead that you'll then have to feed one by one into the printer when you want to use them. Instead, create a dummy letterhead document with your letterhead at the top and a few words in the font you use for letters below it. Here's a sample, using Fluent Fonts' Monterey and Monterey Medium, from CasadyWare:

Jack Twiller
512 Pet-de-Loup Boulevard
Halitosis ND 58353
701/ 555-1941

Month 00, 1989

Dear

**very
hot
tip**

Save this document as *letterhead* or some similar name. Then every time you want to write a letter, open it and immediately *Save As...* under whatever name is appropriate for the letter you're going write.

Then select *Month 00* and change it (unless the date actually happens to *be* Month 00), then place the insertion point after *Dear* and begin writing. When you print out the letter, the letterhead will print out at the top.

You can (and probably should) have more than one letterhead for use with different sorts of letters (business, personal, etc.)

If you have a specialized signature, you can either make it the last item in your dummy letterhead document or drop it in from the Scrapbook or SmartScrap. Here's one I use:

Of course there's no need for you to feel limited to something as stodgy as this.

(The gorilla was drawn by master Mac artist Mei-Ying Dell'Aquilla and is available on the ClickArt Personal Graphics disk from T/Maker.)

🍎 *text does it better* (CJW)

I initially save any writing I do as straight (ASCII) text. This has several advantages. First, nearly all utility programs, including spelling and grammar checkers, can handle text files, whereas many of them choke on proprietary formats like Word's Fast Save.

Second, you can use Style sheets (as in Word or Page-Maker) to add formatting later. This lets you ignore font styles and other formatting considerations while you're writing, so you can concentrate entirely on content.

A third benefit is that text-only files are significantly smaller than their formatted counterparts. You'll be able to put more files on a disk, and it will cost you less to send the files over phone lines.

ᗡ *selecting large amounts of text* (DC)

*esp. for
beginners*

When you want to select a large amount of text, your first impulse may be to start at the beginning and drag until you reach the end, waiting patiently as you scroll through your document. To speed things up, try the shift-click method:

[Click] the pointer at the beginning of the text you want to select, then use the scroll bar to move to the end of the selection, hold down the [Shift] key, and [Click] the pointer where you want the selection to end. All the text between the two clicks will be selected.

This technique also works if you start at the end of the selection and shift-click at the beginning. (Shift-clicking is a general Mac tip that works with many applications. For more details, see the entry on it in Chapter 4.) Word offers a number of other ways to select large amounts of text. See the entry *basic selection commands* in the Word section below.

ᗡ *estimating the number of words in a document* (AN)

To get the most accurate word count of a word processing document, use one of the many spelling checkers that give you this information. But if you don't need to be absolutely precise, you can just divide the number of characters by six.

Some people divide by five, but it's hard to figure how they arrive at that number, since anywhere this side of third grade there are more than five characters in an average word. I'm sure of that because for many years I used a word processing program that gave me both word and character counts; I divided one into the other countless times—in order to decide this very issue—and always came up with a number very close to six. Since I don't use a lot of fancy, sesquipedalian words (except for that one), most normal writing should average about the same. (Maybe they came up with five characters per word by not counting spaces. That might explain it.)

Since Word displays the number of characters in a document in the lower left corner of the screen immediately after you save, all you have to do is divide that figure by six. (There's also a desk accessory called Word Count that very quickly counts the number of words and lines in Word documents; it's described in the utilities chapter.)

MacWrite doesn't count words or characters—although you can, of course, get a character count by exiting to the Desktop and using the *Get Info* command. But from within MacWrite you can get the number of K (kilobytes) in the document you're working on (it's in the *About MacWrite...* window on the menu, and that's enough for a quick-and-dirty word-count estimate. Here's how you figure it:

There are 1024 characters in a K (except when someone's trying to sell you a disk drive) and 1024 divided by 6 equals 170.67...for you, 170. So to get the number of words in a document, you can just multiply the number of K by 170.

Here's a table with some convenient (but approximate) conversions:

very hot tip

1K	=	170 words	30K =	5000 words
3K	=	500 words	50K =	8500 words
6K	=	1000 words	60K =	10,000 words
10K	=	1700 words	75K =	12,500 words
15K	=	2500 words	100K =	17,000 words

To make your estimate more accurate, you should subtract some figure for the "overhead" of your word processing program. For example, if you open a new (empty) MacWrite 4.5 document and immediately save it, you'll find that it contains 1148 bytes (although there are no words in it).

As you add rulers and other formatting instructions, the amount of overhead increases. Graphics in particular will inflate the figures for both the number of K and the number of characters in a document, thus throwing your calculations off.

✪ *finding your place in a document* (DC)

When you open a MacWrite document, it displays the screen you were looking at when you last saved it. That isn't always where the insertion point is, or where you were last working. To get to that place, hit the Enter key. (You can also get there by hitting any key that generates a character, but then you have to delete the character when you get there; Enter leaves no mark.) This same technique is also useful when you're looking through a document and have lost track of where you were working.

important warning

But—if you had some part of the document selected when you last saved, it will be deleted (technically, it will be replaced with the Enter character, which is invisible). You can still recover the deleted text with Undo (⌘-Z)—assuming you realize what happened before the next mouse click or keystroke.

very hot tip

For this and other reasons, it's a good idea—except in certain special situations—to never leave part of a MacWrite document selected when you close it. For that matter, it's a good idea never to leave text selected in a document any longer than you have to, even while you're working on it. You might go off somewhere else and forget about it, and then accidentally delete it.

You don't run this danger in Word, because it ignores selected text when saving (that is, if text is selected before you save, it won't be afterwards). But you can't use ⌜Enter⌝ to find your place in a Word document that you've saved, because Word always places the insertion point at the beginning of the document after saving.

⏧ *text markers* (DC)

Few word processors have a specific function that lets you mark places in a document so you can return to them later. But it's easy enough to do that simply by inserting unique characters (like *##1, ##2* and so on, or any other combination of characters that wouldn't appear in normal text). Then you just use the *Find* command to move to these points in your document quickly. This technique will work with any word processing program available for the Macintosh.

⏧ *deleting text without flushing the Clipboard* (DC)

If you're keeping a picture or important text in the Clipboard for later use, it's important not to unintentionally flush the Clipboard's contents by using *Cut* from the Edit menu (or the keyboard shortcut ⌜⌘⌝–X). To avoid this, delete the text by hitting the ⌜Backspace⌝ key rather than ⌜⌘⌝–X. (You can still change your mind and restore what you deleted by choosing *Undo Typing* from the Edit menu or by using the keyboard shortcut ⌜⌘⌝–Z.)

esp. for beginners

⏧ *aligning columns* (DC)

When setting up a table (or anything else with columns in it), always use tabs—never spaces—to align the columns. If you use spaces, the columns will almost never print out straight. (But see the next entry for an even better way to deal with multiple columns.)

esp. for beginners

⏧ *multiple columns* (DC)

MacWrite won't automatically format text in more than one column, and while Word will, it won't show the columns on the screen. Thus in both programs it's very difficult to create tables. One solution is to use a spreadsheet program like Multiplan or Excel to create the table, then paste the information into a word processing document. The tabs you've set in your word processing program will determine where the spreadsheet columns will appear.

If you create tables frequently, you may want to use a DA spreadsheet (there are several available). It's so easy to cut and paste back and forth between it and your word processing document that it's just about as good as having a multiple-column feature built right in.

⚫ *mixing words and pictures* (DC/AN)

Neither MacWrite nor Word nor WordPerfect will let you put text on the same line as a graphic—unless you combine the text with the graphic in the graphics program before you paste it in.

There are a couple of minor exceptions to this generalization. One is that in the header and footer of a MacWrite document, you can place the special icons for page number, date and time on top of graphics and they'll print out there. The second is that you can use Word's side-by-side columns feature and put the picture in one column and the text in another.

The word processing module of Microsoft Works does let you put text on either side of your picture and move it around quite freely with a grabber hand.

⚫ *distorted graphics* (DC)

You may notice some distortion when you paste MacPaint pictures, especially ones that contain circles, into word processing programs. This is because word processors typically squeeze the image of the page to make it narrower, in order to make text look better when printed out on the ImageWriter.

One way to correct this distortion is to choose Tall Adjusted in the Page Setup window. Your text will now print out wider on the ImageWriter than usual, but graphics will look just the way they do when you print them directly from MacPaint.

🍎 *nonproportional printing* (DC)

On rare occasions you may want to produce a Mac document that doesn't have proportional spacing. Just format the entire document in Monaco (or any other monospaced font). The result will look a lot like a traditional typewritten page.

🍎 *recovering trashed MacWrite files with Word* (DC)

If you have a MacWrite document MacWrite itself can't read, try reading it with Word (enter Word, go to the Open list box, open the document and click OK when Word tells you it's converting it). Word is somewhat more sophisticated in this area than MacWrite and will sometimes succeed where MacWrite failed.

🍎 *importing word processing files to the Mac* (DC)

If you need to import a word processing document from another type of computer to the Mac, the first step takes place on the foreign computer. Regardless of the word processing program being used, save the document as a text file. Some word processing programs call text files *ASCII* (which, in case you're interested, stands for *American standard code for information interchange* and is pronounced *ASK-ee).*

If you neglect this step, you almost certainly won't be able to use the document after it gets to the Mac, because most word processing programs embed formatting codes in the text that appear as gibberish on the Mac's screen.

Unfortunately, WordStar won't allow you to save a document as a text file (although it will let you create text-only documents from scratch). If you need to import WordStar documents, you'll be happy to hear there's a public-domain utility called UnWS that strips out the

very good feature

unwanted embedded format commands from the WordStar document. (It was written by Paul Hoffman, who also contributed several tips to this book.)

● *excess carriage returns in imported documents* (DC)

Sometimes when you transfer a document created on another computer into a word processing program on the Mac, you'll find carriage returns ending each line. Since MacWrite, Word and most other Mac word processors only use carriage returns to mark the end of paragraphs, having them at the end of every line will make the text look ragged and strange. So you'll need to remove all the excess ones.

If you're using MacWrite, you'll have to go through the document and remove each carriage return manually, but Word's *Change* command can search for returns and thus will do the job automatically. See the entry on *removing carriage returns from imported documents* in the *Advanced Word tips* section below for details on how to do that.

● *different margin defaults in MacWrite and Word* (DC)

One problem with importing documents from MacWrite to Word is that Word's default left margin is zero while MacWrite's ruler comes preset with an eighth-inch indent. To reset the indent to zero once you've got the document in Word, select the entire document, choose *Show Ruler* and drag the lower of the two little black triangles at the left end of the ruler over to zero.

Basic Word tips

Unless otherwise noted, these tips apply to Word 3.01, although most of them should also work with Word 4 and later versions of the program.

● *the "selection bar"* (AN)

Beginning Word users must often be confused by the term Microsoft uses to refer to the narrow, invisible column to the left of your text (it's used for selecting text; you know you're in it because the pointer changes from an I-beam to an arrow). Although *bar* virtually always implies a horizontal line—so much so that another Microsoft program, Excel, uses it to distinguish a bar chart (horizontal lines) from a column chart (vertical lines)—Microsoft calls this vertical column the *selection bar.*

esp. for beginners

⚫ *nonstandard type sizes* (DC)

Unlike MacWrite, which only lets you enter text in six standard sizes (9-, 10-, 12-, 14-, 18- and 24-point), Word lets you specify anything from 4-point to 127-point (in whole numbers). You specify the point size by choosing *Formats...* on the Character menu (or hitting ⌘–D) and then simply typing it in.

esp. for beginners

⚫ *preventing pointless saves* (DC)

Word has a nice feature that prevents you from wasting time with pointless saves. If you try to save a document that you haven't made any changes to since the last time you saved, Word simply ignores the command.

very good feature

⚫ *new paragraph vs. new line* (DC)

Word can seem like a quirky program when you first start using it, particularly if you're used to MacWrite. One of Word's idiosyncrasies that can cause a great deal of confusion is the way Word handles formatting information.

Word makes a distinction between a new paragraph and a new line. Unlike other word processing programs, Word stores each paragraph's format in the carriage return (generated by hitting the Return key) at the end of each paragraph. You may need to start a new line in a document without starting a new paragraph (and therefore a new format). This is particularly useful when creating a table.

Rather than use the Return key at the end of each line, use Shift Return. This will start a new line, but Word will not treat it as the beginning of a new paragraph and the formatting will stay the same. (This is also known as a *soft carriage return;* the regular one that ends paragraphs is called a *hard carriage return.*)

When you hit ⌘-Y to cause Word to display hidden characters, Word uses ¶ to indicate new paragraphs (hard carriage returns) and · to indicate new lines (soft carriage returns). You can even Search for them. Just use *^p* to represent the new paragraph symbol and *^n* to represent the new line symbol in either the Find or Change dialog box. (See the entry on *searching for special characters* in the *Advanced Word tips* section for more details.)

⁂ *shrinking Word files* (CJW)

very hot tip

To shrink the size of Word files, try using *Save As...* instead of *Save;* when the dialog box appears, uncheck Fast Save and save. This will reduce file size by about 10%–25%. As a side benefit, you'll also eliminate those annoying incompatibilities with programs that can read Word files except when they're Fast-Saved.

⁂ *left and right quote marks* (SZA)

If for some unaccountable reason you're not using Quote Init or QuicKeys to give you left- and right-leaning (" ") quotation marks (for details, see the entry titled *dumb quotes* in the *General word processing tips* section above, or the one on Quote Init in Chapter 8), you can use your word processor's find-and-replace function to replace all your plain (") quotation marks with them.

To do that, you have to assume that every left (also known as an *open,* or *leading*) quotation mark will be preceded by a space—which is almost always the case. (Right—also known as *close,* or *trailing*—quotation marks aren't necessarily followed by a space, since the next character may be a punctuation mark or, in programs like Word, a paragraph marker.)

Given that assumption, you can change to left and right quotes in two passes. First, replace every instance of *(space)* " (that's a plain quotation mark—it's just the italics that are making it slanted) with a left quotation mark, which you get by hitting $\boxed{\text{Option}}$–[. Then replace every remaining instance of the plain quotation mark with a right quotation mark, which you get by hitting $\boxed{\text{Shift}}$ $\boxed{\text{Option}}$–].

very hot tip

⚫ *toggling window sizes (SZA)*

There are four ways you can toggle between a full-screen Word document window and the size and shape window you've created:

shortcut

- $\boxed{\text{Click}}$ on the zoom box *(at the right end of the title bar)*

- $\boxed{\text{Double-Click}}$ on the title bar itself

- $\boxed{\text{Double-Click}}$ on the size box in the lower right corner

- press $\boxed{\text{Shift}}$ $\boxed{\text{Option}}$–] *(right bracket)*

⚫ *window splitting (SZA)*

You don't have to drag the split bar to split a window; $\boxed{\text{Option}}$ $\boxed{\text{⌘}}$–S has the same effect.

shortcut

⚫ *cycling through windows (SZA)*

When you have multiple windows on the screen, use $\boxed{\text{Option}}$ $\boxed{\text{⌘}}$–W to cycle through them (this sends the topmost window to the bottom of the pile).

shortcut

⚫ *keyboard scrolling (SZA)*

To scroll the contents of a window from the keyboard, use $\boxed{\text{Option}}$ $\boxed{\text{⌘}}$–[(left bracket) and $\boxed{\text{Option}}$ $\boxed{\text{⌘}}$–/ (slash). The first is equivalent to pressing the up arrow in the scroll bar; the second is the same as pressing the down arrow in the scroll bar.

shortcut

⚫ $\boxed{\text{⌘}}$ *arrow keys (SZA)*

You can extend the basic arrow-key movements with the $\boxed{\text{⌘}}$ key. Combining $\boxed{\text{⌘}}$ with ← or → moves you to the

shortcut

beginning of the previous word or to the beginning of the next word. Combining it with ↑ or ↓ moves you to the beginning or end of the current paragraph.

(If you're already at the beginning of a word or a paragraph, these commands move you to the beginning of the previous one; if you're already at the end, they move you to the end of the next one.)

the "top of paste" jump *(SZA)*

very hot tip

After you paste something into your document, the insertion point is left at the bottom of the pasted-in material. To jump back to the top, just use the keypad zero. (Since all pastes are done at the insertion point, the top of the paste is always the previous position of the cursor.)

special deletes *(SZA)*

As you no doubt know, the Backspace key (the *delete* key on some keyboards) erases the character to the left of the insertion point. You can also use it to delete whatever amount of text you've selected. But Word has other delete commands as well:

Option ⌘ –F erases the character to the *right* of the insertion point.

Option ⌘ Backspace deletes the previous word—or, if you're in the middle of a word, everything from the insertion point to the beginning of the word.

Option ⌘ –G deletes the next word—or, if you're in the middle of a word, everything from the insertion point to the end of the word.

recovering text Undo can't *(CJW)*

If you've ever deleted or changed something and then changed your mind after the *Undo* command can no longer help you recover it, give this a try:

First, save your current document under a different file name (using the *Save As...* command); this protects you from losing whatever work you've done since the last time you saved. I recommend you call the new file *trash me* and put it right out on the Desktop, rather than in a folder, so it will be easy to find later.

Next, open the original file—let's say it's called *letter*—and resize the two windows so you can read both *letter* and *trash me*. Copy the text you want to recover from *letter* to *trash me*. When you're done, save the updated *trash me* as *letter*. Be sure to put it in the same folder so it will replace the old version of *letter*.

That's all there is to it. When you next quit to the Finder, put *trash me* in the Trash. It will have done its job and you'll no longer need it.

⚫ *eliminating shifting text* (SZA)

If you're typing in the middle of an existing paragraph, it can be really distracting to have the rest of the paragraph shifting to the right and down as you insert text. To avoid this, put a paragraph marker to the right of the insertion point, by pressing Option ⌘ Return . This pushes the rest of the paragraph down and leaves the insertion point where it was.

*esp. for
beginners*

When you're finished inserting text, use Option ⌘ –F (delete right) to remove the temporary paragraph marker; this joins the two paragraphs again.

⚫ *scanning a long document* (SZA)

If you've ever used a real outliner, you'll find Word's Outliner feature clumsy (and that's being polite). But, it is good for something—when you switch to Outline mode, the first line of each paragraph in your document is displayed. This makes it very easy to skim through a long document when you're looking for something.

✦ *not losing your place in a Word file* (PH)

very
hot
tip

If you're editing a document and want to making some changes in another part of it without losing your place, use the following steps:

- Option ⌘]–S to split the screen

- scroll either half and do the work you want

- Option ⌘]–W to return to the window that shows the part of the document you were working on at first

- Option ⌘]–S to close the other window

✦ *keeping headings attached* (PH)

Always select *Keep with next paragraph* for all your headings. This prevents the heading from falling at the bottom of the page and the first paragraph of text at the top of the next page.

✦ *supercharging Change To:* (SZA)

The *Change To:* text box in the Change dialog box (on the Search menu) has a limit of 255 characters, and it doesn't let you specify font or type styles in the replacement text. You can get around both those limitations by inserting the contents of the Clipboard into the *Change To:* box.

To do that, just use ^C—that is, the caret (Shift]–6) followed by the letter c (cap or lowercase, it doesn't matter). This lets you replace something short with something very long, or something plain with something fancy.

For example, say you want to change every occurrence of *Apple* to **Apple**. Make the first occurrence of *Apple* bold, select it and copy it to the Clipboard. Choose the *Change* command. In the *Find What:* box type *Apple* and in the *Change To:* box type ^c. Then click on the *Change All* button and every occurrence of *Apple* in your document will be changed to boldface.

⚫ *the Again command* (SZA)

The Again command—⌘-A—repeats the last command, or the last related group of commands. So if you've applied a bunch of character formats in a row, Again applies all of them; the same goes for paragraph formats. If you've typed a lot of text without stopping for format commands, all the text is repeated, as if you had typed it.

shortcut

For example, let's say you select a word, make it bold and italic, and underline it. Select another word, hit ⌘-A, and that word will be bold, italic and underlined. Or let's say you just applied a Style to a paragraph. Select another paragraph, hit ⌘-A and the Style is applied there too. (For more on Styles, see the entries that begin with *styles vs. Styles* below.)

⚫ *finding again* (SZA)

To find another occurrence of the word, phrase or format you last searched for, you don't have to open the Find or Change dialog boxes again: just press Option ⌘-A.

shortcut

⚫ *the footnote window* (SZA)

To review or edit text in the footnote window, hold the Shift key down while you drag the split bar, or press Shift Option ⌘-S. To close the footnote window, drag the split bar to the top or bottom of the window, or press Option ⌘-S.

You don't have to close the footnote window after typing text into it. You can just Click in the main part of the window to continue working on your document, or use this trick: press 0 (zero) on the keypad and the insertion point will appear in the main document immediately after the footnote reference mark.

⚫ *customizing menus* (SZA)

You can add many commands to (or subtract them from) Word's menus. To add them, press Option ⌘-plus sign (+).

This gives you the *plus pointer,* which looks something like this (only bigger): **+** . (Calling it `Option` `⌘` –plus helps you remember the command, but you don't actually have to hold down the `Shift` key; in other words, `Option` `⌘` –equal sign (=) works just as well.)

Selecting something with the plus pointer (a font from the Character dialog box, say) automatically puts it on the proper menu. You can add anything to a menu that you can select in the Character dialog box, as well as any of the special paragraph formats in the Paragraph dialog box. You can also add:

- Ruler items (like any of the justification, line-spacing and paragraph-spacing options, or the Normal command)

- Section formats (like the number of columns and the First Page Special command from the Section dialog box)

- *Show Hidden Text* (from the Preferences menu)

- Glossary entries

- Styles

When you add items that don't belong in either the Format or Font menu, a new menu—the Work menu—is created to hold them. You can even add documents to the Work menu, by selecting them from the standard Open dialog box with the plus pointer. Having documents on the Work menu saves you the trouble of constantly diving down into a pile of nested folders to get to the document you want.

Pressing `Option` `⌘` –minus gives you the *minus pointer,* which looks something like this (only bigger): **−** . Select something from a menu with the minus pointer and it's deleted. But you can't delete everything—just fonts, sizes, character styles and any command you've added to a menu.

You can add several items to (or delete them from) your menus without having to call up the plus or minus pointer each time. Just hold down the [Shift] key when you click on an item. It will be added or deleted, but the pointer will remain a plus or a minus.

⍝ *sorting order* (SZA)

Word is smart enough to know the difference between numbers and letters and to sort them differently. Word sorts put punctuation marks first, numbers next and letters last. Alphabetical sorting places the uppercase version of a letter before its lowercase equivalent (e.g., *Mac* before *mac*) and puts accented foreign characters in with their unaccented equivalents (e.g., *e* with *é*, *u* with *ü*, etc.) Word is even smart enough to sort alphanumeric combinations in the right way, so you get *9a* and *9b* before *10a* and *10b*.

⍝ *descending sorts* (SZA)

To sort in descending order (highest numbers first or *z* to *a*), hold the [Shift] key down as you select the *Sort* command from the Document menu.

⍝ *basic selection commands* (SZA)

To select:

shortcut

a word   [Double-Click] anywhere in it
(selects space after word as well)

a sentence   [⌘] [Click] anywhere in it

a line   [Click] in the selection bar

a paragraph   [Double-Click] in the selection bar

the entire document   [⌘] [Click] in the selection bar
or press [Option] [⌘] –M

(And, of course—as with virtually all Mac programs—you can also select any amount of text either by dragging across it or by clicking at one point and then shift-clicking at another.)

shortcut

🍎 *using* Shift *to select* (SZA)

If you use any pointer-movement technique with the Shift key held down, you select the area the pointer moves across. So, for example, Shift ⌘ ← selects the last word you typed. (So does Shift Backspace .)

To extend the selection, just hold the keys down. So, for example, holding Shift ⌘ ← down will continue the selection backward, word by word, until you release the keys.

🍎 Option *key selections* (SZA)

very hot tip

Holding down the Option key as you select by dragging lets you select any rectangular area of the screen, regardless of where there's text. This is especially useful when you want to delete, move, format or use the calculation option on columns in a table.

If you want to delete an Option key selection, you have to cut it: you can't use Backspace . (The Mac just beeps at you if you try.)

Note that if any part of a graphic is selected this way, the entire graphic is affected by the deletion or formatting.

🍎 *shift-clicking works by selection units* (SZA)

Shift-clicking to extend a selection works in the original unit of the selection. So, for example, if you command-click to select a sentence, shift-clicking some place else extends the selection to include the whole sentence you've shift-clicked on, regardless of where in that sentence you shift-clicked.

🍎 *pointer-movement shortcuts* (DC)

shortcut

Word displays the list of pointer-movement commands when you type ⌘ –? and then Click the mouse. But here's a chart of all of them, both the documented and undocumented ones. (But for easier ways to move the pointer, see the next entry.)

Holding down ⌘ , Option and the following characters moves the pointer as indicated:

k	left one letter	**l**	right one letter
j	left one word	**;**	right one word
o	up one line	**,**	down one line
p	up one screenful	**.**	down one screenful

Holding down ⌘ , Option , the apostrophe key (') and the following characters moves the pointer as indicated:

k	to start of line	**l**	to end of line
j	back one sentence	**;**	to start of next sentence
o	to top of screen	**,**	to bottom of screen
p	to top of file	**.**	to bottom of file

As mentioned above in the entry on *using* Shift *to select,* adding the Shift key to any of the above commands will select all the text from the pointer's present position to its new position. But since this involves holding down five keys—⌘ , Option , Shift , apostrophe and the character—you may be better off simply using the mouse.

🍎 *using the numeric keypad* (SZA)

The numeric keypad has two modes—one in which it issues commands that move the insertion point, select text and the like (let's call this *command mode)* and one in which it enters numbers into your text (which is called *Num. Lock,* a term imported from the numb world of the PC). The Clear key toggles you between them. When you're in Num. Lock, this fact is noted in the status box in the lower left corner of the window

shortcut

In command mode, the 4, 6, 8 and 2 keys move the insertion point by one line vertically or one character horizontally (in the obvious directions). Adding the ⌘ key to these numbers moves you by one word horizontally and one paragraph vertically.

The corner keys move you in larger increments. For example, 7 moves you to the beginning of the current line, or to the beginning of the previous line if you're already at the beginning of a line. The 1 moves you to the end of the current line or to the end of the next line if you're already at the end of a line. With the ⌘ key, these keys move you backward and forward by sentences instead of by lines.

The other corner keys, 9 and 3, move you backward and forward a screenful at a time. With the ⌘ key, 9 moves you to the beginning of the document and 3 to the end.

The 5 key doesn't do anything by itself, but ⌘–5 jumps the insertion point to the top left corner of the current screen.

Here it all is in diagram form:

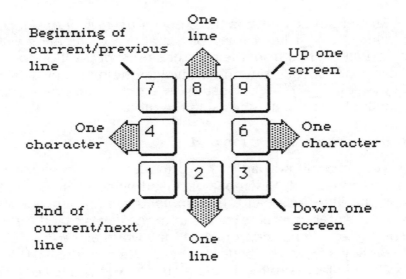

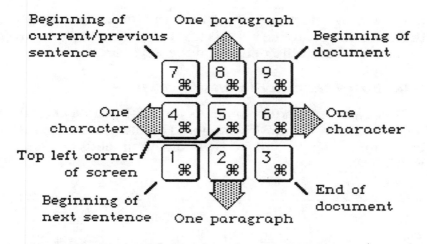

The zero on the keypad is the "go back" control. Say you're typing and see a mistake. You can go to the mistake and correct it, then press the keypad zero to jump right back to where you were. (Word remembers your last four positions, so you can use the keypad zero for even more complicated series of jumps around your document.)

very good feature

Some of the keypad keys select text rather than move the insertion point. And if you hold them down, they extend the selection—you don't have to hold down the Shift key.

* * selects forward, a character at a time

* \+ selects backward, a character at a time

* = selects the line below the insertion point

* / selects the line above the insertion point

Remember, these commands only work if you're *not* in Num. Lock. (For Word's basic selection techniques, see the entry on that above.)

You can also make a selection by pressing the minus key on the keypad. This puts the words *Extend to* in the status box. Press any key that generates a character and all the text between the insertion point and the next occurrence of that character will be selected. (If you already have text selected, the selection will be *extended* to that point.) So a quick way to select everything from the insertion point to the end of the sentence it's in is to hit the minus key (on the keypad) and then the period (on the keyboard).

◆ *keyboard character formatting* (SZA)

esp. for beginners

There are keyboard commands for all of Word's character formats, even if they're not noted on the menu or in the character dialog box. These keyboard commands all begin with Shift ⌘ .

Bold	⌘ – Shift – B	**Shadow** ⌘ – Shift – W
Italic	⌘ – Shift – I	SMALL CAPS ⌘ – Shift – H
<u>Underline</u>	⌘ – Shift – U	ALL CAPS ⌘ – Shift – K
Word <u>Underline</u>	⌘ – Shift –]	<u>Hidden</u> ⌘ – Shift – X
<u>Double Underline</u>	⌘ – Shift – [	Smaller Font ⌘ – Shift – <
<u>Dotted Underline</u>	⌘ – Shift – \	Larger Font ⌘ – Shift – >
~~Strikethru~~	⌘ – Shift – /	Super script ⌘ – Shift – +
Outline	⌘ – Shift – D	Sub script ⌘ – Shift – –

◆ *paragraph formatting from the keyboard* (SZA)

esp. for beginners

Here are the keyboard equivalents for the formats listed in the Paragraph dialog box:

Plain ("Normal")	⌘ – Shift –P	Indent First Line ⌘ – Shift –F
Side-by-side	⌘ – Shift –G	Nest ⌘ – Shift –N
Left Justify	⌘ – Shift –L	UnNest ⌘ – Shift –M
Right Justify	⌘ – Shift –R	Hanging Indent ⌘ – Shift –T
Centered	⌘ – Shift –C	Double Space ⌘ – Shift –Y
Full Justify	⌘ – Shift –J	Open Space ⌘ – Shift –O

Unlike character formats, they don't act as toggles. Sometimes (as with Indent First Line and Double Space), nothing at all happens when you apply the format a second time; sometimes (as with Hanging Indent and Nest), the text is further affected by the command, with margins being moved again, beyond where they had already been moved to.

⬤ *keyboard commands in dialog boxes* (SZA)

Word gives you several ways to choose buttons in a dialog box without having to take your hands off the keyboard. The basic techniques are these:

shortcut

- If there isn't a text field in the dialog box, pressing the key that corresponds to the first letter of the name of a button chooses the button (*c* for *Cancel, o* for *OK,* etc.).

- If there is a text field in the dialog box, you have to hold down the ⌘ key while pressing the first letter of the button name. (This also works even if there are no text fields.)

- In addition to ⌘–C, ⌘–period always selects the Cancel button.

Word also has keyboard commands that let you cycle through the items in a dialog box (be they buttons, text fields or lists).

- To tab from one item to the next, use the decimal point (the period on the keypad) or Tab ⌘ . Items are underlined briefly when you move to them.

- To tab to the previous item (that is, to move backwards through the items), use Shift–decimal point or Tab Shift ⌘ .

- To activate a button once you've moved to it, use ⌘–spacebar or hit the zero key on the keypad.

- To scroll through a list once you've moved to it, use the Backspace and ⌘ keys.

- When buttons are clustered in groups, you can jump from one group to the next by using the arrow keys.

✦ *keyboard control of menus* (SZA)

Word provides for total control of menus from the keyboard. This involves four steps—activating the menu bar (getting it ready for keyboard control), choosing a menu to display (the equivalent of clicking on its title with the mouse), choosing a command from it (the equivalent of dragging down to that command with the mouse), and executing the command (the equivalent of releasing the mouse button). There are various ways to do each of these steps.

To activate the menu bar, press the decimal point (the period on the keypad) or [Tab] [⌘] .

To choose a menu, type the first letter of its name or a number that corresponds to its position on the menu bar. Or you can move to it with the ← and → keys. (After one menu is down, only the arrow keys will take you to another.)

To choose a command, hit the first letter of its name. If more than one command begins with the same letter, repeated pressings of the key will select each command in turn. Or, you can move up or down in the menu with the ↑ and ↓ keys.

To execute the command, press [Return] or [Enter] . (Like almost anything else in Word, you can cancel the procedure at any time by pressing [⌘]–period.)

Keyboard sequences are handy for often-used commands that don't have command keys assigned to them. If you're a decent typist, they take far less time then reaching for the mouse. Here are some of my favorites (you don't type the commas, of course; they're just there to indicate that you don't press the keys at the same time):

Page Preview	period, f, p, [Return]
Save As	period, f, s, s, [Return]
Section	period, f, f, s, [Return]
Sort	period, d, s, s, [Return]

But here's my favorite; it saves a document as text only:

period, f, s, s, [document name], ⌘–F, t, Return , Return

This sequence opens the Save As dialog box, in which you type the document name, then activates the *File Format* button (you need the ⌘ key because there's a text field), then clicks the *Text Only* button (you don't need the ⌘ key because there's no text field in that dialog box), then closes the Format dialog box and clicks on the Save button. *(Editor's note: Isn't Sharon amazing?)*

❤ *plain text* (SZA)

Option ⌘ –spacebar does not remove character formatting: it returns selected characters to whatever you use as the Normal Style. (For more on Styles, see the entries that begin with *styles vs. Styles* below.) To remove character formatting, use Shift ⌘ –Z. To specify plain text in the Character dialog box, click on the Character Formats title above the list of formats.

❤ *leading control* (DC)

Leading (pronounced LEHD-ing, not LEED-ing) is what typesetters call the space between lines of text, and Word gives you a lot of power to control it. To change the leading, go to the Paragraph Formats window (the keyboard shortcut is ⌘ –M) and type the leading you want into the *Line Spacing* box. Be sure to add the letters *pt* after the number so Word knows you're telling it how many points to make the lines (you don't need to type in a space; *12pt* works as well as *12 pt).*

esp. for beginners

So, for example, if you wanted to print out text 11/13 (11–point type on 13–point lines—one of the most common ways to set body copy), you'd first select the text, then go to the Character Formats window and type *11* in the *Font Size* box, then go to the Paragraph Formats window and type *13pt* in the *Line Spacing* box.

❡ *line spacing and paragraph spacing* (SZA)

esp. for beginners

There are two sets of spacing icons on the Ruler, with related commands in the Paragraph Format dialog box—line spacing (the space between the lines within a paragraph) and paragraph spacing (the space before and/or after a paragraph). These options are entirely independent from each other.

❡ *an optional way to cut or copy* (SZA)

You can do the equivalent of a cut (or copy) and paste without using the Clipboard—or the cut, copy, or paste commands—at all. (This can be useful if you have something in the Clipboard and don't want to lose it.)

To move text (and/or graphics) without the Clipboard:

* Select the material you want to move and press Option ⌘ –X. The words *Move to* appear in the status box.

* Click in the spot you want the text moved to, or select the material you want it to replace. (A clicked spot shows as a dotted vertical line; a selection is underlined in gray.)

* Press Return or Enter .

To copy text (and/or graphics) without the Clipboard, follow the same procedure but use Option ⌘ –C instead of Option ⌘ –X (prompt will read *Copy to* instead of *Move to*).

These commands are easy to remember, because they shadow ⌘ –X and ⌘ –C. To remember which key you have to add, think of them as "optional" cut and "optional" copy.

❡ *copying character formats* (SZA)

very hot tip

You can copy existing combinations of character formats (font, size and styles) and apply them either to existing text or to the insertion point, so that they affect whatever you type next.

To copy character formats to existing text:

- Select some text formatted the way you want and press Option ⌘ –V. The words *Format to* appear in the status box.

- Select the text you want the formats applied to. (This second selection is underlined in gray rather than highlighted.)

- Press Return or Enter .

To copy character formats to the insertion point (so that what you type next will have the new formats):

- While nothing is selected, press Option ⌘ –V. The *Format from* prompt appears in the status box.

- Click in any text that's formatted the way you want. The click leaves a dotted vertical line.

- Press Return or Enter . The dotted "insertion point" disappears, the regular insertion point begins blinking again and you can continue typing with the new character formatting.

You can cancel either procedure at any time, getting rid of the prompt in the status box, with ⌘ –period.

⍟ *copying paragraph formatting* (SZA)

To copy paragraph formatting, follow the procedures described in the last entry, with one difference: when you select the text formatted the way you want, Double-Click in the selection bar to select the entire paragraph.

*very
hot
tip*

⍟ *soft and hard hyphens* (SZA)

Word gives a choice of three different kinds of hyphens. A regular hyphen shows up all the time and lets the words it connects be split when it falls at the end of a line. A soft hyphen only appears if it falls at the end of a line. A hard hyphen always appears and won't let its words be split across two lines.

*very good
feature*

To enter a soft hyphen, use ⌘–hyphen. To enter a hard hyphen, use ⌘–tilde (~).

🍎 *run-in headers and footers* (SZA)

very hot tip

The body of a document is automatically adjusted to make room for headers and footers, but you can circumvent this feature. If you have a long, narrow header or footer, you can run down the left or right margin of the page, overlapping the area that "belongs" to the body of the text by defining the header or footer as a *run-in.*

To make a header or footer a run-in, use negative numbers in the paper margin definition in Page Setup. Or, in Page Preview, adjust the header or footer position while holding down the Shift key.

🍎 *using the Ruler* (SZA)

esp. for beginners

The two left markers on the Ruler, which control the left margin and the first line indent, travel together if you grab the bottom one; the top one (the indent) moves separately. To move the bottom (left margin) marker separately, hold the Shift key down while you grab it.

If you want to set a margin or indent to the left of the zero mark on the Ruler, just slide the marker to the left; after an initial hesitation, the window scrolls so you can get to the negative numbers. (To scroll your document beyond the zero mark without moving anything on the Ruler, just hold the Shift key down while using the left scroll arrow at the bottom of the window.)

To change the default tab stops, use the *Page Setup...* command and type the new distance you want in the *Default Tab Stops* box.

The default unit on the Ruler is inches, but you can change it in the Preferences dialog box (you get to it from the Edit menu).

⬤ *styles vs. Styles* (AN)

In its doggedly non-Mac-standard way, Word uses the term *style* to mean a grouping of formats. The problem with this is that virtually every other Mac program use the word *style* to mean a *type style* like boldface, italic, etc. In fact, in most popular Mac programs, *Style* is even the title of the menu of type style options.

esp. for beginners

To help avoid the inevitable confusion between these two uses of the word, we capitalize Style in this book whenever we're using it in the Word sense.

⬤ *defining styles and style sheets* (MB)

(Terminology alert: be sure to read the previous entry before this one.)

The Word manual doesn't make the relationship between formats, Styles and style sheets particularly clear, so I'll give it a try.

esp. for beginners

There are three kinds of formats in Word—character, paragraph and section. To define a Style, you combine a character format, a paragraph format, a ruler and the *Hide ¶* or *Show ¶* command (the section format isn't part of a Style). A group of Styles makes up a *style sheet.* There can be any number of Styles in a style sheet, but only one style sheet per document.

⌘ –T opens the Define Styles dialog box. There Word displays a list of all the Styles in the document's style sheet. When you open a new document, the box lists just two Styles—Normal (the default Style that Word uses with every document) and New.

To create a Style, you click on *New Style.* Type a name in the Style field and then make your selections for character and paragraph formats, ruler and *Hide ¶/Show ¶.* When you're done, click on the *Define* button. That's all there is to it.

⚫ *importing/merging style sheets* (SZA)

If a document has no style sheet, you can import one from another document. If it does have a style sheet, you can merge it with one from another document.

To import or merge, open the Define Styles dialog box and choose *Open...* from the File menu. Select the document whose style sheet you want and click the *Open* button.

Note that when both documents have Styles with the same name, the imported one replaces the current one.

⚫ *changing and creating default Styles* (SZA)

**very
hot
tip**

There are default Styles that Word always uses, like the Normal Style and those used for automatic page numbers and index entries. You can change their definitions and add new defaults of your own.

Why should you want to add your own defaults? Because nondefault style sheets are stored with the document in which they were created (or into which they were imported; see the previous entry for details). So if you create a Style for one document and forget to define it as a default, you'll have to import it into each document you want to use it in.

Changing default Styles is easy. Just hold down the Shift key, choose *Define Styles...* from the Format menu and select the Style you want to change. The names of the default Styles have a bullet (·) in front of them. (If you don't hold down Shift, they won't appear).

Prime candidates for changes are:

- The Normal Style (the default for a new document)

- Page Number (used for the automatic page number)

- Line Number (used with the *number lines* paragraph format)

Page Number and Line Number are based on the Normal Style, so if you change Normal to be Times 10-point, the page numbers and line numbers will also be in that font.

When you change the definition of an existing default Style, paragraphs defined as that Style automatically reflect the changes—but only in the current document and future ones. A pre-existing document using that Style will not show the changes—unless you either open the document, *Select All* and paste it into a new, empty window, or import the new style sheet into it (see the previous entry for how to do that).

♠ *The Apply button* (SZA)

The Apply button lets you see the effect of a formatting change you make in the Character or Paragraph dialog box without closing the dialog box—so you can change it right then if you don't like it. (Note: The Cancel button doesn't cancel the format you apply; it merely closes the dialog box.)

very good feature

♠ *entering and leaving Page Preview* (SZA)

The following sequence of keystrokes will put you into Page Preview mode (do them sequentially, not all at once): decimal point (that is, the period on the keypad), *f, p* and Return . This technique uses Word's keyboard menu-selection techniques, opening the File menu and choosing *Page Preview*. You don't have to wait for the menu to drop— you can type the *p* and Return immediately after the *f*.

shortcut

There are lots of ways to leave Page Preview, but the easiest is to press the 5 key on the keypad.

♠ *adding a page break in Page Preview* (SZA)

To add a page break while in Page Preview, click on the Margins icon, then drag a page break up out of the bottom margin of the page.

⚫ *deleting the automatic page number* (SZA)

To get rid of an automatic page number while in Page Preview, just drag it off the page. It doesn't look like anything happened, but if you click the Margins icon to update the display, you'll see that the page number is gone.

⚫ *double-clicks in Page Preview* (SZA)

shortcut

Double-clicking the page number icon puts the page number in its default position in the upper right corner of the page.

Double-clicking the magnifier icon zooms you into the upper left corner of the left-hand page.

⚫ *printing from Page Preview* (SZA)

Using the *Print* command while you're in Page Preview brings up the Print dialog box preset to print a single page—the one displayed in the Page Preview window (or the one on the left if two pages are displayed).

⚫ *paging and scrolling in Page Preview* (SZA)

shortcut

You don't have to use the scroll controls in Page Preview—you can use keyboard equivalents.

In the regular view, you can change the displayed pages by using any of the following to move back or forwards one page:

- the ↑ and ↓ keys

- the 8 and 2 keys on the keypad

- Option ⌘ –/   and   Option ⌘ –[

- Option ⌘ –O   and   Option ⌘ –comma

- Option ⌘ –P   and   Option ⌘ –period

In addition, you can jump to the first page with ⌘ –9 (keypad) and the last page with ⌘ –3 (keypad).

In magnified view, you can scroll the page around with the four arrow keys, using ⌘ – ← and ⌘ – → to scroll in larger increments. Or use the keypad, with 5 as the center of the action: 4, 6, 8, and 2 scroll the document horizontally and vertically; 7 and 1 are large-increment horizontal controls; 9 and 3 are large-increment vertical controls. (For more details, see *using the numeric keypad* above.)

Not enough for you? Well, you can also use the keyboard to scroll things (just in case you don't have the keypad, or want to leave it in Num. Lock). With the ⌘ and Option keys down, the K, comma, L, and semicolon keys scroll the document in small increments. For large increments, use Option ⌘ + the *J*, semicolon, *P* and period keys.

¢ *sizing and cropping graphics* (SZA)

Dragging the handles on the frame that surrounds a selected graphic resizes the frame, but not the picture. Making the frame smaller than the graphic crops the image, leaving the upper left part of it showing. Making the frame larger centers the picture in the frame.

To change the size of the picture instead of cropping it, hold the Shift key as you drag on the frame. To return a graphic to its original size, Double-Click on it.

¢ *formatting graphic frames* (SZA)

The frames of graphics are treated like characters in Word, so you can apply character formatting to them! Use Outline to show the frame, then use Bold, Shadow or both.

very hot tip

¢ *the graphics dump* (SZA)

To turn any part of a Word document into a *graphic*, select it and hit Option ⌘ –D. This puts a snapshot of it on the Clipboard. Although this feature is meant to allow you to transfer complicated formulas into other programs, it also can be handy within Word, because it lets you distort the text by stretching it. (For more details, see the entry called *creating your own special typographic effects* in the printer chapter.)

very hot tip

printing multiple documents (SZA)

There are two easy ways to print multiple documents:

- Type the name of the file you want printed after the current one after the words *Next File* in the Page Setup dialog box.

- Select all the files by shift-clicking on their icons in the Finder, then choose *Print...* from the File menu.

Print/Merge (DC)

The main document and all files to be merged must be in the same folder.

creating Glossary entries (SZA)

To create a Glossary entry, put it in the document first, then select it, open the Glossary window, name the entry and click on the *Define* button.

You can also make whatever's on the Clipboard a Glossary entry (regardless of what's selected.) To do that, just choose *Paste* from the Edit menu instead of clicking the *Define* button.

storing paragraph formatting in a Glossary (CD)

**very
hot
tip**

Word keeps paragraph-format settings (tabs, justification, line spacing, etc.) in the paragraph symbol (¶) at the end of each paragraph. To copy these settings, first make the ¶s and other format symbols visible by pressing ⌘ -Y. Then select the ¶ (by double-clicking on it), copy it and paste it over the ¶ of any paragraph you want to change the settings of.

An even slicker technique is to save the ¶ as a Glossary entry. Then you can insert it at the end of a paragraph and the paragraph will be formatted instantly. Just store the ¶ in the Glossary with a name that will help you remember what it is. Nothing will be displayed in the Glossary, but be assured that the format is stored.

When you want to use that format, type the Glossary name and press ⌘ Backspace to retrieve the symbol. Position the pointer to the left of the paragraph marker and type the paragraph. (You can also retrieve the paragraph marker from the Glossary to format any existing format.)

⚫ *unusual Glossary entries* (SZA/DC)

A Glossary can store anything you can select in the document. Here are some possible kinds of Glossary entries that may not have occurred to you, but that can be quite useful:

very
hot
tip

- Graphics (for example, a logo or a letterhead).

- Section breaks. All the section definitions (number of columns, page number position, etc.) are stored in the section-break symbol (a double line that runs across the page). Keeping them in the Glossary lets you apply section-formatting options quickly.

- Paragraph formats. As explained in the previous entry, you do this by selecting the paragraph marker (¶) before opening the Glossary window. (Why retrieve paragraph formats from the Glossary instead of using a Style Sheet? Because the Style Sheet includes character formatting, and sometimes you won't want that.)

- Page breaks. The Shift Enter that puts a page break in the document has no menu equivalent. But you can store it in the Glossary and retrieve it by name (which you may want to do if you have a hard time remembering what key combination gives you a page break).

  Here's an even neater trick: since you can add a page break to the Glossary, and since you can add a Glossary entry to the Work menu...yep, you can put a page break into the Work menu so it's there whenever you need it but can't remember the key combination.

[Editor's note: These are cunning kluges, but wouldn't it be easier just to write "Shift Enter = page break" on a piece of paper and put it on the wall?]

For yet another cunning use of the Glossary, see the next entry.

♦ using the Glossary to store character formats *(DC)*

You can use Word's Glossary feature to store character formats as well as words, phrases, and pictures. This is particularly useful for complicated formats like 18-point bold italic outline small caps. All you have to do is copy a single character in the desired format into the Glossary window and give the Glossary a name that will help you remember what it is—*subheads*, say, or *captions*. (Don't worry that the character appears in the Glossary window as plain Chicago; the formats are intact.)

To use the format, just type in the name of the Glossary entry and press ⌘ Backspace to retrieve it. Then select the character (Option Backspace will select it automatically) and begin typing. The character will be replaced with the text you type, and it will all be formatted the way you want it.

♦ miscellaneous uses of the Glossary *(DC)*

You can also use the Glossary to store running heads and frequently misspelled words. For example, if you frequently type *teh* instead of *the*, simply make a Glossary entry *the* with the name *teh*. Then every time you type *teh*, all you have to do is hit ⌘ Backspace to correct the mistake.

Advanced Word tips

Unless otherwise noted, these tips apply to Word 3.01, although most of them should also work with Word 4 and later versions of the program.

♦ standard and nonstandard Glossaries *(SZA)*

When you create a Glossary entry, it's only good for the current session unless it's specifically saved into the Standard (default) Glossary that Word starts with in each session. You'll be prompted to do that when you quit Word, but you don't have to wait till then—just choose *Save* from the File menu while the Glossary window is open.

To save a specialized Glossary as something other than the Standard Glossary, use *Save As...* when the Glossary window is open. To retrieve a nonstandard Glossary, use *Open...* when the Glossary window is open.

To switch from the Glossary you're using to the Standard Glossary (which only has three entries: *New, Date* and *Time*) just open the Glossary window and choose *New* from the File menu. (You don't permanently lose any Glossary entries by doing this.)

● *dynamic dates and times* (SZA)

Date and time entries inserted by the Glossary into a document are static—they don't change once you insert them. For dynamic date and time entries that reflect the time of printing rather than the time of insertion into the document, use the Header or Footer window to make Glossary entries as follows:

- Open the Header or Footer window.

- Click on the date or time icon.

- Select the date or time entry in the window.

- Open the Glossary window, give the entry a name (but not *time* or *date,* since those are taken already) and click on the Define button.

● *table of contents and indexing shortcuts* (SZA)

The way you define a table-of-contents or index entry in Word is very unMaclike. The item (whether it's a word or a phrase) that you want included in a table of contents has to be surrounded by special characters: *.c.* in front of it and a semicolon after it. Index entries have to be marked similarly: *.i.* before the item and a semicolon after.

very bad feature

In addition, these leading and trailing *delimiters* (they mark the boundaries, or limits, of the item) have to be formatted as hidden characters.

You can make the process a little less painful by storing the *.c.* and *.i. dot commands* (living relics from the antique world of CP/M and MS DOS) and the semicolon in the Glossary. Since the Glossary stores formats as well as characters, this saves you both the typing and the formatting.

shortcut

But the thing to do is really automate the procedure with Tempo. Assuming you've stored the table-of-contents leading characters under the name *t* and the semicolon under the name *;*, select any piece of text (anything—it doesn't matter right now) and record the following macro:

⌘–X

⌘, Backspace, t, Return

⌘–V

⌘, Backspace, ;, ⌘, Backspace

This cuts the selected text, puts the Table of Contents leading characters in (from the Glossary), pastes the contents back in and then adds the trailing semicolon. (Without using this cut-and-paste trick, there's no way to be sure you'd get the whole entry: sometimes an entry is a single word, sometimes it's a phrase or short sentence.)

To use the macro, all you have to do is select the text you want as the table-of-contents entry and then play the macro.

(You can, of course, create an equivalent macro for indexing.)

If you don't use Tempo and have to do table-of-contents and Index marking manually, keep in mind you don't have to use the trailing semicolon to mark the end of an entry if it's at the end of a paragraph or if it's followed by a newline character (Shift Return).

⚫ *double-sided Word printouts* (DC)

Nowhere in the LaserWriter or Word documentation will you find instructions for printing on both sides of the paper so that the correct pages will print back-to-back. Here's how you do it:

First print half as many copies of the document as you need. Then arrange them so that the copies of page 2 are on the top, followed by the copies of page 1, followed by page 4, then page 3, page 6, page 5, and so on, continuing to count up by even numbers and subtracting 1 in between. If there are an odd number of pages in your document, set aside the copies of the last page and substitute blank pages for them in the pile.

very hot tip

Place the pile of arranged pages in the paper tray face up, with the top edge of the pages pointing towards the end of the tray that goes into the LaserWriter. Insert the tray and print the other half of the copies.

The same technique works on the ImageWriter II with a sheet feeder. The only difference is how you place the pile of arranged pages (printed on one side)—in the case of the sheet feeder, put them upside down, with the printed side facing you.

❖ *adding crop marks to a Word document* (PH)

Many people use Word to create documents smaller than the standard paper size of 8.5" by 11". When such manu-scripts are sent off to printers (companies with printing presses, that is), they need to know which part of the 8.5 x 11 sheet you want for the page. There are two ways to tell them.

very hot tip

Corner-cropping is when you align the upper left corner of the page to be printed with the upper left corner of the 8.5x11 sheet. Since printers know the length and width of the page, they can just ignore the excess paper on the right and bottom of the 8.5 x 11 sheet.

But sometimes you want to position the page to be printed in the middle of the 8.5 x 11 sheet. To do that, you mark each corner of it with a crop mark which either looks like a corner or a plus sign:

Although corner-cropping is much easier, some printers prefer crop marks.

If you're using Word and a LaserWriter, you can use PostScript commands to produce corner-shaped crop marks on each page. This method is something of a kluge, and doesn't work on ImageWriters or other non-PostScript printers.

First, use the *Page Setup...* command to set the margins so they define the page to be printed. For example, if you're making pages that are 5.5" by 8.5" (the standard size for IBM PC manuals), you'd set your margins to:

Top: 1.25

Bottom: 2.25

Left: 1.63

Right: 2.63

(This gives you margins within the page to be printed of 1/2" on the top and bottom and 5/8" on the left and right.)

Next, type in the following lines and format them with Word's built-in PostScript style (which prevents Word from formatting them and thereby allows PostScript to recognize them).

```
.page. newpath
72 144 moveto 0 9 rlineto 0 -9 rmoveto 9 0 rlineto
72 756 moveto 0 -9 rlineto 0 9 rmoveto 9 0 rlineto
468 144 moveto 0 9 rlineto 0 -9 rmoveto 9 0 rlineto
468 756 moveto 0 -9 rlineto 0 9 rmoveto 9 0 rlineto
stroke
```

Copy this and paste it into the even- and odd-page headers for each section of your document. (Don't type in the ¬'s; they just mean that the next line is a continuation of the one they're at the end of.) If you've set first pages to be special, you'll need to paste it into the first-page header as well.

To modify the PostScript code for pages of different sizes, change the numbers at the beginning of the middle four lines. These measurements are in 72nds of an inch and correspond to the corners of the page to be printed, measured from the bottom right corner of an 8.5 x 11 sheet of paper. Thus 72 144 defines a point one inch from the left and two inches from the bottom of the 8.5 x 11 sheet.

❡ *printing custom envelopes on the LaserWriter* (DC)

The LaserWriter is great for printing stationery. Letterhead is easy, but envelopes can be tricky—especially if you use Word to do them. That's because its commands for margins are so confusing. You can change them both on the Ruler and in the Page Setup window and the effect of one on the other is quite mysterious (and, needless to say, is not explained with perfect lucidity in Word's manual).

But these difficulties are more than made up for by Word's ability to produce type in any point size, not merely in the standard six to nine sizes most programs give you. This is particularly important if you like the way an envelope looks with your name and the return address printed across the end, instead of lengthwise like the name and address of the person you're sending it to, because this format makes copyfitting even more critical.

To center the type across the end of a standard #10 business envelope (and to keep the top of the type from getting cut off by the LaserWriter's invisible image border), create a Word document with the following settings:

- *on the Ruler:* a left margin of 4-7/16" and a right margin of 8-1/2"

- *in the Page Setup window:* a top margin of 0.4"; all other margins set to zero

- *in the Paragraph menu:* center all text

If text gets cut off on either side, reduce the size of the type on that line (one point at a time) until it fits.

For more about printing stationery on the LaserWriter, see the printer chapter.

⚫ *searching for special characters* *(SZA/PH)*

very hot tip

You can search for invisible and other special characters like paragraphs and tabs by using the following *caret combinations* in the text field of the Find or Change dialog box. (You get the caret with Shift –6.)

^n   newline

^t   tab

^p   paragraph

^s   nonbreaking space

^ -   soft hyphen (i.e., Option –hyphen)

^d   section break

^w   white space

^1   graphic

^2   page number mark

^3   current date mark

^4   current time mark

^5   footnote reference mark
(You can only search for this, not add it to your document with the Change command.)

^6   formula mark

Here's an example of how you can use these special characters. Let's say you want to change a table whose lines consist of separate paragraphs (because you pressed Return at the end of each line) into a single paragraph, so that a shadow box will surround the whole table instead of each line. Just select all of the table except the paragraph mark at the end of the last line and replace all the paragraph markers *(^p)* with newline characters *(^n)*.

Or let's say you have to change the indent at the beginning of each paragraph in a document to a tab (as I had to do with the text you're reading right now). First, you select the entire document and adjust the indent marker on the Ruler so there's no indent. Then, you just search for every *^p* and replace it with *^p^t* (you can type them just like that; you don't need anything between them).

❧ removing returns from imported documents *(DC)*

Sometimes when you transfer a document created on another computer into Word, you'll find carriage returns at the end of each line. (Use ⌘–Y to see where all the carriage returns are; they show up as ¶s.) Since Word only uses carriage returns to mark the ends of paragraphs, you'll need to remove all the ones that fall elsewhere. Here's how to do that:

Select the entire document. Now choose *Change* from the Search menu, and change each occurrence of *^p^p* (Word uses *^p* to represent carriage returns) to some unique characters that don't appear anywhere in the document, such as *##*. Click on the *Change All* button.

Next, choose *Change* again and change each occurrence of *^p* to a single space (just use the space bar). Click on the *Change All* button. Now choose *Change* for a third time and change each occurrence of *##* (or whatever you're using) to *^p*. Again, click on the *Change All* button.

All the carriage returns in your document should now be at the ends of paragraphs. (⌘–Y will reveal if any unwanted ones remain.)

❧ recovering from crashes *(DC)*

You may be able to recover a Word document that you've lost in a system crash. After restarting your system, look on the Word disk for a document named *MW0000* (or *MW0001*, *MW0002,* etc.). This is the name Word uses for the temporary file it creates when you're working with a document.

very
hot
tip

If you find such a document, there's at least a fifty-fifty chance you'll be able to recover the text you were working on—if you have a system utility (like ResEdit, Fedit, or

MacTools) that allows you to change the file type. Use the utility to open the document named *MW0000* (or whatever) and change the type from WTMP to WDBM. Then exit to the Desktop and rename the document from *MW0000* to *lost text* or any name you like (as long as it doesn't begin with *MW* followed by four numbers). With any luck, Word will then be able to read the file.

♦ making check boxes (PH)

very hot tip

Word gives you a quick and easy way to include small check boxes in your document. To insert one, give the *Insert Graphics* command (⌘-I). Then press Shift- ← to select the graphic frame that was inserted, and Shift ⌘ -D to outline it.

To make a square check box, grab the black square in the lower right corner of the box and shrink the box to the desired size. To make a rectangular box, shrink or expand the outline with the handles (small black squares) on the right and bottom sides of the box.

As you shrink the box, notice that the status box in the lower left corner of the window shows the percentage of the original size. Shrinking the box as far as it will go, 16%, makes the box just a little larger than standard 12-point letters. For special effect, you can add Shadow formatting to the check box.

If you're going to use the same check box throughout a document, you may want to add it to your Glossary.

♦ creating blank lines on forms (DC)

When designing forms, you usually want to create blanks where people can fill in the information you're requesting. The common way to do this is just to knock out a bunch of underlines (Shift-hyphens). But this method will seldom produce lines of the length you planned, especially on the LaserWriter. Here's a method for producing underlines of an exact length:

Set a plain left tab at the point where the line is to begin, and a right tab with a solid underscore leader at the point where the line is to end. Underscore leaders are chosen in the bottom center of the Tabs dialog box (⌘–T). This will fill the space between the tabs with an underline, and the tabs will keep the line length precise.

🍎 *eliminating blank lines in merge printouts* (DC)

Since the dawn of MailMerge, users have put up with the problem of blank lines in their mailing labels and merge letters. You set up fields for Title, Name, Company, Address, City, State, and ZIP, and the first thing you discover is that half your records have no company name associated with them. In many word processors, this leaves you with no option but to print the labels with a blank line where the company name would go. Officially, Word is no different, but there is a way around the problem.

very hot tip

Word's manual states that each ELSE statement must be enclosed with *guillemets* (which look like this: « » and are pronounced *gee-may).* But if you leave off the last » , Word will not advance to the next line, and blank lines will be eliminated when the document is printed.

The official Microsoft approach shown below will leave you with blank lines if the title, name, or company field is empty:

```
«IF title»«title»
«ELSE»
«IF name»«name»
«ELSE»
«IF company»«company»
«ELSE»
«ENDIF»«address»
«city», «state»   «zip»
```

But the following Print Merge document will not leave blank lines, regardless of whether or not the title, name, or company field is empty:

```
«IF title»«title»
«ELSE
«IF name»«name»
«ELSE
«IF company»«company»
«ELSE
«ENDIF»«address»
«city», «state»  «zip»
```

● *preserving ThinkTank indentation in Word* (DC)

When you convert a ThinkTank document to Word, the first thing you'll notice is that all the indentation is gone. Here's what to do to restore it:

- search for all occurrences of *.head 0 +* and *.head 1?* and delete

- search for all occurrences of *.head 2 ?* and change them to *^t* (which creates a single tab)

- search for all occurrences of *.head 3 ?* and change them to *^t^t* (which creates a double tab)

- and so on for *.head 4?* and as many other levels as you have

Basic MacWrite tips

Unless otherwise noted, these tips should work with both version 4.6 and version 5.0 of MacWrite.

● *maximum screen width* (AN)

Because it doesn't have horizontal scrolling, MacWrite only lets you to see 6-1/8" of text on the screen—if you want the scroll bar to stay its full width—or 6-1/4" if you don't mind a thin scroll bar.

To display the maximum width possible, first move the MacWrite window as far as you can into the upper left corner of the screen (it doesn't come up in that position). Then use the size box to stretch the window as far right and down as possible (either leaving the scroll bar full width or squeezing it down, as you wish). If the ruler isn't showing, choose

Show Rulers on the Format menu. Then move the little black triangles that mark the margins to 1" on the left and to either one or two marks past 7" on the right.

You can still see all your text if the scroll bar cuts the right margin marker in half. But if the marker is any more hidden than that, the last letters on some lines will be cut off.

⚫ *maximum print width* (AN)

Although MacWrite only allows you to display documents on the screen up to 6-1/8" or 6-1/4" wide (without a lot of incredibly inconvenient window-moving), you can print documents up to 7" wide on the ImageWriter. You should only expand the margins to 7" when you're about to print, because it's very hard to edit with lines of text that are wider than the screen.

To expand the margins, drag the MacWrite window way off to the left, then use the size box to stretch it as far to the right as it will go—which will be to 8-1/4". (If the ruler isn't showing, choose *Show Rulers* on the Format menu.) Then move the right margin marker as far right as it will go— which will be to 8". Since you can move the left margin marker to 1", this gives you a print width of 7".

⚫ *minimum tab spacing* (AN)

Tabs in MacWrite can be no closer than 3/16" to each other or to a margin.

very bad feature

⚫ *deleting words* (AN)

Double-clicking on a word in MacWrite highlights the word, but not the spaces on either side. If you [Backspace] to delete the word, you'll have to [Backspace] again to delete the remaining extra space.

very hot tip

The solution? Use *Cut* ([⌘]–X) instead of [Backspace] . This deletes the space to the left of the word along with the word itself.

✎ aligning text (AN)

esp. for
beginners

Text in MacWrite can be aligned four ways:

- flush left (the left margin is straight but the right isn't)
- flush right (the right margin is straight but the left isn't)
- justified (both margins are straight)
- centered

There are two ways to change the alignment. If you're changing the alignment of a lot of text, insert a ruler and click on the appropriate text-alignment box in it. Then go to where you want the alignment to revert to what it was before, insert another ruler and click on the appropriate text- alignment box in it.

If you're changing the alignment of a small amount of text (from a single line to a few paragraphs), it's easier just to select the text and choose the appropriate alignment command from the Format menu. You can also use keyboard commands for each kind of alignment. In version 4.6 of MacWrite (and earlier versions), those commands are:

centered — ⌘-M

flush left — ⌘-N

flush right — ⌘-R

justified — ⌘-J

(The *M* in ⌘-M stands for *middle*—or at least it's helpful to assume it does. ⌘-N is the only one of the four commands that isn't mnemonic, and you can remember that—if your mind is as weird as mine—by telling yourself that the *N* stands for *nonmnemonic*.)

In version 5.0 of MacWrite (and presumably in later versions), those keyboard alignment commands are:

centered — ⌘-\

flush left — ⌘-[

flush right   —   ⌘]–]

justified   —   ⌘]–J

(The mnemonics here are left bracket for left align-ment, right bracket for right alignment and, of course, *j* for *justified.)*

Alignment of text is a paragraph function, which means that these commands change all the text from one carriage return to the next. So to change a whole paragraph (or a single line ending in a carriage return), you don't have to select it all before giving the alignment command—just click anywhere in it.

There is a down side to this. To make a small piece of text at the start of a line automatically align left and another small piece at the end of the same line automatically align right, you have to center or justify the line and then put a lot of spaces in the middle of it—which is what I did to create the middle line of the table above. (But also see the next entry.)

⚫ *right-aligned tabs* (DC)

MacWrite has no built-in right-aligned tab feature, but you can simulate them when needed. All you have to do is insert a ruler, move the right margin 3/16" or more to the right of its present position, and add a decimal tab where the old right margin was. (This will only work for text that doesn't include periods.)

very
hot
tip

⚫ *an easy way to change fonts, styles and sizes* (AN)

Say you're writing a document in 12-point Chicago plain with subheads in 18-point Oblique bold italic. Switching between the two can cost you a lot of keystrokes and trips to the menu bar. But there's an easier way to do it (it may sound a little confusing when you read about it, but just try it).

shortcut

Let's say you just finished typing a paragraph (in 12-point Chicago) and now you want to type a new subhead. Just go to another subhead somewhere nearby and select any character in it. Then copy that character and paste it where you want the new subhead to be, select it, and start to type. What you type will be in the font, size and style of the other subhead (18-point Oblique bold italic, or whatever).

When you're inserting text into some already-existing text (instead of adding it on to the end of a new file you're creating), you often don't have to do any copying. Let's say you've finished typing the subhead and want to go back to your text font. If the text immediately after the subhead is in the text font, just select the first character in it and begin typing. The character you selected will be deleted, so be sure to retype it at the end of what you're inserting.

(The reason for selecting the first character is that the space in front of the text may be in a different font, style and/or size than the text itself. Often it will be the same and all you'll have to do is click in the space, but it's different enough of the time that you're better off always selecting the first letter as a matter of habit.)

This also works if the text immediately before the place where you want to make your insertion is in the font you want. In that case, you begin by retyping the character you selected, then go on to type your insertion.

⬤ *font styles in headers and footers* (AN)

You can have multiple fonts and font sizes in MacWrite headers and footers, but the automatic page number, date and time always print out in the format of the first character. For example, if you boldface the first word of your header, then use plain text for the following lines, the page number will be bold—regardless of the text surrounding it.

very hot tip

One elegant way around this problem is to precede the first character of the header or footer with a space and then simply format that space with the font, style and size you want the automatic features to print out in.

🍎 *defects in MacWrite's search function* (AN)

The *Find...* and *Change...* commands on MacWrite's Search menu won't let you search for carriage returns. In versions earlier than 5.0, they also won't let you do "case-sensitive" searches (that is, they ignore whether letters are caps or lowercase) and sometimes the item found isn't visible on the screen, even after you move the Search window around to get it out of the way.

🍎 *macros in MacWrite* (AN)

AutoMac, QuicKeys, Tempo and Touch·n·Go are all programs that let you create *macro commands* (commands that include two or more smaller commands within them). This can be very useful in MacWrite, particularly in versions before 5.0, which didn't even have a way to save or print from the keyboard.

shortcut

Macros you create generally override built-in keyboard commands. To help you avoid doing that, here are two alphabetical lists of MacWrite's commands (with mnemonics in parentheses and italics, where they exist and aren't obvious). In versions earlier than 5.0:

⌘ +		⌘ +	
b	bold	**o**	outline
c	copy	**p**	plain text
h	superscript *(high)*	**r**	align right
i	italic	**s**	shadow
j	justify	**u**	underline
l	subscript *(low)*	**v**	paste
m	center *(middle)*	**x**	cut *(x out)*
n	align left	**z**	undo

That leaves the following characters available: *a, d, e, f, g, k, q, t, w, y.* You can also use any number, any symbol or any capital letter (i.e., any ⇧⌘ character except the numbers).

In version 5.0, many more keyboard commands were added. Here's a run-down:

⌘ +		⌘ +	
a	select all	**q**	quit
b	bold	**r**	insert ruler
c	copy	**s**	save
d	use ruler	**t**	plain
f	find	**u**	underline
g	go to page ...	**v**	paste
h	show rulers	**w**	close *(write)*
i	italic	**x**	cut *(x out)*
j	justify	**y**	spell word
k	check	**z**	undo
l	find next	**=**	check file
m	check header & footer	****	align center
n	new	**[**	align left *(left [)*
o	open	**]**	align right *(right])*
p	print		

That leaves only *e* available among the lowercase letters, but you can also use any number, most symbols or any capital letter (i.e., any [Shift][⌘] character except the numbers).

♠ *poor man's Glossaries in MacWrite* (DC)

MacWrite has no provision for what Word calls *Glossaries* (pieces of text that can be quickly substituted for a short code you type in), a feature that's quite useful for entering repetitive phrases. One way around this lack in MacWrite works as follows:

Use two or three unique characters as abbreviations for the longer text. For example, you might type *tmb* every time you want the phrase *The Macintosh Bible* to appear. Then, when you've finished entering your text, just use the *Change* command on the Search menu to substitute *The Macintosh Bible* for *tmb* everywhere it appears in the document.

Many people find this technique of using abbreviations more convenient than permanently setting up Glossaries.

❡ *footnotes in MacWrite* (DC)

MacWrite doesn't have a footnote feature, but you can create documents with endnotes with just a little extra effort. Use the Note Pad (or an improvement on it like Super Note Pad or MiniWriter) to store your footnotes as you write, then paste them all at the end of your document.

If you want true footnotes, insert them as you write directly below the line in which they're referenced. When you're finished revising the document, cut each footnote and paste it at the end of the page. This technique works because you're not changing the total number of lines on any page.

If you regularly create documents with footnotes, consider getting Microsoft Word, which has excellent footnoting capabilities.

❡ *underlining just the words* (DC)

When you select some text and choose Underline from the Style menu (or hit ⌘–U), everything, including spaces, is underlined. If you want to underline the words but not the spaces between them, you have to select each word (by double-clicking on it) and underline it individually.

❡ *changing the Ruler in large documents* (AN)

If you've ever changed the formatting of a ruler that controlled a large section of a MacWrite document, you

shortcut

know it can take forever for the document to reformat to the new ruler settings. (It even takes a while if there are no changes, since MacWrite still has to go through and check.) This can get to be pretty frustrating, particularly if you need to make several changes (both margins, the line indent marker and a couple of tabs, say), since you have to wait after each change.

There's an easy way around this—just insert a new ruler right below the one you want to change (either with the *Insert Ruler* command or by cutting and pasting the ruler you want), then change the old ruler. Since there's no text between the old ruler and the new ruler, you won't have to wait for reformatting. When you've got the old ruler the way you want it, delete the new one. The document will now reformat to the new settings, but you'll only have to sit through the process once.

◉ *text formatting in headers and footers* (DC)

esp. for beginners

The text you have in the header and footer of a MacWrite document is not affected by any font, style or formatting changes you make to the text in the body of the document. You have to open the header and footer (from the Format menu) to change their margins or any other of their formatting characteristics.

◉ *trouble printing* (DC)

Sometimes MacWrite won't obey your command to print a document. Usually you get a message that reads *MacWrite cannot print this document,* but other times nothing happens. There are at least four reasons why MacWrite won't be able to print a document.

1. The text is too long. Try printing a few pages at a time.

2. The disk is so full that there's no room for the temporary print file MacWrite creates every time it prints a document. Print a few pages at a time, or delete unneeded files from the disk.

3. The wrong printer resource is selected. Check the Chooser desk accessory to make sure that you've selected the correct printer (ImageWriter, LaserWriter or whatever you're using).

4. The cables aren't properly connected, or the printer is either turned off or "off-line" (not paying attention to what the computer tells it). On the ImageWriter, the Select button toggles the printer between on-line and off-line.

⬢ *title pages* (DC)

To create a MacWrite document with an unnumbered title page, choose *Title Page* from the Format menu. No header, footer or page number information will appear on the first page.

If you want the page right after the title page (the second page of the document) to be numbered 1, choose *Set Page #* from the Format menu and set the number to 0 (zero). (There's one tiny drawback to doing this—you won't be able to print the title page all by itself unless you set the beginning page number back to 1.)

⬢ *printing in reverse order* (DC)

One nice thing about MacWrite is that it outputs the last page first. This saves you having to collate the pages the way you do with Word and many other programs. Of course, if you're printing more than one copy, you'll still have to do some collating (or else print it more than once), but at least the pages will be in the right order. (The LaserWriter II's and many other laser printers automatically put the pages in the right order for you.)

⬢ *"Too many paragraphs for this document"* (DC)

Occasionally MacWrite may give you the above message. That's because it keeps track of carriage returns and rulers rather than words, the way most other word processors do, and limits documents to 2040 paragraphs (i.e., carriage returns).

There is a klugy way around this problem, but it won't work with justified text, and you have to indent the first line of every paragraph. Put the indentation arrow flush with the left margin arrow on the ruler, and set a tab for the indent you want. Then press the Tab key instead of Return to end each paragraph. This will fool MacWrite into thinking you have fewer paragraphs than you do.

✎ *centering text top to bottom* (DC)

Here's a simple way to center text between the top and bottom of the page in a MacWrite document:

1. Remove all blank lines from the top of the page to the beginning of the text.

2. Go to the end of the text you want vertically centered and add returns until you see the page-break marker.

3. Move the I-beam to the middle of the blank lines, select from there to the end of the page, and cut the highlighted blank lines.

4. Move to the top of the page and paste the blank lines you cut.

(This will only work if you've removed the headers and footers, or if they are of exactly the same length.)

Advanced MacWrite tips

Unless otherwise noted, these tips should work with both version 4.6 and version 5.0 of MacWrite.

✎ *leading control in MacWrite* (AN)

Leading is a typesetter's term that refers to the space between lines of text. MacWrite doesn't offer the automatic leading control that Microsoft Word does, but you can exert some limited control over leading by using the following technique:

To change the leading between two lines of text, select a blank space in the second line and change it to a different size. (You're limited to six sizes: 9-, 10-, 12-, 14-, 18- and 24-point.) That line will then adjust itself accordingly. When you're satisfied with the results, repeat the procedure for each successive line of text.

🍎 *making the default window wider* (DC)

If you want MacWrite's window to cover the whole screen without having to stretch it each time you enter the program, you can permanently change its size with the system utility ResEdit. But remember the first rule of ResEdit: only modify a copy, not the original.

Here's how you do it: open MacWrite with ResEdit, open WIND, and change ID=301. New boundsRect should be 38, –58, 337, 550. If wanted, change the ID 302 (header) and 303 (footer) windows to 45, –58, 205, 550.

(Although this trick should work with version 5.0, for some reason it doesn't appear to.)

🍎 *printer delay at end of printout* (DC)

Printing with MacWrite 4.5 on the ImageWriter can be pretty slow, and there's usually an extra delay when the printer gets to the end of your document—it pauses before advancing the paper to the bottom of the last page. The more blank space there is between the end of your document and the end of the last page, the longer the pause.

The solution is to click on the Cancel button (it shows on the screen while you're printing) when the last line of text on the last page has been printed. This makes the ImageWriter scroll the last page out immediately.

🍎 *double-sided MacWrite printouts* (DC)

Both the LaserWriter and the ImageWriter II with a sheet feeder let you print out double-sided copies, but the method varies slightly because on the LaserWriter, MacWrite automatically collates the pages for you, printing the last page first. Here's how to do double-sided copies on both machines so that the correct pages will print back-to-back:

**very
hot
tip**

On the LaserWriter:

First print half as many copies of the document as you need. Then arrange them so that the copies of page 2 are on the bottom, followed by the copies of page 1, followed by page 4, then page 3, page 6, page 5, and so on, continuing to count up by even numbers and subtracting 1 in between. If there are an odd number of pages in your document, set aside the copies of the last page and substitute blank pages for them in the pile.

Place the pile of arranged pages in the paper tray face up, with the top edge of the pages pointing towards the end of the tray that goes into the LaserWriter. Insert the tray and print the other half of the copies.

On the ImageWriter II with a sheet feeder:

First print half as many copies of the document as you need. Then arrange them so that the copies of page 2 are on the top, followed by the copies of page 1, followed by page 4, then page 3, page 6, page 5, and so on, continuing to count up by even numbers and subtracting 1 in between. If there are an odd number of pages in your document, set aside the copies of the last page and substitute blank pages for them in the pile.

Place the pile of arranged pages in the input tray so that you can see the printing, with the top edge of the pages facing down. Print the other half of the copies.

🍎 *inserting text without the mouse* (DC)

If you want to insert some text at a point that's only a few words back from where you're typing, you don't need to move your hand from the keyboard to the mouse and reposition the insertion point. Just backspace to where you want to insert, type in the new text, then hold down the ⌘ and Backspace keys. MacWrite will retype the text you backspaced over.

MacWrite only stores 50 characters deleted with the Backspace key, so if you backspace more than that, you'll lose some text. And, from a practical point of view, if you need to go back more than four or five words, it's probably quicker to use the mouse.

❡ deleting text with the ⌨Enter⌨ key *(DC)*

A very fast way to delete text is to hold down the ⌨Enter⌨ key while selecting it. The text is deleted as soon as you release the mouse button. (This is a little too fast for my taste, but if you have nerves of steel, you may want to give it a try.)

shortcut

WriteNow tips

❡ faster scrolling *(DC)*

When dragging past the bottom of the screen to select text, the closer you are to the bottom of the screen, the faster the scrolling will go.

shortcut

❡ global font-style changes *(DC)*

WriteNow provides an easy way to change the font, size and/or style of identically formatted text throughout an entire document (or any portion you select).

very hot tip

Let's say you've underlined the titles of several books in a document and now you decide that you'd rather italicize them. Position the insertion point at the beginning of the first title and drag (see the previous entry) to select all the text up to and including the last title. Hold down the ⌨Shift⌨ key and choose *Italics* on the Style menu, then choose *Underline*. Each occurrence of an underlined book title will now be in italics.

This same technique works with size and font changes. The important thing to remember in using this tip is that each occurrence you want to change must have exactly the same font, style and size. This feature is not as powerful as style sheets, but it's pretty handy nevertheless.

⚫ *global ruler changes* (DC)

Normally when you make a change to a Ruler, all selected paragraphs are changed. But if you hold down the ⃞Shift⃞ key while changing a ruler, only those paragraphs formatted with exactly the same ruler settings will be affected. (This technique is sort of similar to the one in the entry above.)

⚫ *formatting headers, footers and footnotes* (DC)

To give a document's headers, footers or footnotes the same format as the body of the document, choose *Copy Ruler* (on the Edit menu), then choose *Header, Footer* or *Footnote View*, and then choose *Paste Ruler* (on the Edit menu).

⚫ *bulk document importing* (DC/AN)

shortcut

One of the most annoying features of WriteNow versions before 2.0 was their requirement that you use a separate utility (called *Translator)* to convert documents from other word processors before importing them into WriteNow. If you're still using one of those earlier versions, here's a way to reduce the annoyance a bit.

Put Translator and all the documents you want converted into the same folder. ⃞Shift⃞ ⃞Click⃞ on all of them (including Translator), then ⃞Double-Click⃞ on Translator. You'll still have to select each document to be converted, but when you're done, you can choose the *Transfer to WriteNow* command (on the Transfer menu) to open WriteNow and all the documents you've just converted will open in turn (unless you run out of memory).

⚫ *speeding up spelling checks* (DC)

shortcut

WriteNow's spelling-checker dictionary stays in memory only as long as the Check Spelling window is open, and it slows things down to have to read it from disk. So if you're using floppies and are doing a lot of spelling checks, you can save a lot of time by leaving the Check Spelling window open all the time.

⚜ *bulk editing of the dictionary* (DC)

To add a lot of words to the dictionary, select them all and click on the Learn button. To delete a lot of words to the dictionary, select them all and click on the Forget button.

shortcut

Tips about More

⚜ *about "document window"* (SZA)

The tips in this section reluctantly stick to LivingVideoText's confusing term *document window*. A More document window is not the window that has your outline in it, the one with the close box and the title bar— it's the expandable scrolling area that stores text for a headline.

esp. for beginners

⚜ *keyboard character styles* (SZA)

Since there's no Style menu in More, it's not obvious that you can apply character formatting to selected text with keyboard commands. But you can. The keyboard commands are:

shortcut

Shift ⌘ –B	bold
Shift ⌘ –I	italic
Shift ⌘ –U	underline
Shift ⌘ –S	shadow
Shift ⌘ –O	outline

⚜ *keyboard font sizes* (SZA)

You can make selected text larger with Shift ⌘ –comma, smaller with Shift ⌘ –period.

shortcut

⚜ *document formatting* (SZA)

If you use the Document dialog box when a headline is selected, the formatting you choose applies to all the document windows subordinate to that headline and to its subheadlines.

If you use the Document dialog box when a document is open and active (that's the headline's text area, remember), the formatting changes apply to only that document.

🍎 *headline styles* (SZA)

Style formatting in headlines can work on:

- Selected words in a headline

- Any individual headline

- All the headlines on a given level

To set the style for a group of headlines, you can choose the *Headlines* command from the Format menu and click in your choices of styles. Or just use the keyboard equivalents for styles when you're in any headline: the formatting is applied to the current headline, as well as every other headline of that same level.

To change a single headline, select all the words in it (by dragging, triple-clicking or using the *Select All* command) and then apply the formatting.

To change the style of part of a headline, select it before using the formatting commands.

very hot tip

Basically, remember: if the headline is selected (enclosed in a frame), formatting applies to it and to all the headlines of the same level; if text within the headline is selected (highlighted), the formatting applies to only the selected text.

🍎 *font cycling* (SZA)

shortcut

You can cycle through all the fonts in your System, applying them to headlines or document windows, with [Shift] [⌘] –((left bracket) and [Shift] [⌘] –) (right bracket).

❡ *moving around* (SZA)

To jump right to the Home headline, use `Shift` `⌘` –↑; to jump right to the last headline, use `Shift` `⌘` –↓. `⌘` –↑ jumps you up a windowful at a time, and `⌘` –↓ jumps you down a windowful at a time.

shortcut

❡ *scrolling in document windows* (SZA)

The arrow keys work as expected inside document windows, but you can enhance them:

shortcut

- `⌘` –↑ and `⌘` –↓ move you up and down a windowful.

- `Shift` `⌘` –↑ and `Shift` `⌘` –↓ move you to the beginning and end of the text in the document window.

- `⌘` –← and `⌘` –→ move the pointer a word at a time.

- `Shift` `⌘` –← and `Shift` `⌘` –→ move the pointer a sentence at a time.

❡ *selecting text* (SZA)

You can select text in headlines or in document windows without using the mouse, simply by holding down the `Option` key and using any keyboard command that moves the insertion point. As the insertion point moves, it selects the text it passes over.

shortcut

❡ *triple-click tricks* (SZA)

Triple-clicking on a headline selects all the text in the headline. Triple-clicking in a sentence in a document window selects an entire sentence.

shortcut

❡ *in and out of document windows* (SZA)

`Option` `Enter` –period moves the pointer out of a document window and back into its headline without closing the window. The same command moves you the other way— from a headline into its open document window.

shortcut

☝ exporting options *(SZA)*

When you're ready to Export an outline to another program, the Export dialog box lets you decide whether or not you want to include headline labels. You can define the type of headline labels (and other attributes of them) before exporting in the Print Options dialog box. The options you set for printing apply to exported outlines.

☝ tree charts *(SZA)*

very hot tip

You can put blank boxes in a tree chart just by leaving a blank headline in the outline. If you'd rather have under-lines than boxes in a tree chart, set the height of the box in the Tree Chart Options dialog box to anything less than the height of the current font.

To split a headline into multiple lines in a tree chart box, put a vertical bar (|) where you want the headline to break. The character shows in outline view but disappears in the tree chart box.

☝ clicking buttons from the keyboard *(SZA)*

shortcut

In a dialog box, the first letter of a button's name will click it. For example, if your choices are Yes, No and Cancel, you can simply press *Y, N* or *C.* (⌘–period also works for Cancel.)

☝ automatic Search For: entries *(SZA)*

shortcut

If any text is selected when you use the *Search...* command, it's automatically entered into the *Search For:* text box.

☝ printing centered bullet charts in More *(DC)*

When printing bullet charts, you need to turn on *As Shown When Printed* (in the Bullet Options dialog box) in order to properly center them. Otherwise the chart will be centered on the screen instead of on the page.

⬤ *counting words* (SZA)

You can use More's "search language" to count the words in an outline (or any part of it).

First, select the part you want counted. (Selecting a headline will count all its subheads and document windows; to count the whole document, select the Home headline.) Then type the following in the *Search For:* text box (in the Search dialog box):

[a-z][a-z][a-z]*

Click on the Whole Word and Match Pattern check boxes and the Find All button.

More looks for all whole-word letter sequences of three or more characters. When it's done, it will tell you how many it found—that's the word count. If you want it to count words with one or more characters, or two or more characters, use *(a-z)** and *(a-z)(a-z)**, respectively. (And, of course, you can look for words of four or more characters by using *(a-z)(a-z)(a-z)(a-z))**.

Chapter 11

Data processing

Spreadsheets and related products

♦ *Excel* (AN)

Thanks to its many powerful features and integrated charting ability, Excel has become the standard spread-sheet on the Mac. In fact, in a recent *MacWorld* survey, 89% of the respondents picked it as their favorite.

very good feature

Excel gives you a theoretical worksheet of 256 columns by 16,384 rows (that's more than four million cells, which should be adequate for your personal budget)—although you almost certainly won't need anything like that many.

Although Excel's manual is terrible and some of its dialog boxes confusing, the program is relatively easy to learn and use—especially considering everything it can do. Version 2.0 might be out by the time you read this, but even version 1.5 has some nice enhancements. The macro language and charting function have both been strengthened, page preview is slicker and there's full color support.

Excel is sometimes billed as an integrated program, on the basis of its limited database abilities, but Paul Hoffman considers these to be counterintuitive and "conceptually wrong." He also says the sorting capability is clumsy and feels that it's easier to export data to another database program and then reimport it than to try to use Excel as a database.

Excel dominates its field like no other Mac product but challengers are here (see the entry on *Full Impact* below).

♦ *101 Macros for Excel* (SS)

According to my contacts at Microsoft, only about one out of five Excel users ever creates a macro. *(I never have, for example.—AN)* Apparently, even with the macro recorder, which automates the process, a lot of people find macros scary. *(Or they just don't have the time and patience to plow through that wretched manual to learn something new.—AN)*

*very good
feature*

But you don't have to create your own macros—you can buy ready-to-run ones created by experts, like those in Macropac's collection, 101 Macros for Excel. They range from the simple and obvious (making cells bold or italic) to the interesting (charting a biorhythm or creating a recalculation timer) to the supremely useful (creating a new database or defining hot spots). All in all, they can vastly simplify your day-to-day work with Excel.

Each of these macros can be executed in two or three different ways. First of all, they can be accessed the way any Excel macro can, with the *Run...* command on Excel's Macro menu. Secondly, almost half of them can also be called up with a preassigned [Option] [⌘] combination.

Finally, you can run the Macro Launcher (one of the 101) by pressing [Option] [⌘]–M. This produces the dialog box below. Each macro has a short name (one to three characters long); you simply type it into the dialog box to run the macro. (The one in the illustration, *tg,* toggles grid lines on and off.)

```
╔═══════════════ 101 Macros ═══════════════╗
║                                            ║
║  Enter macro short name and    ┌────────┐ ║
║  Return (or OK)                │   OK   │ ║
║                                └────────┘ ║
║                                ┌────────┐ ║
║                                │ Cancel │ ║
║                                └────────┘ ║
║  ┌──────────────────────────────────────┐║
║  │ tg                                   │║
║  └──────────────────────────────────────┘║
╚════════════════════════════════════════════╝
```

*very good
feature*

101 Macros for Excel gives you a quick reference guide that lists each macro's [Option] [⌘] key and its short name. If the manual's not handy, there's even a macro that will recreate this list for you as an Excel worksheet.

The macros are divided into eight general categories: cursor control; display and window control; format, alignment and border control; editing; calculation, protection and cell identification; formula, table, printing and saving; database and charting; and miscellaneous.

The excellent manual keeps things simple by describing each macro in the same, organized manner. The first paragraph tells you what it does, the second how it works and the third (if any) is set aside for special notes. Since each macro description is completely self–contained, after reading the first four chapters of the manual (37 pages), you can skip immediately to the macros that interest you.

very good feature

Here's what a few of my personal favorites do:

- transpose a row (or column) of data

- swap two columns (or two rows)

- toggle between two hot spots

- tile the windows (horizontally or vertically)

- save all worksheets

- change zeros to blanks

Admittedly, several of the macros—most of those for formatting, alignment and borders, for instance—could easily be created using Excel's macro recorder. Others, however, would require fairly sophisticated macro programming skills. So even if you're a macro hot-shot, this package will save you an enormous amount of work—both in programming effort and in efficiency gained from using the macros. After all, why reinvent the wheel simply because you can?

If you're a macro novice, a careful examination of these macros may be all you need to push you into the elite company of the 20% who "build their own." What better place to start than with 101 carefully debugged and commented examples?

Whether or not you ever write a macro of your own, this excellent package adds enough functionality to Excel to justify its purchase by virtually any user.

⚫ **Excellence and Cobb Group books** (AN)

Getting the most out of Excel takes a lot of advice and one way to get it is by subscribing to *Excellence,* a journal of Excel tips and tricks published by the Cobb Group. It costs $50 a year so you'll only want to do that if you make fairly extensive use of Excel; if you do, *Excellence* should be a real help. The Cobb Group also publishes as number of books on Excel.

⚫ **Full Impact** (SB)

very good feature

The thing Excel has so long been missing is finally here—competition. Ashton-Tate's Full Impact surpasses Excel's power in many ways; it also has a more friendly user interface, with multiple icon bars, custom icon bars, a compass-style navigator and column and row numbers that show in the scroll bars.

Full Impact has excellent formatting capabilities—like variable-height rows and the ability to assign a different font and size to each individual cell. Graphs are faster and easier to do (although Excel can do more kinds) and color is supported throughout. Charts and text blocks can be placed anywhere, even on top of data.

There are many existing prewritten macros and templates for Excel, and it will take a while for Full Impact to accumulate equivalent numbers of them. But the programs are so similar that many Excel resources may work with Full Impact as well. It can import Excel spreadsheets saved in SYLK format and can also import and export dBASE files.

very bad feature

things to come

Unfortunately, both Microsoft and Ashton-Tate share a reputation for truly wretched telephone support. Maybe it's a problem of size (Apple's support is terrible as well). I'd prefer to see these companies get some more people to answer their phones, rather than worry about 256 colors in a graph. *(Since they probably won't, I'm looking forward to Wingz, a high-powered spreadsheet due out from a much smaller company, Innovative Software.—AN)*

MacCalc *(DC)*

If you're not a spreadsheet junkie but do need to use them occasionally, you might be interested in MacCalc from Bravo Technologies. This small (999 rows by 124 columns) and inexpensive ($140) product provides all the power you'll need for simple tasks like balancing checking accounts and doing simple projections.

bargain

But don't expect the sophistication you find in Excel. For example, if text in a cell is wider than the width of the cell, the text won't display in the next cell to the right, even if that cell is empty—the way it does in Excel.

Works' spreadsheet module *(DC)*

Another possibility for the occasional spreadsheet user is Microsoft Works (described in Chapter 15). While not as powerful as Excel, Works' spreadsheet offers most of the important features of Multiplan (Excel's predecessor) and for the extra money you spend, you also get a word processor, a database and a communications program—plus the added flexibility of having all of these applications available from within one program.

bargain

Trapeze *(Michael B. Levy)*

Trapeze has done away with the typical spreadsheet grid. But I find that grid very basic and transportable across systems and applications. I don't like being forced to use natural-language range identifiers. Too often I change titles or am less than consistent in capitalization or spelling. This approach also makes many of the basic spreadsheet tasks very difficult and cumbersome.

Trapeze seems to be aiming at the power user, but I think they've missed the mark; relatively few power users need its capabilities. I was intrigued by this program until I actually began using it; now I feel that it's too complicated to learn and can't recommend it for use at my company. It provides elaborate and elegant solutions to theoretical problems but it doesn't seem to have much to do with the sort of things people do in the real world.

(Michael B. Levy, a controller for a large Silicon Valley company, is a typical power user of spreadsheets and other modelling software.)

Excel tips

These tips work with version 1.5 of Excel and may or may not work with earlier or later versions.

⬥ learning Excel (AN)

*esp. for
beginners*

Like many of Microsoft manual's, Excel's is maddeningly bad. But the program's help screens are pretty good, so use them instead of the manual to learn the program. You'll still have to look things up in the manual (a very frustrating—and usually fruitless—task) but the less time you spend with it, the happier you'll be.

⬥ shortcut to the Scrapbook (MB)

shortcut

To copy an Excel spreadsheet (or part of one) directly into the Scrapbook, simply select the cells you want and hit [Shift] [⌘]–C.

⬥ escaping from cells with invalid formulas (DC)

*esp. for
beginners*

Excel won't let you close a cell until the formula in it meets the program's formatting rules. You'll keep getting a message that says your formula is wrong and you'll be put right back in that cell. This can be maddening when you're working on a complex formula and can't seem to get it right.

To escape, just remove the = (equal sign) at the beginning of the formula. Excel will now treat the entry as text and thus won't analyze it for correctness, allowing you to move on to another cell. After a little while away from the troublesome formula, you may be able to go back to it and spot your mistake.

● *Excel's insistence on certain formats* (PH/AN)

Excel can also be maddeningly insistent on how a date, say, or a percentage, should be formatted. To get around this, start your entry with an option space. This will force Excel to treat the entry as plain text. (For dates, just a plain space will work.) But be aware that while an entry is being treated as plain text, it can't be used in computations.

very hot tip

● *freezing numbers* (SZA)

Let's say you've created a spreadsheet to take care of your checkbook. Instead of typing in every check number, you've created a formula that adds one to the cell above and copied it down a column. That works fine until you have a break in the series (for a deposit, say) or until you do some sorting (to pull out certain expenses, say).

very hot tip

The solution isn't to type in the check numbers one at a time; a computer is supposed to save you time. Fortunately, you can "freeze" the numbers after the formula has created them.

To do that, select the cells that contain the check numbers, cut, [Click] in the cell where you want them to begin (which can be the same place you just cut them from) and choose *Paste Special...* from the Edit menu. [Click] the *Values* button in the dialog box and press [Return] . The cells will now contain actual numbers, not formulas, and so they won't change.

● *printing large worksheets* (DC/AN)

When you're printing a very large worksheet, use forced page breaks to divide it into sections of related data, rather than just letting the program insert page breaks arbitrarily. This makes the printout easier to read, since logically related information is grouped together on the same page, without irrelevant information to distract you. It also lets you print out selected portions of the spreadsheet simply by specifying the pages you want in the Print dialog box.

very hot tip

Another approach is to use the *Set Print Area* command. (To remove a print area you've set up, choose *Define Names* on the Formula menu and delete *Print_Area*.)

🍎 *protecting the structure* (DC/AN)

If you're designing a worksheet that will require the repeated input of varying data, you'll want to protect the cells that contain text or formulas so they don't get accidentally changed during the data-entry process. Here's how to do that:

With the document unprotected, select the cells where the data is to be entered. Use the *Cell Protection* command (on the Format menu) to unlock them. Then choose *Protect Document* from the Options menu. This will lock all the cells that have not been selected.

🍎 *saving time by turning off Automatic Calculation* (DC)

shortcut

When working with large worksheets, you can often save a great deal of time by turning off Automatic Calculation. Just choose *Calculation* from the Options menu and click on the *Manual* option when the dialog box comes up.

Now you can choose when you want the calculations to take place. The simplest way to do that is to hit ⌘ – = (equal sign).

🍎 *rounding* (DC/AN)

very hot tip

Like most other spreadsheets, Excel stores numbers as precisely it can, regardless of how you ask to have them displayed. Say, for example, that the result of a calculation is 31.89624. If you request that the number be displayed without decimal points, it will appear as 32; if you request that it be displayed with two decimal points, it will appear as 31.90. But it will continue to be stored as 31.89624 and that's the value that will be inserted into other calculations if you reference that cell in a formula someplace else on the worksheet.

This can be confusing. Imagine multiplying two cells that display 3 and 6 but have actual values of 2.51 and 5.62. If you ask for the result without decimal points too, you'll get 14 instead of the expected 18. Normally, of course, you want the precision, regardless of the confusion, but if you don't, Excel can be told to use the displayed value—rather than the more precise, stored value—in calculations.

Just choose *Precision as displayed* from the Options menu (but be aware that when you do this, the exact value of the entries is lost; it doesn't come back when you return to full precision).

🍎 *bird's-eye view of worksheets* (DC)

Large Excel worksheets can get really complex, and it's easy to lose the forest for the trees. To regain your sense of the overall structure, try viewing the worksheet in 4-point type (using the *Font* command on the Options menu). Go back to this bird's-eye view whenever you feel lost (you can't actually work on the spreadsheet when the type is 4-point).

very hot tip

🍎 *outlining cells* (AN)

Although it's right there in the Border dialog box (on the Format menu), many Excel users don't realize that they can outline any group of cells they've selected simply by clicking on *Outline*. This is a lot easier than clicking on Left, Top, Right and Bottom all the time.

esp. for beginners

🍎 *hiding part of the worksheet* (DC/Fokko Du Cloux)

You may want to hide part of an Excel worksheet, either because you have sensitive data in it that you don't want to be visible on the screen while you work or so you can move from one column to another without having to use the scroll bar.

To do that, just set the width of the columns you want to hide to zero. Your data will still be there, but it won't be displayed. The only indication that there's a column hidden will be a jump in the letters at the top of the screen that identify each column.

To open up a hidden column, select the columns on either side of it, then choose *Column Width...* from the Format menu. All three columns will assume the width you specify (which means you may have to adjust them back where you want them after the hidden column is revealed).

You can also get this effect with the mouse. When you move the pointer into the row containing the column headers (A, B, C, etc.) and move it sufficiently close to a dividing line between columns, it changes its shape from an arrow into a vertical line with arrows sticking horizontally out of it. This pointer tool lets you drag the right edge of a given column towards the left to make the column smaller. If you move the right edge past the left edge, the column disappears.

very hot tip

Ah, but is there a way to open it again with the mouse? Yes, there is. Drag the vertical-line-with-arrows-sticking-horizontally-out-of-it pointer from left to right over the dividing line that contains the hidden column. When it's just past the dividing line—just before it becomes an arrow again—hold down the mouse button and you'll be able to drag the column open again.

✎ *previews of printouts* (AN)

esp. for beginners

One of Excel's nicer features is the ability to preview on the screen what printouts will look like on paper (you do that by checking the *Preview* box in the Print dialog box). The text is too small to read in the Preview window (unless you're using giant type) but you can zoom in on any part of it by clicking the magnifying-glass pointer. Click again and you're back at the overall view of the page.

You can move around in zoom mode by holding down the Option key. This turns the pointer into a little grabber hand (as in MacPaint) that you can use to move the image around while keeping the text at a readable size.

linked worksheets and recalculation speed *(DC)*

Excel lets you link worksheets, a feature that can be very useful for complex models. That's the good news. The bad news is that linking worksheets can dramatically increase recalculation time, so only do it when it's absolutely necessary.

important warning

special characters in titles *(Fokko Du Cloux)*

To print an ampersand (&) in a header or footer, type *&&* in the text box in the Page Setup window. You have to do that because *&* is normally used by Excel to indicate that the next letter is a command. For example, *&p* produces the page number, *&d* the date and *&f* the name of the file.

esp. for beginners

font of titles *(AN)*

When you print an Excel worksheet, the title appears in the same font as the rest of the worksheet. But when you print an Excel chart, the title is always in Geneva—or in Helvetica if you're printing on a laser printer and have Font Substitution on (see the next entry for why you'd better leave it on in that case).

important warning

printing Excel charts on a laser printer *(AN)*

Always leave Font Substitution on when printing an Excel chart on a laser printer. Because the chart title always stays in Geneva, no matter what you do to the rest of the chart, the program won't be able to print the title if you turn Font Substitution off and the program will crash.

The window on the next page shows the best settings for printing an Excel chart on a laser printer.

```
≡≡≡≡≡≡≡≡≡≡≡≡ Page Setup ≡≡≡≡≡≡≡≡≡≡≡≡
 Paper:   ● US Letter    ○ A4 Letter            ┌─────────┐
          ○ US Legal     ○ International Fanfold │   OK    │
 Orientation:   ● Tall   ○ Wide                 └─────────┘
                                                ┌─────────┐
 Paper Width: [8.5in]   Height: [11 in]         │ Cancel  │
                                                └─────────┘
 Margins:  Top:    [1 in]    Left:  [1.25in]    ┌───────────┐
                                                │Set Default│
           Bottom: [1 in]    Right: [1.25in]    └───────────┘
```

⌘ *easy worksheet navigation* (DC/AN)

shortcut

Navigating around large Excel worksheets can become tiresome. One way to make things easier on yourself is to break the worksheet up into logical parts and use the *Define Name* function from the Formula menu to define each part. Then you can use the *Go To...* command from the Formula menu to go directly to any part of the worksheet that you've defined. (To make the Named Ranges easier to see, you can outline them with borders.)

⌘ *using Excel on a single-drive 512K Mac* (DC)

You can run Excel on a single-drive 512K Macintosh if your worksheets are relatively small. The best method is to create a RAM disk of about 220K and copy a system folder (containing the System, Finder and ImageWriter files) to it. Then set up a floppy with only Excel on it (you can add the Help file, if you like). There'll be plenty of room left on the floppy for most worksheets.

⌘ *importing worksheets from large-screen Macs* (DC/AN)

**very
hot
tip**

If you import an Excel document created on a Mac with an external monitor to a Mac with a 9″ screen, the spreadsheet's window will probably be larger than the screen and you won't be able to resize it because the size box will be off the screen. The solution is simple: just double-click on the title bar and the window will automatically resize to fit the Mac's screen.

♦ *time and date functions* (DC/Fokko Du Cloux)

Use the *NOW( )* function to retrieve the current date and time from the system clock and enter it into a formula as a serial number. Use the following functions to convert the serial number to the format you need:

DAY

WEEKDAY

HOUR

MINUTE

MONTH

YEAR

For example, the formula *=FORMULA("=HOUR(NOW())")* gives you the current hour.

You choose how the date or time appears. For example, if you specify *m/d/yyyy* (with the *Number...* command on the Format menu), you'll get it in this form: *5/12/1989*. If you specify *dddd*, you'll get just the day of the week. *Mmmm* will give you the month written out in full and *hh:mm am/pm* the time in this form: *22:01 pm*.

♦ *using Copy Picture* (DC)

There's a hidden command on Excel's Edit menu called *Copy Picture;* to make it visible, hold down the ⌗Shift⌗ key when you pop down the menu. This will copy the selected portion of the worksheet (along with the relevant row and column headings), in PICT format, to the Clipboard. You can then paste the selection into MacDraw (to manipulate the parts of it individually) or into an application like PageMaker (which lets you stretch or shrink it).

very hot tip

♦ *selecting large areas of a worksheet* (DC/AN)

To select a large portion of a worksheet with the least effort, click on the cell in the top left corner of the range you want to select, then choose *Goto...* on the Formula menu. Specify the cell you want to be in the lower right corner of

shortcut

the selection, then hold down the ⬚Shift key while clicking the OK button or hitting ⬚Return .

To select the whole spreadsheet, click in the box in the extreme upper left corner—that is, above the number *1* and to the left of the letter *A*.

♣ *making x–y scatter charts* (AN)

David Pratt of Los Altos Hills, California, wrote in with a tip on how to make a scatter chart of two or more variables (that is, two value axes instead of a value axis and a category axis). The trick is to use the *Paste Special...* command when you paste them in.

♣ *speeding up macros* (AN)

shortcut

Lee Hinde of Roseville, California, wrote in to tell us that the *Echo(False)* feature greatly speeds up the execution of macros (it particularly makes a difference in long ones). One of his macros that takes two minutes without *Echo(False)* takes just fifteen seconds with it.

Echo(False) works by turning off screen redrawing. (Being able to ignore that saves Excel a lot of time.) By the way, you don't need to reset Echo at the end of the macro so that screen redrawing will be turned on again; Excel does that automatically.

Databases

♣ *two meanings for "database"* (SM)

esp. for beginners

Technically, *databases* are mailing lists and other large collections of data maintained on computers, and *database managers* are the programs that manage them. But in common usage the programs themselves have come to be called *databases* and that's the way the term is used in this section and throughout the book.

❡ databases for the Mac (SM)

The Macintosh has always suffered from an embarrassment of riches when it comes to databases. Databases were some of the first third-party products to appear. Why was that?

The way I heard the story was that in the early days of the Macintosh—late 1983 and early 1984—when Apple was looking for companies to develop software for the machines, they told them, "Don't develop word processors—there'll be plenty of those; do databases." If that's true, Apple's reasons for giving the advice are open to debate. One theory is that they wanted to keep the market for themselves...and for a certain software developer in the Pacific Northwest (no, I don't mean Bigfoot Software).

*gossip/
trivia*

Be that as it may, even now, several years after the Mac was introduced, Mac users who are still looking for a word processor they can love have an uncountable number of databases to choose from. (Oh, I suppose you could count them, but what's the point?)

Before I go on to discuss them, there are a few general matters that should be taken care of.

❡ some useful database terms (SM)

Since I'll be using some database terminology you may not be familiar with, here are a few definitions:

*esp. for
beginners*

A *record* is one item in a database file. For example, in a mailing list, each name and address listing is a record. If your mailing list has 500 names and addresses in it, it contains 500 records.

A *field* is one item in a record. For example, in a mailing list record, you'd have fields for *name, address, city, state, zip,* etc.

A *calculated field* is one whose values are determined by the contents of other fields. For instance, a field called *total purchases* might contain a formula that defines it as equal to *previous purchases + current purchases.*

Databases are called *relational* when they can relate two or more files together. For example, let's say an inventory application contains two files—one that contains the customer information and another that contains the information about the inventory itself.

When a customer buys something, you type in some basic identifying information (her name, say, or her customer number) and the program looks up other data (shipping address, payment terms, etc.) in the customer information file. You can then enter some data about her purchases, like item numbers. For each item number, the program looks up a description (quantity on hand, pricing, weight, etc.) in the inventory file.

It's a rare database that doesn't have that label *relational* slapped on it. You probably don't need a relational database (most people don't) but if you do, make sure the product you buy deserves the label.

A *multiuser* database is one that operates over a network and allows more than one person to access a file at the same time. For example, in a sales and inventory application, one person could enter sales data while another person on a different machine could simultaneously enter inventory data.

Typically, multiuser databases include *record-locking,* which means that only one person at a time can edit a particular record. Other users are prohibited from doing anything more than looking at that record until the first person is done.

⌘ tips on selecting a database (SM)

1. Don't worry about the statistics

If you're looking for a chart in this book that gives you various statistics on these programs—number of records allowed, characters per field, etc.—forget it. I've looked at dozens of those charts over the last couple of years, and none of them has ever given me any help in choosing a database. Who cares if program A will only let you enter

65,536 records but program B will let you enter two or three billion?

Few people ever use even a fraction of the theoretical capabilities of a program. And the charts never really tell you what those numbers mean, or how large amounts of data affect things like the speed of the program. Program B might let you enter ten times as much data but program A may let you work more quickly and easily.

2. Look for flexibility

very hot tip

In choosing a database, try to find one that is as flexible as possible. Don't buy one that won't let you add a field to a file after creating it. You also should be able to change the type of a field after creating the file. For example, you might find that you've inadvertently made the *date* field a text item and therefore won't be able to sort on it. You should be able to change the data type of that field.

3. Little things mean a lot

very hot tip

Look to see what kind of thoughtful small touches the program offers you. For example, it's nice to be able to assign default values to selected fields—so if you're creating a mailing list of people 90% of whom live in—say—Kansas, you can tell the program to make *KS* the default for the state field, instead of having to type *KS* thousands of times. (Then you just tab past the field and *KS* is entered automatically).

Other nice little touches might include being able to customize reports, choose which fields to index or make the current date the default in any date field.

4. So does the ability to transfer information

One of the nice things about the Mac world is the existence of some fairly standard ways of moving data from one program to another. This can be very useful. For example, there's one database file I use quite often that I first created in Microsoft File. Later I wanted to try it out in Filemaker and had a pretty easy time moving the data in. Currently it's in Double Helix, but I've also worked with it in

very good feature

Excel, OverVUE, Word (as *text only,* to check spelling and make some global changes) and in several applications on the PC.

There are many reasons why you might want to move a file around like this. You may need to do some calculations on the data in it, or print it out in a certain form or access it from another database file set up by a different program. Or you may simply have discovered a new program and decide you want to do all your work in it.

very hot tip

Most programs store information in their own special-ized formats. This lets them get at it quicker or offer certain special features. Fortunately, there's a Mac standard for what *delimits* (marks the boundaries of) fields and records; it's [Tab] between fields and [Return] between records. Make sure any database you buy supports this standard format.

5. Buy from a committed manufacturer

very hot tip

This rule applies to software of any kind. Buy from a manufacturer who has a good track record of supporting their products and their customers. Typically, companies that offer good support also offer fairly frequent updates. If they consist of modest improvements, they should be free or very inexpensive; if they consist of complex enhance-ments to the product, they should obviously cost more, but still shouldn't penalize you (in effect) for buying the earlier version.

6. Don't be (too) afraid to spend money

very hot tip

Powerful software costs a lot to create and support. If you can get by with a $50 program, great. But if you really need a $300 one, that $50 is wasted.

Of course, it's important to take price into consideration, but first evaluate your needs as well as you can and try to make sure you're buying enough power. It's almost impos-sible to buy too much power, but it's very easy to buy too little.

7. Look for file templates

If you know somebody who's using a database for the same purposes you want one for, see if you can get a copy of their database file—emptied of records, of course. You can save a great deal of time by not having to reinvent the wheel. Don't be reluctant to pay them something for the template (but if you have to pay a lot, make sure they'll explain it to you and support it).

This works the other way around as well—if you take the time to develop a good application, be sure to let other people know about it.

which database to buy (SM)

That's enough about databases in general. Now let's talk about some specific products. Each of the programs discussed below has its own particular strengths and weaknesses—so much so that a well-stocked software library could include two or even three of them and not be overburdened. A job that's too complex for Microsoft File may be just right for Helix; one that takes too long to develop in Helix may work well in FileMaker; and one where speed is of the utmost importance may demand OverVUE.

FileMaker (AN)

FileMaker has become something of a standard on the Mac; at least most of the people I know use it. Although its organization is a bit unusual and takes some getting used to (see the entry called *basic organization* in the *FileMaker tips* section below), it does the job in a pretty clean and efficient way.

Dale used Filemaker to compile the notes for the first edition and loved it. He found it fast and easy-to-use and it never let him down.

very good feature

The manual for the original FileMaker and for FileMaker+ wasn't very good, but the one for FileMaker 4 is terrific. I've only used it a little but it seems to be well-written and even well-indexed (the impossible dream!). Certainly it looks

very good feature

great—it's a nicely designed, 424-page, *hardbound* book (why don't more companies do that?).

We've been searching for about a year for software to put Goldstein & Blair's mailing lists and other business records on. After looking at a lot of high-end accounting programs (discussed below), we ended up deciding to try FileMaker 4. Although it doesn't come with all the prepared forms and preprogrammed connections we need, it looks like it'll be easier to just do those ourselves than to figure out how someone else did them in some accounting program and then modify them to our needs. I'll let you know (in an update) how it turns out.

We won't be alone in taking this approach. In researching this for us, Carol Pladsen found a winery that keeps it 80,000-name mailing list in FileMaker on a stock SE. Finding a record takes them *two seconds!* (although completely sorting the list takes several hours).

very good feature

One of the things that sold us on FileMaker was the *terrific* support we got from Nashoba Systems, who developed the product and published it for a while (after Forethought and before Claris, the current publisher). I just hope Claris does as good a job!

Here's what Steve Michel has to say about FileMaker:

⚫ *more on FileMaker* (SM)

very good feature

Filemaker is easy to use, provides adequate performance and is very flexible at designing forms on-screen. The way it indexes is unique. With most databases, you choose the fields to be indexed; Filemaker indexes not only every field in the database but every word. This makes it very easy to search for specific entries—you just type in a word to be searched for and the program finds it virtually instantly.

very good feature

FileMaker's Layout function includes helpful tools like *whiskers* (dotted lines that point to a ruler location and make it easy to place things precisely) and has great versatility with text fields (if your field isn't long enough for the text you want to type, FileMaker allows it to expand to accommodate the entry).

FileMaker has relational capabilities—one file can find information in another file and import it. They're not as powerful as those of Helix or Omnis, say, but they're quite adequate for most people. And, with version 4 of the program, it's now multiuser.

FileMaker is most useful for: long text files; applications that require relatively limited relational capabilities; screen forms that resemble paper forms; and small applications that have to run fast.

🍎 *4th Dimension* (AN)

This relative newcomer to the Mac database scene was the favorite of 20% of Macworld's readers (tied with File-Maker). This figure surprised me because I'd heard that 4th Dimension, while quite powerful, was pretty complicated and hard to learn. I'll try to get someone to review it for one of the updates.

very good feature

🍎 *Microsoft File* (SM)

In the first edition of this book, I wrote: "Microsoft brought this program out fairly early in the life of the Macintosh and has...shamefully neglected to provide significant updates to it. (That's what happens when you're successful, I guess. You don't feel the heat of competition and you work less on your products.)

very bad feature

"File doesn't necessarily need a major features update—though...it wouldn't hurt. What File needs, at this late date, is a performance update, one that brings its speed up to par with other programs on the Mac." Almost two years later, that's *still* true.

File was the first Mac database that allowed you to paste pictures into the file. That was one of the big selling points of the program—though I, for one, have never done it and don't know anybody who's needed to do it.

File lets you create many different forms in which to view your data. The forms are very easy to create, but managing them is another story. Each file can have two forms stored with it on the disk. Other forms can be stored separately (by choosing *Save Form As...* from the File menu).

When you're closing a program, File always asks, *Save this Form with the Datafile?* whether or not you've already saved it. Most users are afraid to say No, thinking the form will be lost altogether. But if you say Yes, you lose one of the original files that was stored with the file.

very bad feature

If this sounds confusing, that's because it is. It takes a lot of work to figure this out, and you still get confused. My advice is: if File seems to be the program that's right for you, try working with its forms for a while, and see if you can make any sense out of them.

Version 2.0, promised soon after this book goes to press, will offer more than 120 templates, to make the program easier to use with printed forms; enhanced compatibility with Word, for easier form letters, mass mailings and mailing labels; and support for the Mac II's color capabilities.

File is most useful for: screen forms that resemble paper forms; mailing lists or other simple files; files that incorporate graphics.

♠ *OverVUE* (SM/AN)

In many ways OverVUE resembles a spreadsheet more than a filing program. For one thing, you normally enter data on a spreadsheet-like grid. For another, the program packs impressive power for working on subsets of your data, and for doing calculations on the data. Finally, like a spreadsheet, OverVUE holds your whole file in memory while you're working on it (this limits the document size to some extent, but also allows searches and sorts to happen with blinding speed).

There are some drawbacks to this approach. One is that it's cumbersome to work with forms in OverVUE, both because you have little control over how the form will be designed on the screen and because you can't choose different fonts for the reports (everything is in Monaco).

But the main problem with OverVue is that it doesn't follow the Mac interface. For example, ⌘–Z, which is the command for *Undo* in virtually every other Mac program, shifts a column of data up one row in OverVUE. If you make this mistake and don't catch it instantly, you can completely destroy a whole file. Do that once or twice and you won't care about OverVUE's speed or number-crunching ability.

very bad feature

OverVUE's developer and publisher, ProVUE, is a very responsive company that's apparently coming out with a new database product. We hope it retains OverVUE's virtues and does away with its few, but deadly, vices. (We also hope the new product's manual is as good as OverVUE's was, which was just about the best we've ever seen.)

very good feature

OverVUE is most useful for: amazingly fast sorts and searches; people who need to do a lot of calculations in their database files; people unfamiliar with the standard Mac interface; and files without a lot of text material (long text entries don't display well where you only have one line per record).

Helix, Double Helix, etc. (SM)

Working with Helix is a unique experience, but after you get the hang of it, it's a lot of fun. It uses icons to represent fields, forms, indexes, queries and calculations. And it encourages you to play with your data—that is, to work with it and find new ways of looking at it to get different kinds of information from it.

In addition to being fun, Helix is powerful and makes it easy to do hard things. Odesta has been very good about supporting the product, with very regular (and usually free) product updates, and a vision of a growing line of software that will support almost anybody's database needs in the future. They also offer excellent, free technical support. I've never come away from a phone call with them frustrated.

very good feature

What's the downside? Helix is not one of the fastest database programs on the Mac nor is it one of the easiest to learn. But the most serious problem is its lack of a procedural programming language—which means there is no way to structure what the program does. You can't tell it to *first do A, and then if the user says H, do N.* Although this is a fairly serious hindrance to building serious applications, it's one you can work around.

Helix is most useful for: screen forms that resemble paper forms; complex analysis of data, particularly for business applications like inventory and billing; and files that incorporate graphics.

⌘ *Omnis* (SM)

Omnis offers much the same power as Helix. It's relational and well suited for building complex, powerful applications. But Omnis is a much more traditional database than Helix—both the vocabulary it uses and the user interface feel more like those of an MS-DOS database than Helix's.

Omnis is like Helix in many ways, not just in its capabilities. Both products have evolved through many versions and Blyth Software's commitment to Omnis is obvious from the way they've upgraded it. Omnis started out as a very unMaclike product that used very few of the Mac's features and, despite all the upgrades, it still doesn't seem very Maclike to me.

For example, the last version I saw still didn't support multiple fonts or graphics in files. Fonts aren't important to some people and I recognize that it's easy to get carried away with them, but they're one of the things I like about the Mac and I hate to give them up.

very bad feature

Another problem with Omnis is that its fixed-length fields also waste space. In the twelve-character *city* field mentioned above, *Seattle* would waste five spaces and *Miami* seven, and that begins to take up a lot of room on the disk.

Omnis III does have a lot of power. One of its strongest features is its ability to carry out sequences of commands (*macros,* in other words). You can even install sequences of your own devising in the menus, which is what gives Omnis its unusual ability to create applications for use by clerical personnel and others who don't know all the ins-and-outs of a complex database like Omnis.

very good feature

For example, you could set up a sequence that finds all unpaid invoices more than 60 days old, sorts them by customer name and totals the amount owed by each customer. Then you could install the sequence on a menu with a command name like *60+ by Cust.*

I've heard from friends who use Omnis sequences that once you get used to them, it's hard to imagine a database without them. Even if you're not creating applications for naive users, sequences come in handy: if there's a particular series of commands you use often, you just install it on a menu and save yourself a lot of trouble.

very good feature

Omnis is most useful for creating sophisticated applications for naive or inexperienced users.

dBASE Mac (SM)

For those of you who don't know about dBASE, the program has been around for some time and has gone through many incarnations. It started out as something called Vulcan that ran on some of the first microcomputers. A later version, dBASE II, became the most successful of the CP/M databases.

gossip/ trivia

There were several reasons dBASE's early popularity. For one thing, it wasn't copy-protected. For another, it didn't do anything fancy with the system, so you could run it on just about any terminal.

(One of the curses of the CP/M world was having to configure software for the particular terminal you were using. You'd buy a program and take it home, and then you'd have to wade through an "installation" program that asked you endless questions about how your system was

gossip/ trivia

configured. Even if you knew the answers, you'd find you knew them in, say, Hex, but the program wanted them in Octal. For those of us who suffered through all this, it's something to tell our kids about—like our parents telling us how they had to walk ten miles through the snow to go to school.)

dBASE also became the leading database on the PC. Dozens of books have been published about it and multitudes of consultants make their livings creating dBASE applications for customers who then find they have to keep them on retainer, because nobody but the consultants can understand how to use the applications. (Maybe this accounts for why consultants like dBASE so much.)

very good
feature

dBASE is *hard* to use on the PC. To even speak of a *user interface* in the same breath as dBASE is a contradiction in terms. Early versions of the program presented you with a command that looked like this: .

That's not a typo. That's dBase's infamous *dot prompt.* When you saw it on your screen, you were supposed to tell dBASE to do something. You don't know what command to give? Well, don't type *help,* because there isn't any. And don't look in the dBASE manual, because until recently, it didn't make any sense. Do what everybody else does: Go buy a book on dBASE—and when you can't understand the book, hire a consultant.

In spite of its wretched—virtually nonexistent—user interface, dBASE contained a powerful programming language that could be used to create applications with menu-driven facades that hid the inner workings of the program. Much of dBase's popularity is due to the power of that programming language.

Over the years, Ashton-Tate has improved the program a great deal. Its most recent incarnations on MS-DOS machines have imitated the Macintosh user interface, with pop-down menus and extensive help. Even so, I didn't expect much from the Macintosh version, which is called dBASE Mac, but I was pleasantly surprised.

Like MacPaint and MacDraw, dBASE Mac gives you a palette of icons on the left side of the screen that represent various commands. Like Helix and File, it lets you include graphics in a file. You can even link files together graphically.

very good feature

Even more impressive, its programming language includes all the power of the PC version, with special enhancements for the Mac. dBASE Mac can read files created on PCs but it can't run programs created by the PC version.

dBASE Mac is most useful for relational applications and for creating complex and powerful applications for inexperienced users.

❤ *FoxBASE/Mac* (SM)

Another dBASE lookalike, FoxBASE, can not only run PC dBASE programs but will soon allow users on both PCs and Macs to access the same file! It's also really fast and has a great, Maclike interface.

very good feature

❤ *Retriever* (AN)

This DA database lets you access data while in another application and is thus an ideal place to keep a phone list or the like. Actually, the more I think about it, the ❤ menu is the right place for lots of database files.

very good feature

Retriever gives you all the normal database functions, like searching, sorting, selecting, hiding columns and printing. The publisher's commitment to this product seems genuine; they send a free "maintenance" update (called version 1.01, it fixed a few minor bugs) to all registered users just a few months after the product was released.

very good feature

General database tips

❤ *duplicate database files before working on them* (SM)

It's good practice to keep at least two copies of any database file, and three of any active one. But if you're too

very hot tip

lazy to do that, at least do yourself the favor of duplicating a database file before launching the application to work on it. Most databases keep their files on disk, and constantly update them while you work. So the file you had on disk when you began to work is not the file you'll return to when you're done.

This constant, automatic saving to disk is a good feature, since it means that you don't have to worry about losing any appreciable amount of work if the system crashes. But if you make some changes you later want to discard, you're stuck—unless you made a copy of the file before you started.

Some programs also let you save a file under different names in the course of a long session (for example, Helix has a *Backup As* command). Other programs, like Over-VUE, keep the entire file in memory while you're working on it, so the file remains unchanged until you deliberately save it (but, here again, the only safe course is to keep at least two copies of the file on different disks).

keep written notes as to what does what (SM)

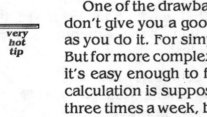

very hot tip

One of the drawbacks of most Mac databases is that they don't give you a good way to document what you're doing as you do it. For simple files, this isn't much of a problem. But for more complex ones, particularly in Helix and Omnis, it's easy enough to forget what a particular report, sort or calculation is supposed to do. I have one file I use at least three times a week, but recently when I went to make some changes to it, I lost a couple of hours' work because I hadn't made extensive notes while I was designing it.

Keeping notes is particularly important if you're designing an application for someone else to use, even if it's just a mailing list. They'll help you to explain it to the person using it, and to yourself when you go to modify it weeks or months later.

It's most convenient to make the notes in a desk accessory. I use Mockwrite or miniWRITER, which are nice text editors. Another good choice is Acta, an outlining desk accessory.

⌘ *use a hard disk* (SM)

A hard disk greatly improves the performance of just about every type of software, but for databases the difference is really incredible. Not only do things speed up, but most databases let you create files as large as the available space on your disk; with a hard disk, this means files can be dozens to hundreds of times larger than they can on a floppy.

FileMaker tips

⌘ *basic organization* (AN)

Although FileMaker is pretty easy to use, it takes some getting used to. First of all, you have to realize that it has three basic *modes;* the kinds of things you do in each of them is different and the program acts differently. To avoid confusion, you always need to be aware what mode you're in.

esp. for
beginners

You switch between modes with the Select menu (there are also keyboard commands). The mode you do 90% of your work in (adding, deleting and editing records) is called—now get this—*Browse.* (Call the Misnomer Hall of Fame! I think we've got a nominee here.)

very
hot
tip

The second basic mode is called *Layout.* That's where you design the various formats in which your data will be displayed on the screen and/or printed out on paper. You can (and should) create layouts both for ease inputting data and in order to generate the kinds of paper reports you need. You can switch between layouts freely without ever affecting the actual data in the file.

FileMaker's third basic mode is *Find.* I wouldn't call this a mode except that when you find records, all the other records in the file disappear (temporarily, of course). This

very
hot
tip

can be very confusing. Before you do other work on the file, you're going to almost always want to *Find All* (also on the Select menu); that returns all the records to you and puts you back in Browse mode.

⚫ *searching for phrases* (DC)

If you type two words into FileMaker's search field, it will find all instances of either word occurring individually. To find occurrences of the phrase only, put an ⌊Option⌋–space rather than a regular space between the words. (This works for more than two words as well.)

⚫ *beware! disaster is just two keystrokes away* (DC)

**important
warning**

Don't let this happen to you. You're furiously entering data into a massive database file. You reach for the ⌊Shift⌋ key to type +, but you accidentally hit the ⌊⌘⌋ key instead. This produces ⌊⌘⌋– = (equal sign), which happens to be the command that tells FileMaker to replace that field in all records with the contents of the field in the current record!

You get a dialog box that gives you two choices: Replace or Cancel. If you absent-mindedly click on Replace, File-Maker dutifully goes about destroying the field in question in every record in the file.

**very
hot
tip**

If this happens, immediately turn off the Mac. (You can use the reset switch too, if you have it installed—whatever's fastest for you.) Then turn the Mac back on (or wait till it restarts) and open the database. If you moved quickly enough, disaster will have been averted, because the inadvertent changes won't have been saved to disk. (But a better solution, of course, is to pay attention when that dialog box comes up.)

⚫ *keeping track of duplicate record entries* (DC)

FileMaker lets you duplicate a given record as many times as you want (with ⌊⌘⌋–M). The trouble is that you can lose count of how many copies you've made. Here's a handy solution:

Use the Find option on the Select menu to find the record you want to duplicate. Then when you duplicate the record, FileMaker will display the exact number of records you've duplicated.

OverVUE tips

⬤ *nonstandard* ⌘ *-Z (AN)*

In every piece of Mac software in the world but one, ⌘-Z is equivalent to the *Undo* command. That one totally nonstandard piece of software is OverVUE—where ⌘-Z shifts a column of data up one row!

very good feature

important warning

Since hitting ⌘-Z gets to be second nature when you use the Mac a lot, you'll find yourself messing up a lot of OverVUE files—with little hope of retrieving your data unless you catch the mistake immediately (that is, before the next keystroke or mouse click). I found this to be so much of a problem that I stopped using OverVUE for that reason alone—even though I loved lots of other things about it.

⬤ *duplicating part of an OverVUE record (SS)*

OverVUE can duplicate either the field or the entire record immediately above the current one, but that's sometimes more (or less) than you want. Here's a simple way to copy more than one field but less than all of them:

Just Shift Click in the field where you want to start copying. This automatically selects it and all the fields to its right. Then simply use ⌘-C to copy the selected fields and ⌘-V to paste them into as many new records as you like.

(The obvious limitation of this technique is that you have to copy all the fields to the right of the one you start with. So if there are twelve fields, say, and you start with the second, you can't copy just 2 through 6—you have to copy 2 through 12.)

♦ *speeding up macros* (AN)

shortcut

Lee Hinde of Roseville, California, wrote in to tell us that the *Hide* command speeds up the execution of OverVUE macros (it particularly makes a difference in long ones). *Hide* works by turning off screen redrawing (being able to ignore that saves OverVUE a lot of time). Don't forget to put a *Show* command at the end of the macro to turn screen redrawing on again.

♦ *stalled printouts in OverVUE* (AN)

OverVUE 2.0 won't print a character it doesn't recognize—like a dash; when the printout gets to such a character, it stalls. The solution is simply to go back into the document and change the troublesome character to a standard one (in the case of a dash, you can use two hyphens).

Helix tips

♦ *make the Abacus icons simple* (SM)

*very
hot
tip*

When you first begin using Helix, there's a tendency to create large Abacus icons, with all the calculations hardwired in. But it's much smarter to make small icons that only do one thing. For one thing, small icons make the Abacus easier to figure out (which is particularly important if you go back to modify something months after you created it). For another, small Abacus icons make Helix run faster. Here's why:

When a particular Abacus icon is used on a form, the results of its calculations are kept in memory—if Helix has to do the same calculation elsewhere on the form. These saved results speed up subsequent calculations, especially of the subtotal and lookup tiles. And the simpler an Abacus icon is, the more likely it is that there'll be another one like it somewhere on the form.

☀ *using text tiles for data transfer* (SM)

The text tiles in the Abacus icon are very handy for handling data transfers. For example, if you want to transfer a list of names and addresses into Microsoft Word for print merging, you'll need to put quotes around any field with a comma in it (because otherwise the comma will be interpreted as separating one field from another). It's easy to build an Abacus that uses the "followed by" tile to put the quotes around the field, and then to create a separate form for exporting the data.

☀ *index judiciously* (SM)

Helix lookups are much more efficient when done on indexed fields. But indexes slow the system down when you're entering (or deleting) data, and take up a lot of room on disk. So examine your indexes often and delete any that aren't being used.

shortcut

☀ *make backups often* (SM)

This is elementary, but bears repeating. Helix data does not always survive system crashes very well (although this seems to be improving as Helix—and the Mac—mature).

**esp. for
beginners**

☀ *document your database* (SM)

Here's another tip that bears repeating. Documenting what goes on inside a Helix program isn't easy. As I mentioned in one of the general database tips above, I use MockWrite or Acta to keep notes about my applications, but with Helix, it's also important to keep a paper record of all your Abacus icons. If you're deleting an Abacus or an index, it helps to have a paper copy of the whole database, so you can find out where everything is used before deleting it.

**very
hot
tip**

Financial and accounting programs

✦ *Managing Your Money* (SS)

very good feature

Although it only came to the Mac in 1988, Managing Your Money has been around on other machines since 1984. It's a mature, well-conceived program that can handle all your home financial activities. *[Andrew Tobias, author of the program (and of books like* The Only Investment Guide You'll Ever Need)*, is one of the clearest and most entertaining writers around. He made sure the program was nonthreatening, easy-to-use and fun.—AN]*

The opening screen/main menu (below) looks like HyperCard. To move to any part of the program, you can click an icon, select a command from a menu or—in many cases—double-click an item on one of the many data entry screens. I initially found this duplication confusing, but the thing to remember is that whatever makes sense usually works. You *can* get there from here—usually by two or three different routes.

After setting up asset-and-liability accounts and customizing the budget categories, you can begin to enter transactions. Each transaction has two components. In the case of money you spent, for example, they're *where did it come from* (checking, savings or cash, say) and *what was it spent on* (groceries, gasoline or whatever).

As you record the bills you've paid and the money received, and update the current value of your investments and possessions, the information is automatically entered into a net-worth statement. A report of your overall financial status (with accompanying graphs) is only a keystroke away. Simply marking items as *tax-related* kicks them into an impressive tax-estimator component, which duplicates major IRS forms and provides on-screen worksheets for the hard parts.

What distinguishes Managing Your Money from its competition is that it's all-inclusive. In addition to the normal check-writing and budgeting functions, it lets you handle IRAs and other investments; do tax, insurance, retirement and college-tuition planning; and perform financial calculations for things like mortgage refinancing, loans and annuities, and bond yields.

very good feature

There's also a "reminder" feature that lets you set reminders, appointments and projects, and specify a frequency for each (one time only, weekly, etc.). I just wish the program would *automatically* let me know that something is pending, instead of expecting me to remember to check my reminders.

The only serious problem I have with Managing Your Money is the price. Is *any* home financial package worth $220? I suppose it depends on how much money you're managing. If the price doesn't bother you and you've made a commitment to keep better track of your money, Managing Your Money will do a fine job of it.

In-House Accountant (SS)

In-House Accountant is a double-entry accounting system that offers invoicing, budgeting, bank reconciliation, check and statement printing and more useful reports than you can shake a stick at. *(Double-entry* accounting requires that each credit transaction be balanced by an equal debit and vice versa. For example, if you make a sale and deposit the money, you'd debit your bank account and credit one or more income accounts *(product sales,* say) by the same amount.

Some of the more useful features include:

- No need to "post" transactions

- Provision for recurring transactions

- On-screen preview of reports and "batch" printing

- Invoicing, statements and aging reports

- Bar and pie charts that compare this year's, last year's and budgeted amounts for any account or group of accounts

- A financial calculator with formulas for present and future value, loan payments, interest and principle, and three kinds of depreciation

Learning to use the program is facilitated by context-sensitive help, a guided tour of the program with sample data, a question-and-answer section in the manual and an introduction to accounting for novices. If you're new to double-entry accounting, you should supplement ·this material with other reading.

Since it uses standard menus and a normal Macintosh interface, you'll spend most of your time learning how double-entry accounting works and setting up a chart of accounts. The issue isn't whether you're a Macintosh novice or expert but whether you're an *accounting* novice.

Because In-House Accountant is designed for account-ants and nonaccountants alike, the program's greatest weakness is its lack of flexibility. Reports—although plen-tiful—can't be customized, invoice and check printing only work on specific forms and data can't be imported from other accounting programs. Still, it *is* easy to use, lists for only $150 and should suffice for many small businesses.

♦ *MOM* (AN)

National Tele-Press's MOM (for *mail order manager)* is an order-entry program written in Omnis that's easy-to-learn, even for novice users. It manages everything from accounts receivable and payable to inventory and sales tax. MOM lets you edit or reverse any transaction you make and you never have to key information in twice—the relevant fields are interconnected and the information is automatically entered in all of them.

We've used MOM at Goldstein & Blair for over a year and National Tele-Press's support has been a delight. There was always a technically knowledgeable person available to return calls, answer user questions and patiently walk people through problems.

very good feature

The problem with MOM is its rigidity. Making changes in how it does things requires customization by a programmer (a certain amount of which is included in the program's price) and although this was always done for us quickly and efficiently, it's nicer to be able to do this yourself.

Still, if you don't want to take the time and trouble to customize a database like FileMaker for your own use, and you want all the connections between files thought through and set up for you ahead of time, MOM is definitely worth considering.

♦ *Flexware, Great Plains, Insight and SBT* (AN)

When Goldstein & Blair grew to the point where we needed something more flexible and powerful than MOM, I first looked at several high-end, modular business accounting packages. (*Modular* means you can buy them in separate pieces: *General Ledger, Accounts Payable, Accounts Receivable, Payroll, Inventory,* etc.)

The first program I considered was SBT. Like most (or all?) of these programs, it's been ported over from the PC. Unfortunately, the Macintosh dBASE clone it was running in had absolutely no Mac feel at all. I quickly dismissed it and started thinking about whether or not I should buy a PC clone and just keep the business records on it.

very good feature

Things have changed now, however. SBT also runs under FoxBASE, a dBASE clone for the Mac that has a great Maclike feel. In that configuration, SBT is definitely worth a look.

Carol Pladsen then looked at three other programs. Here are her impressions:

very bad feature

True to its name, Flexware has very flexible reports, and it's from a company that's been around for many years. But the program operation seemed clunky. For example, you have to call up accounts by customer number, which is both clumsy and slow. One large Flexware user handles this problem by printing out the entire customer file every *week* in alphabetical order and then the order entry people look the numbers up!

very good feature

Great Plains is company with a good reputation and Carol got great technical support on their 800 number. The program itself is easy to learn and use and the documentation is excellent (Carol particularly liked a chapter where all the alert messages were listed in alphabetical order, with explanations of what caused them and what to do about it.)

very bad feature

But there were two problems with Great Plains accounting package—it has a distinctly unMaclike feel and it can't customize reports (although this second problem may be solved by their new Executive Advisor module, which produces all manner of dazzling and informative charts). But the unMaclike feel was enough to make us look elsewhere. (After all, if it's going to feel like a PC, why not save money on the hardware and just *run* it on a PC? Clones just cost a few hundred dollars now.)

very good feature

Insight (from Layered) was the only program we looked at that had a good Mac feel (this was before FoxBASE) and the screens have a clean, uncluttered look. Insight has good sort criteria, good reports and excellent documentation. An additional module is available that makes it easy to export data as ASCII text files.

Unfortunately, Insight is designed for a service, not product, business. There's a one-step billing process that doesn't generate pull tickets, mailing labels or packing slips. So it wasn't for us (as I mentioned above, we ended up deciding to use FileMaker and design our own forms.) But if yours is a service business, Insight may be just the thing for you.

very bad feature

All these programs are expensive, ranging (at current list prices) from $200 to $800 a module (or even more for multiuser versions). Still, if your business needs them, they might easily be worth it.

⬢ *ShopKeeper-4* *(LP)*

ShopKeeper-4 is an amazing "cash register" program designed by Apple retailer Mike Nudd specifically for small, independent, retail businesses. The program comes in single- and multiuser versions and can track over 8000 charge customers and 8000 inventory items.

very good feature

Combined with an APG cash drawer (reviewed in Chapter 7), a hard disk and a bar code reader, it can turn your Mac into a high-tech electronic cash register, just like the ones used in supermarkets and department stores—but at a fraction of the cost. And, in true Macintosh fashion, it's much easier to get started with and to maintain.

When merchandise is received, you enter it on ShopKeeper's supplier invoice screen, which looks just like a supplier invoice. Then you print stock number/price stickers on 3.5" mailing labels and sticker the inventory. When merchandise is sold, all you have to do is copy the stock numbers off the stickers. If a sticker is missing, you can also look up prices and stock numbers right on the screen.

ShopKeeper's data searches are incredibly fast. Given the correct stock number, ShopKeeper fills in a complete item description, enters the current price, calculates tax and discounts, adjusts the inventory, rings up the sale, opens the cash drawer, calculates change and prints the invoice—on plain paper or Deluxe-brand computer forms.

very good feature

The program works with any ImageWriter-compatible printer and even some that aren't ImageWriter-compatible. At the end of the day, ShopKeeper prints detailed sales reports and also totals the register. All this from a program that only costs $300.

If it sounds too good to be true, order the $5 demo disk and see for yourself. You get the full working program with all features enabled (except that it's limited to 50 invoices) and a nicely printed ten-page minimanual.

Miscellaneous data processing software

⬥ *BakerForms* (AN)

BakerForms work with Microsoft Works to let you keep records, generate pertinent reports and print data on a wide variety of standard commercial computer forms. They save you from having to program custom applications and design business forms from scratch. Anyone with normal office experience and minimal Macintosh experience can easily learn to use the program.

There are four modules—accounts payable, accounts receivable, purchase orders and payroll. The accounts receivable module lets you choose between a consultation, manufacturing or field-service business.

The problem is, BakerForms only generates forms; the calculations have to be done separately and entered separately each time. Still, if you have Works already and your business is quite small, BakerForms may be all you need.

Each module costs $50; all four are $170. You can get a $10 demo disk and forms package that shows you how the program works. It lets you do everything but print, so if you enter some actual data and then decide you want to use the program, you won't have to reenter anything.

⚫ *MacInUse* (SS)

If you use your Mac for personal as well as business purposes, the IRS requires records that show how much you use it for each. If you bill for your time, you'll want to track how many hours you spent on each project. If you manage a shared system and are thinking about buying a larger hard disk, you may want to figure out which programs are seldom used so you can remove them from your hard disk, free up space and postpone the purchase.

MacInUse is a simple, elegant solution to each of these needs. Each time you exit a program, it automatically records how long you spent running it. Report templates for presenting the data are provided for MacWrite, Word, WriteNow, Multiplan, Works and Excel.

very good feature

You can just let MacInUse run in the background; there's no need to intervene at any point. When you're ready to examine the data, you select a template and print the report. But you can also enter information (client, project, comments, etc.) each time you run a program.

MacInUse comes with a form that you can use for this purpose. If you need something different, you can customize it by moving adding or editing buttons, check boxes and text fields. You can specify *required* fields (they have to be filled in before you can continue) or enter default text (you get it instead of a blank text field, although you can change it if you want). You can also choose whether this form is displayed before or after each program is run.

On the next page is the custom MacInUse form I have pop up each time I enter a program. I've made MACazine the default client—so I can just skip past that field whenever they're the client.

MacInUse offers a number of installation options, including *minimum time to track* (ignore applications that were open for less than 30 seconds, for example); *track individual Finder accesses (or lump them together); include user name* (for network installations); and *allow over-ride* (keep MacInUse from recording certain sessions). If you want to

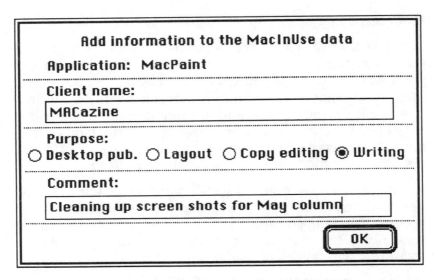

track employee productivity, you can even set it up to run invisibly, so that employees aren't aware of the tracking and therefore aren't biased by it.

In addition to capturing data automatically, you can force a recording by pressing Shift Option ⌘ —M. This lets you switch from one document to another within the same application and record the time spent with each. You can also use this to track desk accessory use (the time spent in them normally isn't broken out from the time spent in an application).

When you dump data into a report template, you get a simple list of every program you ran, the date of the run and so on—in date order. Unless you do some reorganizing, there's no way to know, for example, the total time each program was run. So you'll probably have to spend a fair amount of time customizing reports if you want useful information.

There's one exception to this—the Excel template. A complex macro automatically creates a worksheet with raw data, summary statistics and two charts—percentage of use for each purpose and percentage of use for each application (sorted by purpose). If you run more than a dozen or so programs, however, you may need to play with the chart options if you want to see all the program names. Here's a slightly doctored version of a MacInUse Excel chart:

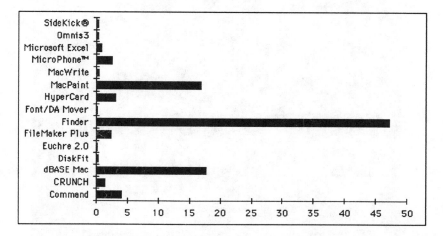

If you want accurate, useful data, you may have to change your Mac habits somewhat. When I get side-tracked, I tend to leave programs open for hours at a time. The reports then show that I spent a disproportionate time in whichever applications happened to be left open. You should quit from programs that aren't actively being used, or shut down the Mac.

I'd love to be able to pull Finder data out of the report, or not record it at all. Who cares how much time is spent in the Finder? But, at present, you'll have to delete those times yourself.

One other potential problem: MacInUse uses the Clipboard to move data into templates; if you have a lot of data, you may get an *out of memory* error. All isn't lost, however. You can always run the template itself and then load the data in with the *Open...* command.

MacInUse works almost transparently. You won't notice any substantial pauses when quitting applications, although there's a slight delay when shutting down. The program is compatible with most networks; the manual discusses how to set it up on AppleShare, MacServe and TOPS. If you need it, it's definitely worth the $80 it costs.

Chapter 12

Graphics

General graphics tips

⚫ *draw programs and paint programs* (AN)

Graphics programs for the Mac fall into two broad categories: bit-mapped *paint programs* and object-oriented *draw programs*.

Paint programs treat the entire screen as a collection of dots. For example, if you want to move something you've drawn, you have to use the Marquee, the Lasso or some other special tool to encircle all the dots that make it up and thus select them as a group.

Draw programs treat whatever you draw as a discrete object. All you normally have to do to select it is click on it. (On the down side, you can't go into FatBits and fine-tune it, removing a dot here and adding one there.)

In general, bit-mapped programs are better suited for artistic tasks and object-oriented programs for business applications like drafting and diagramming. If you do a fair amount of graphics work on the Mac, you'll probably want to have at least one program of each kind in your software library (or a combination *draw/paint program*).

⚫ *"objects" in paint programs* (AN)

When you select a bunch of dots with either ✑ (the *lasso)* or ⌐⌐⌐ (the *selection rectangle* or *marquee),* they behave temporarily like an object (for example, they move together as a unit). The proper name for this collection of dots is the *selection* but I've found it less confusing to refer to it at times as the *object*—although that's technically incorrect.

⚫ *graphic formats* (AN)

Graphics on the Mac can be put in a variety of standard formats that allow them to be transferred between applications. The first of these, and still the standard for low-resolution (72 dots per inch) bit-mapped images, is *MacPaint* format. Higher-resolution bit-maps, like images from scanners, are normally saved in *TIFF (tagged image file format)*.

MacDraw established a standard for object-oriented graphics called *PICT* (from *picture*). *PICT* files use Quick-Draw, the programming routines responsible for the speed with which images move around the Mac's screen, but graphics can also be saved in *PostScript* (the programming language which drives many laser printers and typesetters) or a special structured form of it called *encapsulated PostScript (EPS)*.

There are other formats but those are the major ones right now. Applications vary widely in the number of formats which they can import and export, but at least one program—SuperGlue—recognizes all of them.

⚫ *scaling bitmap images* (CJW)

esp. for beginners

When you shrink a paint image using a bitmap graphics program like MacPaint, FullPaint or SuperPaint's paint layer, adjoining pixels tend to clump together until you have unsightly blotches where once there was finely drawn detail. To reduce it without significant loss of detail, copy it into an object-oriented drawing program like MacDraw (or SuperPaint's draw layer) first and then print it out on a laser printer.

When printing from an object-oriented program, the LaserWriter scales the image starting from a full-size representation in memory, not from the reduced on-screen image. Using a paint program, you'll only get what you see, a printout which will look as muddled as it appears on screen.

⚫ *instant whiteout* (CJW)

In most paint programs, you can change the fill of any area from black to any pattern you want with the Paint Bucket. Be sure to pour directly over the black and be careful that the area you're filling doesn't touch another area you don't want changed. Even a single connecting pixel is enough to cause the new pattern to overflow.

You can use this technique to quickly erase large, solid-black areas by pouring bucketfuls of white paint. This is instant electronic whiteout on a global scale, and is much easier than piecemeal erasing.

🍎 *a kluge for headers and footers* (MB)

Applications like paint and draw programs usually don't let you put headers and footers in your printouts. Some databases and spreadsheets also have this limitation, or at least greatly limit your ability to format headers and footers. If you really need headers and footers, and/or care how they look, simply paste the material you want to print into a word processing program first.

*esp. for
beginners*

Paint programs

🍎 *paint programs* (FT)

Many people mistakenly think that bit-mapped paint programs are passé now that we have draw and PostScript graphics programs. Actually, paint programs give you a range of textures you really can't get elsewhere.

Most paint programs have the same set of basic tools and effects that were in the original MacPaint; where they vary is in their additional features. Here are some extra features I think any good contemporary paint program should have:

- The window should scroll whenever you reach the edge of it, even when you're in FatBits mode.

- You should be able to rotate your selection in increments smaller than 90°—ideally much smaller.

*very good
feature*

- The ability to scale a selection is an important feature. Scaled bit-mapped images don't always look good on the screen, but if you're printing to a LaserWriter, you can get good results. *[Although nowhere near as good as if you scale in a draw program or on the draw layer of a draw/paint program.—AN].*

- You should be able to specify the number of divisions on the rulers and different units of measurement—inches, centimeters, picas, etc.

- The program should display the pointer location on the rulers and show the size of an object as you draw it.

- There should be a grid option to make it easier to line up objects in your drawing.

very good feature

- A paint program should support multiple windows so you can cut and paste between files or work on two drawings at the same time. It should also have a windows menu or a list of opened windows under one of the menus.

- You should be able to hide the tool palettes, so you can expand the window to see as much of the image as possible. FullPaint even lets you hide the menu bar so you can view the full screen.

- Besides the standard Invert, Fill and Trace Edges commands, a good paint program will have other special effects—like the Skew, Distort and Perspective commands in FullPaint and GraphicWorks 1.1 or an "air-brush" paint can like Canvas's.

- Keyboard commands in a graphics program seem almost superfluous but shortcuts for longer methods save you time. I've noticed that I always use the keyboard shortcut to use the grabber hand and to make a copy of an object. The command to constrain objects as you draw them is also important.

⌘ *FullPaint* (DC)

FullPaint looks and acts a lot like MacPaint, and anyone familiar with MacPaint will feel immediately at home with it. In fact, FullPaint incorporates at least 95% of MacPaint's features (versions before 2.0, that is), right down to the obscure keyboard shortcuts that expert users are so fond of. At the same time, FullPaint overcomes several of MacPaint's shortcomings.

For example, it lets you open as many as four documents at a time. You can click on the title bar to cause the window to grow to full screen size. You can move the tool and pattern palettes, or hide them altogether (along with the title bar), so your document takes up the whole screen (which is, of course, where the program's name comes from). If you've ever been frustrated by MacPaint's small window, this feature alone is almost worth the price.

FullPaint also comes with the excellent ColorPrint program that lets you to print multiple color pictures on an ImageWriter II equipped with a multicolor ribbon.

✎ *more on FullPaint* (FT)

FullPaint was the first paint program that came out after MacPaint and had most of the features that MacPaint should have had. Unfortunately, the original publisher failed to update it on a regular basis and, as of this writing, it won't support external monitors (among other things).

very bad feature

FullPaint commands include Skew, Distort, Perspective, Rotate, Flip Horizontal and Flip Vertical, but there's no Free Rotate. Its Mouse Spot feature shows you the exact location of the pointer and the dimensions of the object you're drawing. The program has an invisible grid and a windows menu that lets you switch between different documents, as well as stack or tile them.

The manual deals with all of the menu commands, explains all the features and has a section at the end which lists all of the keyboard commands and shortcuts. The program's current publisher, Ashton-Tate, has a telephone support number and also maintains a forum on Compu-Serve.

If you only need a paint program and not one of the paint/draw programs discussed below, FullPaint is a good deal at $100.

🍎 *MacPaint 2.0* (FT)

Although Russ Wetmore has done an admirable job of extending the original MacPaint, this long-overdue update is disappointing for what it doesn't do. It's now more powerful than FullPaint but it still lacks some features that even desk accessory graphics programs offer.

**very good
feature**

On the bright side, MacPaint 2.0 is easier to use than previous versions. The drawing window is bigger and scroll bars make it easier to move around in. There are tear-off menus and more keyboard commands (although the old ones remain the same). The program's speed has also improved and it's better at catching errors than previous versions or than FullPaint.

MacPaint 2.0 supports as many multiple windows as memory allows but it doesn't have a full window mode like FullPaint's and there's no longer a Show Page command. Although there are no rulers, there's a mouse coordinate indicator like FullPaint's Mouse Spot. Version 2.0 has a grid option, and you can set it for 2-, 4-, 8-, 16- or 32-pixel increments.

While the original, minimalist MacPaint manual only hinted at what the program could do, the manual for 2.0 is much more comprehensive. Claris has a dedicated support number and they've joined the Apple Vendors special interest forum on CompuServe. No significant bugs have been reported.

If you own a previous version of MacPaint and don't have any reason for upgrading to one of the more powerful graphics programs, the update to 2.0 is worth the $25 it costs. To buy it from scratch costs $125, but I think most people would do better with one of the draw/paint programs described below.

Draw programs

🍎 *draw programs* (FT)

Unlike paint programs, whose bit-mapped images are limited to fixed levels of resolution, the objects produced by draw programs can adjust to the resolution of the output device. So if you print them on an ImageWriter, you get 72 dpi; on a LaserWriter, 300 dpi; on a Linotronic 100, 1270 dpi; and so on.

very good feature

Text is handled better in draw programs than in paint programs. You can change the font, style or size without having to reenter the information. Draw programs also give you more printing flexibility because you can specify a drawing size larger than a single page.

very good feature

Draw programs have a fairly standard set of basic commands and tools, modelled after MacDraw's. They can usually duplicate objects, bring them to the front or send them to the back, group or ungroup them, lock or unlock them, rotate them and flip them vertically and horizontally. They also let you align objects with each other or to a grid.

Here are some extra features I think any good contemporary draw program should have (the rarer features are followed by the names of the only programs that currently offer them):

- customizable rulers that let you choose between several different unit settings

- smoothing, unsmoothing, reshaping and rounding corners of a polygon

- importing and exporting to many different formats (including PICT)

- an easy way to reselect the last tool you used

- line widths as narrow as a hairline [Cricket Draw]

- PostScript-generated fill patterns and *fountains* (smooth gradations of gray from light to dark) [Cricket Draw]

very good feature

- aligning objects to a line [Canvas, Cricket Draw, MacDraft]

- seeing the size of an object by clicking on it [Cricket Draw, MacDraw]

very good feature

- "nudge" commands that move an object in increments as small as a pixel [Cricket Draw]

- guides you can lock and snap objects to [Cricket Draw]

- multiple layers for separations, building a drawing a section at a time or combining separate pieces of a drawing [Draw It Again, Sam, MacDraw II]

🍎 *MacDraw* (DC)

The first draw program was MacDraw (then from Apple, now from Claris). Essentially, the program lets you create objects and move them around on the screen to create a drawing. What makes MacDraw so powerful are the rulers, alignment grid, size commands and various other tools that give you precise control over an object's position and size.

One thing MacDraw does well is embellish presentation charts created in Excel or other graphing programs. You can use MacDraw's tools to enhance the title and even change the widths of the bars in a bar graph.

Many people use MacDraw to create professional-looking business forms. MacDraw can also serve as a simple page-makeup program for short documents—as long as you don't need advanced features like kerning and leading.

🍎 *MacDraw II* (AN)

very good feature

This incarnation of MacDraw has a whole slew of power-ful features. For example, you can: zoom from 3200% to 3.12%; rotate objects and text by *tenths of a degree;* size text and leading from 1 point to 127 points; and work on up to 500 separate layers.

things to come

We weren't able to review MacDraw II in time for the book but it will definitely be covered in an update.

⚫ *MacDraft* (FT)

very good
feature

MacDraft is probably the most powerful of the draw programs and is well suited for professional designers. It has more fill and pen patterns than MacDraw and more line options. (The nicest of these is a line with arrowheads at both ends with the length displayed in the middle. MacDraft will automatically center this line on the outside or inside of an object.)

You can rotate objects incrementally and see their size as you draw them. You can even get the size of the object in fractions (1-1/3", e.g.). There are no nudge commands, so you can't move objects in pixel increments. Though you can't customize the ruler, there are scale rulers that let you make an inch equal to anything between 10 and 100 feet.

On the whole, MacDraft works like MacDraw, which makes it easy to learn. It does have a few bugs, however; one particularly annoying one is that a dashed line can't cross page breaks. MacDraft's manual is thorough but, unfortunately, the index is weak. Technical support is good.

MacDraft, which currently costs $240, hasn't been updated as much as its competition but a high-end version of the program, called Dreams, is also available.

⚫ *Cricket Draw* (FT)

very good
feature

Cricket Draw distinguishes itself from MacDraw and MacDraft by PostScript effects like fountains (smooth gradations of gray) and binding text to a line. But it runs more slowly than MacDraw or MacDraft.

In addition to standard tools, Cricket Draw has diamonds, grates, starbursts, and Bezier curves. Some of its PostScript features make it harder to learn than other draw programs, but using Cricket Draw's PostScript functions is far easier than trying to program in PostScript.

very bad
feature

The program's ruler and grid settings are limited and it can't edit a page larger than what's available in the Page Setup dialog box, so it really isn't a professional drafting or engineering tool. Although it isn't buggy, it does have some anomalies. PICT files saved from it have PostScript information imbedded in them, so some programs have trouble reading them. And it can't open Illustrator files.

Cricket Draw gives you access to most dialog boxes and settings by double-clicking on objects. As with FullWrite's interface, this is the ultimate in intuitiveness.

Cricket Draw's manual isn't bad but the commands aren't always explained completely. Telephone support is free except for the toll charges. Updates to the program, which currently costs $300, have generally fixed bugs but haven't expanded Cricket Draw's capabilities.

Draw/paint programs

❖ draw/paint programs (FT)

Programs that combine bit-maps and graphic objects should be integrated so the two layers are easy to understand and use. This isn't always the case (GraphicWorks, for example, doesn't do a very good job of it.) A combination draw/paint program should also be able to save files in several different formats.

❖ Canvas (PH)

very good feature

If you have a lot of drawings in a word processing or desktop publishing document, you'll find a desk accessory called Canvas incredibly handy; it lets you modify the drawings without leaving your application. Canvas has almost all of the features of both MacPaint and MacDraw, as well as some of the innovations of other programs like SuperPaint.

very good feature

Canvas comes as both a desk accessory and a regular application; the application has about 25% more features. Support has been wonderful so far and so has their update policy.

● *more on Canvas* (FT)

At $200, Canvas is one of the most powerful graphics programs available. Its publisher, Deneba Software, has continued to add to the program until it now has all the features you'll find in most paint or draw programs (except for Trace Edges) as well as some you won't.

For example, Canvas lets you magnify or reduce your drawing up to 32 times and edit a bit-map at 72, 150, 216, 300, 635, 1270 or 2540 dots per inch. The Object Specs command shows you all the settings for an object (type, fill pattern, color, pen pattern, pen shape and bit-map resolution) and lets you change any of them you want. There are also Show Size commands that display the size of an object as you draw it.

very good feature

Canvas has 100 pen shapes, four line types, two palettes of fill patterns and an empty third one where you can create your own patterns. There's a MacrObject menu for adding graphic elements you use frequently. You can move or nudge objects with the arrow keys and you can have as many open documents as memory allows.

very good feature

Canvas lets you handle both bit-maps and object-oriented graphics on the screen at the same time. Since it works similarly to the standard draw and paint programs, it's easy to learn. It's not buggy, rarely clumsy, and runs smoothly and quickly.

very good feature

Unfortunately, Canvas's manual is weak; it doesn't explain all the commands thoroughly or in order. But at least Deneba has been good about updating the program.

very bad feature

● *GraphicWorks* (FT)

GraphicWorks rivals Canvas as the most powerful and feature-laden of the draw/paint programs. This $100 program adds some interesting tools and commands to the standard ones—for example, an Airbrush replaces the typical Paint Can. The Airbrush can be set for various amounts of air pressure and spray size, and you can toggle between black and white paint.

bargain

very good
feature

A ⌘ Click splits the window to give you a magnified view of the drawing on the right and a reduced view on the left. There's also a Show Page command. A balloon tool creates cartoon balloons in various styles. A "nudge" command lets you move things in fine increments. You can align panels, easels, drawing tools or balloons to a grid.

very bad
feature

Graphic Works has superior on-line help but it takes a while to learn because you have to create an "easel" before drawing. This is the most cumbersome and counterintuitive feature of the program. The manual clearly explains the commands, contains lots of tips and tricks and includes an excellent reference card. Unfortunately, it doesn't have an index. The publisher, MacroMind, provides free support but you have to pay for the phone call.

SuperPaint 1.1 *(FT)*

very bad
feature

With SuperPaint, the draw tools are in a different layer from the paint tools and you have to flip between the two; this makes using the program less than graceful. Another drawback is that the drawing size can't be larger than a page.

very good
feature

Because SuperPaint has many of the same tools and features as other paint and draw programs, it's easy to learn and use. A LaserBits feature allows you to edit a drawing at 300 dpi.

very good
feature

SuperPaint has nudge commands which move objects in pixel increments, and it can display a reduced full-page view next to an actual-size drawing. The last tool used stays selected and you can select the grabber hand by holding down on the spacebar. You can have as many windows open as memory allows.

The manual is OK but doesn't go into enough detail. The publisher, Silicon Beach Software, provides free technical support, but you pay for the phone call. You can also get information from the company on CompuServe, where they're very active (though they don't have a dedicated forum). This version of the program costs $100 but the much-improved 2.0 version, described in the next entry, costs $200.

SuperPaint 2.0 (SZA)

SuperPaint 2.0 has so many changes and improvements they should have skipped a version number and called it 3.0. Here are some (but not all) of the improvements:

- You can customize the tool palette by adding *plug-in tools* to the basic ones that are always there. Silicon Beach provides a few samples of possible new tools and I expect that third parties, commercial and otherwise, will come up with many more.

very good
feature

- The tool palette now has paging arrows (as the pattern palette always did) so you can flip through your tool collection.

- You can now put the tool and pattern palettes wherever you want, or hide them.

- The Draw layer has Bezier curves, and you can export them to EPS files.

very good
feature

- Edit commands like *Flip* and *Rotate* work on any kind of selection, not just rectangular ones.

- You can rotate Draw text and it's still treated as real text. You can even edit it.

very good
feature

- There are three new selection tools: Selection Oval, Selection Poly and Freeform Selection.

- There are other new tools: an Airbrush with adjustable diameter and flow rate and a Multigon tool that lets you define the number of sides you want drawn.

very good
feature

- Finally, there's Stationery—document templates that always open as *Untitled*, so you don't alter the original by mistake.

Other graphics programs

⚫ *FreeHand, Illustrator, etc.* *(KM)*

Adobe Illustrator was the first program that let you scan existing artwork, save it as a MacPaint file and then trace the resulting image to produce an object-oriented PostScript drawing. Illustrator also lets you shade, scale, tilt, distort, rotate or skew any part of the PostScript drawing without losing definition. When you're done futzing with it, you can print it, at the highest resolution available, on any Post-Script printer, plotter, film recorder or typesetter.

Professional designers immediately recognized Illustrator's potential. Many of them even managed to get the knack of its unintuitive curve-making tools. Most novices, on the other hand, found them intimidating and frustrating. They wanted to be able to trace the intuitive way—freehand (by dragging the pointer along the outline of what you're tracing).

**very good
feature**

Aldus saw the need and introduced a competing program called FreeHand that features a freehand tool, better text manipulation and easier editing. Adobe countered with a considerably enhanced version called Illustrator 88 that includes not only a freehand tool but also one that automatically traces the outline of any object you select. (You can also limit the length of the traced edge.)

**very
hot
tip**

Unfortunately, it's only practical to use auto-trace about half the time—for areas of fine and jagged detail like hair that there's no way you could trace freehand or, on the other hand, for smoothly drawn line art. If you use it for images of intermediate complexity, you'll have to spend more time editing the result than if you'd traced manually.

**very good
feature**

Illustrator 88 also gives you a "blend tool" that can be used to change one shape into another. You just indicate the shapes you want to start and end with and tell Illustrator how many steps you want between the two. The program then smoothly changes shape, color, fill and line as it interpolates transitional shapes. You can also use the blend tool to make repeated copies of the same shape along a specified path.

Another exclusive and powerful Illustrator feature turns a selected object (or objects) into a tiled fill pattern. It's a great way to add textured patterns, design wallpaper or populate a hillside with trees.

very good
feature

With all this power and ease of use, Illustrator 88 sounds like the obvious choice. Unfortunately, it has some problems.

For example, unless you have more than a meg of RAM, Illustrator likes to tell you that you can't finish the rest of a drawing you've spent endless hours creating. It may not even let you save the file. So don't buy Illustrator unless you have two or more megs of RAM in your Mac or plan to make all your drawings very simple.

important
warning

FreeHand also has problems. If you click slightly off the line that defines a drawing path, you'll select the template you're tracing. If you've forgotten to lock it into position, it will probably slide out of register with the rest of the drawing. And if you happen to be zoomed-in for detail, you'll have to go back to the full-page view to deselect it. This happens frequently enough to drive you nuts.

very bad
feature

At least FreeHand lets you rescale and reposition templates. With Illustrator, you can only rescale or move the drawing after it's finished.

FreeHand will grab images from any Mac application you want, but you have to exit the program to do it. Illustrator can only use MacPaint or MacDraw documents as templates, but lets you call them up from within the program.

Both programs give you multiple windows. Illustrator lets you cut and paste between them or trace in one window while previewing final appearances in another. With Free-Hand, changes you make in one window aren't reflected in the other(s). But you can preview and draw at the same time in the same window—something Illustrator doesn't allow.

Aside from these differences, the contest between the two programs comes down to speed and ease of use. Illustrator runs faster, because it keeps a duplicate of your drawing in memory (part of the reason why it's such a RAM hog).

very good feature

The freehand tools in both programs work very well and function nearly identically. Still, Illustrator's implementation is a bit more powerful. You can set the pixel tolerance (in auto-trace too) so that you can make smoother curves with your jittery hands.

The two programs' curve-drawing tools are quite different. FreeHand has three to Illustrator's one—a corner tool, a combination tool (for joining curves to straight lines) and a curve tool that automatically fits curves to any series of points you click on.

In Illustrator, corners, joins and other variations are introduced by unforgiving sequences of clicks and drags that are unnatural and hard to remember. With practice, however, the process can become reasonably quick and efficient (it's a little like learning to rub your head and pat your stomach at the same time).

FreeHand's commands for fill and line variations are more complex than Illustrator's—although once you've gone through the routine, you can pick the same pattern or line from a menu (as long as you stay in the same drawing).

very good feature

FreeHand has automatically graduated fill patterns, whereas with Illustrator you have to use the blend tool to get an approximation of a shaded fill. This gobbles up memory and extends printing time on Linotronic typesetters. And it's hard to visualize how many steps will produce a smooth gray transition.

Both programs give you decent control over text placement, spacing and kerning, and both let you rotate, slant or skew the text.

very hot tip

All in all, it's tough to choose between these programs. If most of your work is with text and logos, FreeHand wins hands down. With it you can make any PostScript font follow any path you can draw, turn it into outline type, add drop shadows and print it in any color or shade of gray.

Pros will probably want to make use of both programs, taking advantage of Illustrator's powerful auto-trace and blend tools, then moving the document to FreeHand for more flexible type handling and quicker editing. Beginners, especially those without spare memory, will find FreeHand simpler.

very hot tip

By the way, there are integrated graphics programs that combine the most-needed basic painting, drawing, tracing and text layout features. LaserPaint comes closest to providing professional-level capability for all these functions but it's fairly complex to use. Draw It Again, Sam, Cricket Draw and Dreams all offer tracing capabilities as well.

✍ *PosterMaker Plus and Laser F/X* (KM)

Stylizing type in a sophisticated way for an ad headline, company logo or letterhead was a job that used to require the talent, skill and steady hand of a trained graphic artist. But then PosterMaker Plus and Laser F/X came along—two programs that stylize type in more ways than all the other Mac graphics and page-makeup programs put together. Between them, there's hardly anything they can't do.

very good feature

PosterMaker works with any Mac-compatible printer, producing lettering as smooth as the printer can make it, while Laser F/X only works with PostScript devices. On the other hand, Laser F/X works with any PostScript font, but PosterMaker Plus's full range of effects are available only with its own five basic typefaces, which have been designed specifically for use in large sizes.

These five fonts can be rotated, skewed, outlined, inlined, drop-shadowed and filled with any of 64 patterns or 64 shades of PostScript gray. Want to make your type curve away into the distance, like the Superman logo, or expand at both ends, like the CinemaScope trademark? No problem. You can also control the weight (thickness) and, if

very good feature

you're outputting to a color printer, specify any of eight colors for each element.

All these tricks let you transform the five standard typefaces into virtually anything you can imagine. But it would be nice if PosterMaker included (or offered as an option) a few fancier fonts. It's also a shame you can't kern.

PosterMaker can make huge posters and banners (up to 21' x 25') with perfectly smooth letters. It can also rescale bit-mapped graphics in 1% increments.

Because PosterMaker uses its own outline fonts, you can preview all its effects on-screen. Because Laser F/X modifies PostScript fonts in the printer, it can't do that. (The calculations take so long it's impractical to show them on the screen.) Instead, you get "greeked" text to show position.

very good feature

On the other hand, Laser F/X's library of effects is more extensive. It can create 30 highly stylized variations on any PostScript typeface. Additional effects are also available, in packages of ten, at $50 a package. You even get *fountains* (where the gray makes a smooth gradation from light to dark).

Two things Laser F/X can't do is wrap text around an object or shape it to make it resemble an object. And, of course, it can't output to a non-PostScript printer.

Both programs will translate files from Paint or Draw format, so you can superimpose lettering over graphics, and both let you save their output as encapsulated Post-Script (EPS) files, for placement in page-makeup or illustration programs.

Since PosterMaker Plus only costs $60, it's the easiest place to start. But if you get serious about this, you'll want to plunk down $100 for Laser F/X as well.

(Editor's note: I haven't tried Laser F/X but I have tried to learn PosterMaker—twice—and I have another view of it. I found it one of the most un-Mac-like and difficult-to-learn

programs I've ever encountered. Nothing works the way you expect and the manual is virtually useless. I'm not stupid, I know the Mac well (not that that's of any help in this case) and I desperately need a program that does what PosterMaker does. Yet twice I simply had to give up in frustration.)

very bad
feature

◉ *Modern Artist* (SH)

Modern Artist (from Computer Friends) was the first color paint program for the Mac II and, at $200 list, it's still the best buy (as of this writing, all other color paint programs cost $500). Since Modern Artist is built on the familiar MacPaint user interface, it's easy to learn, yet it has some pretty powerful features—like Wet Canvas, which lets you smear and blend colors. (The forthcoming Modern Artist II, at $435 list, is supposed to have everything any other color paint program has and more.)

bargain

Modern Artist files can be printed on Shinko printers with Computer Friends' $500 Unigate interface board. A companion program, Color-Sep ($100) lets you make four-color separations from a Postscript screen dump.

◉ *SuperGlue* (AN)

This terrific program (from a terrific company, Solutions International) is a real must if you do desktop publishing or telecommunicate a lot. It lets you copy fully formatted pages between programs or transmit them electronically. In effect, it adds a print-to-disk capability to programs that don't have it. It works as a DA too, so you can view the images from within an application. SuperGlue costs $90 and is well worth it.

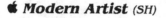

very good
feature

◉ *The Curator* (AN)

This useful picture-filing and -finding DA is described in the *Graphics tools* section of Chapter 8.

MacCalligraphy (FT)

MacCalligraphy's manual describes the program as a word processor (based on the idea that Japanese calligraphy is both writing and painting). I'm not persuaded that it would make a great word processor but it's an intriguing paint program, with tools specifically designed to emulate brushes on paper. A particularly appealing feature is the ability to leave a tail as you end a stroke; to my knowledge, no other graphics program can do this.

The program comes in a wooden box with several sheets of rice paper and its documentation is filled with Japanese art. The manual is quite delightful at times, despite some awkward sentences obviously translated from Japanese. The Desktop of the program's startup disk looks like a Japanese tea room with a treasure alcove.

very good feature

MacCalligraphy is easy to learn, although it takes a while to get used to the way the painting surface picks up ink. The program's tutorials have you practice the strokes of the Japanese character for *eternity* and walk you through drawing bamboo stalks. When you tire of this, there's a "tea break" option that shows you a garden scene as you relax. There are even two short essays that you can read while taking your tea break.

You have to enter a reduced view of your painting to move around in it; this is one of the few complaints I have about the program. I also think the program needs a grabber hand, an essential tool in most graphics programs.

Qualitas Trading Post is the American distributor of MacCalligraphy. They provide free support for the program but you have to pay for the phone call. They've already released one update for MacCalligraphy, so they seem to be committed to keeping it current.

CalendarMaker (AN)

This useful utility is described in the *Miscellaneous utilities* section of Chapter 8.

Clip art

🍎 *beautiful vs. useful?* (AN)

There seems to be an idea afoot that business graphics need to be simple cartoons. Detailed, painterly drawings are seen as somehow frivolous and therefore not business-like. I don't understand this. With the exception of things like charts and graphs, business graphics are *illustrations*. They're there to make something clearer and/or more appealing, and the prettier they are, the better.

It is true, as my esteemed colleague Steve Schwartz points out in the next entry, that some subjects are more likely to be useful than others (although I don't know what he has against farm animals; just because he isn't involved in agriculture doesn't mean other Mac users aren't). But given a choice between a beautiful drawing of a pair of pliers and an ugly drawing of a pair of pliers, a hardware business would be wise to use the former.

Even art that doesn't apply directly to your business can be seen as a challenge. A flyer with a gorgeous picture of a bird on it, say, might well sell more desks than one with nothing on it but minimalist cartoons of desks. I'm not saying you never need simple, practical drawings but beautiful, seemingly irrelevant drawings have their place in business communications too.

very hot tip

🍎 *ClickArt Business Images* (SS)

Given my almost total lack of artistic skills, clip art has always impressed me. I'm fascinated by those intricate, detailed little drawings. Unfortunately, I can seldom find a good reason for using the images found in most clip art packages. Pictures of farm animals, geishas and balloons aren't related to my business and wouldn't impress my clients.

T/Maker, perhaps best-known as the publisher of WriteNow, also publishes the ClickArt line of fonts and clip

very good feature

art. ClickArt Business Images is a collection of abstract icons and symbols that can be used to create your own logos; arrow symbols of different sizes, thickness, etc.; flags of 33 different nations; map symbols (including miniature icons of the 50 states); chart templates; borders and other design elements useful in designing newsletters, company reports and menus; and pictures of computers, food items, livestock, crops, industrial equipment, tools, people in business settings (meetings, presentations, speeches), office workers, symbols for population charts, cars, buses, trucks, bicycles, boats, planes, etc., etc. Here are some samples:

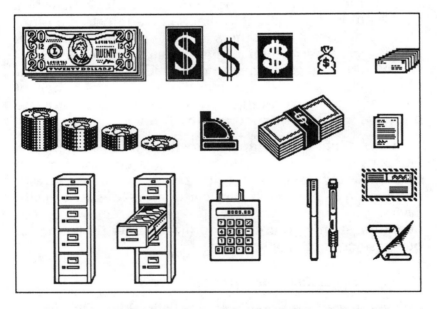

The manual includes several pages of MacPaint tips and a comprehensive index that shows the screen on which each image can be found. This is a truly useful clip art collection and worth its $50 price. It's also available as a HyperCard stack.

🍎 *other ClickArt disks* (AN)

T/Maker publishes a number of other useful ClickArt disks. There's one of holiday images that contains everything from turkeys and pumpkins to flag bunting, easter bunnies and menorahs. My favorite illustration on it is one you could use for a party anytime during the winter (or for a formal party any time of year):

very good feature

There's also a disk of Christian images. It contains one file of 93 crosses, another of 36 stylized signs *(Prayer Group, In Memoriam, Announcing,* etc.) and that just scratches the surface. Any church or religious group should be able to find what it needs for newsletters and flyers in this collection. Here are a couple of my favorites (as you can see, my taste runs toward the elaborate):

very good feature

T/Maker also publishes a four-disk set of clip art in *EPS (encapsulated PostScript)* format, which lets you enlarge or shrink them as much as you want without any loss of detail or clarity. The images vary from the useful to the striking, like the bear shown below. Among the most useful things on the disks are individual drawings of the fifty states (I've shown Louisiana and Alaska, which look particularly good with the drop shadow).

● *Images with Impact!* *(AN)*

This two-disk collection of EPS clip art from 3G Graphics contains a number of basic cartoons like these:

Among the items illustrated are kinds of food, forms of transportation, bears, fireworks, mimes and several everyday objects like a telephone, a cup of coffee and a globe.

● *Japanese clip art* *(AN)*

A Japanese company called Enzan-Hoshigumi has a series of clip-art disks with Japanese subjects. (They also publish MacCalligraphy, described above; both are distributed in the US by Qualitas Trading Co.) Here's an example from a disk of theirs called Year of the Dragon '88:

⬤ *WetPaint* (AN)

very good feature

This is far-and-away my favorite collection of clip art. It contains 24 800K disks, for a total of almost 19 *megabytes* of bit-mapped images. As you can imagine, WetPaint has *everything*.

I'd show you some samples but I like them so much I've used them between chapters and other places throughout the book; they're much more dramatic there than here. (To find them, just look in the index under WetPaint; the page numbers of illustrations are in italics.)

bargain

WetPaint comes in eight three-disk packages that cost $80 each (which amounts to about 3¢ per K for some of the best clip art around). There are four packages in modern style—Classic Clip Art, Publishing, Animal Kingdom and Island Life—and four in turn-of-the-century style—Special Occasions, Printer's Helper, Industrial Revolution and Old Earth Almanac. These last four were previously released as part of the MacMemories collection.

very good feature

Each WetPaint package comes with two desk accessories: ArtRoundup, which lets you open MacPaint files from within another application and edit them with all the usual MacPaint tools, and PatternMover, which lets you edit MacPaint patterns and transfer them between files. WetPaint's manuals are well-written, clear and complete and they contain printouts of all the images on the disks.

MacPaint tips

Unless otherwise noted, the tips in this section work with version 1.5 and version 2.0 of MacPaint, and many will also work in FullPaint, in the paint layer of SuperPaint, etc.

⬤ *double-clicking on tools* (AN)

shortcut

Double-clicking on certain icons in MacPaint's tool palette produces some handy shortcuts, (To use them in version 2.0, you first have to tear off the Tools menu.)

Double-Click on:	to:
🖌	change its shape
✏	enter FatBits
✋	toggle bet. 50% & 100% view
▱	erase the whole window
⬚	select the whole window
a pattern box	change that pattern

✦ Shift key effects *(AN)*

Holding down the Shift key when using certain MacPaint tools produces the following effects:

**very good
feature**

Shift +	lets you:
🖌	paint perfectly straight lines (horizontal or vertical)
✏	draw perfectly straight lines (horizontal or vertical)
✋	move in perfectly straight lines (horizontal or vertical)
▱	erase in perfectly straight lines (horizontal or vertical)
▭	create perfectly square rectangles
the oval tool	create perfectly round circles

✦ *quick FatBits* *(AN)*

The standard way to enter FatBits is to choose it from the Goodies menu. A quicker and more precise way in is to select ✏ (the *pencil*), hold down the ⌘ key and Click in the document. The FatBits window will come up centered precisely on the point where you clicked. In 2.0, this happens in three stages: 200%, 400% and 800% (the last being standard FatBits magnification).

shortcut

♦ quick 〽 *(AN)*

The standard way to select 〽 (known as the *grabber* or simply the *hand)* is to click on its box in the tool palette. This can be annoying when you're moving around the document a lot, because you have to keep going back to the tool palette every time you want to move and then back to it again to select whatever tool you're using to actually do your work. (In 2.0, of course, scroll bars make this less of an annoyance.)

shortcut

There's a much quicker way to get 〽—just hold down the [Option] key. When you're done moving, the pointer will turn back into whatever tool you were using.

♦ quick ℘ *(AN)*

shortcut

You don't have to draw a complete loop around an image with ℘ (the *lasso)* to select it. MacPaint will automatically complete the loop with a straight line between where you start and end.

♦ quick Undo *(AN)*

shortcut

The standard ways to undo the last thing you did are to choose *Undo* from the Edit menu or to use the keyboard shortcut [⌘]–Z. MacPaint offers a third alternative that only requires hitting one key. On ADB keyboards (the ones that come with the SE and the II), it's the *esc* key; on the older Mac keyboards, it's the tilde (~) key (both are in the upper left corner of the respective keyboards).

♦ alternate erasers *(AN)*

very hot tip

When you're erasing unusually shaped images, it's often easier to use ℘ than ⌀ (the *eraser)*, which wasn't designed for fine, detailed work. Just surround the image with ℘ (thereby selecting it) and hit the [Backspace] key. Everything within the shimmering area will be deleted.

very hot tip

When you're erasing large areas, it's often easier to use ⸢⸥ (called the *selection rectangle* or, more popularly, the

marquee) than . Just select the area to be erased with
[ ] and hit [Backspace].

When you're erasing very small details, it's often easier
to use ▟ (the *paintbrush)* than ⬛. Pick a small brush size
(with *Brush Shapes* on the Goodies menu), choose *white* as
the current pattern and simply paint out what you don't
want.

⬥ *moving objects without the background* (AN)

When you select something with [ ] and then move it, a
rectangular chunk of the background moves with it. One
time this looks particularly bad is when you're laying one
object on top of another.

To get just the object and not the background, use ◌
or [⌘][ ] instead. (For more details, see the next entry.) If
you're in a version of MacPaint that doesn't support [⌘][ ]
and you're having trouble getting just the portion of the
picture you want because other things are too close to it, go
into FatBits and use ◌ there.

⬥ *shrinking* [ ] (AN)

Holding down [⌘] while selecting something with [ ]
shrinks the selection down around the object(s) within [ ],
just as if you'd used ◌ instead.

⬥ *printing multiple copies of a single document* (DC)

MacPaint doesn't give you the option of printing more
than one copy of a single document, which means you have
to manually choose the *Print...* command for every copy
you want. Here's a way around that tedious procedure:

In the Finder, duplicate the document you want to print
(using *Duplicate* on the File menu or [⌘]–D). Then select all
the duplicates and choose *Print.* You'll get as many copies
as you made duplicates. (This technique is a bit tedious too,
and it takes up a lot of disk space, but at least you can walk
away from the computer once you've set it up, instead of

*very
hot
tip*

*esp. for
beginners*

*very good
feature*

*very
hot
tip*

having to sit there and issue one *Print...* command after another.

temp files (DC)

MacPaint is one of the many applications that uses temporary files (you never see them because MacPaint closes them when you exit). It needs at least 25K of free space on the disk for these temporary files.

quick quit—don't use it (DC)

important warning

You can exit MacPaint quickly and restart the system by holding down the ⌘ key while choosing *Quit* from the File menu, but it's not a good idea. Quitting like that can scramble the directory on the disk, which means you'll lose all the information on it.

making single copies (AN)

esp. for beginners

You can duplicate objects in MacPaint by copying and pasting them, but there's an easier way to do it. First, use ⌁ or ⬚ to select the part of the picture you want to duplicate, then hold down Option while dragging it. Instead of moving the original, you'll peel away an exact copy. When you have it where you want it, just release the mouse button.

making multiple copies (DC/AN)

very good feature

To make multiple copies of a selected portion of a MacPaint document, use ⌁ or ⬚ to select the part of the picture you want to duplicate, then hold down Option and ⌘ while dragging it. Instead of moving the original, you'll deposit one exact copy after another—until you release the mouse button. (I call this the *deck of cards* or *slur* effect, but the picture below will probably give you a better idea than any words.)

very hot tip

The faster you drag, the less the multiple images overlap. You can also change the rate at which the multiple images are generated by—now get this—changing the line width. (This has to be the most bizarre command in MacPaint.)

The thicker the line you select, the slower the multiple copies will be generated, and thus the less overlap there'll be at any given speed at which you drag the mouse. In other words, to get little overlap, select a thick line width and drag fast; to get a lot of overlap, select a thin line width and drag slowly.

If you want the copies to stay in a straight line, hold down Shift, Option and ⌘ at the same time:

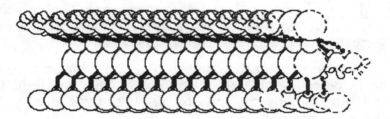

⌘ *stretching things* (DC/AN)

To stretch something, select it with either ℘ or ⬚, hold down ⌘, point to one of its edges and drag. You can create some dramatic effects with the distortion that results.

If you don't want distortion, hold down Shift as well as ⌘ as you drag:

⚫ *Bill Atkinson's three-finger stretch* (DC)

When you've mastered the basic stretching techniques described in the last entry, you may want to try what MacPaint's creator, Bill Atkinson, calls the *three-finger stretch.*

very hot tip

Create a filled rectangle, circle or other shape (by choosing a pattern on the pattern palette and then choosing one of the filled icons on the tool palette). When the object is drawn, select a portion of it with ⌐⌐. Now hold down Shift , Option and ⌘ and drag the image. The selected portion will stretch as you drag it, creating some strange and interesting effects as the pattern distorts.

If you don't want the pattern to distort, choose *Grid* on the Goodies menu before stretching. This is useful for stretching already created objects that aren't exactly the size you want them.

⚫ *resizing images* (DC)

Resizing things in MacPaint is quick and easy. You just select the area you want to resize with ⌐⌐ or ⌐⌐ and then cut it. Next draw a ⌐⌐ that's the size you want the image to be. Then paste the image and it will be resized to fit the ⌐⌐.

One problem with this technique is that it distorts patterns. But with black or white objects, or images made up of lines, it works fine.

⚹ *making images much smaller* (DK)

MacPaint images can be made smaller simply by drawing a ⌐⌐ around them, holding down ⌘ and dragging a corner of the ⌐⌐ inwards. The rectangular proportions can be maintained (*constrained*) by holding down Shift as well as ⌘.

very
hot
tip

There's a major drawback to this technique: if you greatly reduce an image's size, it becomes dark, blurred and indistinct. Here's a step-by-step approach to avoid that pitfall:

1. Put the image to be reduced in a MacPaint window by itself. (If necessary, copy it to a new MacPaint document to do that.)

2. Double-Click on the ⌐⌐ icon in the tool palette. This will select the entire screen.

3. Choose *Invert* from the Edit menu.

4. Choose the *filled* ☐ icon from the palette.

5. Choose the fifth pattern from the left in the top row of the pattern palette.

6. Holding down the Option and ⌘, draw a rectangle that completely covers the image to be reduced. This produces a "mask" effect over the inverted image.

7. Once again, Double-Click on the ⌐⌐ icon and choose *Invert* from the Edit menu. Your original image will now appear as if you were viewing it through a screen.

8. Draw a ⌐⌐ around the image

9. Holding down ⌘ and Shift, place the pointer at the corner of the ⌐⌐ and drag inward.

10. As your image shrinks to different sizes, its quality will vary. It will look particularly good at exactly half its original size.

(This may seem bizarre but it really works. Try it and see.)

⚫ *enlarging pictures to full page* (DC)

It's easier to enlarge a picture to full-page size in a word processor than in MacPaint. Just paste it in and drag it bigger.

⚫ *creating objects with no borders* (DC/AN)

esp. for beginners

You can create filled objects without a black border around them. Just choose the dotted line at the top of the lines palette. Any shape you draw until you change the line width will be borderless.

The same object with and without a border

⚫ *creating dotted lines and outlines* (DC)

very hot tip

To create a dotted line, choose one of the larger line widths, then choose one of the smaller dots as a brush shape. Put a dot on the screen with 🖌, ⌑ the dot and drag it while holding down ⌥Option⌥ and ⌘. With some practice, you can learn to draw dotted circles and other shapes with this technique.

⚫ *shadowing images* (DC)

very hot tip

The *Trace Edges* command (on the Edit menu) is a lot of fun (You can also get it with the keyboard shortcut ⌘–E.) Play with it a bit and then try the undocumented variation I call *shadowing*. Just hold down ⌥Shift⌥ while Tracing Edges. The results look like this:

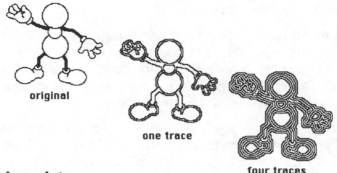

original

one trace

four traces

✎ *tracing pictures* (DC)

Here's a simple technique for transferring pictures from the real world into the Mac that doesn't cost as much—or work as well—as buying a digitizer. Buy some sheets of clear film at an art supply store and trace the image onto one of them with a light-colored pen (the kind that's used for writing on overhead transparencies). Then tape the film onto the Mac screen, with the image centered where you want it, and trace the image carefully with the mouse.

very
hot
tip

Choose a thin *Brush Shape* (on the Goodies menu), but one that's thick enough to be visible behind the trace lines. If the combination you're using isn't working, try tracing the original again with a thinner pen.

✎ *washes* (DC)

To create an image you can see through—in other words, a *wash* effect like you get with watercolor paints—hold down the ⌘ key while you draw over an existing image with 🖌 or 🖌. (You can also use 🖌 or any of the filled shape tools but, for some reason, you have to use Option ⌘ with them.

very good
feature

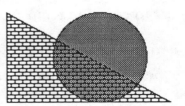

✹ *creating new patterns* (DC)

very hot tip

MacPaint offers two ways to change the patterns in the pattern palette. The better-known method is to edit an existing pattern by selecting *Edit Pattern* from the Goodies menu. But you can also select any part of a MacPaint image and install it as a pattern on the palette.

To do that, simply `Double-Click` on a pattern on the palette that you don't want to keep, then `Click` on the part of the screen that contains the pattern you want to install in its place. (You can also select the pattern on the palette, choose *Edit Pattern* from the Goodies menu and then click on the screen, but why bother?)

✹ *saving custom patterns* (DC)

important warning

When you change the patterns in the pattern palette, the new patterns are associated with the document you're working on, not with MacPaint itself. So if you quit MacPaint without saving the document, they'll be lost.

very hot tip

The easiest way to keep track of the new patterns is to use *Save As...* to store the document with some name like *new patterns 5/12/89,* then erase the contents of the drawing window (double-clicking on ⬜ is the easiest way) so that the document takes up less room. You now have a template with the edited patterns installed that you can use again and again.

important warning

As always with a document you're using as a template, be sure to save your new pattern document under another name immediately after opening it so it will remain untouched on your disk to be used the next time. In fact, it's a good idea to lock the template (with Get Info in the Finder) so you can't save over it using the same name. Finally, don't forget to copy the template to a backup disk.

✹ *using* `Enter` *to manage text* (AN)

When you change the font, size or style of text in MacPaint, all the text you typed since the last mouse click changes to the new setting. This is unlike word processing programs, where the change only affects text you type after you make it. In MacPaint, you have to click with the mouse to start a new text block. But then you have the problem of lining up the old line of text with the new, which is complicated by the fact that they're in different fonts and/or sizes and/or styles.

Fortunately, an answer to this problem is built into MacPaint. Hitting the Enter key stops font, size and style changes from being retroactive. It's as if you clicked the mouse and laid down a new insertion point at the place where you hit the Enter key, except the lines of text line up perfectly. You can press the Enter key as many times as you need to make further changes.

very good feature

text-formatting tricks *(DC)*

One way around MacPaint's habit of treating text as just a bunch of dots (after you've clicked the mouse or hit the Enter key) is to type the text in a note-taking DA-like Note Pad and then paste it into MacPaint.

The text will appear in a ⌐⌐. As you resize the ⌐⌐ (by dragging on it with ⌘ held down), the text will be reformatted to match the new size of the ⌐⌐. As long as the ⌐⌐ is active, you can format the text with any of MacPaint's text options.

This trick is also useful when you paste text in from the Scrapbook. Although it will be in the currently selected font, size and style (rather than what it was in when you wrote it), it will appear in a ⌐⌐ and thus can be formatted with MacPaint's menus or dragged to size with ⌘.

One way to import text with formatting intact is to take a screen shot of it with Shift ⌘ –3). This will create a MacPaint document named *Screen0*. The next screen shot is called *Screen1* and so on up to *Screen9*). Go to the Finder and Double-Click on *Screen0* (which opens MacPaint as well as the document). Select the text you want with ⌐⌐ or ⌐ (you may have to rotate it first), copy it and paste it wherever you want it.

very hot tip

shortcut

⚫ *keyboard shortcuts for formatting text* (DC/AN)

The keyboard shortcuts below change the font and size of text in MacPaint:

shortcut	*effect on text*
⌘ —>	next larger size
⌘ —<	next smaller size
Shift ⌘ —>	next font listed on the Font menu
Shift ⌘ —<	previous font listed on the Font menu
Option ⌘ —>	increases line spacing by one point
Option ⌘ —<	decreases line spacing by one point

Remember that you can only change the text that was entered since your last mouse click. When you click the mouse or press the Enter key, MacPaint forgets that your words are text and treats them as just another pretty picture.

⚫ *thinner outline text* (DC)

very hot tip

The Outline type style makes text wider than plain text and sometimes that makes it hard to fit it into a given area of a MacPaint document. An alternative is to enter the text in plain or bold style, then select it with ⌷ and choose *Trace Edges* (on the Edit menu). This gives you outline text that's no wider than the original plain or bold text.

⚫ *bolder than bold* (DC)

very hot tip

To create characters in your MacPaint documents that are bolder than bold, type them in outline and fill them in with the ⬧ (with the black pattern selected). It sometimes helps to be in FatBits to do this.

⚫ *the sexiest tip in this book* (AN)

very hot tip

From within MacPaint 2.0, hold down Tab and the space-bar while selecting *About MacPaint...* from the ⚫ menu. If you just get a plain About MacPaint box, your copy of the program has been sanitized and you need to find one of the first 20,000 copies of 2.0, the ones that shipped before Claris management became aware of what their deranged programmers were up to.

very
hot
tip

I could have saved you the trouble, of course, by putting a screen shot right here in the book. I debated long and hard about doing that but finally decided that *The Macintosh Bible* is a family book (as its name implies). Anyway, this makes it more of an adventure.

MacDraw tips

Unless otherwise noted, the tips in this section work with version 1.9.5 of MacDraw, but many of them should also work with MacDraw II and later versions of the program.

🍎 *moving horizontally or vertically* (CJW)

You can force an object (or group of objects) to move exactly horizontally or vertically (and nothing in between) by holding down [Shift] as you drag. But be sure to press down the mouse button *before* you hit the [Shift] key or you'll simply deselect whatever object you click on.

*esp. for
beginners*

🍎 *drawing squares and circles* (DC)

To draw perfect squares and circles in MacDraw, just hold down [Shift] while drawing with the □ or the oval tool.

*esp. for
beginners*

🍎 *centering objects on a point* (DC)

Here's a simple way to control the placement of geometric objects (rectangles, ovals, etc.). First draw the object, then cut it, [Click] where you want the center of the object to be and paste.

very
hot
tip

🍎 *putting text in a rectangle* (DC)

The MacDraw manual can be confusing when it describes how to draw a rectangle to use as a border around text. You

esp. for beginners

may think from reading it that you should draw the rectangle, select the text tool, place the insertion point and then type. This method doesn't work.

Instead, draw the rectangle and just start typing, without bothering with the text tool and the insertion point. The text you type will word-wrap within the rectangle.

🍎 *two ways to copy text* (CJW)

very hot tip

If you select a block of text with ▶ in MacDraw, copy it to the Clipboard and then paste it into a page layout or word processing program, it will become a PICT image that can be stretched or reshaped but not edited. (For more on text-stretching, see *creating special typographic effects* in Chapter 6.)

If you select the same text with ⌶ , it will transfer as text and will be editable.

🍎 *retaining (or regaining) the tool used last* (AN)

esp. for beginners

Normally when you draw an object in MacDraw, the tool you're using changes back to ▶ the moment the object is drawn. If you want to use the same tool to draw several objects without having to go back to the tool palette again and again, hold down the ⌘ key while drawing. The tool will persist from one object to the next. (To get back to ▶, just release the ⌘ key.)

very hot tip

If you accidentally let up on the ⌘ key and decide you want the tool back, just hold down ⌘ again and ⟨Click⟩ on the mouse button.

🍎 *taking off the blindfold* (CJW)

very hot tip

Whenever you move objects in MacDraw, they're replaced on the screen by a faint rectangular box. This speeds up screen refreshes and lets you work faster, but it also makes accurate object placement a matter of trial and error.

For more precise control, hold down ⟨Option⟩ (in MacDraw II, ⌘) near the end of the drag, without letting up on the mouse button. You'll see the object you're dragging in full detail, and you'll be able to position it exactly where you want it on the first try.

(You can hold down the key the whole time you're dragging, but this will slow things up. That's why MacDraw gives you just the outline in the first place.)

₡ *resizing very small objects* (DC)

When you need to resize a very small object in MacDraw, you may have trouble grabbing its handles. If this happens, just create a larger object (a simple square or rectangle will do), Shift Click on it and the small object and *group* them (with the *Group* command on the Arrange menu or ⌘ –G).

very hot tip

Now you be able to easily grab the handles of the larger object and resize both objects simultaneously. When you're satisfied with the size of the small object, *ungroup* them (with the *Ungroup* command on the Arrange menu or Shift ⌘ –G in MacDraw II, ⌘ –H in earlier versions) and delete the larger one.

₡ *no pointless saves* (AN)

If you try to save a file that hasn't been changed since the last save, MacDraw gives you a message that reads: *There haven't been any changes since the last save.*

₡ *Print One bug* (AN)

If you select *Print One* (from the File menu) in MacDraw 1.9.5, you'll usually get three copies of your document. Sometimes you'll get other numbers of copies but you'll never get just one (at least I never have).

The workaround (if it's even worthy of that name) is simply to choose *Print...* instead. You can immediately hit Return to request the default values in the Print dialog box, since the default for number of copies is 1. (You don't have to wait for the dialog box to appear.)

⚫ *using smoothing to draw curves* (DC)

**very
hot
tip**

When you use MacDraw's freehand shape tool (the second from the bottom on the palette) to draw curves, you may not be very happy with the results. Instead, try drawing an angular approximation of the desired image with MacDraw's polygon tool (the last one on the palette) and then use the Edit menu's *Smooth* command to curve the edges.

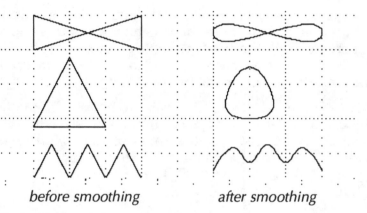

before smoothing   after smoothing

⚫ *Bezier curves in MacDraw* (CJW)

**very
hot
tip**

You can draw and edit curves quickly and accurately in MacDraw without having to struggle with the limitations of the arc tool. The trick is to create the equivalent of a Bezier curve. Here's how you do it:

Draw an open, four-pointed polygon (Double-Click on the fourth point to end the polygon without closing it). While the polygon is still selected, choose *Smooth* from the Edit menu. Then choose *Reshape Polygon*. You'll end up with a Bezier-like curve having two end points and two control points. Dragging these points lets you reshape the curve to fit any path.

For more complex curves, draw the approximate shapes using the freehand tool. When you're done, choose *Smooth* and *Reshape Polygon* from the Edit menu. This will change your irregularly shaped curves into nicely smoothed ones. You can then edit them like any other polygons.

◆ *a template for schedules* (CJW)

Half the time spent preparing schedules in MacDraw is usually spend constructing the grid. So why do it from scratch each time? Here's how to prepare a simple template that's easily customized:

In MacDraw II, turn the Grid feature on (with *Turn Autogrid On,* on the Layout menu), then draw a single vertical line. While it's still selected, duplicate it (⌘-D) as many times as will fit across the page. The lines will be slightly offset, so use the *Alignment...* command on the Arrange menu to line them up.

Next, draw a horizontal line touching the top of the vertical lines. Duplicate it repeatedly until the last line touches the bottom of the vertical lines. Line up the horizontal lines with the *Alignment...* command. Now select all the lines (vertical and horizontal) and group them (⌘-G).

(In earlier versions of MacDraw, you use the same procedure, except the Grid command is *Turn Grid On* (still on the Layout menu) and you don't need the *Alignment...* command, since the lines won't be offset.)

Then save your document as *schedule template* (or whatever) and quit to the Finder. Select *schedule template.* Get Info (⌘-I) on it and check the Locked box.

Now each time you need a new schedule, simply open *schedule template,* ungroup the lines (⇧⌘-G in MacDraw II, ⌘-H in earlier versions), delete any you don't need and regroup those that remain. After setting the correct drawing size and page orientation, choose *Reduce to Fit* (called *Fit to Window* in MacDraw II) from the Layout menu. Grab a corner of your template and drag it to whatever size and shape you want.

Save the revised grid under whatever file name you want to use for the schedule you're creating and you're done! (Well, almost—you still have to fill in the data.)

❡ *adding patterns to MacDraw* (DC)

MacDraw lacks the easy pattern-editing features of MacPaint but you can use ResEdit to create new patterns in it. Open a copy of MacDraw with ResEdit and open the resource *PAT#*. Then open the box that contains the MacDraw patterns. Double-clicking on a pattern allows you to edit it in FatBits mode.

When you have the patterns you want, save and close ResEdit. If you need to use many different patterns, you can keep separate copies of MacDraw on separate disks. If you use this approach, be sure you use the appropriate copy of MacDraw with each document, because MacDraw assigns patterns based simply on where they are on the palette.

❡ *compatible system software for MacDraw II* (AN)

important warning

Claris doesn't recommend running MacDraw II with versions of the System earlier than 6.0 or with versions of the Finder earlier than 6.1.

SuperPaint tips

Unless otherwise noted, the tips in this section work with version 1.1 of SuperPaint, but many of them should also work with SuperPaint 2.0 and later versions of the program.

❡ *switching layers* (SZA)

shortcut

You usually toggle between the Paint and Draw layers by clicking on the icons at the top of the tool palette, but there's also a keyboard equivalent: ⌘ –/ (slash).

❡ *the* 🖐 (SZA)

Pressing spacebar gives you the 🖐 you use to move the document around but if you're working with the I-beam pointer, it just types spaces. At those times, use ⌘ –spacebar instead.

If you hold down ⌷Shift⌷ when you're using the 𓂀, the document will only move horizontally or vertically (whichever way you move first).

⬤ *closing all open windows* (SZA)

If you have multiple document windows open, you can close all of them at once by ⌷Option⌷-clicking in the close box of any one of them. (This is a trick that works in the Finder, too.) If any of the documents have been edited, you'll be asked if you want to save the changes.

shortcut

⬤ *command-drag* (SZA)

Here's another trick from the Finder that works in a lot of programs: you can move a window without making it the active window by holding down ⌷⌘⌷ while you drag it by its title bar.

⬤ *Paint/Draw from Center or Corner* (SZA)

A shortcut for choosing the commands *Paint (Draw) from Center* and *Paint (Draw) from Corner* is to double-click in any of the shape tools in the tool palette.

When *Paint (Draw) from Center* is active, small crosses appear in the centers of the shape tools in the palette.

⬤ *erasing the Paint layer* (SZA)

Double-clicking on the ⬚ erases everything in the Paint layer that's showing in the window. Holding down ⌷Option⌷ and ⌷⌘⌷ while double-clicking on the ⬚ erases the entire paint layer regardless of what portion is showing in the window.

shortcut

⬤ *zooming in and out* (SZA)

You can jump from regular view to maximum magnification (eight times) with either of two shortcuts: ⌷Double-Click⌷ with the 𝄍 in the palette or ⌷⌘⌷⌷Click⌷ with the 𝄍 someplace in the document.

shortcut

♠ ⌷ *tricks* (SZA)

If you hold down ⌘ while you use the ⌷, the ⌷ shrinks down (as soon as you let go of the mouse button) to the smallest size that will enclose all the black pixels of the selected area.

If you hold down Option while you use the ⌷, the selection is lassoed when you let go of the mouse button—and the current tool switches to the ⌇.

♠ ⌇ *tricks* (SZA)

If you hold down Option while you use the ⌇, it won't shrink when you let go of the mouse button. It stays where you traced it, enclosing any white space you selected.

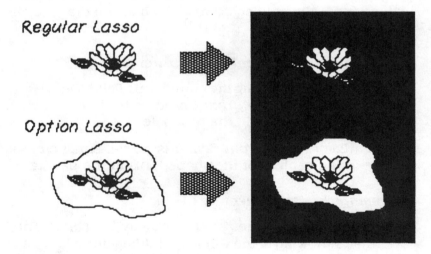

♠ *selecting all* (SZA)

When used on the Paint layer, the *Select All* command (in the Edit menu) normally selects the layer with a ⌷ as large as the page.

If you hold down ⌘ while you choose *Select All*, the ⌷ shrinks to the smallest size possible that encloses all the black dots in the document.

If you hold down Option while you choose *Select All*, everything in the Paint layer is selected.

⚫ *selections in selections* (SZA)

When you've made a selection in the Paint layer with either the ⌐┐ or the ✎, the pointer changes to an arrow as soon as you move it within the selection. (To be precise, within a lassoed selection it only changes to an arrow when you're over a dot.)

If you want to make another selection that begins inside the current selection, you don't have to deselect the current one to do it. Just hold down the [Tab] key. The pointer will stay a ✎ or cross hairs (for the ⌐┐) even when you're within the current selection.

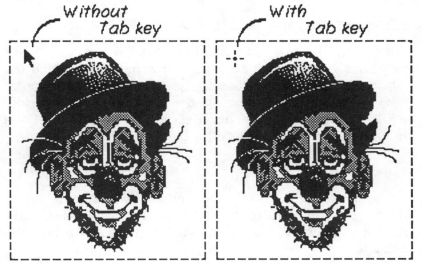

⚫ *Nudge* (SZA)

The *Nudge Left, Right, Up* and *Down* commands in the Options menu move a selection one pixel at a time. They have keyboard equivalents listed in the menu but you can also use the arrow keys.

⚫ *limited pours* (SZA)

When you use the 🖉, it normally fills an enclosed area, even if parts of that enclosed area are not visible in the window. If you hold [Option] when you pour, the paint will pour only into the area that's visible in the window.

❡ *transparent paint* (SZA)

No matter which paint mode you've chosen in the Paint menu (opaque, transparent or paint on black), if you hold ⌘ when using the 🖌 or 🄱, the paint type is temporarily changed to Transparent.

❡ 🄱 *shapes* (SZA)

very hot tip

Did you think the 🄱 was forever restrained to its basic round pattern? So did I, until I very belatedly discovered that if you hold down Option while using it, the spray pattern changes to the currently selected 🖌 shape.

❡ *30° and 60° lines* (SZA)

very good feature

It's second nature to those of us who had MacPaint in the early days to use Shift to constrain movements of paint tools to horizontal and vertical, and to use it to get 90° (horizontal and vertical) and 45° lines with the Line tool. This all works in SuperPaint but you can also get perfect 30° and 60° lines by holding down Option with the Line tool.

❡ *arcs* (SZA)

very hot tip

The Arc tool makes either a wedge (like a slice of pie, if there's a paint pattern selected) or an arc (if the None pattern is selected) but either way, a quarter of an oval is created.

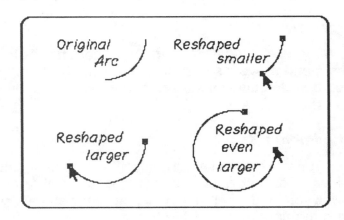

If you want more or less of an arc, you can do it in the Draw layer. Draw an arc, choose *Reshape Arc* from the Draw menu and drag one of the arc's handles to continue the curve or close it down.

✦ adding "corners" (SZA)

When you use the *Reshape Polygon* command on a polygon in the Draw layer, you can not only drag the original "corners" to reshape it but you can also add new corners. Just hold ⌘ down as you move a handle and a new handle will be dragged out of it.

very hot tip

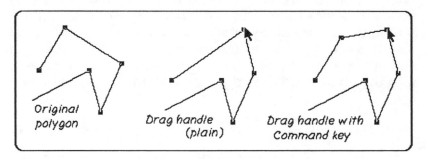

Original polygon

Drag handle (plain)

Drag handle with Command key

✦ text and Enter (SZA)

When you type text in the Paint layer, you can change the size, style, font, justification or spacing of all of it—as long as it's still active (with the insertion point still blinking).

If you want to freeze the formatting attributes of what you've already typed, just click the mouse and start another text block, but then the two text blocks probably won't line up. An easier way is to press Enter. You'll be able to keep typing, but the text before the Enter will be frozen and formatting commands won't affect it.

This lets you do things like insert a bold word in the midst of plain text. Just type plain text, press Enter; choose *Bold*, type the bold text, press Enter; choose *Plain Text* and continue typing plain text. (This trick works in MacPaint as well.)

❡ *pasted text* (SZA)

When you paste text into the Paint layer, it appears as a block inside a selection rectangle. As long as the block is selected, you can use commands in the Font, Size and Style menus to affect it. You can also change the shape of the rectangle: just drag on a corner while holding down ⌘ . As you change the shape, the text inside shifts to fit it.

❡ *text boxes on the Draw layer* (SZA)

When you click someplace in the Draw layer with the I-beam pointer, the initial width of the text box extends from the point of the click to the right edge of the window. Although you can always resize the text box in the normal way (by dragging on a handle), it's easier to start with something close to what you want. So instead of clicking with the I-beam, use it to drag the text box to the width you want.

❡ *pickups* (SZA)

*very
hot
tip*

Here's a trick that works with both the Pattern Edit and Brush Shape dialog boxes:

When the dialog box is open, move the pointer outside the box, press the mouse button and drag the pointer around. Anything beneath the pointer is "picked up" and sent to the edit area of the dialog box. This lets you take any pattern from the screen and make it either a defined pattern in the palette or a brush shape. (This also works in MacPaint.)

You don't have to keep the click inside the document window for the pickup: it works anywhere on the screen.

The pickup jumps in eight-pixel units, so you can pull an actual pattern from a document, or part of one pattern and part of another one next to it. If you want to move freely, you can circumvent the automatic grid by holding down Option before you press the mouse button.

⬢ ⌘ Click **invert** *(SZA)*

In both the Brush Shapes and Pattern Edit dialog boxes, a ⌘ Click in the edit area reverses the black-and-white pixels of the pattern.

⬢ skipping the dialog boxes *(SZA)*

The *Scale Selection...* command in the Edit menu and the *Other...* command in the Size menu have dialog boxes to let you define, respectively, the scaling factor and a nonstandard font size. If you have either of these numbers already set to what you want, you can bypass the dialog boxes entirely: hold down Option when you choose the commands. The last-used sizes will be used again.

FullPaint tips

Unless otherwise noted, these tips refer to version 1.0 .

⬢ similarities to MacPaint *(DC)*

FullPaint incorporates 95% of the features of MacPaint (1.5 and earlier versions) and almost all of them function exactly the same way. So if you're familiar with MacPaint, you can start using FullPaint without missing a mouse click.

This also means that virtually all the MacPaint tips described above also apply to FullPaint. The tips that follow cover a few of the things that are unique to FullPaint (or were before MacPaint 2.0).

⬢ expanding a graphic to fill a page *(DC)*

FullPaint provides an easy method for expanding any graphic to full-page size. Just copy the graphic (with ⌘–C) and open a new document. Triple-click on the ⌐ icon and paste. That's all it takes.

very hot tip

⬢ pasting into the upper left corner *(DC)*

Normally when you paste into a FullPaint document, the image appears in the middle of the window. If you want the

very hot tip

image to be placed into the upper left corner, hold down the [Option] key while pasting.

custom erasers *(DC)*

Here's how to create an eraser of any size you want: First, choose [marquee] from the palette and place the pointer in a blank area of the screen right next to the area you want to erase. Next drag until the [marquee] is the size you want the eraser to be. Then hold down [Option] and [⌘]. Wherever you move the [marquee], it will erase.

Make sure you use a blank area to create the eraser. If you use an area that you've drawn in, [marquee] won't erase but instead will paint the pattern of the original area wherever you move it.

toggling between modes *(DC)*

shortcut

[⌘]–A will quickly toggle you between Menu Mode and Full Screen Mode.

moving the tool and pattern palettes *(DC)*

One of the nice features of FullPaint is the ability to move the tool and pattern palettes to get them out of the way. Just move the pointer to the edge of either palette. When the pointer changes to a hollow cross, you can use it to drag the palette anywhere you want.

shortcut

An even quicker method is to hold down the [Option] key when pointing to either palette; this changes the pointer to a hollow cross without your having to worry about exact positioning.

quick select with [lasso] *(David Goldman)*

shortcut

Double-clicking on an object with [lasso] selects it.

shrink-wrapping with [lasso] and [marquee] *(DC)*

Holding down [⌘] while using [lasso] makes the selection automatically shrink to the edges of the image being lassoed. Holding down ⌘ while using ⌷⌿ makes the selection automatically shrink as close to the edge of the selected image as it can while still remaining a rectangle.

very good feature

🍎 *editing* 🖌 *(DC)*

Creating a custom 🖌 in FullPaint is incredibly easy. Hold down the ⌘ key while double-clicking on the 🖌 icon in the tool palette. That will put you in FatBits mode.

Once you're there, you can move the pointer anywhere on the screen and Click. The brush pattern will assume the shape of whatever you're pointing to. You can then edit the pattern or use it as it is.

From the WetPaint clip art collection.
Copyright © 1988–89 by Dubl-Click Software Inc.
All rights reserved.

Lesson 3 E. Morning Light   © CLEMENT

Chapter 13

Page layout

Desktop publishing programs

✦ why this chapter isn't longer (AN)

Page layout programs (aka *desktop publishing programs*) are evolving faster than just about any other kind. By the time we can give you tips on one version of a program, another version is out. And these versions aren't just "maintenance upgrades"; they're dramatically different— virtually new programs.

That's why, of all the chapters in the book, this one has the fewest tips carried over from the first edition—most of them simply didn't work any more.

A related reason for the relative shortness of this chapter is that desktop publishing products are the last ones we use when we work on a new edition. I could, of course, solicit desktop publishing tips early on in the process, but there's always that great new version coming out—and I certainly don't want to give you tips on the old version, which will be out-of-date by the time you read them.

So I say to myself (every time, I never learn): *We'll be using that new version of PageMaker or XPress on the book itself and will be learning all about it. I might as well hold off on the tips till then.* By the time we're using it on the book, of course, I'm working 16-hour days and don't have time to come up with, or edit, a lot of tips.

Finally, remember that this chapter wouldn't look so short if this book weren't so long, or if I'd made it part of the graphics chapter, as I considered doing. It's a mark of respect to have it stand alone.

✦ which page layout program to buy (AN)

Since page layout programs have price tags ranging from $500 to $800, this is an important question. But evaluating Macintosh page layout software is a little like watching a very close horse race—one program comes out with a new version and pulls ahead of another, only to be passed up when another program comes out with a new version. So the program I'd recommend as I write this may not be the one I'd recommend when you read it.

The easy answer (and maybe the right one) is PageMaker, which is fast becoming the standard in this field. 60% of the respondents in *Macworld's* reader survey named it their favorite desktop publishing program.

very good feature

PageMaker may deserve this status, because it seems to be improving at a faster rate than its competition. Although version 1.2 was very flaky and 2.0a had some problems, we used version 3.0 to this edition of the book and found little to complain about. Many of the annoying, unMaclike (because they were Microsoft-Word-like) features of the program—no font menu, nonalphabetized fonts, etc.— have been eliminated.

PageMaker 3.0 runs pretty smoothly and slickly but there are still frequent "anomalies." For example, my copy of the program has started telling me, every time I load it, that it can't find the supplemental user dictionary. Byron Brown, laying out the pages for this edition, got a series of out-of-memory messages (on a five-meg machine). But the biggest problem was that fonts get handled very differently in PageMaker than in most other programs and we ended up having to reinstall several of them.

The most bewildering bug involved characters in Cairo that print OK at certain times but, for no apparent reason, are partially cut off at other times. We still have to put the final page numbers on that chapter, so I don't know how they're going to come out when we print the page for the final time and send it off to the printer. (If you're curious, take a look for yourself. It's the fried egg and the ice-cream cone in the Cairo printout in Chapter 5.)

PageMaker is, by now, a very complex piece of software. Aldus telephone support is a lot better than it was—even great at times—but it still leaves a lot to be desired. Even at its best, the people there can't begin to figure out problems like the ones just mentioned.

Still, despite PageMaker's quirks and occasional lapses, the 700+-page book you're holding in your hands is proof that it's definitely a usable tool for professional desktop publishing. Given its popularity, it's certainly the safest choice you can make, and it may well be the wisest.

very good feature

XPress is the program to use if you really care about typographic precision (half-point type sizes, for example). Version 2.0 didn't get to us in time to be evaluated for this edition, but Scott Beamer describes its features in the entry below.

Ready,Set,Go! "coulda been a contender" but it switched managers. Its new one, Letraset, isn't keeping the program in shape, and it seems destined to become a has-been, living on its memories.

None of these page layout products has everything I want, or even comes close. But some of that is because the hardware just isn't there yet. That's OK; we're still in much better shape than the PC world. (Desktop publishing on a PC is like trying to tie your shoelaces while wearing gloves and a blindfold. It's possible, but what's the point?)

One last tip: if you're currently shopping for a desktop publishing program, do yourself a favor—don't rush your decision. Look at the latest magazine reviews and try out the products you're considering *extensively* before you buy. If that means you'll have to buy from a store instead of by mail order, and if that costs you a few more dollars, so be it. Better that than spending hundreds of dollars on a product that's not what you need or want.

very hot tip

🍎 *PageMaker 3.0* (AN)

I've talked about PageMaker in general in the previous entry, but here are some specifics on version 3.0. The main improvement (from my point of view) is that you can now pour a long document in and it will automatically create the pages needed and flow the text onto them. It also has easy-to-use style sheets, automatic runarounds (text flowing around graphics), better text exporting to word processing

very good feature

programs, user-adjustable autoleading, support for color and twenty complete page design templates.

Although it still can't do searches and replaces, Page-Maker 3.0 is a slick, professional program that gives you an enormous amount of power.

🍎 *XPress* (SB)

Though PageMaker essentially invented page layout software and dominates the field, Quark XPress has established itself as a high-end ($800 to PageMaker's $600) alternative for people who really care about typographic quality.

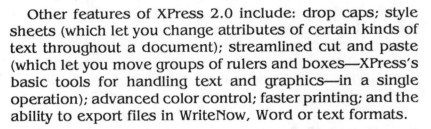

very good feature

The page-layout abilities of the two programs are very similar. PageMaker fans talk about how much they like the user interface and the support Aldus provides (which includes great templates, manuals, newsletters and training courses—all essential for getting the most from programs of this complexity). XPress fans talk about the superior word processing and type-handling capabilities like fractional point sizes (10.5-point type, for example), extremely precise kerning, an excellent spelling checker with word count and links between split sections of text.

Other features of XPress 2.0 include: drop caps; style sheets (which let you change attributes of certain kinds of text throughout a document); streamlined cut and paste (which let you move groups of rulers and boxes—XPress's basic tools for handling text and graphics—in a single operation); advanced color control; faster printing; and the ability to export files in WriteNow, Word or text formats.

XPress was the first layout program on the Mac to do four-color separations. (The quality is fine for line art or spot color, and about that of newspapers for photographic halftones.) Version 2.0 does them in a variety of formats, including CYMK, HBS, RGB and Pantone. You can even import, place, size and rotate 24-bit color images.

Quark also provides a separate utility for transferring XPress files to the Scitex computerized color separation system. The original color photo will be rescanned by the Scitex, which can store a lot more data than a Mac (an 8 x 10 color photo can easily take up 20 megabytes), but the Scitex operator can use your XPress file as a guide to how you want the graphics sized, cropped and placed.

Basic design tips

● *Rule # 1—break the rules* (AN)

Many professional designers would love to have you think that there's a right way and a wrong way to design something. Needless to say, that idea is not merely incorrect but deranged. Designs can't be right or wrong; they can only be better or worse. It's a subjective matter—although that certainly doesn't mean everybody's opinion is equally worth listening to.

The tips in the next entry (and in *Looking Good in Print,* described in the entry after that) are all good, sensible, basic guidelines to good design. But good design is, by definition, not boring (unless you think boredom is good). And yet it's easy to follow *all* those design rules and come up with something that makes phenobarbital seem like a stimulant.

If I had to come up with a design rule, it would be: *Never use Times or Helvetica for anything.* I think it's at least as universal as any of the others you're about to read. But let me give you a more general rule—*Fais ce que voudras* (as my old buddy Frankie Rableais used to say): *Do what you want.*

very
hot
tip

● *C. J.'s design tips* (CJW)

Here are a few general design guidelines I've found useful.

• Mixing more than three typefaces or styles on a page is something a professional designer will do only very rarely.

- Use color to set your publications apart from others. Don't be gaudy. Spot color tastefully applied might be all you need to catch a reader's eye. In a market where color predominates, the absence of color can also be used to good effect.

- Leave plenty of white space to balance your compositions. A cluttered page is likely to be overlooked as being "too busy" to spend time with.

- Organize your message around a dominant visual element. A single large headline or graphic can help to focus your readers' attention; several will probably confuse them.

- Use subheads to break up your text and sustain interest. You can also separate large blocks of text by using well-placed pull quotes. Set them in a different font or type style than the main text.

- Additional emphasis can be given to text and graphics by accenting them with boxes or frames. Drop caps can further heighten interest, but should be used sparingly.

- Design facing pages together. Two pages that look great separately can clash terribly when placed next to each other.

- Above all, be consistent. Consistency lends credibility to your message.

✦ *Looking Good in Print* (SS)

Thanks to desktop publishing software, millions of people now have the tools to create gaudy, unbalanced publications full of klutzy layouts and mismatched fonts. Just as easy-to-use financial software won't instantly make you a CPA, accessible desktop publishing tools won't magically give you taste.

A book called *Looking Good in Print*, by Roger C. Parker, can help. It does a good job of covering design essentials, offers help in selecting typefaces and provides hints for effective use of the tools of the trade. Its heavy use of graphics makes it a quick read.

very good feature

Although this book starts you thinking along the right lines, don't get the impression that knowledge of a few rules (coupled, of course, with a lot of creativity and imagination) will make you a good designer. If you're serious about learning design, treat *Looking Good in Print* as a jumping-off point to other reading and training. As that, it's quite good.

important warning

PageMaker tips

These tips apply to version 3.0. Because the program's changed so much, many of them will not work with earlier versions.

❡ *basic tips* (AN)

Here are some tips for PageMaker beginners:

You can't point to an object (text box, whatever) in PageMaker and get the size of it automatically. But when you move it, *whiskers* that correspond to its edges show up on the rulers. Another easy way to measure its size is to drag guide lines to each of its four edges.

esp. for beginners

You may sometimes have trouble selecting something when a guide is right next to it. The solution is simplicity itself—move the guide away, select the object, then move the guide back when you're done.

When PageMaker underlines a word, it looks like the underlining extends into the spaces on either side. It just looks that way on the screen; it won't happen on the printout.

When you send an object to the back, PageMaker should deselect it. But you have to click somewhere else to do that, which is an annoyance.

When several text blocks are all in the same area, you may have trouble grabbing the one you want. One trick is to grab them at the sides. (You can facilitate that by making one flush left, another flush right, a third centered, and stretching their widths so they extend to different areas on the pasteboard. Of course that's one practical for blocks where the text is all on one line.)

⌘ *easy switching between page views* (CJW)

very hot tip

Forget about using the scroll bars in PageMaker. It's just too hard to get around in your publications that way. *[Is it ever!—AN]* Instead, use [Option] [⌘] [Click] to toggle the screen display between *Actual* size and *Fit in window.*

When you go to *Actual* size, your document is centered around the point where you click. Since you can see the whole page (or pages) in *Fit in window,* it's easy just to figure out where you want to be and then [Option] [⌘] [Click] to get there.

⌘ *viewing the whole pasteboard* (CJW)

very hot tip

If you hold down [Shift] while choosing *Fit in window* from the Page menu, the screen display is reduced so that the entire pasteboard can be seen without scrolling. This makes it easy to use the pasteboard as intended—for temporary storage of text and graphics. [Option] [⌘] [Click] takes you back to Actual view.

⌘ *400% view* (AN)

very hot tip

To see your page at 400% size, hold the [Shift] key down as you choose *200%* from the Page menu.

⌘ *shrinking PageMaker files* (CJW)

PageMaker files tend to be gargantuan, clogging up your disk and costing a fortune if you ever try to send them over phone lines. It's not even uncommon to discover that a PageMaker document you've been working on for a while no longer fits on a single 800K disk.

Fortunately, there's a way to shrink PageMaker files without losing data and without having to use a file-compression program. It could hardly be simpler: just use *Save As...* instead of *Save*. For some bizarre reason, this simple trick will reduce the size of files by as much as 2/3rds, and sometimes even more. (I'm surprised Aldus didn't fix this in version 3.0.)

Open a few old PageMaker documents, note their size and use *Save As...* on them. You'll be amazed.

♦ *some useful keyboard shortcuts* (AN)

This is just a short list of some of the more useful commands that aren't covered in other entries. Commands that are listed on the menus or that are common to many Mac programs have been omitted.

shortcut

> *text*

Shift ⌘ –T	insert thin space
Option ⌘ –P	insert automatic page number
triple Click	select line of text
⌘ Click	select text block
Shift Option ⌘ –>	make text one point larger
Shift Option ⌘ –<	make text one point smaller

> *placed graphics*

Shift	resize proportionally

   (while dragging on graphic handle)

Shift Click	return to original proportions

   (on handle)

✿ *kerning* (AN)

shortcut

To kern a pair of characters (i.e., bring them closer together), hit [Shift] [⌘] [Backspace]. They'll move by increments of 1/48th of em space.

Since an *em space* is the same number of points wide as the font you're using is high, the increments will be one point with 48-point type, a half-point with 24-point type, a quarter-point with 12-point type and so on. (The increments don't have to be even, of course; with 14-point type, they'll be .29167 points.)

To move the characters farther apart (by the same increments), hit [⌘] [Backspace].

✿ *page number reminder* (CJW)

important warning

If you're having difficulty getting automatic page numbering to work, make sure the [Caps Lock] key is up. If it's down, nothing will happen when you type [Option] [⌘] –P.

✿ *a do-it-yourself eraser* (DC)

You can get around PageMaker's lack of an eraser tool by making one of your own. Select the *None* command from the Line menu and the *White* command from the Shades menu, then use either the box or the circle tool to draw an object large enough to hide the area you want to erase.

✿ *PageMaker's font capacity* (AN)

After PageMaker prints a block of text, it flushes the fonts it used out of the laser printer's memory. This should mean that you can have as many fonts in a block as most applications let you have in a whole document. In practice, however, PageMaker doesn't actually seem to be able to handle more fonts than other programs; in fact, it seems to choke on even fewer. Dwight Mayo thinks it's a problem with LocalTalk timing.

Another problem with PageMaker's approach is that it slows down printing, since the fonts have to be downloaded to the printer anew at the start of each block. The way around this is to manually download all the ones you commonly use before you start the job.

shortcut

🍎 *speeding up loading* (SM)

PageMaker can take a while to load and that's often partly because it's searching for its spelling and hyphenation dictionaries. It looks first in the system folder, then in the folder named *PageMaker* and finally in any folders within that folder. Putting both dictionaries in your system folder will speed loading up significantly.

shortcut

Ready,Set,Go! tips

These tips apply to version 3.0. Because the program's changed so much, many of them will not work with earlier versions.

🍎 *too many pasteboards* (CJW)

PageMaker's pasteboard travels with you as you go from page to page, making it easy to store and reuse items without having to cut and paste. But in Ready,Set,Go!, each page has its own pasteboard. Drag something onto it and it disappears from view when you change pages.

very bad feature

This means you should take special care when deleting pages in Ready,Set,Go! If you have something important tucked away on a pasteboard, it's gone forever if you delete that particular page.

important warning

🍎 *speeding things up with shallow windows* (DC)

If you're just checking something at the top of each page (like a page number or a header), you can speed things up considerably by making the window very shallow. Since Ready,Set,Go! will have less to draw, it will bring up each page much more quickly.

This technique also works if you're checking things at the bottom of each page, but you have to click in the scroll bar as each page comes up, to take yourself to the bottom of it. Still, you'd have to do that anyway, and a shallow window still speeds things up.

Chapter 14

Commun-icating with other computers

✦ *the standards* (AN)

In transferring files back and forth while editing this book, almost everyone I dealt with (Macintosh experts all) used MicroPhone. Red Ryder certainly has its fans, as do some other communications programs, but MicroPhone seems to have become the de facto standard for direct computer-to-computer telecommunications. (By the way, all these terms are defined later on in the chapter and/or in the glossary.)

very hot tip

Another de facto standard is Hayes-compatible modems. Non-Hayes-compatible modems are virtually worthless (as I discovered when I tried to sell one). But I don't know a single person who has an actual Hayes modem; everybody gets less expensive ones that use the same protocols.

very hot tip

A third standard is StuffIt, the file-compression utility that virtually everyone uses to speed transmissions (it's also good for maintaining archives that take up less disk space).

very hot tip

A final standard that's evolved is PhoneNET cabling hardware (rather than the regular LocalTalk stuff) in local areas networks. It's cheaper and it lets you use already existing phone wires.

very hot tip

All these products are discussed in more detail below.

Telecommunicating

✦ *telecommunicating on the Mac* (DC)

Telecommunications (computers communicating over phone lines) has a reputation for being one of the least friendly areas of personal computing. That's because it *is* one of the least friendly areas of personal computing. In spite of that, it can be tremendously exciting, useful and fun.

esp. for beginners

Actually, telecommunications on the Mac is a little easier than on other computers. You still have to deal with bizarre terms like *parity* and *stop bits* but some standards have emerged, and most Mac programs walk you through whatever nonstandardized decisions remain.

There was no communications software on the Mac for months after it was introduced. Then Dennis Brothers wrote MacTep and put it in the public domain, and finally the Mac was smart enough to dial the phone.

Perhaps because of this beginning, many the most popular Mac communications programs are shareware. Or maybe it's because bulletin boards and information services are the primary sources of shareware, and thus the people who use communications programs are already tuned into the shareware concept. Whatever the reason, several of the recommended products below are shareware and one of the commercial ones (MicroPhone) was written by shareware pioneer Dennis Brothers.

🍎 *information services* (AN)

Information services like CompuServe and GEnie are discussed in Chapter 16 *(Where to find good information...).*

🍎 *E-mail* (CR)

shortcut

Anybody who has a computer and needs to send stuff to anybody else with a computer should be on an E-mail system (the name is short for *electronic mail).* Once you realize you can send your stuff to someone else in a few minutes instead of a few days, you'll be hooked. Some of the more popular systems are CompuServe and Genie (discussed in Chapter 16) and MCI Mail (discussed below).

(Editor's note: Because I dread having another thing to do each day, I've shied away from signing up on E-mail systems. I transfer stuff directly computer to computer whenever I need to (and in fact most of the contributions to this book passed through my modem several times). But if I had E-mail accounts, I'd have all kinds of people sending me notes and being offended when I didn't have the time

to respond. (I can't even get around to answering regular snail mail—whatever of it gets to me.)

So I disagree with Charlie's blanket recommendation. E-mail is great if you enjoy it, have the time for it and/or need to transfer a lot of stuff on a regular basis. Otherwise, sending files directly from computer to computer takes less time.)

MCI Mail (CR)

MCI Mail lets you send E-mail to other MCI Mail, CompuServe or Telex users; it also will convert your computer messages to paper and have them delivered overnight or by regular USPS snail mail (the advantage in that case being that the letter starts off in the destination city rather than where you live). You can also use the system to access the Dow Jones News/Retrieval database. But MCI Mail is primarily designed to make sending E-mail very easy.

You address mail in most cases simply by typing a user's name (mine is CRubin). You can create and store address lists and then select groups of people to receive your messages en masse. You get an inbox, an outbox and a Desk file (which stores a draft message you have in progress along with messages you've already read). You can create messages by typing them in on-line. There's also a text editor for altering messages before you send them, but it's pretty crude—you're better off deleting your draft and starting over again.

The only charges you pay are for sending messages or accessing Dow Jones News/Retrieval; receiving mail and simply checking for mail only involve the cost of a phone call, and there are local MCI Mail access numbers in every major city. MCI Mail Basic Service is currently $18 a year (which includes about $10 of free message credits), 45¢ for each message up to 500 characters long, $1 for 501-7500 characters and $1 for each 7500 characters thereafter. Access to Dow Jones News/Retrieval is extra, from $12 to $72 per hour, depending on the database you read and the time of day you read it.

If you sign up for MCI Mail Advanced Service ($10 a month plus usage charges), you can store a facsimile of your letterhead and signature—to give your paper mail that personal touch. Basic MCI Mail service is fully menu-driven and easy to use; Advanced Service is command-driven, but the commands are self-evident ones like *Scan Inbox* and *Read Inbox.*

⬤ *Desktop Express* (CR)

very good
feature

Desktop Express is a communications program that lets you transmit graphics, programs or formatted application files to other Desktop Express users via MCI Mail. At last you can send files like this to a mailbox, rather than having to wait for the other person to be available to set up error-checking protocols.

The Desktop Express screen has icons representing separate mailboxes for new mail, opened mail, unsent mail and sent mail. Another icon gives you access to an address book where you can store phone numbers for sending mail to CompuServe and other electronic mail boxes as well as to MCI. A file cabinet icon lets you find mail, delete it or move it to another folder or disk. From this one screen, you can create memos, specify other files to send, address mail, open and read mail, and perform a number of file-management functions.

Once you've stored your own MCI account information and local telephone number, you can click a button and Desktop Express will log on to MCI Mail, check for messages, send any messages you want and then log off, and you can go do whatever you want while it does it. Before you actually tell Desktop Express to dial, you can choose which messages in your outgoing mailbox you want to send and which you want to receive. If you'd rather be involved, you can also call MCI Mail or Dow Jones interactively, and use their normal interfaces.

If you're just sending a short memo, a built-in text editor lets you create it with Desktop Express. But Desktop Express also lets you send any Macintosh file—a formatted document, a program, whatever. It automatically recognizes MacPaint graphics and it comes with ImageSaver, a stripped-down version of Glue that lets you print graphic images from any program to a file that can then be transmitted.

There are some annoying things about Desktop Express. One is its inability to automatically redial telephone numbers. If your local MCI access number is frequently busy (as mine is), you have to keep telling Desktop Express to redial, and that of course eliminates the advantage of automated operation. And unlike Lotus Express, its MS DOS counterpart, Desktop Express won't run in the background and beep you whenever you have an incoming message.

Desktop Express is no speed demon. It occupies 544K, and all that code makes it somewhat glacial. For example, when you click the button to dial MCI, you sit and wait several seconds before your modem actually dials. When the program logs off MCI Mail, it takes about ten seconds for the program to disconnect after it says it's disconnecting. It also takes a long time to open windows showing individual pieces of mail.

Connection costs are another possible drawback. MCI messages 501–7500 characters in length cost $1 and each additional 7500 characters cost another $1. Since Desktop Express makes it possible for you to send formatted files and programs, which tend to be quite large, your MCI bill could get pretty hefty.

While $150 may seem like a lot to pay for access to a service you can reach for free with the modem program you already have, Desktop Express's ability to transfer formatted files, graphics and programs is unique and, depending on your needs, may make the program well worth the money.

✎ *Navigator* (PH)

If you use CompuServe, Navigator is the way to go, especially if you don't want to have to think while the meter

very good
feature

is ticking. It gives you a quick-and-easy method for getting the messages in all the conferences you want to browse; you can then look at them off-line at your leisure.

You can answer the messages you want and create new ones, run Navigator again and have it send all of your responses to the right places in a single step. This sounds like it will save you money but it won't—since using Navigator is so easy, you'll find yourself signing up for many more conferences.

MicroPhone (DC)

very good
feature

MicroPhone, programmed by Dennis Brothers of share-ware fame, walks the thin line between maximum power and maximum user friendliness. Both strengths are obvi-ous in its script feature, which records your every move in a short program you can then install on the menu as a command, in a button at the bottom of the screen, or both.

You could, for example, devise a very complex script that called CompuServe, GEnie and several bulletin boards in the middle of the night (when rates and usage are low) and uploaded and downloaded files based on any number of contingencies. To initiate this flurry of activity, all you'd have to do would be to click on a button or choose a command from a menu.

I do have a complaint about MicroPhone. Its publisher, Software Ventures, have taken longer to fix some bugs than it should have. But their telephone support is good and, in general, this is a fine piece of software.

MicroPhone II (AN)

very good
feature

I hate telecommunicating for the same reason I hate trying to communicate in Urdu—I simply don't know the language. That's why I *do* like MicroPhone, and why I use it exclusively. It translates a lot of telecommunications jargon into English and makes it possible for me to get done what I need to without a lot of research and hacking around.

MicroPhone II has many useful enhancements. It will work in the background under Multifinder, its script language has been expanded and it supports three new transmission protocols that greatly increase file transfer speeds. The price has gone up to $300, which puts it beyond a lot of people's reach, but the added power may well justify it.

● *Red Ryder* (DC/AN)

Red Ryder is one of the most powerful communications programs available. It offers just about every feature you could ask for. Its macro capabilities, while difficult to learn, are extremely flexible, as are its terminal-emulation features (you'll appreciate them if you need to connect your Mac to a mainframe computer).

very good feature

If you have a thorough understanding of the ins and outs of telecommunications, Red Ryder may be just what you're looking for. If you don't, Red Ryder may still be just what you're looking for, because its documentation provides an excellent introduction to the basics of computer communications—and even some of the advanced topics. (But if you're not a telecommunications expert and aren't interested in becoming one, get Microphone instead.)

After years as shareware, Red Ryder is now a commercial product. If you want to get a feeling for what the program is like before buying it, look for version 9.4, the last shareware version; it's still kicking around on bulletin boards, etc. If 9.4's approach appeals to you, pop for the most recent commercial version (10.2, as we write). It's worth the $80 to be up-to-date.

● *Red Ryder* (DK)

Some people say that telecommunications will be seen as the single most important advance of the personal computer revolution of the 1980s—the innovation with the most profound effect on the way we live and work. Whether this is true or not, no other aspect of computing seems to generate as many unyielding opinions. You can no more tell someone which is the "best" telecommunications program than you can tell him or her which is the best religion or the best political party.

It's not clear why this should be. Maybe it's because people use communications programs for personal rather than business purposes, or because they use them almost every day and for a broad spectrum of highly specific tasks.

Some users care more about ease of use and adherence to the standard Mac user interface; others care more about power and speed. But this conflict exists for all kinds of software; why should people have such strong opinions about communications software?

Who knows? For whatever reason, feelings run strong and Red Ryder is at the center of the controversy. Many people have a copy on a disk somewhere. Yet, in some circles, saying you like it invites ridicule.

Red Ryder, in its many incarnations, has been around for almost as long as the Mac itself, and has matured and grown considerably. Back in the days when MacWrite represented the peak of sophistication of Mac software—and Apple had not yet released MacTerminal—MacTep and Red Ryder were introduced (as BASIC programs) to allow Mac users to enter the age of telecommunications.

Red Ryder's developer, Scott Watson, has put the program through dozens of revisions since then. This has actually been criticized by some people. Too much change is unsettling for some and each release has had its flaws, but Watson has shown a true commitment to improving his product.

If you divide users of communications software into two groups—those who use it as a work tool and those with the old-time hacker's spirit, for whom the act of logging on (to almost anything) is an adventure in itself—Red Ryder definitely appeals to the latter group.

very good feature

Red Ryder provides what is perhaps the most powerful procedural language in any communications program on any microcomputer. Even nonprogrammer types can design automated sequences to perform just about every conceivable series of maneuver.

Other communications programs for the Mac, notably SmartCom and MicroPhone, allow the creation of command procedures in a more visually attractive manner, sometimes taking Macness to its cutest extreme. But their procedures lack the flexibility Red offers and they insulate users from the true power of their computers in a way that can only be described as user-condescending.

Red Ryder's commands give more of a flavor of what programming is really like and the excellent documentation makes them accessible to virtually anyone.

Procedure listings are text files and can be created with any text editor, including MacWrite, Word or the MockWrite desk accessory. Red Ryder even has a feature, aptly named *Write a Procedure For Me,* which will watch your activities and responses during a telecommunications session and write the procedure file for you as you work.

The command set includes strings, numeric and time variables, flags, decision-making, user-defined alerts, dialog boxes, pop-down menus and much more. Red Ryder's procedure language is where it leaves the others programs in the dust.

But it's not in the area of power that people fault Red Ryder. Aside from its bulk and department-store variety of features, it's been criticized for its design. Some find the program's user interface less direct and intuitive than the Mac allows. While this may be true, in a larger sense Red Ryder approaches Apple's design philosophy more closely than many other programs, certainly including Apple's own MacTerminal.

It's a principle of good Macintosh software design that Mac programs should employ as little *functional modularity* as possible. Translated into English, this means that, as much as possible, all options should remain available at all times. There should be as few modes (areas of special or limited options) as possible.

Most communications programs flout this principle. They require that the *parameters* (phone number, baud rate, etc.) used to access different remote systems be saved in external files which are only available one at a time. So in order to jump from your Dow Jones News Retrieval settings to those for CompuServe, you must exit the first set and load the next. For some users, such modularity is not much of an inconvenience; for others, it's quite irksome.

very good feature

Red Ryder, however, lets you jump between system settings to your heart's content, without having to open and close parameter files, simply by changing those settings with user-defined macros generated by its powerful command language. This facility gives Red Ryder easy, all-in-one-window operation while you're on-line.

Red Ryder tries to satisfy everyone, and only succeeds in some categories. Even so, dollar for dollar Red Ryder offers a better and fuller mix of features—most of which at least approach the best of their class—than its competitors.

TermWorks and FModem *(DC/AN)*

bargain

These two programs are inexpensive shareware alternatives to commercial communications programs. TermWorks' strengths are simplicity and speed. Although there's no script facility, it does include a dialing directory and macro capability.

very good feature

Its major drawback is that there's no provision for turning off the MacBinary option when doing Xmodem transfers. This isn't a problem if you deal exclusively in Macintosh files (it doesn't matter if you transfer them to another Mac, a PC, a minicomputer or a mainframe, as long as they're eventually used on a Mac). But if you often work with DOS files on your Mac, you'll need to be able to turn off MacBinary and thus shouldn't use TermWorks.

very good feature

FModem is a small, no-frills programs that gives you a lot of major features, including simple macros and VT52 emulation. Its major advantage over TermWorks is that you can turn off the MacBinary option of Xmodem. This is the program to use if you often transfer files between your Mac and a PC. The program is simple, easy to use and quite powerful.

(We don't have addresses for these two products, but they're available from all the usual shareware sources— user groups, bulletin boards, information services, etc.; see Chapter 16 for details.)

🍎 *StuffIt and PackIt* *(AN)*

StuffIt is a virtually indispensable utility developed by Raymond Lau as an enhancement of PackIt. Both programs compress files, so that they're smaller and take less time to send, and combine them into one document, so you can send them all at once. Then they reverse the process at the other end.

shortcut

This file-compression can be really significant if you're paying long-distance charges or information service access fees (even if you're not, the shorter transmission times are a boon to Type-A personalities). File compression is also useful for maintaining archives that take up less disk space.

very good feature

StuffIt is faster than PackIt and more efficient at file compression, making files an average of 25–30% smaller.StuffIt also lets you unstuff individual files, while PackIt makes you do the whole package.

very good feature

If you ever telecommunicate, you need to have StuffIt. For $15, it's an incredible bargain. It's useful to have a copy of PackIt around too, but only to unpack any files you receive that were compressed with it.

bargain

🍎 *QDial* *(DC)*

If you've ever been frustrated by trying to connect to a busy bulletin board, QDial is a DA that you won't want to be without. It continues to dial the number in the background and lets you use your Mac in the meantime (the only thing you can't do is use another communication program).

very good feature

Once you've told QDial what to do, the only indication that it's working is a small icon of a telephone that appears to the left of the Menu each time it dials. When a connection is made, QDial notifies you with an unmistakable honking you've probably never heard your Mac make before. You then choose QDial again from the menu and Click on the Cancel button. QDial holds the connection long enough to start your regular communication program.

QDial works with Hayes and most Hayes-compatible modems, and will store up to five numbers in its dialing directory. You can use standard Hayes dialing commands to control the number of seconds between retries. Although QDial is free, it's not technically in the public domain because the author, Léo Laporte, retains the copyright.

Local area networks

LANs (AN)

esp. for beginners

A *local area network,* or *LAN* (pronounced as one word) as it's frequently called, is confined to a relatively small area and is connected by *dedicated wires* (that is, nothing else runs over them).

On the Mac, LANs are usually connected by LocalTalk hardware or functional equivalents like PhoneNET. (See the entry on PhoneNET in the *Laser printer tips* section of Chapter 6.)

MacServe (Chris Belec)

If you have two or more Macs connected to a laser printer and a hard disk connected to one of the Macs, you should seriously consider MacServe (from Infosphere). It can change your present setup to a fast and convenient information-sharing environment in which all the Macs can share hard disks, laser printers and dot-matrix printers.

MacServe lets you spool print jobs, rank them in order of priority and protect selected portions of the shared hard disk with passwords. All of these features operate without a dedicated disk server or printer server.

very good feature

MacServe requires that each Mac, LaserWriter and ImageWriter on the network have an LocalTalk connector and that at least one of the Macs be connected to a hard disk. Any Mac that's connected to a hard disk that other Macs on the network can use is called a *disk server* or *network host.* Other Macs on the network are called *network users.* You can have up to 30 network users on a MacServe network (plus the network host) but only 16 network hosts.

MacServe requires that each network host be created from a separate copy of MacServe, but no such condition applies to the network users. Therefore if you want to have three network hosts serving the needs of fourteen users, you'll only need to buy three copies of MacServe.

bargain

MacServe doesn't place a limit on the number of hard disks on the network, only on the number of network hosts. But the hard disks of network users can't be accessed by other Macs on the network.

Even ImageWriters that don't have a LocalTalk board can be shared over the network if they're connected to the modem port of a network host (MacServe and LocalTalk use the printer port). Thus you can have as many shared ImageWriters as you have network hosts. (ImageWriters connected to network users can only be used by that Mac.) Making an ImageWriter available to the network and setting up a queue for it takes a few seconds, using the MacServe desk accessory.

MacServe provides print spooling for shared, non-Local-Talk ImageWriters. A problem you can run into with the spooler is insufficient room on the network host's hard disk for the files the spooler creates, but all you have to do is make more room on the disk and things work fine.

very good feature

MacServe provides a very convenient way to share printers. Several users can add jobs to a print queue at the same time, and print jobs are processed without tying up the Mac the printer is connected to.

very good feature

MacServe is easy to install and so stable that I've never seen it crash! It doesn't even lock up network users when the network host suffers a system crash. Other network software (like StarLAN on PCs) goes to pieces if the network host is taken off-line. I was expecting the same from MacServe but once the MacServe host restarts, all the network users can continue right where they left off. It's really incredible to watch.

At the computer store where I used to work, there was a person who had a knack for destroying system files on the Macintosh. To make things worse, when she didn't know how to quit from an application program, she'd simply turn off the Macintosh and turn it on again to reset the system. MacServe survived her abuse every time.

MacServe also performs flawlessly when the reset button on the network host is hit, and it prevents the network host from choosing Shut Down from the Special menu if any of the users have one of the host's hard disk volumes mounted or if there are print jobs in the host's printing queue.

[MacServe can crash, however. Roger Galliett wrote in to say that it seems to happen especially when you try to format several blank disks on the machine you're using as a server.—AN]

MacServe lets you share both information and expensive printing and storage devices. I have trouble imagining an office with multiple Macs that wouldn't profit from having MacServe.

♦ TOPS (AN)

According to a survey of *Macworld* readers, this product is very popular for LANs. For more about TOPS, see the entry on it in the next section.

■ *PhoneNET StarController* (AN)

This high-end product from Farallon Computing lets you connect LocalTalk networks in a star pattern instead of the normal chain. It can support up to twelve separate networks, each incorporating up to 3000 feet of cable, and can be linked with other StarControllers. If you have a big office, this is worth looking into.

very good feature

PC to Mac and back

■ *trading with the enemy* (AN)

If you use a personal computer at work, it probably isn't a Mac. Yes, the ugly reality is that most personal computers are IBM PCs or clones thereof—known generically as *PCs* or as *DOS* (dawss) *machines*, because the operating system they share is called *MS DOS* or *PC DOS* (although *dross machines* might be a more appropriate name).

esp. for beginners

WARNING! HYSTERICAL RANT AHEAD.

There's an ignorant trend afoot to call all personal computers—presumably even Macs!—PCs, as if there were something wrong with the simple and straightforward word *computers.* (The people who use *PC* in that way tend to be the same ones who talk about *software programs*—as if you needed the word *software* to distinguish a program running on your computer from, say, a television program or a drug rehabilitation program.)

gossip/ trivia

Maybe they feel that the *P* in *PC* helps make it clear that you're referring to a personal computer and that without that qualification, you might ask someone what kind of computer they use at home and get an answer like, "Do you mean my *personal* computer or the Cray in the basement?"

This is all by way of saying that—in this book—*PC* refers to an IBM PC or clone, not to a real computer like the Mac.

END OF HYSTERICAL RANT. RESUME NORMAL READING.

Where was I? Oh, yes—the PC you have in your office. Although there's no way around the wrenching feeling in your gut you have to endure every morning when you travel back into the pre-Mac Stone Age of computing, you can at least transfer data back and forth between the office machine and your Mac at home. The tips below tell you how.

direct connection (DC)

very good feature

Transferring files back and forth between a Mac and a PC can be relatively simple, particularly if you can arrange to wire the two machines together directly. A cable is the only hardware you'll need. Simply connect it to the modem port on the back of the Mac and to the serial connector on the PC.

bargain

Next, you'll need a communications program for each machine. For the DOS machine, either PC-Talk or ProComm is an excellent choice. They operate at up to 19,200 baud and both support the error-checking file-transfer protocol called Xmodem. Both are shareware and can be obtained from most computer bulletin boards, commercial services such as CompuServe or PC users groups.

On the Mac you should run software that will transfer at 19,200 baud and that will allow you to disable MacBinary (a special kind of Xmodem file-transfer protocol) when you're doing the transfer. Most communications programs for the Mac meet both requirements—although the otherwise excellent TermWorks doesn't allow you to disable MacBinary.

With both machines set to 19,200 baud, the data moves quite fast.

over the phone (DC)

Lugging machines around can be tedious, so you may prefer to transfer files over the phone. The main differences from the method just described are that you need to add a modem at each end and that data transfer will be slower. (If at all possible, use a modem that supports at least 1200 baud—or, even better, 2400 baud or more.)

Let's assume you have a DOS machine at the office and a Mac at home (the opposite is a bit hard to imagine). Before you leave the office, turn on the PC (if it isn't already on), start your communications program and set it to answer an incoming call.

esp. for beginners

ProComm is particularly well suited for phone transfers, since it has a special option called Host Mode that gives you full access to the files on any disk when you connect remotely, while at the same time providing for extensive password protection so that only you and the people you authorize can access the computer.

When you get home, you just start your Mac communications program and tell it to dial the number of the PC. When you've connected with the PC, it will ask you for your password, then provide you with a menu of files available for transferring *(downloading)* to your Mac. When you've transferred all the files you want, just tell the Mac communications program to hang up. That's all there is to it.

esp. for beginners

When you've finished working with the files, you can call the remote machine and send them back. And, by following the same procedures, you can set the Mac up so you can call it from the PC during the day.

⚫ *what gets lost in the translation* (DC)

If you use both a PC and Mac on a regular basis, you know that they're quite different animals. As a result, there are some limits to what the Mac can do with files transferred from DOS machines.

Two programs that impose very few limitations are WordPerfect and Microsoft Word, because they both have versions that run on PCs as well as Macs. This lets you work extensively on documents on both machines and send them back and forth with little or no loss of formatting.

If you're using another DOS word processing program, you may only be able to enter and edit text; you'll have to remember to save the document as a text file and all your formatting will be lost in the transfers between the machines. (One way around this limitation is to find a word processing program on the PC that offers a conversion utility to Word or WordPerfect format.)

Spreadsheet users are in better shape, thanks to some standards in the industry and to the flexibility of Excel, the most popular spreadsheet on the Mac. The standard spreadsheet in the PC world is Lotus 1-2-3 and you can read 1-2-3 files directly into Excel. After you've worked on the files in Excel you can save them in 1-2-3 format and transfer them back. (The main limitation is that macros written in one product won't work with the other.)

Database files also transfer fairly easily if the PC program uses the Mac standard format of Tab between fields and Return between records. dBASE is a popular PC database and several Mac databases can read PC dBASE files with no conversion.

All this transferring and modifying files can get to be a lot of work. If you're fortunate enough to have Macs at work as well as PCs, you should investigate one of the more direct—and expensive—solutions like TOPS, which is described at some length below.

🍎 *a good book on all this* (AN)

Macintosh Bible contributor Steve Michel has written a good book on this whole topic. Called *IBM PC and Macintosh Networking,* it's published by Howard W. Sams.

🍎 *TOPS* (EA)

With mass quantities of IBM-compatible computers currently installed in corporate America and a growing number of Macintoshes wriggling their way through the back doors, the ability of these two considerably dissimilar computers to chat with one another is becoming—for many—a practical necessity.

TOPS (the name stands for *transcendental operating system)* uses the LocalTalk network that's built into every Macintosh to effect this communication. To allow PCs to join the network, you insert an LocalTalk interface card into one of their available slots. A standard LocalTalk Connector kit for the original Macintosh (from Apple) plugs right into the 9-pin connector on the LocalTalk card.

Once the machines are physically connected, the TOPS network software completes the union on an intellectual level.

When you *publish* a volume (a disk drive, directory or folder) onto the network—that is, when you make it available for others to use—you become a *server.* When you *mount* a server's published volume—that is, when you indicate that you want to use it—you become a *client.* Any computer attached to the network can act as a server, a client or both at the same time. The same software is loaded on each machine, regardless of whether it's intended to be a server or a client.

One of the nice features of TOPS is that PC users continue to use the PC interface—they don't need to learn a lot about Macintosh terms like *icon* and *folder.* And Mac users continue to use the Mac interface—they don't need to learn a lot about PC terms like *DOS prompt* and *subdirectory.*

very good feature

When you mount a published volume (which could be on a machine right next to you or up on the 12th floor), your computer treats it as if it were simply another disk drive attached to your system. On the PC, this means that you have another drive letter to use for saving and retrieving files or for performing any normal DOS command. On the Mac, it means another disk icon appears on the Desktop. When you open the window for this icon, you'll see the mounted volume's files. From the Open and Save As list boxes within an application, you simply click on the Drive button to access the new volume.

The fact that the volume you're using is not actually attached to your system is almost completely transparent to you, since your computer acts exactly as if you were using a local volume (for example, an external disk drive).

With TOPS, file transfer is as simple as copying a file between a local volume and remote volume. For example, let's say you're using a Macintosh and you've mounted a remote volume from a PC server. To transfer a document from your Mac to the PC, you simply drag the file's icon from your Mac disk window to the PC volume icon. Got that? I know it's a bit tricky, so let me repeat it one more time. You drag the file's icon to the PC volume icon.

If you're on the PC side, you transfer a document to a Macintosh simply by copying it to the drive letter that represents the remote Mac volume. Folders on the remote volume will appear to your PC as subdirectories, so you can navigate around the Mac disk using the normal DOS subdirectory commands before copying the file.

very good feature

Actually, in many situations you won't even need to copy your files between computers. Instead, you can simply access files directly from within your applications.

For example, Microsoft Excel reads and translates Lotus 1-2-3 worksheets automatically. Normally, you would first transfer the worksheet onto your Macintosh disk using one of the communication methods discussed above, and then you would load the file. With TOPS, you could leave the file in place on the PC's hard disk. While in Excel, you'd click on the Drive button to access the 1-2-3 files on the remote PC disk and then retrieve one—straight into Excel, right across the network.

Another common use for TOPS is to transfer word processing documents between the Mac and the PC. A program called MacLinkPlus (from Dataviz) can translate documents in WordStar, MultiMate and DCA format over the network and put them in MacWrite format and vice versa. It can also perform many spreadsheet translations—for example from the DIF format common on PC spreadsheets to the SYLK format used by Multiplan and Excel.

TOPS for the PC sells for $390, which includes an LocalTalk card and software. TOPS for the Mac sells for $150. You need a package for each computer on the network, regardless of whether it will be used as a server or a client. You'll also need to get a LocalTalk (or PhoneNET) connector for each computer.

TOPS tips

🍎 an E-mail kluge (DC)

As of this writing, the current version of TOPS has no E-Mail feature, but it's easy to implement one. Simply have each user on the network publish an empty folder bearing his or her name. Then other users simply copy messages (or whatever) to the appropriate folders through the TOPS interface window.

very hot tip

If you need more sophistication than this simple setup, remember that TOPS is compatible with InBox from Think Technologies.

🍎 deweirdifying DOS wp files (DC)

TOPS users often edit ASCII documents on the Mac that were created by DOS. The problem is that these documents often have unintelligible characters when opened in a Mac word processing program.

very hot tip

To create a document with these strange characters stripped out, open the TOPS window, select the original file, decide which volume (disk or folder) you want the converted copy of the file stored in, hold down the Option key and Click on TOPS' *Copy* button.

🍎 making a PC serve the Macs (DC)

If your office has more hard disks connected to PCs than to Macs, you can turn a PC hard disk into a TOPS Mac server with negligible effect on the performance of the PC.

First, set up a directory (called a *volume* by TOPS) on the PC hard disk and call it *MAC* (or *BUD* or *BUSTER*, if you prefer). Make sure it has a copy of the System and Finder on it. Then boot from a Mac without a hard disk using a floppy whose System Folder contains all the files you need to start TOPS. Next, mount the volume called *MAC* from the PC, open it and `Option` `⌘` `Double-Click` on the Finder icon in that volume to make it the active Finder. The Mac can then proceed to mount any other needed volumes.

The advantage of this technique is that the System in the PC volume can contain as many fonts and desk accessories as you want; you're not limited by an 800K floppy. Performance won't be as good as if you were running from a local hard disk but it'll be faster than if you were running from a floppy. The performance of the entire network will also suffer somewhat, because of the frequent transfer of packets of System and Finder data.

Remember that all the Macs using the PC hard disk as a server will need their own copies of the System in their own folders and that TOPS doesn't recommend running more than two Macs from the server at any one time.

★ *using TOPS with Switcher* (DC)

Be sure to mount and publish before running Switcher or, if Switcher is already running, mount and publish in the Switcher window, rather than in an applications window.

★ *multiple users of a single application* (DC)

Most Mac applications were written for a single user. For example, two TOPS users can't mount the same volume and run MacWrite at the same time—there has to be a copy of MacWrite in a separate volume on the server for each user. If your application has help files or the like, you'll also want to duplicate them for each user's folder.

Miscellaneous tips

● *garbage* (SZA)

Intermittent *garbage* (bizarre characters that have no apparent meaning) on the screen when you're communicating with another computer usually means you've got a noisy phone connection.

esp. for
beginners

If you're just typing back and forth, don't worry about garbage as long as you can read through it. But if you're transferring files, garbage will probably ruin the transmission, so hang up and try again for a cleaner connection. Dropping the baud rate (from 1200 to 300, say) sometimes helps too.

If you're getting nothing but garbage on the screen, you and the computer you're connected to are probably trying to communicate at different *baud rates* (transmission speeds). Most programs let you change the baud rate right in the middle of a session, so try that and see if it eliminates the garbage.

● *disabling Call Waiting* (DC)

Many phone companies offer their customers a service called Call Waiting that interrupts calls with brief signals that someone else is calling. You can then easily switch between the two calls. Unfortunately, these signals disrupt data transmissions, thus forcing modem users to choose between giving up the convenience of Call Waiting or gambling on an interrupted connection.

But help is on the way. As local phone companies upgrade their systems by installing electronic switching exchanges, they offer their customers the option of temporarily disabling Call Waiting for the duration of any outgoing call. You just precede the number you're dialing with *70 (on a tone phone) or 1170 (on a pulse phone). When the call is over, Call Waiting automatically comes back.

very
hot
tip

To see whether you can do this on your phone, just try putting the appropriate code in front of a number you're dialing. If the service isn't available, you should get a recorded message that the call can't be completed as dialed.

If you're using an autodial modem (if you don't know, the odds are you are), you have to instruct it to pause briefly between the Call Waiting disabling code and the number you're dialing. Two or three seconds is sufficient. The following command will cause a Hayes-compatible modem to give the code *70, then pause two seconds, then dial the number 555–1212:

ATDT*70,555–1212

(Needless to say, you should substitute whatever number you're dialing for 555–1212.)

important warning

[This doesn't work from a lot of phones (it depends on the switching equipment at your local phone company office). Still, it's worth a try.—AN]

♠ protection against lightning (AN)

important warning

As C.J. Weigand points out in Chapter 7, lightning can hit a telephone pole, come down the wire, pass through your modem and *fry* your computer. If you live in an area where there are a lot of thunderstorms, it's a good idea to disconnect the incoming phone line from your modem when you turn the system off.

(Since lightning hits power poles too, it's also a good idea to pull the plug of the power cord out of the wall socket.)

♠ useful Hayes commands (DC)

There are a slew of powerful and convenient commands in the Hayes manual. For example, putting *ATM1DT* in a dialing command turns on the speaker of any Hayes-compatible modem; *ATM0DT* turns it off. See the Hayes manual for dozens of others.

⚫ *MacTerminal keyboard shortcuts* (DC)

The following keyboard commands are useful for navigating around within MacTerminal:

shortcut

command	*effect*
⌘–H	backspaces cursor one space
⌘–I	moves cursor down one line
⌘–J	moves cursor down one line
⌘–K	moves cursor down two lines
⌘–M	moves cursor to beginning of line

Here's one that doesn't move the cursor:

⌘–G	sounds tone

⚫ *MacTerminal keyboard commands* (DC)

The following MacTerminal keyboard commands are mostly undocumented:

to send	*press*
break	Enter (VT100 mode)
enter	Enter (3278 mode)
escape	` (accent grave)
`	⌘–` (accent grave)
~	Shift ⌘–~
^A thru ^Z	⌘–A thru ⌘–Z
^[	⌘–[or ` (same as ESCAPE)
^\	⌘–\
^]	⌘–]
^^	⌘–6 (no Shift)

^_   ⌘ –? or ⌘ –/

delete   ⌘ Backspace

🍎 *eliminating Tandem's hard carriage returns* (BB)

The Tandem is a line-oriented system, so when you import files from it to the Mac (using a program like MacMenlo), each line ends with a hard carriage return. This means that neither word wrap nor many other formatting features will work properly.

Deleting the hard returns has been a tedious task, now made simple by WriteNow's Translator program. You just launch Translator, choose *Text to WriteNow...* (on the Convert menu), tell the program to treat a blank line (two consecutive Return s) as the end of a paragraph, and stand back.

From the WetPaint clip art collection.
Copyright © 1988–89 by Dubl-Click Software Inc.
All rights reserved.

Chapter 15

Integrated programs and miscellaneous applications

Integrated programs

🍎 *integrated programs* (DC/AN)

esp. for
beginners

The three kinds of applications most commonly used on personal computers are word processors, databases and spreadsheets. *Integrated programs* combine two or more of them (along with graphics, communications or other kinds of software).

The most popular software product of all time, Lotus 1–2–3, is an integrated program, combining spreadsheet, database and graphing. But its success is mainly due to its powerful spreadsheet and only peripherally—if at all—to its rather weak chart program and even weaker filer.

But there are two integrated programs whose success is due mainly to their integration rather than to the strength of one of the programs integrated into them. One is Apple-Works, which runs on the Apple II, and the other is its Macintosh implementation, Works, which has become the best-selling program on the Mac.

🍎 *Jazz* (DC/AN)

The first major attempt to market a full-scale integrated program for the Mac, Lotus' Jazz, was a complete failure—probably because the individual modules were weak. The word processor was actually less powerful than MacWrite and there were no macros (this from a company made rich and famous by macros). Mac owners stayed away in droves, preferring to integrate more powerful individual programs through the Clipboard and Switcher.

Lotus came back with an enhanced version, Modern Jazz, but it met with no more success than its predecessor and was withdrawn.

🍎 *Works* (DC/AN)

Microsoft Works is made up of four *modules*—a word processor, a spreadsheet (with graphing), a database and a communications program. These individual applications are not as powerful as the most powerful individual applications available but neither are they crippled and they work well together.

Since a new version of Works (2.0) is coming out right about when this book is (see the next entry), we won't discuss the capabilities of the modules in version 1.1 in detail. But here are a few general comments.

very good feature

The word processor is fairly graceful and flexible. One area where it really shines is in mixing graphics and text. You can run text on either side of a picture, on both sides of it or even right on top of it.

The spreadsheet is sort of a stripped-down version of Excel and the database a stripped-down version of Microsoft File. Both work fine but their lack of features and flexibility can be annoying.

The communications module lacks many of the bells and whistles found in Red Ryder or MicroPhone (for example, you can't write scripts) but the critical parts are all there, including the ability to do Xmodem file transfers. And it can do something even those powerful programs can't.

very good feature

You can begin a long file transfer, then change to another window and continue working while the transfer goes on in the background. The transfer is slowed when you're working in the other window but being able to continue using your Mac at all while it's doing a file transfer is a great bonus.

very hot tip

Even if you need a more powerful application than the Works module in one particular area, the program may still be adequate for your other needs. Works is a good program for beginning Mac users and for anyone who doesn't need a lot of power. With the money you save buying Works instead of a bunch of stand-alone applications, you can start saving up for a hard disk or a laser printer.

❡ *Works 2.0* (AN)

Works 2.0 makes a good program even better. Here are some of the major changes:

- A spelling checker for the word processor.

- A macro editor for all the modules.

- Draw functions that have been enhanced to the hilt. They're like a mini-MacDraw, and you can overlay the drawings in either the word processor or the spreadsheet. Best of all, the Draw layer includes text boxes that can be tied together for automatic text flow.

very good feature

- More spreadsheet functions to handle times, dates and text.

- Cell notes in the spreadsheet (a text window that's attached to each cell).

- A choice of the font used in the spreadsheet and database.

- A Print Preview function that works in all the modules.

very good feature

- Mailing labels—even two- and three-up, and even on the LaserWriter.

There are lots of minor changes, too, like the addition of decimal and center tabs in the word processor and a title freeze in the spreadsheet. With title freeze, you can keep the first row and/or column showing in the window all the time; in earlier versions, you had to split the window to do that. With the new Works, you can freeze the titles and still split the window, so you can see more things at one time.

For all its improvements, though, Works 2.0 still has a few lapses. For example, although the Report window in the database has an improved interface, especially when it comes to setting the width of the report, it's still not great—they should have redesigned that window from scratch instead of trying to improve the existing one.

Still, Works is an incredibly useful package, and 2.0 makes it even more useful. It's what I recommend to most beginning Mac users, and many never need anything more.

🍎 *WorksPlus Command* (AN)

Tim Lundeen, one of the main programmers responsible for "porting" Works from the Apple II to the Mac, has written two utilities to enhance the program. One is a spelling checker called WorksPlus Spell; it's discussed in Chapter 10. The other is a *macro program* called WorksPlus Command. (If you don't know about macros, see the glossary or the discussion of them in Chapter 8.)

I haven't been able to really put WorksPlus Command through its paces but my general impression is that it works well but is somewhat hard to learn (thanks in part to a not-very-good manual). But since Works is notably poor in keyboard equivalents for menu commands—in the word processing module, for example, there are no keyboard equivalents for *Select All* or for any of the four text-formatting commands *(Left, Centered, Right and Justified)*—a macro program is very much needed. With a redone manual, WorksPlus Command should fit the bill admirably.

General Works tips

🍎 *Works modules* (SZA)

Works is made up of four separate *modules* (subprograms)—the word processor, the database, the spreadsheet and the communications module. This section covers tips that apply to all modules or to the program in general, then I give you specific tips for each module in turn. At the end is a section of tips on combining the modules.

🍎 *version numbers* (SZA)

The Works tips in this chapter all work with version 1.1. Most of them should also work with version 2.0.

❡ *RAM caching and Works don't mix* (CR)

Because Works keeps everything in RAM, the RAM cache you've set on the Control Panel may interfere with large Works workfiles. It's best to set the cache at 64K or 32K—or, better yet, turn it off completely.

very
hot
tip

❡ *double-click for New* (SZA)

When Works' large Open dialog box is on the screen, double-clicking on a module icon has the same effect as selecting it and then clicking the New button. The same trick works in the small dialog box that appears in response to the *New* command in the File menu.

shortcut

❡ *Works' special pointers* (SZA)

Sometimes, you'll notice two unusual pointer shapes—a hollow arrow and an I-beam with a circle in its center (pictured below). The first most often shows up in the spreadsheet module and the second when you're working with large word processing documents.

These special pointers mean that Works is thinking—recalculating in the spreadsheet, for example, or repaginating in the word processor. Unlike the wristwatch, these pointers don't prevent you from continuing to work, but they let you know that what's currently on the screen may be subject to change.

❡ *window zoom* (SZA)

Works gives you five ways to make a window fill the screen or zoom back down to the size, shape and position you set up:

shortcut

- Click on the zoom box
- Double-Click on the title bar

- Double-Click in the size box
- press ⌘–W
- choose the *Small Window / Full Window* command (on the Window menu)

❖ *window cycling* (SZA)

shortcut

You can cycle through opened windows with the keyboard. ⌘–comma brings the window listed at the bottom of the Windows menu to the top of the pile. It also moves that window's title to the top of the window list in the Windows menu. That means that repeated uses of ⌘–comma will cycle you through all the available windows.

❖ *ampersand commands* (SZA)

esp. for beginners

The ampersand (*&*) is used to give formatting commands in headers and footers. To issue the command, just type it in the text box for the header or footer. The following commands are available:

&B	make bold	**&C**	center
&D	insert date	**&I**	make italic
&L	align left	**&P**	insert page number
&R	align right	**&T**	insert time
&F	insert name of file (document)		

(You don't need to use caps for the commands; in other words, *&b* works just as well as *&B*).

If you want an ampersand itself to appear in a header or footer, precede it with another one: *&&*. Only one will be printed.

❖ *current date and time* (SZA)

When you use *&D* or *&T* to insert the current date or time into a header or footer, *current* is the operative word. The time and date you print a document is what will appear in the printout, not the time or date you created or saved it.

❤ *style, size and font in headers and footers* (SZA)

When creating headers and footers in the Page Setup dialog box, you can make text for bold or italic (or both) by using *&B* and *&I* (see the entry above called *ampersand commands* for more details).

These commands only affect the text that follows them in that particular text box; to change the style (and/or size) of all the text in both the header and footer, use the Style menu. (You can also change the font of both the header and footer with the Font menu.)

❤ *exporting text* (SZA)

The *Export* check box in the Save As dialog box saves only the text of your document. You can then import it into another module in Works or into any Mac application that accepts text files.

esp. for beginners

❤ *importing files* (SZA)

To make the *Import* check box in Works' Open dialog box available, you have to first click on one of the module icons; when the *All Works* icon is selected, the Import check box is dimmed.

esp. for beginners

Once the *Import* check box is active and you've put an X in it by clicking on it, you'll see a list not only of Works documents but of all other documents that can be imported into the module you've selected. They include MacWrite and Word files for the word processor, Multiplan and Excel documents for the spreadsheet and text files for all modules.

❤ *sharing information between modules* (SZA)

You can share information between Works' modules in two ways: you can simply cut, copy and paste between them, or you can save a document from one module as an export—or text—file and then import it to another module.

Sometimes the export/import method beats the simpler copy/paste. For instance, importing data into the database module that was originally created in the spreadsheet module automatically creates a database with the right number of fields (equivalent to the spreadsheet columns) and records (equivalent to the spreadsheet rows). If you simply paste the data in and don't have enough fields to hold it, rows of information will be lost.

⚫ *tabs, columns and fields* (SZA)

As you move information from one module to another in Works, keep in mind that:

tabs=columns=fields

That is, a block in the spreadsheet that includes multiple columns can be transferred to the word processor, where the columns will be separated by tabs, or into the database, where each column will be a field. And the same principle applies when going from the word processor into the database and spreadsheet, or from the database into the spreadsheet and word processor.

⚫ *alphabetizing lists* (SZA)

If you need to alphabetize a list in the word processor, paste it into a new spreadsheet, sort it there and then paste it back into the word processor.

⚫ *columns in word processing documents* (SZA)

Use a spreadsheet whenever you have to make a columnar table in the word processor—even if it's all words and no numbers. Columns are easier to manipulate in a spreadsheet and you can paste the whole table into the word processor when you're done.

⚫ *selected form letters* (SZA)

You don't have to send form letters to everyone in a database when you're using the word processor's merge-print function (*Prepare to Merge...* on the Edit menu). If you do a selection in the database (with the *Record Selection...*

command) before you merge-print, form letters will only be generated for the selected records.

♦ *incremental fields* (SZA)

To get incremental number fields in your database (1, 2, 3, say, or 100, 200, 300) without having to type in all the numbers, use a formula in the spreadsheet that says *add 1 (or 100) to the cell above*. Copy it down a column as far as you need to, copy the column and paste it into the database in the appropriate field.

esp. for beginners

♦ *spreadsheet reports* (SZA)

The Report function in the database can't handle anything beyond totals and subtotals across records. If you need more sophisticated reports that show averages, say, or use statistical functions, paste the database information into the spreadsheet and create the formulas there. You can paste it into the word processor for formatting before you print it.

Works word processor tips

♦ *left and right tabs* (SZA)

Left-aligned tabs point right, and right-aligned tabs point left; in other words, the little cross bar shows how the text will lie:

esp. for beginners

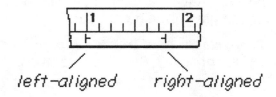

left-aligned   right-aligned

When you click once on the ruler bar, you get left-aligned tab. To change it to a right-aligned one, just click on it—it will do an immediate about-face. You can change it back again by clicking (in other words, it's a toggle). Double-clicking at the outset also gives you a right-aligned tab.

● *automatic entry of search text* (SZA)

shortcut

If any text is selected when you use the *Find...* or *Replace...* command (both on the Search menu), it's automatically entered into the *Find What:* text box.

● *nontoggling Undo* (AN)

very bad
feature

Works' *Undo* command (⌘-Z) doesn't toggle the way it does in virtually every other Mac program. This doesn't sound like much of a problem, but it's amazing how much work you can lose as a result of it. (For example, if you accidentally hit ⌘-Z, you lose all the text you just typed.) Hopefully this will be fixed in Works 2.0.

● *margins vs. indents* (SZA)

As the Works manual tries to make clear, margins are set in the Page Setup dialog box while Indentations—left, right and first line—are set on the Ruler. It may help you avoid confusion if you think of the Ruler as controlling left and right *text* margins while Page Setup denotes *paper* margins.

The zero mark on the Ruler is set wherever the left paper margin is. So with a one-inch page margin and a zero setting on the Ruler, the text begins one inch in from the left edge of the paper. If you set the margin on the Ruler at one inch, the text will begin two inches in from the edge of paper. Paragraphs on a page can have various right and left margins, but the paper margins remain constant.

(This old-fashioned, pre-Mac way of treating margins (a leftover from the primordial ooze of CP/M) is one of Works' weakest points.—AN)

If you put the right margin marker on the Ruler beyond the right paper margin, it turns into a hollow triangle. Since Works won't print anything beyond the paper margin set in Page Setup, you'll lose some text at the ends of your lines.

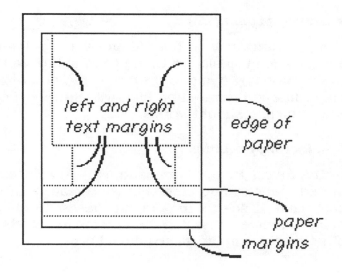

left and right text margins

edge of paper

paper margins

⚫ *page zero* (SZA)

When you use the *Title Page* command, the header and/or footer isn't printed on the first page of the document, but the next page is marked *Page 2* (assuming, of course, that you have a command that reads *Page &p* in the header or footer). To make the second page read *Page 1*, choose the *Set Page # ...* command (on the Format menu) and set the starting page number to zero.

⚫ *page break* (SZA)

You can use Shift Enter instead of the *Insert Page Break* command to put a page break in a document. Both commands insert a manual page break; unlike those inserted automatically by the program, it moves you to a new page regardless of how much text is on the current one.

Manual page breaks can be removed by backspacing over them, but there's another way to do it: Shift Enter acts as a toggle—that is, it also removes a page break if the insertion point is immediately beneath it. (This makes sense if you think of it as issuing the command *Insert Page Break*, because that changes the command on the menu to *Remove Page Break*.)

❖ *drawing room* (SZA)

very
hot
tip

If you turn Draw on but the crosshairs pointer doesn't appear when you place it where you want to start drawing, you're probably trying to draw past the end of the document. Just add some empty lines with the [Return] key and the Draw function should work.

❖ *selecting graphics* (SZA)

very good
feature

The *Select Picture* command ([⌘]–A) selects both imported graphics and elements you create with the Draw command. It selects the graphic closest to the insertion point. Repeatedly issuing the command selects, in turn, other graphics in the same general area.

Works database tips

❖ *date and time* (SZA)

shortcut

You can enter the date or time into any field by pressing [⌘]–D or [⌘]–T.

❖ *ditto fields* (SZA)

shortcut

To enter the same information into a field as is in the same field in the previous record, just press [⌘]–apostrophe. Think of it as [⌘]–ditto (") to make it easier to remember (the " is on the same key, but you don't need to use the [Shift] key for this command).

Remember that if you're using Quote Init, or if you've reassigned keys using QuicKeys or some similar program, you'll have to turn them off for this command to work.

❖ *computed fields* (SZA)

If the results of the calculation in a computed field don't seem to be turning out the way you expect, you may be forgetting something called *priority of operations*. See the entry called that in the *spreadsheet/database tips* section below.

(By the way, these are normally called *calculated fields.* Works, however, uses the term *computed* field.)

⚫ *back and forth* (SZA)

To switch back and forth between the Form view and the List view, you can:

shortcut

• choose the *Show List / Show Form* command (on the Format menu)

• press ⌘ –L

• Double-Click in any empty area of the Form window

• Double-Click in the space in front of a record in the List view to go directly to that record in the Form view

• Double-Click in an empty cell in the List view to go to the currently selected record

⚫ *pasting from the List view* (SZA)

There's a slightly unexpected result when you copy from the database's List view and paste into the word processor or spreadsheet, but it's done on purpose and is very useful. The field names will appear at the top of the pasted columns, even if you didn't select them when copying.

very good feature

⚫ *double-clicking on fields* (SZA)

In the Form view, fields have two distinct parts: the *field name* and the *field data*.

esp. for beginners

Double-clicking in the field name area lets you rename the field; it's the same as using the *Change Field Name...* command on the Edit menu. Double-clicking in the field data area opens the Field Attributes dialog box; it's the same as using the *Set Field Attributes...* command on the Format menu.

In other words:

```
┌─────────────────────────────────────┐
│  Field Name:                         │        Double-click
│  ┌─────────────────────────────┐     │     ┌─────────────────┐
│  │ LastName                    │     │     │ LastName │ Szubin│
│  └─────────────────────────────┘     │     └─────────────────┘
│  ┌──────────┐     ┌──────────────┐   │
│  │  Cancel  │     │      OK      │   │
│  └──────────┘     └──────────────┘   │
└─────────────────────────────────────┘

┌──────────────────────────────────────────────┐
│  Set Field Attributes For LastName            │
│                                               │
│  Type:       Display:      Align:     Style:  │
│  ● Text      ○ General     ● Left     ☐ Bold  │
│  ○ Numeric   ○ Fixed       ○ Center   ☐ Underline │
│  ○ Date      ○ Dollar      ○ Right    ☐ Commas │
│  ○ Time      ○ Percent    ┌──┐                │
│              ○ Scientific │  │ Decimal Places │
│                           └──┘                │
│  ☐ Computed  ☐ Show Day    ┌────────┐ ┌──────┐│
│                            │ Cancel │ │  OK  ││
│                            └────────┘ └──────┘│
└──────────────────────────────────────────────┘
```

⚫ deleting fields (SZA)

If you use *Cut, Clear* or Backspace when a field is selected, the field data, not the field itself, is affected. The only way to get rid of a field is by using the *Delete Field* command (on the Edit menu).

⚫ multilevel sorts in the database (SZA)

very hot tip

Works' spreadsheet lets you sort by up to three columns at a time but its database allows only a single-level sort. If you need a multilevel sort (for instance, records arranged by zip code, by city within zip code and by last name within cities), just do three sorts in reverse order of importance. In other words, in the example above, you'd sort first by last name, next by city and last by zip code.

[This tip will work with any database program, not just Works'.—AN]

♠ *A is for arrange* (SZA)

⌘-S is for *save*, so it can't be for *sort*. Works uses ⌘-A instead (to remember the command, think of *arranging*).

♠ *pasting into empty fields* (SZA)

When pasting information into a database's empty fields (say you're transferring it in from the spreadsheet), be sure to define the field type before you do the paste. If you paste dates into an undefined field, they'll be treated as text and you won't be able to do anything about it (except repaste), since you can't define a field type after you've entered information into it.

important warning

♠ *using spreadsheet functions* (SZA)

Many of the spreadsheet functions can be used in the database's computed fields. For example, you can use the Average function to construct a formula that averages the contents of other fields in the record.

very hot tip

♠ *Find Field... search order* (SZA)

The dialog box that appears when you use the *Find Field...* command (on the Organize menu) says "Find Next Field That Contains:" Notice that it says *next* field. It doesn't start with the current field and record, but goes all the way through the file, back to the start and down to the current field and record, which it searches last.

♠ *Find Field... and Match Records...* (SZA)

The *Find Field...* command displays a record at a time; the *Match Records...* command (also on the Organize menu) searches through the entire database and then displays *all* the records that have fields that match the search criteria.

Neither command is case-sensitive—that is, they pay no attention to upper- and lowercase (search for *Mac* and you'll find *mac* and *MAC* as well). Nor do they care about whole words (search for *Mac* and you'll find *Mac, Macintosh, machine, Machiavellian* and *stomach)*.

🍎 *Record Selection... command* (SZA)

Neither *Find Field...* nor *Match Records...* is field-specific —that is, they'll both find records that contain *John* no matter what field *John* is in. So you'll get first names of *John*, last names of *Johnson*, addresses of *St. John Street*, etc.

But the *Records Selection...* command (also on the Organize menu) lets you specify which field Works should look in. In addition, it lets you decide whether the search criteria *(John)* should be a whole word, part of a word, at the beginning of a word or whatever.

🍎 *stuck in subfiles* (SZA)

When you're viewing and/or working with a subfile created by the *Record Selection...* command, it's hard to tell the difference between that subfile and the main "parent" file. To find out which you're in, look in the Organize menu. If *Record Selection...* is checked, you're working with a subfile; if *Show All Records* is checked, you're not.

🍎 *reports and selections* (SZA)

**very
hot
tip**

If you're working with a subfile created by the *Record Selection...* command and you start a new report, the report initially includes only that subfile. To include all the records in the report, use the *Show All Records* command (on the Organize menu) while the Report window is active. (The main database window will continue to display only the selected records.)

If you use the *Record Selection* command while the Report window is active, the selection rules you create affect only the report. The main database window is independent of rules you create for a report.

✦ *Total-1st Char Field* (SZA)

While it might win a prize for the most poorly phrased Macintosh menu command *(Editor's note: Hear, hear!)*, the *Total-1st Char Field* command (on the TotalsPage menu that comes up when you design a report) is very useful. It creates subtotals on a report when the first character of a field changes instead of when the entire field contents change.

very good feature

This means you could do a subtotal for a column that contains stock part numbers and have the subtotals for all the parts with numbers in the 100's, then those with numbers in the 200's, etc.

✦ *AND and OR hierarchy* (SZA)

When you use multiple selection rules in the Record Selection dialog box and you're mixing ANDs and ORs as connectors between the rules, you have to be careful how you arrange the rules.

very hot tip

For example, if you're looking for customers who owe you more than $200 and also either live out-of-state or have owed the money for more than 60 days, you can't use the following rules:

	Amount is greater than 200
AND	Invoice Date is less than 10/01/88
OR	State is not equal to NY

because Works will interpret them to mean:

[Amount is greater than $200 AND Date is less than 10/01]

OR

[State that is not NY]

In other words, you'll wind up with all the records that don't have NY addresses regardless of what the customer might owe.

The AND connector for a rule always takes priority over the OR connector in a list of rules. Unfortunately, you can't just use parentheses to circumvent this, as you can in a spreadsheet or database formula. Instead, you'll have to redo the rules as follows:

	Amount is greater than 200
AND	Date is less than 10/01/88
OR	Amount is greater than 200
AND	State is not equal to NY

These rules will be interpreted as:

[Amount is greater than 200 AND Date is less than 10/01/88]

OR

[Amount is greater than 200 AND State is not equal to NY]

Works spreadsheet tips

🍎 *clicking on the scroll box* (SZA)

very hot tip

A click in the gray area of the scroll bar shifts the contents of the window up or down by one windowful (and moves the scroll box accordingly). But Works spreadsheets can get so large, and the scroll box can get so close to the top or bottom of the scroll bar, that there's no gray area left for you to click in.

When that happens, just click on the scroll box itself. If it's closer to the top of the scroll bar, it will move up; if it's closer to the bottom, it will move down (and the contents of the window will move accordingly).

(This trick also works in the word processor, but it's not often a document gets so long that you need to use it.)

🍎 *text entry* (SZA)

very hot tip

If you want to enter text that begins with a plus, minus or equal sign, you can't just type it in a cell, since those are *leader characters* that indicate numbers or formulas. So type a quotation mark—a regular, straight one ("), not a curly one—first. The quote mark won't appear in the cell, just in the text field at the top of the screen.

❖ *the Paste Function... command* (SZA)

The main advantage to using the *Paste Function...* command (on the Edit menu) instead of just typing in the name yourself is to make sure it's entered correctly. As an added convenience, the equal sign that signifies a formula is also typed for you, and the insertion point is placed inside the parentheses that follow the function name.

❖ *dates* (SZA)

In the spreadsheet, dates are treated as text. That means you can't sort by date unless you type them just right. January has to be 01, February 02, etc. and the date has to use two digits too (so May 1st would be 05/01).

❖ *freezing numbers* (SZA)

Let's say you've created a spreadsheet to take care of your checkbook. Instead of typing in every check number, you've created a formula that adds one to the cell above and copied it down a column. That works fine until you have a break in the series (for a deposit, say) or until you do some sorting (to pull out certain expenses, say).

very hot tip

The solution isn't to type in the check numbers one at a time; a computer is supposed to save you time. Fortunately, you can "freeze" the numbers after the formula has created them.

To do that, select the cells that contain the check numbers, cut, Click in the cell where you want them to begin (which can be the same place you just cut them from) and choose *Paste with Options...* from the Edit menu. Click the *Values Only* button in the dialog box and press Return . The cells will now contain actual numbers, not formulas, and so they won't change.

⚫ sorting (SZA)

Sorting in the spreadsheet doesn't work like sorting in the database. In the database, you can select a column to sort on in the List view and all the information in the rows (records) stays together. In order for the information to stay together in the spreadsheet, however, you have to specifically select which rows and columns are to be sorted.

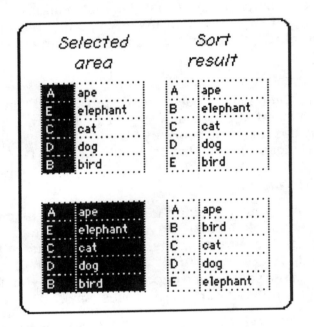

⚫ Go To Cell... vs. Find Cell... (SZA)

Both the *Go To Cell...* and *Find Cell...* commands (on the Select menu) will search for a cell with contents that match what you type in their respective dialog boxes. But only *Go To Cell...* lets you type the name of the cell (A1, say, or V12) you want to go to.

⚫ relative vs. absolute cell references (SZA)

**very
hot
tip**

The default for cell references in formulas is *relative*— that is, cells are normally identified as *three above and two to the right of my present position*. So if you copy a formula to a new cell, or move a cell with a formula in it, the formula will now refer to different cells, as a result of its new location.

Sometimes this is useful (as it would be, for example, in a formula that adds 1 to the value in the cell directly above it). But when that's not what you want, you need *absolute* cell references. They identify cells by their actual locations (4F, X9 or whatever); no matter where you move the formula, it still refers to the same cells.

Absolute cell references are indicated by dollar signs, and you have to put one before both the column and the row (4F, for example). You can type them in yourself or use the *Absolute Cell Ref* command (on the Edit menu).

The absolute reference doesn't have to be for the entire cell. The absolute part of the reference can be just the row, or just the column. So, you can have cell references like A$2 and $B14.

⚫ *blank cells* (SZA)

As far as Works is concerned, any cell that doesn't contain a number is blank—even if it contains text. So, if you use something like the *IsBlank* function, it will return a 1—for *true* ("yes, it's blank")—even if there's text in the cell.

⚫ *copying charts* (SZA)

The charts that Works creates from spreadsheet information can be copied just by choosing *Copy* from the Edit menu when the Chart window is active. You don't have to select the chart first (which is good, since there's no way to select it!).

⚫ *exporting charts* (SZA)

The charts that Works creates are object-oriented. That means if you paste them into a graphics application that handles objects (like MacDraw or SuperPaint's Draw layer), you can edit and move each element separately—change the fill patterns, pull out a slice of the pie, move titles around, etc.

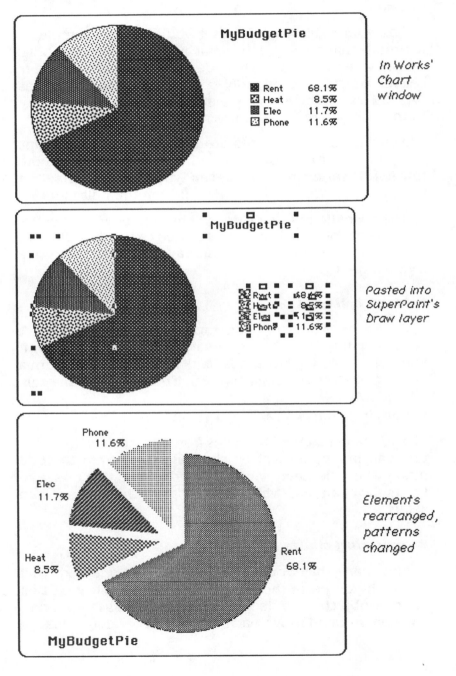

*In Works'
Chart
window*

*Pasted into
SuperPaint's
Draw layer*

*Elements
rearranged,
patterns
changed*

Works spreadsheet/database tips

❡ moving around *(SZA)*

When you're in the List format of the database, it looks a lot like the spreadsheet, and you can use the same techniques to move around in each:

shortcut

command	*moves you*
Tab Shift or ←	left
Tab or →	right
Shift Return or ↑	up
Return or ↓	down

If you select a portion of the grid, your movements will be restricted to it. For example, if you're at the bottom of the selected area and hit the ↓ key (or Return), you'll be wrapped around to the top of the selected area and find yourself in the top cell there.

❡ entering data *(SZA)*

When you enter information into a database field or a spreadsheet cell, it first appears in the text box at the top of the screen (which is called the *Edit bar*). It only gets entered into the field or cell when you leave it and move to another one (by hitting Return , Tab or whatever).

To enter the information without leaving the current field or cell, you can hit Enter or Click on the check mark icon just to the left of the Edit bar. (The X icon there blanks the Edit bar.)

❡ using percents *(SZA)*

Both the spreadsheet and the database understand what you mean when you type the percent sign. So, for example, there's no difference between typing *50%* and *.5*. Works treats them both the same.

♠ priority of operations (SZA)

*very
hot
tip*

When you create a formula for a spreadsheet cell or a computed (calculated) field in a database, you have to be careful how you arrange the mathematical operations. Some operations have a higher priority than others, and are performed first no matter where they are in the formula. If there are multiple operations of equal priority, they're performed left to right.

5+3+2 is a simple example. Because all the operations are additions and are thus of equal priority, the calculation is done from left to right, and the result is 10. Addition and subtraction are also of equal priority, so 5+3–2 is also calculated left to right, with the result being 6.

Multiplication and division are of equal priority to each other but are of higher priority than addition or subtraction. So 5+3*2 gives you a result of 11, not 16, because the multiplication is performed before the addition.

You can circumvent the natural priorities by using parentheses: operations within parentheses take priority over everything else. So if you change the last example to (5+3)*2, the result is 16.

As with other equal-priority operations, if you have multiple parenthetical operations, they're performed left to right. If you have nested parentheses, the innermost parenthetical operations are done first.

On the next page is an example of how it all works together.

♠ too-narrow columns (SZA)

Sometimes a column in the spreadsheet or a field in the database is too narrow to display its contents. If it contains text, Works simply displays as much as will fit in the space provided. (In the spreadsheet, the text will overflow into the next cell if it's empty.) But if it contains numbers, they won't be displayed at all, and you'll get a string of pound signs (#####).

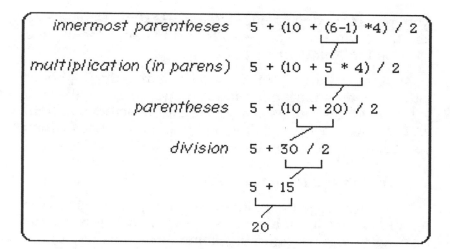

☀ display of numbers *(SZA)*

In the spreadsheet and database, the format you set for numbers affects only their *display*, not their values. So if the number in a cell is 1.239, and you've set the display for two decimal places, you'll see 1.24 (since numbers are rounded, not truncated). But Works remembers that the number in the cell is actually 1.239 and uses that number in any calculation involving the cell. (This is true whether the number is itself the result of a calculation or was entered directly in the cell.)

very good
feature

Works communications tips

☀ dialing *(SZA)*

You can store numbers in the *Dial...* dialog box (from the Communications menu) or you can just type the number you want to dial right in the window. Type *atdt* in front of the number; when you hit Return , it will dial through the modem (unless, like Arthur, you've forgotten to turn it on again).

☀ sending text *(SZA)*

Despite its name, the *Send Text...* command (on the Communications menu) can't send text files, only Works word processor documents. To send a text file, you have to use the *Send File...* command (on the same menu) and click on the *Xmodem Text* button.

Another way to send text is to paste it from the Clipboard into the communications window. It gets treated just as if you typed it in—that is, it appears on the screens at both ends one character at a time (although more quickly than you could actually type it).

🍎 *changing the baud rate* (SZA)

You can change the baud rate even if you're right in the middle of a communications session, by choosing the *Settings...* command (on the Communications menu).

🍎 *control characters* (SZA)

very hot tip

Information services often require that you use *control characters* (key combinations involving the control key) as commands. With most Mac software, you can substitute the ⌘ key for the control key, but in Works, using the ⌘ key triggers a menu command. The ⎇Option key will work, however—even if you're using a Mac-specific service that tells you to use ⌘ –S.

🍎 *hanging up fast* (CR)

shortcut

Either ⌘ – + (plus) or ⌘ – = (equal sign) hangs up the phone. (Both have the same effect; in other words, it doesn't matter if you hold down the ⇧Shift key.)

Miscellaneous programs

🍎 *MacSafe and Sentinel* (SS)

Are you in charge of the company personnel or payroll records? Do you do government work? Perhaps you just have a file or two that you'd prefer no one else see. Security software let you assign a password to files and, if necessary, *encrypt* them (scramble their contents).

The top two contenders in this field are MacSafe and Sentinel. They have a lot in common. Both have extensive on-line help, offer a quick method of encryption as an alternative to DES (the government's standard method) and let you group files into sets. Files in a MacSafe set can share a common password, but have to be encrypted separately. Sentinel's sets can be encrypted or decrypted as a group.

I tested encryption speed with two data files: a 62.5K FileMaker Plus database and a 27K MacWrite document. Each program was tested using its fastest encryption method and using a standard, slower method called DES. As you can see from the chart, Sentinel was the clear winner (to say the least: it took MacSafe 22 to 46 times as long!).

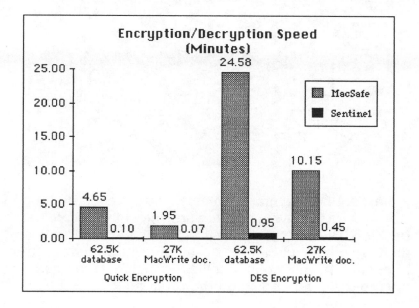

With MacSafe, there's a simpler method for protecting files than encryption—you just create a *safe*, assign it a password and move your documents into it. After the safe has been closed, the documents in it are inaccessible until you enter the password. Moving documents into or out of a safe takes no time at all, since encryption/decryption isn't required. Once a safe has been created, the Finder can't be used to move, duplicate or throw it away. And you can make as many safes as you want.

MacSafe has a "secret compartment" inside each safe where you can also stash files. Like the safe, a secret compartment can be assigned a password, effectively giving you double protection for ultrasensitive files.

Here's what a MacSafe safe looks like. (The icons with 🍎s on them are unencrypted; the one with DES on it is.)

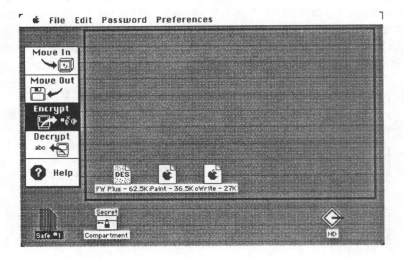

MacSafe has several problems. First, there's nothing to stop you from moving an encrypted file out of a safe to the Desktop. Once it's there, its original icon is restored, and there's no indication that it's still encrypted—until you try to open it. At that point you'll either get an error message or gibberish, depending on the program.

important warning

If you move the file back into the safe, its icon now lacks evidence of encryption. If you attempt to decrypt it and have turned the *Don't allow multiple encryption/decryption* option on, you'll get an error message. The only way to decrypt the file is to turn that option off.

But MacSafe's biggest problem is the snail's pace with which it performs encryptions and decryptions. It's so slow that, for large files, it's just not practical—the safe and secret compartment will have to do.

very bad feature

Perhaps because Sentinel can encrypt so fast, it encrypts *all* files—you can't assign a password without encryption. Icons for files encrypted by Sentinel appear on the Desktop in their original folders bound in chains and secured by a padlock. (There's no need to guess what this indicates.) Here's a sample of how it looks:

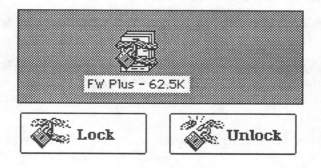

Files can be locked or unlocked individually or in sets—using 4- to 20-character passwords. When locking a set, if Sentinel finds a document that has already been locked with a different password, that document is automatically removed from the set—avoiding the possibility of dual encryption.

Sentinel keeps track of all files that have been unlocked during the current session and refers to them collectively as the *work set*. If you have to run down the hall for a minute, you don't have to relock every open file and set; you can simply lock the work set.

very good feature

So which program is better? They both cost $150. MacSafe is much slower; in fact, unless your files are almost all under 20K, you'll spend a significant part of your computing day waiting for MacSafe to encrypt and decrypt them. I also found Sentinel easier to learn and use.

As far as security goes, the two programs are more or less a wash. MacSafe has a command that displays the current password—so if you leave your computer for a moment with a safe open, someone can find out its password in about two seconds. On the other hand, MacSafe's files can't be copied, deleted or moved the way Sentinel's can, because when they're in safes, they're invisible.

But, all in all, I'd say Sentinel is the best bet for most people.

✦ *security software tips* (SS)

Here are a few tips you may find helpful when working with security software:

important warning

* It's easy to be cavalier when assigning new passwords and to create so many you lose track of them. Remember—if you forget the password, you can kiss the file goodbye.

very hot tip

* If you work with the files as a set, use a password for the whole set. If you use MacSafe, assign a single password to the safe and only use an additional password for the extremely sensitive documents inside it.

* Don't use obvious passwords. One company I worked for used everyone's first names as their passwords into the accounting system. (That's a hard one to crack, huh?)

* Restrict passwords to all caps or all lowercase. It's hard enough to remember them without adding extra complications.

* Unless there's a cryptographer in your office or you're required by contract to use DES, use the fast encryption method for most files.

important warning

* Remember to lock all files whenever you leave your Mac. This is particularly important if you're using MacSafe, because once a safe is open on the Desktop, its password can be displayed with a menu command.

✎ *invisible security* (CJW)

Here's a way to prevent programs stored on your hard disk from being pirated. The trick is to make them invisible (using some utility like DiskTop's Technical level Get Info box). But then how do *you* use them? Well, QuicKeys lets you launch a program with a keystroke combination, regardless of whether its icon is visible. (Both QuicKeys and DiskTop are described in Chapter 8.)

Using this trick gives you full access to all your programs, but no one else who sneaks a peek at your Mac will even know that they're there.

✎ *MacGenogram* (Dean Lobovits)

MacGenogram is a graphics program designed to help family therapists diagram the families they treat, using symbols and conventions developed by Monica McGoldrick and the program's author, Randy Gerson.

Whereas a genealogy deals with the bare bones of a family tree (who begat who, basically), a genogram tries to reveal how a family works psychologically. Its basic components are relationships, not simply the people who make them up.

very good feature

For example, here's a genogram of the Cleaver family:

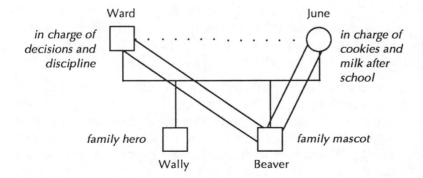

As in a regular genealogy, squares represent males and circles females, X's through either mean *deceased* and solid horizontal lines indicate marriages. Now for what makes a genogram special. In the example above, the dotted line between Ward and June signifies a distant relationship. The double lines between Beaver and his parents represent close relationships. These three relationships form what's called a *family triangle*.

Basically, Beaver's entertaining antics keep Mom and Dad from focusing on the problems of their distant and nonsexual relationship. We also know (although it isn't shown in this particular genogram) that June is dependent on Ward for every decision, that Wally is often a *family hero* who looks after Mom when Dad's not around, and that Beaver is the *family mascot*. This relationship constellation is often found in alcoholic families. You always suspected June was a closet lush, didn't you?

MacGenogram comes with a fascinating sample genogram of Eugene O'Neill's family that shows the recurrence of addictions and suicidal behavior. McGoldrick and Gerson's book, *Genograms in Family Assessment* (Norton, 1985) contains many other interesting genograms, including ones for the families of Sigmund Freud, Scott and Zelda Fitzgerald, Virginia Woolf, Albert Einstein, Thomas Jefferson, Martin Luther King and the Kennedys.

Unfortunately, MacGenogram is a fairly primitive program as far as Mac technology is concerned. It has problems with System 4.2 and Finder 6.0 (and probably later versions as well) and it isn't compatible with Stepping Out or large screens. This last is a significant limitation, since genograms tend to get very big very quickly.

Still, using MacGenogram is a lot easier than drawing genograms by hand, if only because of the ease with which it repositions existing parts of the diagram when you add new information. Although it's mostly of interest to family therapists, MacGenogram may also appeal to laypeople interested in gaining new insights into their own family dynamics.

Chapter 16

Where
to
find
good
information
and
inexpensive
software

Magazines

There've gotten to be so many very good magazines on the Mac that it's almost an embarrassment of riches. The only sensible approach is to buy two or three issues of each of the ones discussed below and decide for yourself whose approach you like the most. It's definitely worth the expenditure of time and money, and you'll probably end up reading at least a couple of them on a regular basis.

*very
hot
tip*

In the case of *MacWEEK*, you don't even have to spend any money; you just fill out their questionnaire. (Since you buy an average of ten Macintosh systems a month, you'll qualify for a free subscription without any problem.) But don't stop there—the others are also worth considering.

bargain

I've listed the magazines in alphabetical order, so no one can say I'm playing favorites. As always, addresses and phone numbers are in Appendix B.

❦ *MACazine* (AN)

Before I say anything about the *MACazine*, I should tell you that its sister company, STAX!, published a HyperCard version of the first edition of this book (and may do the same for the second) and that the *MACazine* has offered (or will offer, depending on when you read this) a sampler of items from this book as a promotional gift to new subscribers.

With that full disclosure out of the way, let me say that I find the *MACazine* to be full of useful, nitty-gritty information that's often missing from other magazines. Although its aimed at users who are slightly more sophisticated than the average, most of its articles are quite readable and accessible—often very much so. *The MACazine's* editor, Bob LeVitus, is one of the best-informed people in the business and also one of the nicest.

*very good
feature*

⚫ *MacGuide* (AN)

very good feature

This is a close-to-exhaustive listing of all Macintosh-related products that exist and the companies that produce them (with names, addresses, phone numbers, etc.). It also has reviews of many products, and scores them on a scale of 100. Readers get a chance to score products as well, so everything doesn't depend just on one reviewers take.

MacGuide comes out quarterly and, as a listee, I get a free copy. But it takes a long time to come. I've come to depend on *MacGuide* so much that I usually go out and buy a copy before the free one arrives.

⚫ *Macintosh Business Review* (AN)

very good feature

Started off as a quarterly, but should be a monthly be the time you read this. As its name implies, it focuses on business (no game reviews, etc.) Its executive editor, Charlie Rubin, is extremely knowledgeable and competent. In fact, I tried to get him to edit this edition of *The Macintosh Bible*, but the *Macintosh Business Review* snatched him away.

⚫ *Macintosh Buyer's Guide* (AN)

This quarterly survey of Macintosh products, published by Redgate Communications, has been around for several years. Like *MacGuide*, its listings are close-to-exhaustive, but there are some categories it leaves out. It's more like a regular magazine, with articles in the front and product listings in the back, and issues have themes (desktop engineering, in the most recent issue).

⚫ *Mac II-specific magazines* (AN)

The Mac II Review is a slick monthly and *The Macintosh II Report* a monthly newsletter. They both cover the II on what I'd call an advanced-user level and are worth taking a look at if you're really into your II.

⬤ *MacUser* (AN)

You'd think a magazine would realize that the free publicity of being mentioned in this book is worth the few bucks a comp (free) subscription costs, but *MacUser* apparently doesn't think so. I finally gave up and just subscribed, but the issues haven't started arriving yet. So my knowledge about *MacUser* is a bit out-of-date. But here it is anyway, for whatever it's worth.

One of the nicest things about *MacUser* are its lists. The two of them I find most useful are the one that tells you the most current version number of virtually every piece of Mac software that exists, and the cumulative list in the back of the magazine that summarizes *MacUser's* reviews of hundreds of products and rates them for you (although this job is now being done at least as well by *MacGuide*).

very good feature

Each *MacUser* also contains a section of tips submitted by users, and usually at least one article full of useful tips on some aspect of an important product. Its editor, Fred Davis, is a brilliant guy who knows a lot about almost everything.

⬤ *MacWEEK* (AN)

As mentioned above, *MacWEEK* is the least expensive of the magazines mentioned here—it's free to qualified people (that is, people its advertisers what to reach; basically, the more computer products you normally buy, the better). Dale Coleman, whose contributions to the first edition of the *Macintosh Bible* are everywhere throughout this edition, works there, currently as Editor-at-Large.

bargain

I find MacWEEK an interesting read, particularly the gossip column, which is called *Mac the Knife*. It's got a lot of very current news and it's generally quite well-written.

very good feature

⬤ *Macworld* (AN)

Macworld is one of the slickest-looking magazines you're ever likely to see (unless you're a fan of European design magazines). It's particularly strong on articles about broad trends in the market, and also has good product reviews. Always a pleasure to read, *Macworld* also provides a lot of good, practical information.

very good feature

They seem to focus on comparisons of all (or all the major) products available in a certain category, which I think is a very useful approach. As I write this, the last two issues have compared large hard disks, accounting packages, plotters, low-cost paint programs, music software and CAD programs. They also listed experts' fifteen favorite desk accessories and their readers' favorite Mac products.

desktop publishing magazines and newsletters *(AN)*

If you're involved in any sort of desktop-publishing, here are some magazines and newsletters you should know about.

Personal Publishing is a monthly out of Chicago that does a good job of covering the field; in fact, if you want to read just one magazine about desktop publishing, this is the one I'd recommend. *The Page,* also from Chicago, is a monthly newsletter (no ads) that's full of useful, practical information and tips you don't find elsewhere. *Verbum* is a slick quarterly that bills itself as a *Journal of Personal Computer Aesthetics;* it covers computer graphics on both the Mac and the PC.

There's also a monthly newsletter called *Desktop Publishing.* Written by Tony Bove and Cheryl Rhodes, two of the most knowledgeable people in the field, it gives you a level of in-depth analysis that's hard to find elsewhere. It's more technical than *Personal Publishing* or *The Page* and aimed at more sophisticated readers. It's also more expensive (about $200 a year as of this writing), but if you need the kind of information it gives you, it's worth it many times over.

User groups

User groups are clubs made up of people who are interested in computers in general, a particular kind of computer, a particular kind of software or even an individual program. They're typically nonprofit and independent of any manufacturer or publisher.

esp. for beginners

User groups are an excellent source of good information—which isn't surprising, since sharing information is their main purpose. Nowhere else are you likely to find so many dedicated people anxious to help you solve your problems, none of whom would dream of charging you a nickel for it.

very good feature

User group meetings are usually open to the public and free. Joining the group normally costs somewhere between $25 and $40 a year and gives you access to the group's library of public-domain software and shareware.

bargain

Large groups often feature guest speakers from the computer industry who describe new products at their meetings, and also have subgroups (called *special interest groups* or *SIGs)* for members with particular interests or needs: beginners, developers, musicians, graphic artists, desktop publishers and so on.

very good feature

Unless you live in a very remote area, finding a local user group shouldn't be hard—especially if there's a college or university nearby. One fast way to find one is to check with an Apple dealer. Any good dealer will know all the local user groups. If you can't find a group in your community, get together with some other Mac users and start one of your own.

very hot tip

⬤ *BCS* (AN)

There are more than forty SIGs in the country's largest user group, the Boston Computer Society (which, as of this writing, has more than 32,000 members) and each of them publishes a newsletter (in addition to BCS's own slick magazine).

*very good
feature*

When you join BCS, you get to choose two SIGs to belong to (more than that cost extra). BCS's Mac SIG has more than 10,000 members and its newsletter, *The Active Window*, is excellent (thanks at least in part to the inspired editorship of Rebecca Waring).

BMUG *(AN)*

bargain

The user group I belong to and depend on as a source of information is BMUG, which has more than 5000 members. Membership is open to anyone and costs $60 a year (as of this writing); their "newsletter," published twice a year and running into the hundreds of 8–1/2 x 11 pages, is worth the price alone.

*gossip/
trivia*

(BMUG was originally called the *Berkeley Macintosh Users Group*; BMUG was just a nickname. But the IRS considers a single-product or single-brand user group a promotional activity of the company, so the name had to be changed to simply *BMUG*.)

To give you an idea of what a large user group meeting is like, I'll describe BMUG's, which is held on the University of California campus every Thursday evening. About 300–400 people come to a typical meeting and their knowledge of the Mac varies from extensive to very limited (although there are many more of the former).

Before the meeting starts, people line up to buy disks and other items like modems that the group sells to members at fantastically low prices. The meetings begin with an open session where people can ask any question they have about any aspect of the Mac, and usually get a definitive answer from someone in the room. When the question-and-answer session is over, one or two guest speakers describe their products (using a Mac that projects onto a giant screen).

Because BMUG is so large and so close to Silicon Valley, it's able to attract representatives of just about every major software publisher and hardware manufacturer, as well as local freelance talent like the ebullient Andy Hertzfeld (who wrote much of the code in the Finder and in MultiFinder, as well as the software that runs on Radius monitors). I vividly remember the night Hertzfeld debuted Switcher at BMUG. When the display on the big screen shot from the application in the first partition to the one in the second, the audience leapt to its feet and cheered.

BMUG maintains one of the most extensive public domain and shareware libraries in the galaxy; their hundreds of disks, which cost only $3 each, contain untold thousands of files. BMUG also publishes *BMUG on HyperCard,* a book that describes some of the better stacks, and a catalog of all known public-domain software on CD ROM. Called (cleverly) *PD ROM,* it costs $100 and takes up *350 megabytes,* which makes it an intellectual undertaking on the order of the *Oxford English Dictionary* or the Great Library at Alexandria before the fire.

very good
feature

⚫ *NABVICU* (DC)

The National Association of Blind and Visually Impaired Computer Users is at Box 1352, Roseville CA 95661, Their phone numbers are 916/ 783-0364 (voice) and 916/ 786-3923 (modem).

Bulletin boards and information services

⚫ *bulletin boards* (DC)

An electronic bulletin board (commonly abbreviated *BBS* for *bulletin board system)* is another good place to tap into the latest rumor mill or get a problem solved. All you need is a modem, communications software, access to a phone line and a little bit of experience.

esp. for
beginners

Bulletin boards are a lot like electronic user groups: you'll find plenty of people there who are willing and able to answer your questions. Most good bulletin boards also have the latest versions of public-domain and shareware

very good
feature

software available for downloading. And for all they provide, they don't charge a penny.

A complete list of every active Mac BBS in the country would take up many pages of this book and would probably be out of date by the time you read it. So we've just listed a few that we have personal experience with. They're among the best in the country and they've all been around for a long time, so they should still be active when you read this. All of them maintain extensive lists of other bulletin boards which they update frequently.

name *sponsor, location*	*phone*
BMUG BMUG, Berkeley	415/849-2684
Check-In Dave Game, Miami	305/232-0393
Desk Toppers Randy Bennett, Chicago	312/356-3776
Mac Boston Steve Garfield, Boston	617/262-9167
Mac Circles Pat O'Connor, Pleasanton CA	415/484-4412
MacFido Tribune Vernon Keenon, San Francisco	415/923-1235

information services (DC)

A final source for good information and inexpensive software is commercial information services like CompuServe, GEnie and The Source. There are two drawbacks to using them; they charge you for each minute you're connected to them, and they present you with a bewildering series of menus that can be frustrating for first-time users (and for many experienced users as well).

Most large information services have Mac special interest groups, which amount to bulletin boards with an area for messages (and for conferences on various subjects) and another area that contains public-domain and shareware software you can download.

The major benefit of using a commercial information service rather than a bulletin board system is that you'll never get a busy signal. If you need some information or a new utility right away, you'll appreciate not having to dial repeatedly just to log on. There are many commercial information services available, but we've found Compu-Serve and GEnie to be particularly good sources for Mac-related information and software.

🍎 *CompuServe* (DC)

CompuServe is an extremely popular service, though its rates are higher than some others. To register, you need to purchase a CompuServe Starter Kit (available at most computer and software dealers for about $40). The kit includes a list of available phone numbers, a login code, and instructions for signing up. You'll also need a major credit card for billing.

very good feature

🍎 *GEnie* (AN)

You'll find most of the same Mac information on GEnie that you find on CompuServe but GEnie's charges are substantially lower.

bargain

🍎 *BIX* (PH)

BIX is an information service run by *BYTE* magazine, one of the oldest technical microcomputer journals. Most of the people who participate in BIX's Macintosh discussion (and they include people who work at Apple and other major Mac companies) are not only technologically knowledgeable but also quite friendly and generous with their time. (But Dale wants to point out that the discussions on BIX can get quite technical; they're definitely not for beginners.)

BIX also offers on-line customer service for Microsoft and some other Mac companies, so you can use electronic mail to report bugs and ask questions, instead of running up your phone bill while on hold.

very good feature

The Macintosh Bible Disk

If you're a member of a user group, or if you regularly log on to a bulletin board or an information service, you have access to all the good public-domain software and shareware you can handle. If you're not (or don't), *The Macintosh Bible Disk* is for you.

It contains almost 800K of the best free and inexpensive programs around, as well as a couple of things from the book: Dictionary Helper, the 1313-word file (described on pages 384–88) that enhances spelling-checker dictionaries, and our MacWrite template for viewing fonts (pp. 147–51).

I can't tell you what else will be on the disk, because we regularly update it as new and better stuff comes out. But I guarantee you'll like what's there; if you don't, just return the disk within 30 days and we'll send you a full refund,, including what it cost you to send it back.

The Macintosh Bible Disk costs $15 from: Goldstein & Blair, Box 7635, Berkeley CA 94707. Add $2 for shipping and tax (if any) in the US; for foreign orders, add $4 in US funds, payable through a US bank. You can also charge it to your Visa or Mastercard; just call us at 415/524–4000 between 10 and 5 Pacific Time.

While I'm at it, I should mention that you can also order copies of this book directly from us (at the same address and phone number). It costs $28 plus $3 shipping and tax (in the US); quantity discounts are also available.

To foreign addresses, add $5 for shipment by surface mail (which also includes the cost of mailing you the updates). For air mail shipment of both book and updates, add $7 for Canada; $8 for Mexico; $12 for the Caribbean, Central America, Colombia and Venezuela; $19 for elsewhere in South America and for Europe (except the USSR); and $27 anywhere else in the world. Be sure to send US funds, payable through a US bank, or charge it by phone.

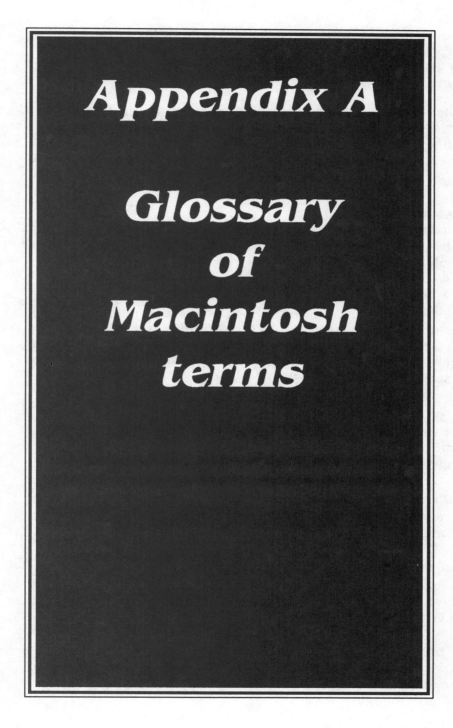

Appendix A

Glossary of Macintosh terms

These definitions only apply the Mac. They may not be accurate if you try to apply them to other computers (or—heaven forfend!—to the world outside computers). Very basic terms (e.g., mouse, keyboard) are omitted.

When a term that's defined in this glossary occurs in the definition of another term, I usually put it in italics—so you know you can look it up if you don't know it (but I don't do that for the most common terms.) Italics are also used for sentences that show how the word is used (see algorithm *for an example).*

accelerator board

A *board* containing a faster *CPU chip* and/or more memory and/or other electronic wizardry to speed up the operation of a computer.

active window

The currently selected window, where the next action will take place (unless the next action is to select another window). The active window is always on top of all other windows, its *scroll bars* are gray and its *title bar* is highlighted (that is, there are six horizontal lines on either side of the title).

ADB *(pronounced as separate letters)*

The *Apple desktop bus* connects the keyboard and mouse to SEs and Mac IIs (not to mention the Apple IIGS). The connections are different than those for the Plus and earlier Macs.

ADB keyboard

A standard Apple keyboard used with the Mac II, the SE and also the Apple IIGS.

Alarm Clock

An Apple-supplied desk accessory that lets you sound an alarm at a given time. (If the Mac is off at that time, the alarm sounds when you turn it back on.)

alert box

A *box* that appears unbidden on the screen to give you some information, and which doesn't require any information back from you. A *bomb message* is one example. Also called a *message box*, although *alert box* is the correct name.

algorithm

The precise sequence of steps required to do something. The first step in programming is figuring out the algorithm. Here's an example of how the word is used: *Both programs produce the same result, but because they use different algorithms, the second one is much faster.*

alpha tester

A person, employed by the company developing a product, who tries to discover bugs in it. Compare *beta tester*.

alpha testing

Early debugging of a product within the company developing it. It's followed by *beta testing*.

alpha version

A version of a program at the point at which it's in *alpha test*. Usually there are several alpha versions. Compare *beta version* and *release version*.

Apple key

Another name for the *command key* (⌘), which has an Apple on it on many keyboards.

Apple (⌘) menu

A menu available both on the Desktop (that is, in the Finder) and from within virtually all applications; its title is an ⌘ at the far left end of the menu bar. The ⌘ menu gives you access to desk accessories and information about the current application. One of the three *standard menus*.

AppleTalk

An old name for *LocalTalk*.

application program *(or simply* application*)*

The software you use to create and modify documents. Some common types of applications are word processors, spreadsheets, databases, graphics programs, page-makeup software and communications programs.

arrow keys

On the standard *ADB keyboard,* four keys (indicated by ↑, ↓, → and ← in this book) that move the *insertion point,* move you through *list boxes* and the like.

arrow pointer

The basic shape the pointer takes—a left-leaning arrow that looks like this: ▶ .

⌈Backspace⌋

This key is called *delete* on many keyboards, but it's indicated as ⌈Backspace⌋ throughout this book. (Why? Because we don't have a neat key caps symbol like that for *delete.)*

baud rate

The number of bits per second. Baud rates are most commonly used as a measure of how fast data is transmitted—by a modem, for example. (In some circumstances, there's a difference between bits per second and the baud rate, but for all practical purposes you can consider them to be the same.) The term comes from the name of a communications pioneer, Baudot.

The most common baud rates are 300, 1200, 2400 and 9600. Which one you use can mean the difference between sanity and three weeks in Bellevue. If you can stand to watch text come on the screen at 300 baud, you either have no central nervous system or you're the Buddha.

BBS

An abbreviation for *bulletin board system.*

beta site

A place where *beta testing* takes place. *We're a beta site for the new version.*

beta tester

A person, not employed by the company developing a product, who tries to discover bugs in it. Beta testers are almost never paid;

they do it for the fun of being in on the development of the product and/or because their work requires that they know what's going on before the product is released. Compare *alpha tester.*

beta testing

Debugging of a product using people outside the company developing the product. Beta testing comes after *alpha testing* and before the *release version* is shipped.

beta version

A version of a program at the point at which it's in *beta test.* Usually there are several beta versions. Compare *alpha version* and *release version.*

Bezier curves *(BEZ-yay)*

Mathematically generated lines that can display nonuniform curvatures (as opposed to curves with uniform curvature, which are called *arcs).* Named after Pierre Bezier, they're defined by four "control points." It's relatively easy to make Bezier curves assume complex shapes and to join their endpoints smoothly, which makes them particularly useful for creating letter shapes and other computer graphics.

bit-mapped

Made up of dots.

bit-mapped font

A font made up of dots and designed primarily for use on dot-matrix printers. Also called an *ImageWriter font.* Compare *outline font* and *screen font.*

bit-mapped graphic

A picture or other graphic made up of dots rather than of objects, like those produced by paint programs like MacPaint, FullPaint and the paint layer of Super paint. Compare *object-oriented graphic.*

board

A piece of fiberglass or pressboard on which *chips* are mounted. Also called a *circuit board.* The connections between the chips are normally printed with metallic ink—in which case it's a *printed circuit board.* The main board in a computer device is called the *motherboard.* A board made to plug directly into a *slot* is called a *card.*

bomb *(or bomb message)*

A message box with a picture of a bomb in it. It appears unbidden on the screen to let you know that a serious problem has occurred with the system software. Bombs usually force you to restart the system. Compare *crash* and *hang.*

(to) boot

To start up a computer by loading an operating system—in the case of the Mac, the System and either the Finder or a Finder substitute—into its memory. The more common Mac term is to *start up* or to *start.* (The name *boot* comes from the idea that the operating system pulls itself up by its own bootstraps—since it's a program that tells a computer how to load other programs, but loads itself.)

box

An enclosed area on the Mac's screen that resembles a window but lacks a title bar. Because it has no title bar, you can't move it. A *dialog box,* a *list box,* a *text box* and an *alert* or *message box* are some examples.

Another use of *box* is in the names of various rectangular icons that control windows. See *close box, size box* and *zoom box* for examples.

A third use of *box* is to indicate a rectangular *button,* as in *check boxes.*

bulletin board *(or bulletin board system)*

A computer dedicated to maintaining a list of messages and making them available over phone lines at no charge. People *upload* (contribute) and *download* (gather) messages by calling the bulletin board with their own computer.

button

On the Mac's screen, an outlined area in a dialog box that you click on to choose, confirm or cancel a command. For example, when you quit from most applications, you get a dialog box that asks if you want to save the current document, and it gives you three buttons to choose from: Yes, No and Cancel.

A button with a heavy border, which is activated when you hit Return or Enter, is called the *default button.* Also see *radio buttons.*

Button also refers to the switch on top of the mouse you use for clicking. When there's a danger of confusion, it's called the *mouse button.*

bye
The standard thing you type to indicate you're ending a telecommunications session. The other person also types *bye* and then you both hang up.

CAD
Computer-aided design (it can refer to both hardware and software).

Calculator
A desk accessory that simulates a simple calculator. You can Cut, Copy and Paste to and from it.

Cancel button
A button that appears in most dialog boxes, giving you the choice of cancelling the command that generated the dialog box.

card
A kind of *board* that plugs directly into a *slot.* Cards have connectors right on their edges, rather than at the ends of a cable.

cdev *(SEE-dev)*
A *cdev* is a utility program that, like an init, must be placed in the system folder to work. Unlike an *init,* it then displays an icon at the left side of the Control Panel, along with the General, Keyboard and Mouse icons. For example, the Mac II has a cdev called Monitor that lets you configure it for a monochrome or color screen. (Cdevs only work on the modular Control Panel used with System version 3.2 and later.)

We tried to find out what *cdev* stands for, but Apple technical support doesn't answer "stupid questions."

CD ROM

A *compact disk read-only memory*—a kind of optical *storage* device (or medium).

check boxes

A group of boxes that work as toggles—that is, when you click on an empty check box, an X appears inside it, turning the option on; when you click on a check box with an X in it, the X disappears and the option is turned off. Unlike *radio buttons,* any or all of a group of check boxes can be on at one time.

character

The generic name for a number, letter or symbol. Included are "invisible" characters like `Tab` and `Return`.

character key

Any key that generates a *character.* Compare *modifier key.*

chip

Silicon is a chemical element found in sand, clay, glass, pottery, concrete, brick, etc. A tiny piece of silicon (or of germanium), usually about the size of a baby's fingernail, is impregnated with impurities in a pattern that creates different kinds of miniaturized computer circuits. This is a chip.

Chips are primarily used as *CPUs* or *memory* and are normally mounted on *boards.*

chip family

A group of related chips, each of which (except, of course, the first) evolved from an earlier one. The *CPU chips* used in Macintosh products are all members of the Motorola *68000* family.

Chooser

A desk accessory used to tell the Mac which printer you want to use, and what port it's connected to.

Chooser resource file

When you place one of these inside your system folder, it displays an icon in the Chooser window. Chooser resource files normally control external devices like printers, or emulate them; some examples are: the ImageWriter and LaserWriter *drivers* that come with the Mac; the ImageSaver file that comes with Desktop Express; SuperGlue, which lets you print formatted files to disk; and AppleShare, which lets you access other volumes on a local area network. There are also custom printer drivers that work as chooser resources.

circuit board

See *board*.

clicking

Pressing and immediately releasing the mouse button. To click on something is to position the pointer on it and then click. A click is the action of clicking.

Clipboard

The area of the Mac's memory that holds what you last cut or copied. Pasting inserts the contents of the Clipboard into a document.

close box

A small box at the left end of the active window's title bar. Clicking on it closes the window. Compare *size box* and *zoom box*.

closing

On the Desktop, closing a window means collapsing it back into an icon. Within an application, closing a document means terminating your work on it without exiting the application.

command

The generic name for anything you tell a computer program to do. On the Mac, commands are usually listed on menus, or are generated by holding down the ⌘ (command) key while hitting one or more other keys. To choose a command from a menu, you drag down the menu until the command you want is highlighted, then release the mouse button.

command character

The combination of the ⌘ (command) key and one or more other characters.

(the) command key

The *modifier key* on the Mac's keyboard that bears the ⌘ symbol. When held down while other keys are struck, the ⌘ key generates commands. For example, ⌘–1 ejects the floppy disk that's in the Mac's internal drive.

command mode

A phrase we use in this book to indicate the opposite of *NumLock*—in other words, the setting on which a numeric keypad, instead of inserting numbers into your document, issues commands for moving the insertion point, selecting text or whatever.

commercial

Said of computer products which are sold for profit through normal distribution channels, with the purchaser paying before taking possession of the product. Compare *shareware* and *public-domain*.

contiguous RAM

RAM that's not split apart by other pieces of RAM used by other programs. Compare *fragmented memory.*

control character

The combination of the control key and one or more other characters.

control key

A *modifier key* on ADB keyboards (but not on earlier Mac keyboards). Widely used in the world of the IBM PC, it mostly wastes useful space on a Mac keyboard.

Control Panel

A desk accessory that allows you to set things like how loud the beeps (and other sounds the Mac makes) are, how fast the insertion point blinks, how fast you have to click in succession for the Mac to recognize it as a double-click, and so on.

copying

Duplicating something from a document and placing the duplicate in the Clipboard. To do that, you select what you want to copy and then choose *Copy* from the Edit menu or hit ⌘ –C.

copy protection

Any of many various schemes for preventing the unauthorized copying of software. They're all a pain (although to varying degrees) and are seldom used any more.

CPU *(pronounced as separate letters)*

The *central processing unit*—the central part of a computer (or other computer device). It includes the circuitry—built around the *CPU chip* and mounted on the *motherboard*—that actually performs the computer's calculations, and the box in which that circuitry is housed.

CPU chip

The heart of a computer (or other computer device). The CPU chip is the main determinant of how fast a computer will run and what software will run on it.

On all Macs through the SE, the CPU chip is a Motorola 68000; on the Mac II, it's the faster and more powerful 68020. (Future Macs will either probably either use the 68020 or the even faster and more powerful 68030.)

crash

A noun and verb which mean that your system has suddenly stopped working, or is working wrong. You normally have to restart. (A *crash* is like a *bomb*, except you don't get a message. Also see *hang*.)

cursor

Unlike more primitive machines, the Mac has no cursor. This term from the prehistoric world of the PC is sometimes incorrectly applied to either the *pointer* or the *insertion point*.

cutting
Removing something from a document by selecting it and then choosing *Cut* from the Edit menu or hitting ⌘–X. What you cut is placed in the Clipboard.

DA *(pronounced as separate letters)*
An abbreviation for *desk accessory.*

daughter board
A *board* that mounts on top of, and connects to, the *mother-board.* Often used for memory upgrades and the like.

decimal point
Although not everybody uses this convention, we find this a convenient way to distinguish the period on the keypad from the period on the keyboard itself (in some programs, like Word, commands only work with one or the other).

default
What you get if you don't specify something different. Often used to refer to default settings (for example, margins in a word processing program, or Speaker Volume on the Control Panel).

default button
A *button* with a heavy border, which is activated when you hit Return or Enter .

delete
What the Backspace key is called on many keyboards.

delimiter
A character that marks the boundary (or limit) of something. For example, the standard for Mac database programs is to use Tab to delimit fields and Return to delimit records.

desk accessory
A program that's always available from the menu, regardless of the application you're using. (It is possible to link a desk accessory to a specific application, so that it won't be available from other applications, but that's a special case.)

desk accessory menu
A common name for the (Apple) menu.

Desktop
Apple's official definition for this term is: "Macintosh's working environment—the menu bar and the gray area on the screen." But in common usage, it refers only to the Finder's Desktop—that is, what the Mac's screen displays when no applications are open.

One way to tell if you're on the Desktop—that is, if you're in the Finder or in some other application—is to look for the Trash in the lower right corner. (Of course, if you're in MultiFinder, the Trash will always be there, unless you've covered it with a window.)

Desktop file
An invisible file that records information like the size, shape and locations of windows.

dialog box
A box on the screen requesting information, or a decision, from you. In some boxes, the only possible response is to click on the OK button. Since this hardly constitutes a dialog, those are more often called *message boxes* or *alert boxes*.

dimmed
When something is *dimmed* (gray) on the Mac's screen, it means that you can't currently access it. For example, commands you can't choose (in a given context) appear dimmed on the menu. When you eject a disk, its icon is dimmed, as are all windows and icons associated with it. Also called *grayed*.

directory
The contents of a disk or folder, arranged by icon, size, date, type, etc.

disk
A round platter with a coating similar to that on recording tape, on which computer information is stored in the form of magnetic impulses. Although the disk itself is always circular, the case it comes in is usually rectangular. The two main types are floppy disks and hard disks..

disk drive

A device that reads information from, and writes information onto, disks. The Mac has one internal drive for floppy disks and can be hooked up to a second (optional) external floppy drive. Many hard disk drives are available for it.

disk window

The window that opens when you double-click on a disk's icon. Also called the *root directory*.

document

What you create and modify with an application—a collection of information on a disk or in memory, grouped together and called by one name. Some examples are a letter, a drawing or a mailing list.

documentation

This term includes manuals, *on-line* tutorials and help files, reference cards, instructional audio cassettes and videotapes, etc.

DOS *(dahss)*

Short for *PC DOS* or *MS DOS*, the operating system used on IBM Personal Computers and compatible machines (which are also called *clones*).

dot-matrix printer

A printer that forms characters out of a pattern of dots, the way the Mac forms images on the screen. Usually each dot is made by a separate pin pushing against a ribbon and then against the paper. *ImageWriter* is the name Apple gives to its line of dot-matrix printers.

dots per inch

A measure of screen or printer resolution; the number of dots in a line one inch long. Abbreviated *dpi.*

dots per square inch

A measure of screen and printer resolution; the number of dots in a solid square one inch on a side. Abbreviated *dpsi* or *dpi2.*

double-clicking

Positioning the pointer and then quickly pressing and releasing the mouse button twice without moving the mouse. Double-clicking is used to open applications and documents (when the pointer is an arrow) and to select whole words (when the pointer is an I-beam).

downloading

Retrieving information from a distant computer and storing it on your own. Opposite of *uploading*.

dpi

An abbreviation for *dots per inch*.

dpsi, dpi²

Abbreviations for *dots per square inch*.

dragging

Placing the pointer, holding down the mouse button, moving the mouse and then releasing the button. If you place the pointer on an object, dragging moves the object. If you place the pointer where there is no object, dragging generates the selection rectangle. If you place the pointer on a menu title, dragging moves you down the menu (and if you release the button when a command is highlighted, chooses the command).

DRAM *(DEE-ram)*

A *dynamic RAM* (memory) chip. *(Dynamic* simply means it loses its memory when you shut the computer off.) Also see *SIMM*.

draw program

A graphics program that generates objects, which are treated as units, rather than a series of dots. Compare *paint program*.

draw/paint program

A graphics program that combines the features of *draw programs* and *paint programs*.

driver

A piece of software that tells a computer how to run an outside device—typically a printer—or that emulates doing that (for example, it might tell the computer how to print a file to disk as if it were sending it to a printer).

Edit menu

In the Finder and in most applications, the third menu from the left. It typically contains commands for cutting, copying, pasting, undoing, etc. One of the three *standard menus*.

ellipsis

This symbol (...) after a menu item is supposed to mean that you'll be asked for more information before the command executes. But it's sometimes used for other things, as in the case of the first item on the  menu, *About the Finder...* (or whatever program you happen to be using), which merely presents you with a message box.

E-mail

Electronic mail; messages sent from computer to computer over phone lines.

encapsulated PostScript

See *EPS*.

[Enter] key

A key on the Mac's keyboard that doesn't generate a character and is used for different purposes by various applications. In dialog boxes and on the Desktop, the [Return] key usually has the same effect as the [Enter] key.

EPS *(pronounced as separate letters)*

Encapsulated PostScript, a format for graphic images that consists of structured PostScript code. Compare *MacPaint, PICT* and *TIFF.*

Sometimes known as *EPSF* (the *f* stands for *file* or *files*). Aside from the fact that the extra letter is unnecessary, it leads to barbarisms like *EPSF files (encapsulated PostScript file files).* This reminds me of people who refer to a long street south of San Francisco as *the El Camino,* which means literally *the the road).* Actually, the offices of Adobe (developer and publisher of Post-Script) aren't far from El Camino; maybe it had an influence.

expansion slot
See *slot.*

facsimile machine
See *fax machine.*

FatBits
A feature, originated by MacPaint, that lets you edit graphics in a magnified view, dot by dot.

fax machine
A device that scans documents, transmits them over phone lines and recreates them at the other end.

field
A specific portion of a *record.* For example, if the record is in a mailing list program, there will be—at least—a name field, an address field, a city field, a state field and field for the zip code.

In the field means anywhere but the factory where a computer— or any piece of hardware—is manufactured. *We've designed this system so just about any repair can be made in the field.*

file
A collection of information on a disk, usually either a *document* or an *application.* (Although the information in a file is normally cohesive—that is, about one thing—it doesn't actually have to be; what makes it a file is simply that it's lumped together and called by one name.)

File menu
On the Desktop and in virtually all applications, the second menu from the left. Within applications it contains commands for opening, saving, printing and closing documents, quitting the application and so on. In the Finder, it contains commands for

opening and closing windows, duplicating icons, ejecting disks and so on. One of the three *standard menus.*

Finder

The basic program that generates the Desktop and lets you access and manage files and disks. Together with the System file and the Mac's ROMs, it comprises what—on other computers—is called the *operating system.* There are many *Finder substitutes,* including *MultiFinder.*

Finder substitute

A program that performs the same basic tasks as the Finder (and usually gives you other capabilities as well).

Fkey *(EFF-kee)*

An Fkey is a small program, like a simple desk accessory, that's activated when you press one of the number keys in the top row of your keyboard while holding down ⌘ and Shift .

The standard Mac commands to eject disks (Shift ⌘ –1 and Shift ⌘ –2) and to save or print the screen (Shift ⌘ –3 and Shift ⌘ –4) are Fkeys. The other number keys—0, 5, 6, 7, 8 and 9— are available to store other Fkey programs. The public-domain program Fkey Manager lets you install or remove Fkeys.

floppy disk

A removable disk that's flexible (although the case in which the actual magnetic medium is housed may be hard, as it is on the 3–1/ 2" floppies used by the Mac). See *disk* for more details.

folder

A grouping of documents, applications and other folders that's represented by a folder-shaped icon on the Desktop. Equivalent to a *subdirectory* on MS-DOS machines.

font

A collection of letters, numbers, punctuation marks and symbols with an identifiable and consistent look; a Macintosh typeface in all its sizes and styles.

Font/DA Mover

A utility program used for installing, removing and moving fonts and desk accessories.

footer

A piece of text automatically printed at the bottom of several pages (although the text may vary from page to page—as it would if it contained page numbers, for example).

footprint

The amount of space a device takes up on the surface where it sits.

fragmented memory

If you open and close lots of applications during a work session, your system's memory gets fragmented—split up into little pieces. This can be a problem, because a segment initially set aside for one application may not be big enough for another. Compare *contiguous RAM*.

function keys

Special keys on some Apple keyboards. The dedicated ones do things like delete to the right, summon help or move you to beginning or end of a document. You can assign tasks of your own choosing to the nondedicated ones.

garbage

Bizarre and/or meaningless characters. When garbage appears on your screen, it means something has gone wrong somewhere.

Get Info window

The window that appears when you choose Get Info from the File menu (or hit ⌘-I). It tells you the size of the file, folder or disk, where it resides, and when it was created and last modified. There's also a space for entering comments and, in the case of a file or a disk, a box for locking and unlocking it.

glossary, Glossary

In English, uncapitalized, a list of definitions like this one. In Microsoft Word, capitalized, a set of abbreviations linked with longer text entries. You type the abbreviation—*wds,* say—followed by ⌘ Backspace , and Word automatically inserts the longer phrase (in this case, *wine-dark sea).*

grayed
Another term for *dimmed.*

hang
A condition where the Mac ignores input from the mouse and the keyboard, usually requiring you to restart the system. Compare *bomb* and *crash.*

hard disk
A rigid, usually nonremovable disk and/or the disk drive that houses it. Hard disks stores a lot of data (generally 20MB or more) and access it very quickly. See *disk* for more details.

hardware
The physical components of a computer system.

header
A piece of text automatically printed at the top of several pages (although the text may vary from page to page—as it would if it contained page numbers, for example).

hertz
One cycle per second. Abbreviated **Hz.** The regular electrical current that comes out of a (US) wall socket is 60 Hz—that is, it alternates sixty times a second. Named after the great German physicist, Heinrich Rudolph Hertz (1857–94). Compare *mega-hertz.*

HFS
A multilevel method of organizing applications, documents and folders on a Mac disk in which folders can be nested (contained) in other folders. Now standard on the Mac. Shorthand for *hierarchical file system.* Compare *MFS.*

hierarchical file system
See *HFS.*

highlighting

Making something stand out from its background in order to show that it's selected, chosen or active. On the Mac, highlighting is usually achieved by reversing—that is, by substituting black for white and vice versa.

hot spot

The actual part of the *pointer* that has to be positioned over something for a click to select it (or have some other effect on it). The hot spot of the arrow pointer is its tip, and the hot spot of the crosshairs pointer is its center (where the two lines cross).

human interface

Another name for *user interface*.

Hz

An abbreviation for *hertz*.

I-beam pointer

The shape (⌶) the pointer normally takes when it's dealing with text.

icon

A graphic symbol, usually representing a file, a folder, a disk or a tool.

ImageWriter

A line of dot-matrix printers sold by Apple as the standard, low-end choice for use with Macs. Also see *LaserWriters*.

ImageWriter font

Another name for a *bit-mapped font*.

incremental backup

A backup in which only the files changed since the last backup are copied.

information service

A large commercial timesharing computer that gives users access to a wide variety of information. CompuServe, GEnie and The Source are three examples.

init *(or **init file**)*

A number of useful utilities now come in the form of an *init* (pronounced *in-IT*, the name is short for *initialization*). To make an init work, you simply put it in your system folder; the next time you start up your Mac, the init is read into the System and alters the way things work. (If you want to see it in action right away, choose Restart from the Special menu.) Compare *cdev*.

initialize

To prepare a disk for use on the Macintosh. If it contains information, initializing will remove it. Disks can be initialized again and again.

insertion point

The place in a document where the next keystroke will add or delete text. The insertion point is represented by a blinking vertical line and is placed by clicking with the *I-beam pointer* or hitting the *arrow keys*.

K

A measure of computer memory, disk space and the like that's equal to 1024 characters, or about 170 words. Short for kilobyte. Compare *meg*.

kerning

Closing up the space between letters in certain combinations— like *A V* or *To*— to make them look better.

LAN *(pronounced as one word)*

Abbreviation for *local area network*.

laser font

Another name for an *outline font*.

laser printer

A kind of computer printer that creates images by drawing them on a metal drum with a laser. The image is then made visible by electrostatically attracting dry ink powder to it, as in a photocopying machine.

LaserWriter
A line of laser printers sold by Apple. Also see *ImageWriters*.

launching
Opening an application.

leading *(LEHD-ing)*
The amount of space from one line of type to the next. Usually measured in *points*.

list box
A box with scroll bars that appears within a dialog box or other window and lists things—files, fonts or whatever. The *Open...* and *Save As...* dialog boxes contain list boxes, and the Font/DA Mover contains two.

local area network
A network of computer equipment confined to a relatively small area—like one office or one building—and usually connected by dedicated lines, rather than by regular telephone lines. Abbreviated *LAN*.

LocalTalk
Apple's *local area network*. It's used to connect Mac's and laser printers, among other things. Previously called *AppleTalk*.

locking
Preventing a file or disk from being changed (until you unlock it). To lock a file, you use the Get Info window. To lock a floppy disk, you move the plastic tab so that you can see through the small hole. On a disk, another name for *locked* is *write-protected*.

LQ
Letter-quality. Said of printers.

MacPaint
In addition to being the first *paint program* on the Mac, MacPaint is also the name of a standard graphics format for low-resolution (72-dpi) bit-mapped images. Compare *EPS, PICT and TIFF*.

macro

A command that incorporates two or more other commands (and/or text). The name comes from the idea that macro commands incorporate "micro" commands.

macro program

Software that creates *macros* by recording your keystrokes and mouse clicks or by giving you a sort of pseudo programming language to write them in.

magnetic media

See *media.*

MB

Abbreviation for *megabyte.*

media

The generic name for floppy disks, hard disks (the disks themselves, not the devices that record on them), tapes and any other substance that stores computer data in the form of magnetic impulses.

meg, megabyte

A measure of computer memory, disk space and the like that's equal to 1024K (1,048,576 characters) or about 175,000 words. Abbreviated *MB.*

Sometimes people try to make a meg equal to an even million characters, usually for sleazeball marketing purposes. We call this smaller "meg" a *minimeg.*

megahertz

A million cycles a second. Used to describe the speed of computer chips (and therefore of the computers built around them). Abbreviated *MHz. The Mac II runs at 16MHz, the SE at 8MHz.* Also see *hertz.*

memory

The short-term retention of information electronically, on *chips.* It disappears when you turn your computer off. Compare *storage.*

There are two main types of computer memory: *RAM,* which is used for the short-term retention of information (that is, until the power is turned off) and *ROM,* which is used to store programs that are seldom if ever changed.

Here are some examples of how memory has grown:

machine	RAM	ROM
original Mac	128K	64K
Mac Plus	1MB	128K
Mac II	1–8MB	256K
LaserWriter I	1.5MB	512K
LaserWriter II NTX	2–12MB	1MB

menu

A list of commands. Compare *palette.* Also see *pop-down menu, pop-up menu, submenu* and *tear-off menu.*

menu bar

The horizontal area across the top of the screen that contains the menu titles.

menu title

Both the name by which a menu is called and the way you access it. Menu titles are arranged across the top of the screen in the menu bar; when you point to one and hold down the mouse button, the menu pops down.

message box

A box that appears unbidden on the screen to give you some information, and which doesn't require any information back from you. A *bomb message* is one example. Also called an *alert box.*

MFS

A single-level method of organizing files and folders on a Mac disk in which folders can't be nested (contained) in other folders.

Originally standard on the Mac, it's been superseded by *HFS*. The name is short for *Macintosh file system*.

MHz
An abbreviation for *megahertz*.

minimegs
Our name for "megabytes" that are figured at one million characters each instead of the standard 1,048,576 characters (1024K).

modem *(MOE-dum)*
A device that lets computers talk to each other over phone lines (you also need a communications program). The name is short for *modulator-demodulator*.

modifier key
A key that modifies the meaning of the *character key* being pressed. The standard ADB keyboard has five: Shift, Option, ⌘, Caps Lock and *control.*

modules
Parts of a program that are separate yet interconnected.

monospaced
Said of fonts where all the characters occupy the same amount of horizontal space. One such font on the Mac is Monaco. Compare *proportionally spaced.*

motherboard
The main *board* in a computer (or other computer device).

mouse button
The button on top of the mouse (used to distinguish it from a button in a dialog box).

mouse cursor
A barbaric substitute for the perfectly adequate—and infinitely more elegant—term *pointer.* Its use can only be attributed to creeping PC-itis in the Macintosh world.

MultiFinder

An Apple that allows several applications, including the Finder, to be open at the same time (although, as of this writing, it doesn't support multitasking).

multitasking

Said of software or hardware that lets you do more than one thing at once.

multiuser

Said of software or hardware that supports use by more than one person.

nanosecond

A billionth of a second. Used to measure the speed of memory chips, among other things. Abbreviated *NS*.

NLQ

Near-letter-quality. Said of printers.

NS

Abbreviation for *nanosecond*.

numeric keypad

A grouping of number keys arranged in a square (and other, associated keys), distinct from the regular keyboard (and usually to the right of it).

NumLock (or Num. Lock)

On keyboards with a *numeric keypad*, the setting in which the keys insert numbers into your document (rather than issue commands). In this book, we use the term *command mode* to indicated *NumLock off*. On most Mac keyboards, there is no key for switching between NumLock and command mode; it's handled by the software instead.

object-oriented graphic

A picture or other graphic where each object, rather than being made up of separate dots (as in a *bit-mapped* graphic) is treated as a unit, as they are in MacDraw and many other drawing and drafting programs.

So if you have a bit-mapped rectangle, you can erase a corner of it (say). But you also have to lasso (or somehow group) all the dots to select it as a unit (in order to move it, for example). An object-oriented rectangle can be selected simply by clicking on it, but you can't cut off a corner of it—it has to remain a square (or at least a four-sided polygon of some kind.

on-line

On, or actively connected to, a computer. For example, on-line documentation appears on the screen rather than in a manual.

(to) open

To expand an icon, or a name in a list box, to a window. With disk icons and folders, this happens on the Desktop. With document icons, the application that created the icon is launched first, then the document is opened within it.

operating system

The basic program that controls a computer's operation. On the Mac, it consists of the *System file*, the *ROMs* and the *Finder* (or a Finder substitute).

[Option]

A *modifier key* used mostly for generating special characters.

option character

The combination of the [Option] key and another character.

outline font

A font designed for use on a laser printer or typesetter. Rather than being composed of separate dots like a *bit-mapped* font, it's made up an outline of the shape of each letter which can be scaled to any size. Sometimes also called a *laser font*. Also see *PostScript font*.

paint program

A graphics program that generates series of dots rather than objects. Compare *paint program*.

palette
A collection of small symbols, usually enclosed by rectangles, like MacPaint's or MacDraw's tool palettes. Compare *menu*.

parameter RAM
A small portion of the Mac's *RAM* that's used to store Control Panel settings and other basic, ongoing information. It's powered by a battery so the settings aren't lost when the computer is turned off (but they are lost if you pull the battery). Sometimes called *PRAM*.

PARC
See *Xerox PARC*.

pasting
Inserting something into a document from the Clipboard by choosing Paste from the Edit menu or hitting ⌘ -V.

patch
A set of instructions you add to a program.

path name
A term borrowed from the PC world. On the Mac, it means all the folders a file is in, listed in order from the largest (most distant) to the smallest. To be precise, a path name should start with the name of the disk all this is taking place on. So, for example, the path name:

hard disk

   personal stuff

      letters

         to family

            Happy Birthday, Rita!

means that the file called *Happy Birthday, Rita*! is in the folder called to *family* which is in the folder called *letters* which is in the folder called *personal stuff* which is on the hard disk called—rather unimaginatively—*hard disk*.

PC

Some people use this term as an abbreviation for "personal computer" and would even call a Mac a PC! We, however, use the term properly—to mean an IBM Personal Computer or a clone thereof. To our ears, calling a Mac a PC is like calling a Mercedes a Buick.

Just to complicate things, *PC* is also used among technical types as a short way of saying *printed circuit*. So a **PC board** doesn't necessarily go into an IBM PC; in fact, there's one in every Mac.

peripheral

Any electronic device connected to a computer—e.g., a printer or hard disk. Usually only refers to something that's either sold by a *third party* or that clearly isn't an integral part of the original system. For example, you wouldn't normally think of the Mac Plus keyboard (sold with the machine) as a peripheral, but you might very well consider a third-party keyboard for the Mac II a peripheral.

pica

A typesetting measure equal (for all practical purposes) to 1/6 of an inch—and exactly equal to 12 *points*.

PICT *(pronounced as one word)*

A standard format for object-oriented graphics. (The name is an abbreviation of *picture.*) Compare *EPS, MacPaint* and *TIFF*.

pixel

Any of the little dots of light that make up the picture on a computer (or TV) screen. The more pixels there are, the higher the *resolution.* (The name is short for *picture element.*) Sometimes simply called *dots*.

point

A typesetting measure equal (for all practical purposes) to 1/72 of an inch. The size of fonts is typically measured in points. Compare *pica*.

pointer

What moves on the screen when you move the mouse. Its most common shapes are the *arrow*, the *I-beam* and the *wristwatch*.

pop down

What the Mac's regular menus actually do. Compare *pull down*.

pop-down menu

The Mac's standard kind of menu (usually—but inaccurately—called a *pull-down menu*). It pops down when you point to the menu title; to keep it extended, you hold down the mouse button. Dragging down the menu highlights each command in turn (except the dimmed ones). Compare *pop-up menu*. Also see *submenu* and tear-*off menu*.

pop-up menu

A Mac menu whose title doesn't appear in the *title bar* and which, as its name implies, pops up rather than down. Pop-up menus appear when you click and hold the mouse button on a box that generates them (which is indicated by a drop shadow around the box). Compare *pop-down menu*. Also see *submenu* and tear-*off menu*.

port

Computerese for a jack where you plug in the cables that connect computers and other devices together. Most Macs have a *SCSI* port, two serial ports (marked for the printer and modem), etc.

PostScript

A page-description programming language developed by Adobe, specifically designed to handle text and graphics and their placement on a page. Used primarily in laser printers and typesetters. Compare *QuickDraw*.

PostScript font

An *outline font* that works with PostScript (although PostScript does also make its own versions of *bit-mapped* fonts when you send them to a PostScript printer.)

PRAM *(pronounced as one word)*
See *parameter RAM*. Don't confuse this with *PROM*.

print buffer
A hardware device that intercepts a print file on its way to the printer and reroutes it to the buffer's own memory, where it's held until the printer is ready for it. This allows you to continue working on other things while the printing takes place.

printed circuit board
A *board* on which the electrical connections between the *chips* are made by printed metallic ink. There's one in every Mac. Also called a *PC board*.

printer driver
A file that tells the Mac how to send information to a particular kind of printer.

print spooler
A piece of software that intercepts a print file on its way to the printer and reroutes it to the disk, where it's held until the printer is ready for it. This allows you to continue working on other things while the printing takes place.

program
A group of instructions that tells a computer what to do. Also called *software* and, by employees of the Department of Redundancy Department, a *software program*.

programmer's switch
A small piece of plastic that, when inserted in the vents on the side of the Mac, allows you to restart the system (using its *reset button*) or access debugging software (using its *interrupt button*).

PROM *(pronounced as one word)*
A programmable *ROM;* one you can change with a special device.

proportionally spaced

Said of fonts whose characters occupy different amounts of horizontal space, depending on their size. Proportional spacing makes fonts much easier to read. Virtually all Macintosh fonts are proportionally spaced. Compare *monospaced*.

public-domain

Said of products you have the right to copy, use, give away and sell, without having to pay any money for the right. Things come into the public domain either because the copyright on them has expired or—as is the case with computer programs—because the copyright holder (usually the author) puts them there. Compare *shareware* and *commercial*.

pull down

What most people—including Apple—say the Mac's standard menus do. But it's not true—they *pop* down.

pull-down menu

The official but inaccurate name for what should be called a *pop-down menu*.

QuickDraw

Bill Atkinson's brilliant programming routines that enable the Mac to display graphic elements on the screen with great speed and agility. Also used for outputting text and images to certain printers. Compare *PostScript*.

(to) quit

To leave an application and return to the Finder (or a Finder equivalent).

radio buttons

A group of *buttons* only one of which can be on at a time (like the presets on your car radio). If you select one radio button, any other that's selected automatically deselects. Compare *check boxes*.

RAM (pronounced as one word)

The part of a computer's memory used for the short-term retention of information (in other words, until the power is turned off). Programs and documents are stored in RAM while you're using them. The name is short for "random-access memory"—although, actually, just about all kinds of memory are accessed randomly these days. Also see *memory, parameter RAM, contiguous RAM* and *ROM.*

RAM cache

An area of memory set aside to hold information recently read in from disk—so that if the information is needed again, it can be gotten from memory, which is much faster than getting it from disk. The size of the Mac's RAM cache, and whether it's even turned on, is set on the Control Panel.

reboot

To *boot* again (that was easy).

record

In a database program, a collection of related *fields.* For example, in a mailing list, a record might consist of the name, address, city, state, zip code and phone number of one particular person or company.

relational database

A database program which is capable of relating information in one file to that in another.

Restart

A command on the Finder's Special menu that *reboots* the Mac—that is, makes it start up again as if you'd just turned it on. Compare *Shut Down.*

release version

The version of a program that's actually shipped to purchasers and stores. Theoretically, all the major bugs are out of it by that point. Compare *alpha version* and *beta version.*

[Return] key

In text, the [Return] key causes the insertion point to move to the beginning of the next line. Elsewhere, it's often used to confirm an entry or a command.

ROM *(pronounced as one word)*
The part of a computer's memory used to store programs which are seldom or never changed. The name is short for "read-only memory," because you can read information from it but can't write information to it the way you can with *RAM*. A ROM chip is often called simply *a ROM*. Also see *memory*.

ROMs *(the Mac's)*
ROMs built into every Mac that contain part of its operating system. They were originally 64K, then 128K, then 256, with each subsequent version containing more stuff.

root directory
The *disk window*—the *folder* that contains all the other folders (and files) on a disk.

sans serif
Said of a font that has no *serifs*.

Save As...
A standard Mac command that lets you save a document under a different name, in a different location, or both. Sometimes it also lets you save the document in a different format.

saving
Transferring information—usually a document—from memory to a disk.

scanner
A device that converts images into digital form so that they can be stored and manipulated by computers.

Scrapbook
A desk accessory that stores material permanently and gives you easy access to it no matter what program you're in.

screen font
The *bit-mapped* version of an *outline font*, used to represent the outline font on the computer's screen.

screenful

The amount of text (or other data) displayed at any given time on the screen. Used when talking about scrolling—e.g., *clicking here scrolls you up one screenful.*

scroll arrow

The arrow at either end of the scroll bar. Clicking on a scroll arrow moves the window's view up or down one line. Pointing to a scroll arrow and holding the mouse button down results in relatively smooth and continuous scrolling.

scroll bar

A rectangular bar that appears on the right and/or bottom edges of a window when there's more in it than what's displayed. Clicking in the gray area of the scroll bar moves the window's view up or down one screenful. Also see scroll arrow and scroll box.

scroll box

The white box in the scroll bar that indicates how what's displayed in a window relates to its total contents. Dragging the scroll box allows you to scroll large distances.

scrolling

Moving through the contents of a window or a list box in order to see things not currently displayed (normally done with the scroll bar). Scrolling is usually vertical, but horizontal scrolling is also possible.

SCSI

An industry-standard interface for hard disks and other devices that allows for very fast transfer of information. It's short for *small computer system interface* and is pronounced *scuzzy* by virtually everyone (officially, you're supposed to say *ESS-SEE-ESS-EYE*). SCSI ports have been standard on all Macs since the Plus.

search path

Where a computer looks for something (i.e., on what disks and in what folders).

selecting

Telling the Mac what you want to be affected by the next command or action. If what you're selecting is in the form of discrete objects, you normally select them by clicking on them. If it's in the form of a continuum, you normally select part of it by dragging across it

The two most important concepts for understanding the Mac are:

- Selecting—in and of itself—never alters anything.

- You always have to select something before you can do anything to it.

(the) selection

Whatever is selected (and thus will be affected by the next command or action). The insertion point is also a kind of selection, because it indicates where the next event will take place (unless you move it).

selection rectangle

On the Desktop and in many applications, a dotted box that appears when you click on an empty spot and drag. When you release the mouse button, the box disappears and everything that fell within it is selected.

serif

A little hook, line or blob added to the basic form of a character to make a font more readable or for decoration. *Serif* is also used as an adjective to describe a font that has serifs; e.g., *Korinna is a serif font.* Compare *sans serif.*

shareware

Software that's distributed on the honor system, usually through bulletin boards, user groups, information services, etc. You're allowed to try it out and give copies to others, and you only pay the (usually nominal) registration fee if you decide you want to continue using it. Compare *commercial* and *public-domain.*

Shift key

Either of two *modifier keys* on the Mac's keyboard that are used to make letters uppercase and for many other purposes (for example, see *shift-clicking*).

shift-clicking

Holding down the Shift key while clicking the mouse button. Shift-clicking allows you to select multiple objects or large amounts of text, depending on the application.

Shut Down

A command on the Finder's Special menu that prepares the Mac to be turned off (or actually turns it off). Compare *Restart*.

SIG *(pronounced as one word)*

A *special interest group* that's part of a larger organization like a *user group*.

SIMM *(pronounced as one word)*

A *single in-line memory module*—a package for *DRAM* memory chips used in many models of the Mac.

68000 *(sixty-eight thousand)*

A *CPU chip* used in the original 128K Mac, the 512K Mac, the Mac Plus, the SE, the original LaserWriter, the LaserWriter Plus, the LaserWriter II SC and the LaserWriter II NT.

68020 *(sixty-eight oh twenty)*

A *CPU chip*, faster and more powerful than the 68000, used in the Mac II, the LaserWriter II NTX and many accelerator boards.

68030 *(sixty-eight oh thirty)*

A *CPU chip*, faster and more powerful than the 68020, which will presumably be used in future Mac products.

size box

An icon consisting of two overlapping boxes, found in the bottom right corner of most windows, that allows you to change the window's size and shape. Compare *close box* and *zoom box*.

slot

A place in a computer where you can install a *card*. Also called an *expansion slot,* since it allows you to expand the computer's capabilities.

software

The instructions that tell a computer what to do. Also called *programs* or, redundantly, *software programs.*

special interest group

See *SIG.*

spooler

See *print spooler.*

standard menus

The three menus—, File and Edit—that appear at the left end of the menu bar in virtually all applications.

startup disk

The disk that contains the System file and Finder the Mac is currently using. You can change it, so it doesn't necessarily have to be the disk you actually started up the Mac with.

storage

The long-term retention of information magnetically (on disks or tapes) or optically (on *CD ROMs*). It persists after you turn your computer off. Compare *memory.*

string

Any specified sequence of characters—a word, a phrase, a number, whatever. The term is usually used in the context of searching and replacing; for example: type in the string you want to find, hit the tab key, then type in the string you want to replace it with.

style

A variation on a font—like bold, italic, outline or shadow. In this sense, it's also called a *type style.* Compare *Style.*

Style

In Microsoft Word and some other programs, a Style is a grouping of formats. In this book, we capitalize this second meaning of the word, to avoid confusion (as much as possible) with *style* (see the previous definition).

submenu

A menu whose title is an item on another menu, and which appears to the right of that menu when you choose its title.

suitcase file (or simply *suitcase*)

This kind of file, identified in the Finder by its suitcase-shaped icon, stores fonts or desk accessories. To open a suitcase file and use the font(s) or desk accessory(ies) in it, you need either the Font/DA Mover or a font/DA management program like Suitcase or Font/DA Juggler Plus.

support

Help with computer problems (either hardware or software), usually in the form of verbal advice. Support should be provided primarily by the vendor that sells you the product and only secondarily by the manufacturer or publisher.

system bomb

See *bomb.*

system crash

See *crash.*

system disk

Any disk containing the system software the Mac needs to begin operation (i.e., the *System file* and either the *Finder* or a Finder substitute).

System file (or simply *the System*)

The basic program the Mac uses to start itself and to provide certain information—like what fonts are available—to all applications. The System file can't be launched like a regular application; instead, it launches itself when you start up the Mac and insert a disk that contains it. Together with the Finder, the System file comprises what—on other computers—is called the *operating system.*

system folder
A standard folder on Mac disks that normally contains the System file, the Finder and other systems software.

system hang
See *hang.*

system heap
The area of memory set aside for storing system information about fonts, DAs, chooser resources, init files, etc.

system software
A catchall term for the basic programs that help computers work; it includes operating systems, programming languages, certain utilities and so on. Some examples of systems software on the Mac are the Finder, the System, the Clipboard, the Chooser, the Control Panel, the Font/DA Mover and printer drivers like the ImageWriter, LaserWriter and Laser Prep files.

tab-delimited
Said of database programs and files that follow the Mac standard of using Tab to separate *fields.*

tab key
In text, the tab key moves the insertion point to the next tab stop. In dialog boxes, database files, spreadsheets and the like, it often moves the insertion point to the next area where information can be inserted (in other words, the next field, cell or whatever).

tear-off menu
A *menu* that you can remove from the *menu bar* and move around the screen like a window. It stays fully extended when detached, so you don't have to pop it down every time you want to use it. Tear-off menus always remain in front of open document windows. Compare *pop-down menu, pop-up menu* and *submenu.*

telecommunications
Transferring information between computers over telephone lines.

template *(TEM-plit, not -plate)*
A document with a special format you use repeatedly. You modify it to the present use and save it with a different name.

text box
An area, usually in a *dialog box,* where you insert text.

third-party
Describes hardware (or sometimes software) made neither by the manufacturer of the major piece of hardware (or software) involved nor by you, the user. For example: a non-Apple hard disk you attach to your Mac, or a spelling checker not published by the publisher of the word processing program you're using it with. (But if you write a small utility program and use it yourself, that's not third-party.)

TIFF *(pronounced as one word)*
A standard graphics format for high-resolution (greater than 72-dpi) bit-mapped images, like those generated by most scanners. The name is an abbreviation of *tagged image file format.* Compare *EPS, MacPaint* and *PICT.*

title bar
The horizontal strip at the top of a window that includes the name and the close box, and tells you whether or not the window is active (it is if the title bar is filled with horizontal stripes). To move a window, you grab it by the title bar.

toggle
Something which turns off and on each successive time you access it. For example, the common type styles (bold, italic, etc.) are toggles, because the first time you choose them from the menu (or with a command), they turn on, and the next time they turn off. Other kinds of toggles are *check boxes* and menu items that switch names (e.g., *Show Ruler, Hide Ruler*).

Trojan Horse program
A program whose sole purpose for existing is to conceal and transport a *virus.*

undo
A standard Mac command (⌘–Z) that undoes the last text that was typed or the last command that was given.(Selecting, scrolling, splitting a window or changing its size or location can't be undone. So, for example, if you type some characters and then scroll the document, undo will remove the characters but won't reverse the scrolling.)

In a well-written Mac program, *undo* is a *toggle,* so you can flip back and forth between two versions of something until you decide which you prefer.

uploading
Sending information to a distant computer from your own. Opposite of *downloading.*

user group *(or **users group**)*
A club made up of people who are interested in computers in general, a particular kind of computer, a particular kind of software or even an individual program. They're typically nonprofit and independent of any computer manufacturer or publisher. Also see *SIG.*

user interface
The way a computer communicates with people; what it's like to use.

utility
A program that performs a relatively simple task—like searching for a specific file on a disk, or counting all the words in a document. Unlike applications, utilities normally don't generate documents.

vaporware
Software that was announced a while ago but still hasn't shipped.

virus

A program whose sole purpose is to surreptitiously invade computers and modify the data on them, usually destructively.

wildcard

A symbol that means *any character* or *any sequence of characters* (just as a wild card in poker can stand for any card). Wildcards are useful in searches.

window

An enclosed area on the Mac's screen that has a *title bar* by which you can move it around). Disks and folder icons open into windows, and documents appear in windows when you're working on them. Compare *box.*

windowful

The amount of text (or other data) displayed at any given time in a window. Used when talking about scrolling—e.g., *clicking here scrolls you up one windowful.*

wristwatch

The shape the pointer normally takes (and should take) when you have to wait for the Mac to do something (although some poorly written programs don't always implement this feature, or do so less often than they need to).

Xerox PARC *(ZEER-ahks PARK)*

Xerox Corporation's Palo Alto Research Center where most of the early work was done on what became the Mac's *user interface.* Often called simply *PARC.*

zoom box

A small box on the right side of the title bar of most windows. Clicking on the zoom box expands the window to fill the screen; clicking again returns it to its original size and shape. (In many Microsoft products, you can do the same thing by simply double-clicking on the title bar.) Compare *close box* and *size box.*

Appendix B

List
of
companies
and
products

Accelerator / Radius

Access Technology
6 Pleasant St
South Natick MA 01760
508/375-1531
   MindWrite
   Trapeze

Acta / Symmetry

Addison-Wesley
Route 128
Reading MA 01867
617/944-3700
   Human Interface Guidelines:
   The Apple Desktop Interface
   and other books written by Apple

Adler, Darin
2765 Marl Oak Dr
Highland Park IL 60035
312/433-5944
   SkipFinder
   StartupDesk

Adobe Systems
1585 Charleston Rd
Mountain View CA 94039
415/961-4400
   Illustrator
   laser fonts *(Benguiat, Optima,*
      Zapf Chancery, many others)
   PostScript

Affinity Microsystems
Suite 425, 1050 Walnut St
Boulder CO 80302
800/367-6771, 303/ 442-4840
   Tempo

Aker, Sharon Zardetto
   (computer writer & consultant)
20 Coutland Dr
Sussex NJ 07461
201/875-6552

Alderman, Eric *(computer consultant & writer,*
   HyperCard programmer)
4798 Geranium Pl
Oakland CA 94619
415/530-8533

Aldus
Suite 200, 411 First Av South
Seattle WA 98104
206/622-5500
   FreeHand
   PageMaker

ALSoft
Box 927
Spring TX 77383
713/353-4090
   DiskExpress
   Font/DA Juggler

Amortize 2.1 / Walsh, Jerry C.

Ann Arbor Softworks
Suite 106, 2393 Teller Rd
Newbury Park CA 91320
805/375-1467
   FullPaint

Anti-Glare Magnification Screen / Sher-Mark
   Products

APG (Upper Midwest Industries)
1601 67th Av North
Brooklyn Center MN 55430
612/560-1440
   APG Cash Drawer

Apple Computer
20525 Mariani Av
Cupertino CA 95014
408/996-1010
   bit-mapped fonts *(Chicago,*
      Geneva, etc.)
   CD Drive
   HyperCard
   ImageWriter printers
   laser fonts *(Times, Helvetica,*
      Courier, Symbol)
   LaserWriter printers
   LocalTalk network
   Macintosh computers
   MacTerminal
   Scanner

Asher Engineering
15115 Ramona Blvd
Baldwin Park CA 91706
800/824-3522 (CA: 818/962-4063)
   quadLYNX Trackball

Ashton-Tate
20101 Hamilton Av
Torrance CA 90502
213/329-8000
   dBASE Mac
   FullPaint
   FullWrite

Autoblack / Itty Bitty Computers

AutoMac III /
   Genesis Micro Software

Autosave DA / Magic Software

Avery International
Consumer Products Division
Azusa CA 91702
    labels for printers and disks

Backdrop / TOPS

Baker Graphics
204 Court St
Box G-826
New Bedford MA 02742
800/338-1753 (MA: 617/996-6732)
    BakerForms

Balance of Power / Mindscape

Batteries Included
30 Mural St
Richmond Hill, Ontario
L4B 1B5 Canada
800/387-6707
    BatteryPak

BatteryPak / Batteries Included

BCS / *see* Boston Computer Society

Beamer, Scott (computer consultant)
180 Stonewall Rd
Berkeley CA 94705
415/848-5923

Becker, Loftus E., Jr
41 Whitney St
Hartford CT 06105
203/523-9558
    Other...

Benguiat (laser font) / Adobe

Berkeley Macintosh Users Group
    former name of BMUG

Berkeley System Design
1708 Shattuck Av
 Berkeley CA 94709
415/540-5536
    Stepping Out

BIX
800/227-2983

Blyth Software
1065 E Hillsdale Blvd
Foster City CA 94404
415/571-0222
    Omnis 3

BMUG
Suite 62, 1442 A Walnut St
Berkeley CA 94709
415/849-HELP, 549-BMUG,
    849-9114
    BMUG on HyperCard
    PD ROM
    public-domain & shareware disks

Bookmark / Intellisoft International

Borderline (bit-mapped font) / CasadyWare

Borland International
4585 Scotts Valley Dr
Scotts Valley CA 95066
408/438-8400
    Reflex
    Sidekick

Boston Computer Society
48 Grove St
Somerville MA 02144
617/625-7080

Bradley, Michael (technical writer)
3825 14th Av
Oakland CA 94602
415/482-2862

Bravo Technologies
c/o DPAS, Box T
Gilroy CA 95021
800/345-2888
    MacCalc

Broderbund Software
17 Paul Drive
San Rafael CA 94903
415/492-3500
    PosterMaker Plus

Bullseye Software
Box 7900
Incline Village NV 89450
702/831-2523
    Fokker Triplane

Business Filevision / Marvelin

Cairo (bit-mapped font) /
    Apple Computer

Calculator Construction Set /
    Dubl-Click Software

CalendarMaker / CE Software

Calligraphy (bit-mapped font) / CasadyWare

Canvas / Deneba Software

Capture / Mainstay

CasadyWare
Box 223779
Carmel CA 93922
408/646-4660
 Fluent Fonts
  (bit-mapped and laser)

Century Software
2306 Cotner Av
Los Angeles CA 90064
213/829-4436
 LaserFonts

CE Software
801 73d St
Des Moines IA 50312
515/224-1995
 CalendarMaker
 DiskTop
 MockWrite
 QuicKeys

Challenger Software
18350 Kedzie Av
Homewood IL 60430
800/858-9565, 312/957-3475
 Mac3D 2.0

Champion Swiftware
6617 Gettysburg Dr
Madison WI 53705
608/833-1777
 Spelling Champion

Chesley, Harry R.
1850 Union St
San Francisco CA 94123
 Packit III

Chicago (bit-mapped font) /
 Apple Computer

Chubby Shadow (bit-mapped font) /
 CasadyWare

C. Itoh Electronics
2025 McCabe Wy
Irvine CA 92714
800/227-0315
 ProWriter printers

Claris
440 Clyde Av
Mountain View CA 94043
415/960-1500
 FileMaker
 MacDraw
 MacPaint
 MacWrite

Clement, Gerald (Macintosh artist)
Diablo Valley Design
7138 Shelter Creek Lane
San Bruno CA 94066
415/589-8806

ClickArt / T/Maker

The Clipper / Solutions International

The Cobb Group
Box 24480
Louisville KY 40224
 Excellence (journal)
 books on Excel

Coleman, Dale (computer writer)
1426 Willard St
San Francisco CA 94117
415/681-1791

Colorprint / I/O Design

Comment / Deneba Software

Complementary Type /
 Software Complement

CompuServe
Box 20212
Columbus OH 43220
800/848-8199 (OH: 614/457-8600)

Computer Cover Company
Box 3080
Laguna Hills CA 92654
800/235-5330 (CA: 800/237-5376)
 computer covers

Computer Friends
14250 NW Science Park Dr
Portland OR 97229
503/626-2291
 Dunn film recorders *(distributor)*
 Modern Artist color paint

printer buffers
program
ribbon re-inkers
Shinko color printers *(distributor)*
SuperChroma video boards
switches
TV Producer video boards

Courier (laser font) /
   Apple Computer

CP290M Home Control Interface /
   X-10

Creighton Development
16 Hughes St
Irvine CA 92718
   Macspell+

Cricket Software
40 Valley Stream Parkway
Malvern PA 19355
215/251-9890
   Cricket Draw

The Curator / Solutions International

Custom Memory Systems
826 N Hillview Dr
Milpitas CA 95035
   DM Capture
   removable hard disks

DataDesk International
7650 Haskell Av
Van Nuys CA 91406
818/780-1673
   HyperDialer
   MAC-101 keyboard

DataFrame (hard disks) / SuperMac

DataPak Software
Suite 507, 14011 Ventura Blvd
Sherman Oaks CA 91423
818/905-6419
   Liberty Spell Checker

Dataviz
16 Winfield St
Norwalk CT 06855
   MacLink

Dayna Communications
Fifth Floor, 50 S Main St
Salt Lake City UT 84144
801/531-0600
   DaynaFile

dBASE Mac / Ashton-Tate

Deja Vu / Mindscape

Dell'Aquila, Mei-Ying
   (Macintosh artist)
3450 Princeton Way
Santa Clara CA 95051
408/246-8875

Deneba Software
Suite 202, 7855 NW 12th St
Miami FL 33126
800/6-CANVAS, 305/594-6965
   Canvas
   Comment
   Spelling Coach

Desk Necessities / MicroSPARC

DeskScene / PBI

Desktop Express / Dow Jones

Desktop Help / Help Software

Desktop Publishing
   (Bove & Rhodes Inside Report)
Suite 600, 501 Second St
San Francisco CA 94107
415/ 546-7722

DiskExpress / ALSoft

DiskFit / SuperMac Technologies

DiskInfo / Maitreya Design

DiskTop / CE Software

dMac III / Format Software

DM Capture /
   Custom Memory Systems

Double Helix / Odesta

Dove Computer
1200 N 23 St
Wilmington NC 28405
800/622-7627
   MacSnap memory upgrades

Dow Jones
Box 300
Princeton NJ 08543
609/452-1511

Dream _(bit-mapped font)_ / CasadyWare

Dreams of the Phoenix
Box 10273
Jacksonville FL 32247
   Phoenix 3D
   Quick & Dirty Utilities
   SetFile

Dubl-Click Software
18201 Gresham St
Northridge CA 91325
818/349-2758
   Calculator Construction Set
   WetPaint _(clip art)_
   World Class Fonts _(bit-mapped)_

Dunn film recorders /
   Computer Friends

Easy3D / Enabling Technologies

EasyView Monitor / Nuvotech

Enabling Technologies
600 S Dearborn
Chicago IL 60605
312/427-0386
   Easy3D

Encore Ribbon
Suite E, 1318 Ross
Petaluma CA 94952
800/431-4969
   laser printer cartridge refills

Enzan-Hoshigumi /
   see Qualitas Trading Co

Ergonomic Computer Products
1753 Greenwich St
San Francisco CA 94123
415/ 673-5757
   screen filters, much else

Ergotron
Box 17013
Minneapolis MN 55417
800/328-9829, 612/854-9116
   MacBuffer
   MacTilt
   The Muzzle

Eureka! / PCPC

Excel / Microsoft

Excellence / The Cobb Group

Exodus Software
Suitge 304, 8620 Winton Road
Cincinnati OH 45231
512/522-0011
   Retriever

Farallon Computing
2150 Kittredge St
Berkeley CA 94704
415/849-2331
   MacRecorder
   PhoneNet
   StarNET

Fedit Plus / MacMaster Systems

Felix / Lightgate

Fifth Generation Systems
1322 Bell Av
Tustin CA 92680
714/259-0541
   PowerStation
   Suitcase

File / Microsoft

FileMaker / Claris

Filevision / Marvelin

Findswell / Working Software

Flight Simulator / Microsoft

Flexware
15404 E Valley Blvd
Industry CA 91746
818/961-0237

Fluent Fonts, Fluent Laser Fonts /
   CasadyWare

Fokker Triplane / Bullseye Software

Font/DA Juggler / ALSoft

Format Software
11770 Bernado Plaza Ct
San Diego CA 92128
   dMac III

Fox Software
118 W South Broadway
Perrysburg OH 43551
419/874-0162
   FoxBASE/Mac

The FreeSoft Company
10828 Lacklink
St Louis MO 63114
314/423-2190
    Red Ryder

FullPaint / Ashton-Tate

FullWrite / Ashton-Tate

General Computer
580 Winter St
 Waltham MA 02154
 617/890-0880
    HyperDrive
    Personal LaserPrinter

Genesis Micro Software
#2, 106 147th Av SE
Bellevue WA 98007
206/747-8512

Geneva *(bit-mapped font)* /
    Apple Computer

GEnie
Dept 02B
Rockville MD 20850
voice: 800/638-9636
data: 800/638-8369

GOfer / Microlytics

GraphicWorks / Mindscape

Great Plains Software
1701 SW 38th St
Box 9739
Fargo ND 58109
701/281-0550

Greene Inc.
15 Via Chualar
Monterey CA 93940
408/375-0910
    QuickDEX

HD Backup / Apple Computer

Helix / Odesta

Help Software
10659A Maplewood Rd
Cupertino CA 95014
408/257-3815
    Desktop Help

Helvetica *(laser font)* /
    Apple Computer

HFS Backup / PCPC

Human Interface Guidelines *(book)* /
    Addison-Wesley

Humanware
2908 Nancy Creek Rd NW
Atlanta GA 30327
404/352-3871
    MacGenogram

HyperCard / Apple Computer

HyperDA / Symmetry

HyperDialer /
    DataDesk International

HyperDrive / General Computer

HyperMedia Group
1832 Woodhaven Way
Oakland CA 94611
415/339-3322

ICOM Simulations
648 S Wheeling Rd
Wheeling IL 60090
312/520-4440
    On Cue

Icon-It! / Olduvai

Images with Impact! / 3G Graphics

InBox / THINK Technologies

Infosphere
4730 SW Macadam
Portland OR 97201
503/226-3620
    MacServe

In-House Accountant / Migent

Innovative Data Design
Suite A, 2280 Bates Av
Concord CA 94520
415/680-6818
    MacDraft

Insight / Layered

Intellisoft International
Box 5055
Novato CA 94948
800/544-MARK
(CA: 415/883-1188)
    Bookmark

International Typeface Corporation
2 Hammarskjold Plaza
New York NY 10017
212/371-0699
    licensed laser fonts

I/O Design
Box 156
Exton PA 19241
800/241-2122
    Colorprint

ITC / see *International Typeface Corporation*
    and/or the name of the particular font

Itty Bitty Computers
Box 6539
San Jose CA 95150
    Autoblack

Jasmine Technologies
55 De Haro St
San Francisco CA 94107
415/621-4339
    Jasmine hard disks

JoliWrite / Widemann, Benoit

JustText / Knowledge Engineering

Kensington Microware
251 Park Av South
New York NY 10010
800/535-4242 (NY: 212/475-5200)Mac II
stand
    7' ADB keyboard cable
    6' Mac II monitor cable ext. kit
    System Saver Mac
    Turbo Mouse

Kent Marsh Limited
Suite 210, 1200 Post Oak Blvd
Houston TX 77056
800/325-3587; 713/623-8618
    MacSafe

Klatzkin, Dennis
    (computer consultant & writer)
2263 Market St
San Francisco CA 94114
415/552-0599

Knowledge Engineering
Box 2139
New York NY 10116
212/473-0095
    JustText

LaPorte, Léo
415/661-7374
415/753-3002
    QDial
    Word Count

LaserFonts / Century Software

LaserSpool / Mac America

LaserView monitors / Sigma Designs

Lau, Raymond
100-04 70th Av
Forest Hills NY 11375
GEnie: RAYLAU
CompuServe: 76174,2617
NYMUG: 212/645-9484
    StuffIt

Layered
529 Main St
Boston MA 02129
617/242-7700
    Insight

Letraset
40 Eisenhower Dr
Paramus NJ 07652
    Ready,Set,Go!

Levco
Suite C203, 6160 Lusk Blvd
San Diego CA 92121
619/457-2011
    Prodigy 4 board for Mac Plus & 512K Mac

Liberty Spell Checker /
    DataPak Software

Lightgate
6202 Christie Av
Emeryville CA 94608
415/596-2350
    Felix

Lisas / The Lisa Shop
    or Sun Remarketing

The Lisa Shop
2438 13th Av S
Minneapolis MN 55404
612/874-8596
　　Lisa (Mac XL) computers & parts

Living Videotext
117 Easy St (!)
Mountain View CA 94043
800/441-7234, 415/964-6300
　　More
　　ThinkTank

Lobovits, Dean
Suite 15, 2955 Shattuck Av
Berkeley CA 94705
415/845-2992

Looking Good in Print /
　　Ventana Press

Lookup / Working Software

Lotus Development
55 Cambridge Pkwy
Cambridge MA 02142
617/577-8500
　　Jazz
　　Modern Jazz
　　1-2-3

Lundeen & Associates
Box 30038
Oakland CA 94604
800/233-6851, 415/893-7587
　　WorksPlus Command
　　WorksPlus Spell

Mac America
18032-C Lemon Dr
Yorba Linda CA 92686
714/579-0244
　　LaserSpool

The MACazine
8008 Shoal Creek Blvd
Austin TX 78758
800/624-2346

MacBottom (hard disks) / PCPC

MacBuffer / Ergotron

MacCalc / Bravo Technologies

MacCalligraphy / Qualitas Trading Co.

MacChimney / Swain, Tom

Macreations
329 Horizon Way
Pacifica CA 94044
415/359-7649
　　The Macintosh II Report

MacDraft / Innovative Data Design

MacDraw / Claris

MacGard / Systems Control

MacGenogram / Humanware

MacGuide Magazine
Suite 500, 550 S Wadsworth Blvd
Denver CO 80226

Macintosh Book of Fonts / SourceNet

Macintosh Buyers Guide /
　　Redgate Communications

The Macintosh II Report /
　　Macreations

MacInUse / Softview

MacLarger / Power R

MacLightning / Target Software

MacLink / Dataviz

MacMaster Systems
Suite 122, 939 E EL Camino Real
Sunnyvale CA 94087
408/773-9834
　　Fedit Plus

MacMemory
2480 N First St
San Jose CA 95131
800/262-2636 (CA: 408/922-0140)
　　MaxChill

MAC-101 / DataDesk

MacPaint / Claris

Mac Pascal / Apple Computer

MacRecorder / Farallon Computing

Macropac International
Suite 168
19855 Stevens Creek Blvd
800/624-0077; CA: 408/996-8143
　　101 Macros for Excel

MacSafe / Kent Marsh Limited

Macs-a-Million /
   Sophisticated Circuits

MacServe / Infosphere

MacSnap / Dove Computer

Macspell+ / Creighton Development

MacTable / ScanCoFurn

MacTerminal / Apple Computer

Mac II Review
Building 112, 240 Sunnyvale Av
Fairfield CT 06430
203/334-0334

Mac3D 2.0 / Challenger Software

MacTilt / Ergotron

MacWeek
Box F
Titusville FL 32780

MacWrite / Claris

Mac XL / The Lisa Shop
   or Sun Remarketing

Magic Software
1706 Galvin Rd S
Bellevue NE 68005
800/342-6243, 402/291-0670
   AutoSave DA

Mainstay
5311-B Derry Av
Agoura Hills CA 91301
818/991-6540
   Capture
   TypeNow

Maitreya Design
Box 1480
Goleta CA 93116
   DiskInfo

Managing Your Money /
   MECA Ventures

Marvelin
Suite 3020, 3420 Ocean Park Blvd
Santa Monica CA 90405
213/450-6813
   Business Filevision
   Filevision

MaxChill / MacMemory

MCI Mail
1900 M St NW, Box 1001
Washington DC 20036
800/624-2255

McSink / Signature Software

MDIdeas
Suite 205, 1111 Triton Dr
Foster City CA 94404
415/573-0580
   hard disk drives

MDIdeas HD-20 & HD-30 / MDIdeas

MECA Ventures
355 Riverside Av
Westport CT 06880
203/226-2400
   Managing Your Money

Micah Storage Systems
Suite B, 60 N College Av
Newark DE 19711
800/782-0097, 302/731-0430
   hard disk drives

Michel, Steve (computer consultant & writer,
   HyperCard programmer)
1027 Pomona
Albany CA 94706
415/528-2418

Microlytics
Suite 716, 300 Main St
East Rochester NY 14445
800/828-6293; NY: 716/377-0130
   GOfer
   Word Finder

MicroPhone / Software Ventures

Microsoft
16011 NE 36th Way
Redmond WA 98052
800/882-8088
(WA & AK: 206/882-8088;
   Canada: 416/673-7638)
   Excel
   Flight Simulator
   Microsoft BASIC
   MS DOS
   Word
   Works

MicroSPARC
52 Domino Dr
Concord MA 01742
617/371-1660
Desk Necessities

Migent
Box 6062
Incline Village NV 89450
800/633-3444
In-House Accountant

Milburn, Ken
(computer consultant & writer)
29 Gate 6-1/2 Rd, Kappas Marina
Sausalito CA 94965
415/331-6926

Mindscape
3444 Dundee Rd
Northbrook IL 60062
800/221-9884 (IL: 800/654-3767)
Balance of Power
Deja Vu
GraphicWorks
Uninvited

MindWork Software
555C Heritage Harbor
Monterey CA 93940
800/367-4334, 408/375-1531
MindWrite

MindWrite / Access Technology

Mobius Technologies
5300 Broadway Terrace
Oakland CA 94618
415/658-2938
SE Silencer

Modern Artist / Computer Friends

Modern Jazz / Lotus Development

MOM / National Tele-Press

Moniterm
5740 Green Circle Dr
Minnetonka MN 55343
612/935-4151
Viking monitors

Monster Cable
101 Townsend St
San Francisco CA 94107
415/777-1355

Monterey *(bit-mapped font)* / CasadyWare

MORE / Living Videotext

MultiFinder / Apple Computer

Multiplan / Microsoft

The Muzzle / Ergotron

National Tele-Press
Box 79
Mendocino CA 95460
707/934-2848
MOM

Nordic *(bit-mapped font)* / CasadyWare

Nuvotech
Suite 204, 2015 Bridgeway
Sausalito CA 94965
415/331-7815
EasyView monitors

Oblique *(bit-mapped font)* / CasadyWare

Odesta
4084 Commercial Av
Northbrook IL 60062
800/323-5423 (IL: 312/498-5615)
Double Helix
Helix

Olduvai
Suite A, 7520 Red Rd
South Miami FL 33143
800/822-0772
Icon-It!

Olympia USA
Route 22
Somerville NJ 08876
201/231-8300
NP30APL and other printers

Omnis 3 / Blyth Software

On Cue / ICOM Simulations

101 Macros for Excel /
Macropac International

Optima *(laser font)* / Adobe

Orcutt, Guy *(photographer)*
4041 NE 22d
Portland OR 97212
503/280-0413

Other... / Becker, Loftus E.

OverVUE / ProVUE

Packit III / Chesley, Harry R.

The Page
Box 14493
Chicago IL 60614
312/348-1200

PageMaker / Aldus

Paragon Concepts
4954 Sun Valley Rd
Del Mar CA 92014
800/922–2993; CA: 619/481–1477
　QUED/M

PBI Software
1163 Triton Dr
Foster City CA 94404
415/349-8765
　DeskScene

PCPC (Personal Computer Peripherals Corp)
6204 Benjamin Rd
Tampa FL 33634
800/622-2888, 813/ 884-3092
　Eureka!
　hard disks *(including MacBottom)*
　HFS Backup

Peripheral Land
47800 Westinghouse Dr
Fremont CA 94538
415/657-2211
　hard disks

Personal LaserPrinter /
　General Computer

Personal Publishing
25W550 (that's not a typo: 25W550) Geneva
　Rd
Wheaton IL 60188
312/665-1000

Personics Corp
Building #2, 2352 Main St
Concord MA 01742
508/897-1575
　VCS

Phoenix 3D / Dreams of the Phoenix

PhoneNET / Farallon Computing

Pina, Larry
147 Meadow Rd
Westport MA 02790
　Test Pattern Generator

PosterMaker Plus /
　Broderbund Software

PostScript / Adobe

Power R
1606 Dexter Av North
Seattle WA 98019
206/547-8000
　MacLarger monitors

PowerStation /
　Fifth Generation Systems

PowerUp / Software Power Co

Prodigy (boards) / SuperMac or Levco,
　depending on the model

ProVUE Development
222 22d St
Huntington Beach CA 92648
714/969-2431
　OverVUE

ProWriters / C. Itoh Electronics

Q&D
see Quick & Dirty

QDial / LaPorte, Léo

quadLYNX Trackball /
　Asher Engineering

Qualitas Trading Co
(Enzan-Hoshigumi)
6907 Norfolk Rd
Berkeley CA 94804
415/848-8080
　MacCalligraphy

Quark
Suite 100, 300 S Jackson
Denver CO 80209
800/543-7711, 303/934-2211
　Xpress

QUED/M / Paragon Concepts

Quick & Dirty Utilities /
　Dreams of the Phoenix

QuickDEX / Green Inc.

QuicKeys / CE Software

Radius
404 E Plumeria Dr
San Jose CA 95134
408/434-1010
  accelerator boards
  monitors

Ready,Set,Go! / Letraset

Redgate Communications
660 Beachland Blvd
Vero Beach FL 32963

Red Ryder / FreeSoft

Reflex / Borland International

ResEdit / Apple Computer

Retriever / Exodus Software

Roundup! / Virginia Systems

Ryan, Tim
  (computer consultant & writer)
Box 6767
Santa Barbara CA 93160

ScanCoFurn (Scandinavian Computer
  Furniture)
Box 3217
Redmond WA 98073
800/722-6263; 206/481-5434
  MacTable & add-on cabinet modules

Schwartz, Steve (computer writer)
7 Grace St
Framingham MA 01701
508/788-0611

Seikosha America
1111 MacArthur Blvd
Mahwah NJ 07430
800/338-2609
  SP-1000AP printer

Sentinel / SuperMac Technology

SE Silencer / Mobius Technologies

SetFile / Dreams of the Phoenix

Set Paths / Snively, Paul F.

Sher-Mark Products
Suite 2R, 521 E 83rd St
New York NY 10028
800/323-1776
  Anti-Glare Magnification Screen

Shinko color printers /
  Computer Friends

ShopKeeper Software
Box 38160
Tallahassee FL 32315
904/222-8808
  ShopKeeper-4

ShrinkWindow / Datamagik

Sidekick / Borland International

Sigma Designs
46501 Landing Pkwy
Fremont CA 94538
415/770-0110
  LaserView monitors

Signature Software
2151 Brown Av
Bensalem PA 19020
215/639-8764
  McSink

Silicon Beach Software
Box 261430
San Diego CA 92126
619/695-6956
  SuperPaint

SkipFinder / Adler, Darin

Slim (bit-mapped font) / CasadyWare

Small Press
Box 3000
Denville NJ 07834
203/226-6967

SmartScrap / Solutions International

Snively, Paul F.
Apt E., 3519 Park Lodge Ct
Indianapolis IN 46205
  Set Paths

Softview
Suite F, 4820 Adohr Ln
Camarilo CA 93010
805/388-2626
 MacInUse

Software Complement
8 Pennsylvania Av
Matamoros PA 18336
717/491-2492, -2495
 Complementary Type laser fonts

Software Power Company
Box 13133
Fremont CA 94539
415/490-6086
 PowerUp

Software Ventures
Suite 220, 2907 Claremont Av
Berkeley CA 94705
415/644-3232
 MicroPhone

Solutions International
Box 989
Montpelier VT 05602
802/229-0368
 The Clipper
 The Curator
 SmartScrap
 SuperGlue

Sophisticated Circuits
Suite 216, 1314 NE 43rd
Seattle WA 98105
206/547-4779
 Macs-a-Million memory upgrades

SoundMaster / Tomlin, Bruce

SourceNet
Box 6727
Santa Barbara CA 93160
805/494-7123
 The Macintosh Book of Fonts

Special Effects (laser font variations) / Century
 Software

Spelling Champion /
 Champion Swiftware

Spelling Coach / Deneba Software

Spellswell / Working Software

SP-1000AP / Seikosha America

StarNET / Farallon Computing

StartupDesk (requires ResEdit) / Adler, Darin

STAX!
8008 Shoal Creek Blvd
Austin TX 78758
800/MAC-STAX
 (TX: 512/467-4550)
 The Macintosh Bible,
 HyperCard edition

Stepping Out /
 Berkeley System Design

Stufflt / Lau, Raymond

Suitcase / Fifth Generation Systems

Sun Remarketing
Box 4059
Logan UT 84321
800/821-3221
 Lisa (Mac XL) computers & parts

SuperChroma video boards / Computer
 Friends

SuperGlue / Solutions International

SuperMac Technologies
295 N Bernardo Av
Mountain View CA 94043
415/964-8884
 accelerator boards
 DataFrame hard disks
 memory upgrades
 Sentinel
 SuperSpool

SuperPaint / Silicon Beach Software

SuperSpool / SuperMac Technologies

Swain, Tom
Suite 117, 2560 Bancroft Wy
Berkeley CA 94704
 MacChimney

Symbol (laser font) /
 Apple Computer

Symmetry
761 E. University Dr
Mesa AZ 85203
800/624-2485 (AZ: 602/884-2199)
 Acta
 HyperDA

System Saver Mac /
  Kensington Microware

Systems Control
Box 788
Iron Mountain MI 49801
800/451-6866
  MacGard Surge Suppressor

Target Software
14206 SW 136th St
Miami FL 33186
800/622-5483 (FL: 305/252-0892)
  MacLightning

Tempo / Affinity Microsystems

Terry, Fred (computer consultant)
2402 Danbury Pl
Lawrence KS 66044
913/749-3802

Thames (laser font) /
  Century Software

ThinkTank / Living Videotext

ThinkTechnologies
135 South Rd
Bedford MA 01730
800/64-THINK, 617/ 275-4800
  InBox

3G Graphics
Suite 6155, 11410 NE 124th St
Kirkland WA 98034
206/823-8198
  Images with Impact!

ThunderScan / Thunderware

Thunderware
21 Orinda Wy
Orinda CA 94563
415/254-6581
  ThunderScan

Times (laser font) / Apple Computer

T/Maker
1973 Landings Dr
Mountain View CA 94043
415/962-0195
  ClickArt Business Images
  ClickArt Christian Images
  ClickArt EPS Illustrations
  ClickArt Holidays
  WriteNow

Tomlin, Bruce
#109, 15801 Chase Hill Blvd
San Antonio TX 78256
GEnie: BTOMLIN
  SoundMaster

TOPS
2560 Ninth St
Berkeley CA 94710
800/222-TOPS, 415/549-5906

Trapeze / Access Technology

Travis, Esther (Macintosh artist)
2728 Yale St
Vancouver, British Columbia
V5K1C3 Canada
604/255-4109

Turbo Mouse /
  Kensington Microware

TV Producer video boards / Computer Friends

TypeNow / Mainstay

VCS / Personics

Ventana Press
Box 2468
Chapel Hill NC 27515
919/490-0062
  Looking Good in Print

Verbum
Box 15439
San Diego CA 92115
619/463-9977

Viking monitors / Moniterm

Virginia Systems Software Services
5509 West Bay Ct
Midlothian VA 23113
804/739–3200
  Roundup!

Walsh, Jerry C., Jr
608 Northampton Plaza
600 Airport Rd
Chapel Hill NC 27514
  Amortize 2.1

Weigand, C. J.
  (computer writer & consultant)
37 Barry Dr / PO Box 647
Gale's Ferry CT 06335
203/464-6188

WetPaint / Dubl-Click Software

Widemann, Benoit
68 avenue d'Italie
Paris, France 75013
  JoliWrite

Word / Microsoft

Word Count / LaPorte, Léo

Word Finder / Microlytics

Working Software
Suite H, 321 Alvarado
Monterey CA 93940
408/375-2828
  Findswell
  Lookup
  Spellswell

Works / Microsoft

WorksPlus Command /
  Lundeen & Associates

WorksPlus Spell /
  Lundeen & Associates

WorldClass Fonts /
  Dubl-Click Software

WriteNow / T/Maker

Xpress / Quark

X-10 (USA)
185A LeGrand Av
Northvale NJ 07647
201/784-9700
  CP290M Home Control Interface

Your Affordable Software Company
1525 N Elston Av
Chicago IL 60622
312/235-9412
  12' and 25' keyboard cables

Zapf Chancery (laser font) / Adobe

From the WetPaint clip art collection.
Copyright © 1988–89 by Dubl-Click Software Inc.
All rights reserved.

Index

Page numbers in italics indicate illustrations (graphics, screen shots or samples of type). Page numbers in boldface indicate important and/or extended discussions, definitions of terms and the like. When both apply, page numbers are in bold italic.

With a few exceptions, items in Appendix A (the glossary), Appendix B (the list of companies and products) and the Acknowledgments aren't indexed. Only the most common, Mac-standard commands (⌘-X for Cut, for example) are listed under the keystrokes that generate them. Other commands are simply indexed under their names.

A

The most useful book I have ever purchased.
ROBERT BARON, NORTHRIDGE CA

By far the most useful and interesting how-to book I've ever seen—on any topic.... A remarkable achievement.
ELLIOT ARONSON, SANTA CRUZ CA

Exceedingly well done. I've acquired just about every help book published for the Mac and yours is the best.
FRED J. KEENE, GREENVILLE ME

The single most useful book in my extensive computer library.
FRANK STOBBE, CARLSBAD CA

Everyone in our office is competing for it.
GEORGE D. HERMANN, PORTALA VALLEY CA

Great book! I have to keep track of who uses it so it won't disappear.
ELLEN TOWNSEND, DUBLIN CA

I've spent the last three months searching for such a book.
JACK COREY, SANTA CLARA CA

Apple should include this with every Mac.
MICHAEL A. SHOEMAKER, LONG BEACH CA

I didn't expect so much humor in a reference book. It's great!
GRETCHEN S. SMITH, REDWOOD CITY CA

Your "Bible" is indispensible. Rarely do you find such a combination of knowledge, common sense and enthusiasm...Congratulations!
JOANNE M. YATES, ST. HELENA CA

Wonderful! It's like having a private teacher.
LEE EVAN BELFIGLIO, BELLEVUE WA

Don't know what I'd do without it.
SUSAN WESEL, WOODLAND HILLS CA

I couldn't manage without it.
SHARYN STILLMAN, LOS ANGELES

Several lifetimes' worth of hints.
ROBERT M. COTE, SANTA MONICA CA

Saved my *** often! Thanks.
KATHY FLETCHER, SAN JOSE CA

Within five minutes of opening it, I had a solution to a problem.
KIERNAN BURKE, BOSTON MA

A tremendous timesaver!
MICHAEL LA BROOY, BRITISH COLUMBIA, CANADA

Paid for itself in one evening's use.
FRED MATICA, PORTLAND OR

Worth $100.
DON CHESTERS, ROSEVILLE MI

Worth a millon.
CHRIS D'ANGELO, WAGONTOWN PA

Although you state that it's not intended to be read cover to cover...I have read it cover to cover—twice!
JUDIE CRUMMEL, SAN FRANCISCO

As good as curling up with a favorite novel.
SUZANNE SLADE, SAN FRANCISCO

Once you start reading it, you can't put it down!
BRAD HOLIFIELD, ANCHORAGE

Addictive reading.
STEVEN MINTA, DAVIS CA

I use it constantly and read it over and over. Thanks!
SYLVIA WILSON, LOS ANGELES

I couldn't put it down.
MARSHA PATO, MILLBRAE CA

My constant companion.
J.T. DOCKING, BRIGHTON, SOUTH AUSTRALIA

A true Bible.
MARY AGAN, PHOENIX AZ

A Godsend. Thanks for writing it.
VALARIE A. SHEPPARD, AKRON OH

I keep it by my bedside—which is more than I can say for the King James version!
LAUREN M. GEE, NEW YORK CITY

Now I can tell my mother I read the Bible every day.
RANDY PREUSS, BURNSVILLE MN

Very useful! A lot easier to follow than the instruction manuals.
KAREN CANTOR, LONGWOOD FL

Written for normal, nontech minds.
GASPAR P. CHACON, SANTA FE NM

I'm a new Mac user and your Bible made a huge difference in my getting comfortable and feeling confident. Thanks!
STANLEY SELIB, SHARON MA

I wish I'd had this book when I first bought my Mac.
RICHARD D. VETTER, AIEA HI

I love the book!
PATRICIA ARNOLD, BAY HARBOR ISLANDS FL
LORI B. BROOKS, SAN FRANCISCO
TOM JAYCOX, REDMOND WA
JACQUES LEVY, NEW YORK CITY
MARK LUHDORFF, SACRAMENTO CA
GEORGE VENETIS, CHICAGO

Great job! Terrific value! Congratulations.
DYKES CORDELL, AUSTIN TX

Super book!

KELLY J. ALIG, EVANSVILLE IN
RICHARD MATHERS, LIVERMORE CA

Very good!

RICHARD M. GILLESPIE, ANAHEIM CA
L.P. HARDING, SANTA CLARA CA
C.G. MILLINGER, STOCKHOLM, SWEDEN
MICHEAL SEBALLOZ, HASTINGS NB
CHARLES EDWARD YOST, REPUBLIC WA

Very, very, very, very, very, very, very, very, very, very good!

DAVID BIANCO, ST. LOUIS

The best!

JOHN FONG, SAN FRANCISCO
MARK A. KATONA, COLUMBUS OH
KEVIN KINE, SIOUX FALLS SD
JANET LEVY, INDIANAPOLIS
CHRISTOPHER C. MASTEN, MONROVIA CA
KATHY PARKER, TOLEDO OH

Very helpful!

SUE FISCALINI, SAN LUIS OBISPO CA
MARILYN JENAI, SARASOTA FL
KAREN LOVINS, BALTIMORE MD
PHILIP PETTY, VISALIA CA
J.P. SAHEURS, ONTARIO, CANADA
KAREN ROUNDS, GRANDVIEW WA

Very useful!

ALLAN CUMMING, DUNEDIN, NEW ZEALAND
GEORGE W. DERUM, PACIFICA CA
M.H. MCCONEGHY, PROVIDENCE RI
BRUCE RYNDFLEISZ, LONG BEACH CA

Extremely helpful!

JOE BAUER, GRAND RAPIDS MI
JUDI JONES. TAMPA FL
BILL SHANAHAN, BLOOMINGDALE IL

Tremendously useful!

JOHN SAITO, HONOLULU

Incredibly valuable!
HISASHI IZUMI, SOMERVILLE MA

Assolutamente indispensabile!
GIANCARLO GENTILE, GREAT NECK NY

Excellent!
J. ALBRECHT, MINNETONKA MN
DAVID K. ANDERSON, MONTROSE CA
KATHERINE E. BELMER, GRANITE CITY IL
SUGIMAN BINSAR, SAN FRANCISCO
ANDREAS BURNIER, SAN FRANCISCO
DAVID J. FISHMAN, NEW YORK CITY
JAMES A. FLYNN, FOND DU LAC WI
VALMORE FOURNIER, SOMERSWORTH NH
GARY L. GALEK, ROCK HILL SC
J.F. HILL, GARDEN GROVE CA
GEORGE GILDAY, AUKLAND, NEW ZEALAND
SCOTT I. HENDRICKSON, SAN DIEGO
BILL HUCKABEE, DELAWARE OH
THOMAS W. JOHNSON, CHICO CA
H. E. JONES, TUCSON AZ
MICHAEL J. KAUFMAN, VALDESE NC
HERB KLINE, MCLEAN VA
ROBERT R. REH, ALTO LOMA CA
KENT J. SHEETS, ANN ARBOR
SUZANNE SLADE, SAN FRANCISCO
DAVID STENZ, DATIL NM
HANK SZERLAG, GROSSE POINTE WOODS MI
LEO W. TAYLOR, SAN ANTONIO
PAUL S. TRUESDELL, GLENDALE AZ
ROBERT VALE, LAS VEGAS
DAVE VAUGHAN, MÜNCHEN, W.GERMANY
PATRICA A. WAITE, WESTCHESTER IL
RICHARD E. WASSERMAN, SCARSDALE NY
STEPHEN R. YOUNG, BELLINGHAM WA

Invaluable!
HOWARD I. ARONSON, CHICAGO
MARK HASKELL, OAK PARK MI

Marvelous!
J.H. CHANG, NEWTOWN SQUARE PA
FRANCISCO PICART, PONCE PR

Wonderful!
BILL ARNONE, SANTA ROSA CA
FRED BENEDETTI, SAN DIEGO
LINDA M. BUIVID, REVERE MA
LISA ANNE NEIL, TROY NY
GENE M. SCHAEFFER, PHOENIX
PAM SALATICH, CINCINNATI

Terrific!
LEE C. BALLANCE, BERKELEY
JAMES D. BAZIN, SUDBURY MA
CHRIS BOYCE, LOS ANGELES
MARGE DELNY, MIDLAND TX
DEE ANN ESPITIA, S. SAN GABRIEL CA
IRIS ETZ, SAN ANTONIO
KATHRINE L.V. ROBINSON, SAN FRANCISCO
DAVID N. SHERRELL, FOUNTAIN VALLEY CA
JAMES R. SOLOMON, HEYWARD CA

Outstanding!
THOMAS E. HOEG, CANTON MI
JULES LAVNER, UPPER MONTCLAIR NJ

Fantastic!
JOHN DIAL, HOUSTON TX
MARK J. GUERETTE, WALNUT CREEK CA
MICHAEL LAMBERT, EULESS TX
IRIS M. SCHMIDT, OROFINO ID

Fabulous!
FREDERIC SWAN, OCEANSIDE CA

Superb!
DR. IRENE M. SKULAS, TOLEDO OH
ROBERT S. RICHMOND, ASHEVILLE NC

Great!

MITCHELL AIDELBAUM, ATHENS OH
EDWARD AMBINDER, M.D., NEW YORK CITY
COL. S.E. ARMISTEAD, FORT KNOX KY
RICHARD S. ARNOLD, STUDIO CITY CA
RICHARD D. BENNETT, PHOENIX
BOB BERRY, VAN NUYS CA
JERRY BLAIR, WALNUT CREEK CA
GAUDENZ BON, AARAU, SWITZERLAND
DAVID J. BROWN, KNOXVILLE TN
DIANE S. BRUCE, CUT OFF LA
NANCY BRUNSON, BLUE LAKE CA
MIMI CHAN, GLENVIEW IL
LAUREN E. CHEDA, REDDING CA
DOUGLAS R. CHEZEM, FAIRFAX VA
NARES CHOOBUA, WEST LOS ANGELES
JOE COHEN, SANTA FE NM
WAYNE COOLEY, VENTURA CA
JACK COREY, SANTA CLARA CA
KRIS. A. CUELLO, SIERRA VISTA AZ
JACK CUTTER, ORINDA CA
DAVID M. DELOACH, HONOLULU HI
NICHOLAS DEPAUL, PALO ALTO CA
P.H. DEWEY, GOODYEAR AZ
MARTIN D. DILL, PORTLAND OR
STEPHEN S. DILTS, SAN FRANCISO
DAVID L. DODD, HOUSTON
PETER R. DUFFY, VICTORIA, AUSTRALIA
JAMES M. EARLY, PALO ALTO CA
CHRIS R. EATON, SAN JOSE CA
MICHAEL A. EFFINGER, UPPER DARBY PA
PETER H. ELLZEY, SANTA FE NM
MARTHA J. ERDMANN, FARGO ND
RON C. ESTLER, DURANGO CO
DAVE FELL, CHICAGO
DR. EDWARD BERNARD GLICK, BROOMALL PA
ELAINE GOLDSTEIN, NEW ORLEANS
LARRY GOTTLIEB, WALNUT CREEK CA
MIKE GREER, CULVER CITY CA
KATHERINE A. GRIFFING, SOUTH NORWALK CT
E.J. GROTH, SCOTTSDALE AZ
NEALE HALL, QUEENSLAND, AUSTRALIA
DEAN HEINBUCH, OKOLONA MS
LORETTA HARRISON, CORVALLIS OR

JEFFREY HERMAN, CUPERTINO CA
MERRILL F. HIGHAM, BELMONT CA
KEITH HOLZMAN, LOS ANGELES
ALLEN S. HORWITZ, CANOGA PARK CA
DEBRA A. JARVENSIVU, ONTARIO, CANADA
RAYMOND JONES, BERKELEY CA
WADE T. JORDAN, M.D., CORSICANA TX
MARY ELLEN KELLY, POCATELLO ID
WALTER M. KELTING JR., SCOTTSDALE AZ
DOROTHY KETTNER, FERGUS FALLS MN
MICHAEL R. KRAINAS, EVERGREEN PARK IL
MORT LANKASKY, SAN LORENZO CA
SHELTON LANKFORD, HOLLIS NH
RICHARD S. LEE, OAKLAND CA
MARIANNE LINS, SAN DIEGO
DANIEL LYNE, NANTUCKET MA
JASPER L. MATHIS, ACTON MA
NEIL M. MCBRIDE, SAN JOSE CA
ZACHARY MILLER, SANTA BARBARA CA
JOHN MURPHY, WOODLAND HILLS CA
MARTHA OELMAN, CHICAGO
LESLIE R. PEAKE, MILWAUKIE OR
CLARE A. POE, FAIR OAKS CA
JEFFREY RENS, LA JOLLA CA
ELAINE ROSENBERG, RADNOR PA
RUDY SCHOLLÉE, TORRANCE CA
DAVID S. SECREST, REDWOOD CITY CA
KURT E. SEEL, ALBERTA, CANADA
ROBERT C. SHEPARDSON, SANTA CRUZ CA
JOAN SHERMAN, CRANBURY NJ
LARRY SILBER, NEW YORK CITY
STEVEN SILVER, SOUTHFIELD MI
RONALD SNEIDER, RANCHO MIRAGE CA
WILLIAM P. SORENSEN, GRAND TERRACE CA
GLEN SPENCE, SAN FRANCISCO
PRISCILLA TREACY, BOSTON
BURTON E. VAUGHAN, RICHLAND WA
DR. M HILDEGARD WALTER, INNSBRUCK, AUSTRIA
LARRY WELLS, KENNEWICK WA
BRAD WEST, EL SOBRANTE CA
J. LARRY YARBOROUGH, FRANKLIN TN

As good as sex.
MARK F. JOSEFF, NEWPORT BEACH CA

More rave reviews

Far and away the best collection of Mac tips around.
Computer Literacy catalog

Written to be read....well-organized....great tables and charts. A useful, fun book.   BMUG Newsletter

The equivalent of many user group meetings in one handy, straightforward book....Although it's designed as a reference book, I found myself reading whole sections of tips at a time.   San Jose Mercury News

Contains almost everything you've wanted to know about the Mac but didn't know who to ask.
Apple Library Users Group Newsletter

I loved the book!....Everyone who owns a Mac should have it.
Bob LeVitus, Editor-in-Chief, The MACazine

*For more reviews, see the back cover
and the first page of the book.
For readers' comments, see pages 752–59.*